Québec

Steve Kokker

LONELY PLANET PUBLICATIONS
Melbourne • Oakland • London • Paris

Elevation

- 1200m
- 900m
- 600m
- 300m
- 150m
- Sea Level

Labrador Sea

Baffin Island

Nunavut

Hudson Strait

Button Islands

Cape Chidley

• Kangiqsualujjuaq

Ungava Bay

• Quaqtaq

• Tasiujaq

• Kangirsuk

Kuujjuaq •

• Kangiqsujuaq

Rivière aux Feuilles

Rivière aux Mélèzes

Rivière Caniapiscau

• Salluit

Lac Nantais

• Ivujivik

Lac Couture

• Akulivik

• Puvirnituq

Lac Payne

Lac Minto

Lac à l'Eau Claire

• Inukjuak

Newfoundland & Labrador

(500)

Labrador City •

Kuujjuaq

Go for an unforgettable dogsled or snowmobile ride above the treeline with Inuit guides in Québec's Arctic.

North Shore

Treat yourself to an unforgettable whale-watching excursion in this region of wild, rugged beauty.

Île d'Anticosti

Be at one with nature here among majestic waterfalls, mysterious caves and white-tailed deer.

• Umiujaq

Lac Guillaume-Delisle

Réservoir Robert-Bourassa

La Grande 3

Lac Sakami

Réservoir Opinaca

• Radisson

• Chisasibi

James Bay

Hudson Bay

James Bay

Venture to Québec's final frontier to gawk at its enormous hydroelectric power stations and breathe in the pure, northern air.

Parc d'Aiguebelle

Go canoeing among magnificent canyons and gorges in the middle of Québec's old gold rush territory.

55°W · 60°W · 65°W · 70°W · 75°W · 80°W · 85°W

60°N · 55°N

55°N

QUÉBEC

Îles de la Madeleine
Find yourself on a slice of heaven, walk along the endless beaches and go kite surfing!

Gaspé Peninsula
Get bowled over by the spectacular coastal scenery, take a hike in Parc de la Gaspésie and see what's so special about a pierced rock in Percé.

Saguenay
Be stunned by the splendor of the Northern Hemisphere's southernmost fjord - and then take a hike atop or a boat ride along it!

Québec City
Experience North America's most European city. Cobblestone streets and Old World charm are sure to enchant.

Eastern Townships
Follow the footsteps of the American Loyalists who settled most of this lovely area of rolling hills, lush wineries and charming villages.

Montréal
Feel the energy of one of the continent's funkiest cities through its cultural diversity, social hotspots and wild festivals.

Mont Tremblant
Speed down one of the continent's best ski hills or plunge into the stunning wilderness of Parc du Mont Tremblant.

Ottawa
Discover Canada's capital and most visited city, skate along the Rideau Canal and rub roses with the Prime Minister.

Hull
Learn that Canadian history can be fascinating at the Museum of Civilization, then hike and bike your heart out in Gatineau Park.

ATLANTIC OCEAN

0   100   200 km
0   60   120 miles

Québec
1st edition – August 2002

Published by
Lonely Planet Publications Pty Ltd ABN 36 005 607 983
90 Maribyrnong St, Footscray, Victoria 3011, Australia

Lonely Planet Offices
Australia Locked Bag 1, Footscray, Victoria 3011
USA 150 Linden St, Oakland, CA 94607
UK 10a Spring Place, London NW5 3BH
France 1 rue du Dahomey, 75011 Paris

Photographs
Many of the images in this guide are available for licensing from
Lonely Planet Images.
W www.lonelyplanetimages.com

Front cover photograph
Rue Petit, Québec City (Andre Jenny)

ISBN 1 74059 024 4

text & maps © Lonely Planet Publications Pty Ltd 2002
photos © photographers as indicated 2002

Printed by SNP SPrint (M) Sdn Bhd
Printed in Malaysia

Contents

2   Contents

THE LAURENTIANS   138

OUTAOUAIS   157

OTTAWA   170

EASTERN TOWNSHIPS   182

MONTRÉAL TO QUÉBEC CITY   206

QUÉBEC CITY   228

CHARLEVOIX, SAGUENAY & LAC ST JEAN · 264

NORTH SHORE & ÎLE D'ANTICOSTI · 292

LOWER ST LAWRENCE · 314

GASPÉ PENINSULA & ÎLES DE LA MADELEINE · 331

QUÉBEC MAP INDEX

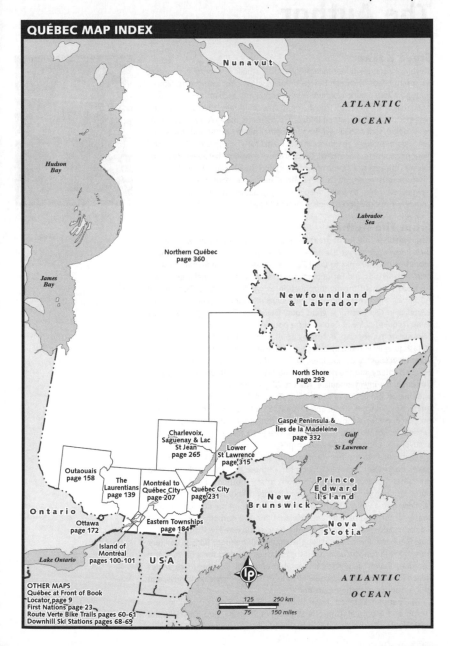

Nunavut

ATLANTIC OCEAN

Hudson Bay

Labrador Sea

Northern Québec
page 360

James Bay

Newfoundland & Labrador

North Shore
page 293

Charlevoix,
Saguenay & Lac
St Jean
page 265

Gaspé Peninsula &
Îles de la Madeleine
page 332

Gulf of St Lawrence

Lower
St Lawrence
page 315

Outaouais
page 158

The
Laurentians
page 139

Montréal to
Québec City
page 207

Québec City
page 231

Prince
Edward
Island

New
Brunswick

Ontario

Ottawa
page 172

Eastern Townships
page 184

Nova
Scotia

Island of
Montréal
pages 100-101

USA

Lake Ontario

ATLANTIC OCEAN

OTHER MAPS
Québec at Front of Book
Locator page 9
First Nations page 23
Route Verte Bike Trails pages 60-61
Downhill Ski Stations pages 68-69

0   125   250 km
0   75   150 miles

The Author

Steve Kokker

Steve Kokker grew up a moderately good Catholic in Montréal, counting his rosary beads in church before primary school. Yet after being filtered through a Jesuit same-sex high school and a very secular university, all in one of North America's most liberal and culturally diverse cities, he swapped rosaries for other things. He received psychology, then social work degrees at McGill, worked in mental health counseling for a few years, then for eight years was the film critic for *The Montreal Mirror* and *Hour* newspapers. Since 1996, he's partitioned his time between Montréal, Estonia (the ancestral home of his father) and Russia (caretaker of his soul). His numerous writing stints for Lonely Planet since 1998 in all these areas have allowed him to more deeply feel and appreciate each of his three homes. He also authored Lonely Planet's *St Petersburg* guide.

From The Author

I am indebted to a lot of great people I met along the way who shared their knowledge about 'La Belle Province' and made my journey much more beautiful. Thanks to Dani Zbinden in Ste Anne de Portneuf for his help with whales and for finding space in his tent; Yvon Bélanger in Ste Anne de Portneuf for my introduction to whales; Nathalie Decaigny in Auclair for the lovely company; Yvon Ouellet pour mon premier vol; Paul L'Anglais in Québec for a great tour; Guillaume Tétrault, my Saguenay guru; Jacques Racine at Cap au Leste pour les conversations; Jean François Miousse from Gros Cap for turning another page; Lorraine Pes for making Natashquan even more memorable; Nicole at Au Naturel in Sutton for the warmth, wisdom and great talks; Oscar and Hélène in Val d'Or for caribou on my birthday and the hospitality; Martin Chouinard for some German, Russian and irony in Jonquière; Robert 'Mojo' for sharing his favorite place with me on the Îles de la Madeleine; Richard T Wilson in Sutton for language tips; Philippe, Claire and Dominic Steinbach on Île d'Orleans for a magical evening; Nicholas Gaudet in Rimouski for Gaudetism; and Etienne Lessard in Rouyn-Noranda, François Grenier Laroque in Godbout, Eric Lecuyer in Québec and Alex in Jonquière.

Thanks also to my friends and family who helped make the job a bit easier. To Louise 'Tweezers' Treich for all those newspaper clippings; to my father Tony for the lifts to Sutton; to my mother Michelle for supporting the project in so many ways; to Ingrid Thompson for letting me fall deep into a writer's cave; Tom Waugh for letting me take up so much space; Brent Beauparlant and Melanie for the camping gear; James Donovan and Athena 'Soup' for the lesson in hackeysack and camping tips; Stephanie Premji for making Kuujjuarapik happen; Boris Romaguer for lessons in forestry and Swedish; to James DiSalvio for a bit of island paradise; Pavel Sijanov for unbeatable company on the road; James Roach for helping me overcome all odds in the Mauricie's wilderness; and Phil Anson for operatic suggestions.

At Tourisme Québec, huge thanks to Patrice Poissant and Johann Eustache in Montréal, Christine St Pierre in St Flavie, and especially the very talented Michel Bonato on the Îles de la Madeleine.

Thanks also to fellow LP authors, some of whose ideas are reflected in this text: Christine Coste for her formidable, groundbreaking work in Lonely Planet's French edition of *Québec*; Mark Lightbody for his great work in the previous editions of *Canada* and Jeremy Gray for his work on *Montréal*. At LP (US), thanks to Robbie Reid for his continued support and patience, to Tracey Croom, Christine Lee, Emily Wolman and the others who wiped many a sweaty brow over this first edition.

This Book

FROM THE PUBLISHER

The first edition of *Québec* was produced in Lonely Planet's Oakland office. The book was edited and proofed by Christine Lee and Emily Wolman, with the help of Rachel Bernstein, Tammy Fortin, Kanani Kauka and Ben Greensfelder. Robert Reid was senior editor on the project, with some last-minute help from Michele Posner.

Maps were mostly drawn by the legendary Lee Espinole and Carole Nuttall, with help from Graham Neale, Buck Cantwell, and Laurie Mikkelsen. Dion Good, Eric Thomson, Herman So, John Culp, Kat Smith, Patrick Huerta, Rudie Watzig, Sarah Nelson, and Terence Phillippe all lent their expertise as base map editors. Ed Turley provided the data, and Patrick Phelan, Chris Howard, and Timothy Lohnes fixed all technical problems. Bart Wright and Tracey Croom were the senior cartographers, and, as always, Alex Guilbert was king of all map world.

Joshua Schefers artfully designed the color pages and laid out the book with the help of senior designer Tracey Croom. Lora Santiago designed and Margaret Livingston produced the cover. Justin Marler created most of the fabulous illustrations with others drawn by Cyril Anguelidis, Hugh D'Andrade, Hayden Foell, Martin Harris and Kate Nolan. Art Director Susan Rimerman provided support for all. Ken DellaPenta indexed the book.

ACKNOWLEDGEMENTS

Some of the maps in this book are derived from aerial photographs from the collection of the National Air Photo Library/Natural Resources Canada by right of Her Majesty the Queen in Right of Canada.

Thanks

Thanks to the following LP readers who wrote helpful letters:

Dominique Doyle, Paula and Larry Fugman, Rita Lauricella, and Richard Samuelson.

Foreword

ABOUT LONELY PLANET GUIDEBOOKS

The story begins with a classic travel adventure: Tony and Maureen Wheeler's 1972 journey across Europe and Asia to Australia. There was no useful information about the overland trail then, so Tony and Maureen published the first Lonely Planet guidebook to meet a growing need.

From a kitchen table, Lonely Planet has grown to become the largest independent travel publisher in the world, with offices in Melbourne (Australia), Oakland (USA), London (UK) and Paris (France).

Today Lonely Planet guidebooks cover the globe. There is an ever-growing list of books and information in a variety of media. Some things haven't changed. The main aim is still to make it possible for adventurous travelers to get out there – to explore and better understand the world.

At Lonely Planet we believe travelers can make a positive contribution to the countries they visit – if they respect their host communities and spend their money wisely. Since 1986 a percentage of the income from each book has been donated to aid projects and human rights campaigns, and, more recently, to wildlife conservation.

Although inclusion in a guidebook usually implies a recommendation, we cannot list every good place. Exclusion does not necessarily imply criticism. In fact, there are a number of reasons why we might exclude a place – sometimes it is simply inappropriate to encourage an influx of travelers.

UPDATES & READER FEEDBACK

Things change – prices go up, schedules change, good places go bad and bad places go bankrupt. Nothing stays the same. So, if you find things better or worse, recently opened or long-since closed, please tell us and help make the next edition even more accurate and useful.

Lonely Planet thoroughly updates each guidebook as often as possible – usually every two years, although for some destinations the gap can be longer. Between editions, up-to-date information is available in our free, quarterly *Planet Talk* newsletter and monthly email bulletin *Comet*. The *Upgrades* section of our website (W www.lonelyplanet.com) is also regularly updated by Lonely Planet authors, and the site's *Scoop* section covers news and current affairs relevant to travelers. Lastly, the *Thorn Tree* bulletin board and *Postcards* section carry unverified, but fascinating, reports from travelers.

Tell us about it! We genuinely value your feedback. A well-traveled team at Lonely Planet reads and acknowledges every email and letter we receive and ensures that every morsel of information finds its way to the relevant authors, editors and cartographers.

Everyone who writes to us will find their name listed in the next edition of the appropriate guidebook and will receive the latest issue of *Comet* or *Planet Talk*. The very best contributions will be rewarded with a free guidebook.

We may edit, reproduce and incorporate your comments in Lonely Planet products such as guidebooks, websites and digital products, so let us know if you don't want your comments reproduced or your name acknowledged.

How to contact Lonely Planet:
Online: e talk2us@lonelyplanet.com.au, W www.lonelyplanet.com
Australia: Locked Bag 1, Footscray, Victoria 3011
UK: 10a Spring Place, London NW5 3BH
USA: 150 Linden St, Oakland, CA 94607

Introduction

Québec is Canada's largest province, a vast territory three times the size of France, and is also the country's most geographically diverse region. This one province alone encompasses sparsely populated stretches of windswept Arctic tundra in the north, rich and wild boreal forests in the central areas, fertile agricultural land in the south and a maritime climate in the east. In between are majestic waterfalls, sand dunes, fjords, jagged mountain peaks and more meat *tourtières* than you can count.

Québec is not called La Belle Province for nothing. In many areas the scenery is nothing short of breathtaking. Unspoiled Charlevoix is a protected area of natural beauty. The Laurentians boast splendid mountains and year-round resorts. The Eastern Townships, settled by Loyalists, is a gentle, quiet region of farms, lakes and rolling hills. The Gaspésie, in the east, with its rugged shoreline wallops you with its beauty. The northern forests' huge parks offer accessible untamed wilderness, in contrast to the equally beautiful delicate flowers and lichen on the rocks of the far north.

Québec's official motto is *Je me souviens,* but it may as well be *Vive la différence!* The land's diversity makes traveling throughout the province especially exciting. Just a few hours' travel will allow discovery of a region's specificity – not just in terms of its physical characteristics, but in the social sphere as well.

Just as the ordered, tended beauty of the Eastern Townships contrasts with the North Shore's brutish wilderness, so too does the province's human fabric reveal itself to be

equally complex and nuanced. Despite the outwardly homogeneous appearance of the population outside Montréal, it's not hard to notice differences in behavior, customs and attitudes as you cross the province.

It's a long jump from the fashion-conscious attitudes of downtown Montréal's young *poseurs* to the down-home, knee-slappin' screams of the *calleurs* lording over an evening of square dancing in Inverness – yet the two are but a few hours' drive apart. It may seem as if the fishers along the Gaspésie shoreline and the Cree Indians in the north inhabit different worlds, yet they are but two facets of the Québécois cultural landscape.

As the bastion of French culture in North America, Québec is indeed unique, unlike any other area on the continent. The differences go far beyond language to include architecture, music, food, religion and other aspects of daily life.

Even Montréal (pronounced 'mo-reh-al'), where English is still widely used, has a decidedly different air than other cities in North America (Americans have dubbed it 'Paris without the jet lag'), and historic Québec City is noticeably European. While a large proportion of the population is French-speaking and signs are mainly in French, English speakers will by and large not have any problems communicating with the locals – and any confusion that may arise can be considered exotic!

The province is also the cradle of modern civilization in the US and Canada. The continent's first European-founded cities are here (Québec City, Montréal and Trois Rivières are the oldest cities north of Mexico), and there are plenty of opportunities to get acquainted with the continent's modern social origins and history. A stroll on Québec City's Plains of Abraham will take you back to a battle that changed the course of North American history. The Native Canadian populations are in many ways thriving and offer travelers opportunities to delve into their rich cultural traditions.

Discovering Québec is getting in touch with the very roots of North America in a unique social context, surrounded by stunningly beautiful nature.

Facts about Québec

HISTORY
The First Nations

By the time Basque, French and English fishermen were hunting whales and fishing cod in the St Lawrence River in the 15th and 16th centuries, a rich diversity of peoples already existed there. The presence of Native Canadians in Québec goes back at least 11,000 years, after Asian tribes probably crossed over the frozen Bering Strait. There is no clear consensus on when and how this happened, however, as recent archeological finds raise questions about specific dates and routes of migration. In any case, these are the ancestors of Québec's ten present-day Native Canadian groups. The northern-dwelling Inuit (once called Eskimos) are thought to descend from another wave of Asian peoples who arrived after the first. They have been living on the territory at least since 3000 BC.

European Explorers

For the Native Canadians, the 'great' landing of Jacques Cartier in 1534 was nothing more than another foreign ship in the river. However, the leader of this crew seemed fond of putting French names to islands, rivers and mountains, on which he had a habit of planting crosses. That he 'took' the land in the name of the French king meant little to the local natives. At first.

Nothing of a permanent nature arose out of Cartier's exploits. Sixty years later, Pierre Chauvin arrived to begin trading with the indigenous peoples and opened the first fur trading post at Tadoussac. Permanent habitation started only after Samuel de Champlain, also of France, founded a settlement at Québec City (then called Stadacona) in 1608 and almost single-handedly attempted to establish French roots. These new lands were seen as a great potential source of revenue for France. Even colonial aspirations fell under the shadow of commerce as companies and bourgeois investors financed several expeditions in the hope of turning profits.

De Champlain allied himself with the Montagnais (today's Innu) and the Hurons. The Compagnie des Cent Associés was formed by Richelieu in 1627, essentially to divide the lands between those who could exploit them for commercial purposes. Trade aggravated intertribe conflicts, and rivalries between the Iroquois and Hurons intensified into fierce battles. Though huge profits were wrested from the land's resources, the companies cared little about colonization, so in 1663 Louis XIV personally took over the administration of what became France's first colony in the North America. He sent over several hundred *filles du Roi* (King's daughters), socially disadvantaged single girls (mostly illegitimate offspring of bourgeois women, orphans and prostitutes) to marry the French settlers and start populating the colony.

European Settlement

As New France was officially established it had only 3000 settlers, and the English colonies in the south already had 100,000. The creation of the Hudson Bay Company in England exacerbated the struggle for control over the fur market. By 1690 war between the two powers affected the colonies once again. In that year, a fleet under General Phips attacked, but Count Frontenac saved the day. The white population of Canada then stood at 15,000 (while in New England it had doubled to 200,000); indeed in hindsight, one of France's 'mistakes' was its inconsistent and incomplete method of colonization, compared to Britain's. France decided much later than Britain to treat their North American territories as veritable colonies and send settlers to ensure their interest, and they paid the price by having a much less formidable presence on the continent.

Through the rest of that century there were occasional disputes with the English, but by 1759 the English, with a final battle victory under General James Wolfe on the

Plains of Abraham, won possession of the colony. The following year Montréal capitulated as 17,000 British troops under Lord Jeffrey Amherst advanced upon the city. This was the same charming Amherst who 13 years earlier had donated hundreds of smallpox-infected blankets to Native Americans in Pittsburgh in an effort to, according to his letter to Colonel Bouquet, 'try every method that can serve to extirpate this execrable race.' The Treaty of Paris of 1763 made British dominion official.

The arrival of some 50,000 British loyalists fleeing the American Revolution paved the way for the formation of Upper (Ontario) and Lower (Québec) Canada, with almost all the French settlers in the latter region. The Loyalists did not want to be governed by the French civil law that ruled the colony.

In 1834 Louis Joseph Papineau and his followers published *Les Quatre-Vingt-Douze Résolutions (The 92 Resolutions),* a long list of demands placed to the British government that would affirm the rights of French speakers in Canada. When these were rejected outright in 1837, a series of rebellions took place, centered in the Richelieu Valley east of Montréal. In November the so-called Patriots scored a victory over British troops near the town of St Denis. It was their only major victory. The Brits returned, torched the town, and hanged 12 Patriots in early 1839, forever squashing organized armed rebellion.

Inevitable struggles of power and status between the two language groups erupted up to and after 1840's Act of Union, which unified Upper and Lower Canada. The Canadian Confederation was born in the British North America Act of 1867, joining Ontario, Québec, New Brunswick and Nova Scotia under one central government, with provincial authority and government structures also recognized.

Modern Québec
The early and middle portions of the 20th century saw Québec change from a rural, agricultural society to an urban, industrialized one whose educational and cultural base, however, still relied upon the Catholic Church, which wielded immense power and authority. Under the patriarchal control of premier Duplessis (see 'Québec's Little Dictator'), Québec became archly conservative.

The 1960s decade of questioning also brought the so-called Quiet Revolution, during which all aspects of French society were scrutinized and overhauled.

During this period Québécois began to assert their sense of nationhood. Under Jean Lesage's Liberals, a number of reforms were set into motion: A mixed and free education system, obligatory for everyone until 16, was instituted; a system of social protection was developed; unions gained clout; hydroelectric companies were nationalized; culture was stressed in an effort to underline the province's distinction; and intellectuals and extremists alike debated the idea of sovereignty from Canada.

From 1963 to 1970 the Front de la Libération du Québec (FLQ), a group dedicated to the 'liberation' of Québec from what were considered the colonial powers of Canada, committed a series of terrorist acts against symbols of English Canadian dominance. In that period, 200 bombs were exploded – inside mailboxes in Westmount (Montréal's most affluent and largely English neighborhood), at Eaton's department store and at the foot of General Wolfe's statue in Québec City (see 'The Trouble with Jamie' in the Québec City chapter). The crystallizing nationalist consciousness of the Québécois was also evidenced by the cheers that greeted French president Charles de Gaulle's infamous cry of *'Vive le Québec libre!'* ('Long live a free Québec!') during a visit to Montréal in 1969.

The Separatist Movement
Though the idea of self-government has existed in Québec since the 18th century, it was only with the Quiet Revolution that groups devoted to the cause got organized. In 1960 the Rassemblement pour l'Indépendance National (Assembly for National Independence) was founded, and in 1968 the Parti Québécois was formed.

Things got very tense during the October Crisis of 1970, when members of an FLQ cell kidnapped British diplomat James Cross in Montréal, issuing their manifesto and a list of demands. Provincial cabinet minister Pierre Laporte was kidnapped by another FLQ cell five days later. Prime Minister Pierre Trudeau resorted to invoking the War Measures Act and sending military troops to Montréal to keep the peace. With sweeping powers, police made hundreds of arrests, often dragging people with even a hint of an FLQ connection out of their homes in the middle of the night. Laporte

Québec's Little Dictator

Dubbed *Le Chef* (The Chief), Maurice Duplessis exercised extreme control over most areas of Québec society as its premier from 1936–39 and 1944–59. The Québec Liberal premier in 1935, Louis Alexandre Taschereau, was a rather corrupt capitalist whose open-door policies with regard to foreign ownership and investment incensed a young Paul Gouin, who founded the idealistic and nationalist L'Action Libérale Nationale (roughly: National Liberal Action).

Duplessis, a lawyer from Trois Rivières and leader of the moribund provincial Conservative Party, smelled a chance for political success and allied himself with Gouin to oust the Liberals. In 1936 Taschereau resigned after a corruption scandal, and Duplessis outmaneuvered Gouin to take control of the newly christened Union Nationale. Using a platform incorporating Gouin's best ideas, he won the 1936 elections.

In office, he did not deliver on his socialist campaign promises, refusing to nationalize hydroelectric companies or to control gas, bread and coal prices. He let big companies, foreign and domestic, have free reign of the market. One of his most infamous acts was the passing of the Padlock Law in 1937. Ostensibly a move to fight communism, it gave the government the power to shut down any company it viewed as a threat to its survival. It was used mainly to intimidate union and labor organizations and to seize so-called subversive literature. Superstitious and paranoid, Duplessis announced his most important decisions on Wednesdays, the day of his favorite saint, St Joseph.

Duplessis continued to coddle big business (and enjoy its graft) at the expense of workers. In the late 1930s he set fair wages so low that some employers lowered worker wages to adhere to the law. In the late 1940s he sold off iron ore at a grossly undervalued $0.01 per ton (which companies outside the province turned into megafortunes). Then, in 1949 and the mid-1950s, he had police crack down brutally on striking miners in Asbestos, who were protesting low wages and unbearable working conditions.

Part of the reason he stayed in office so long was his public face of Québec nationalism, always protesting against federal intervention in Québec's affairs. Yet all the while he proved to be a friend and protector of big business and allowed the powerful Catholic Church to maintain dominion over society's mores.

Duplessis' name is today most often uttered with the word 'orphans' after it. There were so many thousands of children abandoned by their unwed mothers and placed in orphanages during his time in office (in a strict Roman Catholic society it was one of the worst social sins to have a child out of wedlock) that an entire group has emerged known as the Duplessis Orphans. Many were sent into insane asylums thanks to a funding scam led by the church, individual doctors and the province itself to get federal monies. There, many children were exposed to physical and sexual abuse.

In July 2001 the provincial government offered a $37.5 million settlement for the victims of this forced institutionalization – only for those who were interned between the ages of 6 and 12, however, leaving thousands of others to continue to deal with their tragic history.

The province uttered a collective sigh of relief at Duplessis' death in 1959.

was murdered, Cross was eventually set free, and the army left in January 1971, but nothing was the same after the incident.

In 1976, the Parti Québecois came to power, headed by the charismatic René Lévesque, and in 1980 the first referendum

on Québec separatism was held. The 'No' side won with about 60% of the vote.

After many decades of attempts, the Constitution was repatriated from Britain in an agreement signed by Trudeau and Queen Elizabeth II in Ottawa. At first most provinces opposed it, fearing a reduction in provincial authority, but in the end all except Québec reached an agreement and signed the deal. To this day Québec has not signed the new Constitution, which includes a Charter of Rights and Freedoms (though it has its own).

The Liberal party won elections in 1985 and 1989, for a time allaying federalist forces' fear of the country's breakup. However, Premier Bourassa tightened language-use restrictions and fought for a 'special status' for Québec in a constitutional amendment in the Meech Lake Accord (1987). He got it. The accord, however, died in 1990 because of disagreement by other provinces over this and other of its clauses. The Bloc Québecois party was formed under Lucien Bouchard to further the separatist cause in the federal government. He later headed the Parti Québecois but was denounced as 'a soft sovereignist,' dubbed the first Anglophone premier of Québec because he spoke English at home with his American wife.

In 1994 the Parti Québecois returned to power under Jacques Parizeau and held another referendum in 1995 with a confusingly worded question on sovereignty. This one was a nail-biter, and the 'No' side won by less than 1%, by a mere 53,000 votes – fewer than the number of spoiled ballots. Parizeau made headlines by declaring that they had lost, 'but by what? By money and the ethnic vote.' True, some 60% of Francophones voted in favor of separation, while a vast majority of Anglophone, immigrant allophones and Native Canadians voted against it. However, allegations of xenophobia among the Parti Québecois were merely amplified by this and other comments.

By 2001 the issue of separation, while still officially advocated by the Parti Québecois under Bernard Landry, was no longer topical. Landry, not nearly as popular as Lévesque, saw support for his party slip in the wake of forced municipal mergers and accusations by a revived Liberal party

Fleur-de-Lis

The most visible symbol of Québec is the white lily flower on a blue background – it's been on the provincial flag since 1948 and can also be seen painted onto cheeks and biceps during St Jean Baptiste celebrations. Since the 12th century this symbol has been one of French royalty, the monarchy's emblem, first used on battle shields, later incorporated into France's coat of arms. Joan of Arc carried a banner depicting the fleur-de-lis as she led troops to victory over the English in support of Charles VII's quest for the French throne.

The flower's pointed top, like a spearhead, is also as a symbol of power, while its three petals represent the Holy Trinity, suggesting God's power is with the people as well. Its religious ties go back to a legend that says an angel presented Clovis, the king of the Franks, with a lily upon his conversion to Christianity.

The white lily was officially adopted as the Assemblée Nationale's emblem in 1963, and the white lily in a blue square has been the provincial government's official emblem since 1975.

under Jean Charest of fiscal mishandling and social irresponsibility. While sovereignty association with Canada is supported by about 43% of the population, the notion of an independent Québec is less attractive to a younger generation with more global concerns focused on the economy and environment. Indeed, apprehension over globalization will have a greater effect on the future of the separatist cause than the strategies born from a very distant-seeming Quiet Revolution.

GEOGRAPHY

With a total landmass of 1.67 million sq km, Québec would be the 18th-biggest country in the world if it ever did separate. It is three times the size of France, seven times the UK. There are one million lakes on its territory, 130,000 rivers and 9000km of coastline. Water occupies 25% of the province's surface, with 200,099 sq km of freshwater (16% of the world's freshwater resources). Forest covers 51% of Québec's landmass.

The highest peak is Mont d'Iberville (1652m), in the far north Torngat mountain chain on the border of Labrador, Newfoundland. There the mountain is known as Mount Caubvik because Newfoundland objected to Québec's naming it in honor of the ruthless 18th-century explorer who led several destructive rampages in Newfoundland. Caubvik was an Inuit who accompanied British trader Cartwright to England in 1772.

The St Lawrence Seaway is one of the world's great water systems, and reaches to the heart of North America. The St Lawrence River is Québec's spinal cord. It is 65km wide at its estuary and flows 3800km from its source in the Great Lakes to the Atlantic Ocean. It was formed out of an enormous ocean basin during the last ice age and has maintained its shape and course ever since. The major rivers that feed it are the Outaouais, Saguenay, Richelieu and Manicouagan.

Québec is divided into 20 tourist regions: Nunavik, Baie James (James Bay), Abitibi-Témiscamingue, Outaouais, Laurentides (Laurentians), Lanaudière, Laval, Mon-tréal, Montérégie, Cantons de l'Est (Eastern Townships), Centre du Québec (Central Québec), Chaudière-Appalaches, Mauricie, Saguenay-Lac St Jean, Charlevoix, Québec, Bas St Laurent (Lower St Lawrence), Côte Nord (North Shore, itself composed of Manicouagan and Duplessis), Gaspésie and the Îles de la Madeleine (Magdalen Islands).

CLIMATE

Because of its vastness, Québec has three climactic zones: continental in the south and middle, sub-arctic in the Lower North Shore and James Bay, and arctic in the far north. In summer or winter, a few hours drive north from Montréal can bring about noticeable differences in temperature.

Although global warming has taken the edge off the winter, daily temperatures in Montréal average between -20°C and -5°C, with spells of -25°C or colder. Humidity can make such temperatures bone chilling. Québec City is usually a few degrees colder than Montréal. One of the coldest spots is Schefferville, which has known -50°C temperatures.

Overall, Québec ranks with Kamchatka, in Russia's Far East, as among the planet's snowiest winter spots. Montréal can expect about 2m of the white stuff per year; points north of Québec City get double that.

In summer it's not unusual in the southern regions to suffer under 30°C to 34°C temperatures. In the Gaspésie and points farther north, summer nights can still be chilly.

Winter and summer are the seasons that mark the climate the most; spring and autumn tend to be quite short. In the Gaspésie and North Shore, for example, it's not unusual to see snow in May (in Blanc Sablon, they celebrate the passage of icebergs in June!). In the south, summer often begins in earnest like a hammer, but takes a softer, slower approach in the north and east, where July and August are the warmest months. On the Magdalen Islands, however, temperatures stay warm throughout September.

On the whole, while residents complain equally loud about cold and heat, most are

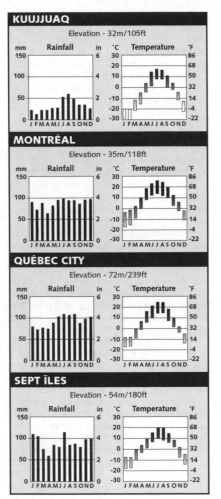

KUUJJUAQ
Elevation - 32m/105ft

MONTRÉAL
Elevation - 35m/118ft

QUÉBEC CITY
Elevation - 72m/239ft

SEPT ÎLES
Elevation - 54m/180ft

happy to enjoy the diversity that four seasons bring.

ECOLOGY & ENVIRONMENT

While it is the beauty and wildness of its nature that provides visitors with their strongest experiences, Québec has a troubled past with regard to the management of its natural resources.

Forestry

Forests are Québec's pride and, along with hydroelectricity, main economic motor. In the Québec manufacturing sector, one out of every seven jobs is forest-related. This sector is the main source of economic activity for some 250 Québec municipalities. Each year, the forestry industry generates over \$10 billion and counts for 20% of the province's total output. There are 65,000 people directly involved in the forestry industry.

However, over a century of exploitation and clear-cutting have left forests in a pitiable state. While tourists are likely to see only the province's splendid parks and reserves, another reality exists inland from main roads. A flight from Rivière du Loup to Matapédia, or north of Chibougamau, for example, would provide a view of roads, rivers and lakes with bands of trees around them and evidence of clear-cutting in between.

The provincial government owns 91.8% of the forested land in Québec. Yet while they retain titular control, forestry companies are in many ways the forests' masters. In 1934 the forest concession system was introduced, which gave forestry companies free reign in the territories they owned. Around 1974 the provincial government took responsibility of the management and development of the forests but still guaranteed companies all the timber they wanted. In 1987's Forest Act, the forests were divided into common areas (about 130), in which maximum harvesting volumes were allocated to companies, who had to ensure sustainable management.

These acts did little toward the implementation of effective reforestation policies, however, and major firms essentially control forest management. In 1997 songwriter Richard Desjardins made a documentary entitled *Erreur Boreale* (Forest Alert), which featured shocking scenes of clear-cutting and delineated how government and big business have been happy bedfellows at the ecosystem's expense for decades. The film inspired a huge reaction among the public, and to this day remains much discussed – and, within the forestry industry, much maligned.

The government made an effort to improve its reforestation policies in the 1990s. However, tree planters affirm that what is printed on Québec City's pieces of paper is not reflective of the reality, and that reforestation is helter-skelter and ineffective. This is partially due to the meager wages these front-line workers receive – $0.06 per tree planted. The companies that hire them get $0.22 per tree planted. There have been no wage increases for planters since 1955, though every other sector in the forestry industry has enjoyed healthy raises.

Finally, as many parks, wildlife reserves and protected areas as the province boasts, they represent less than 3% of Québec's landmass. Half of this lies above the 50th parallel in caribou migratory zones. Québec's amount of protected territory is the smallest in Canada, where the national average is just under 5%; in New Zealand it's 18%; the suggested world average is 8%. More distasteful to the public is the sad fact that a number of the Réserves Fauniques (wildlife reserves) have been partially exploited by the forestry industry.

Pollution

Québec is the world's second largest exporter of asbestos, which is less impressive when you take into account that many countries have banned the cancer-causing substance. By 2005, when the EU will ban all asbestos-containing products, the mineral will have claimed 200,000 lives in the US. In Québec, in order to keep some 1500 jobs and two asbestos mines (in Asbestos and Thetford Mines), the provincial government announced in 2001 that it will buy six times more asbestos-enriched bitumen than in previous years to pave road surfaces throughout the province. While brief exposure is likely harmless (to visit Thetford Mines or Asbestos, for example), citizens aware of this are not so comfortable with the idea of it permanently on their streets.

While some cleanup has gone on in some of the province's waterways (see 'River, Heal Thyself' in the Montréal to Québec City chapter), others continue to register high levels of toxins. In October 2001, out-of-province investigators proved that the fish in three lakes north of Chibougamau contain abnormally high levels of cyanide, mercury, PCP and other toxins. The Native Canadians living there have developed illnesses after eating contaminated fish. Since 1999 the lake's fish had shown physical abnormalities like having one eye or unformed gills. Only after the outside investigation did the government issue a warning to locals about eating fish.

About 40% of the pollutants in the St Lawrence originate in the Great Lakes region in Ontario and the US. Much of Canada's heavy industry is concentrated in this region, and their waste, combined with the industrial pollutants released by factories in US cities like Milwaukee, Detroit, Chicago and Cleveland, create problems for marine life upriver. Shipping also carries a serious pollution risk. The wave action caused by ships and deballasting puts stress on the river's ecosystem, and every year several hundred thousand cubic meters of sediment have to be dredged from one location to another in the St Lawrence Seaway. Additionally, one-third of the river's wetlands were lost to farming between 1945 and 1976.

Conservation

Montréal was the site of a historical environmental accord: the Montréal Protocol on Substances That Deplete the Ozone Layer, signed in 1987. More recently, the city hosted high-level international meetings on biosafety, the issues surrounding the trade and regulation of genetically modified foods.

In general, pollution levels are respectable throughout most of Québec, and it is considered a safe, healthy place to live. As more programs on ecotourism and environmental issues are given at universities, the number of people interested in conservation and protection issues is increasing every year. Along the St Lawrence, as more areas fall under government protection, a slight increase has been witnessed in the bird population after decades of decline.

FLORA

Québec encompasses five life zones: hardwood forest, mixed forest, boreal forest, taiga and tundra, the last occupying 27% of the province's land mass in its northern extremes. Some 74% of Québec's forests are of the boreal type, made up of black spruce, jack pine, balsam fir and tamarack. The maple tree species, including the famous sugar maple whose sap is magically transformed into delicious maple syrup (see 'Maple Syrup & the Sugar Shack' in the Facts for the Visitor chapter), is seen mostly south of the St Lawrence. You'll also find the rarer yellow birch, Québec's official tree.

Québec is home to some 6800 plant species.

FAUNA

There are 653 species of animal wildlife in the province, including 199 fish species, 326 bird species and 91 mammal species. Of these, 76 vertebrate species are considered rare or threatened. For your comfort, 25,000 species of insects also live on this territory.

Bird watchers come from far and wide to set sight on a fantastic variety – the golden eagle and snowy owls are especially prized. The shores of the St Lawrence River feature puffins, black ducks, great herons and marsh wrens. The northern gannet, seen on and near Île Bonaventure off Percé, is another impressive bird with unexpected habits (see 'Dive-Bombing Gannets' in the

Curse of the Puffin

Nature threw a few curveballs to an irresistibly cute bird that is seen most frequently on the islands of the Mingan archipelago. They're so striking, in fact, they steal the show from the already impressive limestone pillars on which they perch themselves. These birds, dubbed 'parrots of the sea' and 'friars' for their appearance, make popular pinups, often making the pages of calendars and posters. They sport a black back, white stomach, bright orange webbed feet,

Look out! I'm coming in for a landing!

and an orange, bluish and yellow bill. Their eyes have red rings and blue plates around them.

Yet like a mythological character in a morality play, or like Narcissus who loved his image too much, these birds are condemned to a few awkward moments. First, they exhibit their attractive, colorful features only during mating season. In winter they lose their color, and their faces go very dark. Their appearance changes so significantly that most people think they are a different species.

Nature's sneakiest trick, however, was making them pretty terrible flyers. Their extra-small wings make it hard to take off gracefully – they have to start flapping before they throw themselves off a cliff – and they must flap 300 to 400 times a minute just to stay in the air. Their feet drag heavily during flight. In short, they make flying seem like a great effort. For a short period each spring, when they shed their wing and tail feathers, they can't fly at all. Yet as if flying wasn't straining enough, their landings are even more of a chore. They often crash into the water or tumble onto land, running or stumbling into standing puffins who, presumably, can sympathize.

They are very good underwater swimmers, however, and can grab several small fish at once to bring them home to their nest.

Gaspé Peninsula & Îles de la Madeleine chapter). The eagle owl, a protected species, has been Québec's official bird since 1987 – it can be seen in the St Lawrence River valley as it migrates south from the Arctic tundra in the fall.

The forests are home to black bears, wolves, deer, porcupines, lynxes, coyotes and moose (watch out for these while driving – in a collision, you and your car will lose out just as much as the moose). Polar bears roam Nunavik, mainly around Ungava Bay, but they've been spotted as far south as Kuujjuarapik. There are also caribou (up to a million!) in the far north and in the Parc de la Gaspésie. Keep an eye out for shy beavers, Canada's national animal.

There is plenty of marine life as well. There are millions of seals (best spotted on the ice at the Îles de la Madeleine), thousands of cetaceans (dolphins, porpoises, whales), and countless fish. Tens of thousands of Atlantic salmon return to Québec's rivers and streams to spawn every year, and some of them make it as far west as the Ottawa River.

PARKS & RESERVES

Aside from federally owned and operated parks and conservation areas, the province administers over 40 areas dedicated to nature conservation. The provincial parks (Parc du Bic, for example) are geared toward ecotourism, open to the public for small access fees, and, for extra fees, offer recreational activities such as canoeing, kayaking, rafting, hiking, biking and camping in the wild, and events like full-moon hikes and campfire nature talks.

The Réserves Fauniques (wildlife reserves) have a mandate to conserve and protect the environment and to make these spaces available to the public. The reserves are known mostly to hunters and fishers, who can practice their sports there with the appropriate licenses and permits, but more and more tourists are discovering them as less-crowded alternatives to the provincial parks. The same gamut of charged-for activities is on offer, but in reserves there are fewer services such as information centers, canteens and guided tours.

Both provincial parks and wildlife reserves are run by the Société des Établissements de Plein Air du Québec (Sépaq) (☎ 418-890-6527, 800-665-6527, Ⓦ www. sepaq.com). The parks and reserves tend to be very well run, with clearly marked trails and clean facilities. Their range is vast and impressive. From the miniscule Parc de Miguasha (see the Gaspé Peninsula & Îles de la Madeleine chapter), one of the world's most important sites for Devonian fossils, to the sprawling Réserve Faunique la Vérendrye (see the Northern Québec chapter), five times larger than the state of Rhode Island and boasting a limitless expanse of forests and rivers, each park and reserve offers an array of sporting options and accommodations. Some of the most popular parks include the Parc du Mont Tremblant (see The Laurentians chapter), for its excellent canoeing options, and the Parc de la Gaspésie (see the Gaspé Peninsula & Îles de la Madeleine chapter), with its magnificent mountain ranges and roaming caribou.

Federally administered parks (Forillon National Park, for example) are run by Parks Canada (☎ 418-368-5505, 800-463-6769, Ⓦ www.parkscanada.gc.ca), which often programs excellent educationally oriented events run by highly knowledgeable staff. It also offers a full range of outdoor activities. Though provincial parks can provide information and services in English, you'll find English more often used at these national parks. They also tend to have more information sessions, displays and possibilities for guided tours. Some of the most frequented include Forillon National Park (Gaspésie), for its splendid seascapes and views of the Appalachian Mountains plunging into the sea, and the Mingan Archipelago National Park Reserve (North Shore), for the opportunity to explore islands marked by unique rock formations and rare bird populations.

See regional chapters for details on specific parks and reserves.

UNESCO SITES

Out of 690 Unesco World Heritage Sites on the planet, 13 are in Canada, and two in Québec: Québec City's Old Town and the Parc de Miguasha, on the lower Gaspésie shore.

Out of the 411 Unesco Biosphere Reserves in the world, 11 are in Canada, three of which are in Québec: the entire Charlevoix region (see that chapter), Lac St Pierre (see the Montréal to Québec City chapter) and the Parc du Mont St Hillaire (see the Eastern Townships chapter).

GOVERNMENT & POLITICS

Québec has more than a dozen political parties, but only three are represented in the 125-seat provincial parliament, called Assemblée Nationale (National Assem-

Municipal Mergers

As of January 1, 2002, the map of Québec is set to change in the implementation of a series of municipal mergers throughout the province. That means that Montréal will administratively be turned into a megacity, uniting 105 on- and off-island municipalities. It also means that some other cities will officially lose their names (Jonquière and Chicoutimi will be merged into one Ville de Saguenay, for example).

While the government is hoping to save costs, amalgamate public services and downsize, the move has been extremely unpopular with a majority of the population. Several (unsuccessful) court cases were brought against the province, spearheaded by groups (mainly but not exclusively Anglophone-dominated sectors of Montréal) worried about a decrease in quality of municipal services.

Tourists will be unaffected by the forced mergers. While names of certain small towns and villages will be changed, it will be done gradually, with the original names printed in this book valid, only in some cases as sectors of a larger town instead of towns in their own right.

bly). The leader of the party that gets the most votes in elections becomes minister. The Parti Québécois (PQ), which advocates separation, has 72 seats in the assembly and is led by Premier Bernard Landry. The party was formed by René Lévesque in 1968 with the goal of bringing independence or sovereignty association to Québec.

The Parti Libéral du Québec (PLQ; Liberal Party of Québec), led by Jean Charest, is the Federalist Party and has 49 seats. A single seat is held by the forlorn Parti de l'Action Démocratique du Québec (Democratic Action Party of Québec), which is separatist but very conservative. Three seats were empty in 2001, and opinion polls indicated that if elections were called, the Liberals would win with a majority (they have not been in power since 1994). At press time, elections were scheduled for 2002.

The British electoral system in place throughout Canada places more emphasis on the number of seats a party holds, achieved by winning local 'ridings,' or districts, than the overall vote.

At the federal level, Prime Minister Jean Chretien is a Member of Parliament for the riding of St Maurice in Québec. In the November 2000 election, voters elected his Liberal Party to a third consecutive five-year term, unprecedented in post-WWII Canadian politics. They took 172 seats in the 301-seat House of Commons, one of the two levels of federal parliament. Québec gets to elect 75 of these seats.

The Bloc Québécois, formed by Lucien Bouchard in 1991 to further the cause of separation at the federal level, has seen its representation in Ottawa decrease from 54 seats in 1991 to 44 in 1997 to 38 in the last elections of 2000.

In 2001 the provincial government began responding to accusations of xenophobia in its hiring policies. Despite its demographic makeup (see Population & People), Québec's government's employees count only 2.1% immigrants, 0.7% Anglophones and 0.4% First Nations peoples. Also in that year they launched an equal employment opportunity proposal that calls for an increase in the number of immigrants, handicapped and Native Canadians in government posts to 25%.

ECONOMY

Montréal suffered a deep recession in the early 1990s, and poverty was a major problem: Nearly one in four Montréalers lived below the poverty line. The widespread relocation of companies to Toronto due to uncertainties over Québec's separatist tendencies made things even worse.

The situation was much improved by the millennium's end. Unemployment in the province, which had risen to the double digits, was down to 8.7% in early 2001 (Canada's average is 7%). Montréal's economy grew by 4% in 2000, and inflation was down to about 2%.

The province's economy is made up of its forestry (see that section, earlier), pharmaceutical, aerospace, agricultural, hydroelectric, metallurgy, tourism, information technology as well as multimedia industries. Mining brings in $3.6 billion annually, agriculture $1.7 billion. The province's hydroelectric output is 14.4% of the global production.

However, by the end of 2001, partially as a result of the September terrorist acts in the US and the resulting 'war on terrorism,' and partially due to other factors, the North American economy slowed into what looked like a recession.

POPULATION & PEOPLE

There are 7,400,000 official residents of Québec, accounting for 24% of Canada's population. It's the second most populous province after Ontario. Approximately 83% are Francophone, 8% Anglophone, 8% allophones (those whose first language is neither French nor English, including Italians, Greeks, Portuguese, Vietnamese and Haitians, all mainly concentrated in Montréal), 1% Native Canadian and Inuit (For more on Native Canadians, see the First Nations section). About 46% of the population lives in or around Montréal, and about 80% live in urban centers along

the St Lawrence River. Nearly all of the province's people of color live in Montréal and Québec City – the rest of the province is markedly homogeneous.

Québec has one of lowest birth rates in the developed world (0.3; the national average is only 0.8), and receives only 15% of Canada's new immigrants (compared to Ontario's 55%). Life expectancy for women is 81 years, for men 75, slightly lower than the national average.

EDUCATION

Education in Canada is a provincial responsibility and thus there are different systems in place across the country. School in Québec is obligatory from age six to 16. Instruction is free not only through secondary school, which ends in grade 11, but also into community colleges called Cégeps, which last two years. There are 67 Cégeps in the province, 11 other specialized colleges, as well as 62 private Cégeps (25 of which receive some form of provincial funding).

There are six universities in the province. L'université de Laval, l'université de Montréal and l'université de Sherbrooke teach exclusively in French, and McGill, Concordia, and Bishop's give courses mainly in English. L'université de Montréal, with some 60,000 students, is the largest French university outside of France. McGill, founded in 1821, is still reputed to be one of Canada's finest universities, though its renown has been overshadowed by the University of Toronto. There is also one state university, l'université de Québec, with 11 campuses across the province.

English and French education is still drawn apart on religious lines, between Roman Catholic (French-language) and Protestant (English-language) school boards. Since 1972 all education from kindergarten through high school must be in French, unless for a child with one parent who was educated in English in Canada.

[continued on page 29]

FIRST NATIONS IN QUÉBEC

Beginning in the late 1960s and increasingly throughout the 1990s, Canada's First Nations (the preferred term to describe all aboriginal groups; you'll also hear 'Native Canadian' and the French 'Amérindien') have been asserting their presence in the political and social spheres. They make up one of the most fascinating aspects of today's Canadian cultural landscape. A journey through Québec offers plenty of chances to get acquainted with the groups that have shaped the country's destiny more than is often recognized. In terms of place names alone, six Canadian provinces and countless towns and geographical features come from Native Canadian words, including the word 'Canada' itself!

While Canada never knew outright genocide on aboriginals as transpired in the US, other methods of cultural and social repression were utilized. As Pierre Trudeau put it to Marlon Brando in 1978 when the actor was appealing for funding for a film project about indigenous people, 'There are differences in the way we treated our natives. You hunted them down and murdered them. We starved them to death.'

Native Canadians started sounding a major political voice in protest to a scrapped 1969 federal law that would have abolished reserves and enforced assimilation. A series of land claims followed, many of which are still before the courts. To this day, protests against Canadian big industries like gas and oil exploration that threaten the ecology or lifestyles of First Nations continue across the country, often in the form of roadblocks.

There are 11 First Nations living in Québec. Eight of them belong to the Algonquin cultural and linguistic group, two to the Iroquois (Mohawk and Huron-Wendat), while the Inuit form a distinct group. Together they number 71,500, just under 1% of the total population. This percentage will skyrocket in the next generations, however, as today, half of all Native Canadians living on reserves are under the age of 25.

Standard of living issues among the First Nations remain controversial. Despite tax breaks and government subsidies, issues like outstanding land claims and the struggle for autonomy are compounded by high rates of unemployment, alcohol dependency, violence, suicide and the loss of traditional culture. Québec was the last province to give aboriginals the right to vote – this came, incredibly, only in 1969. Many Native Canadians feel that little has essentially changed in the government's perspective since an 1871 speech made in Manitoba by the province's lieutenant governor to a group of Native Canadians about to sign the first major treaty with the government:

> Your Great Mother (Queen Victoria) wishes the good of all races under her sway. She wishes her red children to be happy and contented…She would like them to adopt the habits of the whites, to till land and raise food, and store it up against a time of want.

In 2001 the federal government was in the process of renegotiating changes to the outdated Indian Act of 1876. The system of funds distribution, for one thing, appears to have many holes in it. Over $7 billion in grants and handouts are given annually to the nation's 600 native bands, yet many Native Canadians continue to live in dire poverty.

If embarking on First Nations–organized tours, it's good to keep in

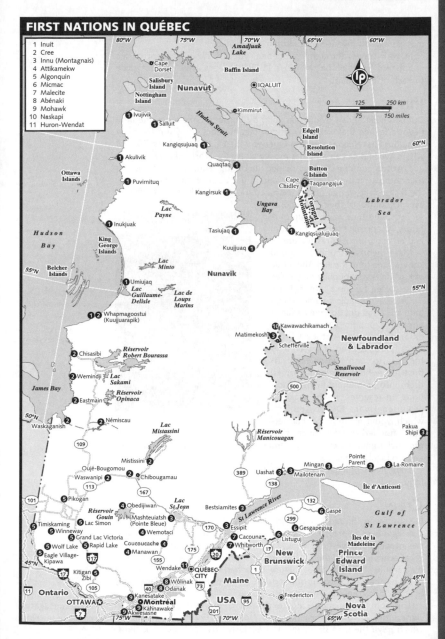

FIRST NATIONS IN QUÉBEC

1 Inuit
2 Cree
3 Innu (Montagnais)
4 Attikamekw
5 Algonquin
6 Micmac
7 Malecite
8 Abénaki
9 Mohawk
10 Naskapi
11 Huron-Wendat

mind that the locals have a more relaxed rhythm of doing things that may jar against mile-a-minute urban sensibilities.

In your travels throughout Québec, you are likely to meet or see members of some of the province's 11 First Nations. Here's a brief guide to each of the groups.

Innu

Dubbed Montagnais (Mountain Folk) by European explorers, the Innu have reclaimed their original name in recent years. They are the most populous First Nations group in Québec with 14,300 members, 70% of whom live in nine communities mostly along the North Shore. They are a dynamic community that helped incoming Europeans set up fur trading posts in the 17th century, and in the 20th century were among the first to take charge of their own communities. They were the first to assume control of their educational services, and they have set up outfitters, shopping malls, a museum and an ecotourism infrastructure.

Many people around the world know of the Innu through the music of Kashtin, a very popular singer (see Music, later, for more information).

Once a nomadic people, many Innu still head out on long caribou-hunting expeditions into their traditional territories – at least those areas not destroyed or affected by the forestry and hydroelectric industries, which originally forced them into permanent living conditions on reserves. In the wake of proposed Hydro Québec projects which would see more of their territory flooded or taken over, they are currently negotiating with the provincial government an agreement that would outline land rights and political autonomy.

Their first language is Innu, then French. *Kwe kwe* means 'hello' in Innu.

Cree

In some ways the most visible First Nations group in the province, the Cree number some 13,100 in nine communities along James Bay and in the interior northwest of Lac St Jean. Visibility came in the form of political activism. When the Québec government first made approaches to the community in the 1960s (before, there had been virtually no contact between them), it was out of the desire to build the massive James Bay hydroelectric complex – on traditional Cree hunting territory.

The community mobilized to defend their rights, and in 1975 signed the historic James Bay and Northern Québec Agreement, which gave them $135 million and exclusive use and hunting rights

Left: The Innu and French languages are seen along the North Shore.

to northern lands. In 1984 they signed the Cree-Naskapi Act with the federal government, which for these two groups replaced the Indian Act of 1876. More formidably, in the early 1990s the Cree successfully blocked another Hydro Québec megaproject on rivière Grande Baleine (Great Whale River) in a brilliant campaign that brought them to Ottawa and New York City. They successfully lobbied for New York State to cancel its $17 billion contract to buy electricity from Québec (partly by bringing Robert Kennedy Jr up north for some rafting!), and the $7 billion project withered away along with Hydro Québec's international reputation.

In 2001, however, they agreed to sign another deal that would allow further hydroelectric development in the James Bay area. Impetus to do so is mainly economic – many say that through bad investments, the community has little money left to solve serious problems of alcohol addiction, a high unemployment rate, violence and suicide in some of their problem villages like Chisasibi.

The group remains highly organized, owns an airline and is slowly making forays into ecotourism. The second language, after Cree (which is written in syllabics, like Inuit), is English. *Watchiya* means 'hello, welcome'; *Taan aa ihtiyin*? is 'how are you?'

Mohawk

Another group with high visibility is the Mohawk nation, which numbers about 11,000 in three communities in southwestern Québec. Kahnawake is just across the Mercier bridge from Montréal, Kanesatake is 53km west of Montréal at Oka, and Akwesane straddles the Québec, Ontario and New York borders. Being so close to urban centers, many Mohawk have integrated to some degree with Québécois society.

In 1990 Mohawks made headlines around the world when residents of Kanesatake took up armed resistance to fight the building of a golf club on land they considered sacred, near Oka. Residents of Kahnawake also participated in what became one of Canada's biggest land claim crises and led to military intervention. It was led by a controversial Mohawk subgroup, the Warriors, who had previously operated illegal casinos and smuggling operations on other reserves. However, public opinion backed their claims. The several-week standoff left one policeman dead and resulted in Ottawa buying the land in question to give back to the Mohawks. It cooled things down, but many issues remain unresolved.

Mohawks, part of the Iroquois cultural and linguistic group along with the Huron-Wendats, are the only survivors of the once mighty Five Nations of Iroquois groups. They practiced 'slash and burn' agriculture and lived in longhouses with up to 20 to 30 families living together. Traditionally they had the reputation of being fierce fighters, expert navigators and excellent construction workers on skyscrapers! They run their own schools and businesses, and have their own police force, the Peacekeepers.

Most Mohawk speak English as a first language, then Mohawk and French.

Inuit

In Nunavik, the most northerly and most remote region of the province, 9200 Inuit (a word meaning 'person') live in 14 villages, spread hundreds of kilometers apart with no roads to link them. Each village is administered by an elected mayor. Kuujjuaq (pop 1800), on the south tip of Ungava Bay, is considered the 'capital.' These were the last peoples to have regular contact with whites, and while the fur trade affected their lives as early as the 18th century, it wasn't until the mid–20th century that federal services began to play a dominant role in their everyday lives. They abandoned their traditional hunting weapons only in the last two generations.

In a short time, the Inuit have formed a co-operative that controls the distribution of food and goods in their territory, they run their own airline and outfitters, and they have developed a system to promote and distribute their unique arts, crafts and clothing in the south. Their signing of the James Bay and Northern Québec Agreement with the Québec government in 1975 kick-started their economy: They were given $90 million, and they invested the money well. Within a few decades they have undergone an almost total transformation in lifestyle. However, like their playful language Inuktitut (written in syllabics), the Inuit are flexible and adaptable.

While the cooperative has its share of problems and corruption, while the community struggles to maintain its traditions despite the onslaught of seductive Western culture, and while the Nunavik communities debate whether to push for total self-government (like the Inuit of Nunavut in Northern Canada), the Inuit still live on the land their forefathers hunted 4500 years ago.

A few words: *ai* ('hello'); *nakurmiik* ('thank you'); *Qiujavunga* ('I'm cold').

Algonquin

Only about half of Québec's 8300 Algonquin live in their nine reserves in the Abitibi-Témiscamingue and Outaouais regions; the rest live in cities like Senneterre and Val d'Or. Many still preserve their nomadic tradition by spending the wintertime hunting in camps in the vast forests of the region.

In the late 1980s and early 1990s the Algonquin signed preliminary agreements with the provincial and federal governments on land claims that have yet to be ratified.

Algonquin is spoken in the communities, with French or English being the second language.

Left: The Inuit created the *inukshuiit*, stone statues shaped like people, to aid them in caribou hunting. See 'The Inukshuk,' in the Northern Québec chapter, for details.

Attikamekw

Some 5300 Attikamekw (pronounced 'ati-ka-MEK') live in three communities in the Haute Mauricie region around La Tuque. Europeans charmingly dubbed their ancestors, the O'pimittish Ininiwac, *Têtes de boules* (Ball Heads), probably referring to their hairstyles. They were actually known as such until 1972!

Their history was particularly difficult – almost completely decimated by disease and Iroquois massacres in the 17th century, a few families sought refuge with the Cree until they joined with survivors from near Lake Superior to settle in the forests of central Québec. In the early 20th century, however, they were forced to concede territory and relocate as the forestry industry began the merciless exploitation of the region's natural resources.

The Attikamekw administer their own education, health and social service programs, but have several unresolved claims with the federal and provincial governments. They are also involved in sustainable management programs for the forests in their area, and own 55% of the Donahue Inc sawmill on their territory. They had been making maple syrup for centuries before they taught the Europeans how to do it, so we have them to thank for Canada's best-tasting export.

Micmac

The only aboriginal people with a true maritime tradition, the Micmac number about 4550 people in the Baie des Chaleurs region of the Gaspésie. Some also live near the town of Gaspé, and another 15,000 live in the maritime provinces. During Canada's colonization period, they were in close contact with the French, with whom they allied against the British.

Known for their intricate craftsmanship, producing ash and sweetgrass-woven baskets, they are also involved in tourism ventures and manage several salmon-fishing outfitters.

Huron-Wendat

This nation has had a troubled history that saw it reduced from a powerful confederation of over 30,000 members to just 300 in half a century by epidemics and vicious intertribal warfare. The Iroquois launched a campaign of extermination against its members in 1648–49 and nearly wiped them off the map. Originally centered in the Great Lakes region, the surviving families reestablished themselves in Québec in 1650, first on Île d'Orléans and then at Wendake, north of Québec City, where they remain. They were the main allies of the French in the early days of the fur trade, and many converted to Christianity at the time. Today the Huron-Wendats number 2900, 1100 of whom live in Wendake.

While they have lost their original language (most speak French as a first language) and culture through generations of intermarriage, they have also fought hard to regain as much as they can. The word 'Canada' comes from the Huron-Wendat word *kanata,* meaning 'village, settlement.' Their tourist village (see Wendake in the Québec City chapter) is now widely visited, and their local economy is healthy thanks to a snowshoe-making factory.

In 1990 the federal government upheld a 1760 treaty granting the Huron-Wendat nation the right to freely practice their religion and customs on their lands. The terms for implementing this are still being worked out.

Abenaki

The Abenaki arrived in Québec in the 17th century from the New England states, eventually settling in two regions on the southern shores of the St Lawrence River. Today there are about 2000 Abenakis, only 380 of whom live in the villages of Odanak and Wôlinak. The rest live and work in surrounding areas like Trois Rivières, and all speak French. There have been some efforts to revive their language, but with little success.

As a community, they are involved in arts and crafts, tourism and run an outfitter in the Haute Mauricie. *Kwai* in Abenaki means 'hello.'

Malecite

This group had been nearly erased from the map before undergoing a revival in 1987. A nomadic tribe, their traditional territory was the Lower St Lawrence between Lévis and Rimouski. A reserve was formed in 1827 near Isle Verte, but in 1869 the territory was ceded to the government under pressure from the local population, who wished to cultivate these fertile lands. Malecites, unused to permanent settlement, didn't seem interested in doing it. After this, the community scattered to different areas and integrated with the larger population.

In 1987, 130 Malecite gathered, elected a chief and decided to re-constitute the nation. Two years later the provincial government officially recognized them as Québec's 11th aboriginal nation. Today they own territories near Rivière du Loup and Cacouna, where many are active in arts and crafts. They number about 650, but do not live on reserves. Their first language tends to be French.

Naskapi

Québec's smallest First Nations group, the Naskapi, number only 560, all of whom live in the isolated community of Kawawachikamach, north of Schefferville. They are traditional caribou hunters who used to live with the Inuit near Kuujjuaq. In efforts to improve their living conditions, they resettled several times before choosing their present location in 1978, moving there in 1984. That year, the federal Cree-Naskapi Act granted them administrative autonomy and $9 million, which they used wisely. Good thing, as the closing of mines in Schefferville in 1982 essentially shut down economic activity in the region, and the Naskapi had to struggle even harder to survive.

They are considered the greatest experts in caribou hunting, and much of their artistic products are made from caribou skin, bones and antlers. Their territory, where taiga and tundra meet, is prime caribou migratory land. They also excel at adventure tourism in the far north and operate outfitters.

Naskapis speak their original language, and most also speak English and French.

[continued from page 21]

ARTS

Dance

Every year, it seems as if there's another new dance festival or performing arts troupe to expand Québec's fertile contemporary dance scene. Increasing numbers of new choreographers pour out of schools or migrate to Montréal, the country's dance capital – and competition is fierce. Newcomers and better-known experimentalists can be seen at Studio 303, which also mounts events such as IMF, a group of improvisers.

Montréal's most famous dance soloist is Margie Gillis, who has been performing for over a quarter of a century. You can catch her exploring contemporary experiments or breathing new life into works by Leonard Cohen and George Gershwin. Choreographers on the cutting edge include Suzanne Miller, Allan Paivio, Lin Snelling, Hetty King, Lina Cruz and Lydia Wagerer.

Carbone 14 (founded by Gilles Maheu) and La La La Human Steps (founded by Édouard Lock) have both been around since 1980 and are among the most exhilarating creative modern troupes on the continent – any show of theirs is bound to be an experience. Carbone 14's *Le Dortoir* and La La La's *Salt* are particularly memorable.

Montréal boasts several ballet troupes with international reputations. Les Grands Ballets Canadiens attracts large audiences to the Place des Arts with evergreens such as *Carmen* and *The Nutcracker*.

Music

Québécois have more of a tendency to focus on lyrics in the music they take to heart than the rest of their North American neighbors. Most popular have been those performers whose lyrical contributions are at least equal to their musical talents. Partially this is due to the tradition of the *chanson*, or folk song, which deepened in the 1960s during the Quiet Revolution's consciousness-raising. Down-to-earth songs sung in local dialect about local issues and feelings were ways to harvest a sense of a distinct community and cultural connectedness.

Francophone Music Until the 1960s Québec was more receptive to pop from France, with stars such as Johnny Halliday and Charles Aznavour topping the charts. But in the 1960s and 1970s a new generation of Québécois singers emerged with their own brand of pop, mixing traditional Québec folk songs with rock, pop and chanson elements.

Gilles Vigneault painted a portrait of the province in more than 100 recordings between 1960 and 1996 (see 'Québec's Most Loved *Pays*an' in the North Shore chapter). Along with legends Félix Leclerc, Raymond Lévesque and Claude Léveillé, Vigneault is the most prominent of a generation of songwriters who advocated independence for Québec. Another veteran *chansonnier* is Jean-Pierre Ferland.

Harmonium released only three albums in the 1970s, but are to this day considered to embody the soul of Québec in their music. Highly orchestral, at times experimental with their folk-rock tunes, their lyrics touched an emotional chord during the period of nationalist consciousness-raising; it's a chord that's still resounding today among fans young and old. They often performed in the US in the mid-1970s and had a cult following there as well. Highly recommended to accompany your journey throughout the province are their first two albums, *Harmonium* and *Les cinq seasons*. The music blends seamlessly with the landscape.

Offenbach and Beau Dommage (with Michel Rivard) are other popular bands from the 1970s.

Jean Leloup has a strong fan base, and his concerts generate a frenzy sometimes bordering on hysteria. He scored a modest hit across Canada with *1990,* and his latest CD, 2001's *Les fourmis,* showcases his continued evolution, embracing blues, improvisation, and kick-ass rock and roll.

Another artist in every good Québécois' collection is Richard Desjardins. His lyrics reflect nature and philosophy more than politics, and his simple, folky tunes have won the hearts of young and old. Fans say *Boom Boom* is his best. Daniel Boucher became a hot name in 2000 with his *Un bon Québécois*.

Three bands in the rock-folk tradition whose energy knows no bounds are Les Colocs, Loco Locass and La Bottine Souriante, the last being a fun group that believes in the power of the fiddle. All three are phenomenal live.

Other well-known names include Roch Voisine, Daniel Bélanger, Laurence Jalbert, Richard Séguin, Robert Charleboix, Kevin Parent, Diane Tell, Diane Dufresne and Nanette Workman.

Anglophone Music Céline Dion, from the town of Charlemagne, 30km east of Montréal, was a star in Canada long before her superstar status in the US and 'My Heart Will Go On' from the movie *Titanic*. In 1983 she became the first Canadian to get a platinum record in France. Although her worldwide success followed fame in the US, many remember how she turned down a Félix Award (the Québec equivalent to the Grammy) for English-Speaking Artist of 1990 with the words 'I am not an Anglophone artist.'

Another international name in English music from Québec is Bran Van 3000, fronted by James DiSalvio and James Donovan. Their big hit *Drinking in LA* from their first CD *Glee* knew modest success in the US and Europe, and their second effort,

Vive Céline Dion!

Discosis (2001), was one of the bravest, most conceptual releases of the year.

Leonard Cohen is no doubt the world's most revered Montréal songwriter (see 'The Spirit of St Leonard'). Rufus Wainwright, the son of poet Loudon Wainwright III and singer Kate McGarrigle, is a Montréaler whose brand of piano- and guitar-driven pop folk has spawned a cult following in the US, particularly after 2001's excellent, highly personal *Poses*.

On the pop side there's Corey Hart, whose *Boy in the Box* album enjoyed success throughout North America in the 1980s. Men Without Hats, known around the world for their hits 'The Safety Dance' and 'Pop Goes the World,' also hail from Montréal and remained creative even beyond commercial success.

In the 1970s Montréal was a big producer of disco music, with dozens of dance songs shaking the booties of people across the continent. Gino Soccio, Geraldine Hunt, Freddie James, Martin Stevens, Voggue, Cheri, France Joli and Patsy Gallant all had hits in the US and Canada.

Other Kashtin is a very popular Innu singer whose music is known around the world. His tour de force first CD, *Innu,* incorporates elements of traditional music.

Lhasa, singing in Spanish, surprises with her passionate global sound.

Legendary pianist Oscar Peterson is Montréal's most famous jazz musician, known for his dexterity and dazzling speed on scores of recordings. Other high-profile jazz names include screech trumpet star Maynard Ferguson, vocalist Karen Young, pianist and vocalist Diana Krall and pianist Oliver Jones.

As for personalities on the classical-music scene, the Orchestre Métropolitain's 26-year-old new director, Montréaler Yannick Nézet-Séguin, is among the youngest to lead a major orchestra in Canada.

Montréal's best-known classical composer is Jean Papineau-Couture, whose works are noted for their modernism in the tradition of Stravinsky. André Gagnon has released dozens of albums of soft classical piano music, notably *Le Saint Laurent* (1977).

The Spirit of St Leonard

Leonard Cohen is one of the world's most eclectic folk artists, and doubtlessly Montréal's most respected musical export. Born here in 1934, he studied English literature at McGill, then at New York's Columbia University. After a false start in the music business, he published several volumes of poetry and two novels, *The Favourite Game* (1963) and *Beautiful Losers* (1966), each of which sold over one million copies.

His songwriting eventually garnered him much attention with three spectacularly confessional first albums, *Songs of Leonard Cohen* (1968), *Songs from a Room* (1969), and *Songs of Love and Hate* (1970), literally poetry in motion. His compositions carry an aura of romantic, semi-suicidal despair, but also a great deal of self-deprecating humor and psychological insight.

A second wave of musical output in the 1980s produced *I'm Your Man* (1988) and *The Future* (1992), which made him hip all over again to a new generation. In recent years he has been living in California and turned his attention to Buddhist philosophy, which no doubt calmed his soul enough to come out with his most unhurried work yet, *Ten New Songs* (2001).

Literature

In the first part of the 20th century, the peasant novel, which sprung from a general idealization of country life, took root in Québec. Land and religion were the main values for French-speaking people who felt denied nationhood. *Maria Chapdelaine* (1913), by Louis Hémon, is the most famous example of this period, and touched a contemporary nerve in its dealing with the decision many were tormenting over – to move to New England to work in factories or take up agriculture in Québec. Honoré Beaugrand's *Jeanne la Fileuse* was about a young woman who had moved to the US.

The church punished by way of censure, attack and funding withdrawal those authors who dared dismiss clerical values. Émile Nelligan and authors and poets of the École Littéraire de Montréal risked such punishment by producing highly individualistic works exploring inner desires, which the church found threatening. Up until the end of WWII, rural life was the main source of inspiration for novelists, even as it was slowly disappearing from real life.

In 1948 a group of artists and writers signed the *Refus Global* (Global Refusal), a manifesto to counter traditional, orthodox constraints in art. More experimentation ensued. Gabrielle Roy's *Bonheur d'Occasion* (The Tin Flute; 1945) is a classic in Canadian literature, and won Roy prizes in Canada and France. In this and later works, she poignantly depicted the lives of Montréal's poor to point to larger societal ills.

In the 1960s the consequences of not asserting nationhood were spelled out in popular works like Hubert Aquin's *Prochain Épisode* and Jacques Godbout's *Le Couteau sur la table*. Never was the point that the French occupy a disadvantaged position as a result of colonization driven deeper than in Jacques Vallières' autobiographical *Nègres blanc d'Amérique* (White Niggers of America; 1969).

An important author who wrote in the street vernacular called *joual* and explored the role of women in Québec's transforming society is playwright Michel Tremblay. *Les Belles Soeurs* (1968) is his signature piece. Anne Hébert is another major novelist, notably for *Le Temps sauvage*, *Kamouraska* and *Les Fous de Bassans*.

On the English side, Mordecai Richler was certainly the best known author from Québec. *The Apprenticeship of Duddy Kravitz*, *Joshua Then and Now* and *St Urbain's Horseman* are regarded as Canadian classics. Much of his early work depicted life in Jewish tenements and delis of 1950s Montréal. His later essays blasted the separatist movement.

The Montréal Group of poets caused a renaissance of Canadian poetry during the 1920s and 1930s by advocating a break with traditional landscape poetry. Its members – who included AJM Smith, AM Klein, Leo

Kennedy and Francis Reginald Scott – encouraged realism, metaphysical complexity and expressionist techniques already used by Ezra Pound, TS Eliot and others. Smith's *Book of Canadian Poetry* (1943) is regarded as a landmark work.

Other familiar names include novelist-essayist Hugh MacLennan and poet Irving Layton. Montréal first became a character in its own right in MacLennan's *The Watch That Ends the Night* (1959). Set in the 1930s, the city becomes a love object in and of itself, and there are wonderfully descriptive passages about rue Ste Catherine. He was the first author to take the risky, self-confident step of situating Canadian novels in specifically Canadian settings, instead of de-emphasizing locale to make them more palatable for international audiences.

Mavis Gallant has been a major literary voice since she published her first stories in the mid-1940s. Though she has called Paris home since 1950, many of her stories have reflected life in wartime Montréal, where she had a miserable childhood – rejected by her parents, she was placed in 17 schools, some lorded over by infamously fearsome nuns. Most of her stories have been published in *The New Yorker,* and in the early 1980s she received some of Canada's highest literary awards. Her *Home Truths: Selected Canadian Stories* (1981) includes some of her best Montréal-themed narratives.

In the realm of theater, David Fennario's *Balconville* scrutinizes the lives of middle-class Montréalers whose summer holidays are limited to their balconies. He strove to forge community ties on the basis of class, not language, emphasizing how exploiters and exploited spoke both languages.

Painting

Québec has produced mainly landscape artists, though in the past several decades, this is much less true than it used to be. Clarence Gagnon (1881–1942) is known for his subtle snowscapes, moving depictions of rural life around Baie St Paul and later Impressionistic works; the work of Jean-Paul Lemieux (1904–90) is more somber. In the early 20th century Horatorio Walker

(1858–1938) captured urban and country scenes of the Victorian era.

Adrien Hébert (1890–1967) and Robert Pilot (1897–1967) became famous for their snowy portraits of Montréal and Québec City. Their lively street scenes were a departure from the romantic classicism that was popular among the previous generation of painters, which included William Brymmer (1855–1925) and Antoine Plamondon (1804–95).

Paul-Émile Borduas (1905–60) and Jean-Paul Riopelle (b 1923) went a step further with their convictions. By cosigning the Refus Global in 1948, they rose against the era's traditional Canadian landscape painting and dedicated themselves to abstract art.

Marc-Aurèle Fortin (1880–1972) became famous for his watercolors of the Québec countryside, particularly the treescapes of the Laurentian Mountains and Charlevoix. His portraits of majestic Dutch elms along Montréal avenues recall the era when the trees were not yet ravaged by disease.

Cinema

The Québécois film industry is the envy of the rest of Canada. Easily the most vibrant cinema industry in the country, it also has a guaranteed homegrown audience. While most English Canadian films flop at the box office, some Québec films have outstripped even major American releases and entered cultural lore profoundly.

Québec cinema has a long tradition going back to the 1930s, such as Maurice Proulx's documentaries about the colonization of the Abitibi region. It wasn't until those magical 1960s, however, when the cinema's form became freer, and, with the main focus on words and ideas, film became a powerful medium and channel for national affirmation.

The late 1960s and 1970s produced Québécois-cinema classics like *Mon oncle Antoine,* by Claude Jutra, considered by many as the best film ever made in Canada; *Kamouraska,* also by Jutra; *Isabel,* by Paul Almond; and *La vraie nature de Bernadette,* by Gilles Carle. All incorporated landscape into their stories.

In the 1980s local cinema burst onto the international scene with the highly acclaimed *Le Déclin de l'empire américain* (The Decline of the American Empire), by Denys Arcand, which casts a wry, light look at male/female relationships. Arcand also took a dig at the Catholic Church with *Jésus of Montréal,* which revolves around a modern production of the Passion Play. Jean-Claude Lauzon's *Un zoo la nuit* and *Léolo* put surrealism and psychoanalysis in a high-speed blender.

François Girard's stylish epic *The Red Violin* weaves together five stories about a single violin as it travels through three centuries and the hands of prominent owners. The film won an Oscar for best original score in 1998. Girard also directed the beautiful *Thirty-Two Short Films about Glenn Gould,* which provided insight into the reclusive pianist's mind.

Feminism and female sexuality continue to be strong themes among Montréal's women directors. Lea Pool's *Emporte-Moi* (Set Me Free) is a drama about the emotional consequences of a young girl's emerging sexuality. Her earlier works, like *La Femme de l'Hôtel* (1984) and *Anne Trister* (1985), were also concerned with these themes. Margaret Wescott produced a powerful chronicle of lesbian history in *Stolen Moments.*

Pierre Falardeau has been one of the industry's most controversial figures, mainly for his strong takes on some of Québec's thorniest issues, like the October Crisis *(Octobre),* the Patriot's revolt *(15 février 1839),* and the French people's place in English Canada, effectively paralleled in 1989's excellent *Le party.* His 1981 comedy *Elvis Gratton* is one every Québécois has seen.

Pierre Perrault is another major force in Québec cinema. His fascinating *cinéma vérité* documentaries of the 1960s, some with Michel Brault, explored the lives of those in remote communities. Some were so evocative they're called *films-poèmes.* His 1982 *La Bête Lumineuse* (The Shimmering Beast) is a standout, ostensibly about a moose hunt but really about buddyship and the Québec soul.

Animation and multimedia technologies have become something of a Montréal specialty, thanks in large part to the success of Softimage, a company founded by Daniel Langlois, a special-effects guru and former director. Softimage created some of the first 3-D animation software and was behind the special effects used in *Jurassic Park, Godzilla* and *Titanic.* Frédéric Back won an Oscar for his beautifully animated *The Man Who Planted Trees.*

Québec has also produced several high-profile actors, including William (Captain Kirk) Shatner and Geneviève Bujold, who starred in a variety of films in Canada and abroad, including *Anne of the Thousand Days,* for which she received an Academy Award nomination. One of the biggest TV and film stars is Roy Dupuis, an actor with as much talent as sex appeal.

SOCIETY & CONDUCT

In general, French Québécois tend to be down-to-earth and not big on ceremony or pretense. People switch over to the informal personal address *tu* much more quickly here than in France, where the formal, polite *vous* is more dominant in social interactions. There is a sense of not wanting to show oneself as better than others, and many project an earthy quality of straightforwardness often missing in their Anglophone counterparts. Francophones also have a reputation of being more fun-loving and raucous at get-togethers than their more reserved English neighbors.

French usually greet each other with a kiss on each cheek (often resulting in much-parodied air kisses). Between men this is seen less often. English Montréalers have adopted this habit to some degree, though a kiss on one cheek usually suffices for them. This occasionally results in comical head bobbing when people greeting each other are unsure whether to give one or two kisses, or none at all.

Though most tourist facilities in the province, from information kiosks to B&Bs, will understand English to some degree, you'll get much further in personal interactions if you initiate contact with French-speakers with a phrase or two in French (see the Language chapter). They'll take it as a sign of politeness and respect.

RELIGION

In the 17th-century's mad dash to colonize France and England's new territories, religion was to play a major role. In their bids to convert the native population, each country's churches used their respective faiths in an often-deadly power struggle between Catholicism and Protestantism. The Native Canadians were caught in the middle.

The church's role in Québec's history, exploration and social development – right up until the 1960s – cannot be underestimated. If the endless reams of place names beginning with 'Sainte' don't convince you, perhaps the dozens of roadside crucifixes and statues of Jesus or Mary lining roads and ornamenting lawns throughout the province will.

Catholicism has always reigned mighty here (about 86% of the province's population is listed as Catholic) because of French domination but also reinforced by Italian, Greek and Polish immigrants. On the Protestant side (8% of the population), the Anglican church has predominated – their churches can be found from Montréal to Nunavik. Montréal also has a sizeable (3%) Jewish population, including a large Hassidic Orthodox community. Immigrants from Asia and North Africa have introduced Hinduism and Islam, respectively, to Québec.

The church has played an ever-lessening role in Québécois society since WWII, but especially after the Quiet Revolution.

LANGUAGE

The most divisive issue in the province has traditionally been language. Although nearly 10% of the population speak a language other than English or French at home, the difference between the 'two solitudes' (French and English) becomes especially marked when addressing this issue. In early 2001 a large-scale survey of language attitudes in Montréal conducted by the Missisquoi institute underscored the varying perceptions of the English and French-speaking communities. Asked whether the French language is threatened in Québec, 61% of Francophones and 22% of Anglophones agreed. Yet asked whether the future of English in the province is threatened, 66% of Anglophones and only 14% of Francophones agreed.

The French may have long dominated the social spheres, but traditionally it was the English who ran the businesses, made decisions, held positions of power and accumulated wealth. As the Québec separatist movement gathered pace, the Ottawa government sought to assuage Francophones by passing the Official Languages Act in 1969, which required all federal services to be offered in French and English. Only then did Canada become officially bilingual.

By the 1980s most positions of power in the province were held by the French, leading to other social groups complaining of discrimination and favoritism. Indeed, in 2001 the provincial government was scrambling to counteract accusations of racism by increasing its representation of minorities (Anglophones, immigrants and First Nations) in government positions from a negligible 3.2% to 25%.

As conflict-ridden as the language debate has been over the years, it has also led to a level of functional bilingualism, which has given Montréal charm and dynamism. Most of the 19% of Montréalers whose mother tongue is English are conversant in French, and many immigrants have become trilingual. Fewer Francophones today than in the 1970s feel that their language is threatened.

To get to this state, some strict language laws were introduced, starting timidly with Law 63, introduced in 1969 by the PLQ under Jean Lesage, which stated the need to protect the French language. In 1973 Robert Bourassa's Law 22 upped the ante, making French Québec's official language and limiting the choice of schooling. The law was excoriated by Anglophones who felt violated and by Francophones who felt it didn't go far enough.

In 1977 the PQ's Law 101 made French the only language permitted in business and social affairs, including commercial signs and posters. An *Office de la langue française* was set up to ensure that only French was used and visible in the province (though in practice this meant in Montréal and surrounding areas). By the late 1980s complaints by the English community led the Supreme Court to denounce Law 101 as unconstitutional. Later the UN would also denounce the law as infringing on individual rights.

In reaction, Bourassa's PLQ first allowed English on indoor signs in very limited conditions, then eventually adopted Law 86 in 1993, which softened Law 101 and permitted English on indoor and outdoor signs as long as French letters were two-thirds larger than English. Later PQ governments never scrapped the law, though in campaign speeches they promised to.

The legacy of these laws was an exodus of many Anglophone residents and businesses from Montréal and a deepening division between the two language groups. There were also many cases where French-only enforcement bordered on hysteria: bricks through windows of a Second Cup coffee store and shops with words like 'Sale' in their windows; forcing English workers in English companies to communicate with each other in French, to use French computer programs and address their Canadian or US business partners in French first; renaming dozens of lakes and mountains to eradicate English-sounding names; citizens reporting on Eastern Townships' stores or motels that had any kind of English-only signs, etc.

However, the measures have been successful in asserting the predominance of French in all levels of Québec society. Most English sympathize with this and feel that it is right that French be the official language. In retrospect, such laws were the natural reaction (if at times overreaction) of a people who for centuries were not made to feel *chez nous* (at home). A harmonious balance seems to have been struck in Montréal in any case, where the city's true face of bilingualism is showing once again.

For more information about the French spoken in Québec, see the Language chapter.

Facts for the Visitor

SUGGESTED ITINERARIES

If your time is limited in Québec, it would be best to give your trip a theme. In other words, focus. If it's Québécois culture you want, discover Montréal and Québec City, catch a folk concert, eat a few traditional meals and visit a Native Canadian reserve. Nature lovers will want a minimum amount of time in the cities to better concentrate on the national and provincial parks. For outdoor adventure, pick your favorite region and plunge into its wilderness. Bird and animal lovers can easily fill up a few weeks with exotic excursions.

Any extensive travel plans in Québec need to take the area's size, diversity and seasonal weather conditions into consideration.

One Week

With only seven days in Québec, you'll limit yourself to Montréal and Québec City, possibly with a few excursions to their surrounding areas. Within the cities themselves, there are veritable world-class attractions and sites, museums and great areas for strolls, not to mention Montréal's seductive cosmopolitan charms. From Montréal, you can easily make day trips to the elegant Eastern Townships for some wine tasting and sumptuous scenery or to the Laurentians for a taste of their grand, rolling mountains and wide open spaces. From Québec City, it's only a 90-minute drive to the Charlevoix region and its undulating valleys and superb views onto the St Lawrence river. From either city, it's possible to spend at least one night in a nearby provincial park or wildlife reserve.

Two Weeks

With two weeks, you'll be able to push out farther beyond the two main cities, though the North Shore, Gaspésie, Îles de la Madeleine and northern Québec will remain difficult if not impossible to fit in.

It would be a tight fit, but from Montréal, you can head to Hull, then north through the Outaouais region and back south through the Laurentians and Lanaudière. Then continue on to Québec City, passing through Trois Rivières. From Québec City, travel as far east as Tadoussac and spend a few days in its surrounding areas, including a trip up the Saguenay River. Pick up one of the ferries to the south shore and return to Montréal via the Lower St Lawrence and Chaudière-Appalaches regions.

Three Weeks

An extra week will allow you to spend more time in the above-mentioned regions, as well as permit a trip deeper into the Saguenay region, farther up the North Shore, or to the Gaspé Peninsula. Alternatively, push farther north into the Abitibi-Témiscamingue and James Bay regions. Yet another recommended option is a trip north of Trois Rivières toward La Tuque, to spend time in forests of beautiful, remote wilderness.

One Month or More

Though a month is still not enough to cover the entire province properly, four weeks will give you enough time to get to the Îles de la Madeleine, a true gem. From Gaspé, it's just a 40-minute flight. Count on spending at least four days there. Or, from the North Shore you could head to the wild Île d'Anticosti. If you have two weeks to spend in this area, you can take the Nordik Express boat to the distant fishing communities on the North Shore. Alternatively, you can arrange a trip up to the far north, to the Inuit communities in Nunavik.

PLANNING
When to Go

Québec is truly a year-round destination. Its reputation for punishing, blistering winters has been, for the most part, much exaggerated. Sure, -40°C temperatures *are* possible in the far north, but the climate in the south is generally milder than people assume. Plus, think of the reputation as a hardcore adventurer you'll have after returning from Québec in February!

If you're planning to spend your time skiing and visiting the cities, a winter visit won't present any major hurdles. Winter tourism is increasing with many outfitters offering dogsledding, downhill and cross-country skiing, fishing and other winter outdoor activities. Also Canada's ballet, opera and symphony seasons run through the winter months.

Spring, summer and autumn are all ideal for touring. The far north is best in summer as daylight hours are long. Many of the country's festivals are held over the summer (one notable exception being Québec City's Winter Carnival; see that chapter for details). While summer arrives in Montréal by May, in the areas north and east of Québec City the official summer season is considered to last from St Jean Baptiste Day (June 24) to Labour Day (first Monday in September). While every year new efforts are being made to extend the tourist season beyond these dates, the farther away you get from major centers, the greater your chances are of finding some attractions either closed or operating on shorter hours. However, advantages are the slower pace, lack of crowds and lower prices.

'March break' is a mid-month, weeklong intermission for elementary and high school students. Many people take this as an opportune time for a holiday, and all trains, planes and buses are generally very busy.

For campers, July and August are the only reliably hot months. However, because the

weather is usually great, the last two weeks of July have the disadvantage of being the so-called 'construction holiday.' This is when factories and heavy industries close down and all their workers – and families – go on vacation. Tourist sites can be unpleasantly jammed at this time, and lodging is often booked solid – plan accordingly.

Maps

Good provincial road maps are available from local tourist offices. Many general maps are given out free, and there are more detailed foldout maps and road atlases (recommended if you'll be doing a lot of driving) on sale. Bookstores generally sell both provincial and city maps. Gas stations often have road maps as well.

The Canada Map Office (☎ 613-952-7000, 800-465-6277, ⓦ www.nrcan.gc.ca) produces heaps of topographic maps of anywhere in the country.

What to Bring

Travelers to Canada have no real need for any special articles. Those with allergies or particular medical ailments or conditions should bring their customary medicines and supplies. Extra prescription glasses and/or contact lenses are always a good idea, as is having a copy of your prescription with you. A small travel alarm clock is useful.

Those planning trips out of the summer season should bring a number of things to protect against cold. Layering of clothes is the most effective and practical way to keep warm. Two sweaters – one thin and one thick – and something more or less windproof and/or waterproof is recommended. On particularly cool days a T-shirt under a long-sleeved shirt and then a combination of the above is quite effective. Gloves, scarf and hat should be considered depending on where you're going and are mandatory in winter.

Sunglasses are a must as well, as are a pair of binoculars if you're planning to do any bird or whale watching.

Even in winter a bathing suit is always good to throw in the pack. A collapsible umbrella is a very useful, practical accessory. A

Québec is prepared for winter – are you?

good, sturdy pair of walking shoes or boots is indispensable.

For English-language speakers planning on spending some time in Québec, a French/English dictionary or phrasebook should be considered, although these are widely available new and used in Montréal and Québec City.

Drivers traveling long distances should have a few basic tools, a spare tire that has been checked for pressure, a first aid kit, a flashlight and a blanket and candle (in case you get stuck in cold areas). A mobile phone is handy in emergencies – check with your provider to find out which areas of the province are covered. A few tapes or CDs may help pass the hours driving in remote areas where there's nothing on the radio but static (see Music in the Facts about Québec chapter for some suggestions).

RESPONSIBLE TOURISM

The best way to appreciate the nature you've come to explore in Québec is, first and foremost, to respect it. Sadly, much of the province's forested land and waterways have been pillaged and misused for over a century and contributing to this, even in small ways, would further damage the already fragile ecosystem. In the past ten years there has been a greater push toward conservation and nature protection, together with the development of an eco-tourist infrastructure. This has opened up an impressive array of opportunities to appreciate the local flora and fauna by delving into inland wilderness and observing sea life and birds in their natural habitat, which slowly but surely has become cleaner in recent years.

There are many ways to help preserve the province's incredible natural resources. Primarily this means reading and respecting the rules and regulations of the places you choose to visit, particularly the national and provincial parks, wildlife reserves and other conservation areas. All have these guidelines in English. Conservation societies, which offer guided tours of fragile areas such as bird nesting and mating grounds, will clearly explain the dos and don'ts of the

tour. Otherwise, think unselfishly and follow common sense (see 'Considerations for Responsible Hiking & Camping' for general tips while you're outdoors).

Whale watching is one of the province's big tourist draws. If you're planning on doing some observing of your own, see the Activities chapter for ways you can do so responsibly.

If you decide upon a dogsledding trek, visit the organization first. This activity has grown in popularity in recent years and has led to some enterprises keeping dogs in less than ideal conditions. Ask to see the kennels. Do the animals live in cramped cages, lying in their own feces? Are the cages four-sided metal (with only a grid for a floor)? Is the trainer aggressive with them? Are the treks done with very large packs of dogs (over 40 running together)? If so, it's best to express your dissatisfaction and leave for another, responsible person offering the same service – they shouldn't be hard to find.

Socially, Québécois tend to be laid-back and open-minded. However, you should try to remain sensitive to the political beliefs of some of the people you will meet. You might be surprised, for example, at some people's unwillingness to call themselves Canadian, only Québécois. Avoid bringing up potentially touchy subjects like nationalism and colonization unless you have sufficient time to discuss them fully.

TOURIST OFFICES
Local Tourist Offices

Since the late 1990s, the provincial government has increased its budget allocations by the tens of millions to promote tourism. As a result, Québec has one of the best-organized tourism infrastructures in the country. Every large city and town, as well as most small towns and villages, has at least one tourist information office. Toll-free, central phone numbers allow you to get help no matter where you are. Thick guide booklets are published every year for each region and are chock-full of information.

Considerations for Responsible Hiking & Camping

Trash

Carry out all of your trash. If you've carried it in, you can carry it out. Don't overlook those easily forgotten items, such as aluminum foil, orange peel, cigarette butts and plastic wrappers. Empty packaging weighs very little anyway and should be stored in a dedicated trash bag. Make an effort to carry out trash left by others as well.

Never bury your trash: Digging disturbs soil and ground cover, and encourages erosion. Buried trash will more than likely be dug up by animals, which may be injured or poisoned by it. It may also take years to decompose, especially at high altitudes.

Minimize the waste you must carry out by taking minimal packaging and no more food than you will need. If you can't buy in bulk, unpack small-portion packages and combine their contents in one container before your trip. Take reusable containers or stuff sacks.

Don't rely on bought water in plastic bottles. Disposal of these bottles is creating a major problem, particularly in developing countries. Use iodine drops or purification tablets instead.

Sanitary napkins, tampons and condoms should be carried out; they burn and decompose poorly.

Washing

Don't use detergents or toothpaste in or near watercourses, even if they are biodegradable.

For personal washing, use biodegradable soap and a water container (or even a lightweight, portable basin) at least 50m away from the watercourse. Disperse the wastewater widely to allow the soil to filter it fully before it finally makes it back to the watercourse.

Wash cooking utensils 50m from watercourses using a scourer, sand or snow instead of detergent.

Erosion

Hillsides and mountain slopes, especially at high altitudes, are prone to erosion. It is important to stick to existing tracks and avoid shortcuts that bypass a switchback. If you blaze a new trail straight down a slope, it will turn into a watercourse with the next heavy rainfall and eventually cause soil loss and deep scarring.

If a well-used track passes through a mud patch, walk through the mud; walking around the edge will increase the size of the patch.

Avoid removing the plant life that keeps topsoil in place.

Fires & Low-Impact Cooking

Don't depend on open fires for cooking. The cutting of wood for fires in popular trekking areas can cause rapid deforestation. Cook on a lightweight kerosene, alcohol or Shellite (white gas) stove, and avoid those powered by disposable butane-gas canisters.

Fires may be acceptable below the tree line in areas that get very few visitors. If you light a fire, use an existing fireplace rather than creating a new one. Don't surround fires with rocks, as this creates a visual scar. Use only dead, fallen wood. Remember the adage 'the bigger the fool, the bigger the fire.' Use minimal wood, just what you need for cooking. In huts, leave wood for the next person.

After use, ensure that you *fully* extinguish a fire. Spread the embers and douse them with water. A fire is only truly safe to leave when you can comfortably place your hand in it.

Wildlife Conservation

Don't buy items made from endangered species.

Discourage the presence of wildlife by not leaving food scraps behind. Place gear out of reach and tie packs to rafters or trees.

Do not feed the wildlife, as this can lead to the animals' becoming dependent on handouts, to unbalanced populations and to diseases such as 'lumpy jaw.'

Tourist offices are often staffed by trained students who can assist you in getting information, making tour and lodging bookings, and assuring that you find your way to the nearest sugar shack, wine yard, wildlife refuge or *dépanneur*. It is highly recommended to make them your first stop whenever entering a new town.

The head tourist office is in downtown Montréal (☎ 514-873-2015, 877-266-5687, W www.tourisme.gouv.qc.ca, 1001 rue du Square Dorchester), near the corner of rue Peel and rue Ste Catherine. This is a great place to start your trip, get information about every region of the province, book tours and even have a shower.

The main limitation with these offices (and the government tourist guides and websites) is that they will dispense information about only those organizations that pay an annual membership fee to a provincial tourism association. While many businesses find it worthwhile to do so (the publicity they get out of it is considerable), some smaller firms cannot afford or justify the hefty fees, and others are simply uninterested in being part of the association. This means that the guide booklets, as helpful as they are, are essentially advertisement, and that you will not be told about a significant proportion of motels, hotels, restaurants and other services in your area. Independent exploration will yield more surprises than you can find at the tourist offices.

Each of Québec's 20 administrative regions (plus Nunavik) has several permanent tourist offices as well as other, smaller, seasonal ones. In general, the permanent offices are open 8am or 9am to 7pm or 8pm from mid-June to early September, and 9am to 5pm the rest of the year. The seasonal offices are open from mid- or late June to early or mid-September, usually from the hours of 8am or 9am to 7pm or 8pm.

The text mentions many of the province's tourist offices. Here is a list of the main offices for each of Québec's regions, along with their website addresses, which are good sources of all kinds of information.

Abitibi-Témiscamingue (☎ 819-762-8181, 800-808-0706, W www.48nord.qc.ca)

Centre du Québec (☎ 819-364-7177, 888-816-4007, W www.tourismecentreduquebec.com)

Charlevoix (☎ 418-665-4454, 800-667-2276, W www.tourisme-charlevoix.com)

Chaudière-Appalaches (☎ 418-831-4411, 888-831-4411, W www.chaudapp.qc.ca)

Duplessis (North Shore) (☎ 418-962-0808, 888-463-0808, W www.tourismecote-nord.com)

Eastern Townships (☎ 819-566-4445, 800-355-5755, W www.tourisme-cantons.qc.ca)

Gaspésie (☎ 418-775-2223, 800-463-0323, W www.tourisme-gaspesie.com)

Îles de la Madeleine (☎ 418-986-2245, W www.ilesdelamadeleine.com)

James Bay (☎ 418-745-3969, 888-745-3969, W www.municipalite.baie-james.qc.ca)

Lanaudière (☎ 450-834-2535, 800-363-2788, W www.tourisme-lanaudiere.qc.ca)

Laurentians (☎ 450-436-8532, 800-561-6673, W www.laurentides.com)

Laval (☎ 450-682-5522, 800-463-3765, W www.tourismelaval.qc.ca)

Lower St Lawrence (☎ 418-867-3015, 800-563-5268, W www.tourismebas-st-laurent.com)

Manicouagan (North Shore) (☎ 418-294-2876, 888-463-5319, W www.tourismecote-nord.com)

Mauricie (☎ 819-536-3334, 800-567-7603, W www.icimauricie.com)

Montérégie (☎ 450-0069, 866-469-0069, W www.tourisme-monteregie.qc.ca)

Montréal (☎ 514-873-2015, 877-266-5687, W www.tourisme-montreal.org)

Nunavik (☎ 819-964-2876, 888-594-3424, W www.nunavik-tourism.com)

Outaouais (☎ 819-778-2222, 800-265-7822, W www.tourisme-outaouais.com)

Saguenay-Lac St Jean (☎ 418-543-9778, 800-463-9651, W www.tourismesaguenaylacsaintjean.qc.ca)

Québec City Region (☎ 418-649-2608, W www.quebecregion.com)

Tourist Offices Abroad

Aside from Canadian embassies and consulates (see that section, later in this chapter), you may obtain general travel information and publications about Québec from the following offices:

France
Délégation du Québec: (☎ 01 40 67 85 00,

e qc.paris@mri.gouv.qc.ca), 66 rue Pergolèse, 75116 Paris

Germany
Agence Culturelle du Québec: (☎ 030 308 76571, e berlin@quebec-info@mri.gouv.qc.ca), Friedrichstrasse 108-109, 10117 Berlin

Japan
Délégation du Québec: (☎ 03-3239-5137, e qc.tokyo@mri.gouv.qc.ca), Nissei Hanzomon Building, 5th Floor, 1-3 Kojimachi, Chiyoda-ku, Tokyo 102-0083

Mexico
Délégation du Québec: (☎ 05-250-8222, e qc.mexico@mri.gouv.qc.ca), Avenida Taine 411, Colonia Bosques de Chapultepec, 11580 Mexico DF

UK
Délégation du Québec: (☎ 20-7766-5900, e qc.londres@mri.gouv.qc.ca), 59 Pall Mall, London SW1Y 5JH

USA
Délégation du Québec: (☎ 617-482-1193, e francois .lebrun@mri.gouv.qc.ca), 31 Milk St, 10th Floor, Boston, MA 02109-5104
Délégation du Québec: (☎ 212-397-0200, e qc.newyork@mri.gouv.qc.ca), 1 Rockefeller Plaza, 26th Floor, New York, NY 10020-2201
Bureau du Tourisme du Québec: (☎ 202-659-8990, e qc.washington@mri.gouv.qc.ca), 1101 17th St NW, Bureau 1006, Washington, DC 20036-4704

TRAVEL AGENCIES

Travel CUTS, known in Québec as Voyages Campus, has seven locations in Montréal, including the main office (☎ 514-843-8511, W www.travelcuts.com), 1613 rue St Denis. It sells ISIC and ITSC cards, (cheap) plane tickets and travel insurance, and it also sets up working holidays and language courses.

Run by Hostelling International, the Boutique Tourisme Jeunesse (☎ 514-844-0287), 4008 rue St Denis, sells books, maps, travel insurance, ID cards and plane tickets. It's open 10am to 6pm Monday to Wednesday, 10am to 9pm Thursday and Friday, 10am to 5pm Saturday and noon to 5pm Sunday. The travel service is closed Sunday.

The American Express Travel Agency (☎ 514-284-3300), 1141 boul de Maisonneuve in Montréal, is open 9am to 5pm weekdays.

VISAS & DOCUMENTS
Passport

For US and Canadian citizens, a driver's license is usually sufficient when entering in a car, be it your own or a rental, via land border crossings. However, a certificate of birth, citizenship or naturalization – a passport is best – is now required for bus and train passengers. Prior to the September 2001 terrorist attacks in the US, passports were required only when flying to and from the US. Permanent residents of the US who aren't citizens should carry their green card, and US citizens arriving from somewhere other than the USA should have a passport.

Visas

Visas aren't required for visitors from nearly all Western countries. However, you need to apply for a visa if you're from Hong Kong, Korea, South Africa, Taiwan, developing countries or most of Eastern Europe. Visa requirements change frequently, so it's a good idea to check with the Citizen and Immigration Canada call center in Montréal (☎ 514-496-1010) to see if you are exempt. Best is to consult W www.cic.gc.ca for up-to-date information.

Single-entry visitor visas ($75) are valid for six months (meaning that you must enter the country within the six-month time period shown on your visa), while multiple-entry visas ($150) can be used over a two-year period, provided that no single stay exceeds six months. You are permitted to stay in Canada for six months from your date of entry, unless the immigration officer at your point of entry writes a separate date on your visa. Extensions, which cost the same as the original visa, must be applied for at a Canadian Immigration Center one month before the current visa expires. A separate visa is required for visitors intending to work in Canada.

A passport and/or visa does not guarantee entry. The admission and duration of a permitted stay is based on a number of factors, including being of good health, being law abiding, having sufficient money and, possibly, having a return ticket out of the country.

If you are refused entry but have a visa, you have the right of appeal at the Immigration Appeal Board at the port of entry. People under 18 years old may be refused entry if they don't have a letter from a parent or guardian indicating acknowledgement and support of their travel plans to Canada.

Travel Insurance

Travel insurance can cover you for medical expenses, luggage theft or loss, and cancellation or delays in your travel arrangements. The policies handled by Travel CUTS (Voyages Campus in Québec; see Travel Agencies, earlier) or other student travel organizations are usually a good value.

Driver's License & Permits

A driver's license from your home country is also valid in Canada. An International Driver's Permit (IDP) comes in handy, however, when dealing with the police and car rental companies. An IDP can be obtained for a small fee from your local automobile association – bring along a passport photo and a valid license.

US citizens should get a Canadian Nonresident Interprovince Motor Vehicle Liability Insurance Card, which will prove financial liability if you're involved in an accident. It's available in the US only – contact your insurance agent.

Hostel Cards

A Hostelling International (HI) card is necessary at official *auberges de jeunesse* (youth hostels) – of which there are 17 in Québec. The card also entitles you to small discounts at non-HI hostels, museums, restaurants, attractions and shops. One-year cards are available at HI hostels for $35 (free for youth under 18). Contact the Canadian branch of HI for more details (☎ 800-663-5777, W www.hihostels.ca).

Discount Cards

An International Student Identity Card (ISIC) can pay for itself through half-price admissions, discounted air and ferry tickets, and cheap meals in student cafeterias. In Montréal, ISIC cards are issued by Voyages

Campus and other student travel agencies for $16 (see Travel Agencies, earlier). The International Student Travel Confederation is another good source for ISIC cards. See also W www.isic.org for more information and lists of discounts.

If you're under 26 but not a student, you can apply for a GO25 card, issued by the Federation of International Youth Travel Organizations (FIYTO), which entitles you to much the same discounts as an ISIC and is also issued by student unions or student travel agencies. It also costs $16.

Teachers, professional artists, museum curators and certain categories of students are admitted to some museums for free. An International Teacher Identity Card (ITIC) costs $16 (surprise) and may be obtained through the International Student Travel Confederation.

Copies

Before you leave home, you should photocopy all important documents (passport and visa, credit cards, travel-insurance policy, air/bus/train tickets, driver's license etc). Leave one set of copies with someone at home and keep another with you, separate from the originals.

You can also store details of your vital travel documents in Lonely Planet's free online Travel Vault. Your own personal password-protected Travel Vault is accessible online from anywhere in the world. See W www.ekno.lonelyplanet.com.

EMBASSIES & CONSULATES
Canadian Embassies & Consulates

For embassies and consulates not on the following list, consult the Department of Foreign Affairs and International Trade (W www.dfait-maeci.gc.ca/english/missions/menu).

Australia
   High Commission: (☎ 02-6270-4000, 09-309-8516) Commonwealth Ave, Canberra ACT 2600; W www.canada.org.au
   Consulate: (☎ 02-9364-3000, Visa Immigration Office 02-9364-3050), 111 Harrington St, Level 5, Quay West, Sydney, NSW 2000

France
Embassy: (☎ 01 44 43 29 00), 35, avenue Montaigne, 75008 Paris; **W** www.amb-canada.fr
Consulate: (☎ 04 72 77 64 07), 21, rue Bourgelat, 69002 Lyon

Germany
Embassy: (☎ 30 20 31 20), Friedrichstrasse 95, 12th Floor, 10117 Berlin; **W** www.dfait-maeci .gc.ca/~bonn/

Ireland
Embassy: (☎ 01-478-1988; after hours ☎ 01-478-1476), Canada House, 65/68 St Stephen's Green, Dublin 2

Japan
Embassy: (☎ 03-5412-6200), 3-38 Akasaka 7-chome, Minato-ku, Tokyo 107-5803; **W** www .dfait-maeci.gc.ca/ni-ka/contacts/tokyo/menu-e.asp

Netherlands
Embassy: (☎ 070-311-1600), Sophialaan 7, 2500 GV, The Hague; **W** www.ocanada.nl

New Zealand
High Commission: (☎ 04-473-9577), 61 Molesworth St, 3rd Floor, Thorndon, Wellington; **W** www.dfait-maeci.gc.ca/newzealand/ welcome-e.asp

UK
High Commission: (☎ 020-258-6600), Canada House, Consular Services, Trafalgar Square, London SW1Y 5BJ; **W** www.canada.org.uk
Immigration Information: (☎ 09068-616644), 38 Grosvenor St, London W1X 0AA
Consulate: (☎ 0131-220-4333), Standard Life House, 30 Lothian Rd, Edinburgh, EH1 2DH Scotland
Consulate: (☎ 0131-220-4333), 378 Strandmillis Rd, Belfast, BT9 5BL Northern Ireland

USA
Embassy: (☎ 202-682-1740), 501 Pennsylvania Ave NW, Washington, DC 20001; **W** www.canadian embassy.org
Consulate: (☎ 617-262-3760), 3 Copley Place, Suite 400, Boston, MA 02116
Consulate: (☎ 212-596-1600), 1251 Ave of the Americas, Concourse Level, New York, NY 10020-1175

Many other US cities have Canadian Consulate Generals; see **W** www.dfait-maeci.gc.ca/ english/missions/menu.htm.

Consulates in Québec

Only the main consulates are listed here – all are in Montréal; check the yellow pages for a detailed list. Australian citizens should call

---

Your Own Embassy

It's important to realize what your own embassy – the embassy of the country of which you are a citizen – can and can't do for you if you get into trouble. Generally speaking, it won't be much help in emergencies if the trouble you're in is remotely your own fault. Remember that you are bound by the laws of the country you are in. Your embassy will not be sympathetic if you end up in jail after committing a crime locally, even if such actions are legal in your own country.

In genuine emergencies you might get some assistance, but only if other channels have been exhausted. For example, if you need to get home urgently, a free ticket home is exceedingly unlikely – the embassy would expect you to have insurance. If you have all your money and documents stolen, it might assist with getting a new passport, but a loan for onward travel is out of the question.

---

the Australian High Commission (☎ 613-236-0841) in Ottawa, which is home to principal diplomatic representations to Canada.

Cuba (☎ 514-843-8897) 1415 avenue des Pins Ouest

France (☎ 514-866-6511) 1 Place Ville Marie

Germany (☎ 514-931-2277) 1250 boul René Lévesque Ouest

Japan (☎ 514-866-3429) 600 rue de la Gauchetière Ouest

Netherlands (☎ 514-849-4247) 1002 rue Sherbrooke Ouest

UK (☎ 514-866-5863) 1000 rue de la Gauchetière Ouest

USA (☎ 514-398-9695) 1155 rue St Alexandre

CUSTOMS

If you're entering Canada by car, you should know that vehicles that look suspiciously full are likely to be searched. Keep the car's weight to a minimum, and stow your belongings in the trunk.

Adults 18 and older can bring in 1.14L of wine or liquor (or a case of beer), 200 cigarettes, 50 cigars and 200g of tobacco – all are cheaper in the USA, incidentally. You can also bring in gifts valued up to $60 plus a 'reasonable amount' (up to the agent's discretion) of personal effects. Most fruit, vegetables and plants can be confiscated. Boats powered by motors under 10hp can be brought in without special licenses.

Don't get caught bringing in drugs – including marijuana and hashish – as sentences can be harsh. Mace, pepper spray, pistols and firearms (except hunting rifles) are also prohibited.

For the latest customs information, contact the Canadian embassy or consulate in your home country.

MONEY

All prices quoted in this book are in Canadian dollars ($) unless stated otherwise. The strong US dollar gives American visitors a favorable exchange rate, although Canadian federal and provincial taxes cut into that buying power.

For financial travel services, visit American Express (☎ 514-284-3300), at 1141 boul de Maisonneuve, open 9am to 5pm weekdays.

Currency

Canadian coins come in one-cent (penny), five-cent (nickel), 10-cent (dime), 25-cent (quarter), $1 (loonie) and $2 (toonie) pieces. The gold-colored loonie features the loon, a common Canadian waterbird. When the toonie was introduced in 1996, Canadians made a sport out of separating the aluminum-bronze core from the nickel outer ring.

Paper currency comes in $5 (blue), $10 (purple), $20 (green) and $50 (red) denominations. The $100 (brown), larger bills are uncommon and might prove difficult to change.

Exchange Rates

At press time, exchange rates were as follows:

country	unit		Canadian dollar
Australia	A$1	=	C$0.84
European Union	€1	=	C$1.38
Japan	¥100	=	C$1.18
New Zealand	NZ$1	=	C$0.69
UK	UK£1	=	C$2.25
USA	US$1	=	C$1.58

Exchanging Money

Currency exchange booths often offer superior exchange rates to most major banks, though all banks will change money of most major currencies. Airport and train and bus station booths, however, tend to offer unfavorable rates compared to their center-city counterparts.

Cash & Personal Checks Most Canadians don't carry large amounts of cash for everyday use, relying instead on credit and debit cards. Unlike in the US, shops and businesses rarely accept personal checks.

Traveler's Checks American Express, Thomas Cook, Visa and MasterCard are the best traveler's checks to use, either in US or Canadian dollars. They offer good exchange rates but not necessarily better than those offered at ATMs. Traveler's checks in Canadian dollars will be accepted as cash at most hotels, restaurants and stores.

American Express and Thomas Cook offices don't charge you for cashing their own traveler's checks. Otherwise, Banque de Montréal and Scotiabank charge the lowest fees.

If your traveler's checks are lost or stolen, call the appropriate toll-free phone numbers: American Express (☎ 800-221-7282), Thomas Cook (☎ 888-823-4732), Visa (☎ 800-227-6811). Keeping a record of the check numbers (separate from the checks!) will help you get a swift refund.

ATM & Credit Cards ATMs tend to offer superior exchange rates, and most also give you a cash advance through your Visa or MasterCard. Montréal has plenty of ATMs – not only in banks, but also in pubs, convenience stores and hotels – that are linked to the international Cirrus, Plus and Maestro networks. Many charge a $1.50 fee per use, and your own bank may levy an extra fee – check before leaving home.

Major credit cards like Visa, MasterCard and American Express are widely accepted throughout the province, at stores, restaurants and hotels, large and small. Diner's Club is also welcome in major restaurants.

International Transfers Telegraphic transfers are not very expensive, but despite their name, they can take several days to reach their destination. Be sure to specify the bank and the branch address where you'd like to pick up your dough.

It's quicker and easier to have money wired via American Express (☎ 800-668-8680), which charges a fee of US$50 for a US$1000 transfer. Thomas Cook's Money-Gram service (☎ 800-926-9400) is also popular. A transfer should go through within 15 minutes.

Costs

By North American standards, Québec is a cheap place to visit, though it boasts some of the highest taxes in Canada. Gasoline taxes are highest here, and only Prince Edward Island and Ontario have a higher sales tax than Québec, which is the winner in the Highest Personal Income Tax category. Generally, however, most goods and services are not significantly higher than in other provinces. If you're on a tight budget, you could scrape by on a mere $30 to $40 a day by staying in hostels, cooking for yourself and limiting your entertainment. Staying in a cheap motel or B&B, eating in budget restaurants and allowing yourself a few drinks in bars could easily run you up to $90 a day. Eating your main meal at lunch rather than dinner can save a lot of money. Car rentals start at around $40 per day. Remember that most posted prices don't include taxes.

Tipping & Bargaining

A tip of 15% of the pretax bill is customary in restaurants. A few restaurants may include a service charge on the bill for large parties. Tipping is expected for bar service too; while the 10% to 15% rule should work in these situations, many people go overboard, feeling cheap if they don't leave $1 for a $4 beer or $3 Coke.

Tips of 10% to 15% are also given to taxi drivers, hairdressers and barbers. Hotel bellhops and redcaps (porters) at airports and train stations should get a minimum of a dollar or two per item.

Taxes & Refunds

The federal goods and services tax (called TPS in Québec and GST in the rest of Canada) adds 7% to just about every transaction. Québec also charges a provincial sales tax (TVQ) of 7.5%, which – to the ire of the general populace – is also levied on the TPS (ie, taxing a tax).

Visitors are eligible for refunds on TPS paid for accommodations and nonconsumable goods (ie, not food or drink), provided you spend at least a total of $200 and apply for the refund within one year of purchase. However, the catch is that each eligible receipt must be for $50 or more. Tax paid on services or transportation is not refundable. You must keep the original receipts and have them stamped by customs before leaving the country. Instant cash refunds of up to $500 can be obtained at land border crossings with participating duty-free shops. Otherwise, you'll need to mail a tax-rebate form (widely available at shops and hotels) with your stamped receipts.

POST & COMMUNICATIONS
Post

The national mail service, also known as Canada Post/Postes Canada (☎ 800-267-1177, **W** www.canadapost.ca), is neither quick nor cheap, but it's reliable. Standard 1st-class airmail letters or postcards cost 48¢ to Canadian destinations and 65¢ to the US (both are limited to 30g). Those to other destinations cost $1.25 (limit 30g).

Telephone

For toll-free, local directory assistance, dial ☎ 411. For long-distance directory assistance, dial 1 + area code + 555-1212, which is also free.

Bell Canada, one of Canada's regional phone services, serves all of Québec. Rates are low for local use but tend to be costly for long distances, more expensive than in the US.

There are a variety of pay phones. Ones operated by Bell Canada cost 25¢ for an unlimited-time local call. Others may charge 35¢, or charge 25¢ for the first three minutes only. All Canadian business and residential phones are billed a flat monthly rate for local calls, so don't feel guilty about the cost of using a friend's telephone if you're making local calls.

The peak and off-peak periods for long-distance calls depend on the country being called. The cheapest rates apply between 6pm and 10pm on weekdays and all weekend, while peak rates are charged weekdays during business hours.

Remember that hotels charge dearly for telephone use – often 50¢ or more for a local call.

Toll-Free Numbers Many businesses and tourist organizations provide toll-free numbers, which begin with 800, 888, 866 or 877 and must be preceded with 1. Some numbers are good throughout North America, others only within Canada and still others in just one province. You won't know until you dial.

Phone Cards There's a wide range of local and international phone cards. Lonely Planet's eKno Communication Card is aimed specifically at travelers and provides cheap international calls, a range of messaging services and free email. You can join eKno online at ⓦ www.ekno.lonelyplanet .com, or by phone from Canada by dialing ☎ 800-294-3676. To use eKno from Canada, dial ☎ 800-808-5773.

For local calls, you're better off with a local card. Bell Canada and Telus, two major phone service providers, sell prepaid cards in denominations of $10, $20 and $50 that work only in public telephone booths, while Bell Canada's Allô! card can be used from both public and private phones. You'll pay hefty connection charges for long-distance calls (generally $1.54 to $1.75) and the per-minute rates are nowhere near as good as those offered by other phone cards.

Many local phone cards offer rates better than Bell's. The cards, sold at many convenience and magazine stores and good in both public and private phones, have catchy names such as Ci Ci, Nuvo and WOW, and they come in denominations of $5, $10, $20,

$30 and $50. For instance, Nuvo charges a flat 5.6¢ per minute for calls between Montréal, Toronto, Ottawa and Vancouver; 7.5¢ for calls to the US and UK; and 9.3¢ for calls to Australia and New Zealand. There's no connection charge. These are available at *dépanneurs* and newspaper stands in Montréal and Québec City but can be used anywhere in the province. Read the card's posters to verify that there are no hidden charges. Most do not have connection fees, and while money sometimes seems to disappear mysteriously from them, they are still good deals.

Fax & Telegram

Fax machines are available to the public at major hotels and post offices and at a range of small businesses like photocopy centers. Typically, sending a fax within North America costs $2 for the first minute, $1 for the following; for overseas faxes, count on $3 to $4 for the first minute, $1.50 to $2 for each minute after that. To receive a fax the charge is usually $0.50 per page. Hotels will charge significantly higher rates.

Even in the cyber age, you can still send telegrams. To do so, contact AT&T Canada (☎ 800-387-1926).

Email & Internet Access

Major Internet providers have local dial-up numbers in Montréal. It's a good idea to open a free Web-based email account, which will allow you to email from cybercafés and other access points. Lonely Planet's eKno offers just such a service. See ⓦ www.ekno.lonelyplanet.com.

Internet cafés and other access points are listed throughout this book. In general, the local tourist information office should know where the nearest access point is. Many of them have a terminal set up for brief use by tourists. Failing this, the main public library in town will usually offer free access. Also, a pilot project by Canada Post placing a computer terminal in many small-town post offices is set to expand – drop in the local post office to see if there's one waiting to be used.

INTERNET RESOURCES

The World Wide Web is a rich resource for travelers. You can research your trip, hunt down bargain airfares, book hotels, check on weather conditions or chat with locals and other travelers about the best places to visit – or avoid!

There's no better place to start your Web explorations than the Lonely Planet website (W www.lonelyplanet.com). Here you'll find succinct, up-to-date summaries on traveling to most places on earth; e-postcards from other travelers; and the Thorn Tree bulletin board, where you can ask questions before you go or dispense advice when you get back. You can also find travel news and updates to many of our most popular guidebooks, and the subWWWay section links you to the most useful travel resources elsewhere on the Web.

Websites are cited throughout this book. For a list of major festivals throughout the province, take a look at Communication Canada's web site at W www.infocan.qc.ca/calendar/qc/index_qc_e.html. Following are some general English-language sites with many useful links:

Canada Tourism Commission – W www.canada tourism.com

Tourisme Québec – W www.bonjourquebec.com

Montreal Gazette – W www.montrealgazette.com

Mirror Magazine – W www.montrealmirror.com

Montréal Bars & Restaurants – W www.bar-resto .com

BOOKS
Lonely Planet

Lonely Planet's *Canada* is the essential companion if you're touring the country; it offers itineraries for everything, from a road trip to a raft trip. *Montréal, Toronto* and *Vancouver* are the definitive guides to exploring those cities, and Lonely Planet's *French phrasebook* is a best-selling and handy primer for *la langue française*.

For the true Francophile visiting Québec, or simply those who want to brush up on their French reading skills, LP publishes a very complete French-language guide to this city.

Guidebooks & Travel

There are a few good specialist guidebooks to Montréal. A good, easy-to-digest guide with insights into history, society and architecture is *Montréal Up Close: A Pedestrian's Guide to the City* (1998), by Kirk Johnson and David Widgington. Exhaustively researched, the book features numbered walking tours on color foldout maps based on aerial photographs.

Although it has nothing to do with crustaceans, the best-selling *Lobster Kid's Guide to Exploring Montréal* (2000) has 150-odd activities perfect for families in Montréal and its environs. The author, John Symon, has also written a similar book for Ottawa-Hull.

Jan Morris, a Welsh travel writer who has written about many cities around the world, published *City to City* in 1990. Written after traveling Canada coast to coast, it's a highly readable collection of essays of fact and opinion about 10 Canadian cities, including Montréal. This book also appeared under the title *O Canada: Travels in an Unknown Country.*

History & Politics

A Short History of Québec (1993, revised 2000), by John A Dickenson and Brian Young, is good for anyone looking for a general introduction to the province. Focused on the social and economic development of Québec (but far from dry), it stretches from the pre-European period all the way to the constitutional struggles of the present.

For a history of Québec from an unashamedly nationalistic point of view, *The History of Québec; A Patriot's Handbook,* by Léandre Bergeron, is the seminal text. Originally published in 1971, the book minces no words as it goes through the history of the colonization of Québec. It's a real treat to read in these politically correct times and opens readers' eyes to historical facts seldom spoken about.

If you enjoy photojournalism, *Montréal's Century* (1999) provides a gripping account of the news and people who shaped the city in the 20th century. The collection was assembled and published jointly by the *Montréal Gazette* and *Journal de Montréal*. It's hard to put down once you start leafing through.

Peter C Newman, who is primarily a business writer, has produced *Caesars of the Wilderness* (1987), an intriguing history of the Hudson's Bay Company, beginning with the early fur-trading days.

For insights into the lives of Canada's indigenous inhabitants, *Native Peoples and Cultures of Canada* (1995), by Allan Macmillan, includes both history and current issues. The seminal work on the topic, however, is *The Indians of Canada* (1932), by Diamond Jenness. It has been reprinted many times. Originally from New Zealand, the author spent years living with various indigenous peoples across the country.

General

Montréal in the Literary Imagination: Storied Streets (2000), by Bryan Demchinsky and Elaine Kalman Naves, looks at the city through the eyes of writers and poets, including Charles Dickens, Harriet Beecher Stowe and Mark Twain, as well as contemporary scribes.

For an Anglo-Saxon take on living in Québec, *Feeling Comfortable* (2000), by Martha Radice, examines the decline of Anglo-Saxon influence in Montréal and its effect on the English-speaking residents over the past few decades. This readable university study includes dozens of interviews with Anglo Montréalers.

The Hockey Sweater (1979), a short story by Roch Carrier, strikes a chord with most Canadians. A Toronto Maple Leafs sweater is given to a Montréal Canadiens fan and becomes a symbol of friction between the country's Anglo and French populations.

David Foster Wallace's hilarious cult novel *Infinite Jest* (1996) is set in the near, bleak future: New England has become the US's dumping ground for toxic waste, and marauding Québec revolutionaries, called the Wheelchair Assassins *(Les Assassins des Fauteuils Rollants)*, wage terrorist warfare, striving for an independent Québec.

For an excellent book on the history of Québécois cinema, see Janis L Pallister's *The Cinema of Québec* (1995).

To feel nostalgic about Québécois cooking once you get back home, pick up Julian Armstrong's *A Taste of Québec* to find out how to make those eggs in maple syrup or blueberry upside-down cake you'll surely crave after your trip. Also check out Micheline Mongrain-Dontigny's series of books detailing regional specialties of Québec, like *La Cuisine Traditionnelle de la Mauricie, 150 Recettes pour le Saguenay-Lac St Jean* and *La Cuisine Traditionnelle de Charlevoix*.

FILMS

Montréal is an ideal city for shooting movies. It has an abundance of atmospheric locations that are ready-made for Hollywood productions, especially in Old Montréal. The strong US dollar, excellent technical facilities and proximity to New York also make Montréal a convenient bargain for American filmmakers, who dominate the scene.

The 500-plus cinema and TV films shot partly or entirely in Montréal include Sergio Leone's epic *Once Upon a Time in America* (1983), with Robert De Niro and Elizabeth McGovern; *12 Monkeys* (1995), Terry Gilliam's twisted sci-fi flick starring Bruce Willis and Brad Pitt; *Batman & Robin* (1997), with George Clooney and Chris O'Donnell as the caped crusaders; and the spine-tingling thriller *Wait Until Dark* (1967), with Audrey Hepburn and Richard Crenna. And let's not forget *Jesus of Montréal* (1989), directed by Québec's own Denys Arcand, in which an unorthodox production of the Passion Play sparks a bitter conflict with the Catholic Church.

NEWSPAPERS & MAGAZINES

The daily *Montréal Gazette* is the major English-language newspaper, with good coverage of national affairs, politics and the arts. The Friday and Saturday editions are packed with entertainment listings. Outside Montréal, the other English-language newspaper of note is Sherbrooke's *The Record,* serving the Eastern Townships.

You'll also often see Toronto's national dailies *Globe & Mail* and *The National Post.*

Readers of French should have a look at both the federalist *La Presse,* the largest-circulation French daily in the province, as well as the separatist-leaning *Le Devoir. Le Journal de Montréal* is a popular French-language broadsheet.

Maclean's is Canada's weekly news magazine; it's quite thin but high quality. Not unlike its US cousin, the monthly *Canadian Geographic* carries excellent articles and photography on a range of Canadian topics, from wildlife to weather.

RADIO & TV

The Canadian Broadcasting Corporation (CBC) airs national and regional broadcasts on both radio and TV. It runs more Canadian content in music and information than any of the private broadcast companies – much like the BBC in Britain.

CBC Montréal (88.5 FM in Montréal) is the local flagship for news, educational and cultural programs in English. Tune in between 9am and noon on weekdays for *This Morning,* a show offering a well-rounded view of the nation's opinions.

There are local AM and FM stations all across the province, with regional stations spinning more of a musical variety than can be heard on Montréal's rather dismal offerings.

The CBC also operates a French radio and television network under the name Radio-Canada (95.3 FM in Montréal and TV channel 4). The other major national TV network is the Canadian Television Network (CTV, channel 11). It's the main commercial channel, and it broadcasts a mix of Canadian and US programs, as well as a popular national news program every night.

Québécois can readily tune into TV and radio stations from the US, and often do.

TIME

Québec is on Eastern Time (EST/EDT), the same time zone as New York City, Toronto and Miami. When it's noon in Montréal, it's 9am in Vancouver and Los Angeles, 1pm in Halifax, 5pm in London, 6pm in Paris, 2am (the following day) in Tokyo and 3am (the following day) in Sydney. Only the Îles de la Madeleine are on Atlantic Time (one hour ahead of the rest of Québec).

Canada switches to Daylight Saving Time (which is one hour later than Standard Time) on the last Sunday in April, making the daylight hours lusciously long. Standard Time returns on the last Sunday in October.

Official times (train schedules, film screenings etc) are often indicated using the 24-hour clock, also known as military time (eg, 6:30pm is represented as 18:30); French-speakers use this system almost exclusively.

ELECTRICITY

Canada, like the US and Mexico, operates on 110V, 60-cycle electric power. Non-North American visitors should bring a plug adapter for their own small appliances. Note that gadgets built for higher voltage and cycles (such as 220/240V, 50-cycle appliances from Europe) will probably run more slowly, and tape recorders not equipped with built-in adapters may function poorly.

Canadian electrical goods have a plug with two flat, vertical prongs (the same as the US and Mexico) or sometimes a three-pronger, with the added ground. Most sockets can accommodate both types.

WEIGHTS & MEASURES

Canada officially changed from imperial measurement to the metric system in the 1970s. Though weather, distance and speed limits are always designated in metric, people will still sometimes talk in feet, inches and pounds.

Measurements in this book are given in metric. For help converting, see the chart on the inside back cover.

TOILETS

That dirty word is rarely used by English-speakers in Canada, who prefer 'washroom,' 'bathroom' or 'restroom' (although French-speakers have no qualms about saying *les toilettes).* Public washrooms are virtually nonexistent, but most department stores and shopping complexes have facilities. You can also duck into a café, restaurant or museum and ask politely (with a hint of urgency) to use the washroom.

HEALTH
Predeparture Planning
Canada is a typical First World destination when it comes to health. No vaccinations are required from visitors unless you're coming from an area with a history of certain diseases – immunizations against yellow fever or cholera are the most likely requirements. However, some routine vaccinations are recommended for all travelers. They include hepatitis B, polio, tetanus and diphtheria, and sometimes measles, mumps and rubella. These vaccinations are usually administered during childhood, but some require booster shots. Check with a doctor before you go.

It's a good idea to pack a basic medical kit (an antiseptic, aspirin or paracetamol, bandages etc). If you're packing medication, bring copies of your prescriptions to avoid problems at customs.

Medical Treatment
There are no reciprocal healthcare arrangements between Canada and other countries, so non-Canadians have to pay up front for treatment and get reimbursed by the insurer later. Consider taking out travel insurance to cover any eventual expense (see Travel Insurance, earlier).

Pharmacies
The Pharmaprix and Jean Coutu pharmacy chains have branches all over the province and are well stocked. Many also stock beverages and snack food.

Water
Montréal tap water, and generally tap water in other areas, is safe to drink. If you intend to be out in the wild on outdoor excursions, the simplest way to purify water is to boil it thoroughly – a vigorous five-minute boiling should be satisfactory, even at high altitudes (where water boils less quickly).

HIV/AIDS
Catie (☎ 800-263-1638) runs a Canada-wide HIV/AIDS help line that is open 10am to 6pm weekdays and until 7pm Tuesday, Wednesday and Thursday. Staff provide information and advice on relevant topics, such as transmission risks, the side effects of certain drugs and alternative therapy.

Info-Sida (☎ 514-521-7432), 1000 rue Sherbrooke Est, gives out information on prevention and treatment, as well as referrals to relevant social and medical organizations. Its bilingual staff are available 9am to 5pm weekdays.

WOMEN TRAVELERS
Québec holds high standards for women's safety, especially when compared to major US cities. Still, the usual advice still applies – avoid walking alone late at night, especially in North Montréal.

It's illegal in Canada to carry pepper spray or mace. Instead, some women recommend carrying a whistle to deal with potential dangers. If you are sexually assaulted, call ☎ 911 or the Sexual Assault Center (☎ 514-934-4504) to report the crime and/or for referrals to hospitals with sexual-assault care centers.

GAY & LESBIAN TRAVELERS
Canada's national attitude of social tolerance has made Montréal a popular getaway for lesbian, gay, bisexual and transgendered travelers for decades. The main center of Montréal's gay community is the Village, though a younger generation is more and more spending time in mixed or non-sexual-orientation-designated clubs and hangouts. Gay Pride Week, organized by Divers Cité (W www.diverscite.org), takes place in late July and early August, often attracting over half a million spectators for their Pride Parade.

Gai Écoute (☎ 514-866-0103) and Gay Line (☎ 514-866-5090, 888-505-1010) provide information, counseling and referrals to organizations within the gay community. Gai Écoute is staffed 11am to 11pm daily; Gay Line 7pm to 11pm daily. These hours, however, are not always reliable. For a complete list of local gay events, call the 24-hour Gay Event Line (☎ 514-252-4429). The Gay and Lesbian Association of UQAM is at ☎ 514-987-3039.

The monthly magazine *Fugues* (W www .fugues.com) is a mostly French-language gay guide, including listings and events. Though gay clubs and events outside Montréal and Québec City are rarities, you'll find a few listed here.

Columbia Fun Maps (W www.funmaps .net) produces gay/lesbian oriented map/brochures for cities across North America. The Montréal guide, for example, also includes information on Québec City.

DISABLED TRAVELERS

Most public buildings in Québec are wheelchair accessible, including tourist offices, major museums and principal attractions. A very wide array of other attractions, restaurants and hotels also have ramps and other facilities suitable for the mobility-impaired (even the youth hostel on the Îles de la Madeleine is wheelchair accessible). Unfortunately, access to the Métro is difficult, as most stations don't have elevators to the platforms.

Most of the wildlife reserves have chalets in the forest equipped for the mobility-impaired. The La Mauricie National Park and the Parc de Frontenac have special trails for wheelchairs; the Centre de la Nature in Mont St Hillaire has wheelchair-adapted facilities and rents special wheelchairs made for slightly rugged terrain; and the Festival International de Lanaudière offers special transport to Joliette for the handicapped.

VIA Rail will accommodate people in wheelchairs with 48 hours' notice. Long-distance bus lines will assist passengers and take wheelchairs or any other aids, providing that they collapse and fit into the luggage compartments. Guide dogs for the visually impaired are allowed on passenger cars at no extra charge. Airlines are accustomed to dealing with disabled passengers and provide early boarding and disembarking as a standard practice – Air Canada is extremely well equipped.

Kéroul (☎ 514-252-3104, W www.keroul .qc.ca) is a well-known agency specializing in mobility-impaired travel, offering attractive packages to destinations in Québec and Ontario. It also publishes the bilingual *Accésible Québec* for $13 ($14 from the US, $20 from Europe, including postage), which is a guide to 300 disabled-accessible hotels, attractions and restaurants in the province.

SENIOR TRAVELERS

Visitors over the age of 65 (often 60) can qualify for discounts on transportation and many attractions, parks, museums, historic sites and cinemas. Some hotels and motels may also offer reductions. Carry your passport, driver's license or other photo ID to prove your age.

USA-based Elderhostel (☎ 978-323-4141, 877-426-8056, W www.elderhostel.org), 75 Federal St, Boston, MA 02110-1941, specializes in inexpensive, educational packages for people 55 years or older. Regular programs include field trips to Québec City, the art and architecture of the Eastern Townships and French-language courses. Accommodations are in university dorms or the like.

For people over 50, the Canadian Association of Retired Persons (CARP; ☎ 800-363-9736, W www.fifty-plus.net) offers information on RV, mobility-impaired and discount senior travel, as well as savings on car and travel insurance. An annual membership costs $16. Members of the US-based American Association of Retired Persons (AARP) can take advantage of many CARP services.

TRAVEL WITH CHILDREN

Traveling successfully with children of any age requires preparation and effort. Lonely Planet's *Travel with Children,* by Cathy Lanigan, can give you some valuable tips.

In Montréal, kids are given discounted admission at major attractions, sometimes up to half off. Family passes (for two adults and two children) are usually a better deal.

Front desks at hotels can also recommend babysitting services if they're not available in-house.

It's easy (though can be costly) to keep kids entertained in the summer at the La

Ronde amusement park on Île Ste Hélène in Montréal and at Village Vacances in St Gabriel de Valcartier north of Québec City. There are zoos and mini zoos across the province. Whale watching will leave an indelible impression. The largest cities have museums and attractions of interest to children, and the opportunity to go ice skating or have a swim in a lake is never far away.

DANGERS & ANNOYANCES

In general, Québec is a safe place. Although there are motorcycle gangs and brawls occasionally break out in large and small towns alike, tourists need not worry unduly about encountering violence.

Since the mid-1990s, the number of people living on the street has risen dramatically due to various social and political factors. Montréal has a serious problem with homeless people; in some cases these are people with mental illnesses trying to cope with few services. The numbers of beggars – young, old, male, female – often surprises both residents and visitors. While the situation will likely engender a mix of emotions and concern, generally there is no specific danger.

Bears & Buggy Bêtes

A serious problem encountered when you're camping in the woods is the animals – most importantly bears – who are always looking for an easy snack. Keep your food in nylon bags, tie the sacks to a rope, and sling them over a branch away from your tent and away from the tree trunk, as most bears can climb. Hoist it up high enough, about 3m, so a standing bear can't reach it. Don't leave food scraps around the site and never, *ever* keep food in the tent.

Don't try to get close-up photographs of bears and never come between a bear and its cubs. If you see any cubs, quietly and quickly disappear. If you do see a bear, try to get upwind so it can smell you and you won't startle it. While hiking through woods or in the mountains in bear country, some people wear a noisemaker, like a bell. Talking or singing is just as good. Whatever you do, don't feed bears – they lose their fear of people and eventually their lives to park wardens.

Blackflies and mosquitoes can also be murder – they seem to get worse the farther north you get. There are tales of lost hikers going insane from the bugs. This is no joke – they can make you *miserable*. Some people are allergic to blackfly bites and will develop a fair bit of swelling, but other than the unsightly welt, there is no real danger. The potential trouble is in the cumulative effects of scores of them, though this hazard is mainly psychological.

Try to minimize the amount of skin exposed by wearing a long-sleeved shirt, long pants and a close-fitting hat or cap. As a rule, darker clothes are said to attract biting insects more than lighter ones. Perfume, too, evidently attracts the wrong kind of attention. Take 'bug juice' liquid or spray repellents. Two recommended names are Muskol and Off; the latter also has an extra-strength version known as Deep Woods Off. DEET, an ingredient often used in repellents, should not be used on children. There are brands without it.

June is generally the worst month for bugs, and as the summer wears on they disappear. The bugs are at their worst deep in the woods. In clearings, along shorelines or anywhere there's a breeze you'll be safe, except for the buzzing horseflies, which are basically teeth with wings.

Mosquitoes come out around sunset; building a fire will help keep them away. For campers, a tent with a zippered screen is a necessity.

If you do get lost and are being eaten alive, submerge your body in water if you are by a lake or river. This will give you time to think clearly about where you are and what to do. Lemon or orange peel rubbed on your skin will help if you're out of repellent.

Pedestrians should take special care at crosswalks in Montréal. Technically drivers are required to stop, but don't bet your life on it.

EMERGENCIES

Almost anywhere in Québec, dial ☎ 911 for all police, fire, accident and medical emergencies. When in doubt, call ☎ 0 and ask the operator for assistance. For non-emergency police matters, consult the local telephone book for the phone number of the nearest station.

Should your passport get lost or stolen, contact your nearest consulate (see the Embassies & Consulates section, earlier, for contact information), which will issue a temporary replacement and inform you when and how to go about getting another official one, if you need it (depending upon your travel plans).

LEGAL MATTERS

Driving motorized vehicles, including boats and snowmobiles, while under the influence of alcohol is a serious offense in Canada. Offenders could land in jail overnight, followed by a court date, a heavy fine and a suspended license. The blood-alcohol limit is set at 0.08%.

In Québec, the legal drinking age is 18. It's an offence to consume alcohol anywhere other than in a residence or licensed premises, which puts parks, beaches and the rest of the great outdoors technically off-limits.

Parking regulations are strictly enforced, and fines are stiff ($30 minimum) – even for an expired parking meter. Be sure to check the signs: Some are incredibly specific and forbid *stationnement* (parking) a couple of days (or even hours) a week.

If you're charged with an offense, you have the right to public counsel if you can't afford a lawyer. For less serious matters, the McGill Legal Information Service (☎ 514-398-6792), 3480 rue McTavish, Bldg 320, Room 21G, Montréal, is staffed by law students who dispense free information and suggestions for whatever bind you're in.

BUSINESS HOURS

Standard business hours are 9:30am or 10am until 6pm Monday to Wednesday; on Thursday and Friday, many shops stay open until 9pm. Many larger retailers, especially department stores, stay open until 9pm every night on weekdays. Most stores commonly open on Saturday, and some on Sunday, from 10am to 5pm.

Convenience stores tend to remain open 24 hours, as do some gas stations, supermarkets and drugstores (chemists). Post offices are generally open 9am to 5pm weekdays, but outlets in retail stores stay open later and on weekends. Banking hours are usually shorter, from 10am to 4:30pm Monday to Thursday, to 5pm or 6pm Friday. Only some branches are open Saturday morning.

PUBLIC HOLIDAYS & SPECIAL EVENTS

On national public holidays, banks, schools and government offices close, and most museums and other services close Sundays. Holidays falling on a weekend are usually observed the following Monday.

The summer season opens with Victoria Day in late May (in Québec this has recently come to be known as the Fête du Dollard – it was done to remove the British associations to the holiday, but ask anyone on the street and they'll draw a blank as to why it's now called Fête du Dollard), and closes with Labour Day weekend, in early September. These two dates also mark the opening and closing of many businesses, attractions and services (though some open only after St Jean Baptiste Day, Québec's national holiday, June 24), and more limited hours of operation for others.

Canadian Thanksgiving (similar to the US holiday but held earlier, on the second Monday in October) is really a harvest festival. The traditional meal includes roasted turkey.

Halloween (originally a Celtic pagan tradition) is a time for costume parties. Nightclubs in particular are often the scenes of wild masquerades.

The following public holidays are celebrated in Québec:

January 1 – New Year's Day
Late March to mid-April – Good Friday & Easter Monday
May 24 or nearest Monday – Victoria Day
June 24 – Jean-Baptiste Day
July 1 – Canada Day
First Monday in September – Labour Day
Second Monday in October – Thanksgiving
November 11 – Remembrance Day
December 25 – Christmas Day
December 26 – Boxing Day

While not a statutory holiday, National Aboriginal Day falls on June 21, the first day of the summer solstice, when Canada's heritage of First Nations, Inuit and Métis cultures is celebrated at public and private institutions.

WORK

Employers hiring casual workers often don't ask for a permit, but visitors working legally in the country have Social Insurance numbers. If you are working without one and get caught, you will be told to leave the country.

The Student Work Abroad Program (SWAP) offers 3500 working holidays every year for people 18 to 25 years of age from nearly 20 countries, including Australia, Britain, France, Japan, South Africa, the US and New Zealand. Participants are issued with a one-year, nonextendable visa to work anywhere in Canada. Most 'Swappers' find jobs in the service industry as waiters, hotel porters, bar attendants or farmhands. SWAP Canada (e swapinfo@travelcuts.com) and student travel agencies can provide details.

ACCOMMODATIONS
Camping

There are campgrounds all over Québec – federal, provincial and privately owned. Government sites are often better maintained and offer more services, though this is not always the case. Sépaq, the body in charge of administering all provincial parks

and wildlife reserves, runs many memorable campgrounds, while others seem overpriced. All cost between $17 and $28 per site, depending on the number of services (water, electricity, firewood) requested. Toilet and shower facilities are available at nearly every park and wildlife reserve, though not necessarily at every campground in them.

In national parks, camping fees range from $15 to $24.

Park access fees are generally included in the price of the campground. If you enter a park and decide to camp there later, the entrance fee will be deducted from your camping fee.

Private campgrounds are generally geared to trailers (caravans) and recreational vehicles (RVs). They often have more services such as swimming pools and other entertainment facilities.

Government parks usually open in early to mid-June and start closing in early September for the winter. Dates vary according to the location. Some remain open for maintenance even when camping is finished and they might let you camp at a reduced rate. Other places, late in autumn or early in spring, are free. The gate is open and there is not a soul around. Still others block the road and you just can't enter the campgrounds although the park itself can still be visited.

For more information, see 'Considerations for Responsible Hiking & Camping' on page 39.

Hostels

There are some excellent hostels in Québec much like those found in countries around the world. There are two hostelling groups operating in Canada geared to low-budget visitors. They represent the cheapest places to stay in the country and are where you'll probably meet the most travelers.

The oldest, best known and most established hostelling association is Hostelling International (HI) Canada (☎ 613-237-7884, fax 613-237-7868, w www.hostellingintl.ca). This national organization is a member of the internationally known hostelling association. Through the text of this book these hostels are referred to as HI Hostel. Their symbol is an evergreen tree and stylized house within a blue triangle. Nightly costs range from $15 to $23 with most around $18. At many, nonmembers can stay for an additional $2 to $5. A membership can quickly pay for itself and has now been built into the system so that after a few stays you automatically become a member.

In July and August space may be a problem at some Canadian hostels, so calling ahead to make a reservation is a good idea. Reservations must be made more than 24 hours in advance and you need a credit card to pre-pay.

Other hostels operate in Québec, some run by Backpackers Hostels Canada, and some are privately run. Rates are similar to those run by Hostelling International.

Another advantage of staying at hostels is that some of them organize outdoor activities such as canoeing, climbing, boating, skiing and hiking expeditions as well as city walks.

YM-YWCAs The familiar YM-YWCAs are for the most part slowly getting out of the accommodations end of their operations in Canada. They are tending to concentrate more on fitness, recreation and various other community-oriented programs. That said, many still offer good lodging in a style between that of a hostel and a hotel, but prices have been creeping up.

YM-YWCAs are clean and quiet and often have swimming pools and cheap cafeterias. They are also, as a rule, very central, which is a big plus, and they are open all year. Some offer hostel-style dormitory accommodation throughout the summer. Many are mentioned through the text under Budget in the Places to Stay sections.

The average price for men is from $25 to $40 a single, and usually a bit more for women. Sharing a double can bring the price down to quite a reasonable level. Also, some places permit couples and these doubles are fair value.

Universities Many Québec universities and nearly all Cégeps (the Québec equivalent to pre-university college) rent out beds in their residence dormitories during the summer months. The 'season' runs approximately from May to some time in August with possible closures for such things as large academic conferences. Prices vary between $20 and $30 a day and, at many places, students are offered a further reduction. Some will charge a small surplus for bedding. Campus residences are open to all including families and seniors.

Reservations are accepted but often aren't necessary. Breakfasts are occasionally included in the price; campus cafeterias tend to close down during the summer months. Other campus facilities, such as the swimming pool, are sometimes available to guests.

Guesthouses & B&Bs

Another alternative is the tourist home. These may be an extra room in someone's home but are more commonly commercial lodging houses, rented more often by the week or month.

B&Bs are an established part of the accommodation picture and continue to grow in number. In Montréal and Québec City associations manage some B&Bs, while in other places they are listed directly with tourist offices. Some operate year-round, while others only are open for several months during summer.

Prices of B&Bs vary quite a bit, ranging roughly from a minimum of $30 for a single to $120 a double with the average being from $55 to $75 for two people.

The more expensive ones generally provide more impressive furnishings and décor. Many are found in classic heritage houses. Rooms are almost always in the owner's home and are clean and well kept. Note that smoking is almost always prohibited. Some places will take children and the odd one will allow a pet. Breakfast can vary from light or continental to a bonanza of pancakes, cereals, eggs and baked beans with maple syrup. It's worth inquiring about the breakfast before booking.

Several guidebooks dealing exclusively with B&Bs across the country are widely available in bookstores.

Motels

In Québec, as in the rest of Canada and the USA (lands of the automobile), motels are ubiquitous. Mostly they are simple and clean, if somewhat nondescript. Many can be found dotting the highways and clustered in groups on the outskirts of larger towns and cities. They usually range from $40 to $80 for singles or doubles, and, all considered, can end up being the best value for your money.

Prices tend to go up in summer or when a special event is on. Off-season bargaining is definitely worthwhile and acceptable. This need not be haggling as in a Moroccan market; just a simple counter-offer will sometimes work. Unlike most better hotels, many motels remain 'mom and pop' operations and so retain more flexibility and often reflect more of the character of the owners.

The Choice motel/hotel chain – seen from coast to coast – includes the Comfort Inn (☎ 800-228-5150) and Econo Lodge (☎ 800-553-2666) lines. They are moderately priced, not the cheapest, not the most expensive but always reliable and good value. The rooms are plain and simple but spotless and always well maintained. The benefit of the chain system is that it allows for reserving a room anywhere through toll-free telephone numbers. Another oft-seen, quality chain is Super 8 Motels (☎ 800-800-8000).

Some motels offer 'suites.' This usually means there is a separate second bedroom (good for those with children) but may mean there is a sitting room with TV and chesterfield set apart from the bedroom. It may also mean there are some cooking facilities. Many offer (and advertise on their roadside signs) a Jacuzzi.

Hotels

Many of the continent-wide hotel chains are represented in Montréal and Québec City and offer the expected level of service and comfort. Most will offer specials for weekends and holidays, and it's worth inquiring about these in advance. Doubles usually begin at $70, and for junior suites or larger, apartment-style rooms with kitchen facilities, expect to pay between $100 and $150.

There are many other quality hotels spread out across the province, and while many will charge over $100 for a double room, you can almost always be assured that you're getting something special, be it in terms of location or décor. This is especially true at some of the province's standout hotels, like the Château Frontenac in Québec City.

FOOD

Good food is one of the main pleasures in many areas of Québec. Montréal and its fine restaurants sit at the top of the list, with dazzling variety of sumptuous world cuisine at reasonable prices. Québec City also has its share of excellent restaurants and cafés.

Seafood is a local specialty in the Lower St Lawrence, Gaspésie, Îles de la Madeleine and North Shore regions. Lobster (which is fished from mid-May to mid-July), snow crab, shrimp, herring and trout make great meals in restaurants or as a roadside picnic. Freshwater salmon is another treat in these areas. In the Far North, Arctic char is king.

Throughout most of rural Québec, dining choices are more limited, and sometimes it seems like all there is to choose from is hamburgers and *poutine* (see 'The Cult of Poutine,' in the Montréal to Québec City chapter, for a description of this, er, delicacy). Diners and fast-food joints (called *casse croûtes*) litter the landscape across the province – but don't overlook them completely. Even in cheap diners it's sometimes possible to find decent seafood, for example. At the very least it's filling.

Fresh fruits like apples, blueberries, cherries and strawberries are abundant in their respective seasons and find their way into tasty pies. Farmers' stands are often seen along highways and secondary roads.

Québec also produces excellent cheeses, in particular Oka and cheddar.

Note that on many restaurant menus the term entrée refers to what some English-speakers call appetizers, and mains are what some call entrées.

Québécois Cuisine

Traditional food in Québec has a home-made, country taste to it and tends to be robust and very filling (read: heavy!). Québécois cuisine tends to very simple, relying on only a few major ingredients per recipe. Historically this is said to have come about as a result of the shortages of resources faced by the early pioneers. Unlike French cuisine it lacks the flair of presentation and experimentation of contrasting ingredients, and there tend to be very few spices used. Instead, several ingredients and a few spices are combined to come up with to-the-point, hearty meals that rarely disappoint. Many visitors agree that Québécois cooking is superb 'comfort food.' It's cooking for and from the heart.

Beans are usually served as a side dish with meals, even breakfast. Pork finds itself into many recipes in one guise or another, as do potatoes. A steaming bowl of thick pea soup has been known to begin many traditional meals. Maple syrup and sap are sometimes used in meat stews but most often show up in desserts. Vegetables play a major role, but rarely without the company of meat. While there are juicy vegetable ragouts (called *bouilli de légumes,)* meat takes primacy in Québécois cuisine; in some dishes, like shepherd's pie or *tourtière,* the closest you'll get to a vegetable is potatoes and maybe corn and carrots. (Supposedly a specialty of the Lac St Jean region but found everywhere, *tourtière* is a meat pie made with different ground meats, onions, parsley, celery and sometimes carrots. Occasionally a dash of nutmeg brings it to life.)

Cretons is a must-try, a delicious pâté made from ground pork spiced with nutmeg. You'll also find excellent pork and vegetable ragouts (like a stew) in traditional restaurants.

French fries in Québec, where they are known simply as *frîtes* or *patates,* are unbeatable, especially those bought at the small roadside chip wagons.

Desserts are also abundant, like blueberry pie, pecan pie, and the very yummy sugar pie *(tarte au sucre,* which can be found across the province). *Pudding chaumeur* (which translates as Unemployed's – or Poor Man's – Pudding) is a thick-as-brick white cake drenched in maple syrup.

First Nations Food

Native Canadian foods, based on wild game such as deer (venison), caribou and moose, are something to sample if the opportunity presents itself. Sometimes these meats are served with blueberries. Sometimes the Cree eat porcupine or beaver, but you won't find these on restaurant menus. The Inuit love beluga whale skin, which they cut into strips and chew raw, like gum. You won't find this in restaurants either, as belugas are not allowed to be hunted except by First Nations peoples – just as well anyway, as it tastes horrid!

Much of the fish First Nations eat is home-smoked. In many of the reserves, the teepees you notice on front lawns are for just that purpose.

Bannik (also spelled bannock) is a tasty traditional bread made from different grains or from corn flour. Sometimes dried raisins, nuts, almonds, dates or prunes are added.

Sagamité is a traditional soup made from a corn flour base, into which fish and meat (fresh or smoked) and spices are added. Makushan is usually reserved for special feasts. Made from potatoes and fish or meat, it was traditionally served as part of the ritual of returning from the hunt.

One of the best places to sample some Native Canadian food is at Onhoüa Chetek8e, a Huron village in Wendake, north of Québec City.

DRINKS

In Montréal and many other places in Québec, most people drink their coffee strong, preferring espresso to the bland, drip variety served in diners.

Apart from the mainstream Canadian beers such as Molson or Labatt's, Québec is home to a number of good regional and microbrews with limited distribution. Some of the tastier froths include Boréale, St Ambroise and Belle Geule; for a doomsday

Maple Syrup & the Sugar Shack

Intimately tied to the very notion of Canada is the country's most recognized export, maple syrup. And nowhere is maple syrup tied more deeply to traditional ways than in Québec. Some 75% of the world's maple syrup comes from Québec, where it brings in over $100 million annually.

It was the Native Canadians who first taught Europeans how to make the sweet syrup from maple sap (they would bring it to a boil by tossing hot rocks from a fire into a pot full of sap). Each tribe has their own legend concerning it. Algonquins say that it was discovered when a wife decided to cook her husband's meat in maple sap. Micmacs say that a woman who left a pot of maple sap boiling too long accidentally discovered maple syrup. The Iroquois had it that a wife cooked her husband's meat in maple sap, thinking it was water – the sweet result so pleased hubby, he decided to look into it...

Europeans began making maple syrup in the early 18th century. By the 19th century, cultivating the sap and transforming it into syrup had become a part of Québécois heritage.

Every summer, starches accumulate in maple trees. When the temperature dips below zero, enzymes turn the starch into sucrose. The sugar maple (native to North America) has more of these enzymes than other species, though sap from red and black maple trees are also used in maple syrup production. In early spring, when the daytime temperatures creep above zero, this sweet sap starts to flow. Sap is sucked out through a series of tubes called Sysvacs, which snake through a maple grove to machines that cook it into a syrup. The different grades produced depend on how long it is cooked and to what temperature (to make taffy, for example, the sap must cook to 26°C above boiling point). Maple syrup always contains between 66% and 67% sugar.

Sugar shacks became part of the Québécois experience in the early 20th century. These are places near maple groves, opened for a month or so in February and March, where the maple tradition is experienced at its best. The 'taffy pull' is the most fun – you scoop up some snow, put it on a plate and have some steaming syrup from a piping caldron poured onto it. It hardens as it hits the snow, and it can then be twisted onto a Popsicle stick and sucked and chewed until you feel the need to do it all over again. In addition to the taffy pull and having a look around the syrup-making operations, you can be treated to a hearty Québécois meal.

Some sugar shacks are mentioned throughout this book. Any tourist information office can recommend others. One that's worth highlighting is the **Cabane á Sucre Jean Renaud et Fils** (☎ 450-473-3943, Ⓦ *www.jean-renaud.qc.ca, 1034 boul Arthur Sauvé (Rte 148)*, in Ste Eustache, near Montréal just west of Hwy 13 on the site of a family-run maple grove that's been operating since 1865. The cafeteria-style dining room here is not what you'd call rustic, but the enormous variety of food makes up for it in a big way. There's a huge buffet table or set meals of traditional Québécois meat-heavy food (turkey, beef, chicken and a 'sausage cocktail') and ten kinds of desserts.

kick, try Fin du Monde (End of the World), which is 9% alcohol. Expect to pay $3 to $5 at a bar or pub for a pint.

Wine is expensive by comparison, with bottles costing from around $9 in the supermarket and $20 in restaurants for a basic, drinkable vintage. You'll find plenty of Californian, French, Italian, Chilean and other New World wines, but you'd better know your stuff if Québec wine is on offer:

The industry is young, and much of the tipple tastes like it.

SPECTATOR SPORTS

Catholicism and ice hockey are regarded as national religions in Québec, but baseball also attracts a fair number of fans. Ironically, although the internationally renowned Habs (Montréal Canadiens) and Expos have fallen upon hard times in their leagues,

Montréal's dark-horse football team, les Alouettes, is riding an unexpected wave of popularity.

Hockey

The Montréal Canadiens, which call Montréal's Centre Molson home, have won the coveted Stanley Cup 24 times, but the last time was in 1993 – and the Molson family did the unthinkable by selling the team in 2000. Still, Montréalers have a soft spot for the Habs, and if you're in town during the season, don't miss the opportunity to see a game.

The once-renowned Québec Nordiques ceased to exist in 1995, when they were sold to Denver and became the Colorado Avalanche, who took the Stanley Cup in 1996 and have been doing very well ever since.

Outdoor and minor league hockey games are some of Québec's most memorable sporting affairs – earsplitting cries of *but!* (goal) fueled by thermoses of mulled wine for the outdoor games, and hyperventilating parents shouting from the rafters at the indoor ones, provide the backdrop. During the winter, informal matches take place just about wherever a pond has frozen over and public rinks are set up.

The Ligue de Hockey Junior Majeur du Québec (or, amusingly, the Québec Major Junior Hockey League; w www.lhjmq.qc.ca) has games in smaller towns throughout the province, and some of the most impassioned playing can be seen in these games – often they're more fun than going to a Habs' match. Pre-season and season games can be

seen from mid-August through March. Some of the more popular teams are Les Foreurs (Val d'Or), Les Voltiguers (Drummondville) and L'Océanic (Rimouski). Check out the league's great website for game times and locations.

Baseball

Montréal's National League baseball team, the Expos, has fallen on hard times, and few fans bother to attend games at the Stade Olympique anymore. At press time, the future of the club was still uncertain. A number of minor free agents were signed for the 2002 season, foreshadowing nothing special for the already beleaguered club.

Football

The Alouettes, the once-defunct football team of the teetering CFL (Canadian Football League), have begun filling the house since it moved to the Molson Stadium at Montréal's McGill University. Rules are a bit different from American football: The field is bigger and there are only three downs. The championship game, known as the Grey Cup, is played in late November. For tickets, contact the Alouettes Billeterie (☎ 514-254-2400, 646 rue Ste Catherine).

Grand Prix Racing

Formula 1 racing is rare in North America, so the Circuit Gilles Villeneuve (see the Montréal chapter for details) is deemed a world-class event. It draws thousands of tourists to Montréal every year.

Activities

Dipping into Québec's wilderness is more than highly recommended – a trip to the province wouldn't be complete without partaking in at least some of the region's myriad outdoor sporting activities. It offers without question one of the continent's widest arrays – from snorkeling and kite surfing on the Îles de la Madeleine to ice fishing and dogsledding in the Arctic north.

The Tourisme Québec offices across the province have general information booklets on parks, historic sites, outdoor activities and adventure tour operators. For more details on individual sites and activities mentioned here, see the specific chapter in question.

HIKING

Québec has a virtually limitless array of hiking possibilities, with well-marked trails, ranging in difficulty from beginner to expert, throughout the province. Generally, the most interesting trails are inside national and provincial parks and wildlife reserves. Their welcome centers can furnish you with detailed maps of the trails showing campsites and rest stops. Many will offer organized guided hikes, often with naturalists, geologists or botanists. These can greatly enhance your appreciation of the surrounding nature, and are generally offered on a daily basis from mid-May through late October. A number of easy hiking trails are wheelchair accessible.

Be sure to note the elevation of your proposed trail – if it's high enough, make certain you'll have something warm to throw on should temperatures fall or if the

ROUTE VERTE BIKE TRAIL

wind picks up. Overnight trails will have simple refuges set up along the way.

Many cities and towns also have hiking and walking trails within their urban limits. Notable examples are Montréal, Québec City, Trois Rivières and Tadoussac.

In 2001, the Québec part of the **International Appalachian Trail** opened up in the Gaspésie, connecting to other trails in New Brunswick and the US down the eastern coast all the way to Florida. See the Gaspé Peninsula & Îles de la Madeleine chapter for more details.

CANOEING & KAYAKING

Beautiful memories are guaranteed by taking part in Québec's vast network of navigable waterways. Every national and provincial park and wildlife reserve offers canoe and kayak rental for about $20 to $30; if you plan to make this a main activity, you may save money by buying one. Many of the circuits are popular with canoe-campers and

weekend nature-seekers, but others take you deep into wilderness and may necessitate portage from lake to lake.

The Fédération Québécoise du Canot et du Kayak (☎ 514-252-3001, Ⓦ www.canot-kayak.qc.ca, 4545 avenue Pierre de Coubertin) can provide tons of useful information and has lists of organized group excursions. They also publish (in French) guides to canoeing in Québec.

Sea kayaking is increasingly popular along the north shore of the far eastern St Lawrence River area, especially around the lovely Mingan archipelago. A superb website for those interested in river or sea kayaking is Ⓦ www.out-there.com/kyk_pq.htm. It lists and describes (in English) the main kayak routes in the province.

WHITEWATER RAFTING

Whitewater rafting is popular in specific places throughout the province. Prices for a half-day of rafting are upwards of $60, with longer excursions costing more but usually including a lunch in the price. Some of the more popular places are on the rivière Mattawin, along the rivière Jacques Cartier near Québec City, the rivière Rouge near Montréal and on the Ottawa River in the Outaouais region.

CYCLING

Cycling in Québec has exploded in popularity over the past 10 years. In 1990 there were a handful of organized biking activities; today there are over 65. Now the province is basking in its growing reputation as one of the best places for cycling in all of North America. Each year, the **Tour de l'Île**, in Montréal, attracts some 35,000 cyclists for a 64km circuit; popular side events include the Un Tour La Nuit, a nighttime circuit through downtown, and events geared toward children. Montréal is regularly voted the continent's best, safest city for cycling by cycling magazines, and the Tour de l'Île is even in the Guinness Book of World Records as the biggest of its kind in the world (one year 45,000 cyclists took part).

[continued on page 67]

A WHALE OF A TIME

One of Québec's biggest and most thrilling tourist draws is whale watching. In many areas of the world, people sail for hours to open seas to find the world's largest, most graceful mammals. Not here. The St Lawrence River is regarded as one of the best places on the planet to observe the gentle creatures, as there are so many whales accessibly close to the shore. In fact, there are thousands of North Shore and Gaspésie residents who can spot them through their windows as they sip their morning coffee.

The main reason for the area's abundance of whales – and what led European whalers here well before Jacques Cartier 'discovered' Canada – is the area's abundance of plankton and the krill that feed on it. Unappetizing for us perhaps, but paradise for the finback, minke, humpback, blue and other baleen whales (those with a sieve-like device made of keratin extending from their upper jaws used to filter food) who take to it like a cat to catnip.

There are underwater peaks and valleys where the freshwater Saguenay flows into the salty St Lawrence. Large masses of plankton carried along by strong horizontal currents from the St Lawrence estuary and Gulf hit a sudden rise in the seabed at the rivers' confluence, where it suddenly gets pushed upward toward the surface – where happy, hungry whales wait for it.

This phenomenon has meant that not only do international marine biologists come to the area (to study, among other things, echolocation in belugas and inter-communication between blue whales), but also that hordes of tourists are a given. Even the most jaded among us is a sucker for whales. Who can remain blasé before a whale propelling itself out of the water? Who isn't moved by the sudden sight of a giant dorsal fin emerging from the waves, by that poetic flip of the tail, by the pffoosh sound of a whale breath?

Tourism means big, big business to an area that otherwise would receive, sadly, a modicum of visitors. It's estimated that whale watching brings in over $40 million to the North Shore region. Without it, the town of Tadoussac would be crippled; others farther northeast, as well as communities in the Lower St Lawrence and Gaspésie, would suffer as well.

That watching whales go about their business has been turned into a big industry is not necessarily good news for the whales themselves, who could no doubt do without the extra attention, flashbulbs and cries of 'Oh my gawd, look!'

Types of Whales

Aside from many smaller cetaceans like white-sided Atlantic dolphins and white-beaked dolphins, there are five species of whales you are most likely to see in the St Lawrence estuary, in the river and where it becomes a gulf and sea. Sperm (*cachalot*) and right (*baleine franche*) whales have also been spotted, but rarely.

Beluga (*béluga*) whales are the smallest species of whale, typically measuring about 4.5m meters long and weighing over 1000kg, or 1.1 metric tons. They usually live in groups (called pods) of 20 to 100. Belugas belong to the toothed subgroup of whales and feed on capelin, smelt, herring, crabs and shrimp. They are pale beige or white and are characterized by a protuberant forehead and a mouth that looks caught in a perpetual grin.

Minkes (*petit rorqual*) can grow to 10m and weigh as much as 7250kg. Fast swimmers, they are also the most likely to approach boats (fishermen swear that young minkes approach whenever there are young children aboard) and love to show off by hurling themselves out of the water.

Finbacks (*rorqual commun*) are the second largest animals on the planet, reaching 24m in length (at birth they're already 6m long!) and weighing up to 72,500kg. The spray from their breath can jet out as high as 7m. They feed in groups when preying on small fish, but alone when filling up on krill.

Humpbacks (*rorqual á bosse*) average 15m in length and 28,000kg, and are characterized by dorsal protuberances and denticulated tails. Though slow swimmers, they are known to fly through the air at times, and during mating season will engage in lobtailing, slapping the water several times with their tails while holding themselves in an inverted position.

Blues (*rorqual bleu*) are the planet's largest mammals. The ones in the northern hemisphere, slightly smaller than their southern counterparts, reach 27m in length and can weigh up to 150,000kg (150 tons) – that's nearly as long as three train cars and as heavy as 30 elephants! Their hearts are the size of a VW Beetle. In one mouthful, a blue whale can take in 45 tons of water, and it eats about 4 tons of krill per day.

Above: A blue whale's heart is the size of a Volkswagen Beetle.

What They Won't Tell You

There are now over 50 licensed boats from the north and south shores converging around the Tadoussac area. In 1983, there were eight. Some have been known to chase troupes of whales to give tourists a thrill. Whales sometimes cut themselves against propeller-driven boats. Large boats disturb their feeding, mating and rearing cycles. Even when large boats do not approach menacingly, the noise they emit can result in a modification of the whales' natural process of building energy reserves.

Yet boats and Polaroids are only part of the problem. While commercial whale hunting is no longer an issue in the St Lawrence, the effects of past hunting are still seen today. Most of the world's countries ceased whale hunting after the International Whaling Commission's 1986 call for a moratorium of commercial hunting on baleen whales, as well as of the sperm whale. Yet by the 1970s, when international conservationists began to lobby in earnest, hunters had already killed 90% of the world's largest whales. Norway and Japan are the only countries that currently openly engage in commercial whale hunting. In 1999 Russia planned to recommence its commercial whaling, but called it off.

64 A Whale of a Time

The beluga is an endangered species in the St Lawrence, where they were hunted throughout most of the 20th century. The government used to offer $15 per kill. Incredibly, in the 1940s, bombs were dropped on schools of belugas, as it was thought (mistakenly) that they were responsible for reductions in salmon and cod stocks. Their population plummeted from about 5000 around 1900 to about 500 in the 1970s, when hunting ceased. Their population is thought to have stabilized since then, perhaps slightly risen. Estimates of current numbers of belugas range from 500 to 1000, though some scientists say it could be another decade before it's possible to be certain of the overall trend in their population.

Toxins and pollutants also threaten cetacean health and survival by compromising their immune systems. Whales are on a high level on the food chain and so are vulnerable to the pollutants accumulated along the way. It's estimated that St Lawrence whales have toxin levels eight times higher than those living around Iceland. Belugas seem particularly vulnerable to noxious elements, as they are the only cetacean species to use the St Lawrence for both feeding and breeding. Some beluga carcasses have even been treated as toxic waste.

A number of behavioral changes have been noted in St Lawrence cetaceans in the last few years, and local fishermen report a remarkable decrease in the number of whales seen in the Tadoussac region since about 1999. While only several years ago it was common to see a group of up to 30 finbacks feeding together, now they are most often seen either feeding alone or in much smaller groups. They have also been seen to travel or feed alongside blue whales, a behavior previously only rarely observed. While at least 75 finbacks of the North Atlantic population are known to come to the St Lawrence, only about 20 to 30 are identified each season.

Blue whales are more typically seen farther east, from Les Escoumins to Ste Anne de Portneuf (a deep underwater furrow lies close to the shore there), though the giants have been sighted all along the North Shore. Approximately 70 visit the St Lawrence each spring and summer. Blue whales are officially considered a threatened species, and they may number as few as 500 in the North Atlantic. Worldwide their population is estimated at about 9000, and their long-term survival is far from assured – before large-scale whaling, their numbers were closer to 200,000.

As for minke whales, the only species that never spends any part of the winter in the St Lawrence (blues and finbacks have been sighted in December and January), their total numbers are estimated to be several dozen at most.

Above: 'And they think they're watching *us*!'

Unfortunately exact figures are not possible to come up with, and not only because counting techniques are fraught with logistic problems. Estimates vary depending on their source. There is a huge financial interest on the part of boat-tour operators and even some research organizations in the region not to show a decrease in whales (which might scare off tourists), while alarmists and those resentful of the profits pulled in by others tend to announce a decrease. Confusingly, there is evidence to support either side.

Some locals theorize that many whales have begun feeding away from Tadoussac partly because of the great number of boats congregated there (in 2001, more boat tours than usual were forced to sail an extra 15 to 20 minutes eastward to better their chances of spotting the whales). Aside from tourists disturbing their feeding cycles, it is suspected that illegal winter whale hunting of mammals that would normally return for spring and summer feeding in the St Lawrence might be occurring out on the open seas of the North Atlantic.

What You Can Do

Should whale watching be encouraged? Absolutely! Seeing these marvelous, highly intelligent creatures is enough to sensitize many to their plight. However, choosing to do so conscientiously should be part of the experience. See the North Shore, Lower St Lawrence and Gaspé Peninsula & Îles de la Madeleine chapters for details on the kinds of expeditions offered.

The most ecosensitive way to whale watch is to stand on the coastline. This may not sound exciting, but where there's deep water near the shore, like at Cap du Bon Désir and Les Escoumins, your chances of spotting them surface, very close up, are excellent.

The most thrilling way to conscientiously whale watch can be unnerving to the unprepared, but going out in a sea kayak into waters where whales feed will make you feel on top of the world. However, many areas in the region have very strong currents, making this inadvisable for those without sea kayaking experience.

If you go by boat, try for a Zodiac that holds a maximum of 12 people. The smaller the better; more exciting for you, less disturbing to the whales. It can get chilly, though, so dress warmly.

If you must go with a big boat tour, ask people coming off a previous one what they saw – they are the best indicators of whether or not you're likely to see any. Try to pick a calm day – this could greatly affect your chances of seeing whales.

You may also approach fishermen in whatever village you may find yourself and ask them to take you out – they often know things the official guides don't, and you're practically guaranteed a unique time!

Finally, joining a scientific research team can provide a unique and enriching experience to deepen your knowledge and ensure close contact with whales. The Minganie Research and Interpretation Center, in Longue Pointe de Mingan, offers six-hour outings with researchers, while the Swiss Whale Society, who have a camp at Ste Anne de Portneuf, offers two-week assistantship programs; see the North Shore chapter for details.

Where to Do It

Although the highest concentration of whales has traditionally been at the confluence of the Saguenay and St Lawrence Rivers, blues are more likely to be seen between Les Escoumins and Ste Anne de Portneuf. Belugas get as far west as St Siméon, and other whales are spotted all along the North Shore to the Mingan archipelago. Along the Gaspé Peninsula is another good area, particularly off Forillon National Park. Tours that depart from Lower St Lawrence towns like Trois Pistoles all cross the river to the north side.

Is It Safe?

As excited as people get to be close to whales out on the open sea, many can't help but wonder if the next time it surfaces it will be under their boat. Whales will not purposely go after a boat or a human. The only reported incidents involving a seeming whale 'attack' have been with orcas (which live along the Pacific coast), which have on occasion gone after divers mistaking them for seals, but even they are released once the orca realizes its error. There have been rare incidents of a whale starting to surface under a boat (in this case it will cease to surface and swim away), but the chances of this happening are slim. Despite the carnage humans have wreaked on their world, whales remain the gentlest giants the planet has ever known.

[continued from page 61]

Across the province, the **Route Verte (Green Trail)** is an ongoing system of bike trails on and off major roads that may become the world's longest bike trail when its 2400km are complete (see map on pages 60–61). Many sections are finished and are enjoyed by thousands each year. It takes in some of the loveliest sections of the Eastern Townships, the Laurentians and Charlevoix regions, among others. In Outaouais there is an extensive system of trails near Hull and stretching north through Gatineau Park.

Vélo Québec, at the Maison des Cyclistes (☎ 514-521-8356, Ⓦ www.velo.qc.ca, 1251 rue Rachel Est), in Montréal, is the province's best place for anyone planning on making cycling a part of their trip. Not only do they rent bikes there (from $25/day) but they organize events and guided excursions, give information about which city taxi companies will pick you up with your bike, and offer invaluable tips on how to plan your trip. See their website for more information and for details on the Route Verte.

There's some wicked mountain biking at Bromont and Mont Ste Anne. Beginners can content themselves with Gray Rocks, near Mont Tremblant in the Laurentians.

All bus companies will transport your bikes, usually for a $15 surcharge. However, it must be packed into a box or bag. At Parbus, inside Montréal's main bus station, bike boxes are sold for $5. One company, Limocar (☎ 450-435-6767), which serves destinations in the Laurentians between Montréal and Mont Laurier, does not require boxed bikes and transports them for free.

FISHING & HUNTING

By and large, a permit is required for any fishing and hunting in the province, where such activities are limited to wildlife reserves and areas called ZECs. Both are administered by Sépaq. Permits are valid for a day or an entire season and can be purchased at welcome centers, where daily catch limits will be explained to you.

Salmon fishing, especially on the North Shore and in the Gaspésie, is renowned and has attracted anglers from around the world for generations. Ice fishing is another exotic activity – hardy fishers set up a makeshift shack on the ice, cut a hole through it and sit on a wooden bench, sometimes near a radiator (and plenty of beer), waiting for dinner to nibble.

DIVING & SNORKELING

There are superb diving and snorkeling opportunities in the St Lawrence River, particularly along the North Shore and on the Îles de la Madeleine but also in the Lower St Lawrence and Gaspésie regions. People travel from around the world to engage in snorkeling here. In places, the river bottom is reputed to be as spectacular as anything found in the Caribbean.

The Fédération Québécoise des Activités Subaquatiques (☎ 514-252-3009, Ⓦ www.fqas.qc.ca, 4545 avenue Pierre de Coubertin), in Montréal, is an excellent source of information and keeps detailed records of all the snorkeling and diving centers in the province. They can even tell you where to engage in a game of underwater hockey!

SKIING & SNOWBOARDING

In winter, Québec is one of North America's prime ski meccas, with excellent slopes in the Laurentians (north of Québec City and Montréal) and south of Montréal, close to the US border at Mont Orford and Sutton. See the Downhill Ski Stations map for details on the main ski hills. Tourisme Québec has a *Ski Québec* guide and a *Winter Getaway* booklet, in which various hotel/ski packages are listed.

There are some 150 downhill ski hills in the province, many small but some among the continent's best. Mont Tremblant is Canada's second busiest ski hill, after British Columbia's Whistler. Many resorts have lit runs for nighttime skiing. Equipment rental is always an option; skis average about $27 per day, $38 for snowboards. Day lift tickets are usually between $25 and $50. Snowboarding is wildly popular as well, and boards can be rented at nearly all downhill ski stations. One of the most popular places for snowboarding is at Mont Ste Anne,

DOWNHILL SKI STATIONS

SKI STATION	TOWN	TELEPHONE
1 Ski Gallix	Gallix	418-766-7547
2 Mont Ti-Basse	Baie Comeau	418-296-8311
3 Mont Jacques Cartier	Parc de la Gaspésie	418-763-7811
4 Mont Béchervaise	Gaspé	418-368-2000
5 Mont Kanasuta	Arntfield	819-279-2331
6 Mont Vidéo	Barraute	819-734-3193
7 Mont Lac Vert	Hérbertville	888-344-1101
8 Mont Fortin	Jonquière	418-546-2170
9 Le Valinouët	St David de Falardeau	800-260-8254
10 Mont Édouard	L'Anse St Jean	418-272-2927
11 Parc du Mont St Mathieu	St Mathieu de Rioux	418-738-2298
12 Centre Mont Biencourt	Biencourt	418-499-2445
13 Centre Val Neigette	Ste Blandine	877-735-2299
14 Parc du Mont Comi	St Donat	418-739-4858
15 Parc Régional Val d'Irène	St Irène	418-629-3450
16 Parc Régional du Mont Grand Fonds	La Malbaie	877-665-0095
17 St Pacôme	St Pacôme	418-852-2430
18 Centre de Ski Municipale	La Tuque	819-523-2204
19 Le Massif	Petite Rivière St François	418-632-5876
20 Mont Ste Anne	Beauré	418-827-4561
21 Station Touristique Stoneham	Stoneham	418-848-2411
22 Le Relais	Lac Beauport	418-849-1851
23 Massif du Sud	St Philémon	418-469-3676
24 Vallée du Parc	Grand Mère	800-363-1639
25 St Mathieu Les Cantons	St Mathieu du Parc	819-539-6140
26 Station Touristique La Crapaudière	St Malachie	418-642-5171
27 Mont Orignal	Lac Étchemin	877-335-1551
28 Mont Gleason	Tingwick	888-349-2300
29 Mont Adstock	St Méthode	418-422-2242
30 Mont Ste Marie	Lac Ste Marie	800-567-1256
31 Vorlage/Edelweiss	Wakefield	818-459-2301
32 Mont Cascades	Cantly	819-827-0301
33 Camp Fortune	Chelsea	819-827-1717

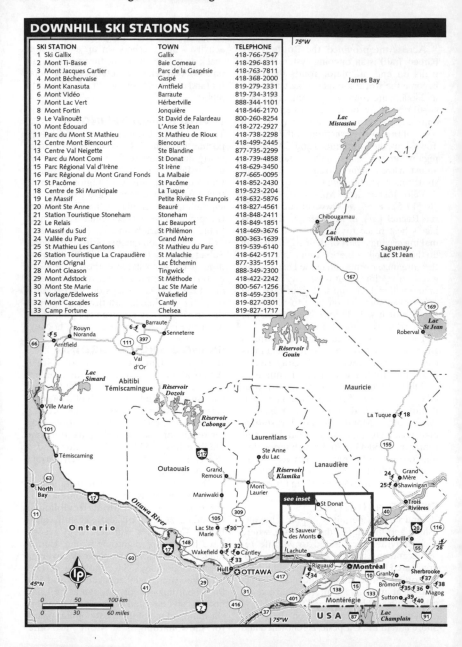

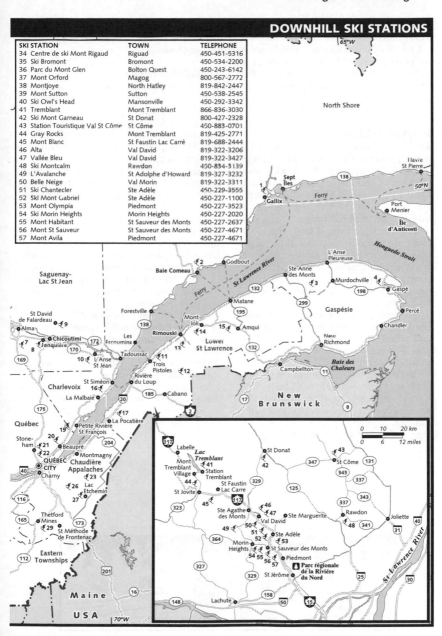

DOWNHILL SKI STATIONS

SKI STATION	TOWN	TELEPHONE
34 Centre de ski Mont Rigaud	Riguad	450-451-5316
35 Ski Bromont	Bromont	450-534-2200
36 Parc du Mont Glen	Bolton Quest	450-243-6142
37 Mont Orford	Magog	800-567-2772
38 Montjoye	North Hatley	819-842-2447
39 Mont Sutton	Sutton	450-538-2545
40 Ski Owl's Head	Mansonville	450-292-3342
41 Tremblant	Mont Tremblant	866-836-3030
42 Ski Mont Garneau	St Donat	800-427-2328
43 Station Touristique Val St Côme	St Côme	450-883-0701
44 Gray Rocks	Mont Tremblant	819-425-2771
45 Mont Blanc	St Faustin Lac Carré	819-688-2444
46 Alta	Val David	819-322-3206
47 Vallée Bleu	Val David	819-322-3427
48 Ski Montcalm	Rawdon	450-834-3139
49 L'Avalanche	St Adolphe d'Howard	819-327-3232
50 Belle Neige	Val Morin	819-322-3311
51 Ski Chantecler	Ste Adèle	450-229-3555
52 Ski Mont Gabriel	Ste Adèle	450-227-1100
53 Mont Olympia	Piedmont	450-227-3523
54 Ski Morin Heights	Morin Heights	450-227-2020
55 Mont Habitant	St Sauveur des Monts	450-227-2637
56 Mont St Sauveur	St Sauveur des Monts	450-227-4671
57 Mont Avila	Piedmont	450-227-4671

outside Québec City. The Snow Surfing World Cup is held there each December.

Cross-country skiing is top-rate across the province as well. There are excellent trails at Gatineau Park and along the Parc Linéaire du P'tit Train du Nord trail, in the Laurentians. Trails usually have an access fee, but this is rarely more than $10.

SNOWMOBILING

What better place to go snowmobiling than in the province that boasts the vehicle's birthplace? Québec is laced with some 33,000km of skidooable trails; it would take a year to cover them all traveling 100km a day. These trails cross through the entire province, are well-maintained – and well-policed. The signed speed limits (usually 60 km/h) are enforced by police riding snowmobiles no doubt faster than yours. Speed freaks get around the law by sometimes veering slightly off-trail – say, by even a meter – as the police have jurisdiction over the trail only.

The Québec Federation of Snowmobile Clubs (☎ 514-252-3076, W www.fcmq.qc.ca, 4545 avenue Pierre de Coubertin), in Montréal, is a great source of information for snowmobile enthusiasts. Their good website has lots of info, links and helpful maps. Also in Montréal, Nonavor (☎ 514-276-7500, W www.nonavor.qc.ca, 4534 avenue de l'Esplanade) organizes snowmobiling, as well as camping, dogsledding and boating excursions, mainly in Québec's northern regions.

Skidoo rental usually costs about $150 per day, plus gas, so it can be a costly though exciting sport.

DOGSLEDDING

Dogsledding has been gaining in popularity in recent years, and there are now dozens of (small and large) organizations across the province offering this service. It's wise to ask many questions before heading out, and ideally a preliminary visit would be advised – not only to check out the facilities, but also to see if the dogs are kept in decent conditions (for more information, see the Responsible Tourism section in the Facts for the Visitor chapter).

Usually sleds are led by Malamutes or Huskies, in groups of four, six, 12 or sometimes as many as 20. Unless you're an experienced dogsledder, the dog's master will steer. Prices range from about $40 for a three- to four-hour expedition to about $130 for a full-day deal, including a meal and perhaps lodging.

Aventures Nord Bec (☎ 418-889-8001, W www.aventures-nord-bec.com, 665 rue St Aimé), in St Lambert, offers excursions. For a fairly comprehensive list of several organizations offering dogsledding expeditions throughout the province, from within an hour's drive of Montréal or Québec City to James Bay, see W www.toile.com/Quebec/commerces_et_economie/Produits_et_services/Sports_et_loisirs/Plein_air/Traineau_a_chiens.

Getting There & Away

AIR

Some simple nuts-and-bolts knowledge about the airline business can save you a bundle of money when buying tickets. The summer months and Christmas holidays are the most expensive seasons; buy early, as advance booking of 14 to 21 days (also known as APEX) reliably produces the best fares. One-way tickets are rarely a bargain, except from Asia. Avoid flying on Fridays and Sundays, and take 'red-eye flights' (in the early morning or late evening). Keep an eye out for standby fares, as well as for specials posted by airlines and travel services on the Web.

Montréal has two airports. Dorval, 20km west of downtown, serves most domestic, US and overseas flights. Mirabel, 55km northeast of downtown, serves mostly charter flights.

Departure Tax

Montréal's Dorval Airport levies a very unpopular 'improvement tax' of $15 on all international flights before you leave (unpopular as it's still one of the most unsightly and worst-organized international airports in North America). Mirabel got in on the fun in 2001 and instituted a $10 departure tax. These are payable at a special payment counter.

Within Canada

Air Canada and its affiliates, such as Air Nova, dominate the home market. For the best deals, check with Travel CUTS (see Travel Agencies in the Facts for the Visitor chapter), the travel section of the *Montréal Gazette* or the *Globe and Mail,* and the Web.

From Vancouver, low-season seat sales to Montréal can be remarkably cheap (around $250), but prices balloon to between $400 and $500 in summer. Along the heavily traveled Toronto-Montréal route, roundtrip fares start as low as $120, including tax – cheaper than the train or bus. From St

John's, Calgary and Edmonton, roundtrips range between $300 and $350 in the low season to around $500 in summer.

The USA

Discount travel agents in the USA are known as consolidators, although you won't see a sign on the door saying 'Consolidator.' San Francisco is the ticket consolidator capital of America, but some good deals can be found in Los Angeles, New York and other big cities.

Council Travel is America's largest student-travel organization, with around 60 offices in the USA; its head office (☎ 800-226-8624, Ⓦ www.ciee.org) is at 205 E 42 St, New York, NY 10017; call for the office nearest you. STA Travel (☎ 800-777-0112, Ⓦ www.statravel.com) has offices in Boston, Chicago, Miami, New York, Philadelphia, San Francisco and other major cities; call for office locations. People younger than 26,

---

Warning

The information in this chapter is particularly vulnerable to change: Prices for international travel are volatile, routes are introduced and cancelled, schedules change, special deals come and go, and rules and visa requirements are amended. Airlines and governments seem to take a perverse pleasure in making price structures and regulations as complicated as possible. You should check directly with the airline or with a travel agent to make sure you understand how a fare (and ticket you may buy) works. In addition, the travel industry is highly competitive, and there are many lurks and perks.

The upshot of this is that you should get opinions, quotes and advice from as many airlines and travel agents as possible before you part with your hard-earned cash. The details given in this chapter should be regarded as pointers and are not a substitute for your own careful, up-to-date research.

---

students and teachers save up to 50% on many routes through these agencies.

Ticket Planet (W www.ticketplanet.com) is a leading ticket consolidator in the USA and is recommended.

Direct flights between major US and Canadian cities are abundant. Air Canada links Newark and New York City with Montréal. The lowest roundtrip fares, often matched by major US carriers, start at US$220. From Boston, roundtrip fares as low as US$160 are available. Royal Air Maroc flights from New York to Montréal start at around US$140.

From Chicago, United Airlines offers roundtrip tickets starting at US$270, as do Air Canada, Canadian Airlines, Northwest and Continental.

Los Angeles is usually the cheapest West Coast gateway to Montréal. Air Canada and many US carriers have roundtrip fares starting at US$450 from Los Angeles and US$500 from San Francisco or Seattle.

Weekly travel sections of the *New York Times, Chicago Tribune, San Francisco Chronicle* and *LA Times* are great sources of cut-rate airfares. Air Canada and many US airlines advertise cheap Internet fares that are available only on their respective websites; these fares are often posted midweek.

Cuba

Many American visitors to Canada make a side trip to Cuba. Air Transat offers good deals from Montréal to Havana, with fares starting at $500 roundtrip. Cubana and Air Canada are also competitive.

Australia & New Zealand

Air Canada, Air New Zealand, Qantas and United Airlines all have regular flights from Australia, most with a stopover in Hawaii or the continental US. For a roundtrip flight, expect to pay A$2350 to A$2750 in the high season and A$2250 to A$2450 in the low season.

Flights from New Zealand to Montréal are limited, with only American Airlines offering direct service. Expect to pay about NZ$2466/2607 for a roundtrip ticket from Auckland in the low/high season.

In Australia, STA Travel (☎ 131-776 Australia-wide, W www.statravel.com.au) is a major dealer in budget fares. Flight Centre (☎ 131-600 Australia-wide, W www.flight centre.com.au) is another option. Smaller agencies often advertise in the Saturday travel sections of the *Sydney Morning Herald* and the Melbourne *Age*.

UK & Continental Europe

Montréal is well served from Europe's main airports. Air Canada offers the most flights, but there's plenty of competition, including Air France, British Airways, Continental, KLM, SAS and United Airlines.

From London, return fares start as low as £231/280 in the low/high season, taxes included. US Airways and British Airways often offer good deals. Prices shoot up during peak periods – standard fares around £500 aren't uncommon.

Cheap airfares appear in the travel pages of the weekend broadsheet newspapers, as well as in *Time Out,* the *Evening Standard* and the free magazine *TNT*. A popular discount travel agency geared toward students (but not exclusively) is STA Travel (☎ 020-7361-6161, W www.statravel.co.uk), which has many offices, including one at 86 Old Brompton Rd, London SW7.

You can also fly to the eastern US and travel by bus or train to Montréal (an eight- to 10-hour journey from New York City). A bevy of airlines offer heavily discounted flights to New York from Europe's air hubs. Roundtrips from London to NYC can be picked up for as low as £150 to £175 in the low season; from Paris, fares start at 1800FF.

Frankfurt, continental Europe's busiest airport, is a good departure point, as many flights on route from Asia to London make a stopover there. Roundtrip tickets to Montréal can cost as little as DM595/1249 in the low/high season.

Roundtrip flights from Paris to Montréal range from 2400FF to 4500FF; tickets from Amsterdam cost about f600 to f1100.

If your schedule is flexible, flying standby can be very reasonable. Airhitch (☎ 01 47 00 16 30 in Paris, ☎ 800-326-2009 in the US; W www.airhitch.org) specializes in this sort of thing and can get you to or from the northeastern US for US$169 plus taxes.

Asia

Flights from Asia to Canada are either eastbound, connecting through Vancouver or major US gateway cities (Detroit, Chicago, New York City), or westbound, via Europe and connecting through London, Frankfurt or Paris.

Air Canada, Japan Airlines, Northwest and American Airlines offer some of the

Air Travel Glossary

Alliances Many of the world's leading airlines are now intimately involved with each other, sharing everything from reservations systems and check-in to aircraft and frequent-flyer schemes. Opponents say that alliances restrict competition. Whatever the arguments, there is no doubt that big alliances are the way of the future.

Courier Fares Businesses often need to send urgent documents or freight securely and quickly. Courier companies hire people to accompany the package through customs and, in return, offer a discount ticket that is sometimes a bargain. However, you may have to surrender all your baggage allowance and take only carry-on luggage.

Fares Airlines traditionally offer 1st-class (coded F), business-class (coded J) and economy-class (coded Y) tickets. These days, there are so many promotional and discounted fares available that few passengers pay full fare.

Lost Tickets If you lose your airline ticket, an airline will usually treat it as a travelers check and, after inquiries, issue you with another one. Legally, however, an airline is entitled to treat it as cash, so if you lose it, then it could be gone forever. Take very good care of your tickets.

Onward Tickets An entry requirement for many countries is that you have a ticket out of the country. If you're unsure of your next move, the easiest solution is to buy the cheapest onward ticket to a neighboring country or a ticket (from a reliable airline) that can later be refunded if you do not use it.

Open-Jaw Tickets These are return tickets used to fly out to one place but return from another. If available, this can save you from having to backtrack to your arrival point.

Overbooking Since every flight has some passengers who fail to show up, airlines often book more passengers than they have seats. Usually excess passengers make up for the no-shows, but occasionally somebody gets 'bumped' onto the next available flight. Who is it most likely to be? The passengers who check in late. If you do get bumped, you are normally offered some form of compensation.

Reconfirmation Some airlines require you to reconfirm your flight at least 72 hours prior to departure. Check your travel documents to see if this is the case.

Restrictions Discounted tickets often have various restrictions – such as mandatory advance payment and penalties for alterations or cancellations. Others have restrictions on the minimum and maximum period you must be away.

Round-the-World (RTW) Tickets These tickets give you a limited period (usually a year) in which to circumnavigate the globe. You can go anywhere the carrying airlines go, as long as you don't backtrack. The number of stopovers or the total number of separate flights is decided before you set off, and these tickets usually cost a bit more than a basic return flight.

Ticketless Travel Airlines are gradually waking up to the realization that paper tickets are unnecessary encumbrances. On simple one-way or roundtrip journeys, reservations details can be held on computer, and the passengers merely show identification to claim their seats.

Transferred Tickets Airline tickets cannot be transferred from one person to another. Travelers sometimes try to sell the return half of their tickets, but officials can ask you to prove that you are the person named on the ticket. On an international flight, the name on the ticket is compared with the name on the passport.

lowest fares from Japan, starting at ¥91,000 roundtrip, excluding taxes. Asiana and Korean Air fly roundtrip from Bangkok for as low as B41,600. Fares jump if you're flying from Hong Kong (HK$13,250) or Singapore (S$3270) – try Asiana, China Airlines, Eva Air, Korean Air or Thai Airways.

Bucket shops in Bangkok, Hong Kong and Singapore undercut the airlines by far.

Buying Tickets Online

Purchasing tickets online has become increasingly popular in the last few years, as consumers take advantage of discounts and appreciate the convenience of doing research on the Web. While sometimes nothing beats talking to a travel agent in person, other times it's great not to have to wait forever on the phone while on hold. There are many organizations offering full- and reduced-fare tickets online. These are a few that we recommend.

American Express Travel
    W www.americanexpress.com/travel
Atevo Travel
    W www.atevo.com
Biztravel.com Inc
    W www.biztravel.com
CNN Interactive Travel Guide
    W www.cnn.com/travel
Miscrosoft Expedia
    W www.expedia.com
Orbitz
    W www.orbitz.com
Priceline
    W www.priceline.com
Travelocity
    W www.travelocity.com

There are also online travel agencies that specialize in cheap fares:

Travel Hub W www.travelhub.com
Cheap Tickets W www.cheaptickets.com
Lowest Fare.com W www.lowestfare.com
Yahoo Travel W http://travel.yahoo.com

One-way fares are steeply discounted; a flight from Bangkok to Toronto, sometimes with a stopover in the US, might cost only B15,000. Some travel agencies are of the cut-and-run variety, so ask around before you buy.

Airlines

The following is a list of international airlines that serve Montréal. You can also see the 'Air Line Companies' in the English section of the yellow pages.

You can call airport information (☎ 514-394-7377) 6am to 10pm daily for details on departures and arrivals at Dorval and Mirabel Airports.

Air Canada   (☎ 514-393-3333)
    W www.aircanada.ca
Air France   (☎ 514-847-1106)
    W www.airfrance.com
Air Transat   (☎ 877-872-6728)
    W www.airtransat.com
American Airlines   (☎ 800-433-7300)
    W www.aa.com
British Airways   (☎ 514-287-9282)
    W www.britishairways.com
Continental Airlines   (☎ 800-231-0856)
    W www.continental.com
Delta Air Lines   (☎ 800-325-1999)
    W www.delta.com
Japan Airlines   (☎ 800-525-3663)
    W www.japanairlines.com
KLM   (☎ 514-397-0775)
    W www.klm.com
Lufthansa   (☎ 800-563-5954)
    W www.lufthansa.com
Northwest Airlines   (☎ 800-361-5073)
    W www.nwa.com
Royal Airlines   (☎ 888-828-9797)
    W www.royalairlines.com
Sabena   (☎ 800-955-2000)
    W www.sabena.com
Singapore Airlines   (☎ 514-748-2769)
    W www.singapore-airlines.com
United Airlines   (☎ 800-241-6522)
    W www.unitedairlines.com
US Airways   (☎ 800-428-4322)
    W www.usairways.com

LAND
Border Crossings
During the summer and on holiday week-ends, waits of several hours are common at major US/Canada border crossings. The busiest is at Rouse's Point (New York State). The smaller crossings are almost always quiet, including Abercorn and High-water (4km south of Mansonville) in the Eastern Townships from Vermont's Rtes 105 and 101, respectively, and Hemmingford via New York's Rte 22. Increased security at border crossings after the September 2001 terrorist attacks in the US has not caused excessive delays for visitors, mainly because of a corresponding decrease in traffic.

Bus
Allow about 45 minutes before departure to buy a ticket – don't assume the automated ticket vendors will work. Most advance tickets don't guarantee a seat, so show up early to line up at the counter. Note that buses get extremely full around holidays. See the Getting Around chapter for details on the discounts offered on bus tickets.

Montréal's Central Bus Station (Station Centrale de l'Autobus) is at 505 rue de Maisonneuve Est. All major lines for Cana-dian and US destinations depart from there.

Within Canada Voyageur (☎ 514-842-2281, W www.voyageur.com/info.htm) run express buses to Ottawa ($31, 2¼ hours) every hour on the hour from 6am to midnight daily. About ten other buses a day head to Ottawa but make local stops along the way.

Coach Canada (☎ 705-748-6411, 800-461-7661) run buses between Montréal and Toronto ($86, 7 hours, 7 daily), via Kingston. There's also a bus to Vancouver via Ottawa, Sudbury and Calgary ($327, 71 to 75 hours, 1 daily).

SMT (☎ 800-567-5151, W www.smtbus.com) and its subdivision Acadian (W www.acadianbus .com) operate buses between Montréal and

Moncton, New Brunswick ($105, 14½ to 16 hours, 3 daily), where other connections are possible to Sydney and Halifax, in Nova Scotia. A ticket from Montréal to Halifax costs $125; the trip takes 20 hours.

For cross-country journeys, Greyhound (W www.greyhound.ca) also offers the Canada Coach Pass, which comes in many varieties, including seven- ($244/218 adult/ student), 15- ($364/324), 30- ($414/367) and 60-day ($554/491) variations (all prices do not include a 7% tax).

The USA Vermont Transit Lines (☎ 514-842-2281, 802-864-6811 in USA, W www .vermonttransit.com) runs buses out of Montréal to Burlington ($33, 2½ hours, 5 daily) and Boston ($87, 7 hours, 5 daily).

Greyhound (☎ 514-842-2281, 800-231-2222, W www.greyhound.ca) has buses to/ from New York City ($105, 7¾ to 8½ hours, 6 daily). Greyhound Ameripass holders travel free between Montréal and Boston or New York.

Train
Canadians feel a special attachment to their 'ribbons of steel' – even though they don't take the train very often. These passenger services, operated by VIA Rail Canada, ar-guably remain Canada's most enjoyable (and romantic) way to travel.

Long-distance train travel is more ex-pensive than the bus, and reservations are

Canada's 'ribbons of steel' offer a scenic and romantic journey.

important, especially for weekend and holiday travel. Five days' notice drops the fares by as much as 40%, except on Friday and Sunday. Students, seniors and children also get discounts, but there are usually no special roundtrip or excursion fares.

Montréal's Gare Centrale is the local hub of VIA Rail (☎ 514-989-2626, 416-366-8411 in Toronto, Ⓦ www.viarail.ca). Service is best along the so-called Québec City–Windsor corridor, which includes Montréal, Ottawa, Kingston, Toronto and Niagara Falls. Drinks and snacks are served from aisle carts, and some trains have a dining and bar car.

VIA Rail's overnight service between Montréal and Toronto is a treat. Trains leave at 11:30pm nightly except Saturday, arriving at 8:20am with a complimentary breakfast the next morning. Standard one-way fares in a sleeper cabin start at $91, taxes included. At other times the service takes five hours, and the price rises to $113 without five-day advance purchase.

Canrailpass For those who are traveling a lot, VIA Rail offers the Canrailpass, which is good for 12 days of coach-class travel within a 30-consecutive-day period. The pass is good for any number of trips and stopovers from coast to coast. Reserving early is recommended, though, as the number of seats on the train set aside for pass holders is limited. Free seat reservations can be made up to six months in advance. You can buy the Canrailpass in Canada or in Europe (ask a travel agent or a VIA Rail outlet) but there's no difference in cost.

For travel between June and mid-October, this pass costs $678/610 adult/student. From mid-October to May it costs $423/381.

Canrailpass holders may be entitled to discounts at car rental agencies, at Gray Line for bus tours and at some hotels.

Amtrak This railway, which is the US equivalent of VIA Rail, offers cut-rate passes and information on its services at many Canadian train stations.

Amtrak has a twice-daily service between Montréal and New York City (US$54 to US$61, ten to 12 hours), one of which goes through St Albans, Vermont. Reservations are needed for all trains. For information about fares and schedules, contact Amtrak (☎ 215-824-1600, 800-872-7245, Ⓦ www.amtrak.com).

Car & Motorcycle
Continental US highways link directly with their Canadian counterparts along the border at numerous points. These roads meet up with the Trans-Canada Highway, which runs directly through Montréal. From Boston to Montréal, it's about 490km, or about 4½ hours; from Toronto, it's 540km, or a little over five hours.

Visitors with US or British passports are allowed to bring their vehicles into Canada for six months. For information on car rental and parking, see the Getting Around chapter.

Driveaways One of the best driving deals in North America is Driveaway. Basically, you drive someone's car to a specific destination because the owner has had to fly or doesn't have the time, patience or ability to drive a long distance.

In Montréal, Driveaway (☎ 514-489-3861, 800-647-7992, Ⓦ www.driveaway.com) is located at 345 avenue Victoria. Once you're matched with a car, you put down a deposit of $200 to $300 and get a certain number of days to deliver the vehicle. Call the office three to four days before your planned departure. Ask about what happens if the car breaks down, and get this information in writing. Most cars offered are fairly new and in good working order. Driveaway is open 9am to 5pm weekdays.

Ride Sharing Autotaxi (Ⓦ www.autotaxi.com) is a Québec-based Web bulletin board for ride sharing. The registered drivers' routes, schedules and contact details are all posted online. A shared ride between Montréal and Toronto usually costs around $40.

ORGANIZED TOURS

Suntrek (☎ 707-523-1800, 800-786-8735, Ⓦ www.suntrek.com) offers two- to five-week trips – most are city-and-sights oriented, but there are also a few geared toward outdoor activities.

TrekAmerica (☎ 973-983-1144, 800-221-0596, in the UK ☎ 01295-256777, Ⓦ www .trekamerica.com) runs three-week Canada Frontier tours starting in New York or Seattle and hitting Montréal, Toronto and Vancouver along their transcontinental route. Prices usually start at US$1200.

The HI youth hostels also run tours and special-event trips year-round. See Ⓦ www.hihostels.ca.

Getting Around

If you're not on an organized tour, there are only two ways to get around Québec: public or private transportation. Private transportation includes riding a bicycle – a feasible, eco-friendly option. Driving your own car is the most common way to go, and will give you much-appreciated flexibility and allow you to see more of the province. Gasoline prices are higher than in the US but considerably lower than those in Europe.

Public transportation – mainly bus and train – is a reliable option. Service in Québec is reliable and on time. For many small towns or out-of-the-way destinations, however, infrequent or nonexistent service may create frustrations.

No matter your chosen mode of transport, it makes sense to do as much planning as possible when setting out to discover an area as vast as Québec.

AIR

There are many inter-provincial flights, which can be an option for those who have the luxury of saving hours of travel in exchange for a bundle of cash. In general, air travel is not cheap within Québec (partially as many of the passengers fly for business-related reasons) and can cost astronomical sums for travelers flying to the province's northern reaches. That said, with enough advance planning, some flights (especially to the Îles de la Madeleine) might end up being cost effective. Low-season flights are always cheaper; most booking agents will define high season as stretching from mid- or late June through early September, and again around the Christmas and New Year's holidays. Some will have shoulder seasons just before and after these dates, with *really* low season usually being between October and December and from February through April.

Air Canada (☎ 800-630-3299, 888-247-2262, Ⓦ www.aircanada.ca) and its regional airlines Air Nova (☎ 800-272-9662, 888-247-2262, Ⓦ www.airnova.ca) and Air Alliance

serve airports at Montréal, Québec City, Bagotville, Val d'Or, Rouyn-Noranda, Mont Joli, Gaspé, Îles de la Madeleine, Baie Comeau and Sept Îles. To qualify for an excursion fare, bookings must be made seven days in advance and include a Saturday stay. Sometimes a lower fare is available with 14-days advance booking. They have regular seat sales, so it's worth checking out their websites.

Roundtrip flights between Montréal and Québec City in summertime are about $250 with advance booking. For roundtrip flights from Montréal to Val d'Or, count on $200 to $300. To get to the Îles de la Madeleine from Montréal, a roundtrip ticket can cost as little as $388 in low season and $460 in summer to over $600 without seven-days advance notice.

There are several small airlines serving the North Shore. Aviation Québec Labrador (☎ 418-962-7901) runs flights from Sept Îles to the small communities all the way to Blanc Sablon, as well as north to Schefferville. A roundtrip flight between any two towns will cost around $300.

Three airlines serve northern Québec's: the Abitibi-Témiscamingue, James Bay and Nunavik regions. Air Creebec (☎ 800-567-6567, Ⓦ www.aircreebec.ca), First Air (☎ 800-267-1247, Ⓦ www.firstair.ca) and Air Inuit (☎ 800-361-2965, Ⓦ www.airinuit.ca) link southern and northern Québec. See the Northern Québec chapter for details, but count on at least $1500 roundtrip from Montréal to any village in Nunavik.

Some small airports may charge a departure tax. The airport in Gaspé, for example, will expect an extra $10 to fly from it, payable just before your flight.

BUS

Buses provide a reliable and relatively cheap mode of transportation, slightly cheaper than trains and with more frequent service. Generally, buses are punctual, safe and clean.

Several bus companies operate in Québec and serve every corner of the province. If different companies serve the same town, they stop at the same bus station. Information about bus routes is given by each town's bus station. Montréal's Central Bus Station (Station Centrale de l'Autobus; ☎ 514-842-2281), 505 rue de Maisonneuve Est, can provide information about all routes in the province.

Each company offers similar discounts. Students and seniors over 60 are given a 25% to 30% discount, and children under 12 ride for half price. Some companies offer a 25% discount on same-day returns, others offer specials on a return within ten days. All prices listed in this book are the regular, adult one-way fares. See the Activities chapter for information about transporting bicycles on intercity buses.

A Route Pass that offers unlimited travel throughout Québec and Ontario for 7/14/18 days costs $204/232/290 and is available between mid-May and mid-December from any bus station. This allows you to hop on and off buses along any route as many times as you like within the time limit. The 18-day pass is also good for travel to/from New York City. There are some restrictions; for example, you can't travel back and forth between two cities countless times.

It's advisable to arrive at least a half-hour before departure time, particularly on weekends. If possible, purchase tickets in advance. It's also wise to inquire whether your desired route has an express bus service – traveling time between, say, Montréal and Ottawa or Québec City can be greatly reduced by avoiding the milk runs! Prices on express buses are the same as on the regular runs.

All main bus stations in the province offer a minimum of services – telephone, washroom, cafeteria (or automated junk-food machines!). Most bus stops are located just outside a *dépanneur* (convenience store) or diner. Take your own picnic whenever possible, as the long-distance buses stop at highway service-station restaurants where you pay an awful lot for even more awful plastic food.

In summer the air-conditioners on buses can be far too effective. Take a sweater on board. Smoking is not permitted.

TRAIN

Train service in Canada is under the dominion of VIA Rail (☎ 888-842-7245, 800-361-5390, Ⓦ www.viarail.ca). The VIA logo is nearly synonymous with train travel. Taking the train is slightly more expensive than the bus, with generally less frequent service, but it's also more comfortable and often far more scenic.

Purchasing your ticket five days in advance can save you at least 30% off regular fares ($48 versus $60 from Montréal to Québec City, for example), and train fares listed throughout the book reflect this discount. Children two to 11 years old travel at half the economy fare, and children 12 to 17 get a 35% discount, as do seniors over 60 and students with a valid International Student Identity Card (ISIC). Seniors can also take advantage of special services such as priority boarding, special meals and occasional discounts. Consult VIA Rail's extensive website for current specials or to verify current prices.

VIA Rail also sells the Corridor Pass, which offers ten days of unlimited travel between Québec City and Toronto (connecting Montréal and Ottawa) for $228/205 adult/student.

If you're heading to the Gaspé Peninsula, be sure to check your arrival time – trains from Montréal tend to arrive past midnight in that area, and while taxis will be waiting to pick you up, you'll need to have your lodging pre-arranged to avoid middle-of-the-night confusion.

For travel in the greater Montréal region, GO commuter trains (☎ 514-869-3200) serve the suburbs from the Gare Centrale and Gare Windsor. Fares in Zone 1 (which includes Dorval Airport) are covered by all Métro and bus tickets; for destinations in other zones, buy a supplement at the ticket counters or at automated ticket machines. Note that commuter trains to Dorval Airport are infrequent, and services end in the early evening.

CAR & MOTORCYCLE

Though not the most ecologically sound option, traveling the province by car is the most convenient one. Major and minor roads are well maintained (Montréal's notorious potholes do not spread out across the province!). Directions are better indicated on road signs between cities than within them. Most major routes have frequent rest stops, often at scenic spots, and are usually set up with information panels. While all road signs in Québec are unfortunately in French only, this fact should not make it any more difficult to get to one's destination. Having a good road map or atlas is always advisable – these are available at bookstores and tourist information offices across the province.

There are no tolls to pay in the province on roads or bridges with only one exception: the small bridge leading to the entrance of the Réserve Faunique du St Maurice, north of Trois Rivières.

All speed limit signs are written in metric. The usual speed limit on intercity routes is 100 km/h (60 mph). Highways are indicated by blue numbered signs, routes (major roads) by green numbered signs.

The Ministère des Transports has a great website (W www.mtq.gouv.qc.ca) where road conditions are listed for every main road in the province. Updated frequently, especially in wintertime, its information is available in English.

Road Rules & Safety Precautions

The use of seat belts is compulsory throughout Canada and the fines for not wearing them are heavy. There are speed traps all across the provinces, even on long, straight roads with light traffic on the North Shore and in the far north. Most traffic police work partly 'on commission' and therefore likely will be thinking primarily of their pockets as they listen stone-faced to your myriad excuses while writing out a fat ticket.

All provinces require motorcyclists to drive with the lights on and for them and their passengers to wear helmets.

Driving Distance (in miles)

	Toronto	Baie Comeau	Chibougamau	Chicoutimi	Gaspé	Hull	Îles de la Madeleine	Matane	Mont Laurier	Montréal	Québec City	Rivière du Loup	Sept Îles	Sherbrooke	St Agathe	Trois Rivières
Baie Comeau	1224															
Chibougamau	1124	676														
Chicoutimi	1000	315	363													
Gaspé	1476	290	990	649												
Hull	399	866	767	660	1116											
Îles de la Madeleine	1818	669	1356	994	839	1465										
Matane	1182	516	706	354	288	831	669									
Mont Laurier	607	909	640	693	1150	208	1511	874								
Montréal	546	670	696	464	919	205	1272	636	238							
Québec City	802	412	515	211	694	449	1042	406	477	254						
Riviére du Loup	982	241	495	157	490	631	837	200	665	433	206					
Sept Îles	1449	228	917	543	517	1096	871	232	1118	900	650	466				
Sherbrooke	693	654	717	448	904	349	1257	620	384	147	237	420	886			
St Agathe	600	769	763	557	1015	201	1375	739	140	103	338	539	984	248		
Trois Rivières	688	545	570	338	824	328	1173	522	345	142	130	320	768	154	210	
Val d'Or	713	1060	412	747	1443	429	1804	1153	293	531	775	958	1302	677	428	638

Traffic in both directions must stop when stationary school buses have their red lights flashing – this means children are getting off and on. In cities with pedestrian crosswalks, cars must stop to allow pedestrians to cross.

Québec (along with New York City) has until recently been the only place in North America to forbid a right turn on a red light. From August 18, 2002, a right turn on red will be permitted across Québec except for the island of Montréal (where drivers are less trustworthy). Until that time, it is permitted in 26 municipalities including the cities of Chicoutimi, Jonquière, Val d'Or and Drummondville. A large green sign with a hand sticking out of a traffic light indicates that a right turn on a red light is permitted; the same sign in red, and with a bar across the traffic light indicates that it is not permitted.

A valid driver's license from any country is good in Canada for three months, and an International Driving Permit, available in your home country, is cheap and good for one year almost anywhere in the world. You can't drive in Canada without auto insurance.

Driving in areas where there is heavy snow is best avoided, but if you do, it may mean having to buy snow tires. Many Canadian cars have four-season radials. If you get stuck, don't stay in the car with the engine going; every year people die of carbon monoxide suffocation by doing this during big storms. A single candle burning in the car will keep it reasonably warm.

In parts of the province, wildlife on the road such as deer and moose are a potential hazard. Most run-ins occur at night when animals are active and visibility is poor. In areas with roadside signs alerting drivers to possible animal crossings, keep your eyes scanning both sides of the road and be prepared to stop or swerve. Often a vehicle's headlights will mesmerize the animal, leaving it frozen in the middle of the road. A direct collision with a moose can be deadly – for both of you. Try flashing the lights or turning them off, as well as using the horn.

Rental

Every city and town has car rentals available, and shopping around for the best rates could save you lots of money. Generally, count on about $30 to $40 a day for a weekly or monthly rental, $40 to $60 for a daily rental. Be sure to ask about mileage limits – if you're planning to drive from Montréal to the Gaspésie, North Shore or Nunavik, they can add up very quickly, and paying 10 to 25 cents per extra kilometer incurred could get frightfully expensive. If this is an issue, try different companies – there's always one that will offer unlimited mileage.

Call the toll-free reservations numbers of large chains like Avis (☎ 800-879-2847, W www.avis.com), Budget (☎ 800-268-8900, W www.budget.com), Dollar (☎ 800-800-4000, W www.dollar.com), Hertz (☎ 800-263-0600, W www.hertz.com) and National (☎ 800-227-7368, W www.nationalcar.com) to compare prices.

Then call smaller companies to see if they'll give you a better deal. Enterprise (☎ 800-325-8007, W www.enterprise.com) has an impressive 23 locations across Canada, Discount (☎ 888-636-9333, W www.discountcars.ca) has ten and Rent-a-Wreck (☎ 800-327-0116, W www.rentawreck.ca) has eight. See the Getting Around section in the Montréal chapter for details on local branches of these companies.

Note that rates are not consistent within any company and each outlet is run independently. Rates vary from city to city, location to location. Downtown usually offers cheaper rates than the airport.

Weekend rates are often the cheapest and can include extra days, so building a schedule around this can save a lot of money. 'Weekends' in car-rental lingo can mean three or even four days. For example, if you pick up a car Friday morning and return it before midnight Monday, it may be billed as just three days.

Beware that prices can be deceptive. The daily rate may be an enticing $29, but by the time you finish with insurance, gasoline (fill it up before taking it back or you pay the rental company's gas prices plus a fee for labor), the number of kilometers, provincial sales tax, GST and any other bits and pieces, you can be handed a pretty surprising bill. Make sure you know all the extra costs.

Some companies require you to be over 21 years of age, others over 26. You may be asked to buy extra insurance depending on your age, but the required premiums are not high. Insurance is generally optional. Check to see if your car insurance at home includes rentals or offers a rental clause. Doing it this way is cheaper than buying the insurance from the rental agency.

Parents should note that children under 18kg (40lbs) are required to be in a safety car seat which must be secured by a seat belt. The big-name rental companies can supply seats at a small daily rental fee. Outside of the major cities it may take a couple of days for the outlet to come up with one but the cost is the same.

Purchase

Older cars can be bought quite cheaply in Canada. Look in the local newspaper or, in larger centers, the weekly *Buy & Sell Bargain Hunter Press, Auto Trader* or an

Three Little Words

Many tourists wonder what the three words written on every license plate in the province, '*Je me souviens,*' mean. When they're told 'I remember,' they usually go silent. Not as straightforward as 'The Sunshine State,' that's for sure, though Québec's equivalent, *La Belle Province* (The Beautiful Province), is another motto. But what makes Québécois so proud of their good memories?

The slogan was first added to the provincial coat of arms in 1883. Author Eugène Taché, the architect of Québec City's Parliament Building, intended it to prolong the memory of a people and its hardships. Of course, it can be interpreted in various ways, but most agree the slant is sociopolitical. The words speak of a permanent recognition, though it may remain unstated, of the fact that the French of Québec have been victims of colonialist policies and denied nationhood.

In 1939 the provincial government adopted 'Je me souviens' as its official slogan.

equivalent, all of which can be bought at corner variety stores. Private deals are nearly always the most economical way to buy a car. Used-car businesses must mark up the prices in order to make a profit. Generally, North American cars are priced lower than Japanese and European cars.

For those who prefer a semi-scientific approach to car buying, take a look at Phil Edmunston's excellent *Lemon-Aid,* an annual book published by the Canadian Automobile Protection Association. It is available in stores and libraries, and details all the used cars on the market, rates them and gives rough price guidelines. Haggling over car prices, whether at a dealership or at someone's home, is the norm. Expect to knock off hundreds or even a thousand dollars depending on the value of the car.

For a few months driving, a used car can be an excellent investment, especially if there are two of you. You can usually sell the car for nearly what you paid for it. A fairly decent older car should be available for under $4000. West Coast cars last longer because salt does not have to be used on the roads in winter, which means the cars rust less quickly.

You will need Canadian auto insurance. Bring a letter from your current insurance company indicating your driving record. In addition to making a transaction easier, this might entitle you to some discount as it makes you a more credible risk. You will also need an International Driver's License. Call an insurance broker (check the Yellow Pages phone book) in Canada and they will find you a company offering temporary insurance, say three months. In order to get the insurance and then a plate for the vehicle, you will need an address in Canada. That of a friend or relative will suffice. You should also have your passport.

Insurance costs vary widely and can change dramatically from province to province. As a rule, the rates for women are noticeably less than for a man of comparable age and driving record. If you're planning a side trip to the USA, make sure the insurance you negotiate is valid over the border, too. Also remember that rates are linked to the age and type of car. A newer car may cost more to insure but may also be easier to sell.

Ride Sharing

Allô Stop (☎ 514-985-3032, ⓦ www.allostop.com), which originated in Québec, is a company that acts as an agency for car sharing. It unites people looking for rides with people who have cars and are looking for company and someone to share gasoline expenses. It is a good service that has been around for years.

Autotaxi (ⓦ www.autotaxi.com) is a highly recommended Web-based bulletin board for ride sharing in all corners of the province and has great deals. See the Getting Around section of the Montréal chapter for more details.

Gasoline

Gasoline (petrol), or simply gas (*gaz* in Québec), varies in price across the country with the highest prices in the far north and on the east coast. In the east, the prices are highest in Québec, Newfoundland and Labrador. Drivers approaching Québec from Ontario should top up the tank before the border. Those arriving from the USA should always have a full tank, as the low US prices will never be seen in Canada.

In general the big cities have the best prices, so fill up in town. The more remote a place, the higher the price is. Major-highway service stations offer no bargains and often jack up the price on long weekends and at holiday time in order to fleece captive victims. Gasoline is always sold by the liter. On average a liter of gasoline costs about $0.60, or about $2.70 per imperial gallon. The Canadian (imperial) gallon is one-fifth larger than the US gallon.

Credit cards are accepted at service stations, many of which are now self-service and will not accept large bills at night. The large cities have some service stations that are open 24 hours, but you may have to search around. On the highways, truck stops stay open the longest hours and some have showers you can use.

Canadian Automobile Association

Known as the CAA (☎ 514-861-7575, 800-686-9243, ⓦ www.caa-quebec.qc.ca), this large organization, like its counterpart, the American Automobile Association (AAA), provides assistance to member motorists (check in your country of origin to see if there are reciprocal agreements). The services provided include 24-hour emergency roadside assistance, trip planning and advice, and it can supply travelers checks.

If you have a decent car the association's help may not be necessary, but if you have bought an older car to tour the country the fee may well be invaluable, and after one or two breakdowns will have paid for itself – towing charges are high.

BICYCLE

This mode of transport is equally popular in and out of the cities. Québec has thousands of kilometers of well-maintained cycleable routes throughout the province, with many service points (tourist information kiosks, restaurants, restrooms) along the way. Some of the more popular regions with cyclists include the Eastern Townships, Laurentians (especially the Parc Linéaire P'tit Train du Nord) and the Gaspé Peninsula. Rentals are easy to find all over the province.

Bus companies, VIA Rail and an increasing number of taxi companies offer bicycle transportation for a small additional fee. Anyone planning to do a significant amount of cycling in the province should first consult Vélo Québec (☎ 514-521-8356, ⓦ www.velo.qc.ca) for a wealth of information and invaluable maps. See the Activities chapter for more details.

HITCHHIKING

Readers' letters indicate there have been no problems hitchhiking in Canada, however, hitchhiking is never entirely safe in any country in the world, and we don't recommend it. Travelers who decide to hitch should understand that they are taking a small but potentially serious risk. People who do choose to hitch will be safer if they travel in pairs and let someone know where they are planning to go. Hitchhiking in Québec is generally an acceptable mode of transport, though not as popular as in other parts of Canada. On main roads, it never takes too long to get a lift.

Out of the big cities, stay on the main highways. Traffic can be very light on the smaller roads. Always get off where there's a service station or restaurant and not at a side road or farmer's gate.

Around towns and cities, pick your spots carefully. Stand where you can be seen and where a car can easily stop. A foreign T-shirt, like one with 'University of Stockholm' on it, might be useful. Some people find a cardboard sign with large clear letters naming their destination can be a help.

BOAT

The magnificent St Lawrence River, as well as the over a million lakes and rivers in Québec, will surely entice you out onto their waters. An excursion along the fjord of the rivière Saguenay, around the magnificent islands of the Mingan archipelago, around the Îles de la Madeleine or to the islands along the coast in the Lower St Lawrence are just some of the possibilities available for a memorable boat outing in Québec.

Boat is the only mode of transport (aside from airplane) to reach the isolated fishing communities of the lower North Shore. It's also possible to travel all the way from Montréal to the Îles de la Madeleine, with several stops along the way to take in the stunning Gaspé coastline.

From Sorel near Montréal all the way along the St Lawrence to Matane, there are a number of ferries that regularly cross the river, transporting both passengers and cars almost year-round. See regional chapters for more details about these ferry services.

ORGANIZED TOURS

While organized tours may appear anathema to the bold, independent traveler, there are a number of fine outfits in Québec that can do much to enrich your time in the province. Depending on your interests, they can help plan all or a small part of your trip and ensure a healthy dose of outdoor activities. This can potentially save on costs and many organizing headaches.

Always make sure you know exactly what sort of tour you're getting and how much it will cost. If you have any doubts about the agency or the company it may be dealing with, pay your money into what is called the 'tour operators escrow account.' The law requires that this account number appear on tourist brochures (you may have to look hard). Doing this protects you and your money should the trip fall through for any reason. It's a good idea to pay by check because cash is always harder to get back; write the details of the tour, with destination and dates, on the front of the check. On the back write 'for deposit only.'

The organization that gets the best marks from our readers is the Moose Travel Company (☎ 905-853-4762, 800-816-6673, Ⓦ www.moosetravelco.com), operated out of Ontario. Run by a fun-loving and well-organized bunch, they set up trips to the Charlevoix and North Shore regions in their own minibuses. You can jump on and off the bus as often as you like, allowing you to spend time in any of their stops (Tadoussac, Stoneham and Baie St Paul are popular), then hop on another tour bus when you're ready to meet new travelers and continue to your next destination.

Between May and October they have three departures a week from their numerous points of departure – their Québec tours generally leave from Montréal – and they'll drop you off at the door of your intended destination. A pass good for the entire summer costs about $240. They also issue some rail passes and organize trips across Canada.

Guide Aventure (☎ 418-549-7512, 800-465-7512, Ⓦ www.guideaventure.com), based in Chicoutimi, is another excellent outfit which offers a variety of sporting activities in some of Québec's most remote areas. They organize hiking expeditions in the Groulx Mountains (halfway between Baie Comeau and Labrador), canoe and kayak trips near Mistassini, dogsledding treks through the Saguenay region and a wide range of other trips. Some of their excursions cost up to $1700, with meals and lodging included, but you'll be assured a good time with expert guides.

The Swiss Whale Society (W www.isuisse .com/cetaces) organizes two-week summertime whale-watching and researching scientific expeditions. They are based in Ste Anne Portneuf, north of Tadoussac on the North Shore. These cost about $1200 (course, accommodation and equipment included).

The Canadian Universities Travel Service Ltd (Travel CUTS; ☎ 514-843-8511, W www.travelcuts.com) runs various trips and outings that include activities like hiking, cycling and canoeing. Budget tours usually start at about $59 a day. It can also arrange ski and sun-destination holidays.

Wawaté (☎ 819-824-7652), based in Val d'Or, offers canoe and kayak expeditions in Abitibi and in the Réserve Faunique la Vérendrye, as well as dogsled treks deep into the Abitibi forests. Count on paying about $110 for a full day's dogsled expedition, but they also offer packages including meals and winter forest camping

Cime Aventure (☎ 418-534-3133, 800-790-2463, W www.cimeaventure.com) are based in Bonaventure in the Gaspé Peninsula and offer rafting and kayaking expeditions (from $20 to $69 typically for the shorter excursions) and snowshoeing in the Parc de la Gaspésie. They have dozens of packages on offer, with tours lasting from several hours to several days. They also sometimes organize dogsled and snowmobile expeditions in northern Québec.

Montréal

☎ 514 • pop 3.4 million

Some cities take a bit of getting used to – you need time to know and appreciate them – but not Montréal. It's a friendly, romantic place where couples kiss on the street and strangers talk to each other, an interesting and lively blend of things English and French, flavored by the Canadian setting. There are 3.4 million people in Greater Montréal – it's the second largest city in Canada after Toronto – and about 10% of all Canadians and over 40% of Québec's population lives here. Two-thirds of the population are French, making it the largest French-speaking city outside of Paris, but the downtown core is surprisingly English.

To the visitor, it is the mix of old with new and the *joie de vivre* that is most alluring. French culture prevails, giving the atmosphere a European tinge, especially for visiting Americans, who have dubbed the city 'Paris without the jet lag.' Yet it's also a modern North American city with great nightlife and 4000 restaurants.

The interaction of the English and French gives Montréal some of its charm but is also responsible for some continuing conflict. The French may have long dominated the social spheres, but traditionally it was the English who ran businesses, held positions of power and accumulated wealth. As Québécois awareness increased, this changed, and the French are now well represented in all realms of life. In fact, some recent laws are reactionary in their discrimination against 'languages other than French.' The English, and other ethnic groups, are now voicing the need for balance and equality.

Regardless of these difficulties, Montréal exudes a warm, relaxed yet exciting ambience. It's as if the city itself has a pride and confidence in its own worth. The city has a reputation for fashion *savoir-faire,* but this is not limited to the moneyed – a certain flair (though sometimes in the form of 'attitude') seems to come naturally to everyone.

Highlights

- Lose yourself among Old Montréal's cobblestone streets and marvel at the Basilique Notre Dame
- Wander around Le Plateau and photograph the colorful houses and long staircases
- Enjoy boulevard St Laurent's multiethnic shops all day and its swank clubs all night
- Ice skate at the Vieux Port or bike along the Lachine Canal
- Let it all hang out at Mont Royal's Tam-Tam Sundays

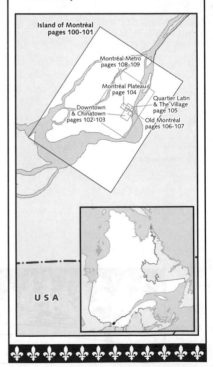

HISTORY
Founding of Montréal

Little is recorded about the pre-European history of Montréal, but it is well established that aboriginal societies of North America had developed for centuries in isolation from European influences. Long before the French arrived in Québec, the Algonquin, Huron and Iroquois shared the area – not always peacefully.

On October 2, 1535, Jacques Cartier became the first European to set foot on the Island of Montréal, landing on the north side to be greeted by the local Iroquois. Cartier was led to the summit of the mountain, which he named Mont Royal (leading, perhaps, to the city's present name – see 'The Naming of Montréal'), and planted a cross in tribute to his sponsor, King François I. Below him to the south lay a large, walled village called Hochelaga, on the site of present-day Montréal. Fur trading soon emerged as a lucrative venture.

More than seventy years later, another great explorer, Samuel de Champlain, shared Cartier's vision of riches and glory from the New World. However, when he arrived in 1611, three years after founding Québec City, he found no trace of Hochelaga or of the Iroquois who had lived there. Undeterred, Champlain made plans to set up a fur trading post at Place Royale on the Island of Montréal, but he had to postpone the project due to ferocious attacks by the Iroquois Confederation on the French, who were allied with the Huron and Algonquin.

In 1639 a French tax collector named Jerome Le Royer, sieur de la Dauversière, formed a company in Paris to establish a settlement on the Island of Montréal. Two years later the company sent a group of Catholic missionaries, led by Paul de Chomedey, sieur de Maisonneuve, to convert the 'Indians' to Christianity. On May 17, 1642, de Maisonneuve set up a religious mission named Ville Marie on what is now Place Royale; this is considered Montréal's official birthday.

Ville Marie soon became a booming fur trading post and also prospered as a religious center and an exploration base. By the early 18th century Ville Marie had become Montréal, the commercial hub of France's North American empire, Nouvelle France. By 1710 the town had 3500 inhabitants. Its location on the St Lawrence River made it an important trading center and linked it to the fur country, as well as to valuable forests along the Ottawa River.

The British Conquest

The British had been battling the French for some time and took Québec City in 1759. The French moved their capital upstream to Montréal, but to little avail: British troops led by General Jeffrey Amherst captured the city the next year, followed by droves of English settlers.

Soon the rebelling American colonies were after the city. In 1775 General Richard Montgomery took Montréal without firing a shot. Benjamin Franklin and other American diplomats tried to win French-Canadian support against the British. Their efforts failed, however, because most French Canadians viewed the war as a quarrel between Britain and its colonies. Montréal was in the

---

The Naming of Montréal

It is commonly assumed that 'Montréal' derives from the name Mont Royal, its trademark mountain. However, there is some evidence that the city was named by French King François I after the Archbishop of Monreale in Sicily, who lobbied to have Spanish and Portuguese claims to the New World annulled by the pope. Then there was Giovanni Battista Ramusi, who published a work in Italian on explorer Jacques Cartier's discoveries and translated 'Mount Royal' as 'Monte Real.' Last but not least, at the time of Cartier's voyage, there were a dozen-odd towns in France called Montréal – most with some kind of fortress on an elevated site. The Pontbriant family owned one such French castle, and son Claude just happened to be with Cartier when he climbed the mount. Hmmm…

hands of the revolutionary forces only until the British beat back another group trying to take Québec City, at which time the revolutionaries fled.

English-speaking merchants gradually gained control of the town's economy; this was made easier by the departure of many French merchants to the 'Old Country' after British troops captured the city in 1760.

19th-Century Growth

By the early 1800s Montréal's population had risen to 9000. The St Lawrence River had been established as the main passenger route into Canada, and Canada's first steamboat, the *Accommodation,* sailed from Montréal to Québec City in 1809.

The Canal de Lachine was opened on the south side of Montréal in 1825. The route provided a detour for vessels around the treacherous Lachine Rapids, which led to a sharp increase in travel and trade between Montréal and the Great Lakes area, though many cargo ships chose to bypass Montréal and continue farther. Shipping replaced fur trading as the chief industry, and the city's port flourished.

In 1832 Montréal was incorporated as a city. From 1844 to 1849 it served as the capital of the United Provinces of Canada, triggering a further influx of settlers, including Loyalists, Irish, Scottish and English. In 1852 the majority of its burgeoning population (by now 58,000) was English speaking, but it remained this way only until 1866. Nonetheless, the English-speakers retained control of the economy and gave the city its first university, McGill.

Investment by wealthy English merchants helped make Montréal a major industrial center, and many factories were built along the Canal de Lachine. Thousands of immigrants from Italy, Russia and Eastern Europe, as well as French Canadians from other parts of Québec, came to Montréal to find work, and ethnic districts began to form. By 1870 more than 100,000 people – about half of French ancestry – lived in the city.

Founded in Montréal, the Pacific Railway Company completed the country's transcontinental railroad in 1885. This brought more prosperity to Montréal, and the population topped 260,000 by the end of the 19th century. By 1900 Montréal was the commercial and cultural center of Canada. In the early part of the 20th century there came a huge influx of Jewish Europeans – even today, Montréal has the largest Jewish population in Canada (about 100,000).

Modern Montréal

By the early 1950s Montréal's population had passed the one million mark. Mayor Jean Drapeau drew up plans for grand projects that would change the face of the city. He had plenty of time to do so: Except for a three-year period in the late 1950s, Drapeau remained mayor right into the mid-1980s. He was sometimes touched by scandal, and critics dubbed him 'Emperor,' claiming he was megalomaniacal. Whatever his faults, Drapeau remained popular and helped to develop Montréal's international reputation.

In 1958 the city embarked on a huge redevelopment program, which over the following decade included construction of a new subway system and the underground city (see 'The Underground City' in the Shopping section).

The skyline altered dramatically during the 1960s. Private developers razed old structures in the area and replaced them with banks, upmarket hotels and office buildings. The two tallest skyscrapers in Montréal, the 49-story Royal Bank of Canada Building and the 47-story Place Victoria, were built during this period. (They won't get much taller, either: City law forbids new buildings from being taller than Mont Royal, which is 233m high.)

As the area now called Vieux (Old) Montréal lost its function as a business center, the focus of downtown moved slightly north to around the Ville Marie shopping complex and Dorchester and Victoria Squares. It was also in the 1960s that Montréal lost its place as Canada's economic capital to Toronto, which had been growing at a faster pace for decades.

New expressways were laid out and the Métro built in time to serve visitors to the 1967 World's Fair, which attracted over 50 million people during what's considered Montréal's finest hour. In 1976 the city hosted the Summer Olympics, for which it built a grand new sports stadium whose troubled construction history continues to this day.

An economic recession in the early to mid-1990s made Montréal a depressing place – rue Ste Catherine was plastered in For Sale or Closed signs, construction ground to a halt, there was a nearly 10% housing vacancy rate, and spirits were sinking along with the employment rate. Tensions between Federalists and Separatists reached a peak in 1995, when a second referendum on separation was barely won by the Federalist camp.

The gloom has reversed itself full force. By 2001 Montréal had a 0.7% vacancy rate, a lower unemployment rate than Toronto's, North America's highest percentage of college students (outstripping Boston) and over $1 billion of construction projects underway. Despite another threat of recession in late 2001, the economy is robust (4% growth in 2000), with multimedia, aerospace, telecommunications, biopharmaceutical and information technologies in the forefront. Rue Ste Catherine is once again seething, with no rental sign in sight.

The city routinely ranks in the top 20 places to live on the planet, according to the United Nations' annual Human Development Index (HDI), which takes into account several factors such as literacy, environmental pollution, life expectancy and earnings. In 2000 *Details* magazine rated Montréal as the best city in the world to live in. Things haven't looked and felt so good in the city since Expo '67.

POPULATION & PEOPLE

With almost 3.4 million residents, Greater Montréal accounts for about 46% of Québec's total population. The city proper numbers just over one million. About 77% of Greater Montréal's residents were born in Canada. Since the end of WWII, hundreds of thousands of immigrants have settled in the city, creating a rich patchwork of languages and cultures.

About 60% of Montréalers have French ancestors; those of British descent now make up only 5% – less than half of what the figure was in the 1960s. People from about 80 other ethnic groups call the city home. Italians account for almost 7% of the total population. Other significant groups, in order of size, are Jews, Greeks, Haitians, Chinese and Portuguese. More than a quarter of Montréalers are descended from more than one group.

Montréal is one of the most functionally bilingual cities in the world, where more and more people speak in half-English, half-French sentences, switch comfortably from one to another and, despite cultural and social divisions, benefit from both cultures.

ORIENTATION

The city occupies the Island of Montréal, roughly 40km long and 15km wide, at the confluence of the Ottawa and St Lawrence Rivers. The narrow rivière des Prairies flows along the northern shore, separating Montréal from the Île de Jésus and the city of Laval. Bridges link all sides with the mainland.

The Island of Montréal's most striking landmark is the Mont Royal, a 233m-high extinct volcano known locally as 'the mountain.' The core of the city is actually quite small and lies below in the southern central section of the island.

Montréal is an easy place to navigate, thanks to its grid system of streets, which is roughly aligned east-west and north-south. (The grid is actually skewed left of true north, but the locals ignore this niggling detail.)

INFORMATION
Tourist Offices

Montréal and Québec province have one central phone number for tourist information offices (☎ 873-2015, 877-266-5687, W www.bonjourquebec.com). The airports also have information kiosks that are open year-round.

Centre Infotouriste (Map 2), the city's main tourist information office, 1001 rue Square Dorchester, is right downtown. Staff are friendly and will supply you with information on all areas of Montréal and Québec. Hours are 9am to 6pm (until 8pm from June to early September). The center also has a bookstore, currency-exchange counter and Internet terminals, and the staff can arrange guided tours and car rentals. Hotel reservations are provided free of charge.

The other main tourist office (Map 5; W www.tourism-montreal.org), 174 rue Notre Dame Est, is in Old Montréal, not far from Place Jacques Cartier. It's busy, but the staff is extremely helpful. Hours are 9am to 7pm daily from late June to early October and 9am to 5pm the rest of the year.

There's also a tourist information booth (Map 5) at the entrance to the IMAX Theatre/Centre iSci complex on Quai King Edward. It's open 10am to 7pm daily in the summer.

Exchanging Money

Rue Ste Catherine downtown has oodles of bank branches.

Currencies International (Map 2; ☎ 392-9100), 1230 rue Peel, offers good rates. It's open daily to 9pm weekdays, to 8:30pm Saturday and to 6pm Sunday. Uniglobe (Map 2; ☎ 845-5849), 1385a rue Ste Catherine Ouest, is another good bet. They charge a 2% commission, 1% for HI cardholders. The head office of Thomas Cook (Map 2; ☎ 284-7388), which can exchange money and issue traveler's checks, is inside the Eaton Centre, 705 rue Ste Catherine Ouest.

At Dorval Airport, there are foreign-exchange desks in the departures and arrivals sections. To find an ATM after you arrive, take the escalator to the departures level.

Post & Communications

Post The national mail service, Canada Post/Postes Canada (☎ 800-267-1177; W www.canadapost.ca), is neither quick nor cheap, but it's reliable. Standard 1st-class airmail letters or postcards cost $0.46 to Canadian destinations and $0.55 to the US

(both are limited to 30g). Those to other destinations cost $0.95 (limit 20g).

The main post office (Map 2; ☎ 846-5401) is at 1250 rue University. There are also many smaller branches around Montréal. Stamps are often available at newspaper shops, variety stores and hotels.

Poste restante (general delivery) is available at Station Place d'Armes (Map 5), 435 rue St Antoine, Montréal H2Z 1H0. It's open 8:30am to 5:30pm weekdays. Mail will be kept for two weeks and then returned to the sender. American Express and Thomas Cook (see Exchanging Money, earlier) will also hold mail for their customers – showing one of their traveler's checks may be enough to qualify.

Fax & Telegram Bureau en Gros (Map 5; ☎ 875-0977), an office-supply store at 770 rue Notre Dame Ouest, charges $0.89 for sending a fax within Canada or to the US, $2 to Europe and Australia and $3 elsewhere. It's open 24 hours daily.

Even in the cyber age you can still send telegrams. To do so, contact AT&T Canada (☎ 800-387-1926).

Email & Internet Access The central public library (Map 4; ☎ 872-5923), 1210 rue Sherbrooke Est, offers Internet access on its 12 terminals for free with a two-hour limit. Other public libraries around town are also equipped for free Web surfing.

Chapters bookstore (Map 2; ☎ 849-8825), 1171 rue Ste Catherine Ouest, charges $2 for 20 minutes. It's open 9am to 11pm daily.

Cybermac (Map 2; ☎ 287-9100), 1425 rue Mackay, is a pleasant Internet café with 11 terminals in modern cubicles. It charges $5.75 per hour and is open 9:30am to 10pm weekdays, noon to 8pm Saturday. Cyber-Ground (Map 3; ☎ 842-1726), 3672 boulevard St Laurent, has the funkiest interiors and charges $8 an hour. It's open from 10am to 11pm weekdays, 11am to 11pm weekends.

Internet Resources

Websites are listed throughout this book (see the Internet Resources in the Facts for the Visitor chapter). The following is a list of English-language sites on Montréal with many useful links:

Tourism Montréal
  W www.tourisme-montreal.org
Montréal Gazette
  W www.montrealgazette.com
Mirror Magazine
  W www.montrealmirror.com
Montréal Bars & Restaurants
  W www.bar-resto.com
Montréal Online
  W www.montrealonline.com

Travel Agencies

Travel CUTS, known in Québec as Voyages Campus, has seven locations in Montréal, including the main office (Map 4; ☎ 843-8511, W www.travelcuts.com), 1613 rue St Denis. It sells International Student Identity Cards (ISICs) and cheap plane tickets, and it also sets up working holidays and language courses.

Run by Hostelling International, the Boutique Tourisme Jeunesse (Map 3; ☎ 844-0287), 4008 rue St Denis, sells books, maps, travel insurance, ID cards and plane tickets. It's open 10am to 6pm Monday to Wednesday and Saturday, 10am to 9pm Thursday and Friday, and 10am to 5pm Sunday.

The American Express Travel Agency (Map 5; ☎ 284-3300), 1141 boulevard de Maisonneuve, is open 9am to 5pm weekdays.

Newspapers & Magazines

The daily *Montréal Gazette* is the major English-language newspaper, with good coverage of national affairs, politics and the arts. The Friday and Saturday editions are packed with entertainment listings. Toronto's *Globe & Mail* and *The National Post,* two national dailies, are also on sale everywhere.

Readers of French should have a look at both the Federalist *La Presse,* the largest-circulation French daily, as well as the Separatist-leaning *Le Devoi. Le Journal de Montréal* is a popular French-language paper.

Montréal has four free independent weeklies well worth picking up for detailed coverage of the city's entertainment scene and the occasional piece of investigative journalism. The English-language ones are *The Montreal Mirror* and *Hour;* their French counterparts are *Voir* and *Ici.*

Medical Services

The best hospital option for English-speaking patients is the Royal Victoria Hospital (Map 2; ☎ 842-1231), 687 avenue des Pins Ouest. Admittance to the emergency ward at this hospital costs $310. Walk-in service at one of the city's many CLSCs (community healthcare centers; call ☎ 527-2361 for the address of the one nearest you) costs $110. Expect to pay the charge in cash and up front, as checks and credit cards are not usually accepted.

The Pharmaprix chain has branches around town, including one at 1500 rue Ste Catherine Ouest (Map 2; ☎ 933-4744). It's open 8am to midnight daily. There's a 24-hour location at 5122 chemin de la Côtes des Neiges (☎ 738-8464).

OLD MONTRÉAL (MAP 5)

This area, called Vieux Montréal in French, is the oldest section of the city and dates mostly from the 18th century. The main streets are rue Notre Dame, which runs past the Basilique Notre Dame, and rue St Paul. The narrow cobblestone streets divide old stone houses and buildings, many of which are now home to intimate restaurants and boutiques. The waterfront is never far away.

Old Montréal is a must for romantics and architecture lovers, and, as the once financial center of Canada, it offers an attractive contrast to the modern-day downtown core. It can get stiflingly crowded in peak season, however, and driving there is not recommended – you're unlikely to find a parking spot.

The Old Montréal tourist office is at the top of Place Jacques Cartier. Ask for the 36-page *Old Montréal Walking Tour* booklet (in English or French; $6), which points out noteworthy spots.

To get to Old Montréal by Métro, get off at the Square Victoria, Place d'Armes or Champ de Mars stops.

Place Jacques Cartier

In summer this square, now the area's focal point, is filled with visitors, vendors, horse-drawn carriages and musicians. The plaza was laid out after 1803, the year a château on the site burned down and a public market was set up in its place. At its north end stands the Colonne Nelson (Nelson's Column), a (fiberglass replica of a) monument erected by the British to the general who defeated the French and Spanish fleet at Trafalgar.

One little oddity is the statue of an obscure French admiral, Jean Vauquelin, in the square north across rue Notre Dame; it was put there later by the French as an answer to the Nelson statue.

Hôtel de Ville

The Hôtel de Ville *(City Hall; ☎ 872-1111, 275 rue Notre Dame Est; admission free; open 8:30am-4:30pm Mon-Fri)* towers over Place Jacques Cartier to the east. It was here, in 1967, that French leader Charles de Gaulle cried *'Vive le Québec libre!'* ('Long live a free Québec!') to the masses from the balcony, fueling the fires of the Québec Separatist movement (and straining relations with Canada for years).

The design is pure Second Empire from 1878, but after a fire destroyed the building in 1922 it was remodeled after the city hall in Tours, France. There are occasional exhibits in the main corridor.

Château de Ramezay

Opposite the Hôtel de Ville is the Château de Ramezay *(☎ 861-3708, 280 rue Notre Dame Est; adult/student $6/4; open 10am-6pm daily June-Aug, 10am-4:30pm Tues-Sun Sept-May)*, which was the home of the city's French governors for about 40 years in the early 18th century. Benjamin Franklin stayed here during the American Revolution while fruitlessly attempting to convince the Canadians to join the cause.

The building has housed a great variety of things since, but it is now a museum with a collection of 20,000 objects – paintings, engravings, costumes, photos, tools and other miscellany from Québec's early history.

Three Courthouses

Along the north side of rue Notre Dame Est near Place Jacques Cartier, no fewer than three courthouses stand together. The most fetching is the neoclassical **Vieux Palais de Justice** *(Old Palace of Justice; ☎ 393-2721, 155 rue Notre Dame Est)*, Montréal's oldest courthouse (1856) and now an annex of the nearby Hôtel de Ville. It's a popular backdrop for wedding photos.

Built in the 1920s, the **Édifice Ernest Cormier** *(100 rue Notre Dame Est)* was used for criminal trials before being turned into a conservatory of dramatic arts. The ugliest of the lot is the oversized **Palais de Justice** *(Palace of Justice; ☎ 393-2721, 1 rue Notre Dame Est)*. It was built in 1971, when sinister glass cubes were still in fashion.

Bonsecours Market

Designed by architect William Footner and inaugurated in 1847, this imposing old market *(☎ 872-7730, 350 rue St Paul Est; open 10am-6pm daily)*, was the main market hall until the 1960s, when local supermarkets effectively drove it out of business. Since 1992 it has served as a hall for exhibitions and shops selling arts and crafts, leather goods and designer clothing.

Place d'Armes & Basilique Notre Dame

The other major square in the area is Place d'Armes, which has a monument to the city's founder – Paul de Chomedey, sieur de Maisonneuve – in the middle. On the south side of the square stands Montréal's standout attraction, the famous Basilique Notre Dame *(☎ 842-2925, 110 rue Notre Dame Ouest; admission free; open 8:30am-5:30pm Mon-Sat, 1:30pm-5pm Sun; Sun mass 8am, 9:30am, 11am & 12:30pm)*.

In 1823 the Sulpicians, a group of French Catholics who came to America to escape the threat posed to their church's survival during the French Revolution, decided to enlarge the small parish church on the site as an answer to the much larger Anglican cathedral on rue Notre Dame (destroyed by fire in 1856). James O'Donnell, a New York architect of Irish Protestant background, designed what became the largest church north of Mexico.

Big enough to hold 5000 people, the church has a magnificently rich interior, with an explosion of wood carvings and gilt stars painted in the ceiling vaults. The altar is backlit in weird and wonderful colors. The massive Casavant organ, with 5772 pipes, is used for concerts throughout the year, particularly during Christmastime. A new, religious multimedia sound and light show has begun *(adult/child & senior $10/7; 6:30pm & 8:30pm Tues-Sat)* in the basilica re-creating the history of the sacred building.

In the back is the small **Chapelle du Sacré Coeur** *(Sacred Heart Chapel)*, which was added in 1888. It's also called the Wedding Chapel because of the countless nuptials held there – there's a waiting list of up to two years.

The basilica's Musée de la Basilique is closed indefinitely.

Vieux Séminaire de St Sulpice

Just east of the basilica, in the city's oldest building, is this seminary, which was built by the Catholic order of Sulpicians after they arrived in 1657. The clock, which has wooden innards, was a gift from Louis XIV in 1701 and is believed to be the oldest working clock in North America. The seminary is closed to the public.

Chapelle Notre Dame de Bonsecours

This church *(☎ 282-8670, 400 rue St Paul Est; admission free; open 10am-5pm Tues-Sun)* is also known as the Sailors' Church because of the several models of wooden ships hanging from the ceiling. In the adjoining **Musée Marguerite Bourgeoys** *(adult/senior & student/child $5/3/2; open 10am-5pm Tues-Sun),* the vignettes tell the story of Montréal's first teacher and the founder of the Congregation of Notre Dame order of nuns. From the church tower (reachable via the museum), there's an excellent view of the port.

Place Royale

In the west end of Old Montréal is the square where Ville Marie, Montréal's first small fort town, was built at a time when the fighting with the Iroquois Confederacy was lengthy and fierce. During the 17th and 18th centuries, this was a marketplace; it's now the forecourt of the Veille Douane (Old Customs House) and is linked to the **Musée Pointe à Callière** *(☎ 872-9150, 350 Place Royale; adult/student $9.50/5.50; open 10am-5pm Tues-Fri, 11am-5pm Sat & Sun),* which provides an excellent archeological and historical study of the beginnings of Montréal.

For the most part, the museum is underground, in the ruins of buildings and an ancient sewage/river system. Montréal's first European cemetery is here, established just a few years after the settlement itself. Gravesites are presented like a working dig. The lookout at the top of the tower in the new building provides an excellent view of the Vieux Port. The tower can be visited without paying the museum's entry fee.

Vieux Port

The Old Port waterfront is a district of riverside redevelopment that is still evolving and changing as construction and ideas blossom. Each year, a range of temporary exhibits or shows are featured. It covers 2.5km of riverfront and is based around four *quais* (quays) or piers. The **Promenade du Vieux Port** is a recreational path along the river from rue Berri west to rue McGill. Cruise boats, ferries, jet boats and speedboats all depart for tours of the river from the various docks.

A summer tourist information booth (☎ 496-7678, 800-971-7678) can be found at the entrance to **Quai King Edward** – pretty much in the center of things, at the foot of boulevard St Laurent.

This pier is also home to the **IMAX Theatre** *(☎ 496-4629, 800-349-4629; adult/student $10/9; open 10:15am-7:15pm daily)* and the latest addition, the sparkling **Centre iSci** *(☎ 496-4724; adult/student $10/9; open 10am-6pm Sun-Thur, 10am-9pm Fri & Sat),* a science and entertainment center. Something of a cross between a workshop and a video arcade, the iSci has interactive games (eg, a 'fight' with a computer virus), a high-tech 'life lab' and lots of educational screen-based displays. Combined tickets with the IMAX are also available. Check out the huge **flea market** *(marché aux puces)* here as well.

At the **Quai Alexandra** is a huge port and container terminal. Also here is the Iberville Passenger Terminal, the dock for cruise ships that ply the St Lawrence River as far as the Îles de la Madeleine. Nearby is the **Parc des Écluses** (literally, Park of Locks), a site of open-air exhibitions.

The **Quai Jacques Cartier** features restaurants, an open-air stage and a handicraft center. The Cirque du Soleil, Montréal's phenomenally skilled troupe of acrobats, performs here on occasion. Trolley tours of the port area depart from here. The Navette Vieux Port–Les Îles ferry departs from here to Parc des Îles, particularly popular with cyclists (bikes can be taken on the ferry).

At Cité du Havre, a narrow promontory between Old Montréal and Île Ste Hélène connected with the island by the Pont de la Concorde, is the city's most recognizable residential complex, **Habitat 67**. Moshe Safdie designed it for the World Fair as an experiment in residential modernism: a futuristic, more livable apartment block. The modular design (concrete blocks stuck together helter-skelter) feels dated but is a bold, bizarre feat by any standards. The best views are from behind. The units sold for $50,000 each in 1967; they're now valued anywhere from $225,000 to $700,000.

Just east of Quai Jacques Cartier is the **Parc du Bassin Bonsecours**, a grassy expanse enclosed by a waterway criss-crossed with footbridges. In the summer you can rent the cute paddleboats (equipped with a mock steamboat funnel) by the half-hour for $4; in winter it's full of ice skaters.

At the northeastern edge of the historic port on the Quai de l'Horloge stands the striking white **Sailors' Memorial Clock Tower** *(Tour de l'Horloge;* ☎ *496-7678)*, now used as an observation tower and open to the public. It also has a history exhibit. Just north of here is a bike path, which stretches southwest toward the Canal Lachine.

DOWNTOWN (MAP 2)

Nestled among the skyscrapers of downtown Montréal are the city's finest museums and several grand churches, many of which are within easy walking distance of each other and accessible via the Métro.

Museums

Tourist offices (see that section, earlier) sell a museum pass ($20), which covers entry to 25 museums and galleries over a two-day period – it generally pays for itself after two museum visits. Note that many Montréal museums are closed Monday.

Musée des Beaux Arts The Museum of Fine Arts *(☎ 285-2000, 1379 rue Sherbrooke Ouest; temporary exhibits: adult/student $12/6; permanent collection: admission free; open 11am-6pm Tues & Thur-Sun, 11am-9pm Wed)* is the city's main art gallery.

The Beaux Arts (pronounced 'bose-ar') museum is split into two sections, the modern Jean Noël Desmarais Pavilion on the south side of the street, and the Renata and Michael Ornstein Pavilion on the north side. Connected to the Ornstein Pavilion is the Stewart Wing, also known as the Musée des Arts Décoratifs, which features decorative art displays and handicrafts from the 20th century.

Both north and south sides split up the permanent collection with temporary shows, but most visitors flock to see the more famous works by European and American artists in the Jean Noël Desmarais Pavilion, including paintings by Rembrandt, Picasso and Matisse, and sculptures by Henry Moore, Alberto Giacometti and Alexander Calder. In the older north wing (1912), which used to constitute the entire museum, the focus is on Inuit and Native Canadian art.

There are guided tours in English on Wednesday at 2:30pm and 5:30pm. Admission is half-price from 5:30pm to 9pm on Wednesday.

Musée d'Art Contemporain Located in the Place des Arts complex (see Concert Halls, below), the Museum of Contemporary Art (☎ 847-6226, 185 rue Ste Catherine Ouest; adult/student/child under 12 $6/3/free; open 11am-6pm Tues & Thur-Sun, 11am-9pm Wed) displays pieces from their permanent collection of more than 6000 works. It's the country's only major gallery that focuses on contemporary art, and nearly two-thirds of the displays are dedicated to Québec artists, such as Paul Émile Borduas. Other featured artists include Picasso, Max Ernst, Andy Warhol, or Piet Mondriaan. The temporary shows are often outstanding.

In mid-2001 this was the setting of a public nude shoot by the photographer Spencer Tunnick, where over 2000 Montréalers showed the world what they were made of, in the name of art. The concrete esplanade around the fountains outside the museum was transformed into a sea of flesh. It was the largest urban turnout for one of Tunnick's shoots to date.

There's a free English-language tour at 6:30pm Wednesday; tours are also given in English at 1pm and 3pm on Saturday and Sunday. Admission is free 6pm to 9pm Wednesday.

Centre Canadien d'Architecture The
Canadian Center for Architecture (☎ 939-7000, 1920 rue Baile; adult/student $6/3; open 11am-6pm Tues & Wed & Fri-Sun, 11am-9pm Thur), is both a museum and working organization promoting architecture, its history and its future in an impressive modern complex.

It may sound dry, but most people find at least some of the displays of interest. Part of the building has been created around **Shaughnessy House**, a wealthy businessman's residence built in 1874 (get a good view of the gray limestone annex from boulevard René Lévesque out back). Highlights in this section include the solarium and a wonderfully ornate room with intricate woodwork and a fireplace.

Don't miss the **sculpture garden** on the south side of boulevard René Lévesque. More than a dozen sculptures of varying styles and sizes – even more impressive lit up at night – are scattered about a terrace overlooking parts of south Montréal.

Students get in free all day Thursday; adult admission is free 5:30pm to 8pm Thursday.

Musée McCord The McCord Museum of Canadian History (☎ 398-7100, 690 rue Sherbrooke Ouest; adult/student/child $8.50/5/2; open 10am-6pm Tues-Fri, 10am-5pm Sat & Sun) is the city's main history museum, though not very large, dealing mostly with eastern Canada's early European settlement from 1700. One room exhibits the history of Québec's indigenous people – one of the best of its kind in the province; another displays highlights of the museum's collection, including Canadian costumes, textiles, decorative and folk art.

A highlight of the huge photograph collection is the collection by William Notman, who, with his sons, photographed Canadian people, places and activities from 1850 to 1930. The 2nd-floor room entitled 'Turning Point: Québec 1900' neatly encapsulates French-Canadian history in Québec.

Sunday workshops at 2pm are geared toward children. Admission is free 10am to noon Saturday.

Musée Juste pour Rire The Just for Laughs Museum (☎ 845-4000, ₩ www .hahaha.com, 2111 boul St Laurent; admission $8; open 11am-6pm Tues & Thur-Sun, 11am-9pm Wed), is meant to be a useful addition to the Quartier Latin, and the seat of the summer comedy festival. You'll see film clips, and there's a humor hall of fame – but unless you enjoy slapstick, forget it. There are frequent special events and shows in the cabaret theater.

Churches
Cathédrale Basilique Marie Reine du Monde The Cathedral of Mary, Queen of the World (☎ 866-1661, boul René Lévesque Ouest at rue de la Cathédrale; admission free; open 7am-7:30pm Mon-Fri, 8am-7:30pm Sat & Sun) is a smaller but still magnificent version of St Peter's Basilica in Rome – scaled down to one-quarter size because of the structural risks of Montréal's severe winters. Built between 1870 and

1894, this landmark provided another symbol of Catholic power in what was the heart of Protestant Montréal.

Inside, the neobaroque altar canopy is the main attraction, fashioned of copper and gold leaf and with fantastic swirled roof supports. This too is a replica of Gian Lorenzo Bernini's masterpiece in St Peter's. The overall impression is far more elegant than that of the more famous Basilique Notre Dame. The 13 sculptures of Christ and the apostles over the entrance are sculpted in wood and covered with copper, and are brilliantly illuminated at night. Locals like to fool tourists by telling them the statues are of famous Montréal Canadiens hockey players!

Cathédrale Christ Church Next to La Baie department store, the Christ Church Cathedral (☎ 843-6577, 1444 avenue Union) provides a much-needed dash of Victorian style (and a green lawn) on busy rue Ste Catherine Ouest. Built from 1857 to 1859, the church was modeled on the Protestant cathedral in Salisbury, England – architect Frank Will's hometown. The interior is sober, but the stained-glass windows by William Morris' workshops add cheery relief.

St James United Church Perhaps it's fitting that this Gothic-style church (☎ 288-9245, 463 rue St Catherine Ouest) is fronted by gaudy neon signs in the thick of the shopping district. Otherwise you'd easily miss this house of worship, because stores and offices are built into the façade – only a narrow passageway from rue Ste Catherine Ouest leads into the church itself. This place shows how Montréal has grown: The entrance once overlooked a garden where traffic now crawls by. Free organ concerts are held at 12:30pm on Tuesday in the summer.

McGill University

This school (☎ 398-4455; 845 rue Sherbrooke Ouest) is one of Canada's most prestigious learning institutions, with over 15,000 students. Founded in 1828 by James McGill, a rich Scottish fur trader, the university has a fine reputation, especially for its medical and engineering programs. Many campus buildings are showcases of Victorian architecture. The campus is rather nice to stroll around or stop for a midday picnic.

Bourse de Montréal

Although once a powerhouse of Canada's stock and bond trading, the Bourse de Montréal (Montréal Exchange; ☎ 871-2424, 800 Place Victoria; admission free; open 8:30am-5pm Mon-Fri) no longer trades stocks and is the country's exchange for derivatives (ie, futures and options). There are interactive displays and presentations, and guides in the gallery explain the sign language that traders use.

Dow Planetarium

The Dow Planetarium (Montréal Planetarium; ☎ 872-4530, W www.planetarium.montreal.qc.ca, 1000 rue St Jacques; adult/senior & student/child 5-17/child under 5 $6.50/5/3.25/free; English shows 2:30pm Tues-Sun, 7:15pm Thur-Sun) is in a 20m-high dome and offers 50-minute programs on the stars, space and solar system via a celestial projector.

MONT ROYAL AREA

One of the nicest areas to walk around in is the Plateau Mont Royal, which extends east of Mount Royal, north of rue Sherbrooke. Having sprung to a new life in the 1990s, it is now among Canada's most densely populated areas. Charming with its funky shops and 19th-century homes with ornate wooden or wrought-iron balconies, pointy Victorian roofs and exterior staircases (the streets between avenues Prince Arthur and Duluth are the most striking), it's best just to wander around in.

Parc du Mont Royal (Maps 2, 3)

Montréal's pride and joy is the Parc du Mont Royal (☎ 872-6559, W www.lemontroyal.qc.ca), known as 'the mountain' (see 'How Green Was My Mountain'). The highest point in the city at 263m, it is topped by the **Chalet du Mont Royal**, where the most popular lookout in the city is located. About a kilometer northeast of the lookout stands Montréal's famous steel **Cross of Montréal**, erected in 1924 on the very same spot as the

View of the mighty St Lawrence, Montréal

Pointing the way on Montréal's Rue University

Glowing architecture, Montréal

ALLAN MONTAINE

Hôtel de Ville, Montréal

WAYNE WALTON

McGill University, Montréal

EDDIE BRADY

Waving to the Laurentian river dwellers, Biodôme, Montréal

one set up in 1643 by city founder de Maisonneuve. It's lit up at night and is visible from all over the city.

Occasionally big bands play on the huge balcony at the Chalet du Mont Royal in summer, reminiscent of the 1930s. Meanwhile, every Sunday from early afternoon to late evening a scene more reminiscent of the 1960s unfolds around the **Georges Étienne Cartier monument** on avenue du Parc, one of the park's main entrances. Dubbed 'Tam-Tam Sundays,' it regroups several hundred people of the type grandma might not have approved of and their tam-tams (bongo-like drums) for several hours of tribal playing and spontaneous dancing. It's become an institution. If the rhythms don't announce its location, flare your nostrils and wait for the wafts of funny-cigarette smoke to lead you to it.

The parking lot to the north at the **Observatoire de l'Est** serves as another major

lookout also known as the Belvédere Camillien Houde. It's a popular spot for amorous couples (the parking lot fills up on summer nights) and students on graduation night. You can walk between the two lookouts via the park trail in about half an hour.

To reach the park from downtown, enter via the staircase at the top of rue Peel, or behind the Georges Étienne Cartier monument on avenue du Parc. By car, there are paid parking lots off boulevard Côte des Neiges. By public transport, take bus No 80 or 129 from Ⓜ Place des Arts to the Georges Étienne Cartier monument or bus No 11 from Ⓜ Mont Royal. This runs through the park and stops near the Observatoire de l'Est.

Cemeteries
To the north of Parc du Mont Royal lie two enormous cemeteries: the Catholic **Cimetière de Notre Dame des Neiges** (☎ 735-1361, 4601

How Green Was My Mountain

Known as 'the mountain,' this charming, leafy expanse was designed in the early 1870s by Frederick Law Olmstead, the architect of New York's Central Park, Boston's Franklin Park and Washington's Capitol Grounds. The impetus came from a public campaign against the exclusive use of the territory by bourgeois residents in the Golden Square Mile to the south. The city gave in, spent $1 million to buy or expropriate the private land, and hired Olmstead, who then designed the park with egalitarian principles, opening it up as a healthy respite to people from all walks of life.

Inaugurated in 1876, **Parc du Mont Royal** has become the city's best and biggest park, with 60,000 trees and nearly half a million shrubs spread over 494 acres. It is home to 700 plant species, representing 25% of all flora in Québec, and 150 species of bird, which is half the species in the province. The lush rolling landscape is great in the summer for jogging, picnicking, horseback riding, bicycling and playing Frisbee; in the winter there's skating, tobogganing and cross-country skiing. Some of the walking trails provide views of the city.

The **Chalet du Mont Royal** and the lookout opposite have great views of the city. Built in 1932, this grand white villa with bay windows houses canvases depicting scenes of Canadian history.

Lac aux Castors (Beaver Lake) was laid out in 1948 in a former marsh as part of a work-creation project. You can rent paddleboats on the lake, and in winter it freezes over for skating. The slope above has a mini ski lift (for kids), which operates when it snows.

Since 1990 a restoration project has revamped many sectors of the park, improving trails, planting trees and repairing the chalet, though you might still notice some of the destruction left behind by 1998's ice storm, when tens of thousands of trees in the park collapsed.

'The mountain' still fulfils Olmstead's ideals of democratizing public space: Every day of the year, you'll see thousands of Montréalers seeking pleasures of all kinds in 'that thar hill.'

boul Côte des Neiges; open daylight hours) and its smaller Protestant counterpart to the east, **Cimetière Mont Royal** (☎ 279-7358, 1297 chemin de la Forêt; open daylight hours). The former has a fascinating bunch of mausoleums that emit solemn music, including that of Marguerite Bourgeoys, a nun and teacher who was beatified in 1982 (see Chapelle Notre Dame de Bonsecours, under Old Montréal, earlier). The office of the Cimetière de Notre Dame des Neiges (see the map signs at the entrances), open 8am to 5pm weekdays and 9am to 3pm weekends, has brochures for self-guided tours around that cemetery.

Oratoire St Joseph

The gigantic St Joseph's Oratory (☎ 733-8211, 3800 chemin Queen Mary; admission free; open 6am-9pm daily), completed in 1960 and based on and around a 1916 church, honors St Joseph, Canada's patron saint. The size of the Renaissance-style building is a marvel in itself and commands wonderful views on the northern slope of Mont Royal. It's also a tribute to Brother André, a monk said to have healing powers; piles of crutches testify to this belief. Brother André's heart, which is on view here (can't you see its purity?), was stolen some years ago but later returned intact.

Inside the oratory there's a small **museum** (admission free; open 10am-5pm daily) dedicated to Brother André, who was beatified in 1982. There are free guided tours in several languages at 10am and 2pm daily in the summer. Sundays feature organ concerts at 2:30pm. From ⓜ Côtes des Neiges, walk or take bus No 16 to the oratory. The more repentant among you may wish to climb the 283 front steps on your knees, as sinners regularly do, reciting a prayer on each step; indeed, the depth of devotion in those who frequent the oratory is palpable.

Holocaust Memorial Centre & Saidye Bronfman Centre

Northwest of the cemeteries, the small Montréal Holocaust Memorial Centre (☎ 345-2605, 5151 chemin de la Côte Ste Catherine; ⓜ Côte Ste Catherine; admission free; open 10am-4pm Mon-Fri), provides a record of Jewish history and culture from pre-WWII Europe and holds seminars, exhibitions and other events. Next door, the Saidye Bronfman Centre (☎ 739-2301, 5170 chemin de la Côte Ste Catherine; open 9am-9pm Mon-Thur, 9am-4:30pm Fri, 10am-5pm Sun) is a Jewish art and performing arts center with a gallery of contemporary art.

OLYMPIC PARK (MAP 6)

Ask any Montréaler and you'll find that scandal, indignation and tales of corruption envelop the buildings of Olympic Park (☎ 252-8687, 4141 avenue Pierre de Coubertin; ⓜ Viau; adult/student $5.50/4.50; English-language guided tours 12:40pm and 15:40pm daily). Still, the complex, built for more than $1 billion for the 1976 Olympic Games, is magnificent.

The showpiece is the multipurpose **Stade Olympique** (Olympic Stadium), which has a capacity of 80,000 and is often referred to as the 'Big O' – or, more recently, 'The Big Owe.' Finally completed in 1990, the complex has required a laughable litany of repairs. Only a year later, a 55-ton concrete beam collapsed during a football game; in 1999 a section of the snow-covered roof caved in on top of an auto show. In theory, the 65-ton roof can be lifted via the tower cables, but you won't see it in action: High winds have torn holes in the roofing fabric, and the system, still undergoing repair, is plagued by mechanical problems. The stadium still manages to host games of the Montréal Expos baseball team, concerts and trade shows.

A cable car runs up the tower of the **Olympic Stadium Funicular** (☎ 252-8687, 3200 rue Viau; adult/student/child $10/7.50/5, with tour $12/8/8; open 10am-5pm daily), which overhangs the stadium and is the world's tallest inclined structure (190m). Up top is a glassed-in observation deck, which affords outstanding views of the city and beyond for a distance of 80km. The **Centre Sportif** is an impressive swimming complex

MONTRÉAL

with six pools, diving towers and a 20m-deep scuba pool (see the Activities section, later in this chapter).

The **Tourist Hall**, at the cable car boarding station, is a three-story information center with a ticket office, restaurant and souvenir shop.

If you're seeing several attractions at Olympic Park, a combination ticket is the best value *(adult/senior & student/child $15.75/11.75/8)*. The guided tour of the grounds is worthwhile – you'll appreciate having taken the time. It covers the Biodôme, Jardin Botanique, Insectarium and the Montréal Tower. The entire site is in huge Parc Maisonneuve.

Biodôme

Housed in the former Velodrome cycling stadium in the Olympic complex, the Biodôme *(☎ 868-3000, 4777 avenue Pierre de Coubertin; adult/student/child $10/7.50/5; open 9am-5pm daily)* re-creates four ecosystems and houses approximately 4000 animals and 5000 plants. Under one roof you can amble through a rainforest, polar regions, the Laurentian Shield woodlands and the Gulf of St Lawrence's ocean environment. Though some sections shine (the rainforest, for example), other sections are decidedly underwhelming.

A free shuttle runs between the Biodôme and the Jardin Botanique.

Jardin Botanique & Insectarium

Though each of these attractions has its own entrance, they are located on the same huge territory; one admission price is good for both venues.

Opened in 1931, the 81-hectare Jardin Botanique *(☎ 872-1400, 4101 rue Sherbrooke Est; adult/senior & student/child $10/7.50/5; open 9am-5pm daily winter, 9am-7pm daily rest of year)* is now the world's third-largest botanical garden after those in London and Berlin. Some 21,000 types of plants are grown in 30 outdoor gardens and 10 climate-controlled greenhouses (where cacti, banana trees and 700 species of orchid grow). The landscaped **Japanese Garden**, with its traditional pavil-

ions, tearoom and art gallery, is a popular draw; the grouping of bonsai is the largest outside Asia.

Whether you love or hate creepy crawlies, the collection of bugs from around the world at the Insectarium, located inside the Botanical Gardens, will intrigue you. Some popular ones include the tarantulas and scorpions, but don't miss the dazzling outdoor Butterfly House, which includes some of Québec's native species. Once a year, sometimes in spring, sometimes fall, biologists don chef hats for a popular Insect Tasting festival of gourmet bugs. Some 25,000 people come to munch on cooked locusts, ants and worms of varying degrees of plumpness!

Mmm, protein.

Château Dufresne

Built for the Dufresne brothers in 1916, this lavish hotel *(☎ 259-9201, 2929 avenue Jeanne d'Arc; adult/senior & student/child $5/4/2; open 10am-5pm Thur-Sun)* is inspired by the Petit Trianon at the Versailles palace in France. Restored in 1976, this national monument has a stunning interior, including furniture, art and other decorative objects collected by its owners. Exhibitions are also held here.

MAP 1 ISLAND OF MONTRÉAL

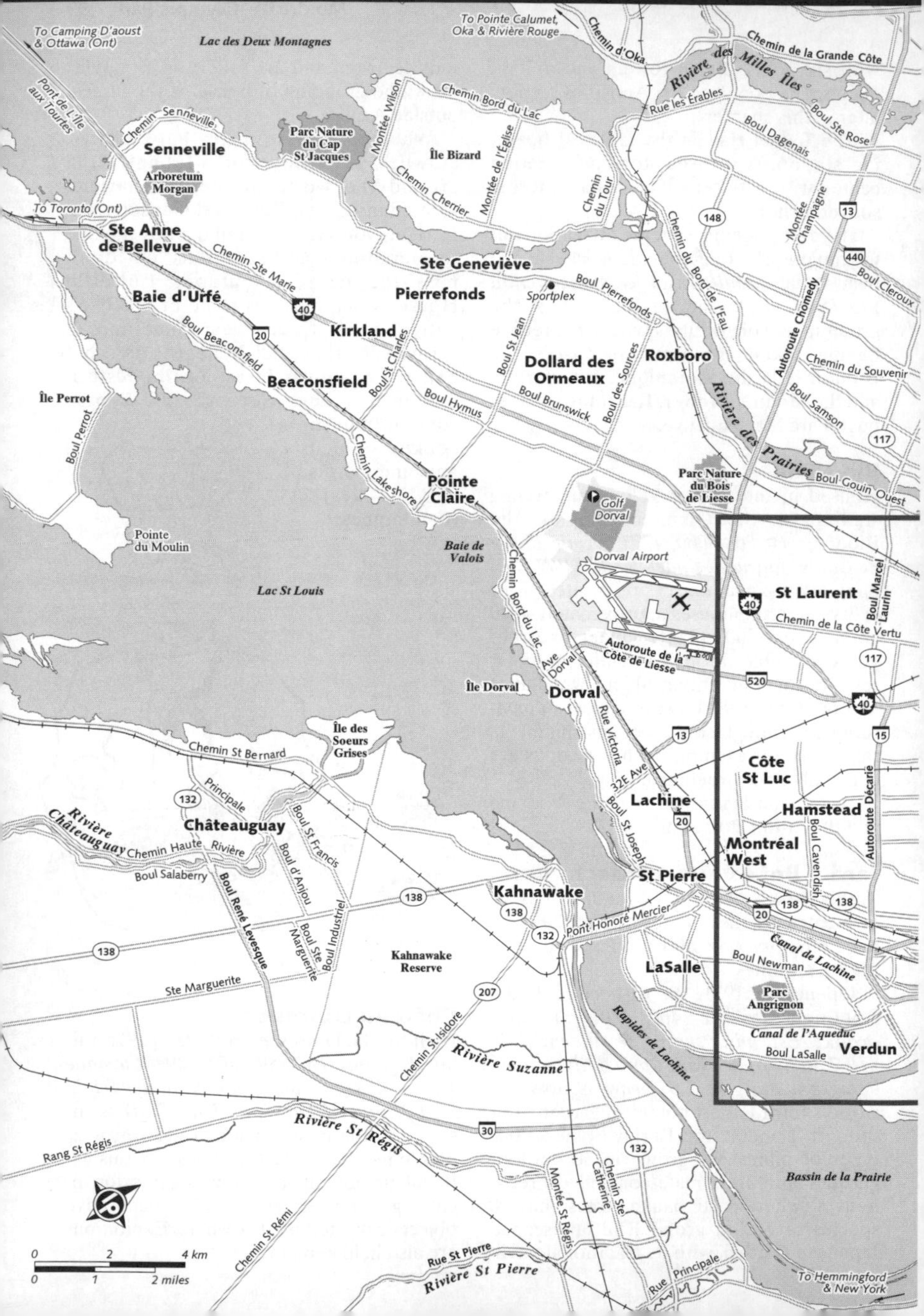

To Camping D'aoust & Ottawa (Ont)

Lac des Deux Montagnes

To Pointe Calumet, Oka & Rivière Rouge

Chemin d'Oka

Rivière des Milles Îles

Chemin de la Grande Côte

Chemin Bord du Lac

Chemin Wilson

Rue les Érables

Boul Ste Rose

Boul Dagenais

Pont de l'Île aux routes

Chemin Senneville

Senneville

Île Bizard

Montée de l'Église

Chemin Cherrier

Parc Nature du Cap St Jacques

Montée Champagne

13

440

Boul Cleroux

Arboretum Morgan

Chemin du Tour

Chemin du Bord de l'Eau

148

Autoroute Chomedy

Ste Anne de Bellevue

Chemin Ste Marie

Ste Geneviève

Boul Pierrefonds

Chemin du Souvenir

To Toronto (Ont)

Baie d'Urfé

40

Pierrefonds

Sportplex

Boul Samson

117

Kirkland

20

Boul St Jean

Chemin St Charles

Dollard des Ormeaux

Boul des Sources

Roxboro

Rivière des Prairies

Boul Gouin Ouest

Île Perrot

Boul Beaconsfield

Beaconsfield

Boul Hymus

Boul Brunswick

Boul Perrot

Chemin Lakeshore

Pointe Claire

Golf Dorval

Parc Nature du Bois de Liesse

Pointe du Moulin

Baie de Valois

Dorval Airport

St Laurent

Boul Marcel Laurin

40

Lac St Louis

Chemin Bord du Lac

Ave Dorval

Autoroute de la Côte de Liesse

Chemin de la Côte Vertu

117

Île Dorval

Dorval

520

40

15

Île des Soeurs Grises

Rue Victoria

13

Côte St Luc

Chemin St Bernard

32E Ave

Lachine

20

Hamstead

Autoroute Décarie

Principale

132

Châteauguay

Boul Joseph

Montréal West

Boul Cavendish

Rivière Châteauguay

Chemin Haute Rivière

Boul St Francis

Boul d'Anjou

St Pierre

138

138

Boul Salaberry

Boul René Levesque

Boul Ste Marguerite

Boul Industriel

Kahnawake

138

132

Pont Honoré Mercier

20

138

138

138

Canal de Lachine

Boul Newman

Ste Marguerite

Kahnawake Reserve

207

LaSalle

Parc Angrignon

Chemin St Isidore

Rapides de Lachine

Canal de l'Aqueduc

Boul LaSalle

Verdun

Rang St Régis

Rivière Suzanne

30

132

Bassin de la Prairie

Chemin St Rémi

Montée St Régis

Chemin Ste Catherine

To Hemmingford & New York

0   2   4 km

0   1   2 miles

Rue St Pierre

Rivière St Pierre

Rue Principale

Rivière St Régis

To Mirabel Airport,
St Jérôme & the
Laurentians

344

15

117

Chemin de la Grande Côte

335

Côte Terrebonne

640

Chemin Gascon

Parc Mille Îles

Boul Ste Rose

Boul des Mille Îles

344

337

Boul Curé Labelle

Boul Ste Rose

Ave des Perron

Boul Ste Marie

To St Donat

Terrebonne

125

Boul Bellerose

15

Île de Jésus

Laval

Rang de
l'Équerre

Boul des Laurentides

Montée St François

Rang Bas
St François

To Joliette

125

Boul St Elzéar
Ouest

Boul Daniel Johnson

Autoroute des Laurentides

Boul Chomedey

Cosmodrôme

Boul René
Laennec

Boul St Martin

148

440

25

125

Boul 440

Rivière des Mille Îles

640

Boul de la Concorde

335

19

25

Boul Cartier

Montée du Moulin

Boul Lévesque

see Map 6

Boul Léger

Montréal
Nord

Boul Langelier

Rivière des Prairies

344

Boul Henri Bourassa Ouest

19

Boul Pie IX

Rue Sauvé

Boul Couture

125
25

Boul Armand Bombardier

Boul Henri Bourassa Est

Parc Nature
de la Pointe
Aux Prairies

To Repentigny,
Trois Rivières &
Québec City

15

Ave Papineau

Boul St Michel

St Léonard

Boul Langelier

Lawson

Golf
Course

138

Boul de l'Acadie

Boul St Laurent

40

Autoroute Métropolitaine

Rue Jarry Est

40

Boul Roi René

Ave Marien

Rue Sherbrooke Est

Boul St Jean Baptiste

Rue Notre Dame Est

Boul Graham

Rue St Denis

Rue Jean Talon Est

Parc
Jarry

Ave Papineau

Anjou

Montréal
Est

Île Ste
Thérèse

Mont
Royal

Ave Van Horne

335

Rue Beaubien

Boul Viau

25

Boul Rosemont

Parc
Maisonneuve

Outremont

see Map 3

Rue Hochelaga

see Map 2

see Map 4

Parc du Mont
Royal

Rue Ontario Est

Rue Ste Catherine Est

Parc des Îles
de Boucherville

Boul Marie Victorin

720

Parc
des Îles

St Lawrence River

Pont Tunnel Louis Hippolyte Lafontaine

To Sorel
& Québec City

see Map 5

20 132

132

Île des
Soeurs

15
20

10

Pont
Victoria

134

Longueuil

Boul Fernand Lafontaine

20

Boucherville

Boul de Mortagne

Boul de Montarville

Rue de Montbrun

132

Pont Champlain

132
20

Motel
Champlain

Boul Simard

112

Boul Taschereau

116

Chemin de Chambly

Boul Roland Therrien

Boul Jacques Cartier

Chemin du Tremblay

Rue de Touraine

132
15

10

Ave Victoria

134

Boul Grande Allée

St Hubert

Boul Sir Wilfrid Laurier

112

Chemin de la Savanne de Bretagne

Aéroport de
St Hubert

20

30

To Eastern
Townships
& Vermont

To Québec City

MAP 2 DOWNTOWN & CHINATOWN

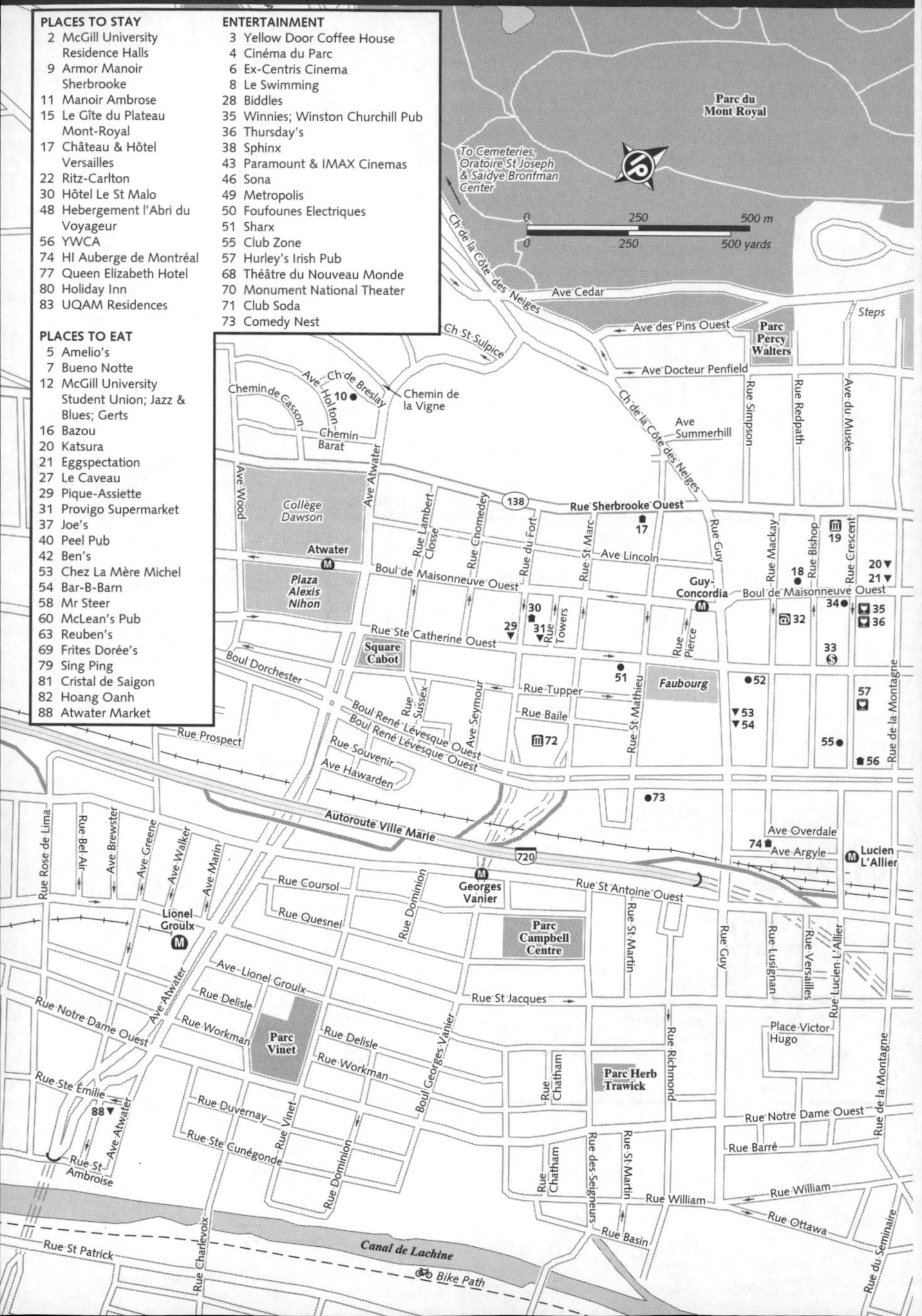

Parc du Mont Royal

To Cemeteries, Oratoire St Joseph & Saidye Bronfman Center

0   250   500 m
0   250   500 yards

Ave Cedar

Steps

Parc Percy Walters

Ave des Pins Ouest

Ave Docteur Penfield

Ch St Sulpice

Ave Summerhill

Ch de Breslay
Ave Holton
Chemin de Casson
Chemin de la Vigne
10
Chemin Barat

Ch de la Côte des Neiges

Ave Wood

Rue Simpson
Rue Redpath
Rue du Musée

Collège Dawson

Atwater

Plaza Alexis Nihon

Ave Atwater

Rue Lambert Closse
Rue St Marc
Rue du Fort
Rue Chomedey

138

Rue Sherbrooke Ouest
17

Boul de Maisonneuve Ouest

Ave Lincoln

Rue Guy

Rue Mackay
Rue Bishop
Rue Crescent

19
18
20
21

Guy-Concordia
Boul de Maisonneuve Ouest

34
35
36

Rue Ste Catherine Ouest

29
30
31
Rue Towers

Rue Pierce

32

33

Square Cabot

Rue Seymour
Rue Sussex

Rue Tupper

Rue St Mathieu

51

Faubourg

52

Boul Dorchester

Rue Baile

53
54

72

55

57

56

Rue de la Montagne

Boul René Lévesque Ouest
Boul René Lévesque Ouest
Ave Seymour
Rue Souvenir

Ave Hawarden

Rue Prospect

73

Autoroute Ville Marie

720

Ave Overdale
74 Ave Argyle

Lucien L'Allier

Rue Rose de Lima
Rue Bel Air
Ave Brewster
Ave Greene
Ave Walker
Ave Marin

Rue Coursol

Rue Dominion

Georges Vanier

Rue St Antoine Ouest

Rue Guy
Rue Lusignan
Rue Versailles
Rue Lucien L'Allier

Lionel Groulx

Rue Quesnel

Parc Campbell Centre

Ave Atwater

Ave Lionel Groulx
Rue Delisle
Rue Workman

Rue Delisle
Rue Workman

Parc Vinet

Rue St Jacques

Rue St Martin

Place Victor Hugo

Rue Richmond

Rue de la Montagne

Rue Notre Dame Ouest

Rue Notre Dame Ouest

Rue Ste Émilie

Rue Duvernay

Rue Ste Cunégonde
Rue Vinet
Rue Dominion

Rue Chatham

Parc Herb Trawick

Rue Barré

88

Ave Atwater

Rue St Émilie
Rue St Ambroise

Rue Charlevoix

Rue William
Rue William

Rue Ottawa

Rue des Seigneurs
Rue St Martin

Rue William

Rue Basin

Canal de Lachine

Rue St Patrick

Bike Path

Rue du Séminaire

MAP 2 DOWNTOWN & CHINATOWN

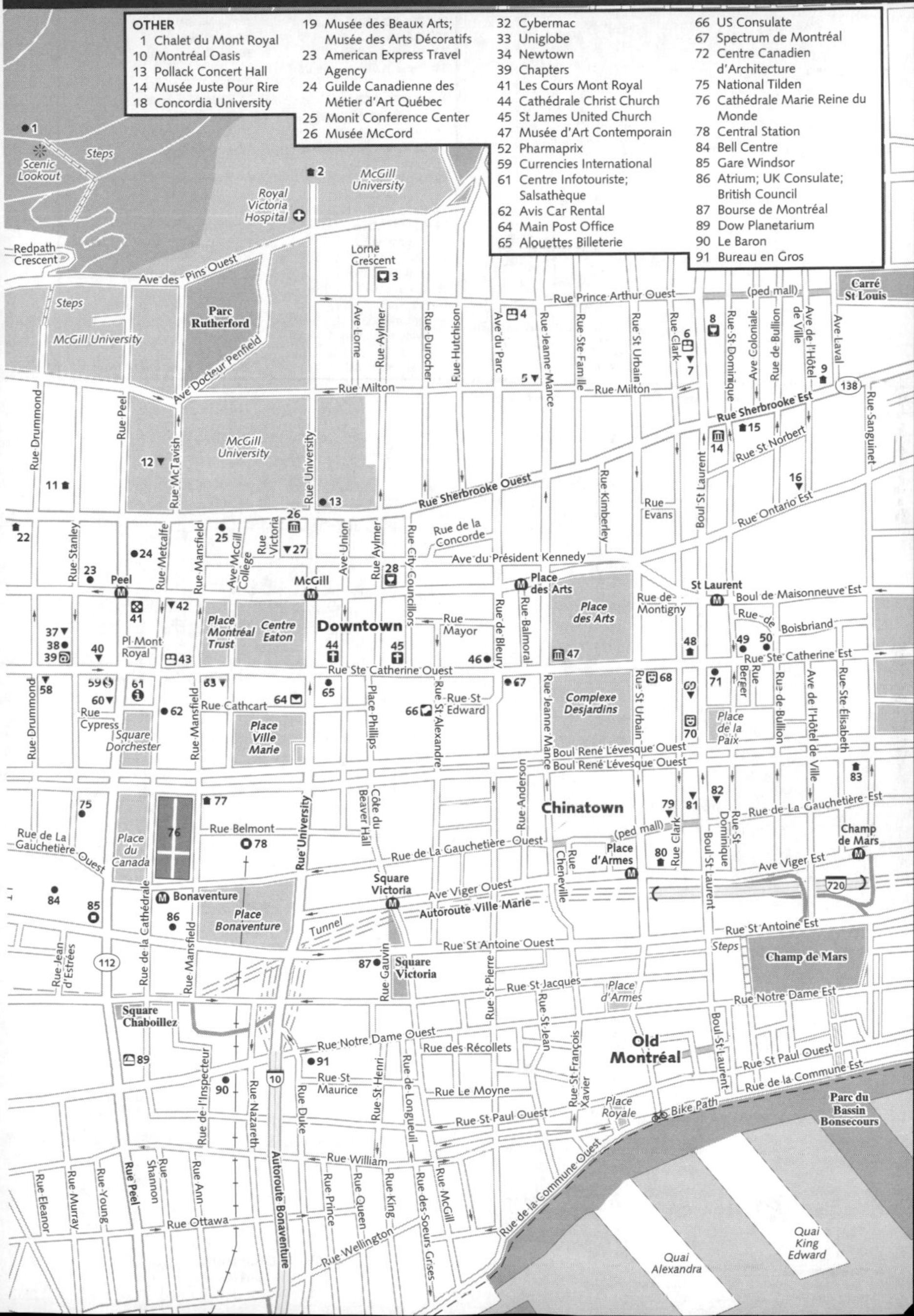

OTHER
1 Chalet du Mont Royal
10 Montréal Oasis
13 Pollack Concert Hall
14 Musée Juste Pour Rire
18 Concordia University

19 Musée des Beaux Arts;
   Musée des Arts Décoratifs
23 American Express Travel
   Agency
24 Guilde Canadienne des
   Métier d'Art Québec
25 Monit Conference Center
26 Musée McCord

32 Cybermac
33 Uniglobe
34 Newtown
39 Chapters
41 Les Cours Mont Royal
44 Cathédrale Christ Church
45 St James United Church
47 Musée d'Art Contemporain
52 Pharmaprix
59 Currencies International
61 Centre Infotouriste;
   Salsathèque
62 Avis Car Rental
64 Main Post Office
65 Alouettes Billeterie

66 US Consulate
67 Spectrum de Montréal
72 Centre Canadien
   d'Architecture
75 National Tilden
76 Cathédrale Marie Reine du
   Monde
78 Central Station
84 Bell Centre
85 Gare Windsor
86 Atrium; UK Consulate;
   British Council
87 Bourse de Montréal
89 Dow Planetarium
90 Le Baron
91 Bureau en Gros

Scenic Lookout
Steps

Redpath Crescent

Royal Victoria Hospital
McGill University

Parc Rutherford
McGill University
Steps
McGill University

Lorne Crescent

Carré St Louis

Ave des Pins Ouest

Rue Prince Arthur Ouest
(ped mall)

Rue Milton

Rue Milton

Rue Sherbrooke Est

Rue Sherbrooke Ouest

Rue de la Concorde
Ave du Président Kennedy

Rue Ontario Est

McGill University

Downtown
Place des Arts

Place Montréal Trust
Centre Eaton

Rue Ste Catherine Ouest

Square Dorchester

Place Ville Marie

Complexe Desjardins

Place de la Paix

Boul René Lévesque Ouest

Place du Canada

Chinatown

Place d'Armes

Champ de Mars

Square Victoria

Place Bonaventure

Autoroute Ville Marie

Rue St Antoine Ouest

Square Chaboillez

Old Montréal

Place Royale

Parc du Bassin Bonsecours

Quai Alexandra

Quai King Edward

MAP 3 MONTRÉAL PLATEAU

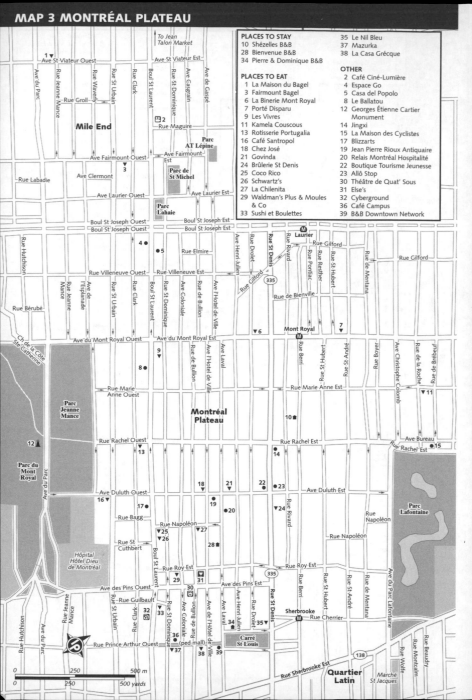

PLACES TO STAY
10 Shézelles B&B
28 Bienvenue B&B
34 Pierre & Dominique B&B

PLACES TO EAT
1 La Maison du Bagel
3 Fairmount Bagel
6 La Binerie Mont Royal
7 Porté Disparu
9 Les Vivres
11 Kamela Couscous
13 Rotisserie Portugalia
16 Café Santropol
18 Chez José
21 Govinda
24 Brûlerie St Denis
25 Coco Rico
26 Schwartz's
27 La Chilenita
29 Waldman's Plus & Moules
   & Co
33 Sushi et Boulettes

35 Le Nil Bleu
37 Mazurka
38 La Casa Grécque

OTHER
2 Café Ciné-Lumière
4 Espace Go
5 Casa del Popolo
8 Le Ballatou
12 Georges Étienne Cartier
   Monument
14 Jingxi
15 La Maison des Cyclistes
17 Blizzarts
19 Jean Pierre Rioux Antiquaire
20 Relais Montréal Hospitalité
22 Boutique Tourisme Jeunesse
23 Allô Stop
30 Théâtre de Quat' Sous
31 Else's
32 Cyberground
36 Café Campus
39 B&B Downtown Network

MAP 4 QUARTIER LATIN & THE VILLAGE

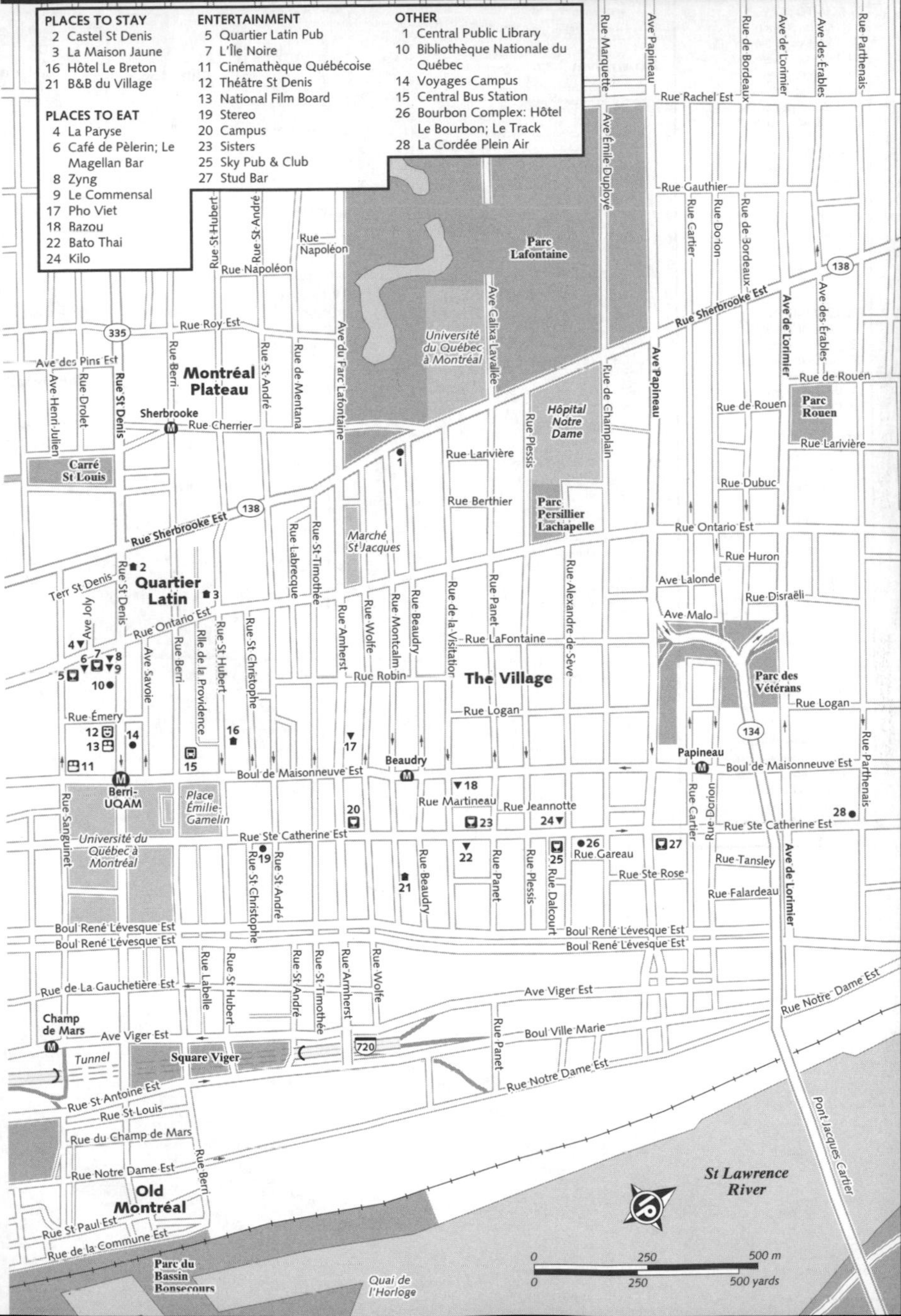

PLACES TO STAY
2 Castel St Denis
3 La Maison Jaune
16 Hôtel Le Breton
21 B&B du Village

PLACES TO EAT
4 La Paryse
6 Café de Pèlerin; Le Magellan Bar
8 Zyng
9 Le Commensal
17 Pho Viet
18 Razou
22 Bato Thai
24 Kilo

ENTERTAINMENT
5 Quartier Latin Pub
7 L'Île Noire
11 Cinémathèque Québécoise
12 Théâtre St Denis
13 National Film Board
19 Stereo
20 Campus
23 Sisters
25 Sky Pub & Club
27 Stud Bar

OTHER
1 Central Public Library
10 Bibliothèque Nationale du Québec
14 Voyages Campus
15 Central Bus Station
26 Bourbon Complex: Hôtel Le Bourbon; Le Track
28 La Cordée Plein Air

MAP 5 OLD MONTRÉAL

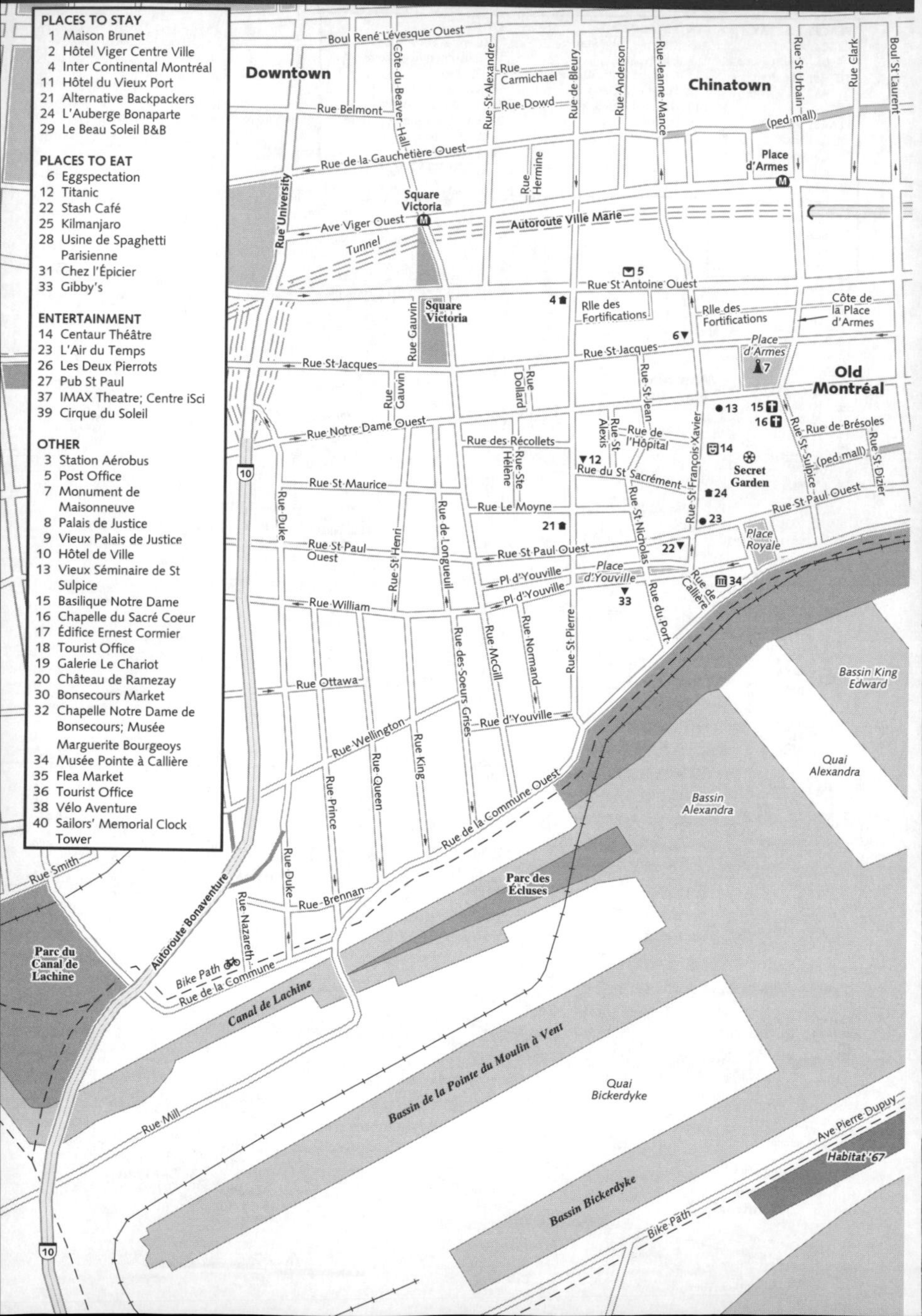

PLACES TO STAY
1 Maison Brunet
2 Hôtel Viger Centre Ville
4 Inter Continental Montréal
11 Hôtel du Vieux Port
21 Alternative Backpackers
24 L'Auberge Bonaparte
29 Le Beau Soleil B&B

PLACES TO EAT
6 Eggspectation
12 Titanic
22 Stash Café
25 Kilmanjaro
28 Usine de Spaghetti Parisienne
31 Chez l'Épicier
33 Gibby's

ENTERTAINMENT
14 Centaur Théâtre
23 L'Air du Temps
26 Les Deux Pierrots
27 Pub St Paul
37 IMAX Theatre; Centre iSci
39 Cirque du Soleil

OTHER
3 Station Aérobus
5 Post Office
7 Monument de Maisonneuve
8 Palais de Justice
9 Vieux Palais de Justice
10 Hôtel de Ville
13 Vieux Séminaire de St Sulpice
15 Basilique Notre Dame
16 Chapelle du Sacré Coeur
17 Édifice Ernest Cormier
18 Tourist Office
19 Galerie Le Chariot
20 Château de Ramezay
30 Bonsecours Market
32 Chapelle Notre Dame de Bonsecours; Musée Marguerite Bourgeoys
34 Musée Pointe à Callière
35 Flea Market
36 Tourist Office
38 Vélo Aventure
40 Sailors' Memorial Clock Tower

Downtown

Chinatown

Place d'Armes

Square Victoria

Square Victoria

Old Montréal

Place d'Armes

Côte de la Place d'Armes

Secret Garden

Place Royale

Bassin King Edward

Quai Alexandra

Bassin Alexandra

Parc du Canal de Lachine

Parc des Écluses

Canal de Lachine

Bassin de la Pointe du Moulin à Vent

Quai Bickerdyke

Bassin Bickerdyke

Habitat '67

MAP 5 OLD MONTRÉAL

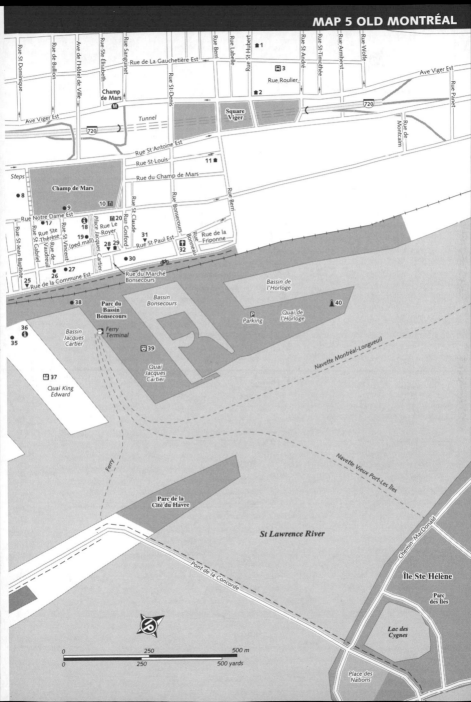

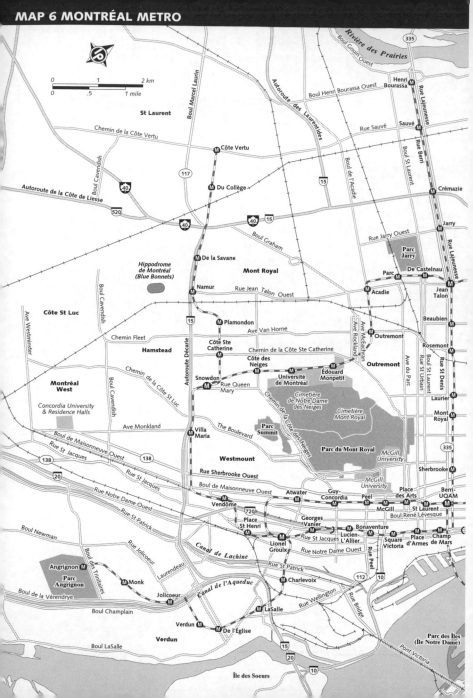

MAP 6 MONTRÉAL METRO

MAP 6 MONTRÉAL METRO

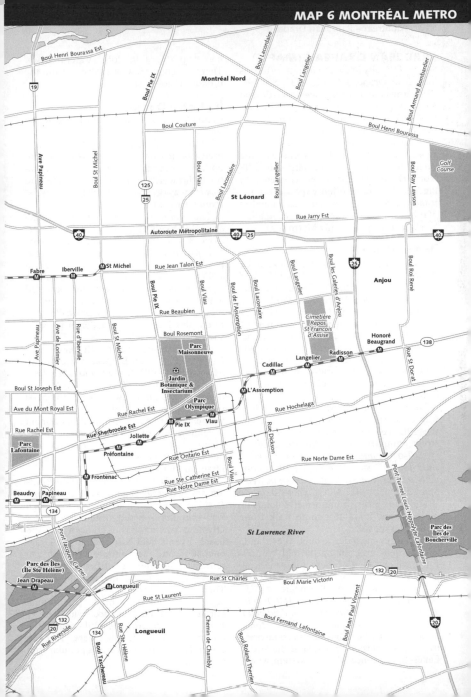

PARC JEAN DRAPEAU (MAP 6)

South of the city in the St Lawrence River is Parc Jean Drapeau (☎ 872-4537, 800-797-4537, W www.parcjeandrapeau.com; ⓜ Jean Drapeau; admission free; open year-round), one of Québec's biggest attractions. It consists of Île Ste Hélène and Île Notre Dame, the sites of the immensely successful 1967 World's Fair: 'Man & His World.' For the event, Île Ste Hélène was enlarged, and Île Notre Dame was completely created with landfill. This park-filled expanse retains some vestiges of the fair and has a number of other attractions. There is an information kiosk near the park's only Métro stop.

Île Ste Hélène

At the northern end of this island is **La Ronde** (☎ 872-4537, 800-797-4537; full/limited admission $29/15.75; open 10am-9pm Sat & Sun May, 10am-9pm daily June–early Sept), the largest amusement park in the province. It has an assortment of bone-shaking rides, including *le monster,* an impressive roller coaster. For the less adventurous, the gentle minirail offers good views of the river and city. A variety of concerts and shows are held throughout the summer.

Near La Ronde there's also an old fort where the British garrison was stationed in the 19th century. Inside the remaining stone ramparts is the **Musée Stewart** (☎ 861-6701; adult/student/senior & child/child under 7 $6/4/4/free; open 10am-6pm daily mid-May–early Sept, 10am-5pm Wed-Sun early Sept–mid-May), where demonstrations are given by uniformed soldiers in period dress. It's a 15-minute walk from ⓜ Jean Drapeau.

Walkways meander around the island, past gardens and among the old World's Fair pavilions. One of them, the American pavilion, in the spherical Buckminster Fuller dome, is now the **Biosphère** (☎ 283-5000, W http://biosphere.ec.gc.ca, 160 chemin Tour de l'Île; adult/senior & student/child $8.50/6.50/5; open 10am-5pm Wed-Mon). Using a range of exhibits and so-so interactive displays, this center explains the Great Lakes–St Lawrence River ecosystem, which

makes up 20% of the globe's water reserves. There's a great view of the river from the upstairs Visions Hall.

Île Notre Dame

Created from 15 million tons of earth and rock excavated when the Métro was built, this artificial island is laced with canals and pretty garden walkways. Things really light up here during the wildly popular international fireworks competition in June and July (W www.lemondialsaq.com; see Special Events, earlier).

The main draw here is the huge, spaceship-like **Casino de Montréal** (☎ 392-2746, W www.casinos-quebec.com; admission free; open 24 hrs), the former French pavilion from the World's Fair. Opened in 1993, the casino was so popular (and earned so much money) that expansion occurred almost instantly. The casino is linked by bridges to an attractive garden called the **Jardin des Floralies**, a wonderful place to stroll.

There's an artificial beach nearby, the **Plage du Parc Jean Drapeau** (☎ 872-6093; adult/child $7.50/3.75, discounts after 4pm; open 10am-7pm daily June 24–late Aug, weather permitting), with room for 5000 people. The water is filtered and treated with chemicals, but many residents remain squeamish about splashing about there. That it is often cramped to capacity doesn't help. Take bus No 167 from the Jean Drapeau Métro station.

Île Notre Dame is also home to the **Pavilion des Activitées Nautiques** (Water Sports Pavilion; ☎ 392-9761; admission free; open 9am-9pm daily), based around the former Olympic rowing basin adjacent to the beach. Events held here include the Dragonboat rowing races in late July. You can rent sailboards and paddleboats; in winter the area becomes a huge skating rink. There's also some cross-country skiing; equipment can be rented. The annual Formula 1 Grand Prix race is held every June at the **Circuit Gilles Villeneuve**, the racetrack named after the Québec race-car driver. The rest of the year, it's popular with inline skaters.

Getting There & Away

If you're driving to the islands, one bridge, the Pont Jacques Cartier, leads to Île Ste Hélène, and another, the Pont de la Concorde, to Île Notre Dame. Consider taking the Métro to the Jean Drapeau stop instead, as island parking fees hit you pretty hard. From the Métro there are buses to attractions on both isles, but walking is almost as fast.

Another option is the Water Shuttle (☎ 281-8000), across the river from the Vieux Port at Quai Jacques Cartier. The shuttle ($3.50 one-way) takes pedestrians and bikes on the 15-minute trip. The first crossing from Quai Jacques Cartier is at 10:35am, with more departures on the hour; the last from Île Ste Hélène is 7:10pm daily (11:10pm Friday to Sunday June through August.)

Alternately, you could bike all the way from Old Montréal on the bike path for free, via Pont de la Concorde.

LACHINE (MAP 1)

The suburb of Lachine, which surrounds the Canal de Lachine, is worth a visit for its history, architecture and general ambience. It's not touristy, it reveals a little of Montréal's roots and culture, and it makes a very good day trip. The side streets behind the impressive College Ste Anne nunnery and City Hall, both along boulevard St Joseph, are perfect for good wandering.

Built between 1821 and 1825, the **Canal de Lachine**, to the southwest of Montréal, allowed boats to circumvent the Lachine Rapids of the St Lawrence River. It was closed in 1970, but the area has been transformed into a 14km-long park that's terrific for cycling and walking. The city of Montréal is also building a marina along the canal near downtown, at the bottom of rue Peel, which will reopen the canal to pleasure boats. Each summer, sections of the canal become living art spaces (☎ 844-9858, Ⓦ www.artefact2001.com), with exhibitions and outdoor sculptures.

The Lachine waterfront is accessible from Old Montréal along the cycling route beside the canal. You can also take the

Métro to Angrignon and then the No 195 bus to 12th Ave.

Fur Trade & Lachine Canal National Historic Site

This historic site (☎ 637-7433, 1255 boul St Joseph; adult/student $2.50/1.50; open 1pm-6pm Mon, 10am-6pm Tues-Sun April–early Sept, 9:30am-5pm Wed-Sun early Sept–Nov) is in an old stone house on the waterfront. The museum tells the story of Canada's fur trade. Trading was done right there because the rapids made further river navigation impossible.

Outside there is a small interpretation center (open 1pm-6pm Mon, 10am-6pm Tues-Sun April–early Sept) that covers the history of the canal . Guided visits are conducted along the canal – you should call ahead to confirm. For more information about the Lachine Canal, call the administrative offices at ☎ 283-6054.

A nearby shop on the canalfront, Claude Brière (☎ 639-7466, 833 boul St Joseph; open 9am-6pm daily), rents out canoes and paddleboats for $12 and $8 per hour, respectively.

ACTIVITIES
Boating

One of the most beautiful spots for boating, canoeing and kayaking is at the **Parc Mille Îles** (Map 1; ☎ 450-622-1020, Ⓦ www.parc mille-iles.qc.ca, 345 boul Ste Rose; adult/child $3/1; open 9am-6pm daily), in Laval, north of Montréal. This park, on the rivière des Mille Îles, has 10 islands where you can disembark on self-guided water tours, and about 10km of the river (including calm inner channels) are open for paddling. There are canoe and kayak rentals ($28/day), and rowboats ($35/day). In winter there's cross-country skiing and skating.

To get there, take the Métro to Henri Bourassa and transfer to the STL bus No 72, which takes you to the park entrance. By car, take Hwy 15 north to exit 16, boulevard Ste Rose – the park is four blocks east.

Cycling

City authorities never tire of pointing out that Montréal was voted North America's most bicycle-friendly city in 1999 by the US magazine *Bicycling*. While you won't find the same concentration of two-wheelers that you would, say, in Amsterdam, the Island of Montréal does enjoy more than 400km of bike paths, a network constantly being expanded. As if to applaud this development, the Tour de l'Île attracts nearly 50,000 cyclists to jockey for position over 65km of paths on the first Sunday in June.

Maps of the city's bicycle paths can be bought at bookstores, but freebies are also available from the tourist offices and bicycle rental shops. One very fine 14km route leads southwest from the edge of Old Montréal all the way to Lachine along the old canal, with a lot of history en route. Picnic tables are scattered along the way, so pack a lunch. Another route covers the Vieux Port area, and yet another the Parc Jean Drapeau. All three are connected.

The lighthearted, good-time Tour de l'Île, on the first Sunday in June, is a major event that attracts 45,000 cyclists. Some riders wear wacky costumes for this long ride around the city. A week earlier, some 10,000 children participate in the Tour des Enfants. For more information, contact La Maison des Cyclistes (☎ 521-8356, 1251 rue Rachel Est) or check Vélo-Tour's site at 🕸 www.velo.qc.ca.

See this chapter's Getting Around section for bicycle rental information.

Ice & Inline Skating

There is year-round indoor ice skating at the gigantic **Atrium** *(Map 2; ☎ 395-0555, 1000 rue de La Gauchetière Ouest; adult/senior & child $5/3; open 11:30am-6pm Tues-Fri & Sun, 10am-10pm Sat)*. Skate rental is available ($4), and there are various children's and adult sessions.

The **Patinoir du Bassin Bonsecours**, inside the Parc du Bassin Bonsecours at the Vieux Port (see Vieux Port), is one of Montréal's most popular outdoor skating rinks *(Map 4; ☎ 496-7678; admission $2, skate rental $6; open 10am-7pm daily)*. There's a nativity scene at Christmastime.

The **Lac aux Castors** *(☎ 872-6559, Parc du Mont Royal; admission free; skate rental $6),*

is another excellent place – it's nestled in the woods near the large parking lot and pavilion at Mont Royal park.

Many bicycle shops rent inline skates too; see the Bicycle section in Getting Around, later in this chapter.

Swimming

The best place to do laps is at Olympic Park's **Centre Sportif** *(☎ 252-4622, 4141 avenue Pierre de Coubertin; adult/student $3.79/3.23; open 6:30am-10pm Mon-Fri, 9am-4pm Sat & Sun)*, which has six indoor pools, wading and diving pools, and a waterslide.

Aside from the unpleasant artificial beach on Île Notre Dame, there are better swimming options at Parc Nature du Cap St Jacques, on the northwest end of the Montréal island, at Oka and at next-door Pointe Calumet (see Around Montréal).

ORGANIZED TOURS

A dazzling array of tours on all forms of transport are offered in Montréal, many departing from the main tourist office (see Tourist Offices, earlier). Check there for more options.

Walking

Worthwhile walking tours are offered by Guidatour (☎ 844-4021), which runs tours of Old Montréal at 11am and 1:30pm daily from late June through September. Old Montréal Ghost Trail (☎ 868-0303) conducts evening crime- and ghost-themed tours led by guides in period costume (read: hard-up local actors). Prices for both are around $12/10 adult/student. Call for more details.

Bus & Boat

Gray Line (☎ 934-1222), at the tourist office on Square Dorchester (Map 2), operates 11 sightseeing tours. The basic city-orientation tour takes 1½ hours and costs $18.50/10 for adult/child. The deluxe bus trip ($45/25 adult/child, 6 hours) is a better value and includes admission to the Biodôme and Jardin Botanique. Yet another trip goes to the Laurentian Mountains, north of Montréal ($69/47). Buses depart from Square Dorchester (Map 2).

Impérial Autocar (☎ 871-4733) offers narrated tours on board an open-top double-decker bus. This hop-on, hop-off tour goes seven times a day and can take up to six hours with stops (just wait for the next bus to hop on). Tickets are $15/12/8 for adult/student/child. There's a more expensive three-hour tour on an air-conditioned bus (no stops). Buses depart from Square Dorchester (Map 2).

The Amphi Tour (☎ 849-5181) offers a surprise: Fitted with a backboard propeller, this bus tours the Vieux Port area for half an hour and then drives into the river. It then cruises the port area for another half-hour. The tour ($18/15 adult/child) departs from Quai King Edward (Map 5) daily from May to October. Reservations are essential.

A couple of companies offer bouncing, soaking jet-boat trips through the nearby Lachine Rapids. Lachine Rapids Tours (☎ 284-9607) has 90-minute trips leaving from Old Montréal. Prices are $49/39/29 for adult/child 13-18/child 6-12. Smaller, faster, less expensive but shorter speedboat trips are also available. Rafting Hydrojet (☎ 767-2230) has rubber-raft trips through the rapids for $34.

AML Cruises (☎ 842-3871) runs river tours from the Quai de l'Horloge (Map 5), at the foot of rue Berri in Old Montréal. The basic two-hour trip around the port, Île Ste Hélène and the Îles de Boucherville (see Around Montréal) leaves at noon and 2:30pm, and costs $22/20/10 adult/student/child. Longer sunset trips and weekend night cruises with a band, dancing and drinks are other options.

SPECIAL EVENTS

Montréal is known as the 'City of Festivals.' Nary a week goes by without some type of festival – cultural or artistic – and most are well organized and a lot of fun.

January & February
Fête des Neiges Two weeks of fun and games at the Parc des Îles celebrating the ubiquitous snow.

June
Le Tour de l'Île A huge cycling event regrouping over 50,000 cyclists for the main 65km race and

many other events. The atmosphere is not heavily competitive and is great fun. See Bicycling, later in this chapter, for details.

Grand Prix Player's du Canada One of North America's only Formula 1 races, the Circuit Gilles Villeneuve is a hugely popular event, held on Île Notre Dame.

L'International Benson & Hedges This international fireworks competition is held twice a week and features splendid displays from around the world. It's held at La Ronde but is visible from many places around the Jacques Cartier bridge.

International Jazz Festival Over 400 concerts held over two weeks of non-stop jazz. See 'Jazzy Montréal' for details.

July
Just for Laughs Comedy Festival For nearly two weeks, everyone in town is giddy because of this fest (☎ 845-3155), which draws in top and some middle and a few bottom acts from around the world. Most performances are in English.

Les Nuits d'Afrique African rhythms overtake the city in a series of great concerts and culinary events.

Les Francopholies de Montréal Over 200 music concerts pay tribute to French-language artists. There are often excellent bands and singers here, and the shows are a lot of fun. Call ☎ 876-8989 for details.

August
Festival des Filmes du Monde The city's biggest, though far from only, film festival (☎ 848-3883) had its heyday in the 1970s and 1980s, before big bad Toronto started a bigger one, but there are always hundreds of great films to see over 10 days.

Marathon de Montréal This race is all embracing, with contestants ranging from the very young to competitors in wheelchairs.

PLACES TO STAY

Montréal's range of accommodations available is impressive, with costs reasonable by national and international standards. Prices often drop in low season. The city's top-end offerings all have various packages and special promos – contact them in advance.

Booking Agencies
There are so many quality accommodations in Montréal, it would be a shame to get stuck in a bad experience. Watch out for

fly-by-night or suspicious-sounding B&B agencies, and if you encounter unreasonably rude service, you can consider registering a complaint at the Centre Infotouriste (☎ 873-2015, 877-266-5687).

If you arrive in town without reservations, the Centre Infotouriste will make bookings for free. You might have to provide a credit card number.

For discounted reservations throughout Québec and discount train fares within Canada, contact Hospitalité Canada (☎ 287-9049, 800-665-1528, **W** www.hospitality-canada.com), 405 rue Sherbrooke Est.

B&B Downtown Network (Map 3; ☎ 289-9749, 800-267-5180), 3458 avenue Laval, has checked over 50 private homes, most of them downtown and in the Quartier Latin, for quality and hospitality beyond minimum requirements. Hosts range from students to lawyers; accommodations range from mansion filled with antiques to Victorian townhouses and penthouses in apartment buildings. Rates start at $45/55 singles/doubles; more luxurious options cost as much as $150.

A similar organization is Montréal Oasis (Map 2; ☎ 935-2312, 3000 chemin de Bresley). Most participant homes are in older houses in the central core, and they pride themselves on the quality of their breakfasts.

Another recommended agency is Relais Montréal Hospitalité (Map 3; ☎ 287-9635, 800-363-9635, 3977 avenue Laval), which provides referrals to B&Bs downtown near Old Montréal.

Budget

Camping There's no camping on the island of Montréal, although several sites are within an hour's drive. See also the Around Montréal section, later.

Camping D'aoust (☎ 450-458-7301, 3844 route Harwood) Tent sites $22; open mid-May–mid-October. Nearly an hour's drive west of Montréal, this bucolic site is on Rte 342 in Hudson. Hiking is good around the site, which encompasses a small farm. Take exit 26 coming from Montréal, or exit 22 coming from Ottawa from Hwy 40; then it's 3km down the road on the right.

Hostels & University Residences Montréal offers myriad budget hostels and dormitory-style accommodations.

Alternative Backpackers (Map 5; ☎ 282-8069, **W** www.auberge-alternative.qc.ca, 358 rue St Pierre) Dorm beds $16/18 off-peak/peak season, doubles $50. Located in a quiet street about 10-minutes walk from the Vieux Port and walkable from the Square Victoria Métro station, there are 48 beds spread over two very colorful, unusually laid-out floors in this converted commercial space. Sheets are $2 extra, and there are cooking facilities.

HI Auberge de Montréal (Map 2; ☎ 843-3317, fax 934-3251, **W** www.hostellingmontreal.com, 1030 rue Mackay) Dorm beds $21/25 member/nonmember, private doubles $52/64; check-in 9:30am-2am. This large, central and well-organized hostel south of boulevard René Lévesque has air-conditioned dorm rooms containing four to 10 beds. Breakfast is offered in the summer, and there is Internet access. The hostel organizes activities and there's a free daily shuttle to the Mont Tremblant hostel (see Mont Tremblant Village in The Laurentians chapter).

Le Gîte du Plateau Mont-Royal (Map 2; ☎ 284-1276, **W** www.hostelmontreal.com, 185 rue Sherbrooke Est) Dorm beds $23, private rooms $45-55. A hostel with a B&B feel, this place is very clean and close to downtown; it offers some self-contained units with cooking facilities.

McGill University Residence Halls (Map 2; ☎ 398-8299, **e** reserve@residences.lan.mcgill.ca, 3935 rue University) Singles $33/40 student/non-student. There are cafeterias and laundry rooms in these residences, a steep walk up near Mont Royal but in a wooded area. For an extra fee, there's access to McGill's superb gym.

UQAM Residences (Map 2; ☎ 987-6669, 888-987-6669, **W** www.residences-uqam.qc.ca, 303 boul René Lévesque) Singles/doubles $35/45, studio apartments $50. These modern, bright rooms receive raves from our readers.

Oratoire St Joseph (☎ 733-8211 ext 2640, **e** pelerinage@osj.qc.ca, 4300 chemin Queen

Mary; **◐** *Côte des Neiges*) Singles/doubles $40/60 with breakfast. West of Mont Royal, pretty, inexpensive rooms are available here at the one of the largest churches you'll ever visit. There are only 13 rooms available, so reserve ahead. To get there, exit the Métro on the west side of chemin Côte des Neiges, turn right, walk to chemin Queen Mary and turn right again. By this time the Oratoire will be visible, looming over the buildings to your left.

YWCA *(Map 2; ☎ 866-9941, fax 861-1603,* **W** *www.ydesfemmesmtl.org, 1355 boul René Lévesque Ouest)* Doubles $62 Oct-May, $69 June-Sept. Montréal's YMCA no longer provides accommodations, but the YWCA allows both men and women in the residences (only women have access to the gym, though). For groups of at least five, bring your sleeping bags and stay for $10 per person in dorm facilities. There's a kitchen on every floor. Dorm rooms have four beds and are not air-conditioned.

Mid-Range
Old Montréal (Map 5) Known in French as Vieux Montréal, the older area of town offers several charming accommodations options.

Hôtel Viger Centre Ville *(☎ 845-6058, 800-845-6058,* **W** *www.hotel-viger.com, 1001 rue St Hubert)* Singles/doubles $45/52-64. In the northern part of Old Montréal, this inexpensive but good hotel has a Victorian shell but a modern interior. It has a wide variety of rooms. The cheapest have color TV, sinks and fans; others have air-conditioning and private bathrooms.

Maison Brunet *(☎ 845-6351, fax 848-7061, 1035 rue St Hubert)* Rooms without/with private bath $58/68. The garrulous owner of this hotel can be found behind the counter amid old-fashioned decor, with touches of sugary rococo. Breakfast is served in the garden, next to a cute fountain.

Le Beau Soleil B&B *(☎ 871-0299, 355 rue St Paul Est)* Singles/doubles/triples $75/90/105. Featuring a lovely upstairs view of Bonsecours Market, this place is a particularly good value – despite the shared baths and the 52 steps, it's worthwhile. The owners

are friendly and personable, and the rooms are homey, if small. They also run the more luxurious **Auberge Bonsecours** at the same address, with singles/doubles for $95-125/160-175.

Downtown & Chinatown (Map 2) Around the central bus station, there are dozens of small hotels with rooms in the $40 to $70 range, particularly up rue St Hubert.

Manoir Ambrose *(☎ 288-6922, fax 288-5757,* **W** *www.manoirambrose.com, 3422 rue Stanley)* Singles $40-50, doubles without/ with private bath $65/85-125. This is a fine place in a quiet, central residential area. Compared to the sterile international hotels, its 22 rooms (some of which are air-conditioned) are a real bargain, even if the decor borders on kitsch.

Pierre & Dominique B&B *(Map 3; ☎ 286-0307,* **W** *www.bbcanada.com/928 .html, 271 Carré St Louis)* Singles/doubles without bath $48/75-85. Located in a row of stone Victorian houses overlooking a busy square, the light, airy bedrooms are decked out in Swedish-style furniture and have a washbasin.

Hôtel Le St Malo *(☎ 931-7366, fax 931-3764,* **e** *stmalo@colba.net, 1455 rue du Fort)* Singles/doubles $50/$68-78. In the western part of downtown, this place offers a good deal, being pleasant and modernly furnished.

Hebergement l'Abri du Voyageur *(☎ 849-2922, fax 499-0151,* **W** *www.abri-voyageur .ca, 9 rue Ste Catherine Ouest)* Singles/ doubles from $52/57, additional guests $10. This is one of the best affordable places around. The totally renovated hotel, with original pine floors and exposed brick, has 30 rooms – each with a sink, fan and TV. Some might find the red-light district too seedy, however.

Armor Manoir Sherbrooke *(☎ 845-0915, 800-203-5485,* **W** *www.armormanoir.com, 157 rue Sherbrooke Est)* Doubles $69-109, with continental breakfast. This is the conversion of two fine Victorian houses into a hotel with 30 rooms. Prices vary depending on room size, but all have private baths (some rooms have Jacuzzis and sumptuous woodwork).

Bienvenue B&B (☎ 844-5897, 800-227-5897, W *www.bienvenuebb.com, 3950 avenue Laval*) Singles/doubles with shared bath $65/75, singles/doubles with bath $75/85. This B&B near Carré St Louis has 12 nicely furnished rooms in a lovely stone Victorian house with wrought-iron balconies.

Shézelles B&B (*Map 3;* ☎ 849-8694, fax 528-8290, W *www.bbcanada.com/2469.html, 4272 rue Berri*) Doubles without/with bath $70/90, studio $120. This place is a bastion of warmth and hospitality, with its paneled walls and large fireplace. The 'love nest' studio apartment, occupying the entire ground floor, is superb and sumptuously furnished. Upstairs are two rooms, one of which has a Japanese sliding door with the bed directly under a skylight.

Quartier Latin & The Village (Map 4) This fun, bohemian area is home to many hotels.

La Maison Jaune (☎ 524-8851, fax 521-7352, W *www.maisonjaune.com, 2017 rue St Hubert*) Singles/doubles without private bath $45/65. This B&B has five rooms appointed in different colors in a pretty yellow Victorian-era building. The quietest room has a balcony overlooking the garden.

Castel St Denis (☎ 842-9719, W *www.castelsaintdenis.qc.ca, 2099 rue St Denis*) Singles/doubles with bath $50/60. Right on lively rue St Denis, this mini hotel has been renovated a couple of times, and is a good value. Rooms all have private baths, TV and air-conditioning.

Hôtel Le Breton (☎ 524-7273, fax 527-7016, 1609 rue St Hubert) Singles/doubles $65/75-80. This hotel is on the western end of the Village, in an excellent location near the bus station, with charming owners. Rates depend on room size and amenities; all come with TV and shower or bath.

B&B du Village (☎ 522-4771, 1279 rue Montcalm) Doubles $70-90, self-contained apartments $130. This gay-friendly place is pleasant, with enclosed courtyard and balconies. There's even a resident masseur for those stressed by shopping and happy hours galore! The larger rooms have TV and bathrooms; all are air-conditioned.

Hôtel Le Bourbon (☎ 523-4679, 800-268-4679, W *www.bourbon.qc.ca, 1574 rue Ste Catherine Est*) Doubles/triples/quads $105/115/135, suites $130-230. Located in the huge Bourbon Complex, an emporia of gay venues including bars and diners, this hotel is a good value – their suites fit four to eight persons. It can be noisy and cruisy till the breakfast hours, though. For circuit party weekends, they're booked months in advance.

Top End

Holiday Inn (*Map 2;* ☎ 878-9888, 99 avenue Viger Ouest) Doubles from $129. This four-star place is on the edge of Chinatown – you can't miss the fake pagodas on the rooftop. It offers above-average luxury for the price, with a health club, indoor pool and sauna. Prices, though, can change from day to day, depending on how booked they are and on time of year.

Hôtel du Vieux Port (*Map 5;* ☎ 844-0767, 888-977-0767, W *www.hotelvieux-port.zip411.net, 756 rue Berri*) Doubles $135, suites $240. This hotel offers special rates for long stays. The modish, 27-room inn is lodged in an 1882 warehouse. It's above a fine pub/restaurant in the heart of Old Montréal. Buffed floors, original wooden beams and views of the Vieux Port set the tone. Prices include access to a pool and a small gym.

Château & Hôtel Versailles (*Map 2;* ☎ 933-8111, 888-933-8111, W *www.versailles hotels.com, 1808 rue Sherbrooke Ouest*) Singles/doubles $120/140. This is a renovated, one-time European-style pension with Old World touches and spacious rooms. It consists of two buildings, the Edwardian-era Château and the more modern Hôtel. The former links four turn-of-the century townhouses, which have snug rooms with slightly outdated decor.

L'Auberge Bonaparte (*Map 5;* ☎ 844-1448, W *www.bonaparte.com, 447 rue St François Xavier*) Doubles $145-185, suites $300, both with full breakfast. Exuding an air of conviviality and relaxation, the wrought-iron beds and Louis Philippe furnishings lend a suitably Napoleonic touch to the surprisingly spacious rooms here. Some suites have a view of the Basilique Notre Dame. Take a virtual tour on the website.

Queen Elizabeth Hotel *(Map 2; ☎ 861-3511, ⓦ www.fairmont.com, 900 boul René Lévesque Ouest)* Doubles $209-299, suites from $300. Prices vary considerably depending on dates, occupancy, etc. The 'Queen E' is world-famous as the site where John Lennon and Yoko Ono wrote 'Give Peace a Chance' during their 1969 nude love-in; in fact, part of their suite is now a room (#1742) that can sometimes be had for as little as $79 (the bed's a pullout, you know), but only when the hotel is full.

Ritz Carlton *(Map 2; ☎ 842-4212, 800-363-0366, ⓦ www.ritzcarlton.com, 1228 rue Sherbrooke Ouest)* Doubles/suites $310/435 May–mid-Oct, $215/245 mid-Oct–May. This has long been *the* place in Montréal for the ultimate splurge. Following a facelift a few years back, even the marble-floored bathrooms are wired for TV and radio sound. If you catch the right moment, the limos out front will disgorge big-shot entertainers and politicians.

PLACES TO EAT

Some people say it's the French background, others put it down to a sin-and-repent mentality of a predominantly Catholic city; whatever the reason, Montréalers also love to eat out. The city's reputation for culinary excellence has Gallic roots, but its more recent cosmopolitanism makes for a veritable United Nations of cuisine. Dining can be such a pleasure in this city, in fact, some *gourmands* come to Montréal for the sole purpose of eating. The choice is bewildering: There are some 4500 restaurants – more per capita than anywhere else on the continent, except New York.

The downtown and Plateau areas have the greatest concentration of restaurants. Spanning the two districts are two major dining strips along boulevard St Laurent and rue St Denis, both of which enjoy a wide range of reasonably priced, high-quality food. The farther north you go, the more quaint and innovative the establishments become.

Chinatown has a bevy of low-cost eateries bunched close together. Greek places are ubiquitous, with a high concentration on rue Prince Arthur Est. On avenue Duluth Est, the Portuguese reign with their wonderful roasted meats and seafood. A vibrant Little Italy has a decent choice of Italian restaurants. The many Vietnamese restaurants are renowned for their authenticity. Add that to the excellent Indian, Lebanese, Thai, even Ethiopian cuisine readily found in the city, and you have a slice of paradise.

Many restaurants have a policy of *apportez vôtre vin* (bring your own wine; BYOW). Lots of these eateries can be found on rue Prince Arthur Est and avenue Duluth Est.

Restaurants

Old Montréal (Map 5) Old Montréal is a fine place to splurge. In fact, it might be a good idea to spend as much as you can. Although some of the city's finest restaurants are in this beautiful area, this is also a major tourist spot, and many of the mid-priced places make delicious-sounding but essentially assembly-line dishes at marked-up prices.

Chez L'Épicier *(☎ 878-2232, 311 rue St Paul Est)* Lunch specials $13-16, dinner mains from $19; open 11:30am-2pm Mon-Fri, 5:30pm-10pm daily; grocery store open 11am-6pm daily. This place combines fine dining with a wine bar and a gourmet grocery store. A three-course dinner – including quirky dishes such as corn and lobster-oil soup and guinea hen seasoned with balsamic vinegar – runs about $40. Yummy ready-to-heat dishes for two can be had from the glass case for under $10.

Usine de Spaghetti Parisienne *(☎ 866-0963, 273 rue St Paul Est)* Mains $6-17; open 11am-10pm daily. Cheap eats with friendly atmosphere can be had here. Meals include fettuccine with baby clams or curried beef-filet medallions (both $14), with all the bread and salad you can eat.

EggSpectation *(☎ 282-0119, 201 rue St Jacques)* Mains $8; open 6am-4pm Mon-Fri, 6am-5pm Sat & Sun. For omelets, crêpes or burgers, try this place.

Gibby's *(☎ 282-1837, 298 Place d'Youville)* Dinner $30-50; open 4:30pm-11pm daily. A snazzy, popular place in a 200-year-old converted stable. The specialties are steak and roast beef, although the lobster and scampi also warrant a visit. Reservations are suggested, especially on weekends.

Stash Café (☎ 845-6611, 200 rue St Paul Ouest) Mains $11-18; open 11:30am-11pm daily. This place serves hearty Polish cuisine in an intimate setting featuring church pews and low-hanging ceiling lamps. Don't be surprised if a customer jumps up and starts to dance with the waiters. A good set meal including standards such as pirogi and borscht costs $14.

Downtown (Map 2) There are eateries every few steps around here. The selection is good as is the variety, though prices tend to be slightly higher and the food a tad more conservative than in the restaurants outside the downtown area.

Katsura (☎ 849-1172, 2170 rue de la Montagne) Lunch $8-14, dinner $27-37; open 11:30am-2:30pm Mon-Fri, 5:30-10pm daily. Amid a blaze of kimonos and stylish decor, sample the excellent lunch, popular with businesspeople. Best is an evening *table d'hôte* at the monumental sushi bar. The Nipponese delicacies are prepared with the greatest care, but the ambience is glacial.

Chez La Mère Michel (☎ 934-0473, 1209 rue Guy) Lunch specials $17, full-course gourmet dinner $40; open 11:45am-2pm Tues-Fri, 5:30pm-10:30pm Mon-Sat. Montréal is renowned for its French food, and this is a fine place to confirm this reputation. The service, the food, the style – everything! – is 1st class.

Le Caveau (☎ 844-1624, 2063 rue Victoria) Three-course specials $13-26, mains $17-28; open noon-3pm Mon-Fri, 5pm-10pm daily. Nestled amid a forest of skyscrapers, the antique-filled Victorian villa that houses this place is an architectural oasis. You'll enjoy the table d'hôte, with fine courses such as glazed snails or marinated salmon.

Pique-Assiette (☎ 932-7141, 2051 rue Ste Catherine Ouest) Mains $6-20; lunch buffet $8, dinner buffet $17; open 11:30am-2:30pm & 5pm-10pm daily. Part of the Bombay House chain, this is one of the oldest Indian restaurants in town. The meats and vegetable curries are sublime (have a peek at the clay pots in the kitchen), and the weekend brunch ($9) will leave your tummy groaning in pleasure.

EggSpectation (☎ 842-3447, 1313 boul de Maisonneuve Ouest) Mains $8; open 6am-10pm Mon-Sat, 6am-6pm Sun. In an attractive converted warehouse, this place has excellent coffees and huge, delicious lunches of omelets, crêpes or elaborate burgers. Their tasty, imaginative dinner specials range from $7 to $12.

Bazou (☎ 982-0853, 2004 avenue l'Hôtel de Ville) Mains $16-27; open 11am-11pm Mon-Sat. Because you BYOW to this branch of Bazou it's cheaper than the more opulent branch in the Village (see that section, later). Sumptuous food (albeit in, shall we say, easily digestible portions) and a quirky, cozy decor make this a winner.

Amelio's (☎ 845-8396, 201 rue Milton) Mains $6-12, Lunch specials $5; open 11:30am-8:45pm Tues-Fri & Sun, 4pm-8:45pm Sat & Mon. In the so-called 'McGill ghetto,' this has been a popular student draw for decades. The portions of pizza and pasta are generous; a medium pizza with salad ($11) is enough to stuff two people.

Bueno Notte (☎ 848-0644, 3518 boul St Laurent) Table d'hôte lunch $12-18, dinner $25-30. More often than not, this elegant place is filled with strutting fashion victims. Because of – or perhaps despite – its poseur clientele, the chefs serve up excellent Italian and international fare, from delicate, savory pastas to sizzling Angus steaks.

McLean's Pub (☎ 393-3132, 1210 rue Peel) Mains $6-15. This has managed to maintain an air of old-style pub (the wood panels, impressive ceiling and fireplace help). The mostly English clientele sure love their Reubens or McLean's subs for $7 to $9.

Bar-B-Barn (☎ 931-3811, 1201 rue Guy) Meals $8-19; open 11:30am-10pm daily. Usually packed at dinner, this place serves the best and biggest spareribs you've ever had. It's small, decked out like a barn-pub, with a zillion business cards stuck in the rafters. It also does good chicken – the only other thing on the menu.

Peel Pub (☎ 844-6769, 1107 rue Ste Catherine Ouest) Mains $3-9; open 8am-3am daily. A favored hangout of McGill students – indeed, it's spacious enough to accommodate the entire student body, and feels as crowded as if it did! The atmosphere is fun and lively, but the star is its bargain-basement food (eg, a quarter chicken and ribs with salad for $7).

Joe's (☎ 842-4638, 1430 rue Stanley) Mains $11-18; open 11am-11pm Sun-Fri, 11am-midnight Sat. This renowned steak house serves meals that include potato or fries and an all-you-can-eat salad bar. The filet mignon special is an especially good deal.

Mr Steer (☎ 866-3233, 1198 rue Ste Catherine Ouest) Mains $6-15; open 7am-11pm daily. This place has been around for nearly half a century. The Mr Steer special (costing precisely $6.72) includes a quarter chicken, burger, hotdog or chili – plus salad, fries and drink. Their calling cards are the Suzy Q fries – curly and deep-fried to perfection.

Chinatown (Map 2) Montréal's Chinatown is small but well entrenched, with a portion of the main street, rue de la Gauchetière, closed to traffic. The food is mainly Cantonese, although spicier Szechuan dishes show up, and several Vietnamese places can be found. Many offer lunch specials as cheap as $6.

Cristal de Saigon (☎ 875-4275, 1068 boul St Laurent) Mains $6-13; open 11am-10pm daily. A Vietnamese diner specializing in satisfying Tonkinoise soups (meals in themselves). It's often packed with local Chinatown residents.

Hoang Oanh (☎ 954-0051, 1071 boul St Laurent) Mains $5-10. Across the street from Cristal de Saigon, this place is famous for Vietnamese submarine sandwiches.

Sing Ping (☎ 397-9598, 74 rue de la Gauchetière Ouest) Mains $8-15, open noon-2am daily. Sing Ping enjoys an excellent reputation, with its huge tables ideal for a good meal with friends before hitting the clubs along rue St Denis.

Quartier Latin & The Village (Map 4) In the last few years, the eating options in this area have improved dramatically. The lively

clientele they attract can be as noteworthy as their food.

Zyng (Map 4; ☎ 284-2016, 1748 rue St Denis) Mains $10-15; open 11:30am-10pm daily. Soup-lovers wax lyrical here, where a bowl of delicious noodles, meat or veggie, costs $5 (your choice of ingredients). The bright, peppy interior makes the flavors even more vivid. Have chocolate-covered lychees for dessert.

La Paryse (☎ 842-2040, 302 rue Ontario Est) Mains $5-10, open 11am-11pm Mon-Fri, noon-11pm Sat & Sun. The thickest, juiciest burgers in town are served with an array of toppings in neo-retro, bright rooms. The homemade fries ($2) and vegetable soups ($2.50) are terrific.

Café de Pèlerin (☎ 845-0909, 330 rue Ontario Est) Mains $7-14. An unassuming space you won't feel like leaving and will find yourself returning to. Decent food, good service and laid-back atmosphere (try the terrace out back) is all you need for a good night out. You can also eat in the attached wood-paneled bar, Le Magellan.

Pho Viet (☎ 522-4116, 1663 rue Amherst) Appetizers $2-4, mains $7-14. Open 11am-3pm, 5pm-9pm Mon-Fri, 5pm-9pm Sat. Because of its excellent Vietnamese food at affordable prices, this is a very popular place. A Vietnamese fondue for two will set you back just $21.

Bato Thai (☎ 524-6705, 1310 rue Ste Catherine Est) Mains $7-17. Open 11am-3pm, 5pm-10pm Mon-Fri, 5pm-10pm Sat & Sun. The ever-fresh ingredients and boat-shaped bar here get rave reviews. Daily specials cost $8, and all main courses are inexpensive (beef curry with coconut milk and basil leaves for $9).

Bazou (☎ 526-4940, 1310 boul de Maisonneuve Est) Lunch $7-10, dinner $15-26; open 11am-11pm Mon-Sat. Based on an automobile theme, this is a fusion restaurant with stylish decor (the high-backed sofas are actually comfy) and a huge dining terrace. The menu spans French, Mexican, Indian and Asian cuisine.

Montréal Plateau (Map 3) This is the dining area of choice for many Montréalers and tourists alike. As you head north from the Quartier Latin, it's slightly seedy, bohemian air gives way to the chichi crowd of upper rue St Denis and boulevard St Laurent, where you'll find some of the city's slickest dining establishments. Just north of there, the pedestrian rue Prince Arthur is a favorite 'restaurant row' with mid-priced eateries, all BYOW.

Farther north, avenue Duluth is a narrow old street (once a red-light district) that has been redone as a restaurant center, but less frequented, more charismatic than rue Prince Arthur, with its painted walls and ethnically mixed populace. Between the two, boulevard St Laurent has many great stops, be it for a Polish sausage or smoked meat, bagel or something fancier.

La Casa Grècque (☎ 842-6098, 200 rue Prince Arthur Est) Mains $7-18, lunch specials $4-14; open 11am-11:30pm daily. Tasty, if unadventurous, dinners can be had at one of the city's legendary eateries.

Mazurka (☎ 844-3539, 64 rue Prince Arthur Est) Mains $5-13; open 11:30am-midnight daily. Some of the best comfort food in the Plateau can be had here, and it's dirt cheap. The daily specials are around $6,

---

Essential Montréal Experiences

In the brain cells of countless foreign visitors, Montréal is genetically fused with the notion of bagels and smoked meat, originally Jewish Eastern European recipes. Aside from the city's other culinary delights, these two form quintessential Montréal experiences which would be plainly sinful not to indulge in during your visit. As Oscar Wilde noted, 'The best way to overcome temptation is to succumb to it.' Dig in!

The Little 'O'

Fans get mighty serious about these round slabs of punctured dough, and debates rage about which bagels are superior – New York City's or Montréal's. From the pavements of Manhattan and Le Plateau to the Web's chat-rooms, people swap taste-test tales, comparing density, saltiness, chewiness, even durability. In the end, sorry guys, it's 'True North' that edges out all competition.

Ever since Isadore and Fanny Shlafman, Ukrainian Jews, opened their first bakery in Montréal in 1915 (which ultimately grew into the legendary Fairmount Bagel), making yeast rings from a recipe they'd brought with them from Kiev, bagels have been part of local yore. A competitor, Myer Lemkomwicz, a Polish Jew, opened his own shop in 1957 (now the Maison du Bagel), and aficionados now debate whether he outstripped the original (many agree!).

Good bagels are available all over town, but why not go for the original?

At *Fairmount Bagel* (Map 3; ☎ 272-0667, 74 avenue Fairmount Ouest) you'll find oodles of variations, including pumpernickel and cumin, sun-dried tomato, and cinnamon raisin bagels. They also make their own matzo boards, New York pretzels (which taste like they've been soaked in the Dead Sea) and 'bozo bagels,' which are triple normal size.

La Maison du Bagel (Map 3; ☎ 276-8044, 263 avenue St Viateur Ouest) has the real deal. A dozen freshly made plain, poppy seed or sesame seed bagels cost $4.25, and they are perfectly crusty, chewy and slightly sweet – worthy of their international reputation. Take bus No 55 north along boulevard St Laurent.

Smoked Heaven on Rye

Debates over bagels seem trite compared to the heated disputes over the origins and authenticity of the other Montréal staple: smoked meat. Termed pastrami outside of Montréal (and don't even dare to put corned beef in the same category!), smoked meat is made by curing a beef brisket with salt, garlic, herbs and spices, then smoking it for several days, and finally steaming it.

featuring pirogi and meat or cheese blintzes. It's a sprawling place, with four levels and paintings from the Old Country.

Le Nil Bleu (☎ 285-4628, 3706 rue St Denis) Mains $7-13. This memorable Ethiopian restaurant is verdantly decorated in bamboo, East African art and even a water-wall. The low ceilings and off-lighting give a cocoon-like feel. All the food – spicy meats, seafood and vegetables – is served on huge pancakes (called bread injera), which you tear off in strips, wrap around your food and eat with your hands.

Sushi et Boullettes (☎ 848-9474, 3681 boul St Laurent) Mains $4-11; open 11am-11pm Sun-Wed, 11am-3am Thur-Sat. This small, unpretentious Japanese eatery dishes up lunch specials such as soup and beef teriyaki ($7) and a dazzling array of sushi and sashimi for $3.25 to $4.25.

Rotisserie Portugalia (☎ 282-1519, 34 rue Rachel Ouest) Mains $6-21; open 10am-9pm daily. Step up to the charcoal grill at the counter at this meatlover's mecca. Its wonderful *churrasco* chicken (marinated and grilled Portuguese-style) costs $16. The menu is short, but everything's succulent.

Essential Montréal Experiences

It was born, by all accounts, in 1908 in Montréal's garment district by one Ben Kravitz, a Lithuanian Jew who arrived in Canada in 1899, according to his grandparent's recipe for curing beef to make it last longer without refrigeration. Eventually, Ben's became a legend. It is still owned by a member of the Kravitz family.

But Schwartz's (also called the Montréal Hebrew Delicatessen) holds the nation's smoked meat crown. Reuben Schwartz, a Romanian Jew, opened his first restaurant in 1927, and today the sandwiches served by the dozens at boulevard St Laurent's landmark deli still use his recipe. The proprietors claim to be the only ones who still smoke their own briskets, using only fresh meat – there's not a freezer in the place! These are cured and smoked for ten days, 14 hours a day, then steamed for three hours before being served.

The frequent line-ups outside the place, which hasn't changed decor in decades (save for the regulation French signs inside), attest to its popularity. There are rich businessmen who fly here from New York for lunch before heading back for an afternoon meeting. One British millionaire has been known to fly over for a meal (a table in the back is cleared out for him). The Rolling Stones, Michael Jackson and Tina Turner are some other famous guests. The staff always stocks extra briskets on American holidays, as they anticipate visiting hordes.

You can find smoked meat in every corner of the province, and some of it, albeit mass-produced and containing artificial ingredients, is mighty good. But want the real thing?

Schwartz's (Map 3; ☎ 842-4813, 3895 boul St Laurent) Lunch mains $5-9; open 9am-12:30am Sun-Thur, 9am-1:30am Fri, 9am-2:30am Sat. Don't bother with the lean cut – medium is what you need for the best taste. While the meat here is a bit drier than at other places, that's only because they use no chemicals to make it artificially juicier. Here you get the full flavor, the real thing.

Ben's (Map 2; ☎ 844-1000, 990 boul de Maisonneuve Ouest) Mains $5-11; open 7:30am-3am Mon-Fri, 7:30am-4am Sat & Sun. Celebrity photos line the walls at this other fixture on the Montréal dining landscape, in this location since 1949. The waiters are creaking old wisecrackers and the kindergarten color coordination of the decor plays tricks with your eyes. There's the classic sandwich ($4.50), lots of smoked meat variations and other food too.

Reuben's (Map 2; ☎ 866-1029, 1116 rue Ste Catherine Ouest) Mains $6-13; open 6:30am-2am Sun-Thur, 6:30am-5am Fri & Sat. With rows of pickled peppers in the window, Reuben's does its eponymous sandwich (smoked meat, sauerkraut and melted cheese) for $7, one of the best smoked meat variations around.

MONTRÉAL

Kamela Couscous (☎ 526-0881, 1227 rue Marie Anne Est) Pizza $6-8, pasta $7-8, couscous $7-14; open 4pm-11pm daily. This inviting little eatery with a split personality specializes in Algerian/Tunisian and Italian cuisine. Its 30-odd varieties of pizza come with a delicious thin crust, and the couscous dishes come in vegetarian, merguez and meat varieties.

La Binerie Mont Royal (☎ 285-9078, 367 rue Mont Royal Est) Mains $6-9; open 6am-9pm Mon-Fri, 7:30am-4pm Sat & Sun. To savor authentic Québécois cuisine in typical Montréal atmosphere, try this place. The tourtières, ragouts, pork and beans and pudding *chômeur* are the great specialties.

Outside the Center A bit of exploring can go a long way in Montréal, as several of the city's best places to eat are in out-of-the-way areas.

Il Mulino (☎ 273-5776, 236 rue St Zotique Est; Ⓜ Jean Talon) Mains $20-35; open noon-3pm Tues-Fri, 5pm-11pm Tues-Sat. This is perhaps the top Italian restaurant in town, right in Little Italy, offering a breathtaking array of specialties. Try the vegetarian starter plate ($10) before moving on to baby lamb chops, so tender they practically cut themselves.

Le Troquet (☎ 271-6789, 106 avenue Laurier Ouest; Ⓜ Laurier) Mains $10; open 9am-midnight daily. People come here, in Mile End, for terrific mussels ($9 to $11) in a very French ambience. The Neapolitan, which consists of sausages and mussels in beer sauce, is great. They also serve panini, soups and salads. There's live jazz and blues on weekends.

Pho Lien (☎ 735-6949, 5703 chemin Côte des Neiges; Ⓜ Côte des Neiges) Mains $5-11; open 5pm-11pm Wed-Mon. In a city with so many excellent Vietnamese restaurants, this is regarded as one of the best. The energy not spent on decor went into the great food here – huge meal soups and authentic *pho* keep customers lining up outside.

Pushap Sweets (☎ 737-4527, 5195 rue Paré; Ⓜ De la Savane) Mains $5-10; open 11am-9pm daily. Out of the way, this little place could be mistaken for a *dépanneur*

from its unassuming appearance. Yet connoisseurs whisper that this family restaurant is the city's top Indian eatery – it's no accident that many of the customers here have been to India. The vegetarian *thali* is superb.

Vegetarian (Map 3) Though most restaurants offer a vegetarian meal, the best places for succulent, healthy food are concentrated in the Plateau.

Café Santropol (☎ 842-3110, 3990 rue St Urbain) Mains $6-12. This is the ideal spot for reading, writing postcards or just plain procrastinating, in its cozy interior or on the garden-like terrace. For over 25 years, it's also been known for its huge, bizarre sandwiches, served with an orchard-full of fruit and salad. There are some meat sandwiches, but veggies are the specialty.

Les Vivres (☎ 842-3479, 4434 rue Ste Dominique) Mains $6-8, brunch $7.25; open noon-midnight Mon-Fri, 11am-midnight Sat & Sun. A granola paradise, a decked-out garage, a diner for tree-hugging lefties – call it what you will, but this vegan co-op serves up delicious food, considering vegans' limited diet. Grab a Kerouac from the shelf, order from your waiter in dreads and skirt, and feast on a BLT (smoked coconut instead of bacon), their Indian plate or succulent homemade bread.

Govinda (☎ 284-5255, 263 rue Duluth Est) Lunch $7, dinner $9; open 11:30am-9pm Sun-Wed, 11:30am-11pm Thur-Sat. Located in the city's Hare Krishna Center, the mini buffet on offer has standard Krishna fare, with a Québécois accent (veggie tourtière and shepherd's pie, for example). The Halava dessert is worth the trip alone.

Le Commensal (Map 4; ☎ 845-2627, 1720 rue St Denis) Average mains $9-15; open 11am-11pm Sun-Thur, 11am-11:30pm Fri & Sat. This was the city's main vegetarian restaurant when the fad began in the 1980s, but is now neither the only one nor the best. Set up buffet-style, the (excellent) food is priced by weight and always comes out way more expensive than it should be. Another outlet is at 1204 rue McGill College.

Cafés

Titanic *(Map 5; ☎ 849-0894, 445 rue St Pierre)* Mains $4-9; open 8am-4pm Mon-Fri. Tucked in a basement, this recommended place caters to a local clientele. The staff and atmosphere are friendly and casual, with artsy exhibits alongside the diner counter and wooden tables. They serve salads, creative sandwiches and pastas.

Kilimanjaro *(Map 5; ☎ 875-2332, 39 rue de la Commune Est)* Mains $5-10. This is probably the nicest café at portside, and the food's a good value too. Grab one of the shaded terrace tables and launch into one of their tasty, oversized sandwiches or burger spreads with side salad.

Chez José *(Map 3; ☎ 845-0693, 173 avenue Duluth Est)* Mains $4-6; open 7am-8pm Mon-Fri, 8am-7pm Sat & Sun. This cramped little place serves up fresh empanadas for just $3. The place is known for its brunchtime crêpes and omelets, but the daily soups ($3) are a real treat (like tomato and blue cheese). People walk miles for their pastries too, made with real butter. The ambience is the real draw here, though, with walls painted in a marine theme, friendly, casual service and an eccentric, bilingual clientele.

Kilo *(Map 4; ☎ 596-3933, 1495 rue Ste Catherine Est)* Meals $6-8; open 11am-midnight daily. With huge pasty faces on its façade, Kilo does creamy cakes and tarts to die for ($3.50 to $6.25), usually baked with a shot of liqueur. It also does hot sandwiches, snacks and salads. This is a great place to people-watch through the ceiling-high windows. Their *original location* (☎ 277-5039) is at 5206 boulevard St Laurent, and is open 5pm to 11pm Monday, 10:30 to midnight Tuesday to Friday and 12pm to midnight weekends.

Brûlerie St Denis *(Map 3; ☎ 286-9158, 3967 rue St Denis)* This place makes superb coffees, roasting the beans on the premises. Try the strawberry cheesecake ($4). The terrace is a great place to hang out.

Porté Disparu *(Map 3; ☎ 524-0271, 957 rue Mont Royal Est)* Mains $4-9; open 9am-midnight daily. Bookworms will love this place, with shelves of volumes against a bare brick wall. Patrons play chess, Scrabble or cards against a background of Québécois CDs and spirited, delightful live music: a Wednesday night jazz trio and Saturday evening *chansonniers* (at 8:30pm). Its philosophical twist shows in the names of its café fare, with sandwiches called 'Optimist' and 'Libertine.'

Fast Food

The city has more than its share of fast-food joints – rue Ste Catherine is lined with all the big chains, plus many Québécois variations. Many serve the infamous *poutine* (see 'The Cult of Poutine' in the Montréal to Québec City chapter). There are food courts in each of the major shopping centers, many with decent world cuisine.

Frites Dorées *(Map 2; ☎ 866-0790, 1212 boul St Laurent)* Mains $2-5; open 7:30am-4am daily. Montréalers take these pedestrian items seriously. Ask for 'toasté all dress,' and you'll get the full Québec dog treatment – relish, mustard and onion, topped with chopped cabbage and on a toasted bun.

Coco Rico *(Map 3; ☎ 849-5554, 3907 boul St Laurent)* Mains $3-6. The appetizing smell from this restaurant envelops the entire surrounding area. It serves salads, but its fame comes from the superb broiled chicken. There are only flimsy barstools and a long counter inside, but most people pick up their orders while cruising the Main.

La Chilenita *(Map 3; ☎ 286-6075, 152 rue Napoléon)* Mains under $5. This slice of heaven is a tiny corner shop with some of the city's best empanadas (13 varieties) for $2 each, steak and chicken-avocado salads, and quesadillas, burritos, fajitas and tacos to go or to eat with the locals there.

Markets

The city's two biggest markets are open 8am to 6pm Monday to Wednesday, until 9pm Thursday and Friday, until 6pm Saturday and until 5pm Sunday. Both have indoor and outdoor sections and are open year-round.

Atwater Market *(Map 2; ☎ 935-5716, 138 avenue Atwater)* Near the Canal de Lachine, this tidy, chichi market has scores of vendors outside and high-class delis, bakeries and specialty shops inside the tiled, vaulted hall under the clock tower. You'll find some of Montréal's best butchers and cheese merchants here.

Jean Talon Market (☎ 277-1588, 7075 rue Casgrain) Located in the heart of Little Italy, this place is more ethnically varied and is the city's largest, most interesting market. There are some 250 market stalls on a huge square ringed by shops stocking produce year-round. The selection is overwhelming, and you're expected to haggle over the fruits, vegetables, potted plants, herbs and (of course) maple syrup. To get there, take the Métro to the Jean Talon stop, or take Bus No 55 north along boulevard St Laurent to rue Jean Talon.

Waldman Plus (Map 3; ☎ 285-8747, 76 rue Roy Est) Open 9am-6pm Mon, 9am-9pm Tues-Sun. For fresh fish there's no beating this Montréal landmark, which supplies many of the city's hotels and restaurants, but you'll still find some extremely good buys. The volume and variety – if not the smell – will make your head spin. It also runs a restaurant next door, ***Moules & Co*** (☎ 496-0540), which serves fish delicacies from mussels to sushi. It's open 11am to 10pm Tuesday to Sunday, and the lunch specials start at $7.99.

Supermarkets

Le Faubourg (☎ 939-3663, 1606 rue Ste Catherine Ouest) Open 9am-9pm daily. For a meal or the makings of one, try shopping around this Parisian-style mall-cum-market. There are bakeries, specialty shops, an abundant fruit and veggie stall, and one of the better food courts upstairs: At ***Tikka*** the Indian food melts in your mouth, and at ***La Maison Bedouin*** the Moroccan fare is delicious – get their fresh mint tea!

Provigo Supermarket (Map 2; ☎ 932-3756, 1953 rue Ste Catherine Ouest) Open 8am-2:15am daily. This large, well-stocked supermarket has wonderful deli counters that offer fried chicken and smoked-meat sandwiches.

In Little Italy you'll find loads of well-stocked groceries, butchers and cheese shops on boulevard St Laurent, a few blocks south of rue Jean Talon. In the Plateau, the section of boulevard St Laurent between avenue des Pins and avenue Mont Royal is another segment that's chock-a-block with specialty and ethnic grocery stores.

ENTERTAINMENT

Even rival Torontonians admit it: Montréal's nightlife is the liveliest in Canada. Nightclubs serve alcohol until 3am – the longest opening hours in the country – and the variety of these establishments is astounding. Most places don't start buzzing until after 11pm, and expect to line up and be mustered.

Traditionally the area around rue Crescent and rue Bishop has been Anglophone territory and eastward more for Francophones. However, for several years now rue St Laurent has become party central for all types and persuasions. Certainly, it is an endlessly more energetic and interesting alternative to the often tacky pick-up cruising bars on rue Crescent.

See the *Mirror* and *Hour* free weeklies for complete listings of what's on. Places des Arts also publishes the monthly *Calendrier des Spectacles* of performing arts events. *La Scena Musicale* is a free monthly devoted to the classical arts. The monthly *Nightlife* is your best bet for hot clubs and music trends. *Fugues* is a free, partially bilingual monthly booklet for the gay and lesbian scene.

Call Info-Arts Bell (☎ 790-2787) for details of theater, shows and other events. For major pop and rock concerts, shows, festivals and sporting events, purchase tickets from the box office or call Admission (☎ 790-1245 or 800-361-4595). Ticketmaster (☎ 790-1111) sells tickets to concerts and theater shows.

Discos & Clubs

Old Montréal (Map 5) Though the neighborhood is a bit touristy and pricey, there are a few places worthy of breakin' out your dancin' shoes.

Les Deux Pierrots (☎ 861-1686, 104 rue St Paul Est) Cover charge around $3; open Thur-Sat, occasionally other nights. A huge two-story club that's been around for the best part of three decades. The public is encouraged to sing along in the French chansons. Their concert space features live rock bands on Friday and Saturday night in summer.

Downtown (Map 2) At night the city center becomes party central at its numerous hip, popular hotspots.

Sphinx (☎ 843-5775, 1426 rue Stanley) Cover charge $6. An alternative/gothic/retro dance bar, this place has varied music (also broadcast on the Web). There may be a line-up, which is usually staged to make the place look even more popular than it is. Some non-goths mix with the standard *Night of the Living Dead* clientele.

Thursday's (☎ 288-5656, 1449 rue Crescent) Open 11:30am-3pm, 6:30pm-2am daily. This singles place has mammoth bars and a dance floor over two levels.

Foufounes Electriques (☎ 844-5538, 87 rue Ste Catherine Est) Café-bar open 3pm-3am daily, dance floor opens 10pm. Students, alternafreaks and all manner of trendies go here, a renowned bastion of underground music (the name means 'electric buttocks'). This place has some bizarre touches – Egypto/sci-fi art, weird backlighting in the aquarium room and a pit (don't ask).

Salsathèque (☎ 875-0015, 1220 rue Peel) Cover charge $5 Fri & Sat; open Wed-Sun. A bright, busy, dressy place featuring large, live Latin bands. Some patrons are phenomenal dancers. There are free salsa lessons on Wednesday night. In summer it's a hangout for the more flexible members of the Montréal Expos.

Metropolis (☎ 844-3500, 59 rue Ste Catherine Est) Open 10pm-3am Fri & Sat. Metropolis has Canada's largest dance floor (capacity 2500). Housed in a former Art Deco cinema, this place features live bands and DJs, bars spread over three floors, and dazzling sound and light shows.

Club Zone (☎ 398-9875, 1186 rue Crescent) Open 4pm-3am daily. Club Zone serves up an eclectic mix of pop to jazz to New Wave lounge – you name it. This is a stage venue with table service and a bar, and there's live music most nights.

Newtown (☎ 284-6555, Ⓦ www.newtown .ca; 1476 rue Crescent) Restaurant and lounge bar open 11am-1am, disco open 9pm-3am daily. Jacques Villeneuve's schmooze emporium (see 'What's in a Name?') is a trendy spot – even the website's super trendy! – that's injected new life into rue Crescent. The food is decent (mains $6 to $17) and the view onto the crowds outside is great. The crowd tends to be in the 25 to 35 range, and fairly well-to-do.

Club Soda (☎ 790-1111, 1225 boul St Laurent) This place is equally varied, hosting jazz acts (such as Ranee Lee, a Sarah Vaughan–style singer) but also avant-garde, heavy metal and other artists in a hall that seats several hundred.

What's in a Name?

Local race-car hero Jacques Villeneuve touched a few sensitive nerves by opening a downtown restaurant with a blatantly English name. Before Newtown even opened in June 2001, several complaints were lodged with the Office de la Langue Française, but the name was exempt from the province's laws on French usage on signs because it had been trademarked.

No matter that it had been the Formula 1 driver's nickname on the international circuit for years – or that the name was a literal translation of his family name – as a show of solidarity, the Iberville, Québec, native was expected to show solidarity and name it Villeneuve. He didn't budge.

In press conferences at the time, when he commented that 'You have to see farther than your nose – it's a big world,' some of the appendages in question got out of joint. Villeneuve, who grew up mostly in Europe, said that it wasn't logical that people get angry at each other for speaking different languages, and that 'Québecers are losing out by being more French than the French.'

Even premier Bernard Landry had to make a statement about the issue, but said he had no problem with the naming of the restaurant/bar complex.

MONTRÉAL

Montréal Plateau (Map 3) There are plenty of clubs along boulevard St Laurent between rue Sherbrooke and avenue Mont Royal. The crowds tend to be young and hipper-than-thou.

Café Campus (☎ 844-1010, 57 rue Prince Arthur Est) Open Mon-Sat. One of the most popular student clubs, with 1980s hits, French rock and live bands. Happy hour ($1 a beer) starts at 8:30pm. Expect young 'uns who can't hold their liquor.

Le Ballatou (☎ 845-5447, 4372 boul St Laurent) Cover charge $7 including one drink Sat & Sun. Open Tues-Sun. Dark, smoky and the most popular Afro-Caribbean nightclub in Montréal. The clientele are multiethnic and the better dancers no doubt double-jointed.

Jingxi (☎ 985-5464, 410 rue Rachel Est) Open Wed-Sat, sometimes Sun. A landmark of Montréal house music, Jingxi attracts legions of 20-somethings to be freeze-framed by the terrific light shows. Their local and imported DJs have great reputations among those in the know.

Blizzarts (☎ 843-4860, 3956a boul St Laurent) Open 8pm-3am daily. There's no sign out front, but this is a cool, discreet music bar where good music is the thing, not pretentious posing. Inventive DJs serve up jazz, funk, hip-hop, roots and dub. There's a small dance floor and lots of sofas.

After Hours Check *Nightlife* for new openings. If you do the after-hours scene, be prepared to witness a massive drug fest – you could probably count on two hands the number of non-dilated pupils in these places.

Stereo (Map 4; ☎ 282-3307, 858 rue Ste Catherine Est) Open 2am-10am Sat & Sun. This is the after-hours club of choice for years – in 1999 *Muzik* magazine voted it the world's fifth-best club and the best in North America. The wicked in-house (Mark Anthony) and imported DJs, excellent sound system and the 60/40% gay/straight mix have been the keys to its popularity. It gets pretty hot around 5am.

Sona (Map 2; ☎ 282-1000, 1439 rue de Bleury) Open 2am-10am Sat & Sun. This

place shines on special theme nights, otherwise it's on the sleazy side, a place reputed to attract off-duty male and female strippers and their hangers-on. Rude staff doesn't help.

Gay & Lesbian Venues (Map 4) The majority of gay and lesbian entertainment is in the Village, along rue Ste Catherine Est.

Sky Pub & Club (☎ 529-6969, 1474 rue Ste Catherine Est) This is a fixture in the gay community. The main floor is a cruisy, immense pub (wear your hippest clothes, they'll be inspected!), which gets crowded, especially on Sunday 'tea dance' afternoons and Tuesday evening drag shows. The club upstairs, with nine separate rooms and 40,000 sq feet of dance floor, takes off very late on weekends.

Le Track (☎ 521-1419, 1584 rue Ste Catherine Est) Open 3pm-3am daily. In the Bourbon Complex, this is a popular disco-bar (especially Wednesday night) with a leather boutique. It sprawls out over three floors.

Stud Bar (☎ 598-8243, rue Ste Catherine Est) Open 6pm-3am daily. This is a leather bar with poor visibility, '80s music and lots of guys with no hair doing karaoke.

Sisters (☎ 522-4717, 1333 rue Ste Catherine Est) Open 9pm-3am. One of the few choices on the lesbian scene. It's got some rough edges – grrrlz belting out Britney Spears tunes – but it's sizzling with 20-somethings looking for fun.

Campus (☎ 526-3616, 1111 rue Ste Catherine Est) Open 3pm-3am daily. The city's premier male strip club (there are five) has the most Chippendales-looking guys in a chrome and disco interior. Drinks are, um, encouraged.

Pubs, Bars & Coffeehouses
Pub St Paul (Map 5; ☎ 874-0485, 124 rue St Paul Est) Cover charge $5. Old Montréal isn't the greatest place to go pub crawling – touristy and expensive. One exception is the Pub St Paul. It affords a terrific view of the port, and has a comfortable ambience and several pool tables.

Winnies (Map 2; ☎ 288-0623, 1455 rue Crescent) This sprawling, split-level place draws crowds with its thumping disco music. Local author Mordecai Richler used to knock back cold ones in the **Sir Winston Churchill Pub** upstairs. It serves so-so food all day (mains $10 to $16), and drinks are half-price from 5pm to 8pm.

Hurley's Irish Pub (Map 2; ☎ 861-4111, 1125 rue Crescent) Open noon-3am daily. A cozy place with live music (usually rock and folk, with great Celtic fiddlers) most nights starting at 9pm. As in many pubs, football and soccer matches are shown on big screens – prepare to join in.

Gerts (Map 2; ☎ 398-3319, 3840 rue Mc-Tavish) Open 9am-1am Mon-Wed, 9am-3am Thur & Fri, 5pm-3am Sat. Gerts, in the McGill University Student Union building, plays DJ-driven R&B, hip-hop, blues and house, with an 'oldies night' thrown in for good measure.

Quartier Latin Pub (Map 4; ☎ 845-3301, 318 rue Ontario Est) This is a cool bar with 1950s lounge-style decor, a small dance floor and a DJ playing New Wave. The front terrace is a great place to watch the world go by.

Le Magellan Bar (Map 4; ☎ 845-0909, 330 rue Ontario Est) Attached to the great Café de Pèlerin (see Places to Eat), this relaxed place plays canned jazz and chansons amid a sprinkling of maritime doodads. Their specialty is rum, and they've got a dozen different kinds.

L'Île Noire (Map 4; ☎ 982-0866, 342 rue Ontario Est) Open 4pm-3am daily. Scotch is the house specialty here, and connoisseurs will be dazzled by the choice. Extremely friendly, even vivacious staff contrast with the low-key ambience and slightly upscale vibes to make this a true delight.

Else's (Map 3; ☎ 286-6689, 156 rue Roy Est) Open 11am-3am daily. You'll seep into the relaxed feel of this place, with dim candlelight, tables to chat over and finger food to keep you going.

Yellow Door Coffee House (Map 2; ☎ 398-6243, 3625 rue Aylmer) Closed summer. This has survived from the 1960s – US draft dodgers once found refuge here. Despite its hippie roots, there's no dope or alcohol here. The program is English-

language folk music, poetry and literature readings, but the schedule is erratic.

Casa del Popolo (Map 3; ☎ 284-3804, W www.casadelpopolo.com, 4873 boul St Laurent) Picking up where the Yellow Door left off, this great space combines a comfortable bar/café serving healthy meals with an English-language performance space (poetry readings, film screenings) and publishing house (their quarterly La Voce del Popolo is a good mix of politics and culture). Check out the schedule of their concert hall, La Sala Rossa, across the street for unusual, interesting fare.

Jazz & Blues Clubs

Biddle's (Map 2; ☎ 842-8656, 2060 rue Aylmer) This is the fixture on the jazz scene. Run by venerable bassist Charles Biddle, it's a tad touristy but fun, with fin-de-siècle décor and musical paraphernalia hanging from the ceiling. His daughter Stephanie can belt out the tunes like the best of them. Prepare to stand in line if you haven't reserved. There's no cover charge, but there is usually a fee to sit at a table (as opposed to standing or sitting at the bar) – ask in advance, they don't always say.

L'Air du Temps (Map 5; ☎ 842-2003, 191 rue St Paul Ouest) This place, with a smoky, spotlit stage girded by a wooden balcony and bar, is the stuff legends are made of. Small groups or solos start at 5pm and the bigger names get on around 9:30pm, when a $5 cover kicks in.

Jazz & Blues (Map 2; ☎ 398-3319, 3840 rue McTavish) In the McGill Student Union building, this usually holds concerts by good student bands. The schedule's on the university's website: www.mcgill.ca.

Pool & Billiards

Sharx (Map 2; ☎ 934-3105, 1606 rue Ste Catherine Ouest) Open 11am-3am daily. Sharx has pool and billiard tables everywhere you look ($9 per hour), rows of TV screens and a post-apocalyptic feel.

Le Swimming (Map 2; ☎ 282-0005, 3643 boul St Laurent) Open noon-3am daily. This homey place has pool tables (thus the name of the place), which are free until 5pm if you order at least one drink per hour. From Thursday to Saturday there's live music.

Classical Music, Dance & Opera

For modern dance, check local listings to see what's on at *Espace Go* (☎ *845-4890, 4890 boul St Laurent*) and *Espace Choréographique* (☎ *521-4493, 2022 rue Sherbrooke Est*). For classical music, check out concerts held at McGill University, which tend to be very good.

The renowned *Orchestre Symphonique de Montréal* (☎ *842-9951*), under the direction of Swiss conductor Charles Dutoit, performs at the Place des Arts (see Concert Halls) from September to May; its Christmas performances of *The Nutcracker* and Handel's *Messiah* are legendary. Check for free summer concerts at the Basilique Notre Dame and in Montréal's municipal parks.

Orchestre Métropolitain de Montréal (☎ *598-0870*) is made up of youngish local musicians and performs at Place des Arts, as well as in the Église St Jean Baptiste, nearby.

The city has two chamber ensembles, the *McGill Chamber Orchestra* (☎ *398-4455*) and *I Musici de Montréal* (☎ *982-6038*), both of which perform at McGill's Pollack Concert Hall (see Concert Halls), and

---

Jazzy Montréal

The **International Jazz Festival** (IJF) is, even in this city of festivals, the 'Big Daddy' of them all. The fest, which began in 1980, now attracts about 1.5 million visitors each year, all crowding into different clubs or jamming the streets around Place des Arts for the outdoor shows. Some of its past highlights have become part of the city's own history, like Pat Metheny's free outdoor shows, or when 225,000 people crowded the streets in 2000 to see the Brazilian group Timbalada play on Brazil's 500th anniversary.

St Cat, the blue saxophone-playing feline, is the mascot of the festival, which in turn attracts some of the biggest cats in jazz – Sonny Rollins, Al Jarreau, Herbie Hancock, Wayne Shorter, Al Dimeola and John Scofield are but a few guests, as well as Montréal's own Oscar Peterson. Big pop 'crossover' artists also put in an appearance (eg, Sting and Rickie Lee Jones), and you'll hear just about everything under the sun, including blues, Latin, Cajun, Dixieland and reggae. Each year the festival picks a theme (Louisiana jazz, for example) and a special section is devoted to it. The festival organizers usually draw the line at inviting more than a few pop artists to ensure the flavor remains jazzy. Many people were wondering, however, why Prince was the star headliner in 2001.

As incredible as the atmosphere can become at times, the fest is known to have had a few 'off' years. Further, a competing, rebel festival has been founded to correct what organizers say are the errors of the IJF. The first occasion of the L'Off Festival de Jazz was in 2000, and it's showing signs of growing. Organizers decry the lack of local talent in the IJF, its growing commercialism, and want to break its monopoly on the jazz scene in Montréal. The IJF counters that there are already over 1000 locals participating annually, and that they work hard to promote them throughout the year.

No matter, now visitors have two great festivals to choose from! The L'Off Festival is held concurrently with the IJF in clubs along rue Ontario near rue St Denis, and in 2001 regrouped some 150 artists for 30 innovative shows. Many of their concerts are free and have been quite popular with the crowds.

The International Jazz Festival has its own Info Jazz Bell line (☎ 871-1881, 888-515-0515) and can be accessed on the Web at Ⓦ www.montrealjazzfest.com. L'Off Festival de Jazz is on the Web at www.lofffestivaldejazz.com.

CHRIS MELLOR

Storefronts in morning, Montréal

KEVIN LEVESQUE

Altar, Basilique Notre Dame, Montréal

EDDIE BRADY

Good pickings at a Montréal market

GEORGI G SHABLOVSKY

Chapelle Notre Dame de Bonsecours, Montréal

A staircase like a wind-carved landscape, Canadian Museum of Civilization, Hull

Skating on 5km of maintained ice, Rideau Canal, Ottawa

neither of which has a strong reputation among cognoscente.

Les Ballets Jazz de Montréal (☎ 982-6771) is a Montréal modern-dance troupe with a sterling reputation in experimental forms, while *Les Grands Ballets Canadiens (☎ 849-8681)* is Québec's leading troupe, performing a classical and modern program throughout the year. They perform in differing venues.

L'Opera Montréal (☎ 985-2258) Tickets $38-105; box office open 9am-5pm Mon-Fri. L'Opera Montréal performs at the Place des Arts, with a mix of local and international talent in standard French and Italian productions like *Faust, Aïda* and *Carmen.*

Concert Halls

Place des Arts (Map 2; ☎ 842-2112, W *www.pda.qc.ca, 175 rue Ste Catherine Ouest)* Montréal's main center for the performing arts first opened in 1963 and now presents an array of concerts and dance in five theaters. The city's symphony plays in the 3000-seat Salle Wilfrid-Pelletier, and ballet, opera and other musical troupes often perform here. The eponymous square is the focal point of the Montréal Jazz Festival, held in June and July.

Spectrum de Montréal (Map 2; ☎ 861-5851, 318 rue Ste Catherine) Box office 10am-9pm Mon-Sat, 10am-5pm Sun. This converted cinema with great acoustics seats about 2000 and hosts comedy, rock and pop concerts.

Pollack Concert Hall (Map 2; ☎ 398-4547, 555 rue Sherbrooke Ouest) This is McGill University's main concert hall and features recitals from its students and faculty year-round. It's in the Victorian building behind the statue of Queen Victoria.

Bell Centre (Map 2; ☎ 932-2582, W *www.centre-molson.com, 1260 rue de la Gauchetière)* Box office open 10am-6pm Mon-Fri, 10am-9pm event days. When not hosting matches of the Canadiens hockey team, the 21,000-seat Bell Centre is *the* downtown venue for big-name shows.

Cinemas

Check W www.cinema-montreal.com for the latest in what's playing where.

Cinéma du Parc (Map 2; ☎ 281-1900, 3575 avenue du Parc) Admission $6. At the Prince Arthur Ouest, this is the last purely English-language repertory cinema in town.

National Film Board (NFB; Map 4; ☎ 283-9000, 1564 rue St Denis) Open noon-9pm Tues-Sun. This is paradise for serious cinephiles. There are regular screenings, but the real attraction is the Cinérobothèque – make your choice, and a robot housed in a glass-roofed archive pulls your selection from one of 6,000 videodiscs. Then settle back into individual, stereo-equipped chair units to watch your personal monitor (students/non-students $2/3 per hour).

Cinémathèque Québécoise (Map 4; ☎ 842-9763, 335 boul de Maisonneuve Est) Admission $4; open 1pm-9pm Tues-Sun. Just south of the NFB, this cinema features French and Québécois avant-garde films, and has a permanent exhibition on the history of filmmaking.

Ex-Centris Cinema (Map 2; ☎ 847-3536, 3530 boul St Laurent) The Ex-Centris is a showcase for first-rate independent films from around the world founded by the creator of Softimage, a Montréal special-effects company. The place is full of high-tech film gadgetry – even the box office cashier interacts with you via a screen when you buy a ticket. Creepy.

Café Ciné-Lumière (Map 3; ☎ 495-1796, 5163 boul St Laurent) Admission free; open 1pm-midnight Tues-Sun. Up in Mile End, Café Ciné-Lumière shows old films for no charge. Don a headset for listening along with your food and drink.

Theater

Centaur Théâtre (Map 5; ☎ 288-3161, 453 rue St François Xavier) This is the center of English-language theater and has a hit-and-miss repertory of classics and experimental fare.

Monument National Theater (Map 2; ☎ 871-2224, 1182 boul St Laurent) Admission $5. This place holds regular rehearsals of dramatic plays by students of the National Theatre School. The programs are mostly in French and cover a range of genres, from Shakespeare to Sam Shephard.

***Théâtre St Denis** (Map 4; ☎ 849-4211, 1594 rue St Denis)* Box office open noon-9pm daily. This theater hosts touring companies of Broadway productions but also features rock concerts and comedians.

***Théâtre de Quat' Sous** (Map 2; ☎ 845-7277, 100 avenue des Pins Est)* This is a wonderful venue for intellectual and experimental drama.

***Théâtre du Nouveau Monde** (Map 2; ☎ 866-8667, 84 rue Ste Catherine Ouest)* This theater specializes in French classics.

***Comedy Nest** (Map 2; ☎ 932-6378, 1740 boul René Lévesque)* Cover charge $3-15 (discounts for students). Shows 9pm Wed & Thur, 9pm & 11:15pm Fri & Sat. The Comedy Nest features talent from all over North America. There's a dash of cabaret – with singers, dancers, musicians, female impersonators and more.

SPECTATOR SPORTS
Hockey and Catholicism are regarded as national religions in Québec, but baseball also attracts a fair number of fans. Ironically, although the internationally renowned Habs and Expos have fallen upon hard times in their leagues, Montréal's dark-horse football team, The Alouettes, is riding an unexpected wave of popularity in their new home (see Football).

Tickets for most sporting events are available from the Admission ticket service (☎ 790-1245), which has various outlets around town, including one in the Berri-UQAM Métro station.

Hockey
The Bell Centre (see Concert Halls, earlier) replaced the smaller Montréal Forum in 1996 as home to the Canadiens of the National Hockey League. The 'Habs,' as the team is called, have won the Stanley Cup 24 times, but the last time was in 1993 – and the Molson family did the unthinkable by selling the team to non-Canadians in 2000. Still, Montréalers have a soft spot for the Habs, and if you're in town during the season, don't miss the opportunity to see a game.

Tickets go on sale in advance during the season (October to April, with playoffs until June). List prices vary ($17 for a seat in the rafters to $130 for rink-side); otherwise, seats are available through the legions of scalpers who begin lingering about noon on game days. After the game starts, you can often negotiate them down to half-price.

Outdoor hockey games are some of Québec's most memorable sporting affairs – earsplitting cries of *but* (goal) fueled by thermoses of mulled wine. Informal matches take place just about wherever a pond has frozen over and public rinks are set up – for example, at Parc La Fontaine (Map 3) or at the Olympic rowing basin of Île Notre Dame, in the Parc des Îles.

You can attend matches year-round at ***Sportplex** (Map 1; ☎ 626-2500, 15540 boul Pierrefonds; adult/child $5/2.50)*, a four-rink complex in the western suburb of Pierrefonds. In the summer, the Montréal Métro AAA Summer Hockey League (☎ 338-1543) organizes frequent matches there for local 'midget' teams – call for a schedule. Take Hwy 40 to exit 52 (boulevard St Jean) and drive 3km north.

Montréalers have a soft spot for the hard Habs.

Baseball

The major-league baseball Montréal Expos (☎ 253-3434, 800-463-9767,  *www .exposmlb.com*) have fallen on hard times, and few fans bother to attend games at the Stade Olympique (see Olympic Park, earlier) anymore.

The owners, led by American art dealer Jeffrey Loria, even considered moving the onetime World Series winners to the US. Gone are the days when the crime rate went down when the Expos played – nowadays, the team can only fill a fraction of the Stade Olympique's 62,000 seats. Some of the star players on their current roster include catcher Michael Barrett and rightfielder Vladimir Guerroro. Tickets ($7 to $23) are available at the box office or from Admission in April to September.

Football

The Alouettes, the once-defunct football team of the teetering CFL (Canadian Football League), have begun filling the house since it moved to the Molson Stadium (Map 2) at McGill University. Grab tickets at *Alouettes Billeterie* (☎ 254-2400, 646 rue Ste Catherine Ouest; advance tickets $17-50; open 9am-5pm Mon-Fri). The season runs from late June through November.

Grand Prix Racing

The annual Grand Prix du Canada is held every June at *Circuit Gilles Villeneuve* (☎ 350-4731, ⓦ www.grandprix.ca; ⓜ *Jean Drapeau*), on Île Notre Dame. Formula 1 racing is rare in North America – the only US event is held in Indianapolis, which was relaunched in 2000 after a 10-year break. Tickets are virtually impossible to get unless you purchase well ahead of time. Expect to pay at least $150 for a grandstand seat.

SHOPPING

Downtown, the east-west-running rue Ste Catherine is the main shopping artery. It is now home to large department stores, specialist clothing stores, consumer-goods shops, restaurants and strip clubs. Swanky boutiques, galleries, jewelry and fur merchants can be found along rue Sherbrooke and, to a lesser extent, the top end of rue Crescent. Rue Notre Dame west of rue

---

The Underground City

When residents answer questions by excited tourists about their famous underground city, the response tends to be, 'Huh? Oh yeah, that...' Essentially a string of office buildings, shopping centers, food courts and Métro stations extending about 3km north-south along 29km of corridors, locals appreciate the alternative it provides for pedestrians on cold winter days. They don't think of it as anything special.

Fact is, it's unique in the world. Over 2000 shops are linked by a jumble of tunnels, escalators, corridors and stairways. It's not only practical but an attraction in itself. On blustery days you can still have a walking tour of the city, only underground, and still take in some main sites.

Between the Monit Conference Center (Map 2) 1000 rue Sherbrooke Ouest, opposite McGill University, and the Inter Continental Montréal (Map 4) 990 rue St Antoine Ouest, near Old Montréal, you'll pass through shopping centers like Cours Mont Royal (which used to be the luxurious Mount Royal Hotel, gutted in 1988), Place Montréal Trust (with one of North America's highest water fountains), the 47-story Place Ville Marie (which opened in 1962) and Place Bonaventure (the continent's second-largest indoor trade mart, with an exhibition hall the size of four football fields).

Also accessible underground are the Molson Stadium, the Queen Elizabeth Hotel, Central Station, several Métro stations, an unknown amount of MSG in all the Chinese fast-food kiosks, and lots of places to drop cash.

A detailed map can be obtained at the main tourist information office. You can also take an original walking tour of part of the underground city with one of the original architects of the Métro system. Call Visite Jean Dumontier (☎ 388-8623) for schedules.

Guy is the place for the serious antique collector.

Boulevard St Laurent and avenue Mont Royal are the meccas of hip fashion and music shops, and have some budget stores. Rue St Denis has some quirky places, starting with headshops in the Quartier Latin. In Old Montréal, rue St Paul Ouest has a slew of art galleries. And don't forget the Underground City, which connects over 2000 shops (see 'The Underground City').

Guilde Canadienne des Métier d'Art Québec (Map 2; ☎ 849-6091, 2025 rue Peel) Open 10am-6pm Tues-Fri, 10am-5pm Sat. This place has a small and somewhat expensive collection of works by Québec artisans and other Canadiana, as well as Inuit prints and carvings. There are rotating exhibits from the country's best artisans, including prints, sculptures and crafts. It is the city's first art gallery.

Galerie Le Chariot (Map 5; ☎ 875-6807, 446 Place Jacques Cartier) Open 10am-6pm Mon-Sat, 10am-3pm Sun. There's an enormous selection of Inuit and First Nations art here, including prints, necklaces, walrus tusks, sculptures and more moccasins than you can shake a whalebone at.

Le Baron (Map 2; ☎ 866-8848, 932 rue Notre Dame Ouest) For survival, sporting and leisure gear, this is the top address in town. Backpack buyers should set aside a few hours just to look.

La Cordée Plein Air (Map 4; ☎ 524-1106, 2159 rue Ste Catherine Est) East of rue De Lorimier, this enormous sports and adventure emporium has a dazzling but pricey array of equipment for all outdoors activities.

GETTING THERE & AWAY
Air
Montréal has two airports. Dorval, 20km west of downtown, serves most domestic, US and overseas flights. Mirabel, 55km northeast of downtown, serves cargo and charter flights.

Montréal's sickly-looking Dorval Airport (Map 1) levies an 'improvement tax' of $15 on all international flights before you leave, a major irritant to locals who haven't seen much improvement since 1996, when this supposedly temporary tax was levied. The special payment counter takes cash or, if you've spent all your Canadian dollars, major credit cards. Mirabel Airport charges a $10 'improvement tax.'

Airport information can be reached at ☎ 394-7377, 800-465-1213 or Ⓦ www.admtl .com. High-season flights to Vancouver are around $500, to Toronto around $300 (though there are often specials as low as $120), to New York City around $250 (again, specials sometimes reduce this by half), and to London around $850.

Bus
The Central Bus Station (Station Centrale de l'Autobus; Map 4; ☎ 842-2281), 505 rue de Maisonneuve Est, is from where most major lines for Canadian and US destinations depart. Buses to the airports and destinations in Québec also depart from there. There are connections with most of the province's destinations, but in some cases a transfer might be necessary. Toward the Gaspésie, buses from Montréal go as far as Rimouski ($80, 7-7½ hours, 3 daily), without a transfer.

Buses to Québec City ($42, 3-4 hours, over 30 daily) come in express, local and long-distance varieties. The locals stop elsewhere along the way, like Trois Rivières ($26, 1¾-2¼ hours, 8 daily), and long-distance ones continue beyond to farther destinations, like Tadoussac ($81, 5½ hours, 2 daily). From Québec City there are many other connections possible.

For out-of-province destinations, see the Getting There & Away chapter.

Train
Montréal's Central Station (Gare Centrale; Map 2) is the local hub of VIA Rail (☎ 366-8411, 888-842-7245, Ⓦ www.viarail.ca). Service is best along the so-called Québec City–Windsor corridor, which includes Montréal, Ottawa, Kingston, Toronto and Niagara Falls.

VIA Rail's overnight service between Montréal and Toronto is a treat. Trains leave at 11:30pm nightly except Saturday, arriving at 8am with a complimentary breakfast the next morning. Standard one-way fares in a sleeper cabin start at $90, tax included.

Amtrak (☎ 215-824-1600, 800-872-7245, Ⓦ www.amtrak.com) runs a daily train between New York City and Montréal (US$52-65, 10 hours), arriving at Gare Centrale (Central Station).

Car & Motorcycle

Continental US highways link directly with their Canadian counterparts along the border at numerous points. These roads meet up with the Trans-Canada Hwy (Hwy 40), which runs directly through Montréal. From Boston to Montréal, it's about 490km, or about 4½ hours; from Toronto, it's 540km, or a little over five hours. Québec City is 2½ hours away.

Ride Sharing & Driveaways

Allô Stop (☎ 985-3032, 4317 rue St Denis, Ⓦ www.allostop.com), the Canadian pioneer among the ride-sharing services, offers lots of rides to destinations in Québec and to the US. Membership for passengers is $6, then you pay a portion of the ride cost to the agency three hours before the trip; the rest goes to the driver. It offers good deals from Montréal, such as Québec City for $15, Ottawa $16, Toronto $35, Gaspé $50, and New York $65. There are even rides all the way to Vancouver – especially in May.

EcoRide (☎ 877-326-7433, Ⓦ www .ecoride.com) operates out of Ontario and at press time had run up against an unfair competition lawsuit there for daring to infringe on bus companies' turf. Check whether they still operate Ontario-Québec routes.

Autotaxi (Ⓦ www.autotaxi.com) is a Québec, Web-based bulletin board for ride sharing in all corners of the province and has great deals.

One of the best driving deals in North America is Driveaway. Basically, you drive someone's car to a specific destination because the owner doesn't wish to. In Montréal, Driveaway (not mapped) is located at 345 avenue Victoria Ave (☎ 489-3861, Ⓦ www.driveaway.com.). Most cars offered are fairly new and in good working order. It's open 9am to 5pm weekdays.

GETTING AROUND

Montréal is a pleasant city to experience on foot, but in the North American tradition of sprawl, things are pretty spread out. You'd often be better off using the city's excellent public transportation system.

When seeking an address, remember that boulevard St Laurent is the dividing point for streets with appendages of *Est* and *Ouest* (East and West). Although the city's grid pattern makes it difficult to get lost, it's slightly off kilter with regard to the compass: What locals refer to as east, for instance, is in fact closer to north.

To/From the Airport

The cheapest way downtown from Dorval Airport is via bus and Métro. Outside the Dorval arrivals hall, catch bus No 204 Est to the Dorval Bus Transfer Station and switch to No 211 Est, which delivers you 20 minutes later at the Lionel Groulx Métro station. You'll wait no more than a half-hour between buses, most often just 15 minutes, and the entire journey should take about an hour. Both buses run 5am to 1am. You can make the trip with only one ticket ($2).

The Québécois Bus Company (☎ 931-9002, 842-2281) runs Aérobus shuttles from Dorval to downtown, stopping at Station Aérobus (Map 5), 777 rue de la Gauchetière Est, and the Central Bus Station (Station Centrale de l'Autobus; Map 4). The 20-minute trip is offered every half-hour daily from 5am to 11pm. One-way/roundtrip tickets cost $11/20. Buses leave from gate 19. At the Station Aérobus, a smaller shuttle will pick you up and drop you anywhere in central downtown, free of charge – an excellent service.

Aérobus shuttles also serve Mirabel Airport; tickets for the one-hour journey downtown are $20/30 for one-way/roundtrip tickets. From the bus station downtown, buses leave three to four times daily weekdays, nine times daily weekends from gate 17.

From Dorval Airport to downtown Montréal, cab fare is a flat $28; from Mirabel, you're looking at about $60. See the Taxi section for more information.

Bus & Métro

Montréal has an modern and convenient bus and Métro system run by STCUM (☎ 280-5653). The Métro is the city's subway system, which runs quickly and quietly on rubber tires, just like the one in Paris. It runs until at least 12:30am, and some buses run all night. Métro stops are indicated above ground by large blue signs with a white arrow pointing down. Berri-UQAM is the main intersecting station, where three lines converge.

One ticket can get you anywhere in the city with a connecting bus or Métro train. On the buses, get a transfer from the driver, and on the Métro, get one from the machines just past the turnstiles. A strip of six tickets (une lisière) costs $8.25, and single tickets cost $2 each. Buses take tickets, transfers or exact cash only – drivers won't give change.

Tourists can purchase day passes for $7 or three-day passes for $14. However, a weekly card (valid from Monday to Sunday) is a better deal ($12.50). Monthly passes cost $47. Cards and passes are swiped through the turnstiles, and tickets are inserted into turnstile slots or dropped at the ticket booth.

A detailed map of bus and Métro stops for all of Montréal, Plan du Réseau (Network Map), is available from any Métro station. You can also call STCUM's itinerary service (☎ 288-6287) to find out the best route to anywhere using the bus, Métro or commuter train.

Train

The GO commuter trains (☎ 869-3200, W www.amt.qc.ca) serve the suburbs of Montréal from Central Station (Gare Centrale; Map 2) and Windsor Station (Gare Windsor; Map 2), on the corner of rue Peel and rue de la Gauchetière Ouest. Fares in Zone 1 (which includes Dorval Airport) are covered by all Métro and bus tickets; for destinations in other zones, buy a supplement at the ticket counters or at automated ticket machines.

Car & Motorcycle

Montréal drivers possess nerves of steel, and you should too if you wish to drive in this town. The rush hours are horrible, lane markings suddenly vanish, and all too often it's like the qualifying heat for Montréal's Grand Prix. Driving the 'Metropolitan' (the Trans-Canada Hwy, Hwy 40, which goes through central Montréal) can be a harrowing experience. Old Montréal, much of downtown and the more popular parts of the Plateau can get very busy – better take the bus or Métro whenever possible.

If you drive downtown, street parking is metered (it's $0.25 for 10 minutes in the center), and there are many public parking lots (about $3 per half-hour).

Car Rental At Dorval Airport there's a counter in the arrivals hall with car rental companies, including Alamo, Avis, Budget, Hertz, National and Thrifty. Budget (☎ 938-1000) also has several locations in town, including Central Station (Gare Centrale; Map 2). You should be able to get a subcompact for around $50 per day with unlimited mileage, taxes and insurance. Similar rates are available at National Tilden (Map 2; ☎ 878-2771), 1200 rue Stanley, and Avis Car Rental (☎ 288-9934), 1225 rue Metcalfe. They tend to charge more but sometimes have good specials.

Rent-a-Wreck (☎ 328-9419), 10625 rue St Gertrude, in North Montréal, charges $46/284 per day/week for its most basic models (stickshift or automatic), all-inclusive and with a $500 deductible ($750 if you're under 25). You get 250km/1500km free per day/week and must pay $0.10 per additional kilometer. Despite the name, the firm rents out recent models. They'll pick you up at Sauvé or St Michel Métro stations.

Taxi

Flag fall is a standard $2.50, plus another $1.20 per kilometer (or $0.44 per kilometer if less than 30km). Waiting time is charged at $0.44 per minute.

Taxi services abound, but ones to try include Taxi Diamond (☎ 273-6331) or Taxi Co-Op (☎ 725-9885).

Bicycle

Bicycles can be taken on the Métro in the last two carriages of the train from 10am to 3pm and after 7pm weekdays, as well as throughout the weekend. The water shuttles to Parc des Îles also take bicycles at no extra charge. For virtually any type of bicycle advice pertaining to Montréal and the region, contact Vélo Québec at the bicycle shop La Maison des Cyclistes (Map 3; ☎ 521-8356, 800-567-8356, ⓦ www.velo.qc.ca), 1251 rue Rachel Est. They organize several excellent bicycle tours of the city and rent bikes in excellent condition.

Vélo Aventure (Map 5; ☎ 847-0666), at the Vieux Port, charges $7/22 per hour/day for bicycles, $8/25 on weekends. Children's trailers and inline skates are also on offer. There's a major bike path going for miles from right near the shop.

A good place to pick up an inexpensive bike is at Jean Pierre Rioux Antiquaire (Map 3; ☎ 247-1600), 270 avenue Duluth Est. In this filled-to-the brim antique store are always several dozen used bikes for sale. If you find one in good condition, it might turn out to be cheaper than renting one for several days.

On Île Ste Hélène, Plaisirs et Santé (☎ 954-0738), at the kiosk close to the Jean Drapeau Métro station, charges $7.50/20 per 1/24 hours for bicycles. Inline skates are also available.

Calèche

These picturesque horse-drawn carriages seen meandering around Old Montréal and up on Mont Royal charge about $35 per half-hour or $60 an hour for four to five people. Calèches line up, among other places, at the Vieux Port and at Place d'Armes. In winter, sleighs are used for trips up and around Mont Royal; they charge similar rates. Drivers usually provide running commentary, which can serve as a pretty good historical tour.

Around Montréal

PARC DES ÎLES DE BOUCHERVILLE

A green oasis right at Montréal's doorstep, this Sépaq-run park (☎ 450-928-5088, ⓔ parc.boucherville@sepaq.com; admission $3.50; open 8am-7pm mid-May–early Sept, 9am-5pm Apr–mid-May & early Sept–early Oct) makes a great respite from downtown (which, only 10km away, is visible from some spots), especially for canoe-lovers. Five interconnected islands have 22km of hiking and cycling trails, and a pleasant canoe circuit. Day rentals of bikes/canoes/kayaks/13-place rabaska cost $21/29/35/115, taxes included. For bike rental, also consider renting in the city and arriving via ferry or by car.

Every weekend from May to August there are guided activities (in French), boat tours, and theme walks. By car, take Hwy 20, exit 1. A ferry (☎ 281-8000) departs from Quai Jacques Cartier in the Vieux Port hourly in the summer.

KAHNAWAKE INDIAN RESERVE

South of Lachine, where the Pont Honoré Mercier meets the south shore of the St Lawrence, there's the Kahnawake (pronounced gon-a-wok-ee) Indian Reserve, home of 6000 Mohawks. Located about 18km southwest from downtown Montréal, the reserve has a few things to see but looks not unlike something from a Hollywood western. Note that streets have no official names.

In the summer of 1990 the reserve was the site of a standoff between the Mohawks and the Québec and federal governments in a bitter territorial dispute, which made headlines around the world. The residents' support of the Mohawks in Oka exploded into a symbolic stand against outstanding land claims and demands regarding First Nations rights and privileges.

Five Nations Iroquois Village (☎ 450-632-1059, ⓦ www.5nations.qc.ca; adult/child $7.50/5; open 9am-6pm daily May-Sept, 9am-5pm Sat & Sun Oct-April) has maps, information and gives guided tours of the reconstructed Iroquois village behind their main house. There are also several gift shops and galleries – good places to get native arts and crafts. Driving from Montréal, you'll see this site on your left after crossing the Mercier bridge on Rte 138. Look for the large log house.

The **cultural center** (☎ 450-638-0880; $3 suggested donation; open 9am-5pm Mon-Fri), with an extensive library relating to the Five Nations of the Iroquois Confederacy, has a small display dealing principally with this reserve and its history. It's located on the road following the river, to your right after crossing the Mercier bridge.

To get to the area from Montréal, take Hwy 138 west over the Mercier bridge. The reserve is below and to the right, on the riverbank. Then take Hwy 132 and turn off at Old Malone, the main road. You can also take the Métro to the Angrignon station and have a taxi pick you up ($9 one-way; call Five Nations Iroquois Village at ☎ 450-632-1059 to book).

COSMODRÔME

In Laval, North of the Island of Montréal, is the Cosmodôme Space Science Centre (☎ 450-978-3600, 800-565-2267, 2150 Autoroute des Laurentides; adult/student/child $9.75/6.50/7.50; open 10am-6pm Tues-Sun), an interactive museum of space and new technologies. Multimedia exhibits focus on the solar system, satellite communications and space travel. You'll find lots of models of rockets, space shuttles and planets. A multimedia show, 'Reach for the Stars,' simulates space travel with cool special effects on a 360-degree screen.

The center also runs well-regarded youth 'space camps' for one to five days, a sort of mini-NASA training.

The center is about a 20-minute drive from downtown Montréal. By public transportation, take bus No 60 or 61 from Ⓜ Henri Bourassa.

OKA

About 50km west of Montréal, where the Ottawa River meets the St Lawrence, this small town is known for its cheese-making **Oka Monastery** (☎ 450-479-8331, 181 rue des Anges; adult/child $2/free; open 10am-5:30pm daily year-round, guided tours 10am-5pm Tues-Sun late June–early Sept, 10am-5pm Sat & Sun Sept & Oct) dating from the 1880s. Some 70 Trappist monks still live there, but it's open to visitors, who come

to see the religious artworks, a mountain with the Stages of the Cross and several old stone buildings.

In 1990 Oka was the arena of a major confrontation between Mohawk people and the federal and provincial governments. At first a local land squabble, this issue soon came to represent outstanding issues such as land claims and self-government that Native Canadians across the country would like to see resolved properly.

On the edge of the large Lac des Deux Montagnes, the Sépaq-run **Parc d'Oka** (Oka Park; ☎ 514-479-8365, 2020 chemin Oka; admission $3.50; open 9am-7pm daily year-round) offers a bunch of activities, including bathing on a sandy (supervised) beach, sailing, canoeing, kayaking and cycling. Equipment is available for rent. You can also rent cross-country skis and snowshoes for the 70km of trails. There's a swarming campsite ($22 to $30) with a staggering 800 sites – on hot summer weekends, it's full to capacity.

In nearby **Pointe Calumet**, 5km west of Oka, there is a **public beach**, which is always crowded. On Sunday mornings this beach turns into Daylight, an outdoor after-hours club, with hundreds of sweaty club kids who didn't get enough dancing the night before.

To reach Oka from Montréal take Hwy 15 or Hwy 13 to Rte 640 (Ouest), which leads to Rte 344.

RIVIÈRE ROUGE

About an hour's drive northwest of Montréal is the rivière Rouge, one of the best white-water rivers in North America. New World River Expeditions (☎ 819-242-7238, 800-361-5033, ⓦ www.newworld.ca, 100 chemin Rivière Rouge), based in Calumet, Québec (near Hawkesbury, Ontario), offers five-hour **rafting** trips ($84 Mon-Sat, $89 Sun, includes hot-dog lunch) from April to October (reserve ahead); two- to five-day trips are on offer, too. Aside from rafting, they offer 'sportyaking' in inflatable rubber kayaks and horseback riding. Be prepared to go overboard: If your raft doesn't flip by itself in the rapids, the guides will make sure it does. No one leaves disappointed. There's a restaurant-lodge and pool, so you're not exactly roughing it. Staff will explain directions – getting there is a bit tricky.

Another of the many organizations offering adventure rides down this gorgeous, at times wild river is Aventure en Eau Vive (☎ 819-242-6084, 800-567-6881), some 15km north of Calumet toward Rivington. They also offer a range of activities, including **rock climbing**. A rafting expedition should set you back $83.

PARC SAFARI & L'ARCHE DU PAPILLONS

Located in Hemmingford, about 40 minutes south of Montréal, this mainly outdoor Parc Safari (☎ 450-247-2727, 800-465-8724, W www.parcsafari.com, 850 Rte 202; adult/ child 3-10/child under 3 $22/14/free; open 10am-6pm daily mid-May–early Sept) is a great place to bring the kids. Traveling in your car, you spot lions, giraffes, zebras and bears living 'in the wild.' Other areas are walk-through, with feeding and petting zoos, and temporary exhibits. There's a murky wading pool for toddlers on hot days, and numerous on-site services.

Nearby, in St Bernard de Lacolle (on the east side of Hwy 15 via Rte 202) is the Arche du Papillons (☎ 450-246-2552, 20 chemin Noël; adult/child $7.75/6.50; open 10am-5pm daily year-round), a brand-new natural museum dedicated entirely to butterflies. There are some 500 fluttery fellows to be seen here from 50 mostly South American species. Their natural habitats have been re-created judiciously. It makes a nice stopover to or from Parc Safari.

SOUTH RICHELIEU VALLEY

The pretty landscape along the southern end of the rivière Richelieu makes a nice alternate road to Hemmingford or an alternate gateway to the Eastern Townships. For details on the northern part of the Richelieu Valley, see the Montréal to Québec City chapter. Following either Rte 133 and Rte 225 along the east side of the river, or Rte 223 along the west side, will lead you through picturesque, quiet villages.

This route is a historic one – for many centuries it was the only north-south access from Lake Champlain to the St Lawrence, and the British and Americans used it frequently to mount attacks on the Canadian colonies. Consequently, the French and British built a series of forts along the river, some of which can be visited today.

The **Fort Chambly National Historic Site** (☎ 450-658-1585, W www.parkscanada .gc.ca/fortchambly, 2 rue de Richelieu; adult/ student $4/3; open 9am-6pm daily mid-May–early Sept, 9am-5pm Wed-Sun Apr–mid-May & early Sept–Nov) is now a Parks Canada site. It's possible to wander around the restored fort (1665–1709) and check out displays about life in the garrison back then. They also host special events like an old cars exhibit and the popular Festibière beer mini-festival in early September (all the better to evoke life in the old garrison!). The town of Chambly is off exit 22 of Hwy 10 (only 22km east of Montréal).

The **Fort Lennox National Historic Site** (☎ 450-291-5700, W www.parkscanada.gc.ca/ fortlennox, 1 61-ème avenue; adult/child $5/3; open 10am-6pm daily mid-May–early Sept, 10am-6pm Sat & Sun early Sept–early Oct) is a smaller stone fort on the island of Île aux Noix. Built by the British from 1819 to 1829, it was used until 1843, when the Americans were no longer deemed a threat. Rebels of the 1837–38 Patriot's Uprising were imprisoned here. The town of St Paul de l'Île aux Noix is 37km south of Chambly on Rte 223.

To get a glimpse of Québec's tackiest village, continue down Rte 223 and head 17km east along Rte 202 to **Venise en Québec**. Perched as it is on the northern end of Lake Champlain, it *could* have been in some ways reminiscent of Venice, but it's not quite that. From June through August, it's a spectacle in and of itself to see the cramped, commune-like atmosphere where anything goes.

The Laurentians

Between 80km and 150km north of Montréal, this 22,000 sq km section of the ancient Laurentian Shield is a mountainous and rolling lake-sprinkled playground. It's considered Québec's Switzerland, a skier's paradise. The land proved a failure for lumber and mining, but when skiing caught on, so did the area as a resort-land. Today it has the largest concentration of skiable hills in North America; the two most popular, Mont Tremblant and Mont St Sauveur, attract millions of tourists each year. Summer is as busy as winter, with visitors camping, cycling, fishing and swimming. The Parc Linéaire du P'tit Train du Nord (see 'The Race to Colonize the North' for more information) alone offers 200km of bicycle and cross-country ski trails.

The many picturesque French towns, dominated by their church spires and the good scenery, also make the area popular for just lazing and relaxing. It's a perfect spot to take meandering car trips or bike rides through the pretty countryside. Plentiful accommodations and restaurants provide a wide range of services, from elegant inns with fine dining rooms to modest motels. In many areas of the Laurentides (as it's called in French), you're likely to notice fairly high prices. As the playground and country respite for many Montréalers (who call heading there 'going up north,' synonymous with taking a vacation), prices have been driven up by a competition among all tourist haunts to out-chic one another.

Orientation & Information

The Autoroute Laurentienne, also known as Hwy 15, is the fastest route north from Montréal and is the way the buses go. The old Rte 117, running parallel to it, is slower but more pleasant. It takes over north of Ste Agathe des Monts (or simply Ste Agathe), after Hwy 15 ends. While the bulk of this chapter focuses on the Laurentians, it also covers sections of the Lanaudière region,

Highlights

- Bike along one of North America's longest and best-maintained trails, the P'tit Train du Nord

- Ski down the slopes of Mont Tremblant, one of the continent's top ski hills

- Go canoeing or hiking in Parc du Mont Tremblant, the province's oldest provincial park

- Enjoy superb cross-country ski trails around Morin Heights and Val Morin

- Treat your inner self at the beautiful Sivananda Ashram Yoga Camp, in Val Morin

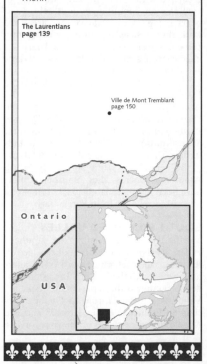

The Laurentians
page 139

Ville de Mont Tremblant
page 150

Ontario

USA

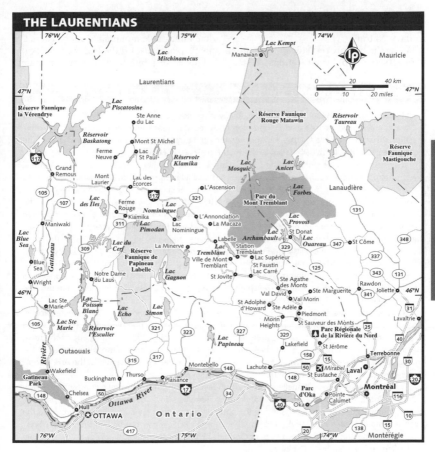

which borders it to the east. Other highways and main routes lead northeast of Montréal directly to Lanaudière.

The region's main tourist office (☎ 450-436-8532, 800-561-6673, ⓦ www.laurentides.com) is at 14142 rue de la Chapelle, in Mirabel. It's a well-indicated turnoff of Hwy 15 (exit 39). Limocar (☎ 450-435-6767) runs daily buses from Montréal bus station to Ferme Neuve, north of Mont Laurier. Most stop in all the towns and villages on the way – inquire about express buses going to your destination.

PARC LINÉAIRE DU P'TIT TRAIN DU NORD

This 200km-long system of bike and cross-country-ski trails stretches the definition of 'park' but provides the area with a great deal of its sporting potential. The park (☎ 450-436-8532; cycling permit adult/under 18 $5/free, cross-country-ski permit adult/under 18 $7/free; open year-round), which was inaugurated in 1996, stretches from St Jérôme all the way up to Mont Laurier, following an old railway line. This is one long, terrific cycling trail, one of the province's best maintained and most scenic. Come winter, it becomes an equally terrific cross-country ski trail.

Along the trail are rest stops, information booths (some in old train stations), restau-rants, B&Bs, and bike rental and repair shops. You pass streams, rivers, rapids, lakes and unbeatable mountain scenery. There are many places just off the trail for a quick dip in a lake or a bite to eat before continuing.

The Race to Colonize the North

The Laurentians may seem like a peaceful, lovely place now, but back in the day, the area saw an intense, albeit covert battle over colonization between the French and the English. What's interesting is that the route to 'victory' was paved along the same path that today serves as one of the province's top bicycle trails, the Parc Linéaire du P'tit Train du Nord.

The first areas to be settled in the Laurentians were the southern reaches, between Montréal and St Jérôme and toward Joliette. Governor Frontenac allotted several strips of land according to the French *seigneurial* (feudal) system from 1673, yet concurrently Anglo-Saxon immigrants of Loyalist and British stock were settling the regions. In 1785, a few townships were allocated for the Anglo colonists, who slowly continued their move northward. (This area was the only one outside of the Eastern Townships to be settled through a British land distribution system.) By 1860, Anglophone immigrants had gotten all the way to St Jovite! Yikes!

Areas farther north held little interest to anyone until the burgeoning forestry industry started flourishing around 1835. Still, the French were watching with some trepidation as American, English, Scottish and Irish immigrants encroached into these lands (the Laurentians, Outaouais and Lanaudière). Further, thousands of French were moving to New England to find jobs in flourishing cotton mills. The door seemed to be wide open for an influx of Anglophone settlers!

No one was more concerned with keeping the region a French one than curé Antoine Labelle, a priest from the parish of the tiny village of St Jérôme. He took it upon himself to curb the Anglo (read: Protestant) infiltration of the area by feverishly promoting French settlement of the area. After helping to found 20 villages, Labelle encountered setbacks as families moved out, having discovered that the land here was not as fertile as previously advertised. Meanwhile, the Anglo communities continued moving northward along the rivière Rouge.

To facilitate settlement, Labelle called for the development of a railway linking Montréal with the Laurentians. After numerous delays and financial troubles, in 1876 the Montréal–St Jérôme line was inaugurated. Six years later, sniffing the potential for success, Canadian Pacific purchased the rail line and extended it to Ste Agathe. In 1888 Labelle's achievements won him the title of Minister of the State and of the Colonization of Québec; he became the first and only priest to ever hold a Parliamentary position in Québec.

The new railway became evermore popular with Montréalers in search of weekend recreation and rest. By 1909 the line reached Mont Laurier. Ski centers opened as the sport became fashionable; the rail line became one of the most frequently used in the country, and many settled in the area.

The 1930s and '40s were the line's heyday, but by the late 1940s the development of Québec's railway system to other parts of the province – coupled with the rise of the Eastern Townships, the Lanaudière region and the northern US as sports and leisure destinations – took clientele away from the Laurentians. In 1969 passenger service on the line was no longer profitable and was halted. Though restarted for a few years in the late 1970s, it was closed forever in 1981; the tracks were removed a decade later. Curé Labelle's idea, however, had paid off: For decades the line had been the region's spinal cord, greatly affecting its settlement.

It's possible to hop on or off the trail at any point along the way, but the paid permits are an enforced policy: Monitors patrol the trail and stop permit-less lawbreakers. Permits can be purchased at any tourist information office or from the patrollers.

Getting There & Around

Taxi de la Rouge (☎ 819-275-3113, 888-893-8356) offers a brilliant luggage transport service to facilitate your travel. For $7, they'll bring your baggage to any campground, B&B, motel or hotel of your choice between St Jérôme and Mont Laurier. Similarly, Vélo du Nord (☎ 888-500-8356) will transport cyclists and their baggage from Montréal (they leave the Maison du Cycliste at 7:15am daily) to St Jérôme, then continue farther north. There are also four campgrounds along the way (noted in the appropriate sections) that offer luggage transport from one to the other.

ST JÉRÔME

☎ 450 • pop 24,400

Just 43km north of Montréal along Hwy 15 is the official gateway to the Laurentians. You can check out a bronze statue of *curé* (priest) Antoine Labelle in front of the Byzantine-style **cathedral** (☎ 432-9741, 355 rue St Georges; admission free; open 7:30am-4:30pm daily year-round). Usually there are excellent temporary exhibits of modern art at the **Centre d'Exposition du Vieux Palais** (☎ 432-7171, 185 rue du Palais; admission free; open noon-8pm Tues, noon-5pm Wed-Sun).

The Parc Linéaire du P'tit Train du Nord also begins here and 5km later passes through the lovely **Parc Régional de la Rivière du Nord** (☎ 431-1676, 1051 boul International; admission $5 per car; open 9am-7pm May-Sept, 9am-5pm Oct-Apr). In the 1880s a pulp mill was constructed in the area, and in 1924 a small hydroelectric station; their ruins can be spotted along the picturesque rivière du Nord. There are 19 scenic cycling, hiking and ski trails through the forest here as well as on-site kayak and canoe rental. The park's proximity to Montréal makes it an excellent day-trip option.

Take exit 45 off Hwy 15 and follow boulevard International.

If all this biking and hiking leaves you yawning and in need of a wilder adrenaline rush, try throwing yourself out of an airplane at 12,000 feet. **Skydiving** is all the rage with Para-Vision (☎ 438-0855, ⓦ http://para-vision .qc.ca, 881 rue de la Montagne), near St Jérôme (exit 43 off Hwy 15). They offer parachute jumps ($240/265 per jump weekday/weekend Apr-Oct, $215 Nov-Mar) with or without instructors. It's one of Québec's best-known skydiving schools, so trust them and don't hesitate when they shout 'jump!'

RAWDON

☎ 450 • pop 9150

Known as one of Québec's most multiethnic towns, Rawdon, in the Lanaudière region 20km west of Joliette, was first settled by Loyalists and Irish immigrants in 1799. Scottish and British followed, and in the 1920s an influx of Slavic immigrants (Russians, Poles and Ukrainians) came along. Reflecting this diversity is the **Centre Multiethnique** (☎ 834-3334, 3588 rue Metcalfe; open 1pm-4pm Fri-Sun), which exhibits these groups' porcelain dishes, costumes, and arts and crafts. Concerts are held from time to time.

Just on the edge of Rte 337, bordering the rivière Ouareau, the **Parc des Chutes Dorwin** (☎ 834-2282, Rte 337; adult/child $3/2; open 9am-7pm daily) is a lovely area for a picnic or short hike. According to Native Canadian legend, the sorceress Nipissingue pushed a young girl, Hiawitha, into the river here. She transformed herself into a waterfall and frightened others with her thunderous sound. If you look closely (or if someone has slipped something in your drink) you can see her profile on the right side of the falls.

Ski Montcalm (☎ 834-3139, ⓦ www.ski montcalm.com, 3294 rue Parc; day pass $18 Mon-Fri, $27 Sat & Sun; open 9am-4pm daily) is a resort with 21 slopes for downhillers and snowboarders.

The local tourist office (☎ 834-2282), open from late June to early September only, is at 3112 1-ère avenue (Rte 337). Rawdon is accessible via Rtes 158, 125 and 337 from Joliette, or via Rte 341 from Hwy 40.

ST SAUVEUR DES MONTS
☎ 450 • pop 7000

Founded in 1854, this is the busiest village in the Laurentians, just 60km from Montréal. There are five major ski hills around the village and in nearby Morin Heights. Simply called St Sauveur (better than its original name, given by the religious curé Labelle: Circoncision, meaning circumcision!), this popular destination is packed year-round. On Sunday afternoons, reams of people walk to and fro on rue Principale. There are many pretty country roads nearby, notably chemin rivière du Simon, accessible via chemin du Village. The residential village of **Piedmont** (pop 2600), just 4km east of St Sauveur, offers good alternate places to stay and eat, and in some ways has become an extension of St Sauveur.

The area's main tourist office (☎ 227-4072, W www.sdeph.org), 605 chemin des Frênes in Piedmont (exit 60 off Hwy 15), is open 8:30am to 7pm Sunday to Wednesday and 8:30am to 8:30pm Thursday through Saturday from late June to early September, and 9am to 5pm daily from early September to late June. A smaller but equally helpful office (☎ 227-2564) is inside Parc Filion in St Sauveur, but it's open only from late June to early September (10am to 6pm daily).

ATMs aren't hard to find, especially along rue Principale. The Royal Bank of Canada (☎ 227-4683) is at 75 rue de la Gare.

Activities
For **biking** and **rollerblading**, wheels can be rented at Sports Denis Parent (☎ 227-2700, 217 chemin Lac Millette; 4-hr rental bike/rollerblades $19/15).

For **skiing**, this is *the* place. **Mont St Sauveur** (☎ 227-4671, 800-363-2426, W www .montsaintsauveur.com, 350 rue St Denis; day pass $34-40; open 9am-10:30pm Mon-Sat, 8:30am-9pm Sun) is the area's largest ski station, with 29 slopes (none classed expert but 15 are difficult), nine lifts, one half-pipe and 213m of vertical drop. There's also snowboarding, snow-tubing, snow-rafting and snowshoeing. In summer, the place turns into a giant but so-so water park with endless lines.

Mont Habitant (☎ 227-2637, W www.mont habitant.com, 12 boul des Skieurs; day pass $22-31; open 9am-10pm daily) is smaller (11 slopes, 183m vertical drop) but day passes are cheaper.

Piedmont has two good options for non-expert skiers. **Mont Avila** (☎ 227-4671, chemin Avila; day pass $24-33; open 9am-10:30pm Mon-Sat, 8:30am-9pm Sun) has 11 slopes, a glade run and three lifts. **Mont Olympia** (☎ 227-3523, 330 chemin de la Montagne; day pass $24-33; open 9am-5pm Sun-Thur, 9am-10:30pm Fri & Sat) is much larger than Avila, with 23 slopes (three double diamond), and a 200m vertical drop.

Special Events
The popular **Festival des Arts** (☎ 227-0427, W www.artssaintsauveur.com) is a 10-day festival beginning at the end of July. The shindig brings in excellent classical and modern musicians and hosts contemporary dance performances.

Places to Stay
Aux Petits Oiseaux (☎ 227-6116, e auxpetit soiseaux@sympatico.ca, 342 rue Principale) Singles/doubles from $60/110. This B&B has a lot going for it, aside from its central location. The spacious foyer is instantly seductive and leads to a back patio and (heart-shaped!) pool. One room has a Jacuzzi. The view onto the mountains is superb, the friendly service is impeccable and the air is smoke-free. What more could you want?

Auberge Victorienne (☎ 227-2328, 119 rue Principale) Singles/doubles $70/75. From the entrance hall to the washrooms, every room here is decorated in Victorian fashion, sometimes quite elaborately. The atmosphere is very welcoming.

Inter Club (☎ 227-7875, W www.interclub piedmont.com, 895 boul des Laurentides) Doubles/suites from $65/85. Located in Piedmont, this place advertises itself as a 'hotel & sports getaway paradise.' Your lodging includes access to a fitness club and pool; an on-site tennis court can be rented. They often have specials and package deals – check their website.

Auberge Mont Habitant (☎ 227-2637, W *www.monthabitant.com, 12 boul des Skieurs*) Doubles $90. Located right at the ski hill, close to a big outdoor skating rink, this place can become party central on winter evenings. The rooms are comfortable, and each is equipped with a kitchenette.

Relais St Denis (☎ 227-4466, 888-997-4766, 61 rue St Denis) Doubles from $90. This top-notch, Victorian-style hotel looks more like a large B&B. It is semi-secluded and has finely cut flower gardens surrounding it and airy, bright rooms. Ask about specials including breakfast and dinner.

Places to Eat

La Brûlerie des Monts (☎ 227-6157, 197 rue Principale) Mains $8-13; open 7am-7pm daily. This place makes for a fashionable coffee break and is a good spot for a light breakfast or lunch. Their hot lunch specials are usually a good deal.

Bentley's (☎ 227-1851, 235 rue Principale) Mains $5-11. This is a popular hangout for those in search of simple, inexpensive grub, like hamburgers, spaghetti and salads.

Le Chalet Grec (☎ 227-6612, 138 rue Principale) Mains $7-14; open 4pm-11pm daily. This is a good and friendly Greek restaurant with a BYO – Bring Your Own (wine) – policy. Brochettes are their specialty.

Vieux Four (☎ 227-6060, 252 rue Principale) Mains $6-13. Locals gather here mainly for saucy and cheesy and heavenly wood-oven pizzas and tasty pasta dishes.

Papa Luigi (☎ 227-5311, 155 rue Principale) Mains $11-18; open 5pm-11pm daily. Fine Italian cuisine is on offer here, along with steaks and seafood dishes.

Getting There & Away

St Sauveur is on the west side of Hwy 15, just off exit 60. Limocar (☎ 435-6767) runs only one daily bus Monday to Saturday to/from Montréal ($14, 1½ hours), but five daily buses go to the Piedmont bus station (☎ 227-2487), at 770 boulevard des Laurentides. From there, grab a taxi to St Sauveur (about $6).

Limocar also offers specials including roundtrip bus tickets to and from Montréal and each of the area's five ski hills daily; see the Activities chapter for more details.

If you're driving, there's lots of free parking in town. Try behind the church if you're stuck.

MORIN HEIGHTS
☎ 450 • pop 2400

This small, dollhouse-like village was founded by Irish settlers in 1885 along the rivière Simon and has remained largely Anglophone. There are five churches and three cemeteries in town, and a slew of appealing cafés on rue Principale. Morin Heights is just 8km west of St Sauveur along Rte 364.

Activities

There's a pleasant, riverside **beach** accessible from rue du Village.

The **skiing** here is simply superb. At **Ski Morin Heights** (☎ 227-2020, chemin Bennett; day pass $24-33; open 9am-5pm Sun-Thur, 8:30am-10:30pm Fri & Sat), there are 23 downhill slopes with a vertical drop of 200m.

The cross-country scene in the area is among the best in the Laurentians, with 47 trails totaling 175km; some trails are

Snowbunnies fly high in the Laurentians.

definitely for experts only. There are several places to hop onto the system of trails, but best enter at the **Centre de Ski de Fond Morin Heights** (☎ 226-2417, 612 rue du Village; adult/child under 18 $7/free; open 8:30am-5pm daily), just off Rte 364.

Places to Stay & Eat

Camping St Adolphe d'Howard (☎ 327-3519, 866-236-5743, 1672 chemin du Village) Tent sites $12. Located 11km northwest of Morin Heights along Rte 329, near the village of St Adolphe d'Howard, this is a good though sometimes crowded campground with hot showers and an on-site convenience store. There are walking and biking trails nearby, and it's not far from pretty Lac St Joseph.

Aux Berges de la Rivière de la Simon (☎ 226-1110, 877-525-1110, 54 rue Legault) Doubles $70-105. This is a great B&B, in a large house dating from 1885, filled with antiques. The cheaper rooms share a washroom while the most expensive boasts a queen-sized bed and spacious bathroom. All the rooms are particularly cozy.

Auberge Swiss Inn (☎ 226-2009, W www .swissinn.ca, 496 chemin de St Adolphe) Singles/doubles $60/65. This small, comfortable hotel with decent rooms has a restaurant that specializes in European sausages and great fondues ($30 for two).

Café de la Rue (☎ 226-1204, 879 rue du Village) Mains $9-18. This nice, relaxed bistro-restaurant offers a standard menu of meats and salads that always please the clientele.

STE ADÈLE
☎ 450 • pop 9450

There are two sides to this village: A rather unattractive modern core contrasts with several streets and the lakeside lined with lovely homes, reminders of a time when this was a main destination for bourgeois holiday-seekers.

Ste Adèle is also known as the birthplace of author Claude-Henri Grignon, who wrote *L'Homme et son péché* (*A Man and His Sin*), a novel that chronicles several generations of 19th-century pioneers of the area. It was

made into a hugely popular radio show in the 1930s, turned into a film in 1949, and from 1956 became one of the most pivotal TV series in Québec history. In 2001, a new film version was directed by Charles Binamé and starred one of Québec's biggest stars, Roy Dupuis.

Things to See & Do

There's a nice public **beach** (adult/child $4/2; open daily late June–early Sept) on the shores of the shallow Lac Rond (exit 67 off Hwy 15). The only museum of note is the **Trainorama** (☎ 229-2660, 1002 rue St Georges; adult/student $6/4; open 10am-6pm Fri-Mon), which tells the story of how the P'tit Train du Nord changed life in the Laurentians.

It's worth checking the schedule of the **Pavillon des Arts** (☎ 229-2586, 1364 chemin Pierre Péladeau) to see what classical concerts are being given. It has a good reputation for excellent concerts.

Activities

Want to do some more **skiing**? There are two hills nearby. **Ski Mont Gabriel** (☎ 227-1100, 1501 montée Gabriel; day pass $24-33; open 9am-10:30pm Mon-Sat, 8:30am-8pm Sun), located halfway between St Sauveur and Ste Adèle, has 13 slopes, including four wicked double diamonds. **Ski Chantecler** (☎ 229-3555, 1474 chemin Chantecler; day pass $28-33; open 9am-10pm Tues-Sat, 9am-4pm Sun & Mon) boasts 23 slopes, a vertical drop of 200m and an impressively large resort area.

A good outfit for **white-water rafting** is Excursions Rivière du Nord (☎ 224-2035, W www.raftingmontreal.com). They also rent canoes ($36/2 persons, including shuttle service) and bikes ($12/4 hours) for combo canoe-bike trips. Their excursions start from the parking lot at the end of rue St Joseph (off exit 67 from Hwy 15). Reservations are a must.

Places to Stay

Aux Dormants du Boisé (☎ 229-1420, W www.auxdormantduboise.com, 1420 rue du Valais) Singles/doubles $55/65. This B&B

feels like a country chalet, with a roaring fireplace, a view of thick forest through the windows and over the terrace, and cozy rooms that make you feel as far from civilization as you can get. From Ste Adèle go 2km north on Rte 370 and turn right onto rue Riverdale; continue on until you get to rue du Valais.

La Belle Idée (☎ 229-6173, 888-221-1313, 894 rue de l'Arbre Sec) Singles/doubles from $40/50. This is a simple, inexpensive B&B with country charm.

Hôtel Mont Gabriel (☎ 229-3547, W www.montgabriel.com, 1699 chemin du Mont Gabriel) Singles/doubles from $150/202. With many types of rooms as well as an in-house health and beauty spa, this luxurious place near the ski hill looks and feels like a villa.

Places to Eat

Sous Mon Toit (☎ 229-3131, 1049 rue Valiquette) Mains $8-17; open 7:30am-11pm daily. This restaurant is a good choice for two things: breakfast (there are numerous delicious egg and crêpe dishes) and dessert. With 26 kinds of filling and over a dozen memorable dessert crêpes, you can't go wrong.

Au Petit Chaudron (☎ 229-2709, 1110 boul Ste Adèle) Mains $6-13; open 6:30am-8pm daily. For a hearty Québécois meal at a mainly local spot, head to this small, friendly place – the oldest restaurant in town.

L'Eau à la Bouche (☎ 229-2991, 3003 boul Ste Adèle) Mains $14-30; open 6:30pm-9pm daily. Renowned throughout Québec as one of the province's finest dining rooms, they emphasize freshly grown produce as well as some organic, fine cuisine and impeccable service. Reservations are a must, as dinners are served only every half-hour on the half-hour.

VAL MORIN

☎ 819 • pop 2000

Nestled among lush mountains is this lovely village whose 'downtown' consists of just a few houses. The excellent cross-country skiing is famous here. The **Centre de Ski Far Hills** (☎ 990-4409, 800-567-6636, chemin du Lac LaSalle; $10 access fee) runs the 96km of magnificently scenic trails, which curve around mountains, across frozen lakes.

In town, an absolute must-see is the **Centre LauRentian** (☎ 322-1668, e garybike@ intlaurentides.qc.ca; open 9am-6pm Sun-Wed, 9am-9pm Thur-Sat). It's a combination bike rental shop ($25/day, $75/week), ski-equipment rental shop (Nordic skis and snowshoes), used bookstore (one of the best selections of English titles outside Montréal!) and café (supposedly just espresso and ready-made snacks, but the owner can whip up a sandwich for you). The shop is filled with little objects that demand attention and has a charming atmosphere.

The bus stop (☎ 322-3097) is at 1054 Rte 117. Four buses a day link Montréal with Val Morin ($17, 2 hours).

Sivananda Ashram Yoga Camp

The most distinguished address in town belongs to this renowned sanctuary (☎ 322-3226, 800-263-9642, W www.sivananda.org, 673 8-ème avenue). Meditation aficionados claim this is the best Sivananda camp on the continent, better run and more beautiful than ones in California. The complex's grounds are just splendid. Outdoor and indoor yoga and meditation courses are given throughout the year, and there are numerous weekend and weekly specials available. Tents are pitched on the hills of a small mountain; a boarded trail leads to the summit, where special events are held and the views are breathtaking. Accommodations range from tents ($35) to summer chalets ($45) to very serene doubles ($70) inside the main building, which they claim is the world's largest construction made of straw bale (though the Raelians in Valcourt, Eastern Townships, also stake this claim for their building in honor of extraterrestrials!).

Places to Stay

Les Jardins de la Gare (☎ 322-5559, 888-322-4273, 1790 7-ème avenue) Doubles with/ without private bath $75/60, including two meals. A charming three-floor country inn in quiet surroundings, this makes for both a great place to stay and an ideal spot for a pause en route. It's under 1km from the P'tit Train du Nord bike trail (at km 38), and there's the beautiful Lac Raymond right out front – you have free use of paddleboats, and you can swim to the public beach on the opposite shore.

Les Florettes (☎ 322-7614, *1803 rue de la Gare*) Singles/doubles $45/65. This home is pretty both outside and inside. In winter, the owners organize cross-country ski excursions by moonlight.

Far Hills Inn (☎ *322-2014*, W *www .farhillsinn.com, 3399 rue du Far Hills*) Doubles from $160. Frequented by well-to-do Americans and tourists from Ontario with impeccable taste, this hotel complex boasts a series of excellent wood and stone chalets and a large choice of organized activities. They frequently offer special rates.

VAL DAVID
☎ 819 • pop 3800

Like Val Morin, Val David is nestled at the foot of mountains and surrounded by beautiful landscapes. As languid as Val David is, however, it feels larger and rushed in comparison. It's a worthwhile break from biking along the P'tit Train du Nord trail, which whizzes right through it, and there are some magnificent places to stay.

The tourist office (☎ 322-2900, 888-322-7030) is at 2501 rue de l'Église, inside the post office. It's open 9am to 5pm Sunday to Thursday and 9am to 6pm Friday and Saturday year-round.

A 1km walk from town, the bus stop (☎ 322-2339) is at 1340 Rte 117. Four buses a day link Montréal with Val David ($17, 2 hours). There's an extra service Friday and Saturday.

Things to See & Do

The **Galerie d'Art Inuit Baffin** (☎ *322-2632, 1337 rue de la Sapinière, 2nd floor; admission free; open 10am-5pm daily*) is more a store than a gallery, but numerous fine pieces of Inuit soapstone carvings are on display.

The art community is alive and well here, as evidenced by the immense popularity of the **1001 Pots festival** (☎ *322-2900*, W *www .parolecommunication.com*), the continent's

largest ceramic exhibit, held from mid-July to mid-August. Japanese-Canadian potter Kinya Ishikawa started the festival in 1989, and now an incredible 100,000 visitors each year appreciate some 25,000 works by over 100 local and international artists.

Activities

Mountain climbing is to Val David what skiing is to other villages in the Laurentians. Passe Montagne (☎ 322-2900 ext 235, 800-465-2123, W www.passemontagne.com, 1760 Montée 2-ème rang) is a mountain-climbing school that offers introductory courses and organizes ice-climbing expeditions. Phénix Sports et Aventures (☎ 322-1118, 877-566-1118, 2444 rue de l'Église) rents climbing gear, as well as mountain bikes and canoes; for $44 you can paddle two hours down the rivière du Nord and bike back.

Pause Plein Air (☎ 322-6880, 877-422-6880, 1381 rue de la Sapinière) is another sports shop offering canoe and bike rental, as well as guided excursions.

Places to Stay

Camping Laurentien (☎ *322-2281, 1949 rue Guerin*) Tent sites $18-24. Alongside Rte 117 just south of Val David, this is a decent campground with some nice, wooded areas.

Le Chalet Beaumont (☎ *322-1972, fax 322-3793, 1451 rue Beaumont*) Dorm beds $18, doubles with/without private bathroom $27/23 per person. This is one of those HI hostels you'll remember for life, about which you'll keep asking yourself, '*This* is a hostel?' Perched atop a wooded hill, it has the look and feel of a luxury country chalet (chopped wood at the entrance adds to its rustic air). The main foyer is as nice as any lodge, only its clientele's jacket labels are more likely to read Columbia rather than Ralph Lauren. The hostel is only 1km from biking and skiing trails (you can ski right out the front door!). The dorm rooms hold two to four persons only, and there's an on-site sauna ($4 per person). Finally, they can pick you up from the bus station – call first. Prices rise about $2 in their high season, December to April.

Au Sapin Rose (☎ *322-5195, 1227 chemin de la Sapinière*) Doubles $55. Right along the P'tit Train du Nord bike trail, this B&B is as convenient as it is comfortable. There's an outdoor pool too.

La Sapinière (☎ 322-2020, Ⓦ www.sap iniere.com, 1244 chemin de la Sapinière) Doubles from $270. This historical hotel has been nurturing its reputation as a top-rate hotel and dining room since the 1930s. It was once a traditional destination for Québecer newlyweds. It still serves up four-star luxury (for those prices, it better!), and its restaurant serves fine cuisine washed down with rare wines from its cellar, which stocks some 20,000 bottles.

Places to Eat

De Bretagne et d'Ailleurs (☎ 322-3761, 2361 rue de l'Église) Mains $5-14; open 10am-9pm Tues-Sun. Lucky are those who discover this unassuming eatery on the village's main street. The French (from France) owner was once the grand chef at the posh Auberge Gray Rocks but decided he wanted a quieter life and moved to Val David. That means he's brought his expertise – and delicious recipes! – to a café-style restaurant where fine cuisine can be sampled affordably. There are salads (warm and cold), crêpes, mussels and calamari, as well as filling, imaginative breakfasts, all served in an atmosphere so laid back you'd think you were still at the Sivananda Ashram Yoga Camp in Val Morin!

La Vagabonde (☎ 322-3953, 1262 chemin de la Rivière) Open 9am-6pm Wed-Sun. This bakery sells mainly fresh breads and pastries but occasionally has pizza slices. Right by the river, it's a nice place to stop in.

Le Grand Pa (☎ 322-3104, 2481 rue de l'Église) Mains $8-16; open 11:30am-2pm & 5pm-8pm daily. A good place for a hearty meal, this relaxed place has wood-oven pizzas, Québécois specialties and Italian dishes. There's often a *chansonnier* singing in the evening.

STE AGATHE DES MONTS
☎ 819 • pop 9000

Before St Sauveur supplanted it as the Laurentian's major resort town, Ste Agathe was *the* place to be. Queen Elizabeth II chose to be here during a wartime retreat in the 1940s, and Jacqueline Kennedy (in her pre-Kennedy days) came here to relax.

Sitting on the edge of the charming Lac des Sables, the village still exudes some of that old-world Anglo-Saxon charm of the English settlers who built it up as an ideal hideaway in the mid-1890s. A number of villas and stately homes around the lake and in the village attest to this era, while the center feels lackluster and rundown. Today, Ste Agathe is the Laurentians' largest town after St Jérôme and can get very busy. While there aren't as many activities here as in other areas, the services are good.

The bus station (☎ 326-6656) is at 200 rue Principale. Five to seven daily buses go to/from Montréal ($18, 1½-2 hours).

Information
The year-round tourist office (☎ 326-0457, 888-326-0457) is at 24 rue St Paul Est. Rue Principale, a western extension of Rte 117, has several banks, ATMs, shops and cafés.

From mid-January through early March, the **Hiver en Nord** festival (☎ 326-8348) organizes a series of daily wintery activities such as ice-castle building and skating.

Things to See & Do
There are three public **beaches** right in town, all of which have paid access ($4). Near the Plage Ste Lucie (beach) at the Quai des Alouettes (where rue Principale runs into the lake), Croisières Alouette (☎ 326-3656) runs 50-minute **lake cruises** (adult/child under 15 $12/5).

About 13km outside of town in the county of St Faustin is the **Centre Touristique et Éducatif** (☎ 326-1606, 5000 chemin du Lac Cordon; adult/student $5/4; open 8am-4:30pm Sun-Thur, 8am-8pm Fri & Sat June-Oct). This marvelous, protected area showcases local flora and fauna. There are walking trails as well as canoe and kayak rental. It's a good place to bring the kids: Every Saturday there are nature-themed activities, and there are some child-oriented information panels on the walks through the forest. There's also an excellent **campground** (☎ 326-9072; $16). To get there from town, head west on chemin Tour du Lac, keep heading west as it turns into chemin du Lac Manitou, then make a left onto chemin du Lac Caribou until it becomes chemin du Lac Cordon.

Places to Stay

Parc des Campeurs (☎ *324-0482, 800-561-7360,* **W** *www.parcdescampeurs.com, 50 rue St Joseph)* Tent sites $23-28. This is a gargantuan campground (550 sites!) on the south side of Lac des Sables, near the Plage Major beach. In winter, you can rent cross-country skis to explore the area's 35km of trails.

Relais de la Sauvagine (☎ *326-5228, 877-326-5228,* **W** *www.lasauvagine.com, 10 chemin Tour du Lac)* Doubles $80. A good deal for the price, this British-style stone country inn has comfortable rooms, each with its own bathroom, and faces the lake.

Auberge La Sauvagine (☎ *326-7673, 800-787-7172, 1592 Rte 329 Nord)* Singles/doubles from $65/90, chalets $130. Run by the same owners as the Relais de la Sauvagine, this place is slightly more upscale, with a stylized rustic décor and riverside location. It's also renowned for its restaurant (dinner runs about $45 per person).

Auberge Le St Venant (☎ *326-7937, 800-697-7937,* **W** *www.st-venant.com, 234 rue St Venant)* Doubles $86-136. Boasting one of the best lake views in town, this small hotel, with nine tastefully decorated and spacious rooms, is one of the most attractive places to stay in the Laurentians.

Places to Eat

Bistro de la Gare (☎ *321-0582, 24 rue St Paul)* Mains $5-8. Right in the old train station doubling as the tourist office, along the P'tit Train du Nord bike trail, this simple café has good, light meals, and $10 full-course lunch specials.

Buona Fortuna (☎ *321-2727, 6 rue Principale)* Mains $8-17; open 4pm-11pm daily. An Italian restaurant with a difference, this cozy place in the center of town serves unique items like ravioli stuffed with caribou, good pasta and seafood dishes, and multicourse culinary extravaganzas for $45. Their three-

course meals go for about $10 during early-bird specials (4:30pm to 6:30pm).

Laurentien (☎ *326-5808, 56 rue St Vincent)* Mains $7-17. An all-purpose destination, this family restaurant serves everything from sandwiches and *poutines* to escargots, veal parmagiana, pastas and brochettes. And let's not forget the bar.

Chic Bar le Times (no ☎, *6A rue Principale)* This local bar has a friendly but grungy feel and sometimes hosts live bands. The main draw is their $1-per-game billiards table and drinks at prices that don't gouge.

ST DONAT
☎ 819 • pop 5300

Located in the neighboring Lanaudière region, St Donat, just 32km northeast of Ste Agathe along Rte 329, shares a similar landscape of lakes and vast mountains. There's even easy access to the Parc du Mont Tremblant, just 11km north (see that section, later, for details). However, it tends to be much less crowded than villages in the Laurentians and as such is a good alternative destination.

The **Centre Ethno-culturel 8atabi** *(pronounced 'wa-TA-bi';* ☎ *424-4411, 303 rue Brisson; adult/child $5/4; open 9am-5pm daily)* is a cultural center focusing on Algonquin culture and traditions. You visit a reconstructed village (in winter you use snowshoes), and there's an opportunity to get a traditional Native Canadian meal.

There are several hiking trails of note, most starting from the southern edge of Lac Archambault. The **Sentier Inter-centre de la Montagne Noire** leads you past the remains of a cockpit from a fallen military plane. A steep 7km trail leads to the mountain's summit (900m), from where there are stupendous views.

Ski Mont Garceau (☎ *424-2784, 800-427-2328,* **W** *www.skigarceau.com, 190 chemin du Lac Blanc; open 8:30am-4pm daily)* is a very decent ski station with 17 slopes and 305m of vertical drop. There's a half-pipe, a snow garden for the kids, and various restaurants and bars. A day pass costs $25 weekdays, $31 weekends.

Camping de la Volière *(☎ 877-688-2289, Rte 125)* Tent sites $19. Located in the Parc du Mont Tremblant, 11km north of St Donat to the end of Rte 125, this great campground lies on the beachy shores of Lac Provost.

Domaine St Guillaume *(☎ 424-5376,* W *www.st-guillaume.com, 467 chemin St Guillaume)* Singles/doubles from $60/100. This is a large, lakeside terrain with separate and fully furnished chalets and condos backing a private beach.

Hôtel Manoir des Laurentides *(☎ 424-2121, 800-567-6717, 290 rue Principale)* Singles/doubles from $75/100. A main manor plus several dozen chalets, all close to the water, offer comfortable rooms and boat rental. It gets very crowded at the end of July.

Only one bus per week joins Montréal with St Donat ($23, 3 hours), leaving Montréal on Friday afternoon and returning Sunday evening.

VILLE DE MONT TREMBLANT
☎ 819 • pop 9000

This is the King of the Laurentians, hands down. With the stunning Parc du Mont Tremblant – an internationally renowned ski hill with all the trimmings – and magnificent scenery in every season, this area draws almost three million tourists per year.

The town of St Jovite was the first of the 20 villages founded by curé Antoine Labelle, in 1879. Later it became the center of the forestry industry, which took over the entire area for many decades and was responsible for much of the region's development; it has remained a mainly administrative town.

Since the late 19th century, Mont Tremblant (the mountain) has been the jewel sought after by first the forestry industry, then by exclusive hunting clubs formed there for rich Americans. In 1937, Philadelphia billionaire Joe Ryan bought the territory and turned it into an exclusive ski resort. Rich sporty types were being flown in on private planes from the US and Ontario. The hill blossomed in the 1940s and '50s and hasn't stopped since.

Now under the administration of Intrawest, the Vancouver company responsible for putting Whistler on the world map, Tremblant is one of the best-known ski hills on the continent, frequently winning prizes as the best ski resort in eastern North America. A fake, pedestrian 'tourist village' of shops, restaurants and condos has been built at the foot of the south side of the mountain, re-creating the feel of a 19th-century village but with 20th-century style and excess. Some original buildings remain close to the mountain; all others were constructed later, some recalling architecture in Old Québec City.

Information
There are several tourist offices in the area. The largest is in St Jovite (☎ 425-3300, e bitr@citenet.net), at 305 chemin Brébeuf; it's open 9am to 7pm daily late June to early September, 9am to 5pm daily the rest of the year. Near Mont Tremblant Village, there's an office (☎ 425-2434) at 1001 Montée Ryan,

---

What's in a Name?

In 2000, several villages were amalgamated under the confusing moniker Ville de Mont Tremblant. This municipality is composed of St Jovite, the main town, mostly an administrative and service center off Rte 117 of limited tourist interest; Mont Tremblant Village, 4km from the ski hill where most tourists shop, stay and eat; and several other small localities.

To further discombobulate people, the ski hill, resort and so-called tourist village is referred to as either Mont Tremblant, Station Tremblant (as used in this guide; 'Tremblant Resort' in English) or more often simply Tremblant. In this text, we divide Ville du Mont Tremblant according to the specific designations; however, they appear bracketed on road signs – for example: Ville de Mont Tremblant (St Jovite). With all these Tremblants running around everywhere – don't forget it's also the name of the actual mountain, which forms part of the provincial Parc du Mont Tremblant – the word seems to lose meaning!

THE LAURENTIANS

THE LAURENTIANS

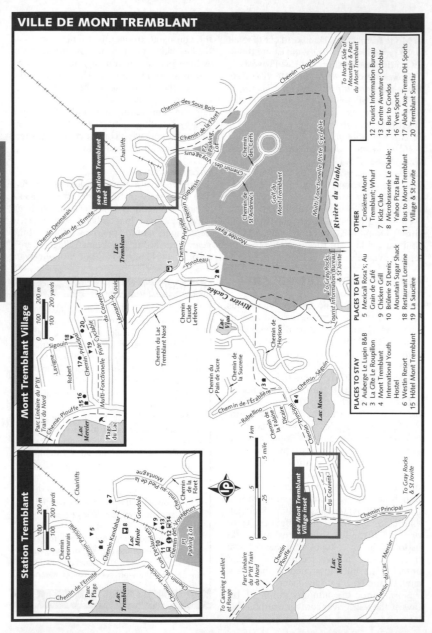

VILLE DE MONT TREMBLANT

Station Tremblant

Mont Tremblant Village

see Station Tremblant inset

see Mont Tremblant Village inset

PLACES TO STAY
2 Auberge Le Lupin B&B
3 La Gîte Le Roupillon
4 Mont Tremblant International Youth Hostel
6 Westin Resort
15 Hôtel Mont Tremblant

PLACES TO EAT
5 Mexicali Rosa's; Au Grain de Café
9 Chicken Grill
10 Brûlerie St Denis; Mountain Sugar Shack
18 Restaurant Lorraine
19 La Saucière

OTHER
1 Croisières Mont Tremblant; Wharf
7 Kidz Club
8 Microbrasserie Le Diable; Yahoo Pizza Bar
11 Bus to Mont Tremblant Village & St Jovite
12 Tourist Information Bureau
13 Centre Aventure; Octobar
14 Bus to Condos
16 Yves Sports
17 Aloha Axe-Treme DH Sports
20 Tremblant Sunstar

at the corner of Rte 327 (which becomes chemin Principal). A tourist information bureau kiosk is in Station Tremblant (☎ 681-3000 ext 46642), on the Place des Voyageurs.

For Internet access, try Au Grain de Café (☎ 681-4567), in the Le St Bernard building of Station Tremblant – though they rob you of $10 an hour for the privilege.

Special Events

The resort hosts a slew of festivals and events all year long. For more details, see ⓦ www.tremblant.com, or call ☎ 88-TREM-BLANT (☎ 888-736-2526).

The most popular celebration is the **Festival International du Blues**, the country's biggest blues festival, held in mid-July. It's three days long and is jam-packed with great talent: In 2001 Colin James, Mel Brown, Sandra Hall and Bad Berger were in the lineup.

Other worthwhile events include the **Molson Ex Pro Challenge**, four days of snowboarding and freeski competitions in early April. **Music in the Mountains**, in the first days of September, is an original assembly of concerts, from classical to contemporary, and a wide variety of events and contests to keep things lively. It's also a good place to celebrate Canada Day (July 1) – as if there aren't that many good places in Québec!

Mont Tremblant Village

This sweet, tiny village barely spreads beyond chemin Principal, the main road on which you'll find all the essential services, as well as a funky youth hostel. The P'tit Train du Nord bike trail slithers beside the village's west side, along the shores of Lac Mercier. Another bike path, which comes right into town, snakes eastward toward the ski hill and takes in some lovely scenery.

Yves Sports (☎ 425-1377, ⓔ yvessport@ qc.aira.com, 1908 chemin Principal) is a well-equipped sports and camping store that rents canoes, bikes and inline skates, and offers an array of guided excursions. For bike rental, count on $23/30 for hybrid/mountain bike. Aloha Axe-Treme DH Sports (☎ 425-0633, 325-0198, ⓔ jwhy69@hotmail.com, 1984 chemin Principal) is a smaller outfit but no less colorful thanks to its eccentric owner. He

THE LAURENTIANS

MARK LIGHTBODY

Cozy Mont Tremblant Village

rents various bikes (none with suspension, though; $15/day), does bike repairs and has lots to say about lots of things.

Places to Stay Run by Intrawest, Tremblant Sunstar (☎ 800-754-8736, W www.tremblantsunstar.com, 2001 chemin Principal) can help find you accommodations of any kind in the area – from campgrounds to luxury condos, chalets and resorts. Though prices for some higher-end options can be stellar, one-bedroom condos can be found for around $100. Sunstar can also arrange transport from Dorval Airport in Montréal.

Camping Labellet et Rouge (☎ 686-1954, *P'tit Train du Nord trail km 98.3)* Tent sites $16. If you're not camping in the Parc du Mont Tremblant, this site, 7km north of Mont Tremblant Village just off the bike trail, is a good option. They can arrange to drive your luggage to other campgrounds farther north or south.

Mont Tremblant International Youth Hostel (☎ 425-6008, W *www.hostellingtremblant.com, 2213 chemin Principal)* Dorm beds $18/21/23 HI member/Canadian nonmember/international nonmember, doubles $48/58 HI member/nonmember, kids under 12 free. A popular, often crowded hostel (reserve as far in advance as possible), it has a kitchen, laundry room, small but lively bar, Internet access and a nice view of the surrounding mountains. It also has a free shuttle service to/from the main hostel in Montréal.

La Gîte Le Roupillon (☎ 429-6402, 877-429-6407, e giteleroupillon@qc.aira.com, 2316 chemin Principal)* Singles/doubles $60/80. One of the best B&Bs around, this chalet-style home with a Cathedral ceiling has a spacious, almost decadedly airy feel. It's just east of Mont Tremblant Village, and in the woods right behind it is a bike trail. The owners' cheeriness matches the positive ambience.

Auberge Le Lupin B&B (☎ 425-5474, 877-425-5474, W *www.lelupin.com, 127 rue Pinoteau)* Singles/doubles $79/109. A combo B&B-hotel, this impeccable log house is a few minutes' walk from the beach on Lac Tremblant, halfway between the village and the resort.

Hôtel Mont Tremblant (☎ 425-3232, 888-887-1111, 1900 chemin Principal)* Doubles from $80. This two-star hotel, right opposite the Lac Mercier beach, has decent and affordable rooms.

Places to Eat The local edible offerings range from family restaurants to romantic bistros.

Restaurant Lorraine (☎ 425-5566, 2000 chemin Principal)* Mains $4-12. Open 6am-10pm daily. A large, no-frills place to get good grub – anything from grilled cheese sandwiches to rib steak, lasagna and that old standby, pizza. There's a kid's menu and a full breakfast menu.

La Saucière (☎ 425-7575, 1991 chemin Principal)* Mains $10-19. Fine French cuisine is the star here, served in a quaint setting. Their full-course daily dinners are a good value.

Station Tremblant

The **skiing** phenomenon here impresses even on paper: 92 slopes (10 expert), vertical drop of 650m, the longest run (La Nansen) of 6km, 248 hectares of skiable terrain and 12 lifts with a capacity to handle over 25,000 people an hour. That's why some 1.2 million people come to Tremblant every winter. Only Whistler gets more.

Accordingly, weekend day passes are considerably higher than at other places: Full-day/half-day passes cost $55/47 for adults, $40/35 for children ages 13 to 17; prices are 30% lower on weekdays. Detractors say that the glitter and glam outshines the slopes at Tremblant and that the prices aren't justified, but most others just get on the snow and have a great time.

There's another ski hill nearby: **Gray Rocks** (☎ 425-2771, 800-567-6767, W *www .grayrocks.com, 525 chemin Principal; adult day pass $25-30; open 8:30am-4:30pm daily).* This much smaller though still pleasant affair, with 22 (mainly intermediate) slopes, is about 5km south of Mont Tremblant Village along Rte 327 (chemin Principal).

Centre Aventure (☎ 681-3000 ext 45564, Chalet des Voyageurs) lays claim to being the biggest renter of skis in North America. Every piece of equipment and stitch of gear is available for winter (and summer!) sports, but beware of next month's whopping Visa bill. A day's rental of skis/snowboard costs $34/37; for hybrid/high-performance bikes it's $30/40.

A glut of other activities are possible onsite or nearby. Croisières Mont Tremblant (☎ 425-1045, 2810 chemin Principal) operates **lake cruises** (adult/child $10-18/5-10) from the main wharf on Lac Tremblant. A central activities center (☎ 681-4848, W www .tremblantactivities.com) takes reservations by phone or online for myriad **watersports** – everything from rafting and sailing to water-skiing and wakeboarding – and **rock-climbing**.

For the less athletic visitor, there's the pedestrian tourist village, which is so colorful it appears candy-coated. It offers distractions and lots of good places to eat or party, if you don't mind that it somewhat resembles an amusement park without the rides. From here you can take a free cable car or the gondola ($12) up the mountain for a panoramic view. Near the foot of the gondola, there's a **Kidz Club** where you can leave the little ones after having them pull maple taffy off snow (no matter the season) in a makeshift *cabane à sucre*, the **Mountain Sugar Shack,** outside the Tour des Voyageurs. And there's always the **beach** at Parc Plage, at Lac Tremblant.

If you're feeling nostalgic once back home, see what's happening at the resort at W www.tremblantwebcams.com.

Places to Stay & Eat Staying here requires big bucks. There are condos, apartments and resort hotels to choose from. You're better to book with Tremblant Sunstar (see the Mont Tremblant Village entry, earlier) or Résidences Mont Tremblant (☎ 800-567-6764, W www.tremblantres .com). Count on a minimum of $250 for double occupancy in a luxury resort, but as little as $90 for a small condo.

Westin Resort (☎ 681-8000, 800-937-8461, 100 chemin Kandahar) Doubles $375. Located on the edge of the tourist village, this five-star luxury hotel pampers you silly.

Chicken Grill (☎ 681-4444, Chalet des Voyageurs) Mains $7-15. A good bet for

good food – and don't worry, their menu is much more exotic than chicken. The upstairs Octobar tends to be the most popular disco/bar in which to unwind after a day on the slopes.

Yahoo Pizza Bar (☎ 681-4616, Vieux Tremblant) Mains $3-9. A trendier-than-thou pizza joint serving slices of the good stuff. They do take-out orders.

Mexicali Rosa's (☎ 681-2439, Le St Bernard) Mains $6-13. A fun though pseudo-Mexican atmosphere greets you here. Try the fajitas.

Brûlerie St Denis (☎ 681-2233, Tour des Voyageurs) Mains $4-8. Mostly salads and sandwiches are on offer here; the real draw is their coffee and desserts.

Microbrasserie Le Diable (☎ 681-4546, Vieux Tremblant) Open 11:30am-3am daily. This relaxed bar has great ambience and serves up local and imported brews.

Parc du Mont Tremblant

One of the province's most spectacular parks (☎ 688-2281, 877-688-2289, chemin du Lac Supérieur; admission $3.50; open 8am-9pm daily), it's also the province's first – it opened in 1894. Covering 1510 sq km of gorgeous Laurentian lakes, rivers, hills and woods, it's divided into three sectors. Rare vegetation (silver maple and red oak, for example) is a distinctive feature of the park; others include hiking and biking trails, canoe routes and wildlife (great blue herons, moose, white-tailed deer, foxes, beavers, black bears…). There are many *campgrounds* in the park, some with amenities but most are basic. Pitching a tent costs $17 to $20.

The most developed area is the Diable sector, whose main feature is beautiful Lac Monroe. Roads are paved and some of the campgrounds have showers. There are incredible hiking trails here, from an easy 20-minute stroll to some with waterfalls to day-long tramps that take in stunning views of majestic valleys. There are bike and nature trails too, as well as canoe rental – a highly rated paddling trip is down the very winding rivière Diable. The Diable sector's main entrance and information center is but 18km east of Station Tremblant.

Farther east, the Pimbina sector is accessible from St Donat. There's also an information center, canoe and kayak rentals, and campgrounds with some amenities. There is swimming at Lac Provost and hiking and biking trails nearby. A highlight in this sector is the **Carcan Trail**, a 14.4km hike to the top of the park's second highest peak (883m), taking in waterfalls and lush scenery along the way.

Still farther east is the Assomption sector, accessible via the town of St Côme, with more trails, secluded cottages and remote camping options. This sector is inaccessible by car in winter, as the roads are not plowed.

The park's wilder interior and far eastern sections are accessible by dirt roads, some of which are old logging routes. Some campsites are accessible only by foot or canoe. The more off-the-track areas abound in wildlife, including bear and moose. With some effort, it's possible to have whole lakes to yourself, except for the wolves whose howls you hear at night. By late August, nights are cold.

Getting There & Around

Limocar (☎ 450-435-6767) buses run from Montréal to St Jovite, Station Tremblant and Mont Tremblant Village at least four times daily ($24, 2¼-3 hours). From St Jovite's bus station there is a free shuttle bus (No 1) to Station Tremblant.

By car from Montréal, take Hwy 15, then Rte 117 (when Hwy 15 ends north of Ste Agathe). Turn north on Montée Ryan, 2km past St Jovite, to head toward Mont Tremblant. As far as parking goes, P2 parking lot is free – if you can find a space – while the slightly more convenient P1 parking lot is paid ($7.50/day).

In town, a free shuttle bus (No 2) goes uphill from Station Tremblant to the condos.

LABELLE & AROUND
☎ 819 • pop 2300

This town, founded in 1880 by its namesake, curé Antoine Labelle, is not of great interest, yet it serves as the gateway to two huge

wildlife reserves. The tourist office (☎ 686-2606), at 7404 boulevard Curé Labelle, is open year-round and can help with making all kinds of reservations. La Douce Aventure (☎ 686-2652, 8 chemin du Camping) offers canoe and kayak expeditions down the rivière Rouge.

The **Réserve Faunique de Papineau Labelle** (☎ 454-2011, 443 Rte 309; admission $3.50; open year-round) is 1628 sq km of wilderness, offering canoe rental, sailing, fishing, 6km of hiking trails and accommodations in chalets and refuges; there is camping as well, but with no services. There are numerous entry points, one of the major ones being close to Labelle: 4km north of town, turn left (west) on chemin La Minerve and follow it to the end (about 15km), where it heads south as chemin des Pionnier. Another entry is via chemin Chapleau from Lac Nominingue. From the Outaouais region, take Rte 315, 321 or 309.

The **Réserve Faunique Rouge Matawin** (☎ 275-1811, 800-665-6527, chemin du Lac Caché; admission $3.50; open daily May-Nov) is somewhat smaller than Papineau Labelle, with 1392 sq km of forests and lakes. It adjoins the Parc du Mont Tremblant to its northwest, with which it shares similar landscape and scenery but with far fewer people. There are ten cabins for rent here, and canoes can be rented for extended trips, but there are no campgrounds per se – only camping sauvage with no services. The easiest access route is north of Labelle via the town of La Macaza; other entrances are via L'Ascension, on Rte 321 north from Rte 117.

LAC NOMININGUE
☎ 819 • pop 2100

Heading north of Labelle, the terrain becomes markedly flatter and the towns less developed – and less touristy. L'Annonciation (pop 3500) may be worth a stop for supplies before heading farther north. The town's tourist office (☎ 275-1622) is inside the old train station, at 682 rue Principale. This is a good place to get information on the entire northern section of the

Laurentians. There are also free concerts here every Friday evening in July and August.

A few kilometers north of town, veer off Rte 117 and head west along Rte 321, which allows you to do a loop around the scenic Lac Nominingue. After 14km you'll come to the municipality of Lac Nominingue, a very pleasant resort town nestled between two lakes and offering a gateway to the **Réserve Faunique de Papineau Labelle**. There's a nice **beach** on chemin des Sureaux in town; 10km out of town, there's a nice, secluded beach arrived at by following chemin Chapleau, then chemin du 7-ème Rang sud.

Lac Nominingue's tourist office (☎ 278-3384 ext 240), at 2150 chemin Tour du Lac, is open 10am to 6pm daily from late June to early September.

Au Boisé du Village (☎ 278-4261, 243 rue Godard) Tent sites $15. This very good campground also offers winter camping. For just $5 per person you can freeze your a** off…that is, enjoy the beautiful snowy landscape and frozen lake. They also offer luggage transport to other campgrounds.

Auberge Villa Bellerive (☎ 278-3802, W www.villabellerive.com, 1596 rue des Tilleuls) Singles/doubles $60/120. Understated luxury is the hallmark of this lovely resort by the lake. There's a private beach and a mini spa, and each room has a kitchenette and is decorated with tasteful elegance.

MONT LAURIER
☎ 819 • pop 8100

The northernmost main town in the Laurentians holds little interest and is even on the somewhat dreary side. However, if you're continuing to the Réserve Faunique la Vérendrye or the Abitibi-Témiscamingue region (see the Northern Québec chapter), you'll need to stock up here first. There are also cheap accommodations here. The tourist office (☎ 623-4544) is at 177 boulevard Albiny-Paquette (Rte 117).

The area south of Mont Laurier, around the town of Ferme Rouge, is quite scenic. There the land rises one last time in the guise of Mont Sir Wilfrid Laurier (783m); otherwise, the terrain is flat, as it is with few exceptions farther north and west.

Le Monde Yvon (☎ 623-9460, 2338 Rte Pierre Neveu) Tent sites $15, chalet doubles $30/person. Just 9km before the end of the P'tit Train du Nord trail, this campground makes a great overnight stop. Right near the banks of Lac des Écorces and the rivière Kiamika, it's a good place for canoeing (you can rent boats there) or just to laze on the beach. There's an on-site convenience store selling organic vegetables. They can also arrange guided tours of the area.

Auberge L'Étape (☎ 623-2400, 800-943-0024, 265 boul Albiny Paquette) Singles/doubles $40/45, suites $72. One of the best of the many inexpensive motels on this strip, this place has very large, if standard,

---

Scenic Drive – Around Mont Laurier

Going north along Rte 117 to Mont Laurier, taking a detour north on Rte 311 then back south on Rte 309 will take you through lovely rural country. Of course, it's a 70km detour, but if you've got time, do it.

On Rte 117, at the town of Lac des Écorces, veer hard right and head north on Rte 311. After 13km you'll come to a covered bridge. Keep going another 17km to the lovely village of Lac St Paul, sitting on a still lake of the same name. After another 7km, at Mont St Michel take Rte 309 back to Mont Laurier. This leg gives you stunning views onto vast plains and farmland with small mountains and rolling hills in the distance. Roll down your window and you'll even catch a whiff of the far north air.

rooms and a large dining room. Suites have Jacuzzi baths.

Dentelle et Croissant *(☎ 623-5363, 309 rue Chapleau)* Singles/doubles from $40/50. This simple home is made welcoming by the gracious owners, very giving and friendly folks who have great respect for their guests' privacy. The breakfasts are notably filling.

Rêve Blanc *(☎ 623-2628, 707 chemin Ferme Rouge)* Doubles from $35. Situated in a forested area by the rivière du Lièvre 12km south of Mont Laurier, this is a dream of a B&B. The rooms are simple but are contained in attractively rustic log houses, and the surrounding nature is very peaceful.

Outaouais

Tucked into Québec's southwest corner – with Ontario as its western border, the Ottawa River (rivière des Outaouais) to the south, the Laurentians to the east and Abitibi-Témiscamingue flanking its northern reaches – the Outaouais (pronounced 'OOH-ta-way') is an interesting blend of influences. Somewhere in this mix, its own personality emerges.

The rivière Outaouais, named by 18th-century Europeans after an Algonquin tribe that resided in the area, forms the region's lifeline. Most of the population is spread out along its shores, which stretch an impressive 1130km. Ontario also exerts its influence in the English nature of many areas in the region. After all, the nation's capital is just across the bridge from Hull, Outaouais' largest metropolitan center.

Aside from the urban center composed of Hull, Gatineau and Aylmer, the 33,000 sq km of Outaouais are divided into three major sections. The lush Gatineau Valley encompasses the pretty communities extending north of Rte 105 all the way to Rte 117, which links the Laurentians and Abitibi-Témiscamingue. Lièvre et Petite Nation (meaning The Hare and the Small Nation), which sounds like a fairy tale, refers to the land extending east toward Montréal (the 'petite nation' in question was the Ouekarinis, an Algonquin tribe from this region who were decimated by the Iroquois). Finally, the Pontiac is the seldom-visited western region, extending to the Ontario border.

Outaouais is a cyclist's dream. Aside from well-marked trails around Hull and through Gatineau Park, the Linear Park trail extends from Low up to Maniwaki, sometimes following Rte 105, sometimes dashing off into the woods. This trails connects with five others totaling over 235km, passing by truly stunning scenery, particularly around Lac Blue Sea. For more information about bicycle trails, contact the

Highlights

- Explore the nation's history in Hull's Canadian Museum of Civilization
- Ride an authentic steam train from Hull to Wakefield along the gorgeous rivière Gatineau
- Uncover your own slice of paradise in Gatineau Park, one of the province's most spectacular
- Bike around stunning Lac Blue Sea
- Set your adrenaline pumping whitewater rafting in the Pontiac region
- Visit the old stomping grounds of Papineau the Patriot at Montebello

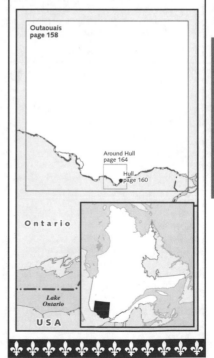

OUTAOUAIS

Société des Parcs Régionaux (☎ 449-6627, ⓦ www.societe-parcs.qc.ca). Any regional tourist office will be able to furnish trail maps.

History

When Samuel de Champlain sailed down Ottawa River in 1613, it was called Mahamoucébé by the Algonquins who lived there. No colonization of the area was permitted (except for part of the Petite Nation sector in the east) as France sought not to disturb the Algonquins, who were needed as allies in the fur trade. This policy didn't change much after the British conquest of 1760. While trappers, missionaries and merchants traveled throughout the area serving their own purposes, it wasn't until the 19th century when settlement began on a large scale.

The political affairs of Europe had a direct effect on the development of this area. Napoleon's Berlin Decree of 1806 effectively forbade Great Britain from gaining access to the forests of the Baltic Sea region, and so England was forced to

look elsewhere for the wood it needed for ship building. What better place to find lumber than in her Canadian colony?

In 1800, Philemon Wright, an American loyalist from Boston, settled with his family (and 25 other farming families he convinced to come with him) in present-day Hull to create a vast agricultural enterprise. In order to subsidize his operations, he heeded England's call for lumber and began extensive forestry operations. Outaouais was soon dubbed 'England's forest reserve.' Thousands of Irish, Scottish, English and American immigrants followed to take part in the burgeoning business. Meanwhile, French Canadians settled only in the Petite Nation region, which had been awarded as a seigneury (a parcel of land given out to be lorded over and tilled under the French regime) since 1674. The pulp and paper industry has continued to be the region's driving motor.

Special Events

February

Winterlude in Hull For the first half of the month, Hull matches Ottawa's more famous Winterlude activities with its own program of snowy fun and games (☎ 595-7400). Sporting, food-related and other events occur in the Parc de la Jacques Cartier, along the riverbank between the Alexandra and Macdonald-Cartier bridges.

June

Artists' Studio Tour Throughout the Pontiac region for a few days in mid-June, this mini-fest (☎ 648-2441) turns artists' studios and workshops into open houses with demonstrations and scheduled events.

July

International Theatre Festival Held in Gatineau, this festival (☎ 986-1292) brings together theatre troupes from around the world for performances. Fireworks and kids' games are also part of the fun.

August

Whitewater Festival Held near Maniwaki in the upper Gatineau Valley, this annual sports event (☎ 449-6627) features descents of the wild rapids of the rivière Gatineau.

September to October

Fall Rhapsody Held in Gatineau Park every weekend from late September through mid-October, this festival (☎ 827-2020, 800-465-1867) celebrates the autumn explosion of color. An arts festival is part of the affair, as are hot-air ballooning, and various concerts and competitions.

HULL
pop 64,000

Hull is as much the other half of Ottawa as it is a separate city (the third largest in Québec). It warrants a visit for more than the famous Canadian Museum of Civilization. In late 2001, the name of Hull was officially changed to Gatineau as part of a political amalgamation agenda of various towns. At street level, this part will be called Hull for many years yet, and that's how it's referred to in this book. Though it has its share of government offices and workers cross the river in both directions each day, Hull feels markedly dissimilar from Ottawa (which is covered in its own chapter). The architecture is different and the population almost entirely French (though it seems more bilingual than Ottawa; more people speak English in French-majority Hull than there are French-speakers in English-majority Ottawa).

Hull used to be known as Ottawa's party central: As soon as boring old Ontario shut down its bars at 1am, the bar-hopping crowd would skip across the bridge and continue the party until 3am. The two cities have since harmonized their closing times (2am, a soggy compromise) to avoid accidents and drunken brawls. Promenade du Portage, easily found from either Pont du Portage or Pont Alexandra, is the main downtown street, with a concentration of bars, restaurants and discos. It's not quite the wild place it once was, but club-goers there still know how to have fun.

Philemon Wright was the person to kick-start settlement in the region (there wasn't any town called Ottawa when he arrived in present-day Hull in 1800). He started a large farm and in 1837 built his humble stone house behind it. Today, that house, at

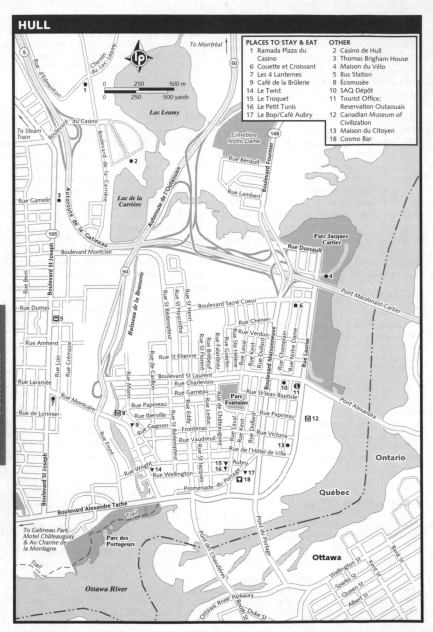

HULL

To Montréal

PLACES TO STAY & EAT
1 Ramada Plaza du Casino
6 Couette et Croissant
7 Les 4 Lanternes
9 Café de la Brûlerie
14 Le Twist
15 Le Troquet
16 Le Petit Tunis
17 Le Bop/Café Aubry

OTHER
2 Casino de Hull
3 Thomas Brigham House
4 Maison du Vélo
5 Bus Station
8 Écomusée
10 SAQ Dépôt
11 Tourist Office; Reservation Outaouais
12 Canadian Museum of Civilization
13 Maison du Citoyen
18 Cosmo Bar

0   250   500 m
0   250   500 yards

Lac Leamy

Chemin du Lac Leamy

Rue d'Edmonton

Boulevard du Casino

Boulevard de la Carrière

Autoroute de la Gatineau

To Steam Train

Rue Gamelin

Rue Berri

Rue Dumas

Rue Amherst

Rue Laramée

Rue de Lorimier

Boulevard St-Joseph

Boulevard Montclair

Rue Lois

Rue Crémazie

Rue Montcalm

Rue Front

Rue Wright

Boulevard Alexandre Taché

Ruisseau de la Brasserie

Lac de la Carrière

Autoroute de l'Outaouais

Cimetière Notre Dame

Rue Bériault

Rue Lambert

Rue Dussault

Parc Jacques Cartier

Boulevard Fournier

Pont Macdonald-Cartier

Boulevard Sacré Coeur

Rue Chénier

Rue Verdun

Rue St-Henri

Rue St-Hyacinthe

Rue Brébeuf

Rue Redempteur

Rue Guertin

Rue Falardeau

Rue St-Florent

Rue St-Étienne

Rue Ste-Hélène

Rue Laval

Rue Kent

Rue Dollard

Rue Champlain

Rue Notre Dame

Boulevard Maisonneuve

Rue Laurier

Boulevard St Laurent

Rue Charlevoix

Rue Garneau

Rue Papineau

Rue Iberville

Rue Gagnon

Rue de Carillon

Rue Morin

Rue Eddy

Rue Leduc

Rue de Châteauguay

Frontenac

Rue Vaudreuil

Rue St-Jacques

Rue Redempteur

Parc Fontaine

Rue St-Jean Baptiste

Rue Papineau

Rue Victoria

Rue de l'Hôtel de Ville

Aubry

Rue Wellington

Promenade du Portage

Pont Alexandra

Ontario

Québec

Ottawa

Maison du Citoyen

Pont du Portage

Pont des Chaudières

To Gatineau Park, Motel Châteauguay & Au Charme de la Montagne

Parc des Portageurs

Trail

Ottawa River

Ottawa River Parkway

Booth St

Duke St

Wellington St

Sparks St

Queen St

Albert St

Kent St

Bank St

OUTAOUAIS

376 boulevard St Joseph, is known as the Thomas Brigham House (named after a later owner) and harbors a computer software company. Its interior staircase is rumored to be haunted, but that's another story. Wright was the driving force behind the nascent forestry industry in Québec, but in his spare time he founded a brewery too – after all, man cannot live on industry alone!

While on the subject of alcohol, the government alcohol shop operates a warehouse here, which sells discounted booze in bulk. The SAQ Dépôt (☎ 777-1955), at 210 rue Champlain (it's just a two-minute stagger to the tourist office) is a rare place in Québec to get cheap liquor.

Information

The super-helpful tourist office (☎ 778-2222, 800-265-7822) is at 103 rue Laurier, a few steps from the Museum of Civilization. Open year-round, they can also give you free day-parking permits to be used around Hull. You can then park your car in Hull and walk to Ottawa, where parking is a headache. In the same complex is Reservation Outaouais (☎ 800-265-7822, W www.western-quebec-tourism.org), a government-sponsored agency that can book hotel rooms and organize package tours – everything from romantic getaways in places with a Jacuzzi to weekend canoeing or rafting adventures.

There's free (!) Internet access and printer service at the Maison du Citoyen (City Hall; ☎ 595-7460), 25 rue Laurier. It's open 10am to 9pm Monday to Thursday, 10am to 6pm Friday. The modern building itself is worth a gander, with its 20m-high glass tower.

The freebies continue (gratis services are one of the perks of visiting government capital areas) at Maison du Vélo (☎ 997-4356), at 350 rue Laurier, which lends out bicycles for free upon presentation of a valid ID. This may be the best deal in the province. Run by a non-profit organization of volunteers who patrol the bike paths, these folks provide information about cycling circuits (there are over 200km of trails in the region) and can even repair your bike if you run into trouble! Plus, they're situated in a beautiful house dating from 1892. The office is open from 9am to 8pm Monday to Friday, 9am to 5pm Saturday and Sunday, from May through October.

Things to See & Do

Canadian Museum of Civilization This is the area's feature museum (☎ 776-7000, W www.civilization.ca, 100 rue Laurier; adult/senior/child $8/6/4; open 9am-6pm Fri-Wed, 9am-9pm Thur May-Oct; 9am-5pm Tues & Wed, Fri-Sun, 9am-9pm Thur Nov-Apr). It's in the large, striking complex with the copper domes, on the river opposite the Parliament buildings. Designed by architect Douglas Cardinal, the building is meant to represent geological shapes, eroded by wind and glaciers. Allow the better part of a day to seriously explore its 100,000 sq m of exhibition space, as do over 1.4 million visitors each year. (The museum is free 4pm-9pm Thur & Fri July & Aug, 4pm-9pm Thur Sept-June).

The museum is principally concerned with the history of Canada. The magnificent **Grande Gallerie** (Grand Hall) of the lower level, with its simulated forest and seashore, explores Native Canadian cultures and offers explanations of the huge totems and other Pacific coastal Native Canadian structures.

Upstairs the **Salle du Canada** presents displays and realistic re-creations tracing the story of the first European explorers of North America, their settlement, and historical developments through to the 1880s. The Basque ship section, complete with the sound of creaking wood in the living quarters, brings to life the voyages undertaken to reach the New World. Be sure to get the free audio tour.

Also particularly good are the Acadian farm model and the replica of the early Québec town square. There are also replicas of a train station, a Ukrainian church from Alberta and the scene of a worker's strike in Winnipeg. Throughout, film and audio clips as well as historical objects help give a more complete picture of various facets of Canadian history.

OUTAOUAIS

The **Salle des Premiers Peuples** (First Nations Hall) has permanent and temporary exhibits on the art – painting, dance, crafts and more – of Canada's native peoples. The entertaining and educational **Musée Canadien des Enfants** (Children's Museum) includes some excellent interactive exhibits designed for the little ones.

Be sure to check out the other halls, which feature excellent temporary exhibits.

Cineplus, inside the museum, shows realistic large-format IMAX and Omnimax films. The IMAX screen is 26m wide and 19m high; the Omnimax screen is 23m in diameter and dome-shaped, hanging overhead. The ever-changing shows are extremely popular, with waits of two to three shows not uncommon, so arrive early for a ticket. Film tickets are purchased separately (admission is not included in the museum ticket); prices vary depending on the show but tend to be around $10.

There is a good cafeteria, which offers, among other things, sandwiches and a salad bar or economical full meals, all served within view of the river and Parliament Hill. The museum bookstore and gift shop are worth a browse. Bus No 8, which runs along Albert St in Ottawa, brings you straight to the museum. If you're driving, there's parking under the building.

Écomusée Much less frequented than the Canadian Museum of Civilization but highly worth a visit is this natural history museum (☎ 595-7790, 170 rue Montcalm; adult/child 4-15 $5/4; open 10am-5pm daily), set up on the premises where Philemon Wright founded his brewery. You might think this museum has bitten off more than it can chew by setting out to explain the origins of our planet, but it does a pretty good job. There are displays on global warming and local geology, but more popular are the 5000 insect specimens on display, a replica of *Styracosaurus albertensis* (a prairie dinosaur) and the earthquake simulation room, which might make you toss your cookies after replicating a 7.0 earthquake.

Casino de Hull This posh gambling hall (☎ 772-2100, 800-665-2274, 1 boul du Casino; admission free; open 11am-3am daily) draws busloads of gambling tourists. There's parking, docking facilities and a helipad. It's somewhat dressy and is situated north of the center, off the third exit after going over the Macdonald-Cartier Bridge from Ottawa.

Steam Train A great way of seeing the stunning scenery of the Gatineau Valley is to ride from Hull to Wakefield on an authentic 1907 steam train (☎ 778-7246, 800-778-5007, W www.steamtrain.ca, 165 rue Deveault; adult/student $29/25 roundtrip; departs Hull at 10am or 1:30pm, depending on the day). In addition to the view, you get two hours to wander around placid Wakefield before heading back.

Places to Stay

Couette et Croissant (☎ 771-2200, 330 rue Champlain) Singles/doubles $55/65. This pleasant B&B is situated close to the Museum of Civilization. The house charms from first sight with its white picket fence and wicker chair sitting invitingly on the porch; the interiors are just as attractive.

Les 4 Lanternes (☎ 777-7755, 888-977-7755, 132 boul St Joseph) Singles/doubles $60/75. A delightful B&B in an old section of Hull, it boasts comfortable decor in an early 20th-century home.

Motel Châteauguay (☎ 595-1000, 877-595-5100, 469 boul Alexandre Taché) Singles/doubles $65/75. This is one of the better motels on this street. For $130, you get a room with a hot tub and a fireplace.

Au Charme de la Montagne (☎ 455-9158, 368 chemin Crégheur) Doubles $55-65. This is a cozy log-cabin-cum-B&B, right on the bank of a lovely little river about 20km west of town (follow Rte 148 until just past Breckenridge). They also organize excellent canoe trips down the Ottawa River.

Ramada Plaza du Casino (☎ 777-7538, 800-296-9046, 75 rue Edmonton) Doubles $220. This swank place is for those who have won lots of money at the nearby casino. It's all about four-star luxury.

OUTAOUAIS

Places to Eat

Café de la Brûlerie (☎ 778-0109, 152 rue Montcalm) Mains $4-8. There are good soups and sandwiches here, but the real attractions are the strong coffee and friendly surroundings.

Le Twist (☎ 777-8886, 88 rue Montcalm) Mains $5-10. This retro café has small meals like hamburgers and salads. Try their specialty, mussels and fries.

Le Petit Tunis (☎ 771-8241, 39 rue Laval) Mains $7-14. This small Tunisian restaurant has a great atmosphere – it's laden with cushions and sofas. There's a lot covering the walls to feast your eyes upon as you wait for the delicious food.

Le Troquet (☎ 776-9595, 41 rue Laval) Mains $6-13. A very popular place to eat a variety of meat, seafood and vegetarian meals, it has a laid-back feel and would be a 'granola' hangout if it weren't for all the government workers here at lunchtime. It turns into an even more popular bar at night. Some nights, it attracts a young (under 20 crowd); other times, the clientele are over 25.

Le Bop/Café Aubry (☎ 777-3700, 9 rue Aubry) Mains $7-16. Another extremely popular place with innovative dishes and friendly staff, this café turns into a bar come evening. There are 2-for-1 beers from 4pm to 9pm daily.

Cosmo Bar (☎ 771-6677, 117 Promenade du Portage) This is a trendy, nicely decorated lounge bar, and is pretty hot at the moment. There are '80s theme nights to keep martini-sipping 30-somethings happy; house and ambient spins other nights.

Getting There & Away

The Outaouais Bus System (☎ 770-3242) operates buses along Rideau and Wellington Sts in Ottawa. From downtown Ottawa, bus Nos 33, 35 and 42 all go to Promenade du Portage. Bus No 8 goes to the Canadian Museum of Civilization.

The bus station (☎ 771-2442) is at 238 boulevard St Joseph. There are ten daily buses to/from Montréal ($35, 3 to 4 hrs), but none is direct; they either do a milk run or go through Ottawa first. There are also three daily buses to/from Maniwaki ($18, 2½ hrs), stopping in the small towns along the way.

AROUND HULL

Only a short drive from Hull are the lush wilderness and nearly limitless outdoor possibilities of Gatineau Park and nearby ski hills. There are also several quaint villages like Chelsea and the area's jewel, Wakefield, which seems to have been time-warped to its present location from the early 20th century.

Gatineau Park

This deservedly popular park (☎ 827-2020, 800-465-1867, W www.capcan.ca/gatineau/, 33 rue Scott; adult/child $4/2; open 9am-6pm daily mid-May–Aug, 9am-5pm daily Sept & Oct) is a 356-sq-km protected area of woods and lakes in the Gatineau Hills, northwest of downtown Hull. It's only a 20-minute drive from the Parliament Buildings in Ottawa, and there's a road leading directly into it from central Hull, off of boulevard Alexandre Taché.

The visitors center (same ☎ and hours) is 12km from Hull, off Hwy 5 in Old Chelsea. On weekends some roads may be closed to cars, and note that parking is charged at the more popular destinations such as Lac Meech and the King Estate.

Things to See & Do The park has plenty of **wildlife**, including about 230 species of birds (such as the great blue heron, turkey vulture and warbler), as well as trails trails trails: 150km for **hiking** and 90km for **biking**. Lac La Pêche, Lac Meech and Lac Philippe have beaches for **swimming** and thus are the most popular. Lac Meech has a nude gay beach.

Canoeing is most popular at Lac La Pêche, where you can rent boats ($9/hour, $25/day). You can fish in the lakes and streams, and the hiking trails are good for cross-country skiing in winter (there are 185km of ski trails). Small Lac Pink is pretty but is off limits for swimming. However, a boardwalk circles the lake for **strolling**.

Also in the park is Moorside, the summer estate of eccentric William Lyon Mackenzie

AROUND HULL

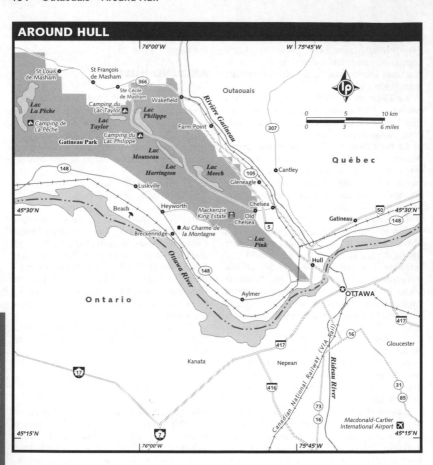

King, Canadian prime minister in the 1920s, late 1930s and early 1940s. Here he indulged his hobby of collecting ruins, both genuine and fake. In 1941, King had bits of London's House of Commons brought over after the German blitz. The **Mackenzie King Estate** (☎ 827-2020, 800-465-1867; adult/child $4/3; open 11am-5pm Mon-Fri, 10am-6pm Sat & Sun mid-May–mid-Oct) is now a museum. An astute politician, King was much interested in the occult and apparently talked to both his dead dog and deceased mother, and consulted mystics to help out on important parliamentary decisions.

Your best bet is to take a stroll of the grounds, beyond the fake ruins through the forest left to grow wild, according to King's wishes. You'll see solid old maple, fir, ash and pine trees.

Organized Tours The Gatineau Park International Hostel (see under Chelsea) organizes overnight or several day bike, canoe, snowshoe and ski excursions through the park ranging in price from $40 to $100, depending on length of desired stay. They run several log cabins on a beautiful, isolated spot on the eastern end of Lac La Pêche.

Places to Stay & Eat There are three campgrounds (☎ 456-3016, 456-3134 to reserve) in the park. These fill up quickly almost any weekend in summer, so reserve ahead of time. There are also rustic refuges with bunk beds for $24 per person.

Camping de La Pêche Tent sites $16. This campground is the far-western sector of the park and is popular with canoe-campers.

Camping du Lac Taylor Tent sites $18. In many ways this is the park's loveliest campground – there are only 34 sites but it's in a dream location where you'll feel thoroughly ensconced in nature. Lac Taylor is perfect for **swimming**, especially under a full moon. Note that sound echoes crisply here, and you're expected to keep things quiet.

Camping du Lac Philippe Tent sites $19. The largest campground in the park, it can hold 300 campers and is great for families.

There's a pleasant tearoom, *Salon de Thé Moorside* (☎ 827-3405), attached to the Mackenzie King Estate residence, with items such as cucumber sandwiches or Black Forest ham on pumpernickel bread. There are no other on-site restaurants; stock up on food in Ottawa, Hull, Chelsea or Wakefield before going to the park for an extended time.

Getting There & Away Public transport does not go directly in the park, leaving you dependent on your car or bike to get you there from Ottawa/Hull. You can consider, however, taking the bus to the Gatineau Park International Hostel (see Places to Stay in the Chelsea section), from where hiking, biking and ski trails lead directly into the park.

Chelsea
pop 6500

Chelsea is the name given to a fusion of small villages just off Rte 105 north of Hull. The region stretches between Old Chelsea, just 12km north of Hull and the main gateway to Gatineau Park, and Farm Point, just south of Wakefield.

This lovely area was built up after 1850, during the golden age of the forestry industry. The population includes a number of parliamentary members and artists galore, and about half are English-speaking.

There are many galleries and artist studios worth visiting. **Reid McLachlan** (☎ 827-4159, 899 Rte 105) is an oil painter whose fanciful works combine a moving realism with playful fantasy. Photographer **Brenda Lee Wilson** (☎ 827-0408, 22 chemin Marie Jo) displays her works at her studio, on the banks of the rivière Gatineau near Gleneagle, north of Old Chelsea. If you're into wood sculptures, check out the work of **Alex MacKenzie** (☎ 827-4336, 1359 Rte 105).

Want a tad more of a thrill? Listen to the masochist within you and brave the nearby **Great Canadian Bungee** (☎ 459-3714, W www.bungee.ca). They boast the highest bungee jump on the continent (200ft above a clear blue lagoon; adult/student $87/67), and their Riptide is a thrilling 1015ft cable slide ($30).

Places to Stay Accommodations in Chelsea are limited, but the one choice is an excellent choice.

Gatineau Park International Hostel (☎ 459-3180, W www.magma.ca/~carman, 66 chemin Carman) Dorm beds HI member/ nonmember $20/24. This HI hostel consistently gets great reviews. It makes an excellent base for exploring Gatineau Park (see that section) and a fine retreat in its own right. With 80 acres linked to the park, there is no end of outdoor possibilities. Cycling, hiking, canoeing and cross-country skiing are all available.

The hostel has its own licensed restaurant and organic greenhouses. Other features are a sauna, fireplace and family rooms. Book ahead as capacity is only 30. By the end of 2002, they'll have a brand-new building combining hotel luxury (restaurant, spa) with a hostel feel (kitchen, many common areas). The double rooms there will cost around $60.

The hostel is near Farm Point, in Chelsea. The Ottawa-Hull-Maniwaki Greyhound bus will let you off right nearby on Rte 105 – you can request the stop when you get on. The more adventurous can get off at Wakefield (request a stop on Rte 105, not in the village itself) and ski or bike along forest trails P17, No 52 and No 57 straight to the hostel (about 5km).

Places to Eat Unlike accommodations, there are several establishments in which to sate your hunger.

L'Agaric (☎ 827-3030, 254 chemin Old Chelsea) Mains $9-16. The French cuisine is excellent here in the charming and rustic surroundings.

Les Fourgères (☎ 827-8942, 783 Rte 105) Mains $19-35. Considered the finest restaurant in the area, it cooks fabulous French cuisine.

Boucanier Chelsea (☎ 827-1925, 706 Rte 105) This store sells smoked fish, fresh seafood and other goodies you can pack up for a picnic.

Wakefield
pop 2000
Founded in 1830, Wakefield is nestled in an incredibly scenic bend of the rivière Gatineau. The main street in town, chemin de la Rivière, is distinguished by the preserved Victorian homes and fine shops that line it. As charming as the village is, thankfully it doesn't have the gentrified, cutesy air that makes some Eastern Townships villages feel cold and elitist. Anglophones are in the majority here (the main street is also referred to as both Riverside Drive and River Road).

Picnic tables are dotted on parkland along the river, perfect spots to have a nibble as you gaze dreamily onto the river. Kayaks and canoes ($35/day) as well as bicycles ($27/day) can be rented at Radisson (☎ 459-3860), 172 chemin de la Rivière, who also organizes nature excursions in Gatineau Park.

There are numerous art galleries in town. Portrait photographer **Hélène Anne Fortin** (☎ 459-2161, 5 chemin Burnside) gives slide shows of her work between 1pm and 9pm daily.

There are three downhill ski stations nearby. **Edelweiss** (☎ 459-2328, chemin Edelweiss Rte 366; day pass $20-31; open 9am-10pm Mon-Sat, 8:30am-4pm Sun) has 18 slopes and a vertical drop of 200m; its longest run is an impressive 1524m. There are also 27km of great cross-country ski

trails. **Mont Cascades** (☎ 827-0301, 448 chemin Mont Cascades; day pass $15-25; open 10am-10pm Tues-Sat, 9am-5pm Sun & Mon) has 16, slightly easier slopes. **Vorlage** (☎ 459-2301, Ⓦ www.skivorlage.com, 65 chemin Burnside; day pass $15-25; open 9am-10pm Mon-Sat, 9am-5pm Sun) is another good choice, with 15 good slopes, even though the vertical drop is only 152m.

Places to Stay & Eat Wakefield has several desirable sleeping and dining options.

Gîte D'Antan (☎ 459-1814, 29 chemin Burnside) Singles $45/50. Near the Vorlage ski station, this small B&B makes a nice retreat.

Motel-Café Algengruss (☎ 459-2885, 831 chemin de la Rivière) Singles/doubles $55/65. Set up in a rustic style with brick walls and omnipresent wood, this is a comfortable, simple option right in town.

Wakefield Mill Inn (☎ 459-1838, 888-567-1838, 60 chemin Mill) Singles/doubles from $85/130. This more luxurious option, outside the center, is known for its excellent service.

Wakefield Bakery (☎ 459-1528, 813 chemin de la Rivière) Meals $5-8; open 6am-8pm Sun-Thur, 6am-9pm Fri & Sat. This great bakery, set up as an old general store, is *the* perfect place for picnic supplies. In addition to sinful desserts, they prepare hot meals to go, often vegetarian or world cuisine.

La Maison Earle (☎ 459-1028, 1 chemin Valley Drive) Mains $6-14; open 7am-11pm daily. With a terrace overlooking the river, this is a great place, even to just hang out. They serve hearty omelets and breakfasts until noon (they understand how it is...) as well as light meals like quiches and salads plus daily specials like lasagna. The bar section is popular at night.

Café Pot au Feu (☎ 459-2080, 794 chemin de la Rivière) Mains $7-14; open 11am-10pm Sun-Thur, 11am-11pm Fri & Sat. Serving the tastiest selections in town is this relaxed place with dishes like lamb and black bean stew ($11). There's a salad bar too.

Getting There & Away A tourist steam train arrives daily from Hull (see that section for details).

Voyageur (☎ 771-2442) runs three daily buses from Ottawa and Hull ($6, 45 mins), which can be flagged for a stop at Wakefield.

BLUE SEA
pop 672
This dream town is about 20km south of Maniwaki, west of Rte 105 (going north, veer onto chemin de Blue Sea at Gracefield). Picturesque and tranquil, the village sits on the south shore of the lake of the same name and is perfect for a quiet day or two. A **biking** trail, the Circle, is a 25km shared asphalt path around the lake, offering nice views. Another trail, the 75km Deer trail, starts nearby and leads inland, past more lakes.

Places to Stay
Camping Manoir du Lac Blue Sea (☎ 465-5351, 888-903-5351, 9 chemin du Manoir) Tent sites $12, family cottages $350/wk. Perched on the northern tip of the lake, this campground also rents paddle boats, motor boats, canoes and surfbikes.

Chez Nap (☎ 771-0739, ⓔ cheznap@ireseau.com, 4 cheminde la Gare) Singles/doubles $45/55. This B&B has a wonderful, harmonious atmosphere. Every room in the house has been transformed into a personalized ode to the co-owner's grandparents (who used to live on this site since 1925), with old photos and furniture completing the picture. Cozy, charming, and boasting a nice veranda for breakfasts, it's also next to a bike trail.

MANIWAKI
pop 4600
This town is the forestry capital of the Gatineau Valley. Half of the population is Algonquin (who call the place Kitigan Zibi), descendants of the Anishnabeg tribe. The **Mawandoseg Kitigan Zibi** (☎ 449-6074, *311 rue Principale Sud; adult/child $4/3; open 10am-5pm Wed-Sun June–early Sept)* is an exhibition center dedicated to preserving and explaining traditional native customs such as canoe building and arts and crafts. There are regular demonstrations, and you can taste some homemade *bannik,* a tasty bread made from different grains or from corn flour, often snazzed up with raisins, nuts, almonds, dates or prunes.

The tourist office (☎ 449-6627) is at 156 rue Principale Sud and can help set you up with everything from a rafting expedition to renting an ATV (zooming around on the quad trails is a popular sport here). Right outside the office is the **Parc du Draveur,** a bit of green space that pays homage to the loggers and raftsmen of the area's forestry industry with a large steel statue by Donald Doiron.

The **Centre d'Interpretation de la Protection de la Forêt de la Feu** *(Interpretative Center for Protection Against Forest Fire; ☎ 449-7999, 8 rue Comeau; admission $2; open 10am-5pm Tues-Sun)* explains the specialized techniques local firefighters have developed to battle forest fires. Their advanced methods, incorporating satellites and computers, are studied by many firefighters from abroad. Part of the exhibit is in the form of a makeshift forest trail.

For rafting, canoe and kayak rentals and expeditions, contact Extrême Plein Air (☎ 441-2726), headquartered in Maniwaki. They also rent a full range of winter-sports gear including skis and snow rafts. All reservations are done by phone.

Places to Stay & Eat
The selection of accommodations isn't so great here, but there are several cheap motels.

Motel Central (☎ 449-6868, 149 rue Principale Sud) Singles/doubles $52/57. Near the tourist office, this is a friendly motel with thoroughly unmemorable but decent rooms.

Auberge du Draveur (☎ 449-7022, 877-449-7022, 85 rue Principale Nord) Singles/doubles $69/79. It's definitely a step up from the Motel Central, but equally unmemorable. Their suite with Jacuzzi is spacious and very nice, and their restaurant is pretty good.

Château Logue (☎ 441-1370, ⓦ www.chateaulogue.com, 12 rue Comeau) Doubles $89, suites $129-164. The top place in town was built in 1887 by Irish businessman Charles Logue, in full-on Second Empire style. There's lots of green space around it, a

OUTAOUAIS

built-in art gallery and a superb restaurant-bar with main courses ranging from $9 to $18. The hotel can organize activities and sports packages.

PONTIAC

This area, just west of Hull, is among Québec's wildest. Aside from Rte 148 snaking timidly along the province's southern border and the small communities that extend from it, the area is a labyrinth of lakes and forests. Accordingly, many people from the Ottawa-Hull region visit for some adventure on the water. Whitewater rafting and canoeing are popular sports in the region.

The town of **Bryson** (pop 740), 86km west of Hull, is on a nice part of land near **Île du Grand Calumet**, named after the calumet, a stone that went into the making of the traditional peace pipe. Back in the days of the steamboat, the town used to be an inland port.

Fort Coulonge (pop 1200), 26km farther west, boasts Québec's second longest covered bridge (le Pont Marchant) as well as the **Chutes de la Rivière Coulonge** (☎ 683-2770, chemin du Bois Francs; adult/child under 12 $5/free; open 8am-8pm daily May-Oct). A small park has been set up around these impressive waterfalls, which descend into a canyon with great force. There are hiking trails, a mini *café* and several old log *cabins* on-site.

Whitewater Rafting

Northwest of Gatineau Park, there are several outfitters who use a turbulent section of the Ottawa River for rafting adventures. Excursions range from a half-day trip to two-day adventures and run from April to October, roughly. No experience is needed and the locations are less than two hours from Ottawa-Hull. Book ahead for weekends, as the trips fill up. You can usually save money by going on weekdays.

Recommended Esprit Rafting (☎ 683-3241, 800-596-7238, W www.espritrafting.com), in Davidson (a tiny village 4km past Fort Coulonge) uses small, bouncy 14-foot, self-bailing rafts and has pickup and delivery

from the Ottawa Hostel and the Gatineau International Youth Hostel. They offer a one-day rafting trip with lunch ($85) and a whole range of longer options and kayaking courses. Good dorm accommodations are available at its rustic river lodge for $20 a night including breakfast and use of canoes and kayaks. You can also camp ($10). If not included in the package, all meals (the barbecue dinners are a treat) are offered: breakfast costs $5, lunch $8 and dinner $17.

Two other reliable organizations are OWL Rafting (☎ 613-646-2263, 800-461-7238, W www.owl-mkc.ca), in Foresters Falls, Ontario, with both wild and mild trips (for thrill-seekers and families), and Aventures Outaouais (☎ 648-5200, 800-690-7238, W www.ottawaadventures.qc.ca), in Bryson, 13km east of Shawbridge. Both offer meals, camping and more expensive cabin accommodations, which should be booked ahead.

Canoeing

Twenty kilometers before Rte 148 slips into Ontario is a great area for canoeing, where the Ottawa River bends around a sharp peninsula and flows around a series of islands. Expéditions Rivière Noire (☎ 778-6347, 613-639-2276), located in Waltham, offers a multitude of canoe trips, from several hours to a week long, all going inland to the wild and beautiful Pontiac landscape.

MONTEBELLO
pop 1140

This lovely village, at the halfway mark between Montréal and Hull along Rte 148, looks markedly different from other Outaouais villages, as it was developed according to the French seigneurial system. From the early 19th century the territory around Montebello belonged to the Québec seminary, under the governance of Louis Joseph Papineau (see 'Papineau the Patriot'). He named the village after his good friend, the duke of Montebello.

The tourist office (☎ 423-5602) is at 502A rue Notre Dame, inside an old train station. It's open from 10am to 6pm daily June through September, 9am to 4pm daily October through May.

Papineau the Patriot

Louis Joseph Papineau was a lawyer when he became Speaker of the Lower Canadian Assembly in 1815. He represented French majority concerns in Québec via the Parti Canadien political party, who were often at odds with the ruling powers in Upper Canada. He also spearheaded opposition to the uniting of Upper and Lower Canada. He knew that unity was merely a method to control potential French opposition and protest. There were 120,000 English in Upper Canada; in Lower Canada, there were 80,000 English and 340,000 French. Through unity, Upper and Lower Canada would have 60 deputies each, assuring English control in government matters.

Papineau won some concessions from London for a time, but parliament strongly objected to his more radical ideas of partial self-government and limiting English interests in Québec, which split his party into moderates and *patriotes*. Still, he held enormous sway with his people and in 1834 convinced Francophones to boycott English institutions and remove their money from English-controlled banks. He was, however, against the armed uprisings that occurred in 1837; In the ensuing pandemonium he fled to the US to avoid arrest.

To many radicals Papineau was considered a sellout, advocating conciliation with the ruling powers via dialogue and threats instead of revolution and rebellion. From the US he went to France and wrote a book on the history of the insurrection in Canada before returning to the Canadian parliament from 1847 to 1854.

Things to See & Do

Manoir Papineau National Historic Site

The history of the area and the French system of seigneurial land allotments is well-explained in this Parks Canada site (☎ 425-6965, 500 rue Notre Dame; adult/child $6/4.50; open 10am-5pm Wed-Sun mid-May–Aug, 10am-5pm Sat & Sun Sept), accessible via the old train station (tourist office). Lord Papineau built this impressive manor, decorated in the Second Empire style, between 1846 and 1850. It remained in his family until a private American club took it over in 1929, at which time its contents were delivered to the University of Toronto, including the 3800 books Papineau kept in his fireproof library on the mezzanine.

On the same site is the **Papineau Memorial Chapel** (☎ 423-5681; admission by donation; open 11am-6pm daily Apr-Nov), built in 1855 by architect Napoléon Bourassa. Eleven members of Papineau's family lay in rest there.

Château Montebello The most elaborate wood log building in the world (☎ 423-6341, 392 rue Notre Dame) is now a luxury hotel. It was built under the auspices of the Canadian Pacific Railway in 1930 using 10,000 red cedar logs to make this star-shaped marvel. It's highly worth a visit, especially to see the inner atrium with its magnificent stone fireplace and wood-paneled balconies.

Parc Oméga This incredible wildlife park (☎ 423-5487, W www.parc-omega.com, Rte 323; adult/child $13/7; open 9:30am-6pm daily June-Sept, 10am-5pm daily Oct-May) covers 1500 acres and features bison, wapitis, moose, black bears, elk, deer, wolves and many other creatures, visible as you drive through a 10km trail inside the park. Through the radio you listen to a guided excursion and hear information about the animals you're checking out. The park is only 3km north of Montebello along Rte 323.

OUTAOUAIS

Ottawa

The capital of Canada evokes mixed emotions – as the nation's capital, it has a statuesque, grand side, yet many visitors consider the city itself less than exciting. Attractive she is, though, as she sits majestically on the south bank of the Ottawa River at the confluence with the Rideau River, and the gently rolling Gatineau Hills of Québec are visible to the north. It's not a terribly lively place, but its streets are wide and clean, and throughout town there's wonderful parkland that acts as a green lung. Another bonus: Most of the land along the waterway is for recreational use.

The government is Ottawa's largest employer, and the stately Gothic-style parliament buildings are attractions in their own right. With its abundance of museums and cultural activities, the city draws five million tourists a year. Many are amused by the traditionally garbed Royal Canadian Mounted Police, known as the Mounties, who patrol on horseback.

HISTORY

The name Ottawa comes from the name of a First Nations tribe who settled on the east side of Lake Huron around 1400. The word itself comes from the Algonquin for 'to trade'; members of the Ottawa tribe were known as traders even before contact with Europeans. There are still about 4000 Ottawa living in Canada, even more in the US.

French explorers arrived as early as the beginning of the 17th century, and missionaries bent on converting the Native Canadians soon followed. The French were dominant in the area, engaging in fur trading and not establishing any major settlements, until the American Revolution sent several hundred Loyalists north.

American Philemon Wright was the area's first settler, setting up shop in present-day Hull (once called Wrightstown). Ottawa was first named Bytown, after Colonel John By, the man responsible for the building of the

Highlights

- Zip along 5km of the frozen Rideau Canal on ice skates in winter

- See Canada's top politicians go at each other's throats during Parliament's Question Period

- Visit the National Gallery, in one of Canada's greatest buildings, and see why it's among the nation's top museums

- Check out some of Canada's oldest Victorian houses in Sandy Hill

- Watch the changing of the guards on Parliament Hill

- Take cover in the fort-com-musuem Diefunbunker, west of town

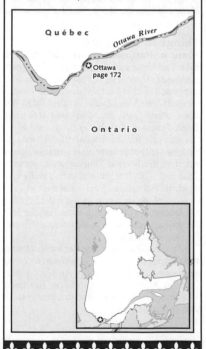

Rideau Canal, the waterway that assured Britain a transport route to the St Lawrence River that didn't go too close to the potentially threatening American border. Bytown and Wrightstown thrived in the first half of the 19th century as forestry centers.

Bytown became Ottawa in 1855. Two years later Queen Victoria chose Ottawa as the capital for her growing colony. She reportedly favored its border location between Upper and Lower Canada, a perfect link between the colony's French and English cultures. There was also a lot of available space to build government buildings. At the time, there was nothing to the small city – only a few stone houses and sawmills littered the landscape. The parliament buildings and Prime Minister Sir Wilfrid Laurier's beautification policies at the end of the century did much to improve Ottawa's looks.

World War II resulted in much growth in Ottawa, as the capital was called upon to act in international affairs. During the war Rideau Hall became the temporary residence of the exiled Dutch royal family – as repayment for the Canadian's kindness, they started a tradition that continues to this day: Holland sends an annual shipment of 100,000 tulip bulbs to beautify the city's parks and green spaces. This generous donation has blossomed into the Canadian Tulip Festival, which sees the city erupt in displays of tulips throughout most of May.

After the war, Jacques Gréber – the man who planned the city of Paris – was in charge of a significant urban renewal project. He removed railway lines from the center, enabling the construction of major new buildings; introduced a green belt around the core; and enlarged Gatineau Park. The green belt was dubbed 'the Capital's Emerald Necklace' and consists of 17,600 hectares of green running about 45km around the city. By century's end, new museums had opened, festivals had been inaugurated and the performing arts scene had grown considerably.

Many of Ottawa's citizens are bilingual, though not as many as in the smaller town of Hull, Québec, which sits across the bridges on the northern bank of the Ottawa River and has been incorporated into Greater Ottawa.

ORIENTATION

Ottawa's central core is quite compact, so walking is a good way to get around. Wellington St, on the western side, is the main east-west street and is home to Parliament Hill and many government buildings. One block south is Sparks St, a pedestrian mall with heaps of shops and fast-food outlets. Bank St crosses Sparks and is the main shopping strip, with many restaurants and several performing arts theaters and cinemas. Just to the west of the canal are Elgin St and large Confederation Square, with the National War Memorial at its center. The gigantic French-style palace here is the Château Laurier hotel.

On the other side of the canal is Ottawa East, with Rideau St as its main drag. The huge Rideau Centre is here, a three-level shopping mall. To the north lies Byward Market, the hub of the restaurant and nightlife district.

Along Wellington St and up Sussex Dr are many 19th-century buildings. Along Sussex Dr between George and St Patrick Sts, walking through the archways or alleys leads to a series of old connected courtyards, where you may find an outdoor café or two.

South of the center, down Bank St, is the Glebe, a more rundown but more hip area where there are used bookshops, antique stores, some alternative clubs and lots of donut shops.

North of downtown, up Sussex Dr and to the left (west) is Nepean Point, at the Alexandra Bridge. The view is well worth the short walk.

There are four bridges across the Ottawa River to Hull. The Pont du Portage (Portage Bridge), which stems from Wellington St on the Ottawa side, plops you out in downtown Hull. (For coverage of Hull, see the Outaouais chapter.)

INFORMATION

The well-stocked, efficient Capital Infocentre tourist office (☎ 239-5000, 800-465-1867, W www.canadacapital.gc.ca) is at 90 Wellington St, opposite the parliament buildings. It's open 8:30am to 9pm daily mid-May to early September, and 9am to 5pm the rest of the year.

OTTAWA

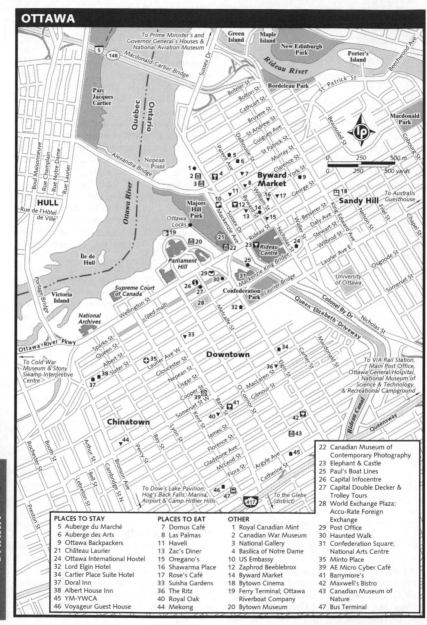

OTTAWA

To Prime Minister's and
Governor General's Houses &
National Aviation Museum

5 148 Macdonald-Cartier Bridge

Green Island
Maple Island
New Edinburgh Park
Porter's Island

Rideau River

Parc Jacques Cartier

Québec | Ontario

Boteler St
Bolton St
Cathcart St
Bruyere St
St Andrew Ave
Guigues Ave
St Patrick St
Murray St
Clarence St
York St

Bordeleau Park

St Patrick St

Macdonald Park

Alexandra Bridge

Nepean Point

Byward Market

Sandy Hill

To Australis
Guesthouse

HULL
Rue de l'Hôtel de Ville

Ottawa River

Majors Hill Park

Ottawa Locks

Île de Hull

Parliament Hill

Confederation Park

Supreme Court of Canada

University of Ottawa

Victoria Island

National Archives

Wellington St

Ottawa River Pkwy

To Cold War Museum & Stony Swamp Interpretive Centre

Sparks St
Queen St
Albert St
Slater St

Downtown

To VIA Rail Station,
Main Post Office,
Ottawa General Hospital,
National Museum of
Science & Technology,
& Recreational Campground

Chinatown

Rideau Canal

Queensway

To Dow's Lake Pavilion,
Hog's Back Falls, Marina,
Airport & Camp Hither Hills

417

To the Glebe
(district)

PLACES TO STAY
5 Auberge du Marché
6 Auberge des Arts
9 Ottawa Backpackers
21 Château Laurier
24 Ottawa International Hostel
32 Lord Elgin Hotel
34 Cartier Place Suite Hotel
37 Doral Inn
38 Albert House Inn
  YM-YWCA
46 Voyageur Guest House

PLACES TO EAT
7 Domus Café
8 Las Palmas
11 Haveli
13 Zac's Diner
15 Oregano's
16 Shawarma Place
17 Rose's Café
33 Suisha Gardens
36 The Ritz
40 Royal Oak
44 Mekong

OTHER
1 Royal Canadian Mint
2 Canadian War Museum
3 National Gallery
4 Basilica of Notre Dame
10 US Embassy
12 Zaphrod Beeblebrox
14 Byward Market
18 Bytown Cinema
19 Ferry Terminal; Ottawa
    Riverboat Company
20 Bytown Museum

22 Canadian Museum of
    Contemporary Photography
23 Elephant & Castle
25 Paul's Boat Lines
26 Capital Infocentre
27 Capital Double Decker &
    Trolley Tours
28 World Exchange Plaza;
    Accu-Rate Foreign
    Exchange
29 Post Office
30 Haunted Walk
31 Confederation Square;
    National Arts Centre
35 Minto Place
39 AE Micro Cyber Café
41 Barrymore's
42 Maxwell's Bistro
43 Canadian Museum of
    Nature
47 Bus Terminal

OTTAWA

Several banks can be found along Sparks St. The Accu-Rate Foreign Exchange, in the World Exchange Plaza, 111 Albert St, 2nd floor, has longer hours and sells traveler's checks. It's open Saturday, too.

There's a post office (☎ 734-7575) at 59 Sparks St, open 9am to 5:30pm weekdays. Poste restante services are available only from the main post office (☎ 800-267-1177), at 1424 Caledon Place, Ottawa, Ontario, K1H 2B6. It's on the east side of the Rideau River, south of Hwy 417, a considerable distance from the center.

Check out ⓦ www.ottawakiosk.com for a good overview of services and attractions in the capital city, together with comprehensive listings. For a list of city festivals throughout the year, see ⓦ www .ottawa-festivals.com.

The AE Micro Cyber Café (☎ 230-9000), 288 Bank St, charges $6 per hour to surf the big ol' Web. It's open 11am to midnight Monday to Friday, 9:30am to 10pm Saturday and 9:30am to 8pm Sunday.

Ottawa General Hospital (☎ 737-7777) is at 501 Smyth Rd. There's also a walk-in clinic, Minto Place (☎ 235-4140), at 344 Slater St between Lyon and Kent Sts.

GOVERNMENT BUILDINGS
Parliament Hill
This striking building (☎ 239-5000, 800-465-1867, 996-0896 tours, Wellington St; admission free; 20-min tours at 20 and 50 mins past the hour, 9:20am-4:50pm daily mid-May–early Sept, 9:20am-3:50pm daily early Sept–mid-May), with its Peace Tower and clock, is home to the Commons and Senate chambers, which can be viewed in session (not during summer). Alongside are the East and West blocks, with their green copper-top roofs. From the top of the Peace Tower, there's an observation deck with a nice view over the city and river. There, the 53-bell Carillon gives mini-concerts at 2pm Monday to Friday in July and August, and at noon Saturday and Sunday from September to June. The **East Block Historic Rooms**, open only in July and August, are four restored Confederation-era rooms in a chamber that was the central government room during Canada's first 100 years.

The building's interior is all handcarved limestone and sandstone, and the **library** is a highlight with its fantastic carved wood and wrought iron. You must reserve for a free 20-minute tour; go to the white tent out on the front lawn in summer, or the indoor desk in winter. Security is tight and includes metal detectors.

At 10am on summer days, the crowds gather in anticipation of the **Changing of the Guard** on the lawns. And summer nights there's a free sound and light show on Parliament Hill – one version in English, one in French.

Pick up a free copy of *Discover the Hill*, with a self-guided tour in and around the buildings.

You may also obtain a pass to sit in on Question Period, the active debate sessions whenever Parliament meets. Just call the House of Commons (☎ 992-4793) or the Senate (☎ 992-4791).

Prime Minister's & Governor General's Houses
You can view the outside of the present prime minister's house (24 Sussex Dr) and take a peek at the property. For security reasons, there is no strolling around the PM's grounds.

Rideau Hall (☎ 998-7113, ⓦ www.gg.ca, 1 Sussex Dr; admission free; visitors center open 9am-7pm daily Apr-Oct), the governor general's pad built in the early 1900s, is just around the corner and up from the river. There are 45-minute walking tours of the residence with stories of some of the goings-on over the years. Tours are offered in summer only; other times of year you are limited to strolling the grounds.

At the main gate there's the small **Changing of the Guard** ceremony, which happens on the hour throughout the day from the end of June to the end of August.

Both houses are northeast along Sussex Dr from the Basilica. Rideau Hall is off Princess Dr, the eastern extension of Sussex.

Supreme Court of Canada
This rather intimidating structure (☎ 995-5361, 301 Wellington St; admission free; open

OTTAWA

9am-5pm Mon-Fri) is partially open to non-litigants. Visitors can stroll around the grounds, lobby and courtroom, and during summer can get a free tour given by a law student; call for the schedule. The rest of the year, reservations are required for tours.

Construction of the home for the highest court of the land was begun in 1939 but not completed until 1946. The grand entrance hall, 12m high, is certainly impressive.

National Archives of Canada

The mandate of this institution (☎ 463-2038, 395 Wellington St; admission free; open 9am-5pm Mon-Fri) is to collect and preserve the documentation of Canada. The vast collection includes paintings, maps, photographs, diaries, letters, posters and even 60,000 cartoons and caricatures concerning Canadian history and people, culled from periodicals from the past two centuries. The exhibition rooms have varying displays.

MUSEUMS
National Gallery

This museum (☎ 990-1985, 380 Sussex Dr; permanent collection admission free, special exhibitions from $8; open 10am-6pm Fri-Wed & 10am-8pm Thur May–mid-Oct; 10am-5pm Wed & Fri-Sun, 10am-8pm Thur mid-Oct–May; closed public holidays mid-Oct–May) is a must. As Canada's premier art gallery, it has an enormous collection of North American and European works in various media, all housed in an impressive building in the center of town. It's just a 15-minute walk from Parliament Hill.

Opened in 1988, the striking glass and pink granite gallery overlooking the Ottawa River was designed by Moshe Safdie, creator of Montreal's Habitat (a unique apartment complex) and Québec City's Musée de la Civilisation. He also renovated Ottawa's City Hall.

The numerous galleries, some arched and effectively colored, display classic and contemporary pieces, with the emphasis on Canadian artists. However, the US and European collections do contain examples from nearly all the heavyweights. The gallery also presents changing exhibits and special shows.

The excellent chronological display of Canadian painting and sculpture not only gives a history of Canadian art but also, in a real sense, provides an outline of the development of the country itself, beginning with the depictions of First Nations life at the time the Europeans arrived.

For a rejuvenating break, two pleasant courtyards offer the eyes and feet a rest. Between them sits one of the gallery's most unusual and most appealing components, the beautifully restored 1888 **Rideau St Chapel**, which was saved from destruction a few blocks away.

On level 2, along with contemporary and international works, is the **Inuit Gallery**, and one room for the display of some of the extensive and fine photography collection.

The entire complex is quite large; you'll need a few hours and you'll still tire before seeing all the exhibits, let alone the changing film and video presentations, lectures and concerts. There's a pleasant café, a restaurant and a very fine gift and bookshop. Underneath the gallery are two levels of parking.

Bytown Museum & the Ottawa Locks

Focusing on city history, Bytown Museum (☎ 234-4570, Rideau St; adult/child $5/3; open 10am-5pm Mon-Sat & 1pm-5pm Sun late Apr–mid-May) is in the oldest stone building in Ottawa. It's east of Parliament Hill, beside the canal – go down the stairs from Wellington St and back to the locks at the river. Used during construction of the canal for storing military equipment and money, it now contains artifacts and documents pertaining to local history.

On the ground floor, Parks Canada runs an exhibit about the building of the canal.

The series of locks at the edge of the Ottawa River in the Colonel By Valley, between the Château Laurier and the parliament buildings, marks the north end of the 198km Rideau Canal, which runs to Kingston and the St Lawrence River. Colonel By, who was in charge of constructing the canal, set up his headquarters here in 1826. Though never fulfilling any military purpose, the canal was used commercially for a while and then fell into disuse. Now the government maintains the locks as heritage parks.

Canadian Museum of Contemporary Photography

On the canal's edge by the Château Laurier, this museum (☎ 990-8257, Ⓦ www.cmcp.ca, 1 Rideau Canal; admission free; open 10am-6pm Fri-Wed & 10am-8pm Thur May–mid-Oct; 10am-5pm Wed & Fri-Sun, 10am-8pm Thur mid-Oct–Apr) sits in a reconstructed railway tunnel. Originally part of the National Film Board, it still houses the photographic research departments and the country's vast photographic archives. The gallery is a bit cramped, but the displays (which change quarterly) are usually outstanding.

Canadian War Museum

This museum (☎ 776-8600, 330 Sussex Dr; adult/senior & student/child $4/3/2, admission free 9:30am-noon Sun; open 9:30am-5pm Fri-Wed & 9:30am-8pm Thur May-Oct, 9:30am-5pm Tues-Sun Nov-Apr) contains Canada's largest war-related collection and traces the country's military history. Check out the life-size replica of a WWI trench. You'll also find multimedia displays and a huge collection of war art.

Royal Canadian Mint

Next door to the War Museum is the mint (☎ 993-8990, 320 Sussex Dr; admission $2; open 10am-2pm Mon-Fri Nov-Apr; Mon-Fri 9am-5pm May-Oct & 10am-2pm Sat June-Aug). Its main job nowadays is to strike special-edition coins, commemorative pieces and bullion investment coins, but this imposing stone building (1908) is also Canada's gold refinery. Tours of the coin-stamping facility are required for entry and are given by appointment.

Canadian Museum of Nature

This museum (☎ 566-4700, 240 McLeod St; adult/student & senior/child $6/5/2.50, half-price then free after 5pm Thur; open 9:30am-5pm Fri-Wed & 9:30am-8pm Thur May-Aug, 10am-5pm Fri-Wed & 10am-8pm Thur Sept-Apr) is housed in the attractive old Victorian building on the corner of Metcalfe St, south of the downtown area. The four-story building, fostering an appreciation and understanding of nature, includes a good section on the dinosaurs once found in Alberta. Also excellent are the realistic mammal and bird dioramas depicting Canadian wildlife. Major temporary exhibits on specific mammal, mineral or ecological subjects are features.

The **Viola MacMillan Mineral Gallery** is excellent, with some of the largest gems and minerals you're ever likely to see. The reproduction mine comes complete with a shaky elevator, and the east-coast tidal zone re-creation is also very realistic.

A separate section of the museum is geared toward children. The museum also has a cafeteria.

Check for more extended hours during summer. Note that the museum is free on July 1, Canada Day.

To get there from Confederation Square, take bus Nos 5, 6 or 14 down Elgin St. Walking from Parliament Hill takes about 20 minutes.

National Aviation Museum

The more than 100 aircraft in this museum (☎ 993-2010, Ⓦ www.aviationnmstc.ca, 11 Aviation Pkwy; adult/senior & student/child $6/4/2; open 9am-5pm Fri-Wed & 9am-9pm Thur May-Aug; 10am-5pm Tues, Wed, Fri & Sun, 10am-9pm Thur Sept-Apr) are housed in a huge triangular building at Rockcliffe Airport, about 5km northeast of downtown along Rockcliffe Pkwy. You'll see planes ranging from a Silver Dart of 1909 and the renowned wartime Spitfire to the most modern aircraft. Displays include aviation-related video games.

National Museum of Science & Technology

This interactive museum (☎ 991-3044, Ⓦ www.nmstc.ca, 1867 boul St Laurent; adult/student & senior/child $6/5/2; open 9am-5pm daily May-Aug, 9am-5pm Tues-Sun Sept-Apr), on the corner of Russell Rd, has all kinds of participatory scientific learning exhibits geared toward children. Try things out, test yourself, watch physical laws in action,

OTTAWA

see optical illusions. Also on display are farm machines, trains, model ships and stagecoaches. The bicycle and motorcycle collections are particularly good. Higher-tech exhibits include computers and communication technologies. Everyone's favorite is running through the gravitationally challenged kitchen.

The large display on space technology is interesting, with an assortment of Canadian space artifacts. An astronomy section has films and slides about the universe; on clear nights, take a peep through the large refracting telescope. Telephone reservations should be made for stargazing.

While popular with all age groups, this place is great for kids. Those without children may wish to avoid weekends and the increased numbers of young ones.

There's free parking at the museum.

OTHER THINGS TO SEE & DO
Byward Market
This lively area north of Rideau St teems with restaurants and pubs. The market building itself (Byward St between George and York Sts) was opened in the 1840s and is packed with specialty shops selling gourmet meats, seafood, baked goods and cheeses. The periphery is lined with vegetable, fruit and flower stands.

Basilica of Notre Dame
This Gothic-style house of worship *(no ☎, cnr Sussex & Patrick Sts; admission free; open 7:30am-6pm daily)*, circa 1839, contains stunning carvings, stained-glass windows, vaulted ceilings and some 200 statues around the altar. Pick up a pamphlet by the door for details of the many features. It's opposite the National Gallery.

Sandy Hill
While Byward Market is the oldest settled area in Ottawa, the region of Sandy Hill is not far behind. Much of it was destroyed or transformed by the expansions of the University of Ottawa, but some old Victorian houses remain as signs of an elite residential area. In Macdonald Park, north of Rideau St between Charlotte and Coburg Sts, you'll find a gazebo, underneath which is supposedly an old cemetery with bodies that weren't transferred elsewhere when the park was developed. The Regroupement des Organisms du Patrimoine Franco-ontarien (☎ 562-5800, Ⓦ www.francoroute.on.ca) have developed a walking tour of the area; their French-language pamphlet can be picked up at the Capital Infocentre tourist office.

ACTIVITIES
In summer, there are **canoe and row-boat rentals** for trips along the canal (from $8/hr) at Dow's Lake Pavilion (☎ 232-1001), Hog's Back Falls (☎ 239-5000, Hog's Back Rd at Colonel By Dr), or the marina on Hog's Back Rd (☎ 736-9894). All are south of the city center.

Ottawa has an excellent parks system with a lot of inner-city green space. There are many **walking**, **jogging** and **cycling** trails as well as picnic areas. You'll even find some fishing. The tourist office has a sheet (with a map) of all the parks and a description of each. Bicycle paths wind all over town; get a map of them, also at the tourist office. For information on bike rentals, see the Getting Around section.

Surrounding the city on the east, south and west, and connecting with the Ottawa River on each side, is a broad strip of connected parkland known as the **Greenbelt** *(☎ 239-5000)*. Within this area of woodlands, marsh and fields are nature trails, more bicycle paths, boardwalks and picnic areas. In the western Greenbelt, 20 minutes by vehicle from the downtown area off Richmond Rd, the **Stony Swamp Interpretive Centre** *(☎ 239-5000)* has a staff naturalist, 38km of hiking, ski and snowshoe trails, and displays about the area. On the eastern side of the Greenbelt is another conservation area, Mer Bleue.

For **whitewater rafting** trips close to Ottawa, see the Pontiac section of the Outaouais chapter.

In winter there's **skiing** as close as 20km from town, in the Gatineau Hills. Two resorts with variously graded hills are Camp Fortune and Mont Cascades. Tow passes are more expensive on weekends.

Gatineau Park has excellent cross-country ski trails with lodges along the way. In warm weather, the park is good for walking and picnicking.

Also in winter, the Rideau Canal is famous as a place where you can **ice skate** along 5km of maintained ice. (You'll even see folks skating to work on it!) Rest spots on the way serve beavertails (see 'Does a Beavertail Taste Like It Sounds?') to go with the hot chocolate, although the beaver must be getting scarce, judging by the prices. Ask at the tourist office about skate rentals.

ORGANIZED TOURS

Capital Double Decker & Trolley Tours (☎ 749-3666, 800-823-6147) Adult/senior, student & child $20/17. This company has a few different options, but note that the trolley is just a bus decorated to look that way and that the vehicle is the only difference between the tours. The narrated tour allows hop-on, hop-off privileges at 20 stops, including some in Hull, and you have the day to do it – a good way to get around. There's a straight two-hour tour and a night version as well. Tickets can be bought from Capital's kiosk, at the corner of Sparks and Metcalfe Sts.

Paul's Boat Lines (☎ 235-8409) Adult/senior/student/child $14/12/10/7. Paul runs 1½-hour cruises on the Ottawa River and Rideau Canal from early May through early October. The ticket booth is on the Rideau Canal opposite the National Arts Centre.

Ottawa Riverboat Company (☎ 562-4888, W www.ottawariverboat.ca) Tours from $31. This company offers a variety of tours, including some cruises and some bus-boat tours of the Ottawa region and along the Ottawa River. They sometimes include admission to the Canadian Museum of Civilization in their prices. Their and other boat tours leave from the ferry terminal, behind Parliament Hill.

Haunted Walk (☎ 232-0344, W www .hauntedwalk.com) Adult/student $12/8. A walking tour designed to give you the creeps, it takes in allegedly haunted areas of the city center and leads you into great, old buildings you wouldn't otherwise think of entering. Tickets can be bought at the booth on the corner of Sparks and Elgin Sts. There are one or two tours every Monday through Saturday evening from May to October.

SPECIAL EVENTS

Ottawa is a year-round tourist destination. Winter here is marked by **Winterlude** (☎ 800-465-1867, W www.capcan.ca/winterlude), a winter festival held on the first three weekends of February in over a dozen locations across town. Sporting events, contests, concerts and fun in the snow are the name of the game.

PLACES TO STAY
Camping

Camp Hither Hills (☎ 822-0509, fax 822-0196, 5227 Bank St) Tent sites $16. This campground is on Hwy 31, 20km south of Parliament Hill. The tourist office has a list of other campgrounds in the area.

Recreational Campground (☎ 833-2974, 800-604-8555, W www.rec-land.com, 1566 Canaan Rd, Cumberland). Tent sites $17.50. A 15-minute drive east along the Ottawa River Pkwy from the city center, this place has plenty of trailers but tent sites too, as well as laundry, showers and an outdoor pool.

Hostels

Ottawa Backpackers (☎ 241-3402, W www .ottawahostel.com, 203 York St) Dorm beds $18, double rooms $55. Sandwiched between two of Ottawa's most interesting regions, Sandy Hill and Byward Market, this hostel is laid-back and friendly.

Ottawa International Hostel (☎ 235-2595, 800-663-5777, fax 235-9202, W www .hostellingintl.on.ca, 75 Nicholas St) Dorm beds members/nonmembers $19/23, private rooms for up to 5 persons members/nonmembers $49/53. This HI hostel is in the old Ottawa jail – check out the gallows at the back – close to the Parliament buildings. It has 130 beds, mostly in the inmates' old cells. Bus No 4 goes from the bus station on the corner of Arlington Ave and Kent St to within two blocks of the hostel; from the train station, bus No 95 does the same thing.

OTTAWA

University of Ottawa (☎ *564-5771, fax 562-5157, 90 University St*) Singles/doubles $22/35 students, $33/40 nonstudents. The University of Ottawa opens its dormitories for visitors from May to August. It has a laundry, swimming pool and cheap cafeteria. It's southeast of Parliament Hill.

YM-YWCA (☎ *237-1320, fax 788-5095, 180 Argyle Ave*) Singles/doubles with shared bath $48/58. This place has good standard rooms, plus there's a cafeteria, gym and pool for guest use.

B&Bs & Inns

Voyageur Guest House (☎ *238-6445, fax 236-5551,* **W** *www.bbcanada.com/avghbb, 95 Arlington Ave*) Singles/doubles $39-49/59-64. On a quiet residential street right behind the bus terminal, this is probably the best low-price option in town. There are six clean rooms with shared bathrooms, and breakfast is included in the price.

Australis Guesthouse (☎ *235-8461, fax 235-8461,* **W** *www.bbcanada.com/1463.html, 35 Marlborough St*) Singles/doubles with shared bath $50/65. This comfy guesthouse is run by a friendly couple and serves bulging breakfasts (included in the price). The owners will pick you up at the bus or train station if arranged in advance. Marlborough St is south of Laurier, about a half-hour walk east of Parliament Hill.

Auberge des Arts (☎ *562-0909, 877-750-3400,* **W** *http://members.home.net/auberge desarts, 104 Guigues Ave*) Singles/doubles $65/70. This place serves great breakfasts to order, and its air-conditioned rooms are nicely furnished. English, French and Spanish are spoken.

Auberge du Marché (☎ *241-6610, 800-465-0079,* **W** *http://members.home.com/auberge dumarche, 87 Guigues Ave*) Singles/doubles with shared bath $65/85. This is an older, renovated house with three rooms; full breakfast is included.

Albert House Inn (☎ *236-4479, 800-267-1982, fax 237-9079,* **W** *www.albertinn.com, 478 Albert St*) Singles/doubles $88-138/98-158. On the downtown side of the canal, this place has 17 well-appointed rooms. It's more expensive than the aforementioned places, but it's in a good location and is a heritage home with all the comforts. The breakfast menu is extensive and included in the price.

Hotels & Efficiencies

Doral Inn (☎ *230-8055, 800-263-6725, 486 Albert St*) Singles/doubles $119/129, units $139. This central spot has decent rooms, plus a few housekeeping units. It runs specials for $89 from time to time.

Cartier Place Suite Hotel (☎ *236-5000, fax 236-3842,* **W** *www.suitedreams.com, 180 Cooper St*) Suites from $129. Prices here are very reasonable for what you get – spacious apartment-style rooms with kitchenette and access to games room, pool and sauna. Twenty-four hours of parking costs $12.

Lord Elgin Hotel (☎ *235-3333, 800-267-4298,* **W** *www.lordelginhotel.ca, 100 Elgin St*) Singles/doubles $145/155. This stately old hotel also has weekend specials where doubles are $110. Parking is free.

Château Laurier (☎ *241-1414, 800-441-1414,* **W** *www.cphotels.ca, 1 Rideau St*) Rooms from $239, suites from $489. The classic Château Laurier is the castle-like place by the canal and a landmark in its own right. Their rates change daily, depending on the season, day of the week, and occupancy rate. Ask for weekend specials and other discounts.

Motel strips line each side of the downtown area, along Rideau St and its extension, Montréal Rd.

PLACES TO EAT
Byward Market & Around

This area is very popular and offers a great selection of places, many with outdoor tables; the place is hopping on weekends. The market building has a good gourmet bagel stand inside.

Shawarma Place (☎ *562-3662, 284 Dalhousie St*) Mains $4-8. These guys do falafel, shawarmas and other Lebanese takeout, with good-value platters available.

Haveli (☎ *241-1700, 39 Clarence St*) Mains $6-10. Excellent Indian food is dished up at the more upscale Haveli. Also try the Kadri beef served in a mini-wok ($10).

Does a Beavertail Taste Like It Sounds?

Shaped like the water-slapping end of Canada's favorite animal, this huge pastry (basically a donut spread out to the size of a small pizza) was created in the late 1970s and has since become associated with skating along the Rideau Canal. Perfect for reintroducing all the calories that you lose skating (and then some!), these hot, doughy delights are often smothered in toppings like chocolate sauce, maple butter, cinnamon sugar (that one's called 'the Classic'), or even smoked salmon or garlic butter and cheese. Even Hillary Clinton, on a winter visit to Ottawa, indulged, and wiped the remains enthusiastically off her face for the attendant press.

These little critters have become so beloved and have so quickly multiplied that they have spread to over 50 locations around North America. They've been spotted by beavertail hunters and lovers at La Ronde in Montréal, at Station Tremblant in Mont Tremblant, at Whistler Mountain in British Columbia and even at the Epcot Center at Florida's Disney World!

Zak's Diner (☎ 241-5866, 14 Byward St) Mains $6-13. This is a 1950s-style eatery with triple-decker burgers ($9.50). It serves breakfast all day and is open late.

Roses Café (☎ 241-8535, 349 Dalhousie St) Mains $6-14, lunch buffet $8. Good, cheap Indian food can also be found at this unlikely named place, which is open for lunch and dinner. The lunch buffet is generous and a good value.

Oregano's (☎ 241-5100, 74 George St) Dinner mains $10. Oregano's is good for inexpensive, varied pasta dishes, and serves an all-you-can-eat buffet dinner. The terrace is the place to be.

Las Palmas (☎ 241-3738, 111 Parent Ave) Mains $9-17. This is a colorful Mexican place with great fajita platters ($17). The cocktails look good but are watery.

Domus Café (☎ 241-6007, 87 Murray St) Lunch mains $9-16, dinner mains $17-26. This place has excellent Canadian regional dishes with fresh ingredients, such as panseared pickerel filet with sweet butter and mashed potatoes ($19).

Downtown & Around

Bank St and its side streets are teeming with numerous restaurants.

Royal Oak (☎ 236-0190, 318 Bank St) Mains from $5. Try this place for British beer and food. It's friendly – and you can play darts.

Mekong (☎ 237-7717, 637 Somerset St W) Lunch mains $6-7, dinner mains $7-15. In the Chinatown area, Mekong does good Vietnamese and Chinese dishes, such as stir-fried scallops and snow peas ($13).

Suisha Gardens (☎ 236-9602, 208 Slater St) Lunch mains from $8, dinner mains from $16.50. Suisha Gardens serves excellent, if somewhat westernized, Japanese food.

The Ritz (☎ 235-7027, 274 Elgin St) Lunch mains $10-11, dinner mains $13-19. Come here for great Italian food – lines of people outside are proof. Lunch specials include items such as phyllo stuffed with sauteed beef and portobello mushrooms.

ENTERTAINMENT

Xpress is Ottawa's main free entertainment weekly; *Capital Xtra* is geared toward gay people. Also check Friday's *Ottawa Citizen* for complete club, cinema and other listings. There are pubs and clubs scattered along Bank St and around Byward Market.

Zaphrod Beeblebrox (☎ 594-3355, 27 York St) This eclectic place is essentially a rock 'n' roll club but with trippy doses of hip-hop, African beats and dance music. Live bands play Tuesday, Thursday, Friday and Saturday nights. Cover charge varies from free to $8.

Elephant & Castle Pub (☎ 234-5544, 101-50 Rideau St) Mains $6-13. Though they serve meals, this is mostly popular as a meeting place and friendly pub, serving

OTTAWA

excellent finger food. Their terrace out back gets crowded around happy hour (5pm to 7pm Monday through Friday), mainly with an over-25 crowd.

Maxwell's Bistro (☎ 232-5771, 340 Elgin St) This spot offers a laid-back bar on the first floor and dance beats on the second, for an over-25 crowd. Their lounge-music Wednesdays are very popular.

Barrymore's (☎ 656-8880, 323 Bank St) This venue features live heavy rock and metal on weekends.

National Arts Centre (NAC; ☎ 947-7000, W *www.nac-can.ca, 53 Elgin St)* The NAC stages dramas and operas, and is home to the symphony orchestra. It also presents a range of concerts and films.

Bytown Cinema (☎ 789-3456, 325 Rideau St) This is where you'll find art-house or underground films. The Making Scenes Gay & Lesbian Film Festival screens here annually in mid-December.

GETTING THERE & AWAY
Air
The surprisingly small Macdonald-Cartier International Airport is 20 minutes south of town. Major airlines serving Ottawa include Royal Air, Air Canada and Canadian Airlines.

Bus
The bus terminal (☎ 238-5900) is at 265 Catherine St. The principal bus lines that serve Ottawa are Voyageur and Greyhound; some 20 buses go to/from Montréal ($29/54 one-way/roundtrip). Other roundtrip fares include Toronto ($117), Kingston ($61) and Sudbury ($170). Students get about 10% off.

Train
The VIA Rail station (☎ 244-8289, 800-361-1235, W www.viarail.ca) is 7km southeast of downtown, at 200 Tremblay Rd near the junction of Alta Vista Rd and Hwy 417, just east of Rideau Canal. There are seven daily trains to Montréal ($44/35 full fare/five-day advance purchase) and four daily to Toronto ($96/77 full fare/five-day advance purchase). The fare to

Kingston (on the Montréal train) is $41/33 full fare/five-day advance purchase. The trains to Montréal stop in Dorval on the way, where you can hop a free shuttle bus to the Dorval Airport. For roundtrip fares only, purchase 10 days in advance for a greater discount. ISIC card holders get a 35% discount.

Car
From Montréal, take Hwy 40 Ouest (West), the Trans Canada Hwy, which becomes Hwy 417 in Ontario. It's about 190km, or two hours by car. In Ottawa, there's free parking in the World Exchange Plaza and the Rideau Centre on weekends. Allô Stop (☎ 562-8248) used to have a popular ridesharing service to Montréal, Québec City and Toronto before they were shut down by the Ontario Transport Commission in a move to protect bus companies. Try calling to see if the decision has been revoked in favor of democracy!

GETTING AROUND
To/From the Airport
City bus No 97 links the Rideau Centre and Slater St with the airport ($2.25). You can also take the Airport Shuttle bus ($9, 25 minutes), which leaves every half-hour from the Château Laurier hotel from 5am to midnight.

Public Transportation
OC Transpo (☎ 741-4390, W www.octranspo .com) runs the Ottawa bus system. One-way tickets cost $2.25 on the bus, but cheaper tickets ($1.70 for one or $8.50 for 10) can be bought from corner stores. Most buses quit around midnight.

A new light-rail transit system opened in 2001 – the O Train, extending southward from Bayview to Greenboro. Tickets are $2 per ride.

Bicycle
Ottawa is an excellent city for bicyclists, with an extensive system of paths in and around town. For rentals, try Cycle Tour Rent-A-Bike behind the Château Laurier, in the parking lot. It's open daily May to

September and charges $20/12 per day/half-day. ID is required. The youth hostel also rents two-wheelers.

AROUND OTTAWA

The Diefenbunker is an underground fort built in the early 1960s to house up to 300 personnel in case of nuclear attack. It's now the **Cold War Museum** (☎ *839-0007, 3911 Carp Rd; adult/senior & student/child $12/10/5; guided tours 2pm Mon-Fri, 1pm & 2pm Sat & Sun)* with displays including air-raid sirens and (defused!) bombs. It's in the village of Carp, about a 30-minute drive west of town.

OTTAWA

Eastern Townships

The Eastern Townships extend roughly from Farnham to the US's Vermont, New Hampshire and Maine borders. Aptly dubbed the 'Garden of Quebec,' the area, nestled in the foothills of the Appalachian mountains, contains some of the province's most scenic countryside. Because of this, and due to its proximity to Montréal, it is a popular destination for urbanites seeking country respites. On summer and fall weekends, the main villages fill up with city folk seeking local produce, antiques, local art and fresh air.

The Eastern Townships boast Québec's most fertile soil. Agriculture has always played an important role here, and the area is the province's apple and wine country. Maple groves also grow in abundance. The forests are mainly deciduous (maple, birch, oak, poplar, walnut), and locals claim that's why there are fewer mosquitoes than in other areas of the province, where coniferous trees are more common (we think that's wishful thinking!).

A popular resort area year-round, there's always something afoot. In spring, 'sugaring off' – the tapping of trees for maple syrup, and then boiling and preparing it – takes place in the region. Summer brings fishing and swimming in the numerous lakes. During autumn, a good time to visit, colors are beautiful as the leaves change, and apple harvesting takes place with the attendant cider production. Skiing is a major winter activity with main centers at Mont Orford and Sutton.

Cycling is extremely popular in the region, with nearly 500km of trails taking in sumptuous landscapes of rolling hills. Pick up the free guide *Cycling the Eastern Townships* and other cycling maps at any of the tourist offices in the area.

In French, the area is called both Les Cantons de l'Est (a literal translation of 'Eastern Townships') and L'Estrie, a more French-sounding term coined by bishop Maurice O'Bready in 1946. Today most

Highlights

- Indulge on local wines, ciders, cheeses – and duck!
- Take a hike in Sutton for some of the best views in southern Québec
- Find out why cloning, ET and nudism go hand in hand at UFOland in Valcourt
- Thunder down the slopes at Sutton, Mount Orford or Owl's Head
- Scream 'eat my dust!' on killer downhill mountain-bike trails in Bromont
- Take a lazy bike or car ride on obscenely picturesque side roads

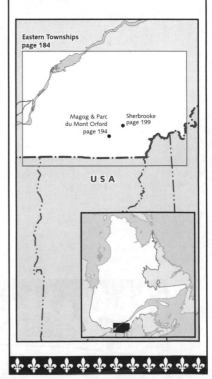

Eastern Townships
page 184

Magog & Parc du Mont Orford page 194

Sherbrooke page 199

USA

Francophones use Cantons de l'Est over L'Estrie, but local residents are called Townshippers in English, and Estriens in French.

This chapter covers the Townships in sections corresponding to official municipal and tourist subdivisions. However, the first section, Apple Route, is technically part of the Montérégie tourist region. It is included here as it is a good, alternative access point to the Townships.

History

Until the end of the 18th century, the area was inhabited solely by Abenaki people, who hunted and built settlements there. Virtually no traces are left of these communities after the vigorous development of the next two centuries. Abenaki place names are the only reminders of this heritage.

In the decades during and after the American Revolution (1776–82), thousands of Loyalists, those who remained loyal to Britain and wanted nothing of an independent United States, fled to and settled in the area, founding towns and industries. In 1792, the British-controlled government of Canada thanked these settlers by allotting them plots of land according to the township system (roughly 260 sq km each). Other areas of Québec had been (from 1534 onward) developed and populated according to the French seigneurial system, which allocated rectangular strips of land radiating out from the St Lawrence River. But by the turn of the 20th century, many of the villages in the Townships were named after British towns or historical personalities.

Moreover, the British-controlled government gave two million acres in the Townships to four English merchants who placed advertisements in American newspapers to sell off the land. Thousands of farmers from New England arrived in the area this way. By tacitly encouraging English-speaking settlement, the government was hoping to anglicize Québec and therefore secure its interests.

Later waves of immigration, brought on by the Napoleonic wars, poverty and epidemics in Europe, led to the arrival of thousands of Irish and Scottish (as well as Dutch, German, Polish and others) into the area.

French Canadians started arriving around 1850, in search of cultivatable lands. Each newcomer must have told two friends about how good things were there, because a decade later they already constituted a quarter of the region's population. They bought up property sold by the Anglophones, who preferred to invest instead in the big industries sprouting up across the Townships and along the St Lawrence River.

Today, Francophones account for about 93% of the population, though the English presence is felt quite strongly in areas like Lennoxville, Knowlton and Sutton. There are still a number of active Protestant churches and there aren't as many names beginning with 'St' as in other regions. In many areas, you'll hear people switching back and forth effortlessly between languages, often in the same sentence.

Furthermore, the architecture throughout the area reflects Anglo-Saxon styles transmuted by a New England heritage. There are numerous red covered bridges, and many houses reflect neo-Gothic, Queen Anne and Second Empire styles.

Orientation & Information

This area's layout is different from any other in the province and is conducive to exploring in zigzag rather than linear fashion. In any case, distances are not great and the landscape is beautiful, so meandering along country roads is a pleasure. Whether by car or by bike, when going from one village to another sampling the local produce, try to take as many side roads as possible to best enjoy the scenery.

The area's main tourist office (☎ 450-375-8774, 800-263-1068) is just off exit 68 of Hwy 10 (at the turnoff for both Granby and Sutton) and is open year-round. There are 23 smaller ones spread out across the region, some of which are open May to September only.

APPLE ROUTE
☎ 450

Spartan, Empire, Cortland, McIntosh, Delicious, Jersey Mac, Golden Russet – take your pick. These and other kinds of apples

EASTERN TOWNSHIPS

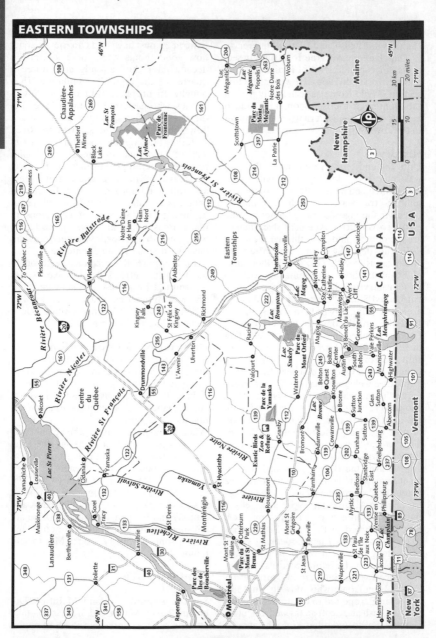

are found in orchards throughout Monté-régie and the Eastern Townships. A high-light is to visit orchards in the fall (September and October) and buy (or, better yet, pick your own) apples. Most cider-producing orchards offer free taste tests. Pick up maps detailing the locations of orchards at local tourist offices. A par-ticularly helpful one is the free, fold-out *Le Circuit du Paysan,* which is also on the web at W www.circuitdupaysan.com.

Parc du Mont St Bruno

Only about 15 minutes from Montréal, this Sépaq-run park (☎ 653-7544, 330 chemin des 25; admission $3.50; open 9am-7pm daily Apr-Aug, 9am-4pm or 5pm Sept-Mar) may be small (only 6 sq km), but there are plenty of activities for the visitor. In winter there's cross-country skiing as well as an adjacent downhill slope (☎ 653-3441, 550 rang des 25); in summer there are pretty walking trails that circle the park's five lakes and guided bird-watching and nature expeditions. There's also a sizeable orchard just beyond the main entrance where you can pick apples. Part of it is an organic orchard, another uses 35% less pesticides than the norm; their goal is to eventually eradicate pesticide use altogether in the entire orchard.

Mont St Hillaire
pop 13,000
This evidently well-to-do town has several notable attractions. The year-round tourist office (☎ 536-0395, 888-736-0395) is at 1080 chemin des Patriotes Nord.

Canada's first Unesco Biosphere reserve was set up here in 1978. This has become the **Centre de la Nature** (☎ 467-1755, 422 chemin des Moulins; adult/child $4/2; open 8am-sunset daily year-round), at the top of the pretty, winding chemin de la Montagne. The preservation area itself is off-limits, but there are 24km of walking trails at your disposal for hiking and cross-country skiing, most of which can be done quickly and rather easily. The Dieppe and Rocky Trails lead to summits where there are nice lookouts.

Along chemin de la Montagne up to the Centre, you'll pass one orchard after another.

Most of these sell their products year-round, but if you visit in September or October, you can go **apple picking** or buy scrumptious fresh apple pies and other yummy products. One of the best orchards to stop at is Les Vergers Petit & Fils (☎ 467-9926, 1020 chemin de la Montagne; admission free; open 9am-7:30pm daily May-Oct, 10am-5pm daily Nov & Dec, 10am-5pm Fri-Sun Jan-Apr). Their boutique is a paradise of local prod-ucts – apple, maple, chocolate, jam – and you can sample some cider here. During apple-picking season, the charming staff organize daylong picnic outings for the kids.

Also worth a stop is the **Maison des Cul-tures Amérindiens** (☎ 464-2500, 510 montée des Trente; adult/child $4/3; open 10am-5pm Mon-Fri, 1pm-5pm Sat-Sun year-round), one of the only museums dedicated to First Nations art and culture in the region. This one is run by non–Native Canadians and the displays are in French only; it's an attempt to acquaint Québécois with indige-nous culture. The displays of First Nations art and traditional methods of maple sap gathering are good, and the museum organ-izes special events.

If you're driving to Mont St Hillaire, which is between Hwys 10 and 20, take either exit 115 off Hwy 20 or exit 29 off Hwy 10.

Rougemont
pop 2500
This is Québec's apple capital; the best-known apple juice in the province, aptly named *Rougemont,* comes from here. Aside from **visiting orchards**, there's nothing to do in this tiny place. For a quick sampler, there are a few McIntosh trees outside the tourist office (☎ 469-0069, 866-469-0069), at 1 chemin Marieville, at the corner of rue Principale (which is Rte 229, coming from Mont St Hillaire). Also check out W www.rougemont .net for details on the orchards in the area.

Probably the best orchard to visit is Cidrerie Michel Jodoin (☎ 469-2676, 888-469-2676, 1130 rang de la Petite Caroline; admission free; open 9am-5pm daily year-round), where you can taste their six differ-ent ciders and get a tour of the premises where they're made. Later you can climb a cleared trail on Mont Rougemont for a great view of the surrounding area.

GRANBY-BROMONT
☎ 450

This area, in the northwestern corner of the Eastern Townships, bridges agricultural and orchard country with the mountainous terrain that characterizes most of the region. Aside from **downhill skiing** at Bromont, the main activity in the area is **cycling**. The Route Verte links many of the most attractive spots in the region, partially by following an old railroad track (see Ⓦ www.granby-bromont.com/sports/velo for more information). Some of the province's best mountain biking is in Bromont.

A popular event is the **Mondial du Vélo** (☎ 534-2453, Ⓦ www.mondialduvelo.com), an annual cycling extravaganza in the last half of August, with events nearly every day. There are rallies, night rides, mountain-bike races, a 24-hour ride, and concerts and parades. All events take place in and around Granby, Bromont and Waterloo.

Granby
pop 45,400

The second largest city in the Townships got its start when families from Vermont and New Hampshire settled here in the 1810s and '20s, founding a flour mill, a sawmill and other small industries. Granby is still a mainly industrial city (plastics, dairy, textile, tobacco) and isn't of much interest in and of itself. An oddly spread-out city, its main attractions lie outside the center. However, some of the town's 40 parks are worth a gander. In Parc Pelletier (on rue Principale, west of the center) a small but much-touted Roman sarcophagus, more than 3000 years old, serves somewhat awkwardly as a fountain.

Things to See & Do The province's most famous zoo is the **Granby Zoo** (☎ 372-9113, 877-472-6290, Ⓦ www.moijezoo.com, 525 rue St Hubert; adult/child 5-12/child 2-4 $20/15/9; open 10am-7pm daily June-Aug, 10am-6pm Sat & Sun May & Sept). Over 1000 animals (250 species) are featured here, most in

The Wrath of Flipper

The Granby Zoo might be loved by thousands of annual visitors, but it has attracted the wrath of such people as Brigitte Bardot and Richard O'Barry, the man who trained Flipper (yes, *the* Flipper!). They have publicly attacked the zoo's $12 million project to open a dolphinarium, which would also enable visitors to swim with the cetaceans.

Defying a North American trend in the last decade to close such facilities, the zoo is unrepentant in the face of protests and statistics showing that up to 40% of captured dolphins die within seven days, and another 40% die within seven years of captivity (in the wild they can live up to 40 years). The zoo even plans to open a similar facility somewhere in Old Montréal.

In 2002 Bardot wrote a critical letter to zoo officials, published in papers around the province, imploring them to reconsider their decisions. O'Barry and animal rights activist groups have made noise too, but the promise of tourist dollars, it seems, rings much more loudly.

For more information on Bardot's activism and its effect on her popularity as well as on the animal-rights cause, see 'What's Wrong with Brigitte?' the Lower St Lawrence chapter.

⚜ ⚜ ⚜ ⚜ ⚜ ⚜ ⚜ ⚜ ⚜ ⚜

cages but some roaming 'free.' As part of the zoo's expansion project, they've installed a small aquapark with wave pool and a controversial dolphin show (see 'The Wrath of Flipper'). The zoo is off Hwy 10 (exit 68). From the town center, follow rue Dufferin until the corner of Rte 139, then turn left.

On the eastern border of town is the sizeable **Lac Boivin**, which becomes a huge skating rink come winter. For bike, canoe, kayak and paddleboat rental, check out Vélo Gare (☎ 777-4438, 71 rue Denison). At the lake's northern tip is the **Centre d'Interprétation de la Nature** (☎ 375-3861, 700 rue Drummond; admission free; open 8:30am-5pm daily year-round), which has walking trails along wetlands and is a good place for bird-watching. There's a **labyrinth** *(adult/child 5-12 $7/5; open 11am-2 hrs before sunset daily late June–early Sept, 11am-2 hrs before sunset Sat & Sun May–late June & early Sept–late Oct)* made from wooden stakes. Its 200 doors are guaranteed to trick you.

About 15km north of Granby is another zoo, the **Exotic Birds Zoo and Refuge** *(☎ 378-6181, ⓦ www.zooicare.com, 2699 Rte 139; adult/child 3-10 $9/5.50; open 10am-5pm daily June–early Sept)*. More than 150 varieties of colorful birds from around the world reside in confined aviaries set up along an outdoor path.

In spring the **Érablier Leclerc** *(☎ 777-7128, 275 rang Brandrick; adult/child $6/4; open 10am-5pm daily mid-Feb–mid-May)* hosts a sugar shack with maple syrup galore, taffy pulls and traditional meals. It's best to call them before coming. Follow Rte 112 to 12km east of Granby, then head north for 2km along chemin Saxby.

Special Events Throughout September, Granby hosts perhaps the province's most renowned **International Song Festival** (☎ 375-7555), bringing in new and established singer-songwriters mainly, but not exclusively, from Québec. Jean Leloup, Luc de la Rochelière and other singers loved by millions of Québécois got started here.

Places to Stay & Eat There are many campgrounds in and around Granby, but the best ones are out of town.

Camping Roxton Pond *(☎ 776-6311, 1563 avenue du Lac Ouest)* Tent sites $16. This campground is on the shores of calm Lac Roxton, a 9km drive north of Granby on Rte 139. There are 52 tent sites, games, a convenience store, and fishing and swimming.

Camping Rivière du Passant *(☎ 539-3835, 330 8-ème rang Ouest)* Tent sites $16-21. Very close to the Parc de la Yamaska and Rte 241, this excellent campground is in moderately wild surroundings, near a rocky river.

Les Trinitères *(☎ 372-5125, 200 boul Robert)* Singles/doubles $20 per person. Rooms have the bare minimum here, but as it's in a monastery, that comes as no surprise.

Motel Les Pins *(☎ 378-0793, 1523 rue Principale)* Singles/doubles from $52/80. This is a decent enough motel near the center of town.

Plus *(☎ 375-1964, 1 boul Mountain)* Mains $6-14. You'll find everything in this restaurant-bar, from pizza and club sandwiches to nachos, quesadillas and BBQ chicken. They also have a kid's menu and inexpensive breakfasts.

Lotus d'Or *(☎ 372-4010, 88 rue Principale)* Mains $6-12. You won't write home about it, but the Vietnamese and Thai food here is quite tasty – even tastier considering their $5 lunch specials.

Getting There & Away Granby is accessed via exit 68 or 74 off Hwy 10. The bus station (☎ 776-1571) is at 111 rue St Charles Sud. National Autocar (☎ 514-842-2281) runs four daily buses between Montréal and Granby ($17, 1½ hours), with three additional buses on Friday and Sunday. The first bus of the day (departing Montréal at 8:30am) stops at the Granby Zoo.

Parc de la Yamaska
Only 10km from the center of Granby is this delightful little provincial park *(☎ 776-7182, 8-ème rang Ouest; adult $5/2.50; open 8:30am-6:30pm daily June–early Sept, 9am-5pm daily May & early Sept–early Oct)*. Centered around the Réservoir Choinière, the activities here are all water-based. Swimming is a big draw. Sépaq, who runs the park, rents out (at rather high prices) surfbikes and canoes ($23 for 3 hours), bikes ($14 for 3 hours) and sailboards ($25 for 3 hours).

Continuing to the end of the 8-ème rang, where it meets Rte 243 just northeast of Warden, there's a small **swimming pond** *(adult/child $5/2)*, set up with a swing and diving board for passersby in need of a quick, fresh dip. The water is clean source water from an underground spring.

Bromont
pop 4400
This town has an air of the well-to-do in its tailored lawns and pristine, wide boulevards bordered by large homes with double

garages. A number of big companies (IBM, Québecor) have major branches here that support the economy. Yet the main driving force behind this community is Mont Brome, which keeps visitors pouring in during winter and summer.

The tourist office (☎ 534-2006, 877-276-6668) is at 15 boulevard Bromont and is open year-round. Pick up their free, foldout, bilingual map, *Circuit du Patrimoine à Bicyclette,* and set out on foot, on bike or by car on a tour of the town's historic buildings. There's a Café Internet (☎ 770-1530) at 40 chemin Compton, which charges $4 per hour.

Activities There are a number of good places to go **horse riding** in the area. Try Équitation Lombart (☎ 534-2084, 374 rue Pierre Laporte; $15/hr; open 9am-6pm daily Apr-Oct), just west of town (exit 74 off Hwy 10).

Mountain biking is hugely popular at Mont Brome's **Ski Bromont** resort (☎ 534-2200, 866-276-6668, ⓦ www.skibromont .com, 150 rue Champlain; mountain-bike day pass adult/child 6-12 $23/17), with its 100km of trails, some very steep and for experts only (there are six double-diamond runs). In 2001 the place hosted the UCI Mountain Bike Masters World Championship. There's a gravel path circling the mountain with access to the trails, which lead up toward the summit. The on-site rental store, Sports Bromont (☎ 534-5858), rents hybrid/tandem/mountain/double-suspension bikes for $27/54/45/60 per day, 10% cheaper for a four-hour afternoon rental.

If it's too hot to eat dust mountain biking, you can join the massive lineups to take several plunges at Ski Bromont's **Water Park** (adult/child $23/17 per day, 50% off after 4pm; open 10am-4pm daily early–late June, 10am-6:30pm daily late June–Aug, 10am-4pm Sat & Sun May–early June, Sept & Oct). In winter Ski Bromont comes alive again as one of the area's top slopes, with 405m of vertical drop and 50% of its slopes classed as difficult or extremely difficult. Count on $38 per day, $27 for night skiing.

Places to Stay Bromont is home to varied accommodations. *Camping L'Estriade* (☎ 776-3864, 1 boul Bromont) Tent sites $15-18. A favorite among cyclists as it's just off the La Villageoise bicycle path, this is a reasonably quiet campground with decent showers and facilities.

Au Bosquet Argenté (☎ 534-0293, 70 rue Champlain) Doubles $70. One of the few affordable B&Bs right in town, this tidy place has a nice view of Mont Brome.

La Maison aux Pignons Verts (☎ 260-1129, 129 rue Adamsville) Singles/doubles $60/80. West of town in the pretty village of Adamsville, this is a warm and friendly B&B in a modern though rustic-styled house with a pool.

Bromont sur le Lac (☎ 534-1818, fax 534-1828, 319 chemin du Lac Gale) Singles/doubles from $60/120. Three semi-luxury chalets in beautiful surroundings by a small lake make a good respite. Activities are possible on-site. They offer package deals including the Water Park and other attractions.

Places to Eat There's good, affordable food in Bromont. *L'Âme du Pain* (☎ 534-4478, 702 rue Shefford) Mains $4-7. At this bakery/café you can find freshly baked goods as well as healthy, light meals.

Confiserie (☎ 534-3893, 679 rue Shefford) Mains $4-8. Also good for light meals and especially for dessert, this place has a built-in chocolate museum (admission free).

Extrier (☎ 534-3562, 547 rue Shefford) Mains $8-16. There's a homey, cozy quality to this small restaurant, which serves a wide array of dishes, from fine starters like snails and smoked trout to very tasty meat and seafood mains. Sunday evenings there's live jazz.

BROME-MISSISQUOI
☎ 450

This region covers a swath from Farnham to Lac Brome, south of Hwy 10 down to the US border, and includes some of the region's top ski slopes and most scenic landscapes. It's also the heart of Québec's wine country, often visited by, er, samplers (they might be more crassly called tipplers!) who go from one winery to another.

Farnham
pop 7900

This is one of the first Townships, named after a town in England from where the first landowner came. There's not much to do here but appreciate some fine neo-Victorian architecture and take a stroll in the **Centre de Nature** (☎ 293-3178, rue Yamaska Est; admission free; open year-round), a central, sprawling and elaborate park that's a nice picnic stop.

From Farnham, head south on Rte 235, passing through the lovely hamlet of **Mystic** (pop 400), the area's gem, known for a huge, red, 12-sided barn. Though the edifice's size is unique in Québec, its circularity was common in the Eastern Townships in the 19th century. People built barns this way because of an Anglo-Saxon superstition that the devil lived in angles and therefore a circular barn would thwart any plans to do evil things to the livestock!

Five kilometers south of Mystic is Bedford (pop 2800), a modern town of limited interest. From there, head east on the pretty Rte 202. In 6km you'll be in Stanbridge East (pop 850), where three 19th-century buildings (the old general store, a mill from 1830 and a barn) now make up the **Musée Missisquoi** (☎ 248-3153, 2 rue River; adult/child $3.50/1; open 10am-5pm daily late May–mid-Oct). This pleasant museum details the area's history through antiques, photographs and bilingual displays. The owners' pride in the area's Loyalist heritage is well apparent.

While in Stanbridge East, check out **Le Ste Jeanne d'Arc** (☎ 877-248-0718, 7 rue River), a medieval restaurant set in an 1861 building that was constructed to house a bank, was converted into a church and finally became a dining hall in 1998. The atmosphere and décor are first-rate, as are the fine meals. Main dishes run about $14 and five-course specials will run you between $25 to $40.

This locality is also the beginning of wine country, so get prepared.

Dunham
pop 3370

It's not hard to notice you're in the capital of Québec's wine region. Not only do wineries line Rte 202 (rue Bruce) east of Dunham, but the tourist office (☎ 295-2621), at 3638 rue Principale, has everything you need to plan your tippling sessions – the free Québec Wine Route map, display bottles of wine (not for sampling, however!), and advice on where to go. Five of Québec's 32 vineyards are located here. The products won't swear you off French and Australian wines forever, but there are a few finds among them.

Wineries To start, try Les Blancs Coteaux (☎ 295-3503, 1046 rue Bruce) which boasts a biological red wine called La Vielle Grange, and L'Orpailleur (☎ 295-2763, Ⓦ www.orpailleur.ca, 1086 rue Bruce), a charming place with 25 lush acres of grape fields, a great staff and the opportunity to personalize your wine bottle labels. Then stagger, er, move on to Domaine des Côtes d'Ardoise (☎ 295-2020, 879 rue Bruce), where there's a nice terrace and nice walking trails behind their main building; Les Trois Clochers (☎ 295-2034, 341 rue Bruce), a smaller venture with a nearby walking trail and sweet, lavender-scented white wine; or Les Arpents de Neige (☎ 295-3383, 4042 rue Principale), where they grow 500 species of wild flowers (many of which go into their white wines).

All wineries are generally open from 9am to 6pm daily, though only on Saturday and Sunday from January to April.

Places to Stay & Eat The only campgrounds around are south of Dunham near Frelighsburg, 9km south along Rte 213.

Camping Écologique (☎ 298-5259, 877-298-5259, 174 Rte 237) Tent sites $18-22. This one is 3km south of Frelighsburg on the banks of the tiny rivière aux Brochets, and practically snuggles up to the US border. It's sizeable (110 sites) but quiet, with lots of wooded areas, good facilities, walking trails and game areas.

Le Pom Art (☎ 295-3514, 888-537-6627, 677 chemin Hudon) Singles/doubles $70/85. This B&B, set up on a hill just southeast of

Scenic Drive – Chemin du Pinacle

About 1km north of Frelighsburg (south of Dunham), take the chemin du Pinacle, which extends east from Rte 239. It's a mostly gravel road that rises onto a plateau affording some stupendous panoramas onto Mont Pinacle (750m) to the south, and in the distance to the east the tall peaks of the Monts Sutton range. You also pass through some farmland that time has forgotten. Few people pass this way, so you'll feel like time's forgotten you, too. There are some well-indicated walking trails along the way (see W www.montpinacle.ca).

Chemin du Pinacle continues about 13km until Rte 139. To continue the scenic drive – quite literally – continue up the hill to the road's end, then make a left (north) onto chemin Scenic and take in great views from on high all the way down to Sutton.

town, is perfect if you're seeking peace and tranquility. The atmosphere is warm and inviting.

La Chanterelle (☎ 295-3542, 3721 rue Principale) Doubles $80. Right in town, this B&B is as lovely inside as it is outside, with a grand white staircase leading to spacious, subtly decorated rooms.

Le Piccoletto (☎ 295-2664, 3698A rue Principale) Mains $9-15. This is a good address for fine dining, with delicious dinner specials and good pasta dishes.

Sutton
pop 2000
One of the region's most popular destinations, the Sutton township, settled by Loyalists from 1799, has as its focal point the Monts Sutton, a string of velvety, round mountains whose highest peak (Sommet Rond) is 950m. Mont Sutton is the name of the area's famous ski resort. The village itself is in the flatlands of a valley; cutesy and filled with arts and crafts stores, it resembles many New England towns of the same size. It fills up on weekends throughout the year – summer for the hiking, fall for the colors, winter and spring for the skiing.

The tourist office (☎ 538-8455), at 11B rue Principale Sud, is open year-round and can supply you with good maps of the many nearby walkable and cyclable trails. There's bike rentals ($25/day) from Vélocipède de Sutton (☎ 538-1048), 17 rue Principale Nord.

Things to See & Do In the village, the Galerie Tournesol (☎ 538-2563, 7 rue Academy) stands out from the other art galleries in town with some truly unique, creative paintings and painted furniture, with the work of Louise André Roberge tinkering playfully on the edge of art naïf.

Some 80km of popular **hiking** trails have been cleared in the thickly forested mountains and are part of a conserved area called the **Parc d'Environnement Naturel** (☎ 538-4085; adult/child $3/2; open daily June-Oct). There's a refuge ($10) to sleep in at 840m (foam mattresses are supplied) and three campgrounds ($5 per person) with no services. The one at Lac Spruce is particularly nice. Get your passes at the tourist office or at the start of the trails, high up chemin Maple, past Mont Sutton ski hill.

If you want to combine hiking with **kayaking, snowshoeing, backcountry skiing** or other activities, the folks at Au Diable Vert (☎ 538-5639, W www.audiablevert .qc.ca, 169 chemin Staines) will ensure a memorable stay. You can rent equipment and go at it alone or take guided kayaking or hiking tours ($25 to 35), camp out ($20 per site), stay in a refuge ($25) or chalet ($85), get a fine meal ($15) or take a combination package. Again, the views are staggering from their trails and campsites. From Sutton, take chemin Scenic all the way until 1km before the pretty village of Glen Sutton.

However, most visitors come for **Mont Sutton** (☎ 538-2545, W www.montsutton.com, 671 chemin Maple), with its 460m vertical drop, nine lifts, incredible 55 trails (including 11 extreme runs) and a bumpy Skill Zone for snowboarders. There's equipment rental, and day tickets for are $39/28 adult/child 6-17 years old; multiday packages are available.

Places to Stay B&Bs dominate Sutton's accommodations scene.

Willow House (☎ 538-0035, 30 rue Western) Singles/doubles $30/50. The cheapest B&B in town is near the center in a large home that could use a few repairs but is comfortable.

Passiflore Inn (☎ 538-5555, 55 rue Principale Sud) Doubles $60-75. It's right on the main street but the spotless interiors of the B&B are gorgeous, some rooms with wood-paneled floors, and you don't hear much traffic from inside.

Au Pic à Bois (☎ 538-3458, 468 chemin Mont Écho) Doubles $75. Situated 6km north of Sutton in the village of Sutton Junction, this B&B offers peace and quiet in lovely surroundings. It's one of the better places in the area.

Auberge La Paimpolaise (☎ 538-3213, W www.paimpolaise.com, 615 rue Maple) Doubles $115. Close to the ski hills, this has a luxury-resort feel (outdoor Jacuzzi and heated pool to boot!) at prices more reasonable than usual. Ask about their B&B special for $38 per person for a one-night stay.

Places to Eat *Alleghanys* (☎ 538-3802, 33 chemin Maple) Mains $6-14. One of the more popular restaurants in town, it has a cozy bar area and chalet-style dining room. Dishes range from sandwiches and steak to creative seafood and vegetarian dishes.

Tartin'izza (☎ 538-4355, 19 rue Principale Nord) Mains $5-11. Mainly a great pizza and pasta place, they also double as an Internet café ($5/hr).

Chez Camil (☎ 538-2456, 1 rue Principale Sud) Mains $4-11. Basically a greasy diner, the food is less recommended than their adjacent bar/disco, where locals challenge each other to pool games and visitors compare their days on the slopes.

Beetle Pub (☎ 538-3779, 19 rue Principale Nord) Mains $6-10. A cozy bar with pub grub, this is a good place to kick back and relax after a day of skiing or hiking.

Getting There & Away Sutton is 12km north of the US border on Rte 139. Take exit 68 off Hwy 10 and head south on Rte 139.

The bus station (☎ 538-2452) is at 28 rue Principale Nord. Autobus Viens (☎ 348-5599, 877-348-5599) runs two daily buses ($15, 1¾ hours) to/from Montréal with an extra service on Friday and Sunday.

Lac Brome (Knowlton)
pop 3200

Lac Brome is the name of five amalgamated towns, with Knowlton the biggest and best known. Situated just south of Lac Brome (the lake, that is), much of the town's history has been tied to this scenic, small body of water. There's swimming just off chemin Lakeside on the south tip of the lake. The main tourist office (☎ 242-2870) is at 696 chemin Lakeside in the Foster section, just north of the lake.

Loyalists settled Knowlton in the early 19th century, and thanks to a successful flourmill and sawmill the town turned into an upper-class residence and retreat by the end of the century. It still retains a chicer-than-thou air, evidenced by the shiny cars paraded down the main street, the pricey art, antique and souvenir shops and fashionable restaurants. It's worth driving around the side streets to look at the stately homes and manors. Otherwise, the town has a sterile, almost cold feel to it.

The town is also famous for its Brome Duck, essentially Peking duck bred only here since 1912 and fed a special diet including soya and vitamins. The result is a tasty bird that's lower in nasty things like sodium, cholesterol and fat than other meats. You can visit the breeding farm's shop (☎ 242-3825; open 8am-5pm Mon-Fri, 10am-4pm Sat & Sun year-round), at 40 rue Center.

The **Musée Historique du Comté de Brome** (☎ 243-6782, 130 rue Lakeside; adult/ child $3.50/1.50; open 10am-4:30pm daily mid-May–mid-Sept), set up in six historic houses, focuses on the Loyalist history of the area, and, oddly, has a WWI Fokker DVII German war plane on display.

Places to Stay & Eat There are quite a few lovely spots to stay in and around Lac Brome.

Majuka (☎ 243-1239, 266 Stage Coach) Singles/doubles $75/90. This is a sublime B&B you'll fantasize about buying as your country house. Made of wood, nestled in woods, overlooking Sutton's mountains and with a freshwater pond good for a brisk swim after a hot sauna, this place is a dream. From Knowlton, head 6km west to Rte 215, drive 2km south to Brome, then another 2km along chemin Stage Coach.

Auberge Knowlton/Le Relais (☎ 242-6886, W www.cclacbrome.qc.ca/ak, 286 chemin Knowlton) Doubles from $90. This Victorian hotel has pretty rooms. Le Relais is a reputed restaurant on the first floor, with very fine regional and international cuisine and a nice terrace; appetizers go for $3 to $7, mains $15 to $22.

Beaver Pond Motel (☎ 243-5369, 26 Rte 243) Singles/doubles $45/55. This simple but comfortable motel is several minutes west of central Knowlton. Though it's on the main road, it's quiet enough to hear the frogs croaking outside.

Papa Spiro (☎ 242-2409, 290 rue Knowlton) Mains $5-14. Great food like souvlaki and pizza is served with little fuss in a diner atmosphere.

Thirsty Boot Bar (☎ 243-0163, 25 Rte 243) Right across the road from the Beaver Pond Motel is this local favorite, frequented by those who find little comfort in the touristy, up-scale Knowlton bars. The sign outside just says 'Bar,' as the Office de la Langue Française kept hassling the owners about their illegal English name (and translating it into *La Bottine Soif* just wouldn't sound right).

Valcourt
pop 3500

North of Hwy 10, the relatively unattractive though widely renowned Valcourt is 47km north of Knowlton. From Hwy 10, take exit 90 and head north along Rte 243.

Valcourt was founded by Loyalist, Irish and Scottish immigrants, but it was a French family by the name of Bombardier who made the town the epicenter of one of the world's most successful enterprises. There is now a whole mystique created around Joseph Armand Bombardier, father of the snowmobile (Ski-Doo) and whose name is carried on some of the world's finest commercial and military aircraft. His inventions are indeed a source of pride to Canadians.

The Bombardier family settled here around 1814. In the early 20th century, Joseph Armand's (who was not yet 15 years old) tinkering had led him to develop a primitive way of traveling across snowy plains in a motorized cart. A real prototype was developed by 1935, and two years later a small factory opened. The war effort called for a military use for his inventions and in 1941, a full-blown factory began operations, which still continue today. While Bombardier wasn't the only or the first to have invented a motorized snow vehicle, he was the first to manufacture one and as such is credited with the invention of the snowmobile.

If there's any doubt about Québécois' deep attachment to the Ski-Doo, it's erased during mid-February's **Valcourt Grand Prix** (☎ 532-3443, W www.grandprixvalcourt .com), the largest gathering of snowmobile enthusiasts in the world.

Things to See & Do Valcourt is visited for two sites of international renown on opposite ends of the social spectrum. At the **Musée J Armand Bombardier** (☎ 532-5300, W www.fjab.qc.ca/museejab, 1000 avenue J-A Bombardier; adult/student $5/3; open 10am-5pm daily May–early Sept, 10am-5pm Tues-Sun early Sept–Apr), you can see early models of Armand's famous snowmobile (and see amusing clips of how they looked in action) and other inventions, and get a tour of the factory.

Valcourt's other residents of world-wide renown ('infamy' might be a more accurate term) are the Raelians. Quite an intriguing bunch, actually (see 'Beam Me Up, Rael!').

On a dusty lot outside town, they've set up a funky museum of sorts, **UFOland** (☎ 532-6864, Ⓦ *www.ufoland.com, 1382 rang 7; adult/child $10/7.50; open 10am-5pm Sat & Sun June, 10am-5pm Wed-Sun July-Aug*), which was constructed out of straw bales in accordance with messages that the movement's leader, Rael, received from extraterrestrials. You'll get a 90-minute tour, visit a life-size UFO replica, learn why genetics and cloning are salient to the Raelians (there's an 8m DNA model to revel at) and be guided to the kitschy souvenir shop.

MEMPHRÉMAGOG

In many ways the most interesting sector of the Eastern Townships, this area is defined geographically by the huge Lac Memphrémagog and therefore offers excellent opportunities to get your fill of water sports. Just as significant is the Parc du Mont Orford, with top-rate facilities to please skiers. There's a major town, Magog, to take care of urban yearnings (at least a few!), and lovely areas where you're highly unlikely to see another tourist, even in the middle of summer. Culturally, the area offers some diversity beyond the usual

---

'Beam Me Up, Rael!'

The Raelians are a quasi-religious cult who believe that humans were invented by extraterrestrials from the planet Elohim. Allegedly, representatives of Elohim's inhabitants paid two visits to Claude Vorilhon (a former automobile journalist and race-car driver now called Rael) in France back in 1973 and 1975 to explain to him the origin of our species. They also convinced him to build an embassy for the Elohim in Jerusalem. As soon as it was built, they would visit our planet as friendly guests and set us all straight as to our true origins.

In 1975 Vorilhon was lucky enough to have met Jesus, Buddha, Confucius and that other great visionary, Joseph Smith. ('Who?' you ask? Ah, ye of little faith, it was he whose own visitations by heavenly creatures led him to found Mormonism!) You see, these were all prophets created by the Elohim to help humanity progress, and they now live happily together on the far-away planet.

Rael dons a spacey white suit and gives lectures worldwide on many topics, including how to awaken consciousness and appreciate the here and now, essential to foster the openness of spirit needed to receive Elohim's messages. This can be achieved, wouldn't you know, through 'sensual mediation' including lots of vigorous masturbation and 'communal orgasms,' and by shedding emotional and sexual inhibitions.

Raelians are also great proponents of cloning, as it was extraterrestrial genetic engineering that created humanity in the first place. In 1997 they founded Clonaid in the Bahamas, a research center whose goal was to clone humans (those interested in cloning themselves had to give only a few sample cells and $200,000). Chased out of the Bahamas, they relocated to the USA, where they were chased away in 2001. They moved operations to another, undisclosed country, but soon after were beat by another company, which first successfully cloned human cells.

Raelians' theory of scientific creationism, which blends beliefs in UFOs and unhindered sensuality, has found some 55,000 adherents in 84 countries. Many of these gather every July in Valcourt, where Rael has set up his personal headquarters, for a two-week Sensual Mediation camp. From all reports, this sounds like a free-love commune of the 1960s. The sexual experimentation tacitly encouraged must certainly open many cosmic pathways to Elohim.

Rael has had less luck building his embassy in Jerusalem. Some Raelians in Switzerland, where there's an especially strong following, tried demanding diplomatic status for Elohim in their Federal Assembly. They were rebuffed when a member of the Assembly stated that the government would expect the opening of a Swiss embassy on Elohim in return.

Anglo-Franco divide, with small Ukrainian and Russian settlements smack in the middle of peaceful woods.

Magog
☎ 819 • pop 14,600

The area around this town was settled after the 1797 arrival of New Englander Ralph Merry III, who founded several flour and saw mills. The tourist office (☎ 843-2744, 800-267-2744) is a busy place, at 55 rue Cabana, walking distance from the wharf and city beach. There are photographs and details of accommodations and restaurants in the area, and you can make free local calls.

In a converted 1881 Methodist church, **Le Vieux Clocher** (*☎ 847-0470, 64 rue Merry Nord*), a theatrical and concert hall, hosts popular Québécois acts all summer. Tickets usually start at $12.

The real attraction here is the lake. There's a small, free **beach** in the middle of town that's often unbearably crowded. At the marina, 200m south of the beach, a number of companies offer **water sports**. Tribord (☎ 868-2222) has a kiosk there and offers parasailing, Sea-Doo (Jetski) rides,

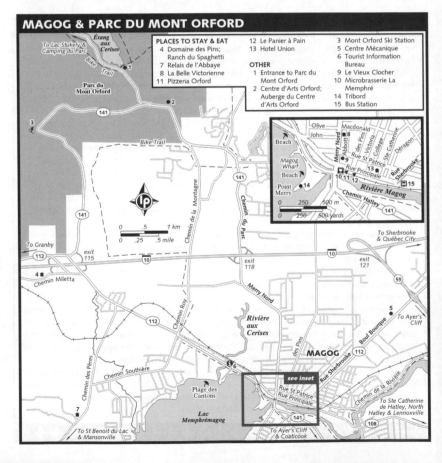

MAGOG & PARC DU MONT ORFORD

PLACES TO STAY & EAT
4   Domaine des Pins;
    Ranch du Spaghetti
7   Relais de l'Abbaye
8   La Belle Victorienne
11 Pizzeria Orford

12 Le Panier à Pain
13 Hotel Union

OTHER
1   Entrance to Parc du
    Mont Orford
2   Centre d'Arts Orford;
    Auberge du Centre
    d'Arts Orford

3   Mont Orford Ski Station
5   Centre Mécanique
6   Tourist Information
    Bureau
9   Le Vieux Clocher
10 Microbrasserie La
    Memphré
14 Tribord
15 Bus Station

waterskiing and a bumpy ride on a Big Banana. Count on prices of at least $25 per hour for these activities. Big boat cruises also ply Lac Memphrémagog from here; cruises start at $27/19 adult/child.

Sea-Doos and their landlocked cousins Ski-Doos can be rented at Centre Mécanique Magog (☎ 868-2919), at 9 boulevard Bourque, a five-minute drive from the center of town. They'll transport your rented equipment free of charge.

A 23.5km **bicycle trail** begins from Magog and ends up at the entrance to the Parc du Mont Orford.

Places to Stay & Eat While there are numerous places to stay and eat in central Magog, it's recommended that you venture out of town for more scenic and varied options. If you have a car, the Parc du Mont Orford makes an excellent alternative to town and offers several accommodations choices.

Hotel Union (☎ *843-3363, 259 rue Principale*) Doubles $30-50. Central and cheap – that's about all it has going for it. Though sometimes that's all you need.

La Belle Victorienne (☎ *847-0476,* Ⓦ *www.bellevic.com, 142 rue Merry Nord*) Doubles $75-95. A daintily elegant and large Victorian house in the town center, this is reputed to be one of the best places in town. You can have your morning coffee in the garden.

Domaine des Pins/Ranch du Spaghetti (☎ *847-4091,* Ⓦ *www.domainedespins.com,*

The Creatures of Memphrémagog

Legend has it that a prehistoric creature nicknamed Memphré lives in Lac Memphrémagog. Sadly, however, just like its feisty cousins in Loch Ness, Lake Champlain and other lakes around the world where monsters supposedly reside, this sneaky bugger has eluded photographers and researchers who could reliably prove its existence.

Still, the 'evidence' is intriguing in a sort of 'hmmm' way. Apparently, when Europeans first arrived in the area, they were warned by the Abenaki not to swim in the lake because a monster resided in it. A petroglyph (mysteries in and of themselves) found in the region, dating back at least 1500 years, apparently, had the figure of a serpent on it. There have been some 230 confirmed sightings of a creature (with a serpentlike head, several humps and a body length of about 15m) in both the US and Canadian sides of the lake.

While many of these sightings were filed by reputable people not stoned out

Don't mess with Memphré

of their minds when they saw *something* in the lake, no documentary proof exists that Memphré lives. Thousands of exploratory dives have found nothing. Keep up to date with sightings – or report one yourself! – via Ⓦ www.interlinx.qc.ca/memphre/ang.

This scenic lake is actually more famous for another creature, one much less shy than the cryptozoological Memphré: the ouananiche, a fresh water salmon whose capture is a main pastime for hundreds of local fishermen. It no doubt tastes better than old Memphré would.

The lake itself has a serpentine shape (which might have something to do with the legend of Memphré in the first place) and covers 103 sq km. It is 42km long (only 2 to 4 km wide) and is surrounded by a rocky and wooded escarpment 240m in height in some places.

3005 chemin Miletta) Singles/doubles $70/95; mains $8-15. Your best choice in Magog is this motel-restaurant combo near the southern tip of the Parc du Mont Orford, not far from exit 115 off Hwy 10. Away from the town bustle, you're treated to excellent views, comfortable rooms and a very good dining room where, as you can tell by the name, pasta reigns supreme.

Relais de l'Abbaye (☎ 450-759-0228, 877-868-5151, 2705 chemin Gendreau) Doubles $80-160. A warm and luxurious mansion-style home in a quiet region west of Magog, this boasts spacious and elegant rooms. The more expensive rooms have fireplace, balcony and/or Jacuzzi. Breakfast and a five-course dinner costs an extra $50.

Pizzeria Orford (☎ 843-6554, 176 rue Principale Ouest) Mains $6-10. Pizzas large and small, plus sandwiches, salads and steaks, are on offer at this local hangout.

Le Panier à Pain (☎ 868-6602, 382 rue Principale Ouest) Mains $4-8. This place builds great sandwiches to take on your day in Parc du Mont Orford and also serves sit-down meals like salads, waffles and full breakfasts, along with excellent pastries and strong espresso.

Microbrasserie La Memphré (☎ 843-3405, 12 rue Merry Sud) Mains $5-11. You sample and purchase some mighty fine local brew here in a nicely arranged brewery-restaurant setting. Pub meals are served as well.

Getting There & Away The bus station (☎ 843-4617) is at 67 rue Sherbrooke. There are 10 daily buses to/from Montréal ($23, 1½-3 hours) and seven extra buses on Friday and Saturday. They leave most hours on the hour from 8am to 11pm from Montréal, but ask if it's an express or local bus – the latter takes twice as long.

Magog is accessible by car off exit 118 from Hwy 10.

Parc du Mont Orford
☎ 819

Just north of Magog (a 10-minute drive), this Sépaq-run, 58-sq-km park (☎ 843-9855, 877-843-9855, 3321 chemin du Parc; admis-

sion $3.50; open daily year-round) is one of the province's best and most diverse, partially due to an arts center and excellent ski station in its territory. These allow the park to have a functional use and be enjoyed by thousands of people even if they don't partake in outdoor activities. Surprisingly, there is no public transport system from Magog to Parc du Mont Orford, so you'll have to rely on wheels – car or bike – to get there.

Flanked by two mountains, Orford (853m) and Chauve (600m), the park is a forested paradise with a major lake (Lac Stukely), rivers and numerous walking trails. There's an 11.5km trail that leads to the summit of Mt Orford. The views from here are very dramatic – on a clear day you can see all the way to Vermont, in the US. Canoe trips up the Étang aux Cerises are popular.

The **Centre d'Arts Orford** (☎ 843-9871, Ⓦ www.arts-orford.org, 3165 chemin du Parc) hosts the **Festival Orford**, a series of highly reputed classical music, theater and dance performances held in July and August. Tickets range from $20 to $30. It's a pleasant place to just drop in as well, and occasionally free exhibits are mounted.

Mont Orford (☎ 843-6548, 800-363-3342, Ⓦ www.mt-orford.com, chemin du Parc; open 9am-4pm daily) is a massive ski station, with 52 slopes and a 540m vertical drop; 75% of the slopes are not classed as difficult, so it's not a place for maniacal thrill-seekers. There are also 56km of cross-country trails. During the last week of September and the first week of October, there's a panoramic chairlift ride to take in the splendid autumn colors (adult/child $9.50/7.50 roundtrip), and Octoberfest is a much-loved Bavarian-beer, song and drinking festival held in early October.

Places to Stay Within Parc du Mont Orford, your accommodations (and eating options) are limited.

Auberge du Centre d'Arts Orford (☎ 843-8595, Ⓦ www3.sympatico.ca/arts.orford, 3165 chemin du Parc) Dorm beds $15/18 HI member/nonmember, doubles $89. Located on the grounds of the Centre d'Arts, this is one of the province's nicest locations for a hostel. The spacious, rustic cabins are available from May through October. There's also a lovely, peaceful hotel, mostly for art lovers who arrive for the concerts and show. Off-season (spring and fall) these rooms can sometimes be had for as low as $21 each.

Camping du Parc (☎ 843-9855, 877-843-9855, 3321 chemin du Parc) Tent sites $19-30, refuges $13. Camping on a site with services can get pricey here, depending on whether you require electricity – plus they also charge $5 to reserve in advance! Parking is another $5. Despite the sense of gouging here, the park has lovely campgrounds, though you're just as well to pitch a tent in the wild ($19).

St Benoit du Lac
☎ 819 • pop 53

That's right, population 53. As in, 53 monks. This lovely area (hard to call it a village), 18km south of Magog on the west side of the lake, is dominated by a **Benedictine monastery** (☎ 843-4080, Ⓦ www.st-benoit-du-lac.com; open 5am-9pm daily year-round), founded here in 1912.

French architect Dom Paul Bellot believed that the structure of the building itself promoted inner harmony. It's an imposing neo-Gothic construction in which the monks practice Gregorian chanting and pray much of the day – that is, when they're not busy working, making cheeses, ciders, maple products and chocolates. The store (open 9am-10:45am & 11:45am-4:30pm Mon-Sat year-round, until 6pm July & Aug), in the basement of the main monastery building, sells their delicious creations. Their cheeses are particularly well-known across Québec – there are 14 different kinds.

Men can sleep at the monastery, though casual overnighters are not encouraged. Usually people come for several days of peaceful contemplation. The charge is a donation. Women are also welcome under the same conditions in an adjacent building, the Villa Ste Scholastica (☎ 843-2340).

Mansonville & Around
☎ 450 • pop 900

Named after a town in Bedfordshire, England, Mansonville and its surrounding area has a special feel to it. This is only partly due to its remoteness (just 7km from the Vermont, US, border). The small tourist office (☎ 292-3109) is at 302 rue Principale. It's open late June through early September, 10am to 6pm daily.

In the nearby village of **Vale Perkins**, a number of petroglyphs have been uncovered in two archeological sites, called Jones and White. These carved stones have been carbon-dated to be 1500 to 1800 years old. What makes them unique is that some of them have been engraved with ideographic

---

Scenic Drive – St Benoit du Lac to Mansonville

Between Mansonville and St Benoit du Lac, the unbelievably scenic drive offers up some stupendous scenery of mountains and the lake, all from pretty country roads sometimes covered by an arc of leafy maple trees. You'll pass the odd cemetery, barns falling romantically apart, a weather vane in the shape of a cow and, near Knowlton Landing, a small area called Vorokhta where 20 Ukrainian families are the only residents.

From St Benoit du Lac, go 2km west on route de la Baie Serpent, turn left onto chemin Cooledge, and stick to your left again, following chemin du Lac until Vale Perkins, where there's a public beach. Mont Owl's Head is nearby. Continue on chemin Vale Perkins to Mansonville.

signs associated with ancient Celtic culture. The symbols B-L signifying the Celt god Baal have been deciphered. This has raised many questions as to how these stones got there – had Vikings made it to the continent earlier than we thought? Did the Native Canadians have some previously unknown link with Celtic culture?

Another anomaly in the Québec landscape is the small Russian **Orthodox monastery** south of Mansonville. It is not open to the public (so be discreet if you go) and services are held there only rarely, as the community is so small. However it's worth a visit to take in the calm isolation of the area and to check out the atmospheric cemetery. To get there head about 4km south on Rte 143, turn east on chemin de l'Aéroport and south on chemin du Monastère.

There's downhill skiing at **Owl's Head** (☎ 292-3342, W www.owlshead.com, chemin du Mont Owl's Head; day pass adult/child $32/25; open 9am-4pm Mon-Fri, 8:30am-4pm Sat & Sun). There are only 27 slopes, but the vertical drop is 540m, there are five double-diamond runs, and the chairlifts can move 10,000 skiers per hour (say goodbye to long lineups!). From the top you can see all the way up the frozen lake to Mont Orford. There is a hotel with doubles for $90.

The bus station (☎ 292-3109) is at 302 rue Principale. One bus a day links Mansonville with Montréal ($18, 2½ hours), with an extra service Friday and Sunday from/to Montréal. The same bus makes stops at Knowlton and Sutton.

Places to Stay & Eat Though the pickings here are slim, you'll be rewarded by lovely, quiet surroundings. The local tourist office can help you find other accommodations options.

Carrefour des Campeurs (☎ 292-3737, chemin Vallée Missisquoi) Tent sites $17-21. This fairly large campground (119 sites) is spread out over 80 wooded acres of land and water and offers canoe rental.

Le Vieux Presbytère (☎ 292-5753, 328 rue Principale) Doubles $75. There are three doubles plus one family room ($90) in this nice home in central Mansonville.

Owl's Bread (☎ 292-3088, 299A rue Principale) Mains $4-9, dinner specials $20-24. This bakery-restaurant sells fresh bread and pastries, and serves hot and cold sandwiches, salads and daily three- or four-course dinner specials like Brome Lake duck.

SHERBROOKE & AROUND
☎ 819

This section covers the area from Sherbrooke, *the* city in the Townships, down to the US border. Lac Massawippi is the major feature here, a picture-postcard perfect (and monsterless) lake. Farther south, around Coaticook, is some of the Townships' most arresting scenery, which, because the area is somewhat out of the tourist loop, is easier to get happily lost in and appreciate *au naturel*.

Sherbrooke
pop 78,100

The administrative and industrial capital of the Eastern Townships is a pleasant, bilingual city, a mix of slightly rundown 19th-century charm in the old downtown sector with its low-key antique shops, newer sectors with modern conveniences and riverside parks. With the Université de Sherbrooke and nearby Lennoxville's Bishop's University, there's a youthful energy to it, and therefore some good nightlife options, too.

Founded on an area called Ktineketolek-wak by the Abenaki who used to live here, its modern development began in the late 1790s with American Loyalists founding a flourmill and sawmill here. An active textile (especially cotton and wool) industry flourished in the mid-19th century.

The tourist office (☎ 821-1919, 800-561-8331) is at 3010 rue King Ouest. Réseau Riverain, the 18km walking and cycling path along rivière Magog, makes an agreeable stroll. It begins at the edge of Parc Blanchard (☎ 822-5890), where there's also a public beach (it's on the south side of rivière Magog, accessed via rue Cabana).

MoMo Sports (☎ 822-3077), 42 rue Wellington Nord, rents many kinds of bicycles.

Things to See & Do The **Centre d'Interprétation de Sherbrooke** (☎ 821-5406, 275

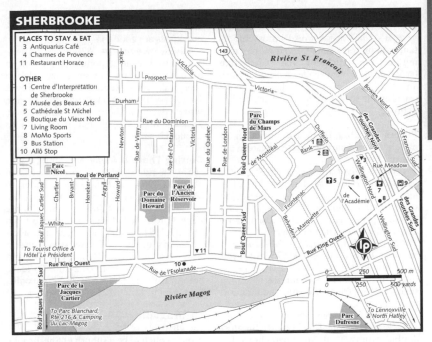

SHERBROOKE

PLACES TO STAY & EAT
3 Antiquarius Café
4 Charmes de Provence
11 Restaurant Horace

OTHER
1 Centre d'Interprétation de Sherbrooke
2 Musée des Beaux Arts
5 Cathédrale St Michel
6 Boutique du Vieux Nord
7 Living Room
8 MoMo Sports
9 Bus Station
10 Allô Stop

rue Dufferin; adult/student $4/2.50; open 9am-5pm Tues-Sun) has a lot to offer. There's an exhibit on the city's history, and it's possible to book a guided city tour or head out on your own with a recorded version ($7). The center is also one of the province's best kept archives, and you'll see many people researching their genealogies or going through old newspapers.

At the **Musée des Beaux Arts** (☎ 821-2115, *241 rue Dufferin; adult/student $4/3; open 11am-5pm Tues & Thurs-Sun, 11am-9pm Wed late June–early Sept; 1pm-5pm Tues & Thurs-Sun, 1pm-9pm Wed early Sept–late June)*, there are decent temporary exhibits along with a permanent display of regional artists and sculptors. Art naïf is well represented here, particularly in the works of Arthur Villeneuve.

The **Cathédrale St Michel** (☎ 563-9934, *130 rue de la Cathédrale; admission free; open 8am-noon & 2pm-7pm daily)* is an impressive Gothic cathedral with 105 stained-glass

works re-creating Old Testament episodes. In the chapel are works by Ozias Leduc.

Window-shopping in the old part of town, along rue Wellington Nord, is pleasant. Boutique du Vieux Nord (☎ 562-4746, 150 rue Wellington Nord) is fun to poke around in and has a junkshop feel with antique-store prices.

Special Events There's usually lots going on in both winter and summer. The **Fête du Lac and Molson Great Canadian Fireworks** (☎ 823-5171) happens in mid-July for six days of fireworks, free concerts and general merry-making. The **World Tradition Festival** (☎ 565-0522, w www.ftmf.qc.ca), in mid-August, is five days of multicultural exhibits and performances centering on dance, music and arts and crafts.

If you're one of the handful of lucky folks to find yourself spending Christmas in Sherbrooke (!), check out the **International Bantam Hockey Tournament** (☎ 569-2319, tibs.qc.ca), which happens between Christmas and New Year's at several arenas here. It's billed as the world's most important bantam tournament. Even more exciting is the **Michelin Ice Challenge** (☎ 560-4270, W www.challengecanada.com), an international car race on the ice that attracts about 30,000 spectators at the end of February.

Places to Stay There are a number of motels on rue King Ouest at the western entrance of the city.

Camping du Lac Magog (☎ 864-4401, 7255 chemin Blanchette) Tent sites $17-24. A nice location near Lac Magog some 12km south of town, there are 135 sites and good swimming. Take Rte 216 out of Sherbrooke and head west on chemin Blanchette.

Charmes de Provence (☎ 348-1147, 350 rue du Québec) Doubles $75. Situated near small Parc de l'Ancien Réservoir, this is a justifiably popular B&B – nice surroundings, friendly owners and a good breakfast.

Hôtel Le Président (☎ 563-2941, 800-363-2941, 3535 rue King Ouest) Singles/doubles from $50/80. Not a bad choice for mid-priced hotels, this one is on a main thoroughfare and has an indoor pool and sauna.

Places to Eat & Drink Thanks to the nearby universities, Sherbrooke's nightlife is well developed, and you'll find lots of late-night action along rue Wellington Nord.

Antiquarius Café (☎ 562-1800, 182 rue Wellington Nord) Mains $7-14; open 10am-5:30pm Mon & Tues, 10am-10pm Wed-Sun. This is a truly amazing place, half antique store, half restaurant, where you can eat surrounded by – even on! – nice works of art and old furniture. Check out the engraved ceilings. There are giant sandwiches and paninis, as well as carefully prepared fish and meat meals. It's also good for a lazy coffee.

Restaurant Horace (☎ 820-1520, 1115 rue King Ouest) Mains $6-15; open 24 hrs. This is a good bet at any time of the day (and the crowd gets pretty interesting come 3am on a

Sunday morning!). Their specialties are seafood and mussels, but their copious breakfasts are good too.

Living Room (☎ 822-3534, 66 rue Meadow) The most popular nightclub in town, it's as good as any same-sized club in Montréal, a hip place for an under-30 crowd. There's a VIP lounge, a large covered terrace, funky décor and friendly atmosphere. Tuesday night's open bar from 9pm to 11:30pm is a hit.

Getting There & Away Allô Stop (☎ 821-3637), the ride-sharing organization, has an office at 1204 rue King Ouest. Rides to Montréal/Québec City cost $9/15.

The bus station (☎ 569-3656) is at 20 rue King Ouest. Ten daily buses go to/from Montréal ($26, 2¼-3½ hours), with an additional six buses on Friday and Sunday. Buses also go to Trois Rivières, Magog and Granby. Local buses (Nos 2 and 82) leave here to Bishop's University, in Lennoxville, from 6am to 1am ($2.25).

Lennoxville
pop 4850

Close enough to be a suburb of Sherbrooke but feeling like it's in another country, Lennoxville is the region's English bastion, thanks to the Anglican **Bishop's University** (☎ 822-9600, W www.ubishops.ca, rue du Collège). Founded in 1843 (it had been Bishop's College from 1834) and styled architecturally after Oxford and Cambridge Universities in England, it has managed to retain an air of the mother country – notably in the certain stiffness that reigns over the rather prim campus.

The campus' architectural highlight is St Mark's Chapel (☎ 822-9718, rue du Collège; admission free; open 8am-5pm Mon-Sat, 10am-5pm Sun, mass 10am Sun). Constructed in 1857 in the perpendicular Gothic style, popular during the 13th-century Tudor period, the chapel is a pastiche of elements recalling churches overseas. The beautiful entrance door's ogival arch recalls one at Trinity College; the windows repeat the arrangement at Salisbury Cathedral. The interiors are beautiful, particularly the wood carvings, but the chapel is too close to traffic to be peaceful.

The **Uplands Cultural and Heritage Centre** (☎ 564-0409, W www.uplands.ca, 9 rue Speid; admission free; open 1pm-4:30pm Tues-Sun late June–early Sept; 1pm-4:30pm Thur, Fri & Sun early Sept–Dec & Feb–late June) is in a neo-Georgian home dating from 1862. Different art and photography exhibits are set up, and afternoon British tea is served summertime for a small fee.

For bicycle, canoe and kayak (single and duo) rentals, check out Le Dépot (☎ 820-2453, 4 rue Massawippi), right on the banks of the rivière Massawippi. A bike trail from here leads 13km to North Hatley. They can arrange for you to bike there and canoe back. Half-day bike/canoe rentals are $20/30.

Lennoxville is only 5km south of Sherbrooke along rue Wellington (Rte 143). Buses Nos 2 and 82 run from Bishop's University to the bus station in Sherbrooke. One bus daily goes to/from Montréal ($28, 2½ hours) with one extra service on Friday and Sunday.

Places to Stay & Eat The accommodations options here are very limited. A few fast-food places line Rte 143 (rue Queen).

Bishop's University Residences (☎ 822-9600 ext 4, rue du Collège) Singles/doubles $16/25 with shared bath, $19/33 semi-private bath. Somewhat austere but clean student residences are available from mid-May to late August and allow you access to the excellent sports facilities and pool. Register at MacKinnon Hall (follow the signs reading 'Conferences').

Lion d'Or (☎ 565-1015, 2 rue Collège) Mains $4-10. This pub-restaurant, on the corner of Rte 143, is a local institution – the university's party central, a place where students mingle, perhaps shoot a game of pool – and it's also a good place to get a meal (sandwiches, burgers, daily specials).

North Hatley
pop 800
On a beautiful spot at the northern tip of Lac Massawippi, this is the cutest of all the cute Eastern Township towns. An epicenter of art galleries and antique shops, this is where the upper classes with artistic inclinations come to shop. Consequently, there's fine dining to boot.

The stately homes attest to its past as a vacation spot for rich Americans who used to partake of the charming ambience via a passenger rail service that once linked Sherbrooke with Vermont. As early as 1880 it could be called a resort town. An American influence is still felt: There are just as many cow paintings and scented candles here as

Scenic Drive – Lennoxville to Coaticook

Cruising from Lennoxville to Coaticook is a driver's paradise. Take a roundabout way of getting there. Head south of Lennoxville on Rte 147 to the village of Compton (17km). Turn east on Rte 208, make a left after 3km on chemin Couture and a left again at chemin Viens and go back to Compton.

Now that you've completed a pretty circle and taken in rolling hills and rustic houses, keep going south but on chemin Cochrane (the road extending off the east side of Rte 147, where the Boni Soir convenience store is). Drive for about 7km, taking in the superb views of valleys and fields and distant mountains to the west. Rejoin Rte 147 by turning west on tiny chemin Riendeau, go south for another kilometer, then head west again on chemin Vaillancourt. You need go only about 1km to the top of the hill to appreciate the gorgeous view of endlessly sloping hills and scenic farmhouses. From there head back to Rte 147 and continue 7km to Coaticook.

anywhere in New England, and rue Principale is even sometimes still referred to as Main St here!

The tourist office (☎ 842-2223) is at 300 rue Mill. They sell the $10 pass you're supposed to buy to use to bike trails in the region (trails are patrolled, but the fine of being on the trail without a pass is the $10 to buy one on the spot). There's Internet access at L'Agora (☎ 842-4701), 35 rue Principale, a used bookstore, publishing house (of a literary magazine) and Internet café without coffee ($6/hr).

Things to See & Do The **Au Gremier de Gife** (☎ 842-4440, 330 chemin de la Rivière) is an art gallery with beautifully painted furniture and creative works by local artists. There's a pleasant tea shop attached to it, and you can sip tea or coffee in the mini–Chinese gardens out front. Another worthwhile art gallery is **Gallerie Jeanine Blais** (☎ 842-2784, 100 rue Principale), which specializes in colorful, fanciful art naïf.

Les Sports d'Eau (☎ 842-2676, 240 rue Mill), adjacent to the parking lots in front of the tourist office, rents bikes/canoes/kayaks/paddleboats for $7/15/10/12 per hour. **Équitation Massawippi** (☎ 842-4249, 4700 Rte 108) provides horse rides through nature for $35 for two hours.

There's alpine skiing at **Montjoye** (☎ 842-2447, 4785 chemin Capelton; day pass adult/student 16-21/child 5-15 $20/16/13; open 9am-10pm daily). Most of the trails are not difficult, and it's a good place to bring the kids – there are children's training courses and lots of equipment for kids to rent. Many runs are illuminated at night. There are good prices for half-day or night skiing.

Places to Stay This is not the place to find inexpensive accommodations, but many of the B&Bs and lodges are sumptuous and boast very pretty views. The tourist office has photos and descriptions of all lodging types.

Serendipity (☎ 842-2970, 680 chemin de la Rivière) Singles/doubles $70/90. North Hatley's least expensive B&B provides pleasant views and an agreeable decor.

Abenaki Lodge (☎ 842-4455, W www.abenakilodge.com, 4030 chemin Magog) Doubles $159-179. This four-star mini-palace has impressive, wood-paneled interiors and spacious rooms decorated with fine rugs and arts and crafts.

Manoir Hovey (☎ 842-2421, W www.manoirhovey.com, 575 chemin Hovey) Doubles from $220, including breakfast and dinner. If four stars aren't enough, here's a five-star, bright white, luxury complex, built according to a model of George Washington's residence on Mt Vernon, Virginia. It sits on the lake and boasts its own beach.

Places to Eat North Hatley is full of quaint restaurants and cafés, though prices here are higher than in other towns in the Eastern Townships. The tourist office has a booklet with photos and descriptions of the local places to eat.

Café Lafontaine (☎ 842-4242, 35 rue Principale) Mains $7-13. You can't go wrong with anything on the menu here, from $5 nachos to a $12 warm salmon salad. The atmosphere is relaxed – just grab a paper and lounge.

Pub Pilsen (☎ 842-2971, 55 rue Principale) Mains $9-13. You can try the Massawippi dark beer in this upscale pub, which serves everything from light snacks to large seafood, meat and vegetarian meals.

Café Massawippi (☎ 842-4528, 3050 chemin Capelton) Mains $10-16. North Haltey's most inventive cuisine is no doubt in this pleasant restaurant, which serves dishes like rabbit spring rolls in pernod sauce for $14 and lamb in chili sauce for $35.

Getting There & Away North Hatley is only 17km east of Magog along Rte 108. However there's a longer, scenic route from Magog: Take Rte 141 12km south, then head north on chemin de la Montagne, which runs parallel to Lake Massawippi. Next, at Ste Catherine de Hatley, head east on chemin de North Hatley–Magog until it rejoins Rte 108; North Hatley is just 2km farther east.

If you're coming from Sherbrooke, head south on Rte 143 until Rte 108. North Hatley is 9km away.

There is no bus service to/from the town.

Hockey-Stick Tape Border

In the municipality of Stanstead, an amalgamation of several small villages straddling the US frontier, a very special notion of 'border' exists. In the village of Rock Island, at the southern end of Rte 143 (off Hwy 55), several buildings, main roads and side streets are shared with Derby Line, Vermont, on the other side. Locals chock up the uneven, illogical border to soused British surveyors who drew it two centuries ago.

The height of absurdity is reached in the village's main cultural building, the 1901 Haskell Free Library and Opera House (☎ 876-2020, 1 rue Church), modeled after Boston's Opera House: The border runs right through it. It has the distinction of being the only US library with no books (they're all in Québec) and the only US opera house with no stage (it's in Canada)!

In the main reading and research area, the US-Canada border is demarcated with a black line made with hockey-stick tape, which runs down the middle of the room (placed a few years ago for insurance purposes – if there's a fire or vandalism in either side, it'll be the responsibility of the appropriate country's insurance company). How perfect that it's hockey tape and not, say, boring old electrical tape! Spectators can also ask for American or Canadian seating for their operas.

The border issue is both a novelty for visitors and a daily reality – and sometimes a headache – for the locals. Sure, they can cross-border shop easily, and many residents keep post office boxes on either side to facilitate mail-order delivery. But there are customs formalities to deal with, as well as the creepy presence of overhead spy cameras set up to spot ne'er-do-wells. People who cross illegally into the US can be fined US$5000 for doing so (though sneaking into Canada is a better deal – the fine's only $200). Security is sure to be beefed up under new border agreements signed by both countries.

Meanwhile, it's a curiosity that locals have learned to live with, and occasionally laugh at, like tripping over the hockey tape and knowing they've crossed an international border.

Coaticook
pop 9000

The entire area around this town is particularly scenic. With rolling hills and stretches of sweet-smelling forest interspersed with farms (this is the province's milk capital, with 300 dairy farms), the roads see little traffic and make for great cycling. The area was settled in the late 18th century but flourished as more Loyalist families arrived and opened businesses, schools and a post office. It receives fewer tourists than do other regions in the Townships, yet is no less beautiful. The tourist office (☎ 849-6669), 635 rue Child, is open 10am to 6pm daily from late June through early September.

You can cross the longest suspension bridge in the world (169m) in the **Parc de la Gorge de Coaticook** (☎ 849-2331, ⓦ *www .gorgedecoaticook.qc.ca, 135 rue Michaud; adult/child $7/4; open 10am-5pm daily*

May–late June & early Sept–Nov, 9am-7pm daily late June–early Sept, 9am-4pm Mon-Wed & 9am-9pm Thurs-Sun Dec–mid-Mar). The bridge towers 50m above an impressive gorge created by the rivière Coaticook coursing through it. There are 10km of hiking and 18.5km of biking trails as well as other surprises inside this wild, lovely and very worth-visiting park.

Places to Stay & Eat The choices in this area are pretty limited, but the places you will find have a quiet, country charm.

Camping de Compton (☎ *835-5277,* ⓦ *www.campingcompton.com, 24 chemin Station)* Tent sites $15. Located 15km north of Coaticook outside Compton, this is one of the province's best campgrounds. Though it's fairly large (180 sites), it's peaceful – guests are gently encouraged to respect each other's privacy. Moreover, it's perched atop a hill overlooking a valley that stretches to distant mountains, so the views are stupendous. The owners are super friendly.

Brise des Nuits *(☎ 849-4667, 142 rue Cutting)* Singles/doubles $55/65. One block from a bike path in Coaticook, this is a charming little B&B that captures the atmosphere of its surroundings.

Coffret de l'Imagination *(☎ 849-0090, 145 rue Michaud)* Mains $6-12. Opposite the Parc de la Gorge, this café-restaurant serves incredible food – killer gazpacho, stuffed crêpes, and meat and seafood dishes – either on an outdoor terrace where birds make more noise than the diners or in a cozy dining room that doubles as a boutique.

MÉGANTIC
☎ 819

This region covers the far eastern section of the Eastern Townships, bordering Maine and New Hampshire. It boasts the highest elevations in the region, with mountains topping 1000m. Some towns around the Parc du Mont Mégantic sit 600m above sea level. Mégantic is also the least visited part of the Townships; one of its greatest attractions is that it is less developed, boasting superb scenery and more breathing space.

Parc du Mont Mégantic

Some 60km east of Sherbrooke and Lennoxville along Rtes 108 and 212, just 5km from the village of Notre Dame des Bois, is this provincial park *(☎ 888-2941, 866-888-2941, 189 route du Parc; admission $3.50; open 9am-11pm daily June–early Sept, 9am-5pm early Sept–May)*.

Dominated by the impressive Mont Mégantic (1105m), the rocky, mountainous park boasts over 50km of altitude **hiking** trails – some bits require expert hiking skills and good boots. Over 120 species of birds live here along with animals like Virginia deer, red lynx and moose. Sépaq, which runs the park, organizes guided activities, nature walks and ecological displays.

In winter the park opens up 10km of **snowshoeing** trails and 40km of beautiful **cross-country skiing** trails. On the full moon every March, a cross-country ski run by torchlight is organized – quite something to remember.

Unique to this park is the **AstroLab** *(☎ 888-2941, W www.astrolab.qc.ca; adult/ child $10/7.50; open noon-11pm daily mid-June–late Aug, noon-5pm Sun-Fri & 7:30pm-11pm Sat mid-May–mid-June & late Aug–early Oct)*, the showpiece of an astronomical research observatory that's one of the largest of its kind in northeastern North America. There is observation (the largest telescope is 1.6m in diameter) as well as multimedia shows about the birth and death of stars.

The activities at the AstroLab are conducted in French unless an English-speaking guide is reserved in advance, but one day in mid-August is reserved for English tours.

Places to Stay & Eat Options in this area are limited.

Camping Altitude *(☎ 888-2206, 121 route du Parc Mont Mégantic)* Tent sites $18. Just 2km from the park's entrance, this is a small (23 sites) but sumptuously rustic campground nestled in the woods at an altitude of 600m. There's a spring for source water.

Aux Berges de l'Aurore *(☎ 888-2715, W www.auberge-aurore.qc.ca, 139 route du Parc)* Singles/doubles $90/110. A top-notch B&B in a Victorian home a few minutes from the park's entrance, each room here has a private bath and views of the mountains. Hearty meals are also served – every morning, a different breakfast is prepared and dinner is a gastronomic delight, usually a six-course affair of caribou, salmon, duck or other delicacies ($32 to $42).

Piopolis
pop 300

This tiny dot on the map, 30km east of Notre Dame des Bois via Rtes 212 and 161, blends harmoniously with its surrounding beauty. It lies on the western shore of Lac Mégantic, and the surrounding hills offer more stunning views. What distinguishes this village, however, is its history. It was founded in 1879 by a group of French Québécois who called themselves the Papal Zouaves. Some 500 of them traveled from Québec to Italy in 1869 to fight for Pope Pius IX in an attempt to save the Papal States from Garibaldi and the Risorgimento. Those who returned were granted land concessions here for their loyalty to the papacy, and they named their new village after the Pope they so cherished.

Aside from pleasant drives around the area, swimming in the municipal beach or enjoying an occasional outdoor concert, there's not much to do here aside from slipping into the easy rhythms of this remote place.

Lac Mégantic
pop 5850

The last sizeable town in the Townships is a fusion of two previous villages dating from the 1880s, one founded by Scottish immigrants, another by Québécois. The tourist office (☎ 583-5515, 800-363-5515) is at 3295 rue Laval Nord.

The several churches are among the town's oldest buildings. The highlight is the 1913 **Église Ste Agnès** *(☎ 583-0370, 4906 rue Laval Nord; admission free; open daily year-round)* with its impressive stained-glass window made in England in the early 19th century; the window was originally destined for London's Church of the Immaculate Conception.

At the **Complexe Baie des Sables** *(☎ 583-3965, 505 Rte 263 Sud; admission free; open daily year-round)*, on the northwestern tip of the lake just outside of town, there are lots of water sports possibilities – swimming, windsurfing and sailing. In winter there's cross-country skiing and tube sliding. The beach can get crowded, but it's still pleasant thanks to the views. There's an on-site **campground** ($19 to $23).

In spring there's a good sugar shack, **Cabane à sucre Mégantic** *(☎ 583-1760, 888-228-1760, 3732 rang 10; adult/child $6/4; open 11:30am-7pm daily mid-Mar–late Apr)*, with taffy pulls on the snow and all sorts of good things to eat.

There are a few accommodations options in the Lac Mégantic area.

Camping Mercier (☎ 583-4923, 680 Rte 161 Sud) Tent sites $16. A low-key campground right by the lake, there's good swimming, and showers and laundry machines.

Aux Trois Lucarnes (☎ 583-4884, 1171 Rte 161 Sud) Singles/doubles $50/60. The least expensive B&B in the area is pleasant. Two bathrooms are shared between three comfortable rooms.

Motel sur le Lac (☎ 583-0293, 800-263-0293, 2000 Rte 161 Sud) Singles/doubles from $70/95, suites $175. Also lakeside, this semi-luxurious complex offers free canoe and kayak rental, and boasts a pool and wide open spaces around it for stretching your legs.

Parc de Frontenac

One of the province's least visited parks *(☎ 418-422-2136, 877-696-7272, 599 chemin des Roy; admission $3.50; open 8am-9pm daily May-Sept)*, it contains 155 sq km of enchanting nature and offers a large array of activities. There are 26km of hiking and cycling trails; bicycle, canoe and kayak rentals; and a great beach (indeed, swimming is possible from almost anywhere along its 65km of shores). Canoeing enthusiasts rave about the circuits and scenery here. There are several **campgrounds** and **refuges** ($19 to $23) for overnight canoe or hiking trips.

Montréal to Québec City

North of the River

This route, along Rte 138, follows closely to the original chemin du Roi (King's Road), one of the first major roads constructed in North America, joining Québec City and Montréal. The route was completed from 1706 to 1737, when the journey took five days by horse; today, using the much duller Hwy 40, the trip takes about 2½ hours.

From Montréal to Berthierville, the 138 passes through the southern part of the Lanaudière region (see The Laurentians chapter for information on the northern ski areas).

A good first stop just after leaving the island of Montréal is the tourist office in Repentigny (☎ 450-657-9914), 396 rue Notre Dame. It's open 9am to 7pm daily mid-May to mid-October, and 9am to 4pm Wednesday to Sunday mid-October to mid-May. On your way out of town, be sure to notice the **Église Notre Dame des Champs** (☎ *450-654-5732, 187 boul Iberville)*, one of the province's most unusual-looking churches. It was built by Frank Lloyd Wright student Roger D'Astous, a Montréaler, in 1963. The bell is made from two large metallic arcs.

Lavaltrie (pop 11,400), 26km northeast of Repentigny, has several flea markets doubling as antique stores (signposted *Antiquités)* along its main street, where you can find World Expo '67 souvenirs alongside religious kitsch, old furniture, odd lamps and a delightful wealth of unneeded objects.

JOLIETTE
☎ 450 • pop 18,000

A quick 25km from Lavaltrie along Rte 131 is the host city of two well-loved festivals.

From the end of June to early August, the **Festival International de Lanaudière** (☎ 759-4343, 800-561-4343, Ⓦ www.lanaudiere.org) brings a series of classical music concerts almost daily to Joliette's churches and main amphitheater. The Montréal Symphony Orchestra, as well as international quartets, choirs and chamber orchestras, form part of

Highlights

- Retrace the path of the *Chemin du Roi,* the continent's oldest road
- Explore the wild tangle of forest and lakes in the Haut St Maurice
- Try a *poutine* in its unofficial birthplace!
- Swing your partner round and round at a folk dance in Inverness
- Relive the province's past at the Village Québécois d'Antan in Drummondville

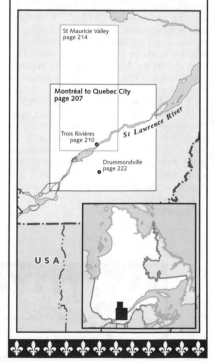

St Mauricie Valley
page 214

Montréal to Quebec City
page 207

Trois Rivières
page 210

St Lawrence River

Drummondville
page 222

USA

an innovative schedule bridging Bach and Bruch with Paderewski and world music. Tickets range from $10 to $42. They also offer a bus service, the Festival Express ($16 roundtrip), which departs from Montréal's main tourist office on weekends.

The **Mémoires et Racines Festival de Folklore** (☎ 752-6798, 888-810-6798, Ⓦ www .memoireracines.qc.ca), held at the end of July in Parc St Jean Bosco, at the end of chemin du Golf Est, regroups Canadian folk musicians with international guests for three days of traditional music and dance. Day tickets are about $20.

The **Musée d'Art de Joliette** (☎ 756-0311, 145 rue Wilfrid Corbeil; $4/2 adult/student; open 11am-5pm Tues-Sun) has a good collection of medieval European religious sculptures.

For something more modern, check out **Les Créations Koppo** (☎ 755-3854, 855 boul Joseph Arthur), a furniture crafts workshop with some highly unusual pieces.

If you're joining the 138 at Berthierville via Rte 158 from Joliette, notice, around the village of St Thomas, 5km from Joliette, a number of tobacco fields (with their checkerboard appearance), identifiable

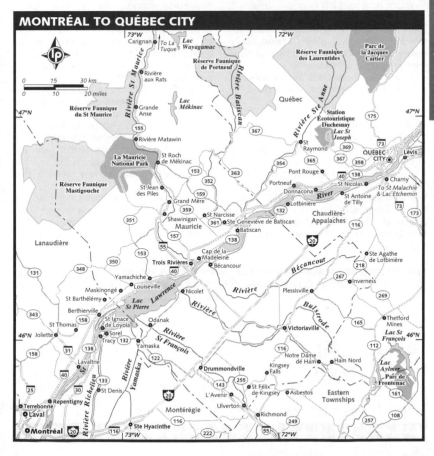

MONTRÉAL TO QUÉBEC CITY

from their slant-roofed drying shacks. Archeological digs in the area have found that the Iroquois cultivated tobacco long before Europeans set foot here.

Places to Stay & Eat

There are several motels on Rte 131, north of Joliette.

Camping Belle Marée (☎ *756-2542, chemin No 4, rang Ste Julie*) Tent sites $18-22. This is a full-service, medium-sized (99 sites) campground some 5km north of Joliette. Follow 131 north to Notre Dame des Prairies, turn left on boulevard Antonio Barrette, then right onto rang Ste Julie.

Château Joliette (☎ *752-2525, fax 752-2520, 450 rue St Thomas*) Singles/doubles $95/105. The nicest place around has a resort feel to it. The restaurant serves good meals throughout the day.

In central Joliette there are a number of cafés and fast-food restaurants around the Place Bourget.

BERTHIERVILLE
☎ 450 • pop 4150

While this town is known as the birthplace of world-famous racecar driver Gilles Villeneuve and for its proximity to the Îles de Berthier (comprising the northern parts of the Unesco-designated Lac St Pierre World Biosphere Reserve), visitors will appreciate the air of faded 19th-century bourgeoisie along the town's once-rich waterfront.

On the southwest corner of Rtes 138 and 158 stands the oldest Anglican church in Québec, the **Chapelle Cuthbert** (1785). The summer tourist office (☎ 836-7336) is conveniently located within. From early September to the end of May, the tourist office is inside the Days Inn hotel (☎ 836-1621, 800-367-6853), 760 rue Gadoury. Throughout the year they offer travel packages including cruises, ice-fishing and wildlife excursions.

Heading south on Rte 158 (rue De Bienville), turn right onto rue Frontenac, the last street before the bridge. Along this charming street are many stately Victorian houses and manors, one of the most impressive being the **Cuthbert Manor**, at the corner of rue Champlain. James Cuthbert was one of General Wolfe's senior aides during the definitive 1760 battle between England and France on the Plains of Abraham. There are numerous cafés on this street also.

The **Gilles Villeneuve Museum** (☎ 836-2714, W *www.villeneuve.com, 960 avenue Gilles Villeneuve; adult/student $6/4; open 9am-5pm daily*) is a shrine to Villeneuve, who became legendary after his death in a 1982 crash, replete with model racecars, simulators and lots of photos. His brother Jacques, also a well-known racer, is also featured.

While most of the **cruises** around the Lac St Pierre Biosphere Reserve depart from the south bank of the St Lawrence (see Sorel, later), the Pourvoirie du Lac St Pierre (☎ 836-7506, 2309 rang St Pierre) are outfit-

---

Scenic Drive – Berthierville to Maskinongé

About 7km east of Berthierville, off Rte 138 turn north on rue Ste Thérèse to St Viateur, make a right on rang York and continue past St Barthélémy, where it soon turns into Rte du Pied de la Côte. Continue until you rejoin Rte 138 at Maskinongé. The original chemin du Roi made this same detour to avoid the spring floods, which used to inundate the lands up to this point. This route, now also part of the Route Verte biking trail, is transporting in its beauty. If the weather's right, you'll see gentle hills on which cows feed happily between centuries-old maples and poplars on one side, and pillowy green fields that stretch as far as the eye can see on the other. Stop in at the Magasin Général Le Brun (see Maskinongé).

ters who offer two-hour bird watching excursions in medium-sized boats for $15 a person upon reservation. Boats leave from their headquarters in St Ignace de Loyola.

Rue de Bienville south ends in the village of St Ignace de Loyola, where the ferry departs to Sorel (☎ 836-4600; one-way passenger/bicycle/car $2/free/$3.35, 6 minutes). Service is year-round, hourly or twice hourly.

MASKINONGÉ
☎ 450 • pop 1050

Rural is the word that defines this town, founded in 1714, spread out along the old chemin du Roi. The one attraction here – aside from the tranquil beauty of the landscape – is the wildly eclectic **Magasin Général Le Brun** (☎ 819-227-2147, 877-427-1272, W www.mglebrun.com, 192 pied de la Côte; adult/child $6/4; open 1pm-5pm Sat-Tues mid-June–early Sept & 1pm-5pm Sat & Sun early Sept–early Oct), 5km from Rte 138.

Strongly worth a detour, this museum, inside an old general store, is as fun as a romp in an antique-stuffed attic. Not only will you learn about what a bustling area this once was when the chemin du Roi passed it by, the artifacts on display and the exuberance of your guide will provide lasting memories. Tours start on the hour. For an English guide, it's better to call in advance. The first Saturday of every month from October to May they host a lively dinner party ($35 per person, bring your own wine).

LOUISEVILLE
☎ 450 • pop 8000

For a rich contrast between elegance and kitsch, make a stop here. The **St Antoine de Padoue church** (1917), at 50 rue St Laurent, is one of the most impressive churches in the province. An opus of marble, it has 67 intricate stained-glass windows and a magnificent cupola painted to represent the seven virtues (temperance, justice, faith, charity, hope, prudence and strength). Note the wooden statue of St Antoine de Padoue out front – apparently it miraculously survived a major fire in 1926.

That's the elegance. For the kitsch, take a drive down rue Notre Dame Sud, which follows the pretty rivière du Loup. You'd think there was a city ordinance requiring residents to place lawn ornaments. Among all the plastic Jesus and Virgin Mary statues are Charlie Chaplin and a happy Mexican farm boy, to name a few.

The **Réserve Faunique Mastigouche** (☎ 819-265-2098, 800-665-6527, 830 chemin des Pins Rouges; admission from $3.50), with over 1600 sq km, provides 140km of rivers fit for a canoe and some 200km of cross-country ski trails. The main entrance is 15km north of St Alexis des Monts, itself 36km north of Louiscville along the 349. Camping and lodging in chalets and refuges are available.

TROIS RIVIÈRES
☎ 819 • pop 48,400

Though this is the second oldest city in North America north of Mexico, you'd never know it now – it resembles a forgotten city in the US Midwest more than it does one borne of a 1634 European outpost. This is largely due to a 1908 fire that destroyed most of the city and forever wiped out most Old Town charms. Still, this is a pleasant midway break between Montréal and Québec City or as a springboard to the wilds of the St Maurice Valley.

Trois Rivières – the name is a misnomer as there are two, not three rivers here. There are, however, three branches of the rivière St Maurice at its mouth, where islands split its flow into three channels. Though Jacques Cartier placed one of his ubiquitous crosses here (on Île St Quentin) in 1535, it wasn't until 1615 that a small trading post was established in the area, and it took until 1634 before a fortification was built and a city born.

The pace of development continued in this slow vein; in the mid-16th century there were but 300 inhabitants. A century later, only some thousand people lived in Trois Rivières. Real growth only started after the industrial revolution in the 1850s, when American investors, eager to reap the fortunes in the densely forested backlands, installed a sawmill. In the early 20th century the city's growth was phenomenal, as sawmills and related factories opened. By the 1920s it was the world's pulp and paper capital. Wood logs were flowing by the millions down the St Maurice toward Trois Rivière's factories.

Today, paper remains an important part of the city's economy, but emphasis has been placed on cultural heritage, and it boasts bona fide tourist attractions and festivals like the **International Poetry Festival** (☎ 379-9813, W www.aiqnet.com/fiptr), in late September. Some 400 activities take place in 80 locations, with poets from around the word arriving to contribute a stanza or two. Trois Rivières cherishes poetry – you'll notice over 300 plaques on buildings throughout downtown

with poems engraved onto them, and every St Valentine Day, the city's mayor places a flower bouquet at the feet of the Statue to the Unknown Poet, in Parc Champlain.

Orientation

Rue Notre Dame and rue des Forges constitute the main arteries of downtown. The oldest remaining sections are south of rue Hart and east of rue Notre Dame, in the areas behind the Parc Portuaire. Rue des Ursulines is particularly attractive. There's a riverfront promenade that's popular for evening strolls (and with skateboarders),

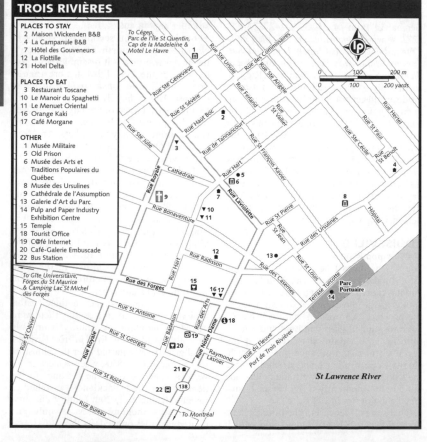

TROIS RIVIÈRES

PLACES TO STAY
2 Maison Wickenden B&B
4 La Campanule B&B
7 Hôtel des Gouveneurs
12 La Flottille
21 Hotel Delta

PLACES TO EAT
3 Restaurant Toscane
10 Le Manoir du Spaghetti
11 Le Menuet Oriental
16 Orange Kaki
17 Café Morgane

OTHER
1 Musée Militaire
5 Old Prison
6 Musée des Arts et Traditions Populaires du Québec
8 Musée des Ursulines
9 Cathédrale de l'Assumption
13 Galerie d'Art du Parc
14 Pulp and Paper Industry Exhibition Centre
15 Temple
18 Tourist Office
19 C@fé Internet
20 Café-Galerie Embuscade
22 Bus Station

from which Bécancour's industrial park and Gentilly's nuclear power station are visible on the opposite shore.

The Parc de l'Île St Quentin and Cap de la Madeleine are accessible via Rte 138 (rue Laviolette heading north), then eastward on rue St Maurice. The south shore is accessible via the bridge on Hwy 55.

Information
The tourist office (☎ 375-1122, 800-313-1123), 1457 rue Notre Dame, is open year-round. Its French-language booklet *Circuit Patrimonial* well explains the oldest, most historic buildings that remain in the city. You'll notice bilingual signs in front of these sites.

There are banks and ATMs throughout the city, with several along rue des Forges between rue Notre Dame and rue Royale. For Internet access, C@fé Internet (☎ 374-1137), 121 rue St Antoine, charges $4.50 per hour. They're open 1pm to 11pm weekdays.

Tickets for **boat cruises** can be bought from the Croisières/Cruises kiosk (☎ 375-3000, 800-567-3737), along the waterfront promenade at the foot of boulevard des Forges. One-day cruises leave for Montréal (during the L'International Benson & Hedges fireworks competition only; see Special Events in the Montréal chapter) and the St Maurice, Saguenay and Outaouais Rivers, among other destinations. There are once- or twice-daily 90-minute regional cruises (adult/child $12/6) as well.

Things to See & Do
Musée des Arts et Traditions Populaires du Québec This museum (☎ 372-0425, 800-461-0406, 200 rue Laviolette; adult/student $6/4; open 9am-7pm daily mid-June–early Sept, 10am-5pm Tues-Sun early Sept–mid-June) presents, in six rooms, a good collection of traditional domestic objects, and material from archeological digs of the area's Native Canadian settlements. The nearby **old prison** (1822) contains a small exhibit.

Cathédrale de l'Assumption This 1858 neo-Gothic giant is the only North American cathedral done in the Westminster style. The interior (☎ 374-2409, 363 rue Bonaventure;

admission free; 7am-noon & 2pm-5pm daily) is just as remarkable, with delicately sculpted wooden statues and gorgeous stained-glass windows made by Florentine artist Guido Nincheri.

Musée Militaire Set in a soldiers' training hall, this museum (☎ 371-5290, 574 rue St François Xavier; adult/student $2/1; open 10am-6pm daily mid-June–early Sept) explores the military history of the region, recalls a few interesting facts (see 'Chasing the Yanks Home') and displays artifacts like old scrapbooks. There's even an original WWII letter from General Montgomery.

Galerie d'Art du Parc Located inside a handsome 1795 manor, this art gallery (☎ 374-2355, 864 rue des Ursulines; admission free; open 10am-5pm Tues-Fri, 1pm-5pm Sat & Sun) often features good temporary exhibits of Québécois artists.

Musée des Ursulines Ursuline nuns (see Old Town in the Québec City chapter for details) first arrived in Québec in 1639 from Italy, with four settling in Trois Rivières in 1697 to found a school and hospital. Their grand, solemn convent, including a chapel, an infirmary and a small school for girls, has seen many reconstructions. Today the former hospital houses a small museum (☎ 375-7922, 🖂 www.musee-ursulines.qc.ca; adult/student $2.50/1.50; open 9am-5pm Tues-Fri & 1:30pm-5pm Sat & Sun May-Nov, 1:30pm-5pm Wed-Sun Mar & Apr) with a fine collection of textiles, ceramics, books and prints related to religion. The chapel has splendid ceiling frescoes by Luigi Capello (1897).

Pulp and Paper Industry Exhibition Centre This museum (☎ 372-4633, 🖂 ceipp@ qc.aira.com, 800 Parc Portuaire; adult/child $3/1.50; open 9am-6pm daily June-Aug, 9am-5pm Mon-Fri & 11am-5pm Sat & Sun Sept) explains why the city was the industry's world capital for so long, and why the pulp and paper business is Québec's economic backbone.

Parc de l'Île St Quentin It's tricky, making an eco-park in the midst of all that industry, but this park *(☎ 373-8151,* W *www .ile-st-quentin.qc.ca; adult/child $3/1, car $1 extra; open 9am-10pm daily May-Oct, 10am-5pm Dec-Mar)* manages nicely. Walking trails, an outdoor pool and game courts make this great for a stroll, bike ride or picnic. The beach opened in 2000 for the first time in decades, but pollution levels are still iffy, and they still periodically forbid swimming. Bus No 2 from downtown comes here.

Forges du St Maurice A Parks Canada attraction, this site *(☎ 378-5116,* W *www .parkscanada.gc.ca/forges, 10000 boul des Forges; adult/student $4/2; 9:30am-5:30pm daily mid-May–mid-Oct)* is on the grounds of Canada's first ironworks, begun in the 17th century. Costumed guides show you around the ruins and explain the important role it played it the city's development – even long after the works closed shop in 1883. Bus No 4 from downtown reaches the site.

Basilica Notre Dame du Cap Located in nearby Cap de la Madeleine, this immense, modern sanctuary *(☎ 374-2441, 626 rue Notre Dame; admission free; 8am-8pm daily, schedule varies)* is a major pilgrimage stop. Though it looks somewhat like a spaceship about to lift off, the interiors are both magnificent and garish, with gold and Calacatta marble its principle elements. The lack of columns or pillars gives the space a daunting feel. From downtown, take Bus No 2.

Places to Stay

Camping Lac St Michel des Forges (☎ 374-8474, 11650 rue du Clairon) Tent sites from $18-25. About 8km from the center (exit 191 off Hwy 55), it's not a bad place to spend a night or two, though it's not very wooded.

La Flottille (☎ 378-8010, e *flottille@ tr.cgocable.ca, 497 rue Radisson)* Dorms $16.50-19.50, private doubles $46. A member of Hostelling International, this is a relatively lackluster hostel, though not far from the center.

Gîte Universitaire (☎ 374-4545, W *www .uqtr.uquebec.ca/gite, 1550 rue Père Marquette)* Singles/doubles $25 per person, May-Aug only. About a 10-minute drive from the center, this separate University residence building is clean, and staying here gives access to the sports complex. Better to reserve in advance, as offices don't always seem to be staffed.

Maison Wickenden B&B(☎/fax 375-6219, 467 rue St François Xavier) Singles/

Chasing the Yanks Home

French or English, Canadians are united in feeling smug whenever they stick it to the Americans. In Trois Rivières, a favorite tale is how they showed those Yanks but good, back in 1776. In those days, Americans were fond of attacking Lower Canada via the Richelieu, Kennebec and Chaudière Rivers. In 1775 they had invaded Montréal and St Jean, and rolled over Trois Rivières on their way to a battle at Québec City, which lasted until May 1776.

During their forced retreat, the Americans stationed at St François du Lac on the south shore before crossing Lac St Pierre to Yamachiche in early June. From there they made their way with a sympathizer to Pointe du Lac, 13km west of Trois Rivières, where they forced a local farmer, future hero Antoine Gauthier, to guide them to Trois Rivières. They figured it would be a piece of cake to seize this little town, compared to fierce battles for Québec City.

Gauthier pretended to sympathize, to hate his British masters. A quick thinker, he told them, 'Let's do it! But we must attack the city by surprise from behind, not from the river!' When he went in to get his coat before setting off, he told his wife to alert the local captain, who made it to Trois Rivières – by river – faster than the Yanks. Under Colonel Fraser and Louis Joseph Godefroy de Tonnancourt, there was time to regroup a small army, who then surrounded and took the Americans by surprise. There were some 200 American casualties in the ensuing battle, the rest taken prisoner, and a dozen wounded British and Canadians.

doubles from \$45/55. This place is conveniently located and has an air of utter tranquility to it – but maybe that's due to the St James cemetery next door.

La Campanule B&B (☎ *373-1133, 634 rue des Ursulines*) Singles/doubles \$50/65. The redbrick house is pretty and welcoming, the interiors homey.

Motel Le Havre (☎ *691-3496, 1360 rue Notre Dame*) Singles/doubles \$35/40. This one's the best of many motels on this street, just beyond Cap de la Madeleine on Hwy 138. It's friendly, clean, simple, and right by the river.

Hôtel des Gouveneurs (☎ *379-4550,* W *www.gouverneur.com, 975 rue Hart*) Singles/doubles from \$80/100. This is as luxurious as you'll get here – the building's attractive, the rooms are ample, and there's an indoor pool and exercise room.

Places to Eat

Most of Trois Rivière's eateries are concentrated on rue des Forges, from the waterfront to rue Royale, and along rue Notre Dame. That's where the nightlife happens too.

Café Morgane (☎ *691-2233, 100 rue des Forges*) A café that's popular round the clock, it has good coffee, and serves sandwiches and salads too.

Orange Kaki (☎ *375-5358, 120 rue des Forges*) Appetizers \$3-8, mains \$8-17. One of the most popular places for a quick lunch or just to hang out on the terrace, the mussels and pasta combo for \$12 is good, as are all the other pastas on the extensive list. The neo-industrial décor is spruced up with wrought-iron sculptures.

Le Manoir du Spaghetti (☎ *373-0204, 1147 rue Hart*) Mains \$10-18. Copious and tasty pasta concoctions are served in a cozy setting.

Le Menuet Oriental (☎ *379-8754, 324 rue Bonaventure*) Lunch special \$8, dinner \$11-16; open 11am-2pm & 5pm-10pm daily. This first-rate Vietnamese restaurant has one of the best full-course lunch specials in the city. The setting is great too. It's best to reserve on weekend evenings, as it fills up.

Restaurant Toscane (☎ *378-1891, 901 rue Royale*) Lunch \$8-13, dinner average \$23.

For atmosphere, this one beats all others. In a 19th-century home, it serves fine cuisine like wild boar with apricots and blueberries (\$27). The balcony terrace adds to the charm.

Entertainment

Many of these cafés and restaurants on rue des Forges stay open late and double as bars.

Café-Galerie Embuscade (☎ *375-0652,* W *www.embuscade.qc.ca, 1571 rue Badeaux*) Open until 3am daily. This art bar is the closest thing to alternative here, feeling both lightly 'goth' and laid back. They don't mind if you bring in your own food.

Temple (☎ *370-2005, 300 des Forges*) This is the official hot nightclub, with pool tables, poseurs and lots of cruising.

Getting There & Away

From Montréal and Québec City, Trois Rivières is easily accessible via Hwys 20 and 40, and via Rtes 132 and 138. From Lac St Jean, take Rte 155 and Hwy 55.

The bus station (☎ *374-2944*), 275 St Georges, is located behind the Hôtel Delta. Orleans Express runs buses to/from Montréal (\$26, 2 hours, 8 daily) and Québec City (\$35, 1¾ hours, 6 daily). There are also buses to/from Shawinigan (\$7, 45 mins, 3 daily) and La Tuque (\$23, 3 daily).

ST MAURICE VALLEY
☎ 819

The 300km from Trois Rivières north to Lac St Jean is one of the final frontiers in Québec. It's also one of its most beautiful areas, with the powerful rivière St Maurice its sturdy backbone. Despite its central location in the province, the region north of Shawinigan, Grand Mère and La Mauricie National Park remains unknown to most Québécois, mostly thanks to a justified reputation as a polluted, industrial area. Yet the area is in the midst of a rebirth (see 'River, Heal Thyself').

The one good outcome of the region's industrialization is a lack of resorts, motels and cottages lining the river's shores, something destined to happen in the next decade. Not far from the main (and only) Rte 155, visitors can still appreciate a relatively pristine forest environment, particularly north of La Tuque. Even the drive itself, as the route winds along the valley, is spectacular, though best done on a weekend to avoid the plethora of huge trucks thundering up and down the roads.

Shawinigan
☎ 819 • pop 18,500

Another instance of a city reinventing itself after the closure of many factories is the interesting case of Shawinigan. The first planned city in Québec, it was founded by American businessman John Alder in 1898, who transformed the area into an industrial

ST MAURICE VALLEY

city. He was impressed with the hydro potential of the 50m-high waterfalls thundering nearby. Eventually, the first aluminum smelter in Canada began there – this became Alcan, the world's second largest aluminum producer. Petrochemical, electrochemical, hydroelectric and textile plants also sprung up. For many years this was Canada's richest city, and one of the only to be protected against air raids during WWII.

The **Cité de l'Énergie** (*City of Energy;* ☎ *536-8516,* W *www.citedelenergie.com, 1000 avenue Melville; adult/student/child $14/12/8; open 10am-5pm Tues-Sun mid-June–early July & early Sept–early Oct, 10am-6pm daily early July–early Sept),* founded in 1997, is a glittering example of Shawinigan's brave face in the advent of the collapse or slowing down of its *raison d'être* – big industry. A small town in and of itself, this theme park incorporates a river cruise, a guided city tour, a 'time machine,' and a truly stunning view of the river valley from the 115m-high observation tower atop an old hydroelectric pylon. Aside from having an interest in industrial themes, visitors are required to understand French, as the tours aren't offered yet in English – unbelievable for a site that attracts 100,000 tourists a year.

It also boasts a multimedia spectacle called *Kosmogonia,* the June 2001 premiere of which was attended by Prime Minister Jean Chrétien, Shawinigan's native son.

The **Parc des Chutes** (☎ *536-0222, Île Melville, off Rte 157; admission free; open year-round)* lets you come face to face with the extraordinary 50m waterfalls that inspired John Alder. They're best viewed in spring, after the dam's floodgates open. You can stand on a boulder at the foot of the dam and marvel.

Getting There & Away There are three buses daily to/from both Trois Rivières ($7, 45 mins) and Grand Mère ($2, 15 mins). One bus a day runs from Shawinigan to La Tuque ($17, 2 hours), with an extra run on Sunday. Three trains a week run to/from Montréal ($24, 2½ hours), continuing from Shawinigan to La Tuque ($17, 2½ hours) and Senneterre ($72, 9 hours).

Grand Mère

☎ 819 • pop 14,100

The main reason for stopping here is to stock up on supplies before heading farther north, and to see a rock. The city gets its name from a rock that the Algonquins called *Kokomis* (your grandmother). The rock, which resembles the profile of an old woman, was once situated on the banks of the St Maurice but was removed to make way for the hydro dam. According to legend, a desperate young woman waiting for her beloved to return from a hunting trip gone awry turned herself into this so she could forever keep an eye out for his return (and what a surprise he'd get if ever he did!). The rock is now in a small park at the eastern end of 6th Avenue.

La Mauricie National Park

This very well may be Québec's best-run and -organized park (☎ 538-3232, 🆆 www .parkscanada.gc.ca/mauricie; adult/student $3.50/1.50). As such, it is also one of its most frequented. The arresting beauty of the nature here, whether seen from a canoe or from one of the many walking trails, is eye-candy for everyone, but particularly for those who don't want to feel completely disconnected from 'civilization.' Among the services offered are a convenience store and two cafés. Some of the campgrounds have as many as 219 sites.

The park covers 550 sq km, straddling northern evergreen forests and the more southerly hardwoods of the St Lawrence River valley. The low, rounded Laurentian Mountains, among the world's oldest, are part of the Canadian Shield that covers much of the province. Between these hills are many small lakes and valleys. The park was created in 1970 to protect some of the forest that was being decimated by the paper industry – at one point, half of the park's current territory was being exploited and two sawmills were operating there.

There are numerous **hiking** trails, from 30 minutes to five days long. These offer chances to spot wildlife while taking in the indigenous flora, brooks and waterfalls (the Chutes Waber, in the park's western sector,

River, Heal Thyself

It's easy to see the difference between the St Maurice and St Lawrence Rivers, as the former forcefully empties into the latter. A high iron content makes the St Maurice's waters jet-black, and from a cruise boat or even from shore, a clear demarcation between these and the St Lawrence's softer hues can be seen. For well over a century the St Maurice, which winds its 563km-long path from the Gouin Reservoir, has been Québec's most maligned, heavily abused major river. Mistreated by industry – pulp and paper, aluminum smelting, hydroelectricity – it was literally choked by logging, which began in 1852 and ended only in 1995 (pulp and paper plants now use wood chips instead of logs).

Generations of loggers (*bûcheux*) rode or pushed millions of logs down the river, through roaring rapids and down waterfalls, to the awaiting sawmills. The forest industry defined the culture, lore, and employment of everyone in the region. Yet this considerably changed the river's ecosystem, making it unsuitable for human activity.

The river has begun to heal itself. With the decline in the global paper market and the historic end of the log drive (after the merciless depletion of the forests' resources), more stringent laws against pollution came into effect, and a cleanup of rotting debris was done. Tests show that the St Maurice has braved its assault relatively well. The unpolluted waters flowing from its source have cleansed many impurities downstream. The river is now even deemed fit for swimming north of Grand Mère, and canoeists and other pleasure boats are making their first appearances again, navigating this robust, incredibly scenic river valley.

are particularly worth the hike), and panoramic views onto delicate valleys, lakes and streams. The longest trail, Le Sentier Laurentien, stretches over 75km of rugged terrain in the park's northern reaches. There

MONTRÉAL TO QUÉBEC CITY

are refuge chalets along the way, but you must arrange to somehow get back to the starting point after finishing the trail (30km along Rte de la Promenade). Plus, there's a $40 charge to complete the trail (reservations ☎ 533-7272).

The park is also excellent for **canoeing**. There are maps of five canoe routes, ranging in length from 14km to 84km, for beginners or experts. Canoes can be rented at three sites ($18 per day), the most popular being Lac Wapizagonke, which has sandy beaches, steep rocky cliffs and waterfalls. There's also fishing for trout and bass.

Cross-country skiing is also possible (adult/child $5/2.50), as is winter camping in heated huts. Call ☎ 888-855-6673 for details.

A variety of activities geared toward children are also offered for a small fee, such as demonstrations and talks about nature.

Places to Stay Camping at designated sites costs $26/22 with/without electricity, and camping in the wild during canoe trips costs $18/14 with/without a campfire. There are also two large chalets in the park (☎ 537-4555), for $22 per person in rooms shared between four to 10 people; the weekend rate is $24 per person.

Getting There & Away No public transportation reaches the park, so you'll need a car. The main entrance is at St Jean des Piles (exit 226 off Hwy 55), and there's another at St Mathieu (exit 217 off Hwy 55). Both entrances are well indicated and connected by the 63km-long Rte Promenade, which runs through the park.

Réserve Faunique du St Maurice

The 784 sq km of this wildlife reserve (☎ 646-5687, 800-665-6527, 3773 Rte 155) offer a more secluded, less-touristed variant to the same kind of wildlife found in La Mauricie National Park. The reserve's visitors center is at Rivière Matawin, 90km north of Trois Rivières. The centerpiece here is Lac Normand, a crystal-clear lake where a rare species of salmon called *kokani* live. A campsite with showers is located here ($19). **Hiking** trails (there are about 44km of them

throughout the reserve) snake around the lake, offering impressive views.

Canoeing ($18 per day) is most popular on the long, thin Lac Tousignant, along which are isolated spots to pitch your tent ($13.50) and several comfortable refuges ($22.50) with bunk beds and woodstoves. After a small portage, you can continue on Lac Soucis and make an 18km (one-way) trip over several days.

Most people come here for hunting and fishing, so the trails and lakes are marvelously uncrowded. The only minus is the $12 fee you have to pay to cross the tiny bridge over the rivière St Maurice, making it Canada's most expensive toll bridge by length. The drive from Trois Rivières, however, is especially scenic. Be sure to stop off at the flea market **Marché aux Puces** (☎ 646-5005, 3660 Rte 155), south of rivière Matawin – an outdoor extravaganza of old furniture, toilets, funky dishes and outlandish owners.

La Tuque
☎ 819 • pop 13,200

The city of La Tuque may well be the smelliest in Québec. The province's largest carton-producing factory spews its noxious muck through tall chimneystacks all day long and tends to give the newcomers headaches; residents hardly notice. The stench comes as a shock after the gorgeous drive to it along Rte 155. Nonetheless, this town, founded in 1911 as a gateway to the exploitation of inland forests, is a good stop on your way to/from Lac St Jean and as a springboard to exploring inland forests.

Named after a hat-shaped hill (*tuque* is the Québécois term for winter woolen hat), this is also the birthplace of one of Québec music and literature's greats, Félix Leclerc (1914–1988), who became a legend in his home province only after huge success in France. There are interpretation panels set up around town to experience La Tuque as he did. His childhood home was 168 rue Claire Fontaine.

The La Tuque tourist information office (☎ 523-5930), open from May to September only, is at 3701 rue Ducharme. The municipal offices (☎ 523-6111, 🌐 www.mrchsm.org,

445 Lacroix) are another good source of information, year-round. Ask for the map of the region's hiking trails.

The **Parc des Chutes de la Petite rivière Bostonnais** (☎ *523-5930, Rte 155; admission free; open 9:30am-7pm)* has an excellent visitors center complete with a sweet-smelling re-created forest trail where 75 exhibits of stuffed animals and local flora acquaint tourists with what they might see in the area. Trails out back lead to a 35m waterfall and hydroelectric dam.

La Tuque is also known, of all things, for its **Festival International de Pétancle** (☎ 676-3476), where lawn bowling lovers creep out of the woodwork to indulge in their craft. More interesting are the **Fête de la rivière St Maurice** (☎ *375-8699),* in August, and the **Classique Internationale de Canots de la Mauricie** (☎ *537-9221),* in late August into early September, two festivals that celebrate the river with canoe races, including a 167km canoe trip to Shawinigan.

Most of La Tuque's restaurants are along rue St François near the train station.

Places to Stay La Tuque offers several accommodations options.

Camping Haut de la Chute (☎ *523-7575, 1555 chemin des Pionniers)* Tent sites $16. This gorgeous spot near the rivière Bostonnais offers crisp, fresh air, a small beach, walking trails and friendly owners.

Auberge La Résidence (☎ *523-9267,* e *aubergelaresidence@simpatico.ca, 352 avenue Brown)* Shared rooms $17/20 HI member/nonmember. A youth hostel in the north end of town (turn west on rue St Michel from Rte 155; it's the fifth street on the right) in what looks like an elementary school isn't exactly unforgettable, but it'll do.

Motel Le Gîte (☎ *523-9501, 1100 boul Ducharme)* Singles/doubles from $55/60. A range of rooms is available at this comfortable motel in the center of town.

Getting There & Away A daily bus (twice on Sunday) links La Tuque to Trois Rivières ($23, 2¾ hours) and Shawinigan ($19, 2½ hours), and a train runs to/from Montréal ($40, 5 hours, 3 weekly).

Haut St Maurice

This region, north of La Tuque to Lac St Jean, spreads deep inland, where the rivière St Maurice curves into a dense forest of lakes, streams and pristine wilderness. Much of the 30,000 sq km are privately owned; there are some 40 outfitters in the area, offering hunting and adventure tourism, often to Europeans who find paradise in these wild expanses (outside of La Tuque, only some 2000 people live in an area nearly the size of Belgium!).

Only a few dirt roads and a train track course through the heart of this land, westward to Senneterre in Abitibi (see 'Scenic Drive – Chemin du Rang Sud-Est'), stopping in miniscule villages, fishing outposts and Native Canadian communities. **Parent** (pop 436) is the main stop on this route, a

---

Scenic Drive – Chemin du Rang Sud-Est

Going north from La Tuque, veer right off Rte 155 onto chemin des Pionniers. This becomes chemin du Rang Sud-Est. Continue past La Bostonnais, stopping to admire the covered bridge (1945). This pretty road follows the pretty rivière La Bostonnais, which at times widens enough to allow a few islets to be seen, and even musters up some gentle rapids. Ducks and geese swim near the banks. It also passes decaying wooden huts and houses with gigantic moose horns proudly stuck to their façades. Continue until the road turns to gravel, at which point double back, cross the second covered bridge, rejoin the 155 and continue north.

supply stop for hunters and fishermen, and a rest stop for snowmobilists and long-distance canoeists.

Otherwise, Rte 155 is the region's only artery. Relentless forest is the main scenery here, broken up by a few small villages on the way, sporting charming covered bridges. **La Bostonnais** (pop 500), 12km north of La Tuque, is the area's most attractive (see 'Scenic Drive – Chemin du Rang Sud-Est').

Lac Édouard (pop 160) is in the middle of nowhere, at the end of a 30km road that heads east from a turnoff 34km north of La Tuque. It's the only easily accessible village in the area that can give visitors a taste of what the wild inland is like: a magnificent lake with bushy islands, scattered cottages, colonies of birds (including herons) and lots of quiet.

See the Charlevoix, Saguenay & Lac St Jean chapter for details on the northern stretch of Rte 155.

If you're interested in a trip inland, you couldn't find better help than the Association des Pourvoyeurs (☎ 676-8824, fax 676-8825, @ natur_mauricie@lino.simpatico.ca, 550 rue St Louis), in La Tuque. The knowledgeable staff, clearly in love with the area, can help navigate you through the wilderness or set you up with an outfitter. There's something for all budgets and means of transportation, and for all interests, be they canoeing, skiing, fishing or just relaxing.

TROIS RIVIÈRES TO QUÉBEC CITY
☎ 418

Between these cities, there isn't much of interest along the main road (see 'Scenic Drive – Rtes 361 & 159'). There are occasional views of the St Lawrence, some villages and, near Québec City, roadside stops for fresh fruit, vegetables and maple products.

Batiscan

This town, 31km east of Trois Rivières, is where explorer Samuel de Champlain first met with the Huron nation. The **Vieux Presbytère** *(Old Presbytery; ☎ 362-2051, 340 rue Principale; adult/student $3/2; open 10am-5pm daily June-Sept)* is worth a stop, with its re-created 19th-century interiors.

Réserve Faunique de Portneuf

This wildlife reserve *(☎ 323-2021, Rte 367; admission $3.50; open year-round)* is 775 sq km of boreal and coniferous forest accessible via Rtes 365 and 367 (Hwy 40 exits 281 and 295, or accessible via the 138 east of Donnacona). During the summer, hiking, rafting and canoeing (nicest area: Lac Lapeyrère) are possible; in winter cross-country skiing and snowshoeing. There's also rock climbing near Lac Bellevue.

Cap Santé & Donnacona

This region is known as a significant salmon migratory pass. This is also where

---

Scenic Drive – Rtes 361 & 159

Just east of Batiscan, head northwest on either branch of Rte 361, either just before or just after the rivière Batiscan, and follow it until Ste Geneviève de Batiscan, where there are great views of the area's surrounding valleys, gentle slopes and the tranquil river itself. Continue to St Narcisse, enjoying the slow rhythms of the landscape. Moraine – very rare in Canada – has shaped the surroundings. From St Narcisse, take Rte 352 east for 10km until St Stanislas, where suburbia seems to meet country living, then follow the 159 south until you rejoin the 138. Here the countryside, awash in maple trees, enchants with rolling hills and dreamy riverbanks. On your way, you'll pass through St Prosper where, on steep chemin Massicotte, there are several sugar shacks to sample some sweets to see you through the day.

Jacques Cartier befriended the Iroquois grand chief Donnacona, leader of the region from present-day Montréal to Charlevoix. Cartier convinced him to let him take his two sons back to France – he may not have found the sought-after passage to China, but his booty, two live 'Indians,' was sure to make him popular back home. Returning on his second voyage of 1534–35, he convinced Donnacona and nine other Iroquois to return to France with him, ridding himself of a potential threat in the lands yet to be exploited (but already seized in the name of King Francis I). All Iroquois died shortly after their arrival in France, yet when Cartier returned on his third voyage, he told the Iroquois that their chief and brothers had become such successful and rich *seigneurs* they did not wish to return. This forever increased Iroquois suspicion and hostility toward the French.

From Donnacona, Québec City is about 30km.

South of the River

COASTAL ROAD

Instead of taking the 132 directly from Montréal, take Hwy 20 and then the 133 north (exit 113) to explore the northern Richelieu Valley until Sorel. The picturesque and historic Rte 133, known as the chemin des Patriotes, extends in the north from Sorel down to the US border along the rivière Richelieu. See the Eastern Townships chapter for information on the southern portions of the area.

An important part of the Patriots revolt (see the Facts about Québec chapter) was centered along the rivière Richelieu, which flows from Lake Champlain to the St Lawrence, as it was an important waterway into the country. It was traveled alternately by the Iroquois, the British and the Americans during attacks on the colony. This was also a heavily francophone region and the birthplace of the Patriot movement in the 1830s, which strove for an independent French-speaking country.

St Denis
☎ 819 • pop 1900
The site of the Patriots' only victory against the British, on November 23, 1837, St Denis today is a quiet, pastoral town. It's hard to imagine the violence it once saw. Founded in 1758, this became a prosperous village, where beaver-skin coats were made and exported to Europe and the southern colonies.

In the tumultuous 1830s it was also where the Fils de la Liberté (Sons of Liberty) were based. Their victorious battle in November 1837, which forced British troops to retreat back to Sorel, was answered mercilessly by the Brits, who were not used to losing battles. They returned two weeks later in the dead of night, set St Denis afire, destroyed all its industries and killed hundreds of its inhabitants. The worst of the fighting occurred on the northern end of the village, around present-day rue Phaneuf.

The **Maison Nationale des Patriotes** *(☎ 450-787-3623, 610 chemin des Patriotes; admission $5/3 adult/student; open 10am-5pm Tues-Sun May-Sept & Nov)* is a well-designed museum that recounts these events and their historical context.

The village is a good place to visit on the Sunday closest to November 23 (often the third Sunday) for the **Fête des Patriotes** *(☎ 450-787-3623)*, a daylong gathering in honor of the fallen heroes, complete with costumed reenactments, singing and other fun.

Sorel-Tracy
☎ 450 • pop 36,300
Originally two towns now fused into one, it's the Sorel side that's of more interest here. Tracy is nothing but a depressed industrial landscape, whereas Sorel has more to offer, despite being an industrial town itself. Situated strategically on the east bank of the Richelieu river where it flows into the St Lawrence, Sorel has had an active history since Samuel de Champlain set up a fortified trading post nearby in 1635. In the 19th and 20th centuries it was an important center of ship construction, and in the last few decades industry has focused on metallurgy and mineral extraction (particularly iron and titanium).

In Sorel's downtown, centered around the Careé Royal (which runs along rue du Roi between rue Charlotte and rue Georges), it's possible to see and feel the traces of a more prosperous past. The view of the grain silos as a background to rusting tankers, visible from rue de la Reine, has a charm of its own. Perhaps due to its proximity to Montréal, the eating options are surprisingly good here too, with a number of restaurants and pubs lining rue du Roi, rue Georges and rue Augusta.

However, most visitors to Sorel use the place as a stepping stone to the Îles de Sorel and the Lac St Pierre World Biosphere Reserve (designated by Unesco in 2000). From Sorel it's possible to take eco-cruises of the largest archipelago in the St Lawrence (103 islands), which boasts the largest heron colony in North America, rare plants and fish, and 288 species of observed birds (116 of these nest in the region). It's hard to believe that such pristine beauty lies within view of factories and metal industries.

The **Centre d'Interprétation de Sorel** (☎ 780-5740, 6 rue St Pierre; admission $3/1.50 adult/student; open 10am-7pm daily July & Aug, 10am-5pm Wed-Fri & 1pm-5pm Sat & Sun Sept-May) acts as a general introduction to the Lac St Pierre region, including its flora and fauna, as well as Sorel's industrial history.

For cruises, Nature Cruises (☎ 780-5740, 877-780-5740, 6 rue St Pierre) runs three three-hour excursions a day. The last, which leaves at 6:30pm, is the most popular as it catches a usually spectacular sunset and includes a light supper. Prices are $30/15 for adults/children, $10 more for the evening excursion. Staff can also organize overnight stays on the islands.

From Ste Anne de Sorel, a village 5km east of Sorel, Tour of the Marshes (☎ 742-3113, 3742 chemin du Chenal du Moine) offers daily tours of the unique, fragile and fast-disappearing marshes in a motorized *rabaska* (traditional Native Canadian) canoe. Prices are $25/15 adult/child, but times vary, so best call in advance.

The regional Tourist Information Bureau (☎ 746-9441, 800-474-9441) is at 92 chemin des Patriotes. The ferry service to St Ignace de Loyola (☎ 743-3258) leaves from Sorel (see Berthierville, earlier, for details).

Places to Stay & Eat The area offers a few fun places to spend some hours.

Motel Le Charentais (☎ 746-5650, fax 746-9406, 13325 rue Marie Victorin) Singles/doubles $43/52. This is the best of several motels on the Tracy side of this street. It's cozy and in a wooded area, near a small beach, and you can also set up your tent on the grounds.

Pub Café St Thomas (☎ 742-9700, 59 rue du Roi). Mains $4-8. There's atmosphere galore in this wood-lined bar, which serves over 100 kinds of beer and 22 coffees. The restaurant section boasts healthy paninis, salads and pizzas, in small or large portions, for a decent price. There's also a wicked collection of 1970s and 1980s board games on the second floor. This is a great place to hang out.

Odanak
☎ 819 • pop 295

One of only two Abenaki reservations, this small village is also home to the only museum dedicated to their culture and traditions, the **Musée des Abénakis** (☎ 450-568-2600, ☎ abenaki@enter-net.com, 108 rue Waban-Aki; adult/student $4/2; open 10am-5pm Mon-Fri & 1pm-5pm Sat & Sun May-Oct). Masks, videos, artifacts and handicrafts tell their story. The sculptures placed outside on pretty parkland are particularly interesting. On the first Sunday in July, the Abenaki hold their annual powwow here.

Nicolet
☎ 819 • pop 7800

Founded in 1672, Nicolet has become a major religious center and is sometimes referred to as the 'town of bells' for all its churches and cathedrals. Frightening in its 1960s modernity is the austere **Cathédrale de Nicolet** (☎ 293-5492, 671 boul Louis Fréchette).

Of far more interest is the **Musée des Religions** (☎ 293-6148, 900 boul Louis

Fréchette; $4.50/1.75 adult/student; open 10am-5pm daily June-Sept, 10am-5pm Tues-Sun Oct-May). The permanent collection is composed of 5000 religious objects and artifacts, including flashy altarpieces; the temporary exhibits, on loan from museums around the world and focusing on world religions, tend to be excellent.

Nicolet to Québec City

From Nicolet to Bécancour and Gentilly, big industry dominates the landscape. Pulp and paper factories of Trois Rivières and Cap de la Madeleine visible across the river face Bécancour's industrial park, Québec's largest, and just east of that, the province's only nuclear power station, **Gentilly-2** *(☎ 819-298-5205, 4900 boul Bécancour; free tours year-round upon reservation).*

East of Gentilly, however, upon entering the Chaudière-Appalaches region, there are nice views of the St Lawrence from Rte 132 as it dips into small green valleys, and the scenery becomes pastoral. It was this region that some of New France's first settlers called home, farming fertile strips of land descending from the river.

In **Lobtinière**, a number of houses date from the 18th and 19th centuries, including a **flourmill** (Moulin de Portage; 1816) and the lovely **St Louis Church** (1845), at 7557 Rte 132.

In Ste Croix is the **Domaine Joly de Lobtinière** *(☎ 418-926-2462, Rte du Pointe Platon; adult/student $8/7; open 10am-5pm daily early May–late Oct),* the 1851 manor house of Québec's first premier. The impressive main house, almost unchanged since it was first built, is surrounded by sumptuous sprawling gardens, giant trees and hiking trails through the forest. Most Sunday mornings there are classical concerts in the garden, a nice accompaniment to morning tea.

There's not much to do in **St Antoine de Tilly**, but this village, founded in 1702, seduces with its simple charms. Several buildings date from the 18th century, including its **church**, from 1788. A stop in the **Fromagerie Bergeron** cheese factory *(☎ 418-886-2234, 3837 rue Marie Victorin; open*

9am-9pm daily July & Aug, 9am-6pm daily Sept-June) is recommended to sample some of their home brands.

The rest of the road to Québec City follows the river closely.

VIA CENTRE DU QUÉBEC

This route follows a path roughly parallel to Hwy 20, but takes minor routes south of it. Not heavily touristed, it offers plenty of surprises.

Ste Hyacinthe
☎ 450 • pop 39,000

Only 42km east of Montréal, but already it's another world. Here, agriculture, horticulture, religion and business combine in a heady mix. Known as Québec's capital of agribusiness, the small city, sprung from a *seigneurie* (a strip of land awarded or sold by the French government before the English Conquest to a *seigneur*, who lorded over the way it was worked and tilled) founded in 1748, boasts a University-level veterinary faculty and many scientific research centers for animal food products. There are also two world-renowned factories producing church organs: Casavant, which invented the electropneumatic organ, and Guilbault-Therrien, which makes mechanical organs called Tourneau.

The principal attractions in town are the **Jardins Daniel Séguin** *(☎ 778-0372, 3215 rue Sicotte; adult/student $5/3; open 10am-8pm Tues-Sun late June–early Sept),* 4 hectares of pretty, thematic gardens (Zen, Louis XIV, etc). They make a nice stop, but are too close to traffic to be relaxing.

On rue Girouard Ouest are several Victorian homes lining the banks of the rivière Yamaska. Also here is the impressive **Monastère du Précieux Sang** *(Monastery of the Precious Blood; ☎ 773-0330; admission free; open 6:30am-7:20pm daily).* The first monastery founded in Canada, in 1861 by Catherine Aurélie, is headquartered in this magnificent church (1876), where wooden pews sit meekly beneath a massive dome ceiling, beautifully painted in rich blues and yellows by European painter Joseph-Thomas Rousseau.

Visitors can see Mother Catherine Aurélie's tomb and take a piece of her death veil for good luck. There has been an ongoing process toward her canonization since 1984, after several postmortem miracles were attributed to her.

Drummondville
☎ 819 • pop 45,500

In many ways, this is the little city that could. After years of being the butt of many regional jokes as an ugly hicksville, Drummondville has reshaped its fate. Its citizens decided to stop the ridicule and build a small city well worth a detour. Now some 50,000 people come here each summer just to see the unique Légendes Fantastiques (see Le Village Québécois d'Antan, below). The **Mondial des Cultures festival** (Ⓦ www.mondialdescultures.com) is one of the province's most renowned cultural gatherings, where artists and performers from around the world converge at the beginning of July for 11 days of multicultural merrymaking.

Although founded in 1815, Drummondville took off only after the 1915 building of two hydroelectric dams nearby. Later, metal processing, pulp and paper, and especially textile plants turned it into a none-too-pretty industrial town. Visitors tended to be businessmen who could smugly hurry home to Trois Rivières or Montréal. Now tourists intermingle with surprisingly hip locals who seem proud to live where they do.

Aside from the city's worthy attractions and quiet downtown, the surrounding area boasts rustic villages, great bike trails, a few beaches and even an emu farm where you can either cuddle or eat the cute Aussie creatures.

Information The tourist office (☎ 477-5529, 877-235-9596), open daily year-round, is at 1350 rue Michaud, accessible from Hwy 20 exits 175 or 177. To surf the Web, head to Infoteck Internet (☎ 477-2888), at 416 rue Lindsay, which charges $5 per hour. It's open 9am to 5pm Monday through Wednesday and Saturday, to 9pm Thursday and Friday.

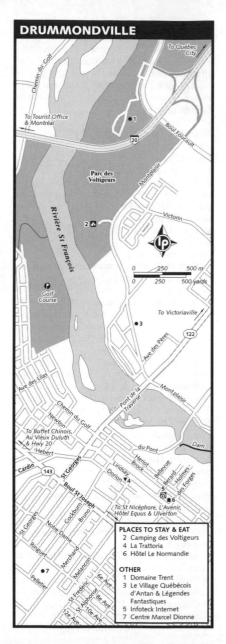

DRUMMONDVILLE

To Québec City

Chemin du Golf

To Tourist Office & Montréal

Boul Foucault

20

Montplaisir

Parc des Voltigeurs

Victorin

2 ▲

Rivière St François

0   250   500 m
0   250   500 yards

Golf Course

To Victoriaville

• 3

Ave des Pères

122

Ave des Lilas

Pont de la Traverse

Montplaisir

Chemin du Golf

Newton

To Buffet Chinois, Au Vieux Duluth & Hwy 20

du Pont

Dam

Hebert

Heriot

Brock

Bellevue

Berard

Holmes

Cardin

143

St Georges

Boul St Joseph

Lindsay

Dorton ▼4

5

6

des Forges

Cockburn

Brunel

To St Nicéphore, L'Avenir, Hôtel Equus & Ulverton

St Georges

Notre Dame

Ringuet

Marchand

Melancon

8e Ave

• 7

Pelletier

St Frederic

Alphonse

10e Ave

12e Ave

PLACES TO STAY & EAT
2 Camping des Voltigeurs
4 La Trattoria
6 Hôtel Le Normandie

OTHER
1 Domaine Trent
3 Le Village Québécois d'Antan & Légendes Fantastiques
5 Infoteck Internet
7 Centre Marcel Dionne

Le Village Québécois d'Antan This reconstruction of early pioneer villages from 1810 to 1910 (☎ 478-1441, 877-710-0267, W *www.villagequebecois.qc.ca, 1425 rue Montplaisir; adult/student/child $17/11/7; open 10am-6pm daily June-Sept)* features some 70 buildings reflecting nine types of architecture over 7km of territory. Guides in period costume put on bread-making and crafts displays, there's traditional food, and kids can feed the animals. Aside from Val Jalbert in Lac St Jean, this is the only place in Québec to get a flavor of what life here used to be like. Every July and August there are nightly performances of **Légendes Fantastiques** (☎ *800-265-5412; adult/child under 12 $33.50-37.50/$16.75-18.75)*, a dazzling multimedia show that's a mix of circus, drama, comedy and high-tech (the immense water screen is a hit) re-creating folklore and timeless tales for all ages.

Domaine Trent This 1848 manor house (☎ *472-3662, fax 472-1628, boul Foucault, Parc des Voltigeurs; admission free; open 10am-6pm daily June-Sept, 10am-4pm daily Oct-May)* was recently expanded into a full-fledged cultural emporium. An exhibition on regional history (the city's first) is filled with 19th- and 20th-century artifacts, there are rotating exhibits by local artists, and the ever popular **Musée de la Cuisine**, inside, explains all you wanted to know about Québécois cuisine. The in-house restaurant serves up delicious local fare as well (best to reserve in advance). Outside, there are 120,000 sq m of parkland to relax in, with picnic areas by the rivière St François, and one of Québec's only natural driving ranges. From Hwy 20, take exit 181.

Au Nid d'Émeu The 'Emu's Nest' (☎ *474-3741, 235 rue Lemaire, St Nicéphore; guided tour $3; open 10am-4pm mid-June–late Aug)* provides an unexpected sight: emus running wild – at least those that have not been canned and pickled! Kids can play with and pet them; adults can buy exotic foodstuff. St Nicéphore is 5km south of Drummondville along Rte 143.

Jardins de Lumières The 'gardens of lights' (☎ *394-3350, 552 1ére rang, L'Avenir; adult/child under 12 $5/free; open 7pm-11pm Fri-Sun July & Aug)* are the brainchild of two creative flower-lovers who transformed their garden into a sweet-smelling museum. Each evening the plants, flowers, and unusual marble and granite sculptures are illuminated with colored lights, producing a hypnotic effect, especially after a few drinks on their licensed terrace. L'Avenir is 15km south of Drummondville along Rte 143.

Moulin à Laine d'Ulverton This wool mill exhibition center (☎ *826-3157, 210 chemin Porter; adult/student/child under 12 $6/5/free; open 10am-4:30pm daily July & Aug, 10am-4:30pm Tues-Sun June & Sept)* is the largest of its kind in Canada, with four floors of displays. Even if you're not aching to dive into the world of wool weaving, the restored 1850 mill in which the museum is housed is worth a visit. Nearby are 5km of wooded trails, a covered bridge and suspended footbridge. Scottish immigrants founded the surrounding village (pop 300) in 1845. Ulverton is 24km south of Drummondville along Rte 143.

Junior Hockey All winter long, Drummondville rallies behind its junior hockey team, les Voltigeurs, and invites spectators in to see them practice and play. For over 38 years the city has hosted the International Midget Hockey Tournament at the end of January. All matches happen at the **Centre Marcel Dionne** (☎ *478-7044, 300 rue Cockburn)*.

Places to Stay One option is *Camping des Voltigeurs* (☎ *477-1360, 800-665-6527, 575 rue Montplaisir)* Tent sites $20/27 without/with full services, 5% higher July–mid-Aug, extra $5 for reservations. This is a Sépaq-administered site with playground and pool, inexplicably overpriced and crowded but conveniently located.

Hôtel Equus (☎ *394-2688*, W *www.hotelequus.com, 714 chemin Gagnon, L'Avenir)* Doubles $74, with meals $68-79 per person.

Located in the woods, a 15-minute drive from Drummondville, this complex makes you feel like you're in a country home. It offers various activities year-round like snowmobile outings, dogsledding, horseback riding and hiking, and also boasts an indoor pool and sauna. Ask about special rates that include tickets to local attractions.

Hôtel Le Normandie (☎ 478-2593, 512 rue Lindsay) Singles/doubles $51/65, including tax. A step up from a motel, this place has standard rooms and a central location.

Places to Eat Try *La Trattoria (☎ 474-0020, 195 rue Lindsay)* Mains $5-11; open 11am-10pm daily. You can look forward to decent Italian food with impeccably friendly service and a nice terrace.

Au Vieux Duluth (☎ 477-2233, 565 boul St Joseph) Mains $7-26; open 11am-11pm daily. This is a BYOW venue that re-creates a bit of a Montréal atmosphere. Look for the buy-one-get-a-second-for-$1 specials. Brochettes and meat dishes are the specialties here.

If only we would've made it to Internationals

Buffet Chinois (☎ 472-4300, 565 boul St Joseph) Lunch $7, dinner $10.50; open 11:30am-2:30pm & 5pm-11pm daily. This place is as Chinese as you'll get in the area. Their seafood is particularly good.

Getting There & Away Buses leave from Montréal's Central Station to Drummondville ($17, 1½ hours, 5-8 daily). From there, the service continues to Victoriaville, Plessisville and Thetford Mines, making local stops in between. There are also trains to/from Montréal ($21, 1¼ hours, 4-6 daily). The train station (☎ 472-5383) is at 263 Lindsay.

Downtown Drummondville is accessible off exit 177 of Hwy 20.

Asbestos
☎ 819 • pop 7000

Take a deep breath and hold it as long as it takes to set your eyes on the world's largest open-pit mine. From an observation deck, you can gaze across this 2km by 350m-deep pit used to extract some 600 tons of cancer-causing asbestos each year (see Pollution in the Facts about Québec chapter). You can't miss the turnoff for the mine and lookout from Rte 255 – there's a gigantic orange truck signaling the way.

The nearby **Musée Minéralogique et d'Histoire Minière** *(Mineralogical and Mining History Museum; ☎ 879-6444, 104 rue Letendre)* explains why this town is the world's 'Asbestos Capital,' and covers the miners' strikes, which played an important role in the development of trade unions in Québec.

Kingsey Falls
☎ 819 • pop 1900

This town, named after a village near Oxford, England, is a good example of a successful marriage between industry and nature. Once a depressing industrial town – it's home to Cascades, Canada's largest paper recycling plant – it has now beautified its core with florid gardens, and boasts the splendid **Parc Marie Victorin** *(☎ 363-2528, W www.ivic.qc.ca/mv, 385 rue Marie Victorin; adult/student $7/4.50; open 9:30am-8:30pm Wed-Sat & 9:30am-5:30pm Sun-Tues June 20–early Sept).*

An hour-long tour of these thematic gardens takes you across 26 sprawling acres, some which have wild Edward Scissorhands–like animal-shaped bushes.

If you're in the mood for chemicals afterward, the park can organize a visit to Cascades, the park's main sponsors.

Victoriaville & Plessisville
☎ 819 • pop 38,100 & 6800

These towns are each considered capitals of two dearly beholden culinary delicacies in Québec – *poutine* (see 'The Cult of Poutine') and maple syrup (see 'Maple Syrup & the Sugar Shack,' in the Facts for the Visitor chapter), respectively.

Victoriaville is the area's largest center, with several strip malls and busy boulevards. Some stately homes from the Victorian period are the only real draw here, like the **Maison Sir Wilfrid Laurier** *(☎ 357-8655, 16 rue Laurier Ouest; adult/student $3.50/2.75; open 9am-5pm Mon-Fri, 1pm-5pm Sat & Sun year-round, closed Monday Sept-June)*. Laurier, Canada's charismatic prime minister from 1896 to 1911, lived here from 1876. Another branch of the museum, the Pavilion Hôtel des Postes *(☎ 357-2185, 949 boul Bois Francs Sud; same admission and opening hours)*, is in a 1910 post office and features permanent and temporary exhibits by local artists. The region's most famous painter and sculpture is Marc Aurèle de Foy Suzor Coté (1869–1937), who studied in Paris art schools when it was still fashionable to do so. His Impressionistic landscapes were particularly well loved.

Plessisville calls itself the 'Maple Capital of the World,' and if you don't believe it, just read the huge sign declaring it as you drive into town. Or stop by in early May for the **Festival de l'Érable** (Maple Festival; W www.erable.org) for a celebration of all things maple. It's the province's second oldest festival after Québec's City Winter Carnival. Or check out the **Musée de l'Érable** *(Maple Museum; ☎ 362-9292, 1280 rue Trudelle; adult/child under 12 $4/2.50; open 9am-5pm daily)*. A smallish display therein explains how maple gathering, and a video shows how technology has changed sap-gathering techniques.

Still, these places don't explain Plessisville's self-knighted worldwide status. This comes from the fact that Citadelle, a company that regroups 2700 maple groves and syrup producers (the largest in the province), is based there and sets the export standards for grades of syrup.

Inverness
☎ 418 • pop 840

This gem of a village, founded by Scottish and Irish immigrants in 1829, shows its roots in unexpected ways, despite the fact that over 90% of its inhabitants are francophone. For such a tiny village, there are a surprising number of churches (three functioning, one a bronze foundry) and cemeteries (13!). In an ode more to western Canada than to Scotland, it also hosts the **Beef Festival** *(☎ 453-2592)*, in the last days of August, replete with rodeo rides, crowning of the Beef Queen, and, of course, a massive barbecue.

More bizarre are the weekly **traditional dance evenings** held throughout the year at the Odd Fellows Hall *(☎ 450-453-2698, 317 rue Gosford; admission $2; 7pm Fri)*. Here, locals swing their pad-ners round and round in wild evenings of dances ranging from the jig (a leftover of Celtic settlers) to American square dancing via the figure dance, the two-step, waltzes and line-dancing.

The tradition of Irish and Scottish folk dancing has been going strong here since 1949. These Friday sessions are chock-full of knee-slapping, hand-clapping, fiddle-playing, accordion-swooshing exuberance where an old-time *calleur* (caller) yells out instructions (in English). Bring your own beer and throw yourself into the fun.

In summertime there are additional square dancing evenings held every second Saturday at Fort Verness *(☎ 453-2400, 1771 rue Gosford)*.

In wintertime there is excellent **cross-country skiing** in the area.

Things to See & Do The Musée du Bronze *(Bronze Museum; ☎ 453-2101, e info@museedubronze.com, 1760 rue Dublin; admission $3; open 10am-5pm daily late June–early Sept)* displays locally sculpted works and shows the workings of its mini foundry.

The **Celtic Way** *(☎ 453-3434, fax 453-3315, e route_celtique@globetrotter.net,*

MONTRÉAL TO QUÉBEC CITY

The Cult of *Poutine*

No historian can trace the exact time and place of the momentous birth of *poutine*. Sad, but we'll just have to live with it. Experts say that Victoriaville is its likely birthplace, a distinction that surely has Queen Victoria (in whose honor the town was named in 1861) thrashing about with indigestion in her grave.

In the last two decades especially, poutine has become something of a Québécois institution, served up in steaming glops in every corner of the province. You can find it in greasy diners just as easily as in spiffy restaurants – hell, you can even order it in McDonald's and Burger King (but we would counsel against it)! The cult of poutine also knows no bounds – there are reports of it cropping up on menus in such faraway lands as British Columbia, Florida and Mexico (wherever Québécois expats land!).

What is this mystery dish, pronounced in the same way as the French say the name of Russia's president? What is this visionary feast that transports tens of thousands of people into culinary ecstasy each day (and their coronary arteries into collective paroxysms of high anxiety)? What gourmet treat comes from the Québécois slang for both 'strange mixture' and 'fat woman'?

Simple. It consists of a pile of French fries (these can be crispy, droopy, thin or thick, but the best are soft and greasy), mixed with processed cheese curds and topped with thin, brown gravy. Add salt as you please, and go for it!

Yet the endless versatility of the poutine cannot be underestimated. Not only can you find an ever-growing array of poutine variations (Italian poutine with spaghetti sauce, Chinese poutine with onions, green peppers and soy sauce, smoked meat poutine etc), the dish has also spawned several spin-offs.

The *galvaude* (from the French verb 'to disturb, to put into disorder') is certain to disturb the digestive process: On top of a thin and soggy hot dog bun sit a small mountain of fries topped with cheese curds, pieces of chopped chicken, coleslaw and gravy, sprinkled with peas. The good news is you won't have to eat for days afterward.

The *guédille* is the least popular poutine cousin, no thanks to the fact that the word in Québécois slang means 'snot' (no joke!). This little repast is essentially a galvaude on Prozac – a hot dog bun covered with fries and sauce.

Both the galvaude and the guédille boast regional differences, sometimes substituting chicken for fish, or peas for corn. This underscores their multifaceted nature, readily adaptable to local tastes and products.

Though the mention of such dishes make many Québécois giggle or snicker (snicker, that is, as they order a second helping!), its defenders proudly state that its nutritional value is better than other North American fast food, and that as comfort food, it can't be beat. There are people plenty serious about poutine – connoisseurs argue that the purest poutine has the cheese curds lying *under* the fries, not placed willy-nilly on top of them, as most places serve them.

There is also fiery great debate as to the dish's origins. Though Victoriaville is championed by some, others fervently bellow that Warwick, a small town 10km westward, is the true cradle of poutine. Most agree, however, that it was known as far back as the 1950s, well before its renown flowered across the Northern Hemisphere.

And despite the groans of disgust the word usually summons in those who mock it, most grumble that it does, at the end of the day, taste pretty good.

If you're passing through Victoriaville and wish to render homage to the city which likely nurtured the discovery of poutine, a good place to do so is at the most popular restaurant/pub around: *Plus* (☎ 819-758-9927, 192 boul Bois Francs Sud).

1813 rue Dublin) has devised a very interesting tourist circuit around Inverness that explains the town's deep-rooted Scottish and Irish heritage. Detailed maps and explanations (in English) are sold for $5 at their office, and they can arrange guided group visits.

Following rue Gosford northeast some 7km from Inverness are the lovely **Parc des Chutes Lysander** (Lysander Falls; 15m high) and surrounding park *(admission free; open 8am-9pm daily)*. Small, uncrowded and serene, it's a perfect place for a picnic.

Places to Stay & Eat *Gîte du Moulin Avant* (☎ 453-2331, 955 chemin Dublin) Singles/doubles $40/50 with huge breakfast. Located 5km from Inverness (towards Plessisville), this maple grove and farm run by some of the nicest folks in the area has walking trails and hosts springtime sugar shacks. There's even a makeshift 'museum' in the garage, full of old farm equipment (ask to see the tobacco cutter). Sample homemade maple products for breakfast. It's best to reserve ahead of time.

Camping des Chutes d'Inverness (☎ 453-2400, 1771 rue Gosford, ⓔ fortinverness@ ivic.qc.ca) Tent sites $17/15 with/without services. Opposite the Fort Verness dance hall and restaurant, and within walking distance of the Lysander Falls, is this pleasant campground.

Camping La Plage (no ☎ , chemin Gosford) Tent sites free, $3 car park fee. Rustic camping as it's meant to be – free and wild. Park your car, find the attendant (if he's not busy organizing weekend raves also held on the spot), enter the forest and look for the fun. There are two beaches – including one for nudists – and no amenities whatsoever, though a dry toilet has been promised for 2002, and perhaps a small nightly fee. It's located 500m past the covered bridge on chemin Gosford toward Ste Agathe from Inverness.

Bronze Café (☎ 453-7999, 1817 rue Dublin) Mains $4-8; open 11am-9pm Tues-Sun. The best place to eat in miles, this oasis of a country kitchen serves up succulent, healthy and simple meals using garden vegetables and grandma's recipes.

Québec City

☎ 418 • pop 672,000

Québec City is the cradle of French culture in North America, the historic heart of Québec. Moreover, it is the province's jewel. Since 1985 the city's entire Old Town has been placed on the UN's prestigious World Heritage List. This walled, old city – the only remaining in the US and Canada – is a living museum, each street a page in the book of French Canada's struggle for survival – even dominion – in British North America. Much of the city's past is still visible, and its many churches, old stone houses and narrow streets make it an architectural gem. As the oldest city in the US and Canada, it boasts many 'firsts' and 'oldests.'

Yet it is also a lively capital with a vibrant population. It has some of the province's, indeed the country's, best museums and is the most 'European' of any city on the continent. Old Montréal has this feel to some degree, as does the French Quarter in New Orleans, but nowhere in North America is the picture as complete as here.

Because of this, Québec City is a year-round tourist mecca. Each year, some four million visitors pass through, a quarter of them from outside Canada. It regularly figures in the top ten most-visited spots in North America on numerous surveys.

As the seat of the provincial government and home to Université Laval, this is the functional center of Québécois consciousness in both its moderate and extreme manifestations. Many of today's 'intellectuals' and politicians speaking for independence are based here.

Although many people are bilingual, the vast majority speak French as a first language, and 94% have French ancestors. This is a tourist town, however, so English is spoken around the attractions and in shops.

The city is also an important port, lying where the St Charles River meets the St Lawrence. It sits on top of and around a cliff, a wonderful setting with views over the river and the town of Lévis (pronounced not as in the jeans but as 'lev-ee') across the river.

Highlights

- Have a blast at the Winter Carnival and tweak Bonhomme's nose
- Spend an enlightening day at Old Town's Musée de la Civilisation
- Snooze like the seals on an ice bed at the Ice Hotel
- Uncover the human tragedy on beautiful Grosse Île
- See the famous wooden sculptures at St Jean Port Joli

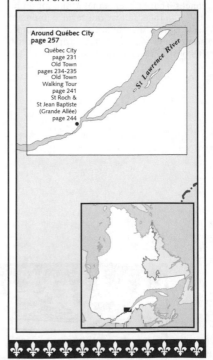

Around Québec City
page 257

Québec City
page 231
Old Town
pages 234-235
Old Town
Walking Tour
page 241
St Roch &
St Jean Baptiste
(Grande Allée)
page 244

HISTORY

One of the continent's earliest settlements, the site of Québec City was already a First Nations village called 'Stadacona' (in the Huron language) when the French explorer Jacques Cartier landed here in 1535 on his second voyage to the New World.

Cartier carried on his naming spree of rivers and bays, erected a cross in the name of the King of France and left in 1536 after having spent a harsh winter. He took with him basketfuls of iron pyrite (fools' gold) and quartz crystals, thinking they may be valuable (from which came the expression *'voilà un diamant de Canada,'* 'there's a diamond from Canada,' meaning 'something fake').

He returned in 1541 with the notion to found a post upstream at Cap Rouge, but this was a failure and it set back France's colonial pretensions in the region for more than half a century.

Finally explorer Samuel de Champlain founded the city for the French in 1608, calling it Kebec, from the Algonquin word meaning 'the river narrows here,' and built a small base at Cap Diamant (Cape Diamond, atop the highest point of which now sits the Citadel, or La Citadelle). He allied with the Hurons to develop the fur trade. Their geographical position in the west and north made them the essential middlemen (essentially they took the Europeans to the lands of plenty, showed them where the catches were particularly abundant and helped the explorers survive in the wilderness) that Champlain needed to ensure a constant supply. By the 1620s the Hurons were supplying up to two-thirds of the furs sent back to France.

In 1619 Champlain was dubbed the King's Lieutenant in Canada, and the following year he built a fort where today's Château Frontenac stands. As there were so few colonists (fewer than 100 until 1630), Cardinal Richelieu devised a scheme that would send 200 colonists a year to Québec City, all of them Roman Catholics, to help with supplying furs and resources to the motherland.

The English seized the city in 1629 but Québec was returned to the French under a treaty three years later and it soon became the center of New France. After the threat of Iroquois attack subsided in the 1660s a period of relative peace followed, allowing the city to develop. Already the city's two sections, Lower Town and Upper Town, were distinguished: the former for business, naval affairs and the residences of workers and lower classes, the latter for higher affairs and bourgeois homes.

Repeated English attacks followed. In 1759 General Wolfe led the British to victory over Montcalm on the Plains of Abraham (although both generals died in the battle). This is one of North America's most famous battles and virtually ended the conflict. In 1763 the Treaty of Paris gave Canada to Britain. In 1775 the American revolutionaries had a go at capturing Québec, but they were pushed back promptly.

In 1791 the divisions of Upper Canada (Ontario) and Lower Canada (Québec and the Atlantic Provinces) were created. In the 1800s Lower Canada became known as Québec, and Québec City was chosen as the provincial capital; it had always been the seat of power in France's territories, so it was a logical move to keep the government there during the divisions. Interestingly, after the union of Upper and Lower Canada in 1841, Québec City was the capital of the United Provinces of Canada in 1851–55 and 1859–65, before Ottawa was finally decided upon as the new capital.

In the 19th century the city lost its status and importance in the shadow of Montréal. When the Depression burst Montréal's bubble in 1929, Québec City regained some stature as far as government matters were concerned. The now-famous Winter Carnival was launched in the 1950s to incite a tourism boom, and since that time the city has become one of the most visited in North America.

In April 2001 the city was the site of the Summit of the Americas, which exploded into mass demonstrations and protests against globalization. Images of 6000 police and 1200 soldiers using water cannons, tear gas, clubs and rubber bullets on protesters were broadcast around the globe. A lasting image was Prime Minister Jean Chrétien on

QUÉBEC CITY

television saying, 'Having a democratic government is an essential condition of membership in the Summit of the Americas' while helicopters hovered overhead and police doused and shot at the crowds behind him.

The graffiti on building walls along rue St Jean and down toward St Roch will long be reminders of the chaos of those days, which forever shook the confidence of thousands in their government. Some photos of the events are viewable at ⓦ www.time.com/time/photoessays/quebecprotest.

ORIENTATION & POPULATION

Québec City itself is home to only 167,000 people and is surprisingly small, covering only 93 sq km, with nearly all things of interest packed into one compact corner. The population most often given of 672,000 takes into account all the surrounding towns and once-separate cities that have been, as of early 2002, fused with Québec. This new, or Greater, Québec City encompasses 9000 sq km (nearly 100 times its original size!) and swallows Ste Foy, Charny, Lévis, Île d'Orléans and Loretteville, among others.

Québec City is much more homogenous than Montréal. A recent census shows, for example, only 3900 people of Asian descent living there.

Part of the city sits on top of the cliffs of Cap Diamant (Cape Diamond) and part lies below. Thus Québec is divided into Upper Town and Lower Town (Haute Ville and Basse Ville, respectively), each with old and new sections. The Citadel, a fort and famous landmark, overlooks the city from its lofty perch on the highest point of Cap Diamant.

The best and maybe only way to orient yourself in this area is simply to walk around (skateboards on the cobblestones just won't do). The northeastern end of Upper Town is still surrounded by a stone wall and is referred to as Old Town (Vieux Québec), whose main rue St Jean is loaded with bars and restaurants. This area is the city's main attraction because of its decidedly European feel, born out of its winding, narrow streets and hidden stairwells.

A well-known Old Town landmark is the copper-topped, castle-style Château Frontenac hotel, dating from 1892. Behind it a large boardwalk called the Terrasse Dufferin edges along the cliff, providing good views over the river. Here you will also find the statue of Monsieur de Champlain, the man who started it all. At the other end of the boardwalk is the wooden slide used during the Winter Carnival (see the Special Events section for details). From here the boardwalk leads to the Promenade des Gouverneurs, a path that runs between the cliff's edge and the Citadel. Beyond the Citadel, outside the walls, is the huge and green Parc des Champs de Bataille, where the battles over Québec took place.

A smart place to start your visit is at the Observatoire de la Capitale (☎ 644-9841, 888-497-4322), at 1037 rue de la Chevrotière. This is an observation deck on the 31st floor of the Édifice Marie Guyart and has great views. It's open from 10am to 5pm daily but from mid-October to late June it is closed Mondays. It's $4 to get in ($3 for students) but is worth it, as it's a great way to get oriented, and there are good historical explanation panels.

Down below the Château Frontenac is Old Lower Town, the oldest section of the city, sitting mainly between the St Lawrence and St Charles Rivers and hugging the cliffs of Cap Diamant. The focal point of this small area, at the northeastern edge of Old Québec, is Place Royale. From here you can walk (it's neither hard nor far) or take the funicular railway ($1.50 one-way) to the top of the cliff of Upper Town. The funicular terminal in Lower Town is on rue du Petit Champlain. Rue Sous le Cap and rue du Petit Champlain, which are only 2.5m across, are two of the oldest streets in North America.

Outside the wall in Upper Town are some places of note, including the National Assembly (legislative buildings) and some tasty restaurants. The two main streets heading west from Old Upper Town are boulevard René Lévesque and, to the south, Grande Allée, which eventually becomes boulevard Wilfrid Laurier. Grande Allée is particularly busy at night with bars and numerous places to eat. The neighborhoods of St Roch and St Jean Baptiste have a more local feel. Heavily residential, these are nonetheless spotted with places of interest, and provide a respite from the hordes of tourists in the Old Town.

Lower Town, lying to the north, south and west of Upper Town, contains residential, business and industrial areas, as well as some vibrant and newly developing social sectors.

Much farther north in Lower Town are the highways leading north, east and west. In this section of the city you'll find a number of motels.

To the extreme southwest of the city you'll see signs for either Pont de Québec or Pont Pierre Laporte. Both bridges lead to the south shore.

INFORMATION
Tourist Offices

There are quite a few tourist information offices throughout Greater Québec. For general information on the Web, check out ⓦ www.quebecregion.com.

The main office is Centre Infotouriste (☎ 649-2608, 800-363-7777), 12 rue Ste Anne, on Place d'Armes opposite the Château

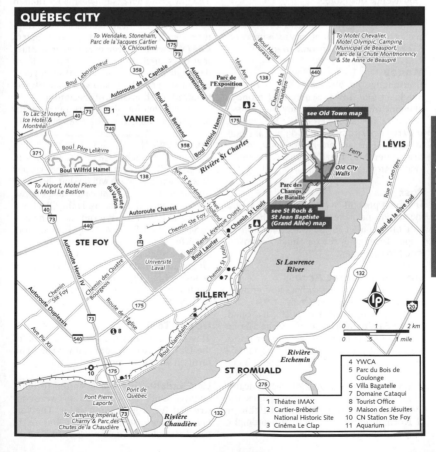

QUÉBEC CITY

1 Théatre IMAX
2 Cartier-Brébeuf National Historic Site
3 Cinéma Le Clap
4 YWCA
5 Parc du Bois de Coulonge
6 Villa Bagatelle
7 Domaine Cataqui
8 Tourist Office
9 Maison des Jésuites
10 CN Station Ste Foy
11 Aquarium

QUÉBEC CITY

Frontenac hotel. The staff are bilingual, friendly (considering the crowds they get at peak times) and well supplied with maps and other information on the city and province. They can also help with booking accommodations and numerous city tours. The office is open from 8:30am to 7:30pm daily June through September; at other months it closes at 5pm.

A second, equally large but less crowded tourist office (☎ 649-2608) is at 835 avenue Laurier, at the entrance to the Plains of Abraham. Yet another office (no ☎), open year-round, is west of town in Ste Foy at 3300 avenue des Hôtels.

Kiosk Frontenac, a booth on Terrasse Dufferin facing the Château Frontenac, makes reservations for all city activities and is the starting point for some tours.

Money

Transchange (☎ 694-6906), at 43 rue de Buade in Old Town, is a central money-changing office; it is open daily. The Caisse Populaire Desjardins (☎ 694-1774), nearby at 19 rue des Jardins, is open daily from 9am to 6pm. ATMs are not hard to find in the city center, and there's one at the main tourist information office.

Post

The main post office (☎ 694-6175) is at 300 rue St Paul, near the train station. There is a post office outlet in the walled section of Upper Town, at 3 rue de Buade, opposite Parc Montmorency.

Email & Internet Access

If you like your surfing with a bit of grunge, try Cyber Bar Étrange (☎ 522-6504), 275 rue St Jean in St Jean Baptiste; it's open 1pm to 3am daily. They only charge $2 per hour, and for that you get to saunter up to the bar and order a beer with the metal-rocker toughies dressed in black who hang out there. If you'd prefer to read your Hotmail surrounded by kids energetically killing each other playing cybergames, try Cybar (☎ 522-0523), at 369 rue de l'Église in St Roch. They're open noon to midnight daily and charge $6 an hour.

For an 'I just wanna check my email' experience, the AL Van Houtte (☎ 692-4909) café, 995 Place d'Youville, just outside the Old Town wall, has several terminals to use for $6 per hour.

Laundry

There are several laundromats in town. A central one is the Lavoir Moderne (no ☎), 17B rue Ste Ursule, where wash and dry are $2 each. It's open 9am to 9pm weekdays and 9am to 6pm weekends.

Gay & Lesbian Travelers

The gay scene here is much smaller than in Montréal and is mostly limited to a few venues along rue St Jean in the St Jean Baptiste area. The annual pride festival, **Divers Cité** (ⓦ www.diverscite.org), held in the first few days of September, is a pretty huge deal, with a series of concerts, art shows and, of course, a *fabulous* parade, which attracts hundreds of thousands of spectators.

For information about bars and community groups, call Gay Line (☎ 888-505-1010).

OLD TOWN

The jewel of Québec City is the Old Town, which is divided into Lower and Upper Towns. Which is which will be sharply felt by the steep hills and staircases; in general, Upper Town is the area inside the Old Town walls and Lower Town is outside of them.

See the Old Town Walking Tour section, later, for a great way to catch many of the must-see sites in this area. Starting in the Upper Town and finishing at a Lower Town watering hole, the tour guides you through the history, architecture and culture of one of Canada's most vibrant urban areas.

Upper Town

This section covers the Old Town areas of the Upper Town, the originally walled and fortified section of the city.

La Citadelle The French started to build on this site in 1750, when bastions were constructed for storing gunpowder. The fort (*The Citadel; ☎ 694-2815, Côte de la Citadelle; adult/child $5.50/4; open 9am or*

10am-5pm or 6pm Apr-Sept, 10am-3pm Oct) was completed by the British in 1820 after 30 years of work and served as the eastern flank of the city's defense system against potentially invading Americans. The irregularly sided structure sits on the plain over 100m above the river at an appropriate vantage point.

Today the Citadel is a bit of Canadiana in the heart of Québec. It's the home base of Canada's Royal 22s (known in bastardized French as the Van Doos), a French regiment that developed quite a reputation through WWI, WWII and the Korean War. There is a **museum** outlining its history and a more general military museum containing documents, uniforms and models situated in a few different buildings, including the old prison at the southeast end. As it is a military base, some sections are closed to the public.

The entrance fee includes admission to these museums and a guided tour; tours run April to October. The **Changing of the Guard** ceremony takes place at 10am daily in summer. The **Beating of the Retreat** at 6pm on Tuesday, Thursday, Saturday and Sunday during July and August is followed by the last tour.

Parc des Champs de Bataille (Battlefields Park)

This huge park runs southwest from the Citadel. Its hills, gardens, monuments and trees take up 108 hectares and are perfect for strolling, biking, rollerblading and cross-country skiing. It may be pleasant now, however the park was once a bloody battleground, the site of a conflict that determined the course of Canadian history. The part closest to the cliff is known as the Plains of Abraham (Plaines d'Abraham), and it was here in 1759 that the British finally defeated the French with both generals, Wolfe of the British and Montcalm of the French, dying in the process. There's a **Wolfe monument** in front of the Musée du Québec (see 'The Trouble with Jamie'), and the **Montcalm monument** stands on rue Grande Allée, west of the military *manège*.

Walking or bus tours of the park depart from the **Discovery Pavilion** (☎ *648-4071, 835*

avenue Laurier; admission free, tours adult/ child $3.50/2.75; open 9am-5:30pm daily year-round), which provides a good starting point to the park. From here you can walk through the park or take a bus tour and decide which sights you wish to see. They also sell combined entrance tickets, which save money if you wish to visit many attractions. Also in the Discovery Pavilion is the **Canada Odyssey** (W *www.odysseecanada.com; adult/child $6.50/5.50)*, a 75-minute multimedia show focusing on the famous battle.

You can also visit **Tour Martello 1** *(Martello Tower 1; adult/child $3.50/2.75; open 10am-5:30pm daily mid-June–early Sept)*, a British defensive structure from 1812. Kids love to run around in here. The Tour Martello 2, on avenue Tache, is open only for special presentations and events.

Southwest of the Discovery Pavilion and about 500m east of the Wolfe Monument, the **National Battlefields Park Interpretive Centre** (☎ *648-5641; adult/child $3.50/2.75; open 10am-5:30pm daily mid-May–mid-Oct, 10am-5:30pm Tues-Sun mid-Oct–mid-May)* focuses on the dramatic history of the park with another multimedia show.

The standout museum in the park – and one of the city's finest – is just west of the Interpretive Centre. The **Musée du Québec** (☎ *643-2150; adult/child $8/5; open 10am-5:45pm daily & to 9pm Wed year-round; closed Mon early Sept–May)* houses the province's most important collection of Québécois art, as well as international paintings, sculptures and ceramics. Included in their collection are works by Riopelle, Borduas, Dallaire and Leduc. Be sure to look out for works by James Duncan and Cornelius Krieghoff, and the statues of Québec's best-loved sculptor, Louis-Philippe Hébert (whose 22 bronze works adorn the façade of the Assemblée Nationale). The museum also has a rich collection of modern art, photographs, drawings and arts and crafts. There are incisive, well-documented thematic and temporary exhibits, and most weeks they screen art films. The old prison nearby is now part of the gallery.

Rollerblading is a great way to get around. Rent wheels (☎ 522-2293; adult/child 2-hour

OLD TOWN

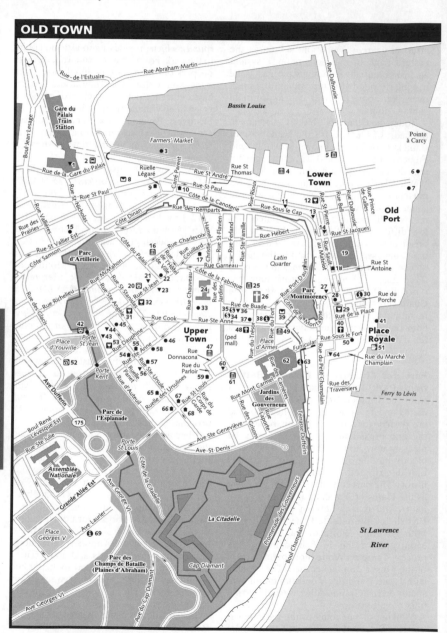

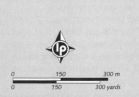

rental $14/10; open 10am-9pm Mon-Fri, 10am-6pm Sat & Sun) from the kiosk at the western entrance of the park, off rue Montcalm. For **cross-country skiing**, there are 11km of trails; call ☎ 649-6476 for info.

Fortifications of Québec National Historic Site The largely restored old wall (ramparts) of Québec City is now deemed a protected site (☎ 648-7016). In fact, you can walk a complete 4.6km circuit on top of it, all around the Old Town. At the old Powder Building beside Porte St Louis, an interpretive center has been set up, which provides a little information on the wall's history. Guided walking tours (90 mins; adult/student $10/7.50) leave from the Kiosk Frontenac, on Terrasse Dufferin.

Parc d'Artillerie Beside the wall at Porte St Jean, Parc d'Artillerie (☎ 648-4205, 2 rue d'Auteuil; adult/student $3.50/3; open 10am-6pm daily), a National Historic Site, has been used militarily for centuries. A munitions factory here made cartridges for the Canadian Forces until 1964 (as proof, there are daily rifle-firing demonstrations). It was a French military headquarters from 1747, and later it housed the British garrison. It's now an interpretive center with a scale model of Québec City the way it was in the early 1800s. In the Dauphine Redoubt, there are costumes and displays about the soldiers for whom it was built during the French regime. The Redoubt, built between 1712 and 1747, is a defense structure designed to protect a prominent point. In this case, the edge of the hill could be well-guarded by the soldiers within. In the officers' quarters there's a history lesson for children.

Musée du Fort Near Place d'Armes this small museum (☎ 692-1759, 10 rue Ste Anne; adult/student $7/4; open 10am-6pm daily April-Oct, 11am-4pm Thur-Sun Feb & Mar) deals with provincial military history. With the aid of a large model of 18th-century Québec City, six sieges and battles are retold using sound and light. The half-hour show isn't bad and comes in English and French versions.

QUÉBEC CITY

Musée d'Art Inuit It may not be very well known, but this museum (☎ 694-1828, 39 rue St Louis; adult/student $6/4; open 9:30am-5:30pm daily) houses one of the best collec-tions of Inuit art in the country. Further, aside from simply displaying its 450 unique works of art, it places them in context. There are works from northern Québec (Nunavik),

The Trouble with Jamie

It strikes some visitors as odd that there are several statues of James Wolfe in Québec City. He was, after all, the British general who led the victorious battle on the Plains of Abraham that wrested the Canadian colony from France once and for all. In the capital of a province that isn't exactly what we could call proud of its, er, British heritage, it's strange to see statues and monuments (and street names) commemorating Wolfe.

Only don't think that Wolfe won his high visibility in this city easily. It wasn't enough that he himself died in the bloody battle of 1759, but statues of him were later bombed, stolen, replaced, kidnapped and taken overseas – what a way to treat a hero!

Let's start with the monument at the place of his death on the Plains. In 1790 a land surveyor placed small, plain marker on the spot Wolfe was said to have died, where Wolfe's army had rolled a stone to mark the spot. In 1832 a small column replaced it, this time with a plaque, yet this soon fell into disrepair. In 1849 officers of the local English garrison took up a collection to replace it with a more fitting 11m column topped with a helmet and sword. Nice! Too bad the cholera epidemic prevented anyone from showing up to the opening ceremony.

This column lasted until 1913, at which time it was replaced by a stone version of the same monument. This one stood sturdy...until it was bombed to bits in 1963 in a nasty show of nation-alist fervor. The provincial government voted to replace it in 1965 (if you can imagine that debate), and today the one that did still stands courageous, if a tad shaken.

A statue of the fallen hero met an even stranger fate. In 1780 a Scot named George Hips ac-quired a beautiful house on the northwest corner of rue St Jean and Côte du Palais. There was a pretty niche above the main entrance where a statue of St Jean Baptiste stood. When Hips moved in he replaced St Jean in one fell, ironic swoop with a statue of Wolfe he had commissioned by two Francophone sculptor brothers named Chaulete (who never admitted to having made it).

So there stood Wolfe as a local curiosity (pride for some, provocation to others) until one fateful summer night in 1838 when a few drunken sailors stole the statue and took it on a round-the-world joy ride. Wolfe no doubt drank rum with his *confrères* on binges in Bermuda and elsewhere before ending up back on his original niche, no worse for wear, a few years later.

Poor Wolfe's statue was beginning to resemble the plot of the Hitchcock black comedy *The Trouble with Harry*, but it wasn't over yet. In 1847 the corner house was demolished and replaced by the one you can see today, and James was moved up to a niche on the second floor, away from the noise below: Downstairs was now one of the city's most popular taverns, the Vaillancourt (Wolfe was still suffering from his round-the-world hangover, you see). In 1898 Bell Canada, the new owners of the house, removed the now crumbling Wolfe for good, giving it to the Literary and Historical Society, at 44 rue St Stanislas, where it remains to this day.

By 1901 a new Wolfe statue commissioned by British Loyalists was back in its original location – there's just no keeping a good general down – until the charged 1960s, that is. In 1964, a year after the Wolfe monument on the Plains of Abraham was blown up, the new owner of this build-ing on rue St Jean received threats of arson unless he removed the offending statue. He did.

Today James Wolfe's statue finally has time to rest, contemplating his view from the inside of the museum at la Citadelle.

Nunavut, Baffin Island and other Inuit areas. Regional differences in themes depicted and materials used are well delineated. The exhibit is an outgrowth of the personal collection of Raymond Brousseau, who started collecting Inuit soapstone carvings in 1960, and features some standout pieces like a tall sculpture made of a narwhal tusk. Allow at least an hour to go through the museum.

Conveniently connected to the museum, the Galerie Brousseau et Brousseau (see Shopping for contact information) sells Inuit sculptures. A percentage of the sales gets reinjected into the local communities where the objects were originally purchased.

Ursuline Convent & Museum This convent (☎ 694-0694, 12 rue Donnacona; adult/student $4/2.50; open 10am-noon & 1:30pm-5pm Tues-Sat, 1:30pm-5pm Sun May-Sept; 1pm-4:30pm Tues-Sun Oct-Apr) is the oldest girls' school on the continent, founded in 1641. There are several buildings on the estate, some of which are restored. The museum deals with the Ursuline sisters and their lives in the 1600s and 1700s, and also displays paintings, crafts, furniture and other belongings of the early French settlers.

At the same address, the lovely **chapel** (admission free; open 10am-11:30am & 1:30pm-4:30pm Tues-Sat & 1:30-4:30pm Sun May-Oct) was built in 1902 but has retained some interiors built in 1723. Buried here are the remains of both Marie de l'Incarnation, the founder of the convent, and General Montcalm. Talk about strange bedfellows! The morbid can take a gander at Montcalm's skull, on display inside the museum.

Cathedral of the Holy Trinity This elegantly handsome cathedral (☎ 692-2193, 31 rue des Jardins; admission free; open 9am-6pm daily May & June, 9am-8pm daily July & Aug, 10am-4pm Sept-mid-Oct) was modeled on London's St Martin in the Fields. Constructed in 1804, it was the first Anglican cathedral built outside the British Isles. The bell tower, 47m high, has an eight-bell chime that competes with attention with the nearby Basilica Notre Dame.

Latin Quarter The Latin Quarter refers to a section of Old Upper Town surrounding the large **Québec seminary** complex, with its stone and wooden buildings, grassy, quiet quadrangles, a chapel and museum. The seminary was originally the site of Université Laval, which outgrew the space here and was moved in the 1960s to Ste Foy. Many students still live along the old, narrow streets, which look particularly Parisian.

The focus of the area is the towering **Basilica Notre Dame de Québec** (☎ 694-0665, 20 rue de Buade; admission free; open 7:30am-4:30pm daily year-round). Samuel de Champlain erected a chapel on this site in 1633. It was destroyed in 1640, and in 1650 a stone church was built in its place. Over the next century the church was enlarged and promoted to the rank of cathedral. Much of it was destroyed in the 1759 battles, then rebuilt by 1771. This got burned down in 1922 and was entirely reconstructed in 1925. The grandiose interiors, however, faithfully re-create the spirit of the 18th century. The remains of Cardinal Laval (beatified in 1980 by John Paul II) lie inside. There is a tacky multimedia show ($7, 5 times daily) that tells the story of the church.

Next door is the excellent **Musée de l'Amérique Francaise** (Museum of French America; ☎ 692-2843, 2 Côte de la Fabrique; adult/student $4/2; open 10am-5pm daily year-round, closed Mon early Sept-late June). Canada's oldest museum, it contains artifacts relating to French settlement and culture in the New World. If your time is limited, head straight to the second floor to watch a superb film – angry, sad, ironic all in one – that successfully makes the viewer empathize with the French side of Canada's history.

The (bilingual) exhibits are also first-rate. Your admission fee grants you entrance into some of the seminary buildings, where religious and other temporary exhibits are held. The free (also bilingual) guided tours will get you into the oldest buildings. If the gates to the left of the Basilica are closed, enter the seminary grounds at 9 rue de l'Université.

Musée des Augustines Describing the lives of the religious nuns who arrived in a harsh, nearly unpopulated Québec in 1639, this museum (☎ 692-2492, 32 rue Charlevoix; admission by donation; open 9:30am-noon & 1:30pm-5pm Tues-Sat, 1:30am-5pm Sun) is situated on the territory of the monastery they built. Three brave sisters originally came to New France to found a hospital, Hôtel Dieu, which for over 350 years has never stopped functioning as a care-giving center. The interesting exhibit features paintings, antique furniture and other works of art.

Le Château Frontenac

This castle-like edifice (☎ 692-3861, 1 rue de Carrières) is said to be the world's most photographed hotel. (It's also the city's top hotel – see Places to Stay for details.) Named after the French governor who challenged invading Americans with 'I'll answer with the mouth of my cannons and the shots of my firearms!,' it is now one of the city's most recognizable features. The Château was built in 1893 by the Canadian Pacific Railway as the most striking of their series of luxury hotels across Canada. New York architect Bruce Price was at the helm. The 17-story medieval tower was added in 1912, but the elevators date from 1893 – they were steam-operated before switching to electricity in 1912. During WWII, Prime Minister MacKenzie King hosted Winston Churchill and Franklin Roosevelt here.

Tours leave every hour on the hour and last 50 minutes (tour reservations ☎ 691-2166; adult/child $6.50/3.75; 10am-6pm daily May–mid-Oct, 1pm-5pm Sat & Sun mid-Oct–Apr). They depart from the base of the staircase next to Bar St Laurent, on the main floor.

Facing the hotel along rue Mont Carmel is the **Jardins des Gouverneurs**, a small park that was part of the Château St Louis, which once stood in Château Frontenac's place. There's a small monument to both Wolfe and Montcalm here.

Terrasse Dufferin

This is the most popular meeting spot in the city, a given on any visitor's agenda. Outside the Château Frontenac along the riverfront, this 425m-long esplanade provides dramatic views over the

St Lawrence River, perched as it is 60m high on a cliff. Its western extremity leads to the Citadel, and on the eastern end a statue of de Champlain is a popular place to arrange meetings. There's also a Unesco monument, placed in 1985, honoring the city's placement on their World Heritage List.

Champlain's statue stands facing **Place d'Armes**, a small square in front of the main tourist information office. This former military parade ground is now a handy city-orientation point.

Rue du Trésor

Between Place d'Armes and the Basilica is this narrow street, jammed with painters and their wares – it's mostly kitschy stuff done for tourists, but scrounge and you'll probably come up with something nice. The makeshift art market has been a tradition since 1950 when students of the fine arts college took to the streets to sell their wares.

Québec Expérience (☎ 694-4000, 8 rue du Trésor; adult/student $7.50/5; 10am-10pm daily mid-May–mid-Oct, 10am-5pm daily mid-Oct–mid-May) is an overstated, grandiose 3-D spectacle that re-creates the history of Québec City in a half-hour of special effects, optical illusions and projections on a water screen.

At the end of rue de Buade is the **Hôtel de Ville** (City Hall; ☎ 691-6467, 2 rue des Jardins; tours adult/student $3/2; tours 9am, 3pm & 3:45pm end June–Aug, 3pm & 3:45pm mid-May–late June & Sept–mid-Oct), built in 1895 on the site of a destroyed college for Jesuits. They had arrived here in 1625 and founded the continent's first school of classical education one year before Harvard was founded. The Brits closed them down in 1759. The present building is interesting architecturally as it exhibits a mix of styles, with American neo-Roman being the predominant one. The small park next to the Hôtel de Ville is used for shows and performances throughout summer, especially during festival time.

The tall building nearby is the **Price Building** (☎ 691-4636, 65 rue Ste Anne; tours adult/child $3/2; open 9am-5pm Mon-Fri), the city's first modern skyscraper, built in

1929. Its impressive Art Deco style is also evidenced in the inner corridors.

Lower Town

This section covers the Old Town areas of the Lower Town, which is well worth exploring. There are several ways to get down. You can take Côte de la Canoterie from rue des Remparts to get to the Old Port and Gare du Palais train station. A second method is to follow the sidewalk beside the Musée du Fort toward the river, and the staircase will lead you down. There's also a funicular (☎ 692-1132; $1.50 one-way) that'll cable-car you down the side of the Cape. It goes from Terrasse Dufferin to Place Royale.

However, most folks walk down the charming and steep rue Côte de la Montagne. About halfway down on the right there is a shortcut – the *escalier Casse-Cou* (Break-Neck Staircase) – that leads down to rue du Petit Champlain. This busy, attractive street is said to be, along with rue Sous le Cap, the narrowest in North America and is also one of the oldest.

Parc Montmorency This small expanse of green is on your way down Côte de la Montagne. In the center is a statue of Sir Georges Étienne Cartier, one of the fathers of the Canadian Confederation. This spot, however, was the site of the first European cemetery in North America north of Mexico. When de Champlain lost 16 of his men to scurvy in 1608, he buried them where the stone cross now stands on the hill just below the park. The idea caught on and the cemetery grew larger until a greedy Cardinal St Vallier had it dug up and removed in 1694 to build a large palace for himself. This was later used to hold government assembly meetings, and later by the provincial parliament until it burned down in 1883. A memorial park then sprung up in its place, vindicating de Champlain's original intentions after all. Can't mess with fate, you see.

Place Royale This is the central and principal square of the Lower Town area, with 400 years of history behind it. Cannons

placed here held off Phips' attacks in 1690. The name is now often used to refer to the district in general. When de Champlain founded Québec, it was this bit of shoreline that was first settled. The entire area has been under renovation and restoration for years and has gotten a sparkling facelift.

The streets are teeming with visitors, people going to restaurants and cafés, and schoolchildren from around the province getting history lessons. There are historic sites to visit, galleries and craft shops, and it's not uncommon to see a bride coming down the church steps either.

On the square are many buildings from the 1600s and 1700s, (overpriced) tourist shops and a statue of Louis XIV in the middle. The tourist information office (☎ 643-6631), at 215 rue du Marché Finlay, can tell you of the many free events, concerts and shows that frequently take place in and around the Lower Town. It also has some historic exhibits.

The **Centre d'Interpretation de Place Royale** (☎ 646-3167, 27 rue Notre Dame; adult/student $3/2; open 10am-5:30pm daily late June–Oct) is a new interpretation center that shows the area as the cradle of French history on the continent.

Église Notre Dame des Victoires Dating from 1688, this modest house of worship (Our Lady of Victories Church; ☎ 692-1650, 32 rue Sous le Fort; admission free; open 9:30am-4:30pm daily), on the square, is the oldest stone church in the US and Canada. It's built on the very spot where 80 years prior de Champlain had set up his 'Habitation,' a small stockade. Inside are copies of works by Rubens and Van Dyck. Hanging from the ceiling is a replica of a wooden ship, the *Brézé,* thought to be a good-luck charm for ocean crossings and battles with the Iroquois. The church got its name after several successful military campaigns against the British (in 1690 and 1711) were waged on the waters nearby. However, no one suggested changing its name after 1759, when the British defeated the French one final time.

Royal Battery This is at the foot of rue Sous le Fort, where a dozen cannons were set up in 1691 to protect the growing town. The Canadian government has a Coast Guard base near the ferry terminal across the street.

Old Port

Built around the old harbor in Lower Town north and east of Place Royale, the Old Port (Vieux Port) is a redeveloped, multipurpose waterfront area still undergoing change and growth. It's a large, spacious assortment of government buildings, shops, condominiums and recreational facilities with no real focal point but a few things of interest to the visitor, including the phenomenal Musée de la Civilisation.

Strolling along the waterfront leads to the **Agora**, a large outdoor concert bowl and site of many summer shows and presentations. A little farther along is a warehouse-style building housing numerous boutiques. Nearby is a large naval training center, and by Bassin Louise is the **Musée Naval de Québec** (*☎ 694-5560, 170 rue Dalhousie; admission free; open 10am-5:30pm daily June-Sept, 10am-4pm Mon-Fri Oct-May*). Tracing the naval history of the city, the museum has displays on WWII tactics and gives an idea of what a sailor's life at sea is like.

Musée de la Civilisation Arguably the province's best museum (*Museum of Civilization; ☎ 643-2158, W www.mcq.org, 85 rue Dalhousie; adult/student $7/4, free Tues Sept-May; open 10am-7pm daily late June-early Sept, 10am-5pm Tues-Sun early Sept-late June*), this is *not* to be skipped! The first striking aspect of the museum is its architecture. Built in 1988, the ensemble was conceived by Moshe Safdie, whose experiments have often been highly controversial (he was the genius behind Montréal's Habitat and Ottawa's Museum of Fine Arts). Here he not only incorporated some existing old buildings into the whole (the Estèbe house dates from 1752), but he used traditional elements of Québécois architecture (slanted roof, stylized garret windows). The exterior staircase is a brilliant work of art in its own right.

Inside, things get even better. There are two permanent exhibits: One focuses on the cultures of Québec's 11 First Nations, and the other, called Mémoires/Memories, is an excellent chronology of life in the province via the objects that defined different eras. You'll see everything from old bars of soap to spinning wheels to a huge neon tavern sign.

The temporary exhibits are usually well-organized and memorable. Moreover they usually deal with very contemporary concerns (globalization, genetics, cloning, etc). A number of displays are interactive, and many are truly innovative (a surprising rarity in our age of technological complexity!).

The museum is so large, it's best to concentrate on several exhibits matching your interests rather than trying to take in a bit of everything. There are English-speaking guides on hand, and many daily activities. Check out their website for periodic virtual exhibits.

Old Port of Québec Interpretation Centre This exhibition (*☎ 648-3300, 100 rue St André; adult/student $3/2.25; open 10am-5pm daily*) is a National Historic Site that details the history of Québec's portuary activities. Before Montréal usurped it in the 19th century, Québec City's port was one of the largest in the world. This center is a large, four-story exhibition depicting the shipbuilding and timber industries, with good displays and often live demonstrations.

Antique Shop District Rue St Paul, northwest of the Place Royale near the Interpretation Center, is the heart of an expanding antique quarter. From Place Royale, take rue St Pierre toward the harbor and turn left at rue St Paul. About a dozen **shops** here sell antiques, curiosities and old Québécois relics. There are also some good little **cafés** along this relatively quiet street. Farther along, along the waterfront on rue St André, is the **Farmers Market** on the right-hand side, where you can find dozens of local specialties, from wines and ciders to honeys, chocolates, herbal hand creams and, of course, maple syrup products. Beyond the market is the **Gare du Palais** train and bus station, constructed in the Château style. It's well worth walking inside just for a gander of its Old World splendor.

L'Îlot des Palais A few minutes walk toward the wall from the train station is this rather interesting historic site (☎ 691-6092, *rue St Vaillier Est; adult/student $3/2; open 10am-5pm daily late June–early Sept).* It's an exhibition set up around actual archeological digs of the Jean Talon – the first city intendant – house, actually a palace built in 1669 originally to be used as a brewery. Platforms lead over foundations, firepits and outlines of several buildings, which Université Laval students uncovered and explored. There's an interpretive center here to supply background information but there is not much in English.

OLD TOWN WALKING TOUR

This proposed walking tour takes in some of the best-known – as well as the lesser-known – corners of Old Town to give you a good idea of life in today's and yesterday's city. See the Old Town section for more details on some sites.

Begin at the top of the stairs of the **Porte St Louis** (St Louis Gate), the Old Town entrance at the end of Grande Allée. There's a nice view onto the National Assembly. The Parc de l'Esplanade, which borders both sides of the Old Town wall, was the site of 18th- and 19th-century military concerts and parades. Go downstairs and proceed along rue St Louis to see some of the city's oldest surviving houses. First, though, check out the tree at the corner of rue St Louis and rue du Corps de Garde – supposedly the cannonball embedded in its trunk has been lodged there since 1759!

At **32 rue St Louis** is a pretty house with slanted roof dating from 1674. **No 34,** next door, is a well-kept domicile from 1676 – well-kept as it now houses one of Québec's most expensive restaurants, Aux Anciens Canadiens (the title of a novel by author

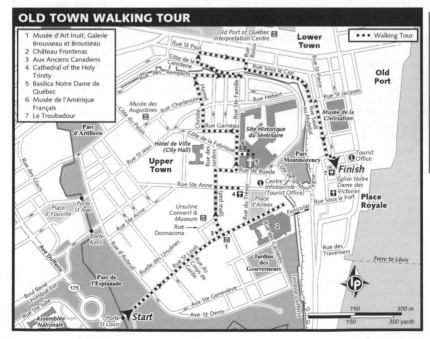

OLD TOWN WALKING TOUR

1 Musée d'Art Inuit; Galerie Brousseau et Brousseau
2 Château Frontenac
3 Aux Anciens Canadiens
4 Cathedral of the Holy Trinity
5 Basilica Notre Dame de Québec
6 Musée de l'Amérique Français
7 Le Troubadour

••• Walking Tour

Philippe Aubert de Gaspé, who lived here from 1815 to 1824). Its steeply slanted roof (51.5 degrees) was typical of 17th-century French architecture. At **No 25** is a house erected in the early 1650s by the then-governor of New France, Louis d'Ailleboust, and later lived in by the Duke of Kent.

We're not going this way, but if you'd like, go to the end of rue St Louis and dip into the **Château Frontenac** to revel in the luscious interior of sculpted wood, Old-World salons and painted ceilings – and the hundreds of tourists in oversized Bermudas with their Polaroids swinging against their I Love Florida T-shirts. Get out quick, come back along rue St Louis and turn right down rue des Jardins. You'll soon come to a **statue of Marie de l'Incarnation**, founder of the **Ursuline Convent** behind you, at 12 rue Donnacona. Note the lovely chapel window, rebuilt in 1902. Marie's statue honors all women who devoted their lives to educate the young in Québec.

If you'd like another little detour, turn right onto rue Ste Anne and you'll see the **Cathedral of the Holy Trinity**. Pop in – it's beautiful inside, very subdued and very, very proper. Continue along rue des Jardins until the brown granite, slightly ostentatious **statue of Taschereau**, the first Canadian cardinal.

Hang a right on rue de Buade, and the splendid **Basilica Notre Dame de Québec** is to your right. Enter the grounds of the **Site Historique du Séminaire** just to the left of the basilica. This used to be the territory of Université Laval. Their faculty of architecture is still located here. Once you enter the courtyard, the largest building opposite you, with the sundial on the wall (still ticking after 227 years!) and the inscription *Dies nostri quasi umbra* ('Our days pass like shadows' – in other words, 'Time is short, so get on with it!'), was the grand Seminary for older students finishing their theological studies. The whiteness of these walls shows how most of Québec once looked – the brightness kept homes cool in the summer and blended with the snow to protect from distant attack in the winter.

Head down rue Ste Famille and make a left onto the narrow, very pretty rue Garneau.

Make a right on the third street, rue Christie, which turns into rue Hamel. Notice the tiny doors on the houses to your right. They said people used to be shorter in the old days, but... The tall wall on your left keeps the cretins away from the grounds of the **Musée des Augustines** and the 1646 Augustine monastery, built for the religious sisters who founded the first European-style hospital north of Mexico nearby in 1639.

At the end of rue Hamel, turn right onto rue des Remparts and follow the wall to the embedded model cannons. Take note of the particularly picturesque houses here, especially Nos 43 and 43½. Most striking is **No 14** (circa 1900), perhaps the apotheosis of eclecticism in Québec. On its façade alone you can see Roman and Gothic arcs, an art nouveau balcony, a renaissance ledge and a medieval chateau tower.

Don't get used to the upper-class air – we're about to descend into Lower Town, where the plebes and undesirables lived. Take the stairs or go around the wall and walk down Côte de la Canoterie, for centuries the main link between Lower and Upper Towns (and classes). Hope Gate stood at the top of the Côte until 1873 to keep the riff-raff from entering uninvited – or from hoping too much.

Make a right onto rue St Thomas and a right onto rue St Paul. A block later, at rue Rioux, veer right again and you'll note an alleyway to your left. This is **rue Sous le Cap**, the narrowest, most cramped and one of the most interesting streets in the city. What today is the back of houses fronting rue St Paul used to be the front entrances of homes along the waterfront – the river used to creep up all the way to rue St Paul at high tide! This was also the red-light district. Many a wealthy merchant would condescend to make his way to the Lower Town to visit one of the several brothels that used to operate on this street.

Walk the length of rue Sous le Cap, looking up at the staircases that shoot up from everywhere, and continue along rue Sault au Matelot, which boasts a few low-key art galleries and antique shops. Where it ends, veer left and continue south on rue St

Pierre for another block, past the minuscule **Parc Unesco**, a reminder that everything you have just seen is part of a Unesco World Heritage site. If you feel like sampling some local brew, end the tour and rest your feet at 29 rue St Pierre, a great cellar bar called **Le Troubadour**, pouring pints in one of the city's oldest houses. Otherwise, if you have the energy to keep going, you're in Place Royale, near the funicular.

OUTSIDE THE WALLS

This section includes areas of Québec City outside the Old Town walls, including the nearby National Assembly, St Roch and St Jean Baptiste. Making these part of your visit and not sticking only to the Old Town will greatly enrich your understanding of the city.

Assemblée Nationale

Back in Upper Town, just across from the Porte St Louis, is the home of the provincial legislature *(National Assembly; ☎ 643-7239,* Ⓦ *www.assnat.qc.ca; admission free; open 9am-4:30pm daily late June–early Sept, 9am-4:30pm Mon-Fri early Sept–late June),* between boulevard René Lévesque and Grande Allée Est, west of avenue Honoré Mercier. This Second Empire structure dates from 1886, built to replace the old parliament building that had burned down in present-day Parc Montmorency. The façade is decorated with 22 bronze statues of important figures in Québec's history, from politicians and cardinals to explorers and colonists.

Free tours are given in English and French. The Assembly sits in the Blue Room; on the ceiling you'll notice Québec's coat of arms with the national slogan *Je me souviens* (see 'Three Little Words' in the Getting Around chapter). The equally impressive Red Room is no longer used as the Upper House. The restaurant is worth a look-see as well.

Outside are more statues and monuments. Along boulevard René Lévesque west of avenue Honoré Mercier are statues of past provincial premiers, the most notable being that of Lévesque himself.

St Roch & St Jean Baptiste (Grande Allée)

These two regions flank Old Town to its northwest and west, respectively, and are both worth exploring on foot. The heart of St Jean Baptiste, part of the Upper Town, is rue St Jean, which extends from Old Town. You are more likely to see locals in this laid-back neighborhood than in Old Town itself. Between avenue Dufferin and rue Racine, rue St Jean is lined with good restaurants, hip cafés and bars, and interesting shops, but the down-to-earth ambience is proof that you're way out of the traditional tourist zone. On the corner of rue St Augustin there's an old Protestant church, **St Matthew's Church**, which functioned from 1771 to 1860. The overrun cemetery doubles as a popular makeshift picnic spot. This area also has several gay bars and shops.

From rue St Jean take any side street and walk downhill (northwest) to the narrow

KEVIN LÉVESQUE

Traditional architecture outside Québec City

QUÉBEC CITY

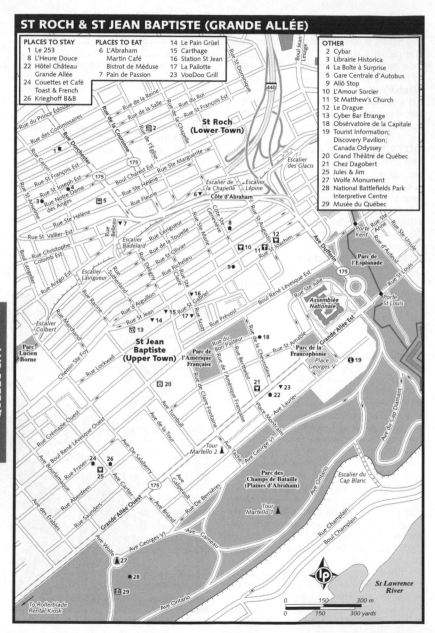

ST ROCH & ST JEAN BAPTISTE (GRANDE ALLÉE)

PLACES TO STAY
1 Le 253
8 L'Heure Douce
22 Hôtel Château Grande Allée
24 Couettes et Café Toast & French
26 Krieghoff B&B

PLACES TO EAT
6 L'Abraham Martin Café Bistrot de Méduse
7 Pain de Passion
14 Le Pain Grüel
15 Carthage
16 Station St Jean
17 La Pailotte
23 VooDoo Grill

OTHER
2 Cybar
3 Librairie Historica
4 La Boîte à Surprise
5 Gare Centrale d'Autobus
9 Allô Stop
10 L'Amour Sorcier
11 St Matthew's Church
12 Le Drague
13 Cyber Bar Étrange
18 Observatoire de la Capitale
19 Tourist Information; Discovery Pavilion; Canada Odyssey
20 Grand Théâtre de Québec
21 Chez Dagobert
25 Jules & Jim
27 Wolfe Monument
28 National Battlefields Park Interpretive Centre
29 Musée du Québec

residential streets like rue d'Aiguillon, rue Richelieu or rue St Olivier. Just as long, outside staircases are trademarks of Montréal architecture, so are these miniature houses scrunched together, some with very nice entrances, typical of Québec City's residential architecture.

Walking down Côte Ste Geneviève you'll get to a steep staircase, the Escalier de la Chapelle. This takes you to Lower Town and to the St Roch district. The areas north and west of here have traditionally been for the lower classes, mainly factory and naval workers. In 1840, St Roch held one-third of the city's population and went through the usual cycles of overcrowding and eventually crime.

In recent years, however, it's been slowly going through a gentrification process. The confluence of impulses is fascinating to witness. Along the main artery, rue St Joseph, are junk shops, second-hand clothing stores and used book shops along with spiffy new cafés. Half-dilapidated buildings stand next to newly repaired ones. Check out the art galleries on rue de St Vallier Est. Definitely an area in transition, St Roch provides a welcome contrast to the manicured aura of Old Town.

Outer Neighborhoods

This section covers worthwhile attractions outside the city center. Refer to the Québec City map for locations.

Cartier-Brebeuf National Historic Site On the rivière St Charles, north of the central walled section of the city, this park (☎ 648-4038, 175 rue de l'Espinay; adult/ student $3/2.25; open 10am-6pm daily mid-June–mid-Sept) marks where Cartier and his men were nursed through the winter of 1535 by the local First Nations tribes. In 1625 the Jesuits established a settlement here. Displays provide information on Cartier, his trips and the Jesuit missionaries.

There is a full-scale replica of Cartier's ship and one of a First Nations longhouse in the park's green but rather unauthentic-looking riverside setting. Native people may be on hand story-telling, demonstrating crafts etc.

By car, take rue de la Couronne north to the Laurentienne Expressway (Hwy 73 north)

about 6km to exit 150. By bus, take either No 4 or No 801 (the faster of the two) to rue Julien, from where you can walk to the park.

Le Bois de Coulonge Park Not far west of the Plains of Abraham are these colorful gardens (☎ 528-0773, 1215 chemin St Louis; admission free), a paean to the plant world. Long the private property of a succession of Québec and Canada's religious and political elite (until 1966 it served as a residence of Canada's lieutenant governor), the area of woods and extensive horticultural displays is now open to the public. It stretches out along the riverfront and is wedged between boulevard Champlain and chemin St Louis with access from the latter only.

Maison des Jésuites South of the center along the river in Sillery, this Jesuit house and Native Canadian site (☎ 688-8074, 2320 chemin du Foulon; admission $2; open 11am-5pm Tues-Sun June-Sept, 1pm-5pm Tues-Sun Oct-May) has a history stretching back 3500 years. The first Jesuit mission was here in 1637 but it continued as a meeting place for the First Nations tribes and acted as a focal point for their relations with Europeans. Low-key displays illustrate the story and clash of cultures. Frances Moore Brooke, the British author of History of Lady Julia Mandeville, lived on these grounds from 1763 to 1768.

Domaine Cataqui Fantastically impressive are the 300,000 sq m of lovely gardens at this site (☎ 681-3010, 2141 chemin St Louis; adult/child $5/4; open 10am-5pm daily Mar-Dec, 10am-5pm Tues-Sun Jan & Feb). This is where the provincial premier holds official functions to bedazzle VIPs. There are nine buildings on the sprawling grounds, all elegant, and it's easy to see how this place was the epicenter of high-class social life in the 1930s. Then, the international socialite Catherine Rhodes lived here together with impressionist painter Percyval Tudor-Hart, a pal of Matisse's. They hosted parties for the city's artistic elite – ah, to be a fly on that wall!

In the main villa are several rooms serving as exhibition halls, mostly focusing on the site's history. Though the site is open year-round, it really is something to see when the gardens are in full bloom.

Villa Bagatelle Not quite as impressive as Domaine Cataqui, this fine house and English garden (☎ 688-8074, 1563 chemin St Louis; admission $3; open 10am-5pm Tues-Sun Mar-Dec) present an example of 19th-century upper-class property and life. In the *très* British garden are some 350 types of plants. The house is largely given over to exhibiting art. Afternoon tea is served.

Aquarium This aquarium (☎ 659-5264, 1675 avenue des Hôtels; adult/student/child $10/7/5.50; open 10am-5pm daily) is in the Ste Foy district. With 340 species of fresh- and saltwater fish and reptiles, there's bound to be something to please the kids here. There are usually two seal shows per day. There's a cafeteria and, out on the grounds, walking trails and nicely set up picnic tables.

ORGANIZED TOURS

There are dozens of area tours to choose from, be they via foot, bus or boat. Check flyers at tourist offices and ask for advice on which would best suit your needs. Following are some of the ones we've tried out and recommend – all of the walking tours are outstanding.

Walking

Paul Gaston l'Anglais (☎ 529-3422, e langlaispaul@yahoo.com) is an affable archeologist who gives the city's best and most thematically diverse walking tours when not zipping around town researching on his bike. His themes include Beer Brewing, Cemeteries of Old Québec, Military Walks, Women's Struggle to Get the Vote and Parks of the City. All cost $8 to $12 for about two hours. His English is a bit rusty, but he manages gracefully.

La Compagnie des Six Associes (☎ 802-6665) has a great staff (a very cheery bunch, they are) and very good walking circuits like the ever-popular Vice and Drunkenness, which creaks opens the rusty door on the history of alcohol and prostitution in the city. Other circuits focus on epidemics, disasters, crimes and prisons in Québec City's past. Tours, which are done in English or French, cost from $12 to $15 and are booked at their kiosk at the main tourist office.

If you don't want a live guide, you can rent a CD player at any tourist office for $10 to $15 and walk different circuits yourself while listening to tours on disc. Call ☎ 990-8687 for more information.

Boat

Québec City is not a particularly good place to take a boat cruise: The choices are limited and the views aren't much better than what you'd get from the cheap ferry to/from Lévis on the south shore. However, at the river's edge near Place Royale you'll see the MV *Louis Jolliet* and other vessels offering cruiscs downriver to the Montmorency and Île d'Orléans waterfalls.

Another company with a smaller vessel, *Le Coudrier* (☎ 692-0107), does 90-minute cruises around Québec City and down the river for $15; they have cheaper one-hour trips too. There are also full-day trips (with a meal), which include Grosse Île (though better tours reach this island from Berthier sur Mer; see that section in Around Québec City). For more information call or see them at quay No 19, along the Old Port dock opposite the Agora.

Other

Cyclo Services (☎ 692-4052, w www.cyclo .services.qc.ca, 160 Quai St André), inside the farmers market near the Old Port, rents bikes but also organizes excellent bike tours of the city and outskirts for small groups ($28 per person). It's a great way to see the city, and the guides are knowledgeable and fun. They frequently give tours in English.

Intégra (☎ 648-8424, 1105 rue St Jean) runs small hiking and camping trips in the countryside surrounding Québec City. Groups are small and the prices good, making access to outdoor activities and historic and cultural sites fun and economical. They can also be contacted through the HI hostel.

SPECIAL EVENTS

Following are some of the major festivals and celebrations held in Québec City.

February

Winter Carnival This famous annual event, the biggest of its kind in the world, is unique to Québec City. The festival lasts for the first half of February, always including three weekends. (If you want to go, organize the trip early as the city gets packed out – and bring lots of warm clothes.) The carnival symbol and mascot is Bonhomme, the frequently seen roly-poly snowman figure with a red hat and wide grin (see 'Bonhomme's Kingdom of Snow'). Featured are parades, ice sculptures, a snow slide, boat races, dances, music and *lots* of drinking. Quite simply, the town goes berserk. Activities take place all over Old Town (many at the Parc de l'Esplanade) and the famous snow slide is on the Terrasse Dufferin, behind the Château. In recent years, some celebrants have become unruly to the point of being problematic at times. Those with children may wish to inquire about participating in particular nighttime festivities.

March

Festival de la Neige Just like in pagan times, people here celebrate the coming of spring with a plethora of activities and general merrymaking. The center of the party happens at Stoneham's ski hill (☎ 848-2411, Ⓦ www.ski-stoneham.com).

June

Fête Nationale de la St Jean Baptiste On the night of June 23 Québec City parties hard. Major festivities are held on the Plains of Abraham (Plaines d'Abraham) as of 8pm. For details see Ⓦ www.snqc.qc.ca.

July

Summer Festival This is held in the first half of July and consists of some 500 free shows and concerts throughout the town, including drama and dance. The tourist office should have a list of things going on. Most squares and parks in the Old Town are the sites of some activity daily, especially the Parc de la Francophonie behind Hôtel de Ville, at noon and in the evening. For more info, call ☎ 888-992-5200 or see Ⓦ www.infofestival.com.

Les Grands Feux Loto-Québec This major fireworks show is held at the Montmorency Falls at the end of July. Call ☎ 800-923-3389 for information.

August

Medieval Festival Events with a medieval theme are featured during this popular, five-day festival, held toward the beginning of the month in odd-numbered years.

International Festival of Military Bands It may feel anachronistic in this city but the Canadian military band plays its heart out, decked out as if it were on Parliament Hill in Ottawa, and invites other military bands from around the world to do the same. You may even see bagpipes! Over 40 free concerts are given in the center of town at the end of August. See Ⓦ www.clicl.net/fimmq for more information.

Québec City Provincial Exhibition Officially known as Expo Québec, the Ex is held around the end of August each year and features commercial displays, agricultural competitions, handicrafts, a blackjack parlor, horse racing and a 'midway,' a large carnival with 55 rides and games of chance. Nearly three-quarters of a million people visit the Expo each year. Parc de l'Exposition (Exhibition Park) is north of the downtown area, off Rte 175.

PLACES TO STAY

There are many, many places to stay in Québec City and generally the competition keeps prices down to a reasonable level. The bulk of the good-value accommodations is in small European-style hotels. Motels and larger downtown hotels tend to be expensive. As you'd expect in such a popular city, the best cheap places are often full. Look for a room before 2pm or phone ahead for a reservation. Midsummer and Carnival time are especially busy, particularly weekends; book as far ahead as you can.

For accommodation assistance, tourist offices are helpful. Don't take their occupancy information as gospel, however. Offices may have a place down as full when in fact a call will turn up a room, as everybody else has ignored it. Nor does the tourist accommodation guide list all the places – a wander around will reveal others.

Budget

Camping There are numerous campgrounds close to town.

Camping Municipal de Beauport (☎ 666-2228, fax 666-2360, 95 rue Sérénité) Tent sites $18. This excellent campground north of

Bonhomme's Kingdom of Snow

More than a simple mascot of the Winter Carnival, Bonhomme acts as a cultural ambassador for Québec in his embodiment of the Québécois spirit – and he's the most important delegate there is from the Kingdom of Knulandis.

Bonhomme is a friendly snowman dressed only in a traditional red Québécois *tuque* (winter hat), an arrowed, colorful belt like those his *coureurs de bois* ancestors wore and the same big, wide smile that all people in Québec wear all winter long (yeah, riiiight!). He came into being with the founding of the Winter Carnival in 1954, and he's developed into quite a phenomenon since then (he sure looks cute on all those merchandising items like dolls and mugs!).

A fantasy world has grown around Bonhomme, making him like a Santa Claus with a Québécois – even Métis – accent. He lives in a land of ice and snow called Knulandis, whose residents are called Knuks; Grrrounches form a minority in the population. In the Knulandis tales, there is a town chief, and ritualistic dances, and natural elements like wind, the moon and the sun all play a formative role in the destiny of their land. The clear references to First Nations' beliefs and customs cleverly link Québec's past and present.

Bonhomme also follows modern customs with impressive skill. A month before festivities begin, he unofficially sneaks into town, throws a big party, then reappears only at the solemn, official opening of the Carnival, in which Québec City's mayor hands him over the keys to the city.

Bonhomme was created in the image of his makers, or at least in the image his makers fashioned for themselves. According to his official description, he is someone who loves to dance and be merry, expresses his feelings through gestures, loves everyone equally and without prejudice, and represents the joy and the hardy spirit with which Québécois handle their winters. The carnival's official literature says there is also a 'certain air of mystery that floats around him, as well as real respect!'

This jolly, traditional fellow also knows how to adapt to societal changes and roll with the punches. In a sign that political correctness has entered even Knulandis, he is no longer surrounded by his Queen (a new one was crowned every year!) and the six Duchesses who used to support his every move and stand around looking as pretty as only female balls of snow could!

Québec City is green, peaceful and just a 15-minute drive to the Old Town. To get there take Hwy 40 or 440 toward Parc de la Chute Montmorency to exit 321 and turn north. Follow the blue and white signs; the park is not too far.

Camping Impérial *(☎ 831-2969, 888-831-2969, 152 route du Pont)* Tent sites $21. On the south shore, just 1km west from the Pont du Québec (Québec Bridge), this small, intimate campground (only 36 sites) has all the conveniences. There are many private campgrounds on this south shore road, particularly west of Québec City.

Hostels Québec City has some of the best-rated hostels in the province.

Centre International de Séjour de Québec *(☎ 694-0775, 800-461-8585, W www .cisq.org, 19 rue Ste Ursule)* Dorms bed $17/21 members/nonmembers, doubles $50. This HI hostel is the most central and popular in town. Despite its massive size (233 beds), it's usually full in summer. This friendly, lively place has rooms that are off creaky, wooden-floored corridors that go on forever. The pleasant cafeteria serves three economical meals. The hostel-run activities are worth looking into, and there's Internet access too. Some travelers report better luck finding a room by showing up in person than by calling.

Auberge de la Paix *(☎ 694-0735, 31 rue Couillard)* Singles $19, sheets $2; includes breakfast. Relatively small and quiet, this place is open year-round and has 60 beds. The European-style building is marked with a peace sign. There are two double rooms at $30 but families are given preference for these. The location is perfect; there is a grocery store, a bar and restaurant mere minutes away. It's best to arrive early (or call ahead) to secure a bed. It's a short walk from the bus/train station but it's uphill all the way.

YWCA *(☎ 683-2155, fax 683-5526, 855 avenue Holland)* Singles/doubles $29/52. The Y, complete with pool and cafeteria, takes couples or single women. There are only 15 rooms, so reservations may be useful. Avenue Holland runs off chemin Ste Foy, which becomes St Jean in the old section. Take bus No 7 along chemin Ste Foy to avenue Holland, then walk south.

Université Laval *(☎ 656-2921, W www.ulaval.ca/sres, 5030 rue de l'Université)* Singles/doubles $25/35, students get about 10% discount; open May–mid-Aug. The university offers decent if small quarters, but the campus is pretty lively even in summers. It's located west of the center where boulevards René Lévesque and Wilfrid Laurier merge. Bus No 800 or 801 from the corner of avenue Dufferin and boulevard René Lévesque will get you there in about 15 minutes.

Mid-Range

B&Bs Bed and breakfasts are popular in Québec City, and there are many to choose from.

Chez Hubert *(☎ 692-0958, e bheber@microtec.net, 66 rue Ste Ursule)* Singles/doubles $85/110. This smoke-free B&B on one of Old Town's prettiest streets is decorated in smart colors and with tasteful furniture.

Le 253 *(☎ 647-0590, e jeanclaude@oricom.com, 253 rue de la Reine)* Singles/doubles $35/45. This is a gay-friendly place with a variety of rooms on the second floor of an old-style St Roch home. The atmosphere is familial and friendly.

L'Heure Douce *(☎ 649-1935, e Jacques.gagnel@simpatico.ca, 704 rue Richelieu)* Doubles $65-75. On a quiet street in St Jean Baptiste, some of the rooms here have a stunning view onto the distant Laurentian mountains. The common room is particularly charming.

Krieghoff B&B *(☎ 522-3711, 1091 avenue Cartier)* Doubles $80. Run by the Krieghoff bar downstairs, this modern B&B still retains an intimate air. It's located on a nice street near Grande Allée, far enough from the busy center to make a respite but close enough to be walkable.

Couettes et Café Toast & French *(☎ 523-9365, W www.quebecweb.com/toast&French, 1020 avenue Cartier)* Singles/doubles $75/85. A nice spot away from the crowds and close to Grande Allée, this place offers tastefully decorated rooms. The owner takes special delight in guests who wish to practice their French over morning toast and coffee.

Motels There are several areas to look for motels. One is in Beauport, about 15km northeast of the city (going north along avenue Dufferin, take Hwy 440 to the boulevard Ste Anne exit, Rte 138; head to the 500-1200s). A bike trail from the city passes nearby. A second area is about 10km west of the center on boulevard Wilfrid Hamel (Rte 138; head west on Hwy 440 to the Henri IV exit). Neither are far or difficult to reach. City buses run to these districts so whether you have a car or not, they may be the answer if you find that everything downtown is booked. Generally prices are higher than you'd pay for motels in other regions.

Motel Chevalier *(☎ 661-3876, fax 666-8062, 1062 boul Ste Anne)* Singles/doubles $55/65. The rooms aren't anything to brag about, but it's a place to sleep. There's a pool, and each room has phone and TV – and 'adult films' is listed as one of their offered services.

Motel Olympic *(☎ 667-8716, W www.motelolympic.com, 1078 boul Ste Anne)* Singles/doubles $69/89. The rooms in this nondescript motel are comfortable enough.

Motel Pierre *(☎ 681-6191, fax 688-9606, 1640 boul Hamel)* Singles/doubles $76/88. This place tries hard. There are a range of room sizes to choose from.

Motel Le Bastion *(☎ 871-9055, 3825 boul Hamel)* Singles/doubles $40/60. This is a good bet, though farther out of the city, close to Rte 73 (which becomes the Pont de Québec farther south). Rooms are comfortable and prices are decent.

Hotels There's also a good selection of affordable and comfortable hotels in the area.

Maison du Général (☎ *694-1905, 72 rue St Louis*) Singles/doubles with shared bath $35/55. This place has 12 rooms, which range in price: The cheaper the room, the fewer extras (like TV) it comes with. The warm welcome you get compensates for the drawbacks.

Manoir La Salle (☎ *692-9953, 18 rue Ste Ursule*) Singles $35, doubles $50-75. The prices in this nine-room place haven't risen in years. Some may prefer the upstairs rooms to avoid having to go through the lobby to the bathroom, as is the case from the ground-floor rooms. Some kitchenettes are available.

Maison Acadienne (☎ *694-0280, 800-463-0280,* W *www.maison-acadienne.com, 43 rue Ste Ursule*) Singles $50-90, doubles $60-129. Across the street, this is a good place, and if you have a small car and are lucky you may get one of the parking spots around the back. A continental breakfast served out on the patio is available for $3.75.

Maison Ste Ursule (☎ *694-9794, 40 rue Ste Ursule*) Doubles $47-87. One of the best deals in Old Town, this small hotel on a quiet street is in a house built in 1756. There are a range of rooms, with shared or private bath, and a pleasant courtyard out back. The art gallery on the first floor is home to a talkative parrot.

Auberge St Louis (☎ *692-2424,* W *www .bonneadressesvxqc.com, 48 rue St Louis*) Singles/doubles from $69/89 including full breakfast. This is another great deal in Old Town, with 27 rooms at reasonable rates. Parking is available but costs extra.

Hôtel Le Clos St Louis (☎ *694-1311, 800-461-1311, 71 rue St Louis*) Singles/doubles from $79/99. This super-renovated hotel has 29 rooms, the cheapest with shared bath; the most expensive, a suite at $195, has a whirlpool. The décor is classic and quite charming.

Hôtel Belley (☎ *692-1694,* W *www .oricom.ca/belley, 249 rue St Paul*) Singles/doubles $80/110. A great place for the young and hip who still like their creature comforts, this place offers spacious, tastefully decorated though sparse rooms, some with brick walls. There have been hotels and taverns in this house since 1868. On the first floor is a wonderful bar, the Belley Tavern, with quirky décor and a jovial crowd.

Hôtel Château Grande Allée (☎ *647-4433,* W *www.quebecweb.com/cga, 601 Grande Allée Est*) Singles/doubles $109/139. On the main restaurant strip, it can get a bit noisy at night, but the Grande Allée location's still great. The red neon sign prepares you for a bit of tack, but the rooms are cozy enough.

Top End

Gîte Côte de la Montagne (☎ *694-4414, 888-794-4414, 54 Côte de la Montagne*) Doubles $150, loft $300. Some rooms have a view onto the Château Frontenac. The gorgeous loft (big enough for six persons) is the standout, fully furnished, with fireplace, views onto the river and the Château and even a sink that swivels around into a toilet!

Hôtel Le St Paul (☎ *694-4414,* W *www .lesaintpaul.qc.ca, 229½ rue St Paul*) Doubles $140. Run by the same people as the Gîte Côte de la Montagne, this is another luxurious place, with warm, intimate rooms with brick walls.

Auberge St Pierre (☎ *694-7981, 888-268-1017, 79 rue St Pierre*) Singles/doubles $125/219, suites $325. Tucked into a corner of Lower Old Town, this is a very high-class hotel but with an intimate feel and no pretense. Not more luxurious than other hotels in this category, this one accents service and extras (like Jacuzzis, down-filled blankets, and wool bathrobes).

Château Frontenac (☎ *692-3861, 800-441-1414,* W *www.fairmont.com, 1 rue des Carrières*) Singles/doubles from $229/369, suites $550-1250. This is *the* place to treat yourself. Expect first-class luxury here from the 650 staff who serve 607 rooms. Each room is different, accounting for the wide price range. They frequently have package deals, which cut prices significantly.

Canada's Coolest Hotel

Spending hundreds of dollars to sleep on a bed of ice may not sound terribly appealing. Well, North America's first Ice Hotel was such a smash success among hardy thrill-seekers in its first year, winter 2000–01, that it was back bigger, better and icier in the 2001–02 season. The concept originated in northern Sweden with a wildly successful project birthed by Absolut Vodka, and they are cosponsors of Québec's Ice Hotel.

It's hard to wrap your head around the concept, but picture a place in which everything is made of ice. Yes, everything – the reception desk, the pen you sign the guest book with, the working sink in your room, your bed, the dishes, the shot glasses (which often come in handy), the bar, the alcohol decanters…am I digressing? It makes sense that firewater is the hottest element here. You need it.

OK, not *everything* is made of ice. There are no ice hot tubs, ice stoves or ice fireplaces, for example. But once inside, no one feels like nit-picking. Visitors say that the bed of ice is not as chilly as it sounds – you sleep in thick sleeping bags on lush deer pelts.

Some 350 tons of ice go into the five-week construction of this perishable hotel. One of the most striking aspects is its size – with over 3000 sq meters, the dimensions merely add an aspect of incredulity to its completion. Already in the entrance hall, it feels strangely overwhelming – tall, sculpted columns of ice support a frosty roof from which hangs a crystal chandelier, and lining the endless corridors are carved sculptures, tables and chairs.

Located about a half-hour drive from central Québec City at Lac St Joseph's Station Écotouristique Duchesnay, it is well-placed to combine an exotic stay with outdoor activities – skiing, snowshoeing, dogsledding, igloo-building and ice fishing. There's also a luxury hotel nearby, so you can enjoy indoor comforts too.

Oh yes indeed, you pay through the nose for all this exoticism. There are many package deals, some including a part-time stay in the luxury hotel, but expect to pay no less than $229 per person per night, based on double occupancy. There are larger suites that fit up to eight people, which are marginally cheaper. For more information contact the *Ice Hotel* (☎ 875-4522, 877-505-0423, Ⓦ www.icehotel-canada.com, 143 route Duchesnay, Ste Catherine de la Jacques Cartier). It's off exit 318 of Hwy 40, west of Québec City via Rte 367.

PLACES TO EAT

As one would imagine, restaurants in Québec City are abundant and the quality generally high. Still, you won't find the same price-quality ratio that Montréal has. A number of Old Town eateries have a herd mentality to keep turnover high and are an odd mix of high- and low-brow cuisine. You're likely to have your duck *à l'orange* or salmon in fennel sauce served with a mound of fries, or your fancy, full-course meal served on a paper placemat that advertises a local boutique or the funicular. Perhaps it just means that things are more down-to-earth here. Many restaurants do boast unbeatable locations, however.

Rue St Jean outside Old Town and other excellent places in St Roch offer viable alternatives, though without the Old World charms.

Old Town

Upper Town The most frequented area of Québec City has a bevy of dining choices – some are tourist traps, but there's a wide selection of flavors to choose from.

Marché Richelieu (no ☎, 1097 rue St Jean) Try making your own meal at this grocery/market, which offers breads from the in-house bakery, fruits, cheeses and even bottles of wine with screw-top lids.

Restaurant Liban (☎ 694-1888, 23 rue d'Auteuil) Mains $3-6. This is a popular place for a quick shish taouk and other Lebanese fast-food favorites.

Casse Crêpe Breton *(☎ 692-0438, 1136 rue St Jean)* Mains $6-11. Near Côte du Palais, this small restaurant specializes in crêpes of many kinds, starting as low as $3.25. It's a favorite because it has been here for years and you can sit right up at the counter and watch them pour and build the tasty crêpes.

Café Buade *(☎ 692-3909, 31 rue de Buade)* Mains $6-14. One of the Old Town restaurants suitable for families, it's right in the middle of everything, just east of rue des Jardins. Their breakfasts are a good deal, usually under $6.

Le Petit Coin Latin *(☎ 692-2022, 8½ rue Ste Ursule)* Breakfast $4-8, mains $12-16. For a French-style breakfast, this small café is near rue St Jean. Open every day, it has croissants, muffins, eggs, café au lait in a bowl (as it's meant to be served!) and low-priced lunch specials. In summer enjoy your nourishment on the outdoor patio.

Aux Anciens Canadiens *(☎ 692-1627, 34 rue St Louis)* Mains $11-23. This restaurant is in the lovely Jacquet House, dating from 1676. Aside from the historical aspect it is noteworthy for its reliance on traditional dishes and typically Québécois specialties. It costs no more than many of the other nice places in town and is one of the few with a distinctly different menu. Here you can sample such provincial fare as apple wine, pea soup, duck or trout followed by maple-syrup pie for dessert. Or try the caribou in blueberry wine sauce. The special *table d'hôte* (fixed-price) menu offered from noon to 6pm is fairly priced from $14 including a glass of wine or beer.

Le St Amour *(☎ 694-0667, 48A rue Ste Ursule)* Mains $14-24. This restaurant has a $35 table d'hôte dinner , value lunch specials and an excellent reputation. The menu offers about a dozen meat and fish dishes daily incorporating delicate sauces. There are even meals made with organic ingredients only. The elegant setting includes an indoor garden.

Lower Town The old and quiet Rue St Paul is this district's main restaurant drag, with several inexpensive places away from the main bustle. The main Farmers Market is on rue St André, not far from Old Port or the train station. Under the covered, open-air building you'll find fresh bread, cheeses, fruits and vegetables, as well as products from across the province. The best time to visit is busy Saturday morning.

Buffet de l'Antiquaire *(☎ 692-2661, 95 rue St Paul)* Mains $5-9. A small, simple place for things like sandwiches or hamburgers at non-tourist prices. It even has a few tables out on the pavement.

Piazzetta *(☎ 692-2962, 63 rue St Paul)* Breakfast $3-8, mains $7-16. Now *this* is a pizza parlor! With beautiful high ceilings, wood-paneled floors and large stone oven into which some 25 types of pizzas get baked, this is heaven. Their pasta dishes are equally good. The surprise is their breakfasts – all eggs and omelets are cooked in the stone oven, so there's not a dab of grease.

Place du Spaghetti *(☎ 694-9144, 40 rue du Marché Champlain)* Mains $8-15. With its attractive patio in the shadow of the looming Château Frontenac, this is one of the best bargains in town, with various pasta dishes including bread and salad from $10 ($8 at lunch). Don't bother with the indoor salad bar; it's very basic and the atmosphere outside is way better.

Le Lotus Royal *(☎ 692-4286, 77 rue Sault au Matelot)* Mains $11-19. This BYOW Asian restaurant serves credible, tasty Cambodian, Vietnamese and Thai dishes, including many vegetarian options.

Aviatic Club *(☎ 522-3555, 450 rue de la Gare du Palais)* Appetizers $6-12, mains $15-24. Set sumptuously inside the already grand Gare du Palais train station, this was *the* hot spot in town in 2001. The dimly lit interior is set up like a lounge and, with their on-site DJs, has a Café del Mar feel to it. The terrace out back is also cozy. Their world cuisine menu is great, of course – appetizers like shrimp in coconut sauce and mains like grilled salmon in orange sauce melt in your mouth. They're famous for their sushi, which on Wednesday nights starts at only $1.25 a pop!

St Roch & St Jean Baptiste (Grande Allée)

West of the old city walls, Grande Allée Est is a popular and lively strip of over a dozen alfresco restaurants. Packed at night, they make a good spot for a beer or lunch if you're out near the Plains of Abraham. All have complete lunch specials for $7 to $10 (from soup to coffee) and most places offer dinner for $12 to $22.

Le Pain Grüel (☎ 522-7246, 375B rue St Jean) Open 7am-5pm daily. A great place in St Jean Baptiste to get freshly-baked bread and mini pizzas. All the golds and browns of the décor – and the smell! – make it a treat just to walk in.

Pain de Passion (☎ 529-0065, 85 rue de St Vallier Est) Open 9am-7pm Mon-Sat, 9am-5:30pm Sun. This incredible, red-bricked eatery from the 1920s is first and foremost a bakery, but along with their breads there are many hot meals ready to take away (or eat in) as well as pastas, sandwiches and ready-made salads. You won't know where to start.

L'Abraham Martin Café Bistrot de Méduse (☎ 647-9689, 595 rue de St Vallier Est) Mains $7-11; open 9am-11pm daily. Good for a quick bite or a bit of lounging, this café boasts an unusual locale, perched on the staircase leading down to St Roch at the bottom of Côte Ste Geneviève. It's also the hangout for the artistic co-op Méduse that lies below, hence the wrought-iron sculptures and art on the wall. It serves mainly sandwiches and salads and good, light hot meals.

Carthage (☎ 529-0576, 399 rue St Jean) Lunch $8, dinner from $12; open 11:30am-2:30pm & 5:30pm-11pm daily. This split-level BYOW Tunisian restaurant has couscous, meat and vegetarian specials, agreeably spicy. The atmosphere is even more memorable than the food, with high ceilings, low tables and cushions for seating.

Station St Jean (☎ 529-6672, 481 rue St Jean) Mains average $7; open 8am-11pm daily. These folks understand the rhythm of the night – breakfasts (over 30 choices of them, and copious ones at that) are served until 4pm! Otherwise their hamburgers are inventive (with smoked meat or salmon) and their fries are great.

VooDoo Grill (☎ 647-2000, 575 Grande Allée Est) Mains $8-17. They call themselves a restaurant-museum, but it's even more than that. In a complex that merges two discos, a bar, a splendid dining room that stretches the concept of exotic décor to its fullest, and a laid-back patio overlooking busy, fashionable Grande Allée, it's an experience just to walk through. It's an especially good place if you like your waitresses in suggestive apparel. Their specialties include wok meals, huge Asian soups, mega salads, and many meat dishes with, er, exotic sauces.

La Pailotte (☎ 522-6226, 821 rue Scott) Mains $10-17. Just south of rue St Jean, this is a good, casual (BYOW) Vietnamese place.

ENTERTAINMENT

Though Québec City is small, it is active after dark with plenty of nightspots – although many change faster than editions of this book. *Voir* is a French entertainment paper appearing each Thursday with complete entertainment listings. Rue St Jean – both inside and outside the Old Town wall – is alive at night. This is where people strut, though there are good places for just sitting and watching those who want to be watched.

Pubs & Bars

Folk clubs known as *boîtes à chanson* are more popular here than in Montréal and can be found along and around rue St Jean. They're generally inexpensive, and foster a casual, relaxed atmosphere in which it's easy to meet people.

Pub St Alexandre (☎ 694-7075, 1087 rue St Jean) This busy Old Town watering hole has 200 kinds of beer (ever tried Chinese, Portuguese, New Zealand or Lebanese beer?) and an array of pub-type grub (mains $4-9).

Chez Son Père (☎ 692-5308, 24 rue St Stanislas) One of the city's best *boîtes à chanson* for years, this has great atmosphere. Here you can catch some newcomers, local acts, and (sometimes) big-name concerts.

Bar Le d'Auteuil (☎ 692-2263, 35 rue d'Auteuil) There's often live music here, spanning styles like blues, jazz and rock.

L'Inox (☎ 692-2877, 38 rue St André) In the Old Port area, this is the city's only brewpub and has a pleasant outdoor patio. A must-visit, you can first tour its small ecomuseum, which shows how and what they brew, and then you can put that knowledge to practical use until the wee hours.

Le Troubadour (☎ 694-9176, 29 rue St Pierre) Set cozily in the cave cellar of one of the city's oldest surviving houses (1754), this is a great tavern with plenty of local brew. For $4 you can sample four different kinds. There are imported beers from 11 countries too. It's a great place to hang out for a few hours.

Jules & Jim (☎ 524-9570, 1060 avenue Cartier) Decorated with stills from Truffaut films, this is a nice place for a quiet drink. It's a short walk from Grande Allée Ouest.

Le Drague (☎ 649-7212, 815 rue St Augustin) The city's gay and lesbian scene is pretty small, and this St Roch venue is its star player: a relaxed bar that spills out into an alleyway when busy and a weekend disco in the basement. Its clientele is mostly male.

L'Amour Sorcier (☎ 523-3395, 789 Côte Ste Geneviève) Open 2pm-3am Thur-Sun. The most pleasant bar on the gay circuit, this St Roch spot is mainly frequented by women but is not exclusive.

Discos

There are lots of dance clubs around town but they change quickly, so ask around. See also VooDoo Grill under Places to Eat – go there to be seen and be seen.

Chez Dagobert (☎ 522-0393, 600 Grande Allée Est) An immense, three-story celebration of energy, this club is popular with an 18-to-30-year-old crowd who love to move and shake. The first floor has a cabaret with often free music or comedy acts, while the dance floor is upstairs.

Fourmi Atomik (☎ 694-1473, 33 rue d'Auteuil) The crowd here would never darken Chez Dagobert's dance floor. This place is more geared toward the underground set, and the music alternates between grunge, rock, punk and ambient.

Performing Arts

Grand Théâtre de Québec (☎ 643-8131, 269 boul René Lévesque Est) In St Jean Baptiste, this is the city's main performing arts center, presenting classical concerts, dance and theater. The building's design and the gigantic epic mural in three parts – *Death, Space and Liberty,* by Spaniard Jordi Bonet – are notable features. Unfortunately you can't see the inside without a ticket to a show, but the good news is that the shows are usually very good! The Opéra de Québec often performs here.

Théâtre de la Bordée (☎ 694-9721, 995 Place d'Youville) Just outside Porte St Jean, this is probably the city's most popular theater. Performances follow a mostly modern repertoire, mixing Québec productions with international ones, both comedy and drama.

Théâtre Capitole (☎ 694-4444, 972 rue St Jean) Just up rue St Jean in Old Town, this is a smaller performing arts center.

Cinemas

Cinéma Le Clap (☎ 650-2527, 2360 chemin Ste Foy) Located in Ste Foy, this cinema shows English, French and other international films, many with subtitles.

Théatre IMAX (☎ 627-4629, 5401 boul des Galeries) This place, in Vanier, shows often-mindblowing large-format and 3-D films featuring digital wraparound sound.

SPECTATOR SPORTS

Most sporting events are held outside the city proper. For winter sports, people head to the multipurpose Mont Ste Anne (see Around Québec City).

In mid-February, an International Pee Wee Hockey Tournament (☎ 524-3311) is held here, regrouping 12- and 13-year-old future big-time slap-shotters from around the world.

Biking enthusiasts can consider participating in the Raid Pierre Harvey (☎ 658-5898), an annual 24-hour mountain-bike race that goes from Chicoutimi to Québec City (290km) in mid-August.

If you're not hardcore enough to participate, the Canadian Championship of Speed

Canoe-Kayak (☎ 569-7713), held at the end of August to early September at Lac Beauport, can be interesting to watch from the sidelines. Over 2000 athletes participate.

SHOPPING

For Inuit art, there's *Galerie Brousseau et Brousseau (☎ 694-1828, 35 rue St Louis; open 9:30am-7pm Sat-Wed, 9:30am-9pm Thurs & Fri)*, adjoining the Musée d'Art Inuit, and *Aux Multiples Collections (☎ 692-1230, 69 rue Ste Anne)*. Both assure that a fair price was originally paid to the artists and that a percentage of sales revenue is returned to the community.

One of several cool junk and secondhand shops in St Roch is *La Boîte à Surprise (☎ 261-8560, 95 rue St Joseph Est)*, where you can find furniture, old games, toys, lamps and all those scratched disco 45s you've been searching for. Nearby, *Librairie Historica (☎ 525-9712, 155 rue St Joseph Est)* is a good used-book shop.

GETTING THERE & AWAY
Air

Airport Jean Lesage is west of town, off Hwy 40, near where Hwy 73 intersects it on its way north. Both Air Canada (☎ 692-0770, 800-630-3299) and Canadian International (☎ 692-1031) serve Montreal, Ottawa and most major Canadian cities. Air Nova (☎ 800-630-3299), a division of Air Canada, has daily flights connecting to Montréal and the Îles de la Madeleine.

Bus

The station (☎ 525-3000) is at 320 rue Abraham Martin, adjacent to the Gare du Palais train station. Orléans Express has buses to Montréal nearly every hour during the day and evening ($42, 3-4 hours). There are regular services to Rivière du Loup and then on to Edmundston, New Brunswick ($45, 5 hours). Rivière du Loup is the connecting point with SMT bus lines for destinations in Atlantic Canada. Intercar bus line runs up the north coast to Tadoussac ($33, 4 hours).

There are no direct buses between Québec City and the US. They go via Montréal.

Train

Odd as it may seem, small Québec City has three train stations (☎ 692-3940, 800-361-1235) with two phone numbers for all of them. The renovated and simply gorgeous Gare du Palais, complete with bar and café, on rue St Paul in Lower Town, is central and convenient. It is used for trains going to and from Montréal ($38, 3 hours) and beyond Montréal westward. Bus No 800 from Place d'Youville runs to the station.

CN Station Ste Foy, southwest of the downtown area, is used by the same trains and is simply more convenient for residents on that side of the city.

The third station, inconveniently on the south shore, about 10km from the river in the town of Charny, is used primarily for trains heading eastward to the Gaspé Peninsula or the Maritimes. Some Montréal trains also use it. Local buses connect to Ste Foy. To Moncton, New Brunswick, overnight trips leave at 10:30pm ($111, 12 hours, Wed-Mon).

Car

All rental agencies here suggest booking at least two days ahead. Budget (☎ 692-3660) is at 29 Côte du Palais as well as at the airport. For compact vehicles the rate is $40 per weekday with 250km, and $30 on a weekend day with 350km. Discount (☎ 692-1244, 800-263-2355) has cheaper rates. Call to find their nearest location.

An alternative to renting a car is ride-sharing. Allô Stop (☎ 522-0056, W www .allostop.com), at 467 rue St Jean, is an agency that gets drivers and passengers together. It also has offices in Montréal, Rivière du Loup and Rimouski among others. See the Montréal chapter's Getting There and Away section for more details.

Ferry

The ferry (☎ 644-3704) between Québec City and Lévis runs constantly – all day and most of the night. The one-way fare is adult/child $2.50/1.75, and $5.60/2.50 for a car/bike. Fares are about 25% cheaper from October to March. Even though the cruise lasts only a few minutes you get good views of the river and cliffs, the Québec skyline and Château Frontenac. The terminal in Québec City is at Place Royale, Lower Town, not far from the Québec harbor.

GETTING AROUND
To/From the Airport

Autobus La Québécoise (☎ 872-5525) shuttles between downtown and the airport for $9. It leaves from major hotels but will make pickups around town if you call at least one hour before flight time. They also have daily service to both Montréal airports.

A taxi from Old Town or Ste Foy is $24.50. Try Taxi Coop (☎ 525-5191).

Bus

The recommended city bus system (☎ 627-2511) costs $2.25 a ride (or eight tickets for $15.25) including transfer privileges. The buses go out as far as Ste Anne de Beaupré, on the north shore. The terminal, Gare Centrale d'Autobus, is at 225 boulevard Charest Est, in St Roch. Stop by for a supply of route maps and information, or call the above telephone number.

Many buses serving the Old Town area stop in at Place d'Youville, just outside the wall on rue St Jean. Bus No 800 goes to the central bus and train station (Gare du Palais), and Nos 800 and 801 go from downtown to Université Laval.

Car

In Québec City driving isn't worth the trouble; you can walk just about everywhere or hop a bus, the streets are narrow and crowded, and parking is an exercise in frustration. But if you're stuck driving, the tourist office has a handy map of city-operated parking lots scattered around the central area that don't price-gouge too much. Use the lots in St Roch, which charge nearly half the price as those in Upper Town. There are a few off rue St Vallier Est; they're a 10-minute hike (up lots of stairs), but you can treat yourself with the money you save.

Bicycle

Vélo Passe-sport (☎ 692-3643), at 77A rue Ste Anne in Old Town, has bicycles and rollerblades for rent. Bikes are about $24 for 24 hours; hourly rates are also offered, as are various guided tours and adventures.

Cyclo Services (see Organized Tours for contact information) does the same and is staffed with super-friendly, knowledgeable folks.

There is a 25km cycling path running to Parc de la Chute Montmorency from Old Port. Another 10km run goes north alongside the rivière St Charles, and there are many more cyclable paths around the area. Some have paid access, others are free. The tourist information office sells a detailed map, *Greater Québec Cycling Trails*, for $3.

Calèche

Horse-drawn carriages (*calèches*) are nice and romantic, but the price isn't: $60 for about 40 minutes.

Around Québec City

NORTH SHORE
Wendake

About 15km northwest of the city is the small town of Wendake, which is of interest because of **Onhoüa Chetek8e** (☎ 842-4308, W *www.huron-wendat.qc.ca, 575 rue Stanislas-Kosca; adult/student & child $7/6; open 9am-5pm daily May–mid-Oct).* (No, that 8 in the name is not a typo! See 'Say 8at?' on page 258) This is billed as a reconstructed Huron-Wendat village. It may look pretty tacky at first glance, with pricey souvenir shops and groups of tourists staring nonplussed at traditional dance displays, but it'll be of interest to anyone with even a passing curiosity about First Nations culture.

A guided tour takes you through a traditional longhouse and into a sweat lodge, and teaches you about their liberal child-rearing practices and beliefs in the meaning of dreams. Call ahead to make sure there are English-speaking guides on duty the day you want to visit. An on-site restaurant serves up bison, caribou, succotash and linguini (for the timid) for $13 to $28. The gift shop sells souvenirs and crafts all done by locals; the money you spend stays in the community.

Paddling in the St Lawrence, Québec City

Château Frontenac, Québec City

Mind your step, Québec City

MARK LIGHTBODY

Take a ride on the wild side, Québec City

ALLAN MONTAINE

Street performers, Québec City

CHRIS MELLOR

Fountain detail, Château Frontenac, Québec City

KEVIN LEVESQUE

Don't miss your train, Gare du Palais, Québec City

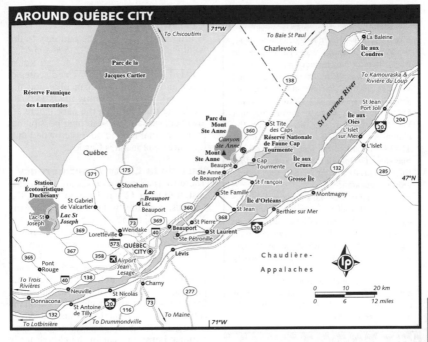

AROUND QUÉBEC CITY

In town there's the **Notre Dame de Lorette Chapel** of 1731, which contains some articles from the first Jesuit mission set up for the Hurons.

To get to Wendake take bus No 800 from Place d'Youville to Terminus Charlesbourg, then transfer to the No 72 and get off at the Grand Teepee.

St Gabriel de Valcartier & Stoneham

St Gabriel de Valcartier, farther north on Rte 371 from Wendake, is a large military base that you can drive through. Also there is the popular **Village Vacances** (*Holiday Village;* ☎ *844-2200, 1860 boul Valcartier*), a mini-city in itself that offers a gamut of summer fun. The most popular section is the huge Aqua Park (adult/child $22/14; open 10am-5pm June, 10am-7pm July–early Sept), which is packed to capacity on hot summer days. Horse riding, rafting and water luging are also possible.

Located at Stoneham is the **Station Touristique** (*Mountain Resort;* ☎ *848-2411, 800-463-6888,* **W** *www.ski-stoneham.com, 1420 chemin du Hibou*), which offers an array of summer and winter activities. There's a good downhill ski station here, used for mountain biking in the summer. All equipment can be rented. It recently had a $200 million facelift in an effort to turn it into one of the province's main ski centers.

Just north of Stoneham is the *Auberge du Jeune Voyageur* (☎ *848-7650,* **W** *www .chez.com/jeunevoyageur, 24 montée des Cassandres*), a combo B&B-hostel that's a lot of fun. They're but a few minutes drive from the Parc de la Jacques Cartier (a drive there costs $3), and they rent bikes and help organize activities. The house itself is very comfortable, and the dorms have their own bathroom. Dorm beds are $18 and singles/doubles are $35/50. Readers rave about the place.

Say 8at?

Like most native North American languages, the Wendat language was first recorded in the written form by religious missionaries. In this case, it was the Jesuits who transformed Wendat, part of the Algonquin linguistic group, from an oral to a written language. Father Jean de Brébeuf wrote the first Wendat catechism after his stay with the Huron-Wendat peoples in 1626–28, and in 1648 he published the first Wendat Christmas story, Le Noël Huron. It was in this story that the mysterious letter 8 made its first written appearance.

Supposed to look like a 'u' sitting atop an 'o,' it is most often written as '8' for simplicity's sake. In the few instances in Québec where a word with this letter is written on a signpost (near Wendake), it always attracts stares. Not only does this letter sneakily mimic a number but it also changes sounds depending on what's in front of it. Before a consonant it's pronounced 'ou' but in front of a vowel it's pronounced 'wa,' like the 'wh' in 'what' and 'where.'

Parc de la Jacques Cartier

Just off Rte 175, about 40km north of Québec City, is this huge wilderness park (☎ 890-6527, 800-665-6527, Rte 175; admission $3.50), ideal for a quick escape from the urban jungle. In less than an hour's drive you can be camping, hiking or biking, or canoeing along the long, narrow and exceptionally scenic rivière Jacques Cartier. The only drawback is that the park's main road follows the river and, unless you go farther inland, cars and vans whiz by as you're canoeing.

Near the entrance an information center provides details on the park's activities and services. Camping equipment, canoes and bikes can all be rented (about $25/day). Simple overnight cabins are scattered throughout the park, and there are *campgrounds* ($18-20). In winter there is cross-country skiing with shelter huts along some of the routes.

Réserve Faunique des Laurentides

A little farther north is the entrance to this wildlife reserve (☎ 848-2422, 800-665-6527, Rte 175; admission $3.50), 7861 sq km of wooded hills and mountains, and scores of lakes and streams. You can hike and fish here, and there are *campgrounds* ($18-20) along the road through the park. There are also very good canoe-camping possibilities in regions that tend to be less crowded than the Parc de la Jacques Cartier.

Parc de la Chute Montmorency

These tourist-trap waterfalls are about 7km east of Québec City in Beauport, along Rte 138, just past the bridge for Île d'Orléans. Yes, these are higher than Niagara Falls, but not nearly as impressive. They are perfectly visible from the main road where they can be seen for free, but many pay hefty fees inside the park (☎ 663-3330, 2490 avenue Royale). There's no entrance fee per se, but parking from the end of April to the end of October is $7.50, and a roundtrip ride on the cable car up the mountain is another $7.50.

To get to the park for free, you have three options: Park your car in the church lot in neighboring Beauport and walk the 1km to the falls; catch the No 800 bus at Place d'Youville in Québec City and transfer at the Beauport terminal to No 50 to the top of the falls or No 53 for the bottom; or bike from Québec City. The cable car doesn't provide the best views – the suspended footbridge right above the falls does. There are also 487 steps running up and down the mountain. In winter, the falls are especially impressive.

From the end of August to early September the **Grands Feu Loto Québec** (☎ 523-3389) fireworks festival is held here. You can also watch the pyrotechnics display from the southwestern tip of Île d'Orléans.

Île d'Orléans
pop 7000

An uncontestable highlight of the region, this island will make you feel eons away from Québec City even though it is visible from many spots in town. This special feel has attracted hundreds of urbanites who have summer, country or even permanent homes here. On summer weekends and during apple-picking season, you'd think the rest of the city was here too – the lines on the bridge can be horrendous.

While it's no longer a sleepy, pastoral farming region, Île d'Orléans remains agricultural and has some beautiful scenery and views onto either shore. One road circles the island, with two running north-south. There are a few windmills and lots of artists' workshops and galleries. Some of the villages have 300-year-old houses and boast other Normandy-style wooden or stone cottages. Parts of it feel like a well-off city suburb that has been transplanted into a forest.

The 34km-long island is divided into six sectors, each with a small village center. Most of the services are concentrated on the western tip, in St Pétronille, but restaurants, B&Bs and attractions are spread out everywhere. The tourist information office (☎ 828-9411, 490 Côte du Pont), visible as soon as you cross the bridge, will tell you what's available in terms of accommodations on the island. They can also set you up with bike rentals (about $25/day).

A tour of the 18th-century **Manoir Mauvide-Genest** (☎ 829-2630, 1451 chemin Royal; admission by donation; open 10am-5pm daily July-Oct, 10am-5pm Sat & Sun Nov–mid-Dec) allows you to step back into another era of the island's history. It's in the middle of St Jean, on the south side.

Places to Stay & Eat There's a wide variety of places to stay on the island, but in summer they book up fast, and on weekends it might be impossible to find space without reservations. If you're really stuck, you can try asking a farmer for permission to pitch a tent on their property – most will agree. The tourist office has photos of places to stay and eat.

Auberge le P'tit Bonheur (☎ 829-2588, e auberge@lepetitbonheur.qc.ca, 183-186 Côte Lafleur) Dorm beds $18. This HI hostel, in a gorgeous stone manor, is in St Jean, on the south shore. They rent bikes and cross-country skis.

Domaine Steinbach (☎ 828-0000, W www .domainesteinbach.com, 2205 chemin Royal) Singles/doubles $65/75. This apple orchard and cider house is one of the most charming places to stop on the island, whether you sleep in their 300-year-old manor or not. Their fine ciders, jams and vinaigrettes, on sale in the main house (where there's also an exhibit on this family industry) are obviously made with love. Bonus: Sampling is encouraged! Also on sale here are the traditional herbs and teas of herbalist Hélène Mathieu (☎ 842-6715), who has a round garden out front. Her nighttime guided tours of the garden are very popular. The rooms are extremely comfortable, and the views across to Charlevoix's mountains are stunning.

Le Relais des Pins (☎ 829-3455, 3029 chemin Royal) Mains $7-14. This is one of the best restaurants serving traditional Québécois dishes anywhere. Truly delicious, reasonably priced country meals like meat and potato pie or vegetable or beef ragout are served in a grand hall, where on weekends you can swing your partner around to folk music for no extra charge. There's a maple grove out back with trails leading down to the river.

Ste Anne de Beaupré

This gaudy little tourist town, a kind of religious theme park, is justly renowned for its immaculate and mammoth basilica (☎ 827-8227, 10018 avenue Royale; admission free; open 8:30am-4:30pm daily). Since the mid-1600s the village has been an important religious site. An annual pilgrimage takes place here in late July, attracting thousands of people; any nearby space becomes part of a huge camp – the camper/trailer park across the street is a great venue for people-watching.

The basilica, begun in the late 1920s, replaced earlier chapels. Note the many crutches inside the door. There's good tilework on the floor, and nice stained glass and ceiling mosaics; there are further chapels in the basement. Yet somehow the priest's sermons, bellowing out of loudspeakers, and the TV monitors flashing instructions like 'Kindly Keep Silent' detract. Outside is a souvenir kiosk with the Blessings Bureau next to it where you can have the priest inside bless the Jesus keychain you've just bought. The customers holding up the line are trying to slip in a spontaneous confession.

Check out the tacky hotel across the street. It's designed like a chapel, stained glass and all! Yet it does have an inexpensive cafeteria. Nearby is the **Cyclorama of Jerusalem** (☎ 827-3101, 8 rue Régina; adult/child $6/3; open 9am-6pm end April–end Oct), not an indoor cycling track but a 360-degree painting of Jerusalem on the day Jesus died.

To get there (and away!) Intercar runs buses up the north shore from Québec City and stops in town.

Mont Ste Anne

A little farther east, 50km from Québec City, Mont Ste Anne (☎ 827-4561, Ⓦ www .mont-sainte-anne.com, 2000 boul Beau Pré) is best known as a ski area. It's the number one hill near Québec City and one of the top slopes in the province – amateurs and experts alike rave about its 600m drop, 56 trails and 13 lifts. In summer there is a gondola to the mountain's summit, or if you're up to it, bicycle and hiking trails wind to the top. There are also 224km of excellent cross-country ski trails, 8km from Mont Ste Anne along Rte 360 around the village of St Ferreol les Neiges.

All equipment can be rented. Downhill skis are $22/17 per day for adult/child 14 to 22, cross-country skis are $15/13, and snowboards are $31/26. Check their website for a full list of prices.

In mid-December the Snow Surfing World Cup is held here. A giant slalom and half-pipes make for snowboarding heaven. In early January the 24-Hours of Mont Ste Anne sees sponsored participants complete as many runs as they can for charity. All throughout April there's a giant sugar shack set up here.

Camping Mont Ste Anne (☎ 827-5281, 800-463-1568, rang St Julien) Tent sites $22-28. More expensive than usual because there's an on-site water and beach slide as well as walking trails, this is one of several places on Rte 138 going east from Québec City through the Ste Anne de Beaupré area.

The Intercar bus line (☎ 888-861-4592) goes by but not into the park en route to Charlevoix, and the camping is quite a distance from the highway. The Hiver Express (☎ 525-5191) is an express bus service from several Québec City hotels to Mont Ste Anne ($22 roundtrip) and other winter destinations, leaving in the morning and returning in late afternoon.

Canyon Ste Anne

Some 6km northeast of Beaupré on Rte 138, in a deep chasm, are the 74m-high Ste Anne waterfalls, at the Canyon Ste Anne (☎ 827-4057, 206 Rte 138; adult/child $6.50 including parking; open 9am-5:30pm May–late June, Sept & Oct, 8:30am-6:30pm late June–Aug) in a natural setting. You can walk around and across them via a series of steps, ledges and bridges. Though busy, this is quite a pleasant spot – less developed and more dramatic than the falls at Montmorency. The water roars loudest in spring but autumn is grand with the surrounding red and gold maple leaves. The site also has a *restaurant*.

Les Sept Chutes

A few kilometers farther east are these waterfalls (☎ 826-3139, 4520 avenue Royale; adult/student $6.50/5; open 9am-7pm daily late June–early Sept, 10am-7pm late May–late June & early Sept–early Oct), at a defunct hydroelectric station and dam. Trails wind along the river past the various falls and through the woods. There's a display about the old power-production facilities as well as a *restaurant* and picnic tables.

Réserve National de Faune Cap Tourmente

Beyond Cap Tourmente village, south off Rte 138, along the riverside is this wildlife area and bird sanctuary (☎ 827-4591, 570 chemin du Cap Tourmente; adult/child $4/2; open 9am-5pm daily) run by Parks Canada. Flocks of snow geese come here in spring and autumn but many other bird species, as well as a range of animals and plants, make these wetlands home. There are meandering walking paths and an interpretation center (watch for the hummingbirds).

SOUTH SHORE
Parc des Chutes de la Chaudière
Just 4km after the Pont Pierre Laporte (exit 130 from Hwy 73) in Charny, this free and very pleasant park, on the site of a former hydroelectric station (a new one, completed in 1999, is nearby) boasts some very impressive waterfalls (35m) and over 2km of walking trails. There's a small photo display showing how magnificent these falls used to be before the stations' construction.

Lévis
pop 45,500
There's not much here for the visitor, as Lévis is a cross between a smallish town and a suburb of Québec City, but the ferry ride over makes for a pleasant mini-cruise and offers nice views of Québec City (see Getting There & Away in that section). The main shops and restaurants are along rue Bégin.

The **Terrasse de Lévis**, up the hill on rue William-Tremblay, is a lookout point inaugurated in 1939 by King George VI and his wife, Queen Elizabeth, the late Queen Mum, with even better views of Québec City and beyond. Between 1865 and 1872 the British built three forts on the south shore cliffs to protect Québec. One, known simply as **Fort No 1** (☎ *835-5182, 41 chemin du Gouvernement; adult/student $3/2.25; open 9am-5pm daily May-Aug, 1pm-4pm Thurs-Sun Sept)* has been restored and operates as a national historic site with guided tours. It's in Lauzon, a neighborhood on the east side of Lévis.

Berthier sur Mer
pop 1260
This small, riverside village, founded in 1672, is of interest mainly as the departure point for the best tours to **Grosse Île** (☎ *248-8888, 800-463-6769)* (see 'Island under Quarantine'). These are given from the marina by Croisières Lachance (☎ 259-2140, 888-476-

7734, 110 rue de la Marina; adult/child $42/34; one to four daily May–mid-Oct). The price includes roundtrip transport to Grosse Île as well as a Parks Canada–guided excursion of the island. Other tour options cruise through the Îles aux Grues archipelago. The boat tours are run by three charming brothers, descendants of seven generations of

---

Island under Quarantine

For over 100 years, from 1832 until as late as 1937, Grosse Île was the major Canadian quarantine station for immigrants coming from Europe. During this time, four million people passed through here and Québec City en route to points across North America.

In 1832 British soldiers returning from India brought cholera along with them, which killed 3500 people in Québec City alone – about 10% of its population. Grosse Île was set up to stop further contagion, and at that it was very effective. The island's most active time was in the late 1840s, when 100,000 Irish came to Canada escaping the potato famine (after a deadly microbe attacked potato crops, which were the only produce left for them to eat after the British government had taken all others for themselves). Many of the Irish brought typhus with them. In the single year of 1847 there were 10,000 people waiting to be hospitalized on the island.

In total, 7553 people died on the island (over 5000 in the summer of 1847 alone), never making it to their dreamed-of destinations. Many of them were of Irish descent, so in 1909 a 14m Celtic cross – the highest one in the world! – was erected as a memorial.

After its original function had run its course, Grosse Île was turned into a secret military research facility. In 1942, it was used to find an anthrax vaccine. In the following decades it was used for biological warfare research and for testing cures to animal maladies. After a big cleanup, the island was designated as a historical site and has been open for tours since 1994.

seamen and captains; passengers are always put in a good mood by their good-humored excursions.

A trip to Grosse Île is undoubtedly one of the most interesting excursions in the province and sheds much light on a little-known aspect of North American history. The tragic histories lived out on the island are cleverly, at times movingly, explained by knowledgeable guides. The tour includes visits to the disinfection chambers, the original hospital and living quarters of the immigrants, and the memorial burial area. You'll also be told about the island's 600 species of flora (21 of them rare).

The water in the St Lawrence River here begins to get salty – the concentration is about 23% and increases gradually farther east.

Montmagny
pop 11,900

This first town of considerable size east of Lévis is a good place from which to visit Île aux Grues (pop 150). The only inhabited island in the 21-island archipelago, as well as the biggest (10km long; Île aux Oies is the northern section of this same island), it has North America's largest unspoiled wetland on its eastern tip. Bird-watchers come here and to Montmagny in spring and autumn as snow geese stop nearby on their migration route. The island is a peaceful, pretty place for leisurely walks along the shore. There is bike rental on the island (about $20). There are ferries (☎ 248-6869; free, 2 or 3 daily) from the marina in the center of town. Other excursions are possible to the archipelago.

The tourist information office (☎ 248-9196) in Montmagny is at 45 avenue du Quai and can help set you up at motels, B&Bs or campgrounds in the area.

Also in town is the **Centre Éducatif des Migrations** (*Migration Educational Center; ☎ 248-4565, 45 rue du Bassin Nord; adult/ student $4/3.50; open 9:30am-5pm daily June-Nov*), a dual-purpose interpretive center with exhibits on migration, both bird and human. The first portion is a display on the Great White Goose. The second presents the history of European migration at Grosse Île and the surrounding south shore. There is an English version.

Places to Stay & Eat There are guesthouses and B&Bs both in Montmagny and on Île aux Grues.

Camping Municipal (☎ 248-8060, chemin du Roi) Tent sites $10. About 2km from the ferry dock on Île aux Grues, this is a small (19 sites), attractive campground with minimal services (there are showers, though).

Les Deux Marquises (☎ 248 4178, 153 rue St Joseph) Singles/doubles $50/70. Located in a large Victorian home, this B&B boasts four spacious rooms, many with slanted roofs, giving them a cozy feel.

La Belle Époque (☎ 248-3373, 100 rue St Jean Baptiste) Singles/doubles $70/90. This small and comfortable hotel in Montmagny has a highly reputed restaurant attached to it. The hotel prides itself on its top-notch service and in maintaining a cordial atmosphere.

St Jean Port Joli
pop 3400

This small but spread-out town, with the big two-spired church right in the middle, is a famous center for the Québec art of woodcarving. Locals call it the 'world capital of wooden sculpture,' and they've got a pretty good case. Just about everything you'd need can be found along avenue de Gaspé, including the central, seasonal tourist office (☎ 248-9196), at 7 Place de l'Église; it's open 9am to 8pm daily June through August and 9am-5pm daily May and September. The impressive church dates from 1890, and the priest's house next door was built even earlier, in 1872.

Excellent examples of woodcarvers' art can be seen in the **Musée des Anciens Canadiens** (*☎ 598-3392, 332 avenue de Gaspé Ouest; adult/child $4.50/2; open 9am-5:30pm daily May, June, Sept & Oct, 8:30am-9pm daily July & Aug*). Ask for a guide booklet in English. The museum contains works by some of the best-known local sculptors, past and present. Some represent local legends, others are on the gaudy side, still others are incredible. The largest piece measures 2½m by 5m. There is a gift shop where browsing without paying is welcome.

More recent carvings in the same and other styles can be seen in the many workshops and stores in and around town. Some carvers specialize in figures, some in religious themes, some in boats and ornate murals. Courses in carving can be taken as well; check with the tourist office for recommendations. Ceramics and textiles are produced and sold here as well but are distant seconds to the number of works in wood.

Faunart *(☎ 598-7034, 377 avenue de Gaspé Ouest; adult/student $4/3; open 9am-6pm daily May, June, Sept & Oct, 9am-9pm July & Aug)* is a gallery/store showing works of art, mainly dealing with animals, in many mediums, by Denis D'Amours and other Québec artists.

Orléans Express buses stop right in the center of town, at the SOS dépanneur across the street from the church. There are buses to Québec City ($22, 2¼ hours, 3 daily).

Places to Stay & Eat There are numerous motels on Rte 132. Campgrounds can be found in both directions out of town, closer heading east.

Camping de la Demi Lieue *(☎ 598-6108, 800-463-9558)* Tent sites $19-23. This huge campground (over 300 places) has a heated pool and all the amenities. At least you won't feel alone!

Auberge du Faubourg *(☎ 598-6455, 280 avenue de Gaspé Ouest)* Doubles from $120. On the west side of town, this is a massive accommodations complex with fairly luxurious rooms and a restaurant.

La Boustifaille *(☎ 598-3061, 547 avenue de Gaspé Ouest)* Appetizers $3-7, mains $5-11. This place is a veritable institution, renowned far and wide. It serves purely Québécois food, and after huge portions of pork ragout, meat tourtière, cheese quiche and maple syrup cake, you'll not need to eat for several days. Don't be shy to clean off your plate with pieces of homemade bread – no one else is.

Charlevoix, Saguenay & Lac St Jean

☎ 418

The three regions covered in this chapter each have their own personalities, subtleties and geographically unique features. Charlevoix is a beautiful, exciting region with endless possibilities for total wilderness immersion; the Saguenay's rhythms are more placid, but the fjord landscape is among the most stunning and dramatic in the province; Lac St Jean slows the pace even more and is mostly flat, defined by its huge lake of the same name. Small wonder, then, why locals from these districts are none too pleased to hear the three lumped together and often tied by hyphens (Saguenay-Lac St Jean) – they look and feel markedly different from each other.

History

Despite their autonomy, the three regions' histories are intertwined and all have remained in relative isolation until fairly recently. Charlevoix was hardly touched until the mid-17th century when the land was divided into seven seigneuries, but even after this it remained inhabited primarily by sailors, fishermen and agriculturists. A lack of social infrastructures meant solitude for the locals, who mainly had to fend for themselves. A main road wasn't completed through the area until 1954. Before then, the only mode of transport (aside from boats, which were landlocked by ice some five months earlier) was by train.

The arrival of the steamboat in 1830 changed Charlevoix's destiny somewhat, bringing in wealthy tourists attracted by the wild beauty of the natural surroundings. By the end of the 19th century, many luxurious homes and resorts had been built to accommodate the floating bourgeoisie.

From the 17th to the early 19th centuries Saguenay-Lac St Jean was the exclusive property of fur traders, who did business with the area's Innu people. The entire area, along

Highlights

- Take a kayak or boat trip along the fjord at Parc du Saguenay
- Take a lazy walk in and around the beautiful village of Ste Rose du Nord
- Step back in time at the re-created village of Val Jalbert
- Go from thick forest to subarctic permafrost along one trail in the Parcs des Hautes Gorges, near La Malbaie
- Discover what's so funny about the Baie des Ha! Ha!, at La Baie

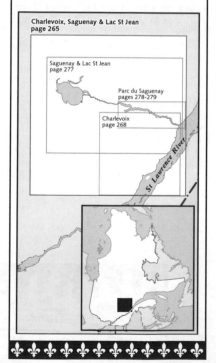

Charlevoix, Saguenay & Lac St Jean page 265

Saguenay & Lac St Jean page 277

Parc du Saguenay pages 278-279

Charlevoix page 268

St Lawrence River

with the North Shore, was known as Le Domaine du Roy, and the French forbade colonization. After the British won Canada from France in 1760, the area became simply the King's Posts, and things didn't change even though the owners were now the Hudson's Bay Company. They controlled and limited all development and population of the territory until 1842.

By then, not only had the vicissitudes of European fashion tastes meant that beaver fur was no longer *à la mode,* but the growing forestry industry was encroaching on these fertile, forested lands. William Price, who by that time already had started developing Charlevoix, set his sights on the Saguenay-Lac St Jean area and made a deal in 1838 with the Hudson's Bay Company to allow for limited settlement. Farmers from Charlevoix, in search of new, cultivatable lands (many had already immigrated to the US to find them) started arriving by the boatful up the Saguenay river to the virgin territory, and colonization was begun in earnest.

Partially because the area was settled by a relatively small number of people, who were themselves subgroups of a small number of

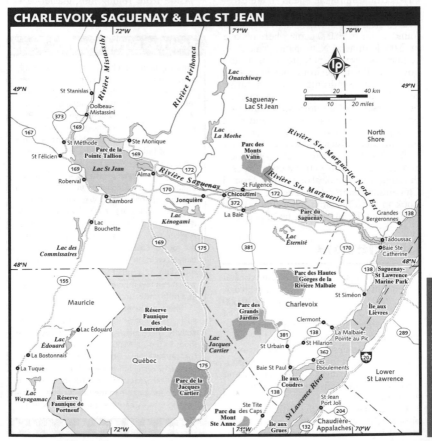

CHARLEVOIX, SAGUENAY & LAC ST JEAN

European settlers, the Saguenay-Lac St Jean region, and to some extent Charlevoix as well, has developed a number of genetically transmitted diseases. This is a distinction locals are less pleased to discuss than the uniqueness of the region's natural beauty. However, there are numerous conditions found either exclusively in this region or in concentrations higher than anywhere else on the planet. Biologists and geneticists from around the world regularly come here to study gene transmission.

Tyrosenemia, a liver disease, affects one in 100,000 people globally, but in the Saguenay-Lac St Jean region one in 20 are carriers, and one in 1846 are affected by it. The neurological disorder Leigh's Syndrome is found in one in 20,000 people; here it's one in 2000. Peripheral Neuropathy, which can render its victims paraplegic, is found nowhere else in the world but here. And Andermann Syndrome, a degenerative central and nervous system disease marked by the absence of the corpus callosum (the bridge between the brain's left and right hemispheres), is more concentrated here than anywhere else in the world.

Besides a relatively small gene pool, another reason for high transmission rates is the large families typical of the area. Around Chicoutimi, families average six siblings. Look in the Chicoutimi phonebook – the family name Tremblay takes up 22 pages!

Charlevoix

Beyond Mont Ste Anne is the scenic coastal and mountain district known as Charlevoix, whose 6000 sq km are home to only 30,000 people. For 200 years this pastoral strip of hilly, flowery farmland counterbalanced with steep cliffs and woods wedged between northern wilderness and the river has been a summer retreat for the wealthy and privileged. Though vestiges of this remain and prices are on the high side it is now a more democratic destination.

Unesco has classed the entire area as a biosphere or heritage cultural and environmental region, and this has meant worthwhile restrictions on the types of permitted developments – as well as a palpable sense of pride on the part of residents.

Charlevoix is an outdoor playground for people from Québec City who enjoy the area for a weekend break or a short holiday destination. It has long been a popular district with artists, and numerous galleries and craft shops may be found in the towns and villages. Inns and less-expensive B&Bs abound and there is no shortage of quality restaurants. Beginning around the middle of September the autumn foliage is remarkable.

Aside from rolling hills, glacier-carved crevices, cliffs and jagged rock faces, the most

Feel the Earth Move?

Charlevoix is Québec's most geologically active area, so don't be surprised if you feel some trembling underfoot. Every year some minor seismic activity is recorded in the region. A particularly active year was 1996, with four earthquakes measuring over 3.0 on the Richter scale – enough to cause some rumbling but not enough to disrupt a pleasant day's hiking.

In 1988 a quake measuring 4.7 originating 35km south of Chicoutimi in an area of no previous seismic activity was felt in Montréal and New York State; it was the largest earthquake in eastern North America since 1935. And in 1925 a whopping 7.0 quake caused the roof of Québec City's train station to partially cave in. In 1971 a small quake caused a mudslide in a small village near Jonquière, which in a few moments enveloped 35 houses in a mud crater and killed over 30 people.

There are several reasons why the area is such a hot spot. Shifting tectonic plates create activity, particularly under the St Lawrence River in the La Malbaie area. As an effect of the retreated glaciers from the last Ice Age, the earth is still lifting here at a rate of 50cm every 100 years. Finally, the meteor crash from so long ago had the effect of destabilizing the area by causing cracks in the bedrock.

unique geographical feature of the area is the immense valley from Baie St Paul to La Malbaie, formed from the impact of a prehistoric meteor. A space rock 2km in diameter and weighing in at 15 billion tons smashed into the earth here at 36,000km/hr some 350 million years ago. The point of impact was the present-day Mont des Éboulements, halfway between the two towns, some 10km inland. The crater it left is 56km in diameter.

Special Events
In addition to the local festivals and special events listed throughout this chapter, here are some dates to remember.

February
Ukatak International Trek This event (☎ 665-4454, Ⓦ www.ukatek.com), apparently the largest winter trek in the world, pits international four-person teams against the rugged climes and nasty weather for a grueling outdoor endurance test.

August & September
Festival Coureur des Bois During the last few days of August and into early September, this festival (☎ 639-2740, 639-1099) explores and re-creates the lifestyles of Québec's truc folk heros, the *coureurs des bois* (the woodsmen, explorers and trappers who opened up much of the land for colonization) with games, performances and exhibits. It's held in St Urbain, north of Baie St Paul.

October
Charlevoix International Rally Supposedly the largest car rally in the world, this annual event (☎ 665-9991) is held in La Malbaie, which is trying to host a race in the World Rally Championship. It's held for four days at the end of October.

PETITE RIVIÈRE ST FRANÇOIS
pop 750
This scenic town's landscape and economy is dominated by **Le Massif** (☎ 632-5876, Ⓦ www.lemassif.com, information office 1350 rue Principale; day pass adult/student/child 7-12 $35/31/21), a huge mountain west of town and a popular downhill ski destination. From the center of town, near the marina, there are great views back onto the mountainous surroundings.

The ski station boasts the highest skiable slope (770m) east of the Rocky Mountains and an average annual snowfall of over six meters. There are 20 slopes for all grades of experience (plenty of black diamonds for you experts!) and three lifts (two chair lifts, one surface). Le Massif gets raves from both skiers and snowboarders. For one thing the views are magnificent, probably the most impressive in Eastern Canada; descending the mountain, you feel like you'll ski right into the frozen St Lawrence. Another much-appreciated aspect is that, in comparison to Mont Ste Anne or Mont Tremblant, this hill is relatively uncrowded. It's also not over developed and touristy, though there is a cozy pub to defrost in after a day outdoors.

There are also several festivals held throughout the year, the most lively being the **Reggae Bash** (☎ 632-5876) every March, where tropical rhythms announce the (eventual) arrival of warmer temperatures.

BAIE ST PAUL & PARC DES GRANDS JARDINS
Heading east along Rte 138 the first urban stop after Québec City is **Baie St Paul** (population 7400), with its old streets and big church. The town's main street, rue St Jean Baptiste, is lined with historic houses, some of which have been converted into galleries and restaurants. Artists' studios and craft shops are scattered around the side streets.

The main attraction here is the splendid **Parc des Grands Jardins**, which covers 310 sq km of territory, much of it taiga. Caribou roam freely here and munch on lichen. If you can't make it farther north in Québec, some areas here will give you a good idea of the vegetation that can be found there. Baie St Paul makes a good launch pad for treks to and through the park, and is where you'll want to stock up on supplies before heading off on expeditions.

Information
The year-round tourist office (☎ 435-4160) is at 444 boulevard Mgr de Laval (Rte 138), just west of town. It's worthwhile stopping here on your way east. Not only are the panoramic lookouts stupendous from this

spot, but attached to the office is the **Centre d'Histoire Naturelle de Charlevoix** (☎ 435-6275; admission free; open 9am-5pm daily late May–mid-Oct, 10am-4pm Sat & Sun mid-Oct–late May). This center has displays on the flora, fauna and geography of the Charlevoix district, detailing the meteorological impact and the area's seismic proclivities. Ask at the front desk for English translations of the displays.

Another tourist office (☎ 435-3681), open June to September only, is in the Art Centre (☎ 435-5654) in the town center, at 4 rue Ambroise Fafard.

Things to See & Do

A major art gallery well worth visiting is the **Centre d'Exposition** (*☎ 435-3681, 23 rue Ambroise Fafard; adult/student $3/2; open 9am-7pm daily June-Sept, 9am-5pm daily Oct-Apr*), with three floors of exhibits of local artists. The Art Centre (see Information) often has shows of Charlevoix painters.

A must-do while in the area is visiting the **Parc des Grands Jardins** (*☎ 439-1227, 800-665-6527; admission $3.50; open 8am-8pm daily June-Aug, 9am-5pm daily Sept-May*), accessible via 381 (30km from Baie St Paul to the visitor's center, 46km to the main en-

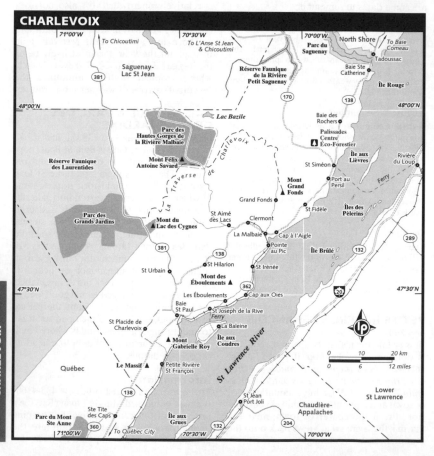

CHARLEVOIX

trance). Run by Sépaq, there are canoe and kayak rentals ($28 per day), and opportunities for *camping* ($19 to $24) and overnight stays in chalets. There is little swimming, but the hike up Mont de Lac des Cygnes (Swan Lake) makes an excellent half-day outing. Sections of the park suffered a forest fire in the early 1990s and camping at Lac Athabaska amid the charred trunks certainly provides a unique perspective. The tireless among you might want to take up the challenge of one of the province's longest and most difficult continuous trails, La Traversée de Charlevoix (see 'Québec's Most Arduous Trail').

Activities

Randonées Nature (☎ 435-6275, W www .charlevoix.net/rando, 41 rue St Jean Baptiste) organizes several types of regional tours. For walkers there's a 4½-hour hike ($22) through Parc des Grands Jardins with a naturist on hand to explain the subarctic landscape. Cyclists can take a two-hour bike tour ($6) of the town and its surrounding areas. Avid sitters can relax with a two-hour bus tour (adult/child 12-18/child under 12 $17/12/7). They also rent bicycles ($20 to $25 per day).

Located at Baie St Paul's marina, L'Air du Large (☎ 435-2066, W www.quebec web.com/airdularge, 210 rue Ste Anne) rents kayaks, canoes, bicycles and paragliders. They'll also give initiation courses for inexperienced sea kayakers and paragliders. Their guided excursions on a 12-place boat explore nearby islands and marine life.

Places to Stay

La Balcon Vert (☎ 435-5587, W www .balconvert.charlevoix.net, 22 Côte du Balcon Vert) Tent sites $17, dorm bed $17, room/ chalet for two $45; open mid-May–mid-Oct. This is an excellent place for spending the night, located east of the town center up the hill, off Rte 362. Watch for the signs; it's only 1km after exiting the village. With its restaurant, bar, woodsy setting, chalets, dorms and campground, it is a retreat, hotel and hostel all in one. It has a fabulous view overlooking the town and surrounding mountains,

Québec's Most Arduous Trail

It stretches 100km from the Parc des Grands Jardins, winds down the great valleys in the Parc des Hautes Gorges and winds up in the Parc du Mont Grands Fonds. If you can hike or ski about 18km a day, it will take you seven days and six nights to cross. It's one of the province's longest continuous trails, arguably its most challenging: La Traversée de Charlevoix.

It demands a fairly experienced hiker or cross-country skier to complete the trek, as there are descents of 200m to 350m into valleys and ascents up to 850m along the way. The scenery, needless to say, is likely to leave you just as dizzy as in awe. There are log huts for overnight stays along the way. Guided treks with experts are possible. For all infomation concerning this trek, call ☎ 639-2284 or see W www.charlevoix.net/ traverse. The Sépaq-run trail office is at 841 rue St Édouard in St Urbain.

and makes a perfect base for exploring the region. The cafeteria has tasty, bargain-priced meals.

Camping du Gouffre (☎ 435-2143, 439 chemin St Laurent) Tent sites $16-23, chalets from $65. On the banks of the shallow rivière du Gouffre outside of town, this is a heavily wooded, rustic campground with numerous services.

Au Clocheton (☎ 435-3393, 877-435-3393, 50 rue St Joseph) Singles/doubles from $45/60. Though it's in the middle of town, this B&B feels nicely isolated because of its sprawling garden, which runs down to the banks of the small rivière du Gouffre. One room in this pretty, Victorian, smoke-free house has its own bathroom; the rest share.

Auberge La Grande Maison (☎ 435-5575, 800-361-5575, 160 rue St Jean Baptiste) Singles $70-225, doubles $130-285. This immaculate red and silver place, covered in flowers, is central and has its own restaurant. The more expensive units are quite luxurious.

CHARLEVOIX

Motels-Chalets Chez Laurent (☎ 435-3895, 888-437-3895, 1493 boul Mgr de Laval) Singles/doubles in motel from $50, fully equipped chalet cottages $125. This is a decent choice, about 20 minutes north of Baie St Paul among a strip of hotels and motels right on Rte 138.

Places to Eat

Le Saint Pub/Microbrasserie Charlevoix (☎ 240-2332, 2 rue Racine) Mains $7-13, full-course meals $13-21. Beer lovers will be foaming at the mouth here in this brewpub, where many meals are infused with the locally brewed malt (beer-marinated smoked meat, salads with beer vinaigrette) and for $4.50 you can try four regional brews in sample sizes. Local cheeses are on the menu too. The friendly atmosphere makes it a popular hangout.

Al Dente (☎ 435-6695, 30 rue Leclerc) Mains $6-15. A large variety of excellent Italian dishes are on offer here, with four kinds of homemade pasta, a dozen tasty sauces and regional specialties like local cheeses and smoked Charlevoix veal. There are several vegetarian meals. Rue Leclerc is the continuation of rue Ambroise Fafard on the north side of the rivière du Gouffre.

Café des Artistes (☎ 435-5585, 25 rue St Jean Baptiste) Mains $5-14. A subdued and cozy café with European pretensions, the favorite here is pizza, though many just pop in for an espresso and dessert.

Getting There & Away

The bus station (☎ 435-6569) is at the restaurant La Grignotte, 2 route de L'Équere (at the corner of boulevard Mgr de Laval), about a 20-minute walk to downtown. There are three daily departures/arrivals to/from Québec City ($15, 1¼ hours) a day with an extra Friday service. There are also three buses daily to/from La Malbaie ($7, 45 mins) and two daily buses going as far east as Baie Comeau ($54, 5½ hours).

ÎLE AUX COUDRES
pop 1400

Quiet, rural Île aux Coudres is what many people disappointed in better-known Île d'Orléans are looking for. It's the gentle, easy-paced kind of place where you go to spend an afternoon and stay for days. Jacques Cartier gave the island its present-day name for all of the *coudriers* (hazel trees) on it. It became a base for whale hunting and is now mainly farmland with a number of small, low-key historic sites, a watermill and a windmill. There are a few museums, but the real pleasures here are in lazy walks along the beach (where you can swim) or a drive around the island. There are several spas here, underscoring the calming effect the island can have on the overwrought.

The tourist office (☎ 438-2930) is at 21 rue Royale Ouest, near the crossroads just beyond the port.

If you're visiting in late June around St Jean Baptiste day, don't be surprised by the odd sight of hundreds of Volkswagen Beetles on the island – it's the annual **Bug Out** (☎ 438-2887), a three-day festival that celebrates the cult of the Beetle, with antiques and new models being shown off.

The **Musée de l'Isle aux Coudres** (☎/fax 438-2753, 231 chemin des Coudriers; adult/student $3.50/3; open 8:30am-7pm daily May-Oct) makes for a pleasant stop, with its antique-shop feel. It chronicles the settlement of the island and has displays on local flora and fauna.

Activities

Cycling is a great way to get around the island, and there are two main places to rent bikes. Close to the port, just beyond the first crossroad, Locations Gérard Desgagnés (☎ 438-2332, 34 rue du Port) has race, mountain and tandem bikes. Their competition, Vélo Coudres (☎ 438-2118, 877-438-2118, 743 chemin des Coudriers), has a better selection. Although their claim to have the 'widest selection of bicycles in North America' is doubtful, they sure do have some strange contraptions here, like the Buddy Bike, with two side-by-side seats on the same bike. They're 5km from the port but if you want to save your energy for bike riding, they run an hourly shuttle from the port to their store, 10am to 5pm in July and August.

For **sea kayaking** trips head to Kayak de Mer (☎ 438-4388, ⓦ www.charlevoix.net/k-iac-de-mer, 783 des Coudriers), on the south side of the island. They offer simple rentals ($29 for a half-day) as well as several excursions – the 90-minute sunset trip is nice, and the more adventurous five-hour excursion includes detailed explanations about the island's marine and bird life.

For the even more audacious, consider participating in the **Grande Traversée** (☎ 438-2568), a two-day canoe race at the end of January. Yes, a canoe race. In January. Over the ice from the mainland. It's a tribute to the bravery of the postmen who used to deliver mail this way in the good ol' days. Five-person teams brave an 8km course over the ice floes.

Places to Stay & Eat

In general the island's places to stay and eat are not very exciting, but there is choice. There are several fast-food diners around, but most of the hotels also serve food.

Camping Sylvie (☎ 438-2420, 191 rue Royale Ouest) Tent sites $12-17, chalets $40. There are canoes and paddleboats for rent here for use on an artificial lake, and there's a beach nearby. There are some nice spots to pitch a tent – look around first before choosing.

Chalets et Camping du Ruisseau Rouge (☎ 438-2128, 779 chemin des Coudriers) Tent sites $15, chalets $75. With simple chalets and some nice, semi-isolated, wooded terrain for camping, this may be your best bet on the island.

Un Petit Coin de Paradis (☎ 438-2979, 877-438-2979, 37 rue Tremblay) Chalets $65, $5 off after 3rd night. Calling it 'a little corner of paradise' is an exaggeration, but the small, split-level cabins in the woods are sweet enough and clean, though mildly run-down.

Hôtel du Capitaine (☎ 438-2242, 888-520-2242, 781 chemin des Coudriers) Singles/doubles $60/100. Nicely managed gardens surround this stately home-cum-hotel, 7km east of the port. Rooms are comfortable, and the salt-water pool does the trick. Their restaurant is open from 8am to 10am (to 11am Saturday and Sunday) and from 6pm to 8pm daily.

Hôtel Cap aux Pierres (☎ 438-2711, 888-554-6003, 246 rue Principale) Singles/doubles from $80/160 including breakfast and supper. Near-luxury suites are on offer here, and the restaurant serves very decent food daily from 7am to 9pm.

Getting There & Away

Ferries (☎ 438-2743) run to the island from St Joseph de la Rive, a lovely 22km drive from Baie St Paul via Rte 362. The pleasant, 3.7km boat trip takes 15 minutes and runs year-round, from 7am to 11:30pm, eight to 24 times daily. The service is free and accommodates cars as well.

LES ÉBOULEMENTS
pop 1000

Heading east from Baie St Paul, take the coastal Rte 362 instead of the 138. It eventually rejoins the 138 but in the meantime you get to enjoy rolling hills and lovely scenery. A bike trail hugs the coast in this area, one of the prettiest in the region.

The scenery is superb around Les Éboulements, with farms running from the town's edge to the river. You may have to stop while a farmer leads cattle across the highway. Note the piles of wood used for the long winters and the many carving outlets. Also note the unusual rock formations – these are the result of a powerful 1663 earthquake. The village is worth a stop, just to soak up its atmosphere.

The **Moulin Banal** (☎ 635-2239, 157 rue Principale; adult/child under 12 $2/free; open 10am-5pm daily May-Oct) is a grain and flour mill that offers a good taste of what 19th-century life was like here. Built in 1790 with an adjacent seigneurial manor, the entire complex has been preserved exceptionally well.

ST IRÉNÉE
pop 650

Just 15km east from Les Éboulements along Rte 362 is this beautiful village surrounded by rounded hills which seem to flow into the river. Famous here is the **Domaine Forget** (☎ 452-8111, ⓦ www.domaineforget.com, 5 rang St Antoine; admission free except

CHARLEVOIX

concerts; open 9:30am-5:30pm plus concert times), an internationally renowned music and dance school that takes in students from around the world.

Composed of three stately buildings, which were once upper-class private residences, the Domaine's riverside grounds can be visited. There is also a small exhibit on the theme of female suffrage in Québec; Thérèse Casgrain, daughter of one of the estate's owners, Rudolphe Casgrain, fought hard for women's right to vote in the province.

The main attractions here, though, are the summer concerts. The lovely Françoys-Bernier concert hall has some of the best acoustics in Canada and plays host to the **Domaine Forget International Festival** (☎ 452-3535, 888-336-7438). Held from late June through late August, this is a series of highly esteemed concerts given by the students, mainly on weekends. Tickets range from about $23 to $30, a good deal considering the talent and surroundings.

Places to Stay

Le Port d'Attache (☎ 452-3307, **e** *rbtrem blay@simpatico.ca, 10 rang St Antoine)* Singles/doubles from $50/63. This is the least expensive of the several B&Bs in the village, situated a short walk from the Domaine Forget. It's a comfortable, smoke-free environment.

Les Studios du Domaine (☎ 452-8111, 888-336-7438, 5 rang St Antoine)* Singles/doubles $60/80. A perfect place to retire after an evening's concert, these studio apartments are set up in large parkland overlooking the river. Some are outfitted with kitchenettes.

L'Auberge des Sablons (☎ 452-3594, 800-267-3594, **w** *www.quebecweb.com/sablons, 290 chemin des Bains)* Singles/doubles from $90/160. The emphasis is on first-rate service here, hence the hefty prices. However, ask about their specials incorporating concerts and meals – it might work better into your budget.

LA MALBAIE
pop 9400

The community of La Malbaie is now an amalgamation of five previously separate villages on both sides of the rivière Malbaie. The main sector, on the west side of the river, is called La Malbaie-Pointe au Pic, designating the two most important towns, now fused together.

The tourist office (☎ 665-4454, 800-667-2276) is at 630 boulevard de Comporté in the village of La Malbaie. Open daily year-round, it can help with information on the entire Charlevoix area.

La Malbaie-Pointe au Pic

Seemingly a small, insignificant village, Pointe au Pic was a holiday destination for the wealthy from as far as New York at the beginning of the 20th century. Dozens of so-called 'white ships,' steamboats masquerading as veritable floating palaces, would sail into Pointe au Pic bringing moneyed, American elite. It was one of Canada's earliest and most popular resort destinations. The scenery, isolation and air of refinement had many visitors building fine summer residences along the shore. One such resident was William-Howard Taft, a former US president, who had a summer home built there. Some of these large, impressive 'cottages' along chemin des Falaises have now been converted into comfortable inns.

In the mid-1960s the era of the luxury liners came to an end, and so too, in part, did Pointe au Pic's international fame.

Attesting to the area's glory – past and present – is the splendor of the **Manoir Richelieu** (see Places to Stay for contact information). The sprawling, romantic hotel dating from 1928 got a $140 million facelift in 1999 and resembles Québec City's Château Frontenac. Today it's filled mainly with busloads of gamblers rabidly partaking of the adjacent, posh **casino** (☎ 665-5322, **w** *www.casinos-quebec.com; open daily year-round)* but is still worth a look. The casino, replete with gaming tables and slot machines, is not overly formal but shorts and jeans are not acceptable. The casino hours are seasonal, but opening hours are 10am or 11am until midnight to 3am; check their website or call for precise times.

The **Musée de Charlevoix** (☎ 665-4411, 1 chemin du Havre; adult/student $4/3; open

10am-6pm daily late June–early Sept, 10am-5pm Tues-Fri & 1pm-5pm Sat & Sun mid-Sept–mid-June) has a small permanent collection on local history, but the major part of the museum is an art gallery with temporary shows. Regional artists, sculptors and photographers display their wares here.

In winter the area is a cross-country skier's heaven. The **Centre de Plein Air Les Sources Joyeuses** (*☎ 665-4858, 141 rang Ste Madeleine, La Malbaie)* is a non-profit organization that has cleared ten cross-country ski trails (totaling 82km), two 5km ice-skating trails, several winter hiking trails

La Malbaie: Heaven for cross-country skiers

and a few ice slides for the kids. Prices are very reasonable: A day ticket for all the activities is adult/child $8/4, skiing alone is $6/3, and skating alone is $1.50/1. There's rental of all equipment as well.

The La Malbaie side of this sector has nothing much of interest for tourists.

Les Quatre Vents
Just 2km east of La Malbaie, in the Cap á l'Aigle sector on Rte 138, is this private garden, considered Canada's biggest and best.

It's open only four Saturdays per summer, and tickets sell out mighty quick. In order to visit the gardens, contact the **Centre Ecologique de Port au Saumon** (*☎ 434-2209, 877-434-2209, 3330 boul Malcolm Fraser; adult/child $5/3; guided tours 10am & 2pm daily July & Aug)*, in St Fidèle (also part of La Malbaie, but 15km east of Pointe au Pic). At their headquarters they have an ecological exhibit that's of particular interest for the kids.

Places to Stay
Camping Chutes Fraser (*☎ 665-2151, 500 chemin de la Vallée)* Tent sites $16-25, chalets from $30 per person. Opened in 1962 this was the first campground in Charlevoix, and it still is one of the best. A small waterfall and hiking and cycling trails do much to beautify the surroundings. There's a pool, mini-golf course and other on-site games, but the grounds are so spacious it doesn't feel *too* crowded – even though there's room for some 300 campers. The chalets are spotless and modern. The campground is just 7km from the casino; cross the bridge going east, turn left (north) on chemin de la Vallée and continue for 3km.

Camping au Bord de la Rivière (*☎ 665-4991, 1510 boul de Comporté)* Tent sites $20. Quite luxurious as far as campgrounds go, this medium-sized place is situated on pleasant terrain by the river in La Malbaie.

Gîte Condor (*☎ 665-3873, 470 côte Bellevue)* Singles/doubles $40/50. One of the less pricey options right in Pointe au Pic, this is a decent, small B&B.

Gîte HM Duchesne (*☎ 665-3619, 615 rue St Raphaël)* Singles/doubles $35/55. A good deal, this simple B&B is charming in a subdued way. They also sell local handicrafts. It's located in the Cap á l'Aigle sector, 10km east of La Malbaie.

Les Mille Roches (*☎ 665-3344,* **e** *gualbert@ charlevoix.qc.ca, 870 chemin des Falaises)* Doubles $60. There's an air of refined simplicity to this charming hotel, inside an 1873 home in La Malbaie. The floors are still wood paneled, the furniture and décor are tasteful and the kitchen is at your disposal. It's less than five minute's walk from the Manoir Richelieu.

CHARLEVOIX

Maison Victoria Inn (☎ 665-1022, 726 rue St Raphaël) Singles/doubles $75/85. This is another good, very nicely decorated, place in Cap á l'Aigle.

Auberge Donahue (☎ 665-4377, www .aubergedonohue.com, 40 chemin du Havre) Doubles $89-219. Located only 200m from the Musée de Charlevoix, this is a lovely hotel that obviously prides itself on its elegance. Its 19 rooms are each differently styled and offer varying levels of comfort.

Auberge des Peupliers (☎ 665-4423, W www.aubergedespeupliers.com, 381 rue St Raphaël) Singles/doubles from $135/195. In Cap à l'Aigle, this fine, old house wrapped with a veranda has one of the top-rated Charlevoix restaurants (lunches average $20, dinners $40 to $55). The hotel sets out to pamper you – and with their prices, they should.

Manoir Richelieu (☎ 665-3703, W www .fairmount.com, 181 rue Richelieu) Doubles from $200. This palatial hotel in La Malabie often has specials for stays of over two days, but no matter, this is break-the-budget territory. An exception to the prices is the Winston bar-restaurant on the ground floor with a low-cost breakfast – a good excuse for checking out the place. Snowmobiles are rented out here too.

Places to Eat

All of the region's hotels (most notably the Manoir Richelieu) have restaurants, bars and cafés in them; many B&Bs will also cook meals. Ask in advance.

Les Délices du Petit Manoir du Casino (☎ 665-8888, 525 chemin des Falaises) Mains $6-12. Decent, standard fare like pastas, meat and seafood dishes are served in this spacious restaurant situated to attract the casino crowd – it's a few meters away.

Café de la Gare (☎ 665-4272, 100 chemin du Havre) Mains $9-16. Located right at the La Malbaie marina, there are nice views from this laid-back restaurant. The menu is limited but the food is good – grilled paninis hit the spot nicely, and their fries are tasty. There are also nachos and the ever-popular mussels and fries.

Club des Monts (☎ 439-3711, 110 Ruisseau des Frênes) This high-kickin' place is one of the liveliest bars in the area, where live bands or solo guitarists play to an audience that tries its darndest to have a good time. Joining in is definitely encouraged. Housed in a bright red and white house from 1860 called the Maison du Bootlegger, the upstairs is where all the action takes place. The food is decent pub fare, with hearty portions.

AROUND LA MALBAIE
Parc des Hautes Gorges de la Rivière Malbaie

This provincial park (☎ 439-1227, 800-665-6527; admission $3.50; open 7am-9pm daily May–early Oct) is still somewhat of an undiscovered gem – relative to other provincial parks, that is. It fell under Sépaq's administration as a conservation area only in 2000, when the once heavily potholed access road leading to it was first paved. The park's 233 sq km have several unique features, including the highest rock faces east of the Rockies, as sheer rock plummets (sometimes 800m) to the calm rivière Malbaie, which snakes off at right angles at times.

A vigorous, calorie-burning climb along the **hiking** trail named L'Acropole des Draveurs (Acropolis of the Log Drivers) takes you 1030m high for some unforgettable views, where mountains repeat themselves to infinity. Count on almost three hours to reach the summit. The Mont des Érables trail is even more adventurous and leads you through several vegetation zones. You begin in a maple grove and end up, 4.5km later, in a permafrost region where rocks are covered with beautiful moss and lichen. However, that means you'll be going straight up and navigating some tricky spots – not for the out of shape. Count on six hours for the roundtrip adventure.

As in other provincial parks, there is canoe and kayak rental (28 per day) and numerous camping options ($19 to $24), including some wild camping right by the banks of the river and accessible only by canoe. There are also cruises ($23) along the river on a 46-seat boat.

Getting There & Away If you're driving east along Rte 138, head north at St Hilarion and follow the signs to the park (it's about a 35km drive from the 138). If you're in La Malbaie head back west along the 138, then go north at the cut-off for St Aimé des Lacs.

Descente Malbaie

About halfway between La Malbaie and the Parc des Hautes Gorges, you'll come upon this adventure outfit (☎ *439-2265, fax 439-5110, 316 rue Principale)*, just north of St Aimé des Lacs. These gluttons for an adrenaline rush will make sure you get more than your feet wet descending some serious rapids (classes I to III) on the rivière Malbaie. The rafting takes about 2½ hours but there are camping options and longer stays are possible. Count on about $50 for the experience; young ones 10 to 16 get a 50% discount.

Parc du Mont Grand Fords

Yet another great opportunity for top-notch **downhill skiing** is at this park (☎ *665-0095, 877-665-0095,* W *www.quebecweb.com/montgrandfonds, 1000 chemin des Loisirs; admission free, day lift pass adult/student/child 6-15 $28/20/18; open as long as there's snow 10am-3:45pm Mon-Fri, 9am-3:45pm Sat & Sun)*. For downhill enthusiasts there are 14 trails (including two expert), and there's a snowboard park, innertube run and snowsurfing track. Ski instructors are available for consultation and there's an onsite babysitting service. There are also some 160km of cross-country trails (adult/student & child $11/9).

To get to the park, cross over the bridge going east from La Malbaie, turn left (north) to Rivière Malbaie, then follow the blue signs. It's about a 15-minute drive.

ST SIMÉON
pop 1460
There's nothing of much interest in this town, which calls itself an ecological village because of the nearby **Palissades Centre Éco-forestier** (☎ *638-3333,* e *ecovillage@qc.aira.com, 502 rue St Laurent; adult/child $3/2; open 9am-8pm daily June-Sept, 9am-6pm Thurs-Sun Oct)*. At this ecological

forest center you can walk on several trails to admire the unusual geological formations.

The center is 13km from the village itself, east of the turnoff to Rte 170 (which leads to the Saguenay area along the south shore of the rivière Saguenay, and to Chicoutimi). There's a 65-minute ferry service (☎ 638-2856) from St Siméon to Rivière du Loup on the south shore of the St Lawrence (see the Lower St Lawrence chapter for details).

BAIE STE CATHERINE
pop 290
This attractive dot on the map is in many ways Tadoussac's little sister (see the North Shore chapter for information about Tadoussac). A number of the same activities offered in Tadoussac are possible from here, and some of the large whale-watching cruises that depart from Tadoussac make a pick-up stop from Baie Ste Catherine's pier as well.

Things to See & Do

The Groupe Dufour Croisières (☎ 692-0222, 22 Quai St André) offer excursions on boats carrying 300-plus passengers, from $45 per person.

Azimut Aventure (☎ 237-4477, W www.fjord-best.com/azimut, 185 Rte 138) is one of the best places to organize kayak expeditions. They're a friendly, professional bunch and tend to attract a clientele who are serious about their water sports. They offer a range of possible excursions, as well as simple rental ($35/day). They'll take care of transporting you to your point of departure (on either side of the Saguenay if you wish to cruise the fjord, or to Les Escoumins if you're more into whale watching). Alternatively they'll pick you up from a specified location if you leave from Baie Ste Catherine. A memorable, two-day trip to Saguenay's L'Anse St Jean will cost $95.

The main point of interest on this side of the river is the **Pointe Noire Coastal Station**, up the hill from the ferry landing. This whale-study post (☎ *418-237-4383, Rte 138; admission free; open 9am-5pm daily mid-June–mid-Oct)*, where the Saguenay and St Lawrence Rivers meet, has an exhibit, a slide show and films, and an observation

CHARLEVOIX

deck with a telescope for views over the mouth of the rivière Saguenay. This is one of the best places, cruises included, to see belugas. They are often seen in the Saguenay very close to shore, especially when the tide is coming in.

Places to Stay

Accommodations here are fine, but for places to eat we strongly suggest crossing over to Tadoussac!

Camping du Fjord (☎ 237-4230, 610 Rte 138) Tent sites $12. With only 30 sites, this is a comfortably intimate campground, with showers. It's much quieter than Tadoussac's main campground.

Gîte de l'Ancêtre (☎ 237-4040, 888-595-4040, 550 Rte 138) Singles/doubles $30/45. This B&B is run by people proud of their small village and who'll delight in letting you in on local history. They can also set you up on fishing trips or other excursions. Meals are on request too.

Hôtel-Motel Baie Ste Catherine (☎ 237-4271, 877-444-7247, 294 Rte 138) Singles/doubles $50/80. A very decent place (cozy with only 16 rooms), rooms are tastefully done up, plus there's a dining room. In winter it's a popular stop for snowmobilers.

Getting There & Away

A free, ten-minute ferry runs around the clock to/from Tadoussac at the northern end of town. Between 8pm and 10pm weekdays and between 1pm and 8pm Saturday, there's a ferry every 20 minutes; at all other times it runs once or twice an hour.

Saguenay

There are two main areas of this region. The first hugs the rivière Saguenay, close to the fjord, and is composed of tiny, scenic villages on both the north and south sides of the river. The second is an urban, industrialized center with Chicoutimi as its pivot. Both have as their lifeline the majestic rivière Saguenay, fed by Lac St Jean. For information about Sacré Coeur see the North Shore chapter.

The fjord itself is 100km long, stretching from Ste Fulgence, just northeast of Chicoutimi, to Tadoussac. Formed during the last Ice Age, the fjord is the most southern in the Northern Hemisphere. As deep as 270m in some places, the riverbed rises to a depth of only 20m at the fjord's mouth at Tadoussac due to a narrowing of the glacier at that point. This makes the relatively warm, fresh waters of the Saguenay jet out atop the frigid, salt waters of the St Lawrence, leading to some unique marine life. The entire waterway is now under protection. The cliffs, some 500m high, are the real stars of the area, jutting dramatically over the river.

Aside from the spectacular fjord, whale watching dominates the tourist sector in this area. See the North Shore chapter as well as the special section on whale watching in the Facts about Québec chapter for tips on how to get the most out of this exciting activity all the while remaining respectful to the ecology and to the whales themselves. Aside from those show-stopping whales, there is plenty of other marine and bird life to enjoy in this very beautiful stretch of the province.

There are so many choices for boat cruises and kayaking that it's best to read through this section in entirety and plan your destinations according to where the activities that best suit you are offered. If you wish to appreciate the fjord's majesty with a few friends quietly on a small Zodiac, for example, you'll feel cheated out of an experience if you settle on a big cruise boat holding 400 people.

Regardless of where you're headed, if you're going out on the water take a lot of clothes no matter how hot it is on shore. It is always breezy on the rivers and the water temperature here is low, even in July. Also, the waters can become stormy very quickly.

SAGUENAY-ST LAWRENCE MARINE PARK & PARC DU SAGUENAY

These parks overlap somewhat and extend into the Saguenay, Charlevoix and North Shore regions – see sections in this and the North Shore chapters for details on local points of entry.

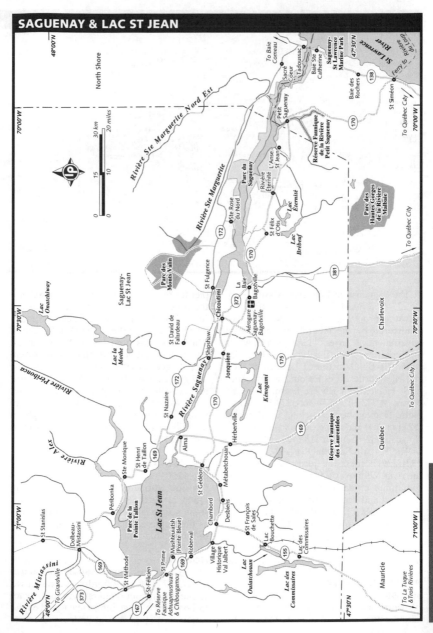

SAGUENAY & LAC ST JEAN

48°00'N

North Shore

70°00'W

St Lawrence River

To Baie Comeau

Tadoussac

Sacré Coeur

Baie Ste Catherine

Saguenay-St Lawrence Marine Park

47°30'N

Ferry to Rivière du Loup

Baie des Rochers

138

St Siméon

To Québec City

70°00'W

Petit Saguenay

170

Rivière Ste Marguerite Nord Est

L'Anse St Jean

Réserve Faunique de la Rivière Petit Saguenay

Rivière Éternité

Parc du Saguenay

30 km

20 miles

15

10

0

0

Rivière Ste Marguerite

Ste Rose du Nord

172

St Félix d'Otis

Lac Éternité

Lac Brébeuf

Parc des Hautes Gorges de la Rivière Malbaie

Lac Ouatchiway

70°30'W

St Fulgence

Parc des Monts Valin

Saguenay-Lac St Jean

381

To Québec City

170

Chicoutimi

La Baie

372

Bagotville

Aéroport Saguenay Bagotville

Charlevoix

70°30'W

St David de Falardeau

Lac la Mothe

Shipshaw

Jonquière

175

Lac Kénogami

To Québec City

St Nazaire

172

Rivière Saguenay

170

Québec

Réserve Faunique des Laurentides

71°00'W

Rivière Péribonca

Ste Monique

St Henri de Taillon

Hébertville

169

Alma

Rivière Ashuapmushuan

Péribonka

169

Parc de la Pointe Taillon

Metabetchouan

St Gédéon

169

Lac St Jean

Chambord

Desbiens

St François de Sales

71°00'W

47°30'N

St Stanislas

Dolbeau-Mistassini

To Girardville

169

Ste Méthode

167

St Prime

Mashteuiatsh (Pointe Bleue)

Roberval

169

Village Historique Val Jalbert

Lac Bouchette

Lac des Commissaires

155

Lac des Commissaires

Mauricie

To La Tuque & Trois Rivières

Rivière Mistassini

48°00'N

373

St Félicien

To Réserve Faunique Ashuapmushuan & Chibougamau

Lac Ouiatchouan

48°00'N

CHARLEVOIX

PARC DU SAGUENAY

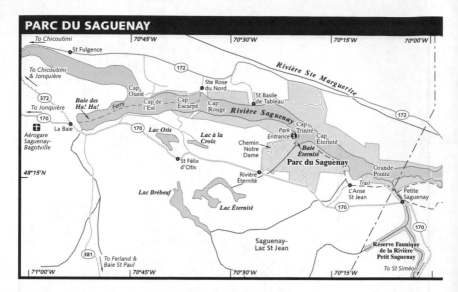

The Saguenay-St Lawrence Marine Park (☎ 235-4703, 800-463-6769) was the first conservation project in Québec to be jointly administered by the federal and provincial governments. It covers 1138 sq km of water and coastline from the Baie des Ha! Ha! (near La Baie) to the St Lawrence, then stretches north to Les Escoumins and south to St Fidèle. Their Rivière Éternité visitor's center (☎ 272-3027, 877-272-5229, 91 chemin Notre Dame) offers canoe and kayak rental ($27 per day) and numerous guided activities. You can camp here for $18 to $25 per night.

The Parc du Saguenay (☎ 272-3008, 877-272-5229) borders the fjord on both sides of the river. With over 100km of splendid trails sometimes opening onto striking views of the fjord and dotted with refuges to spend the night, it's a hiker's delight. This Sépaq-administered park has one of its entrances at Rivière Éternité (☎ 272-1509, 272-3008, 91 chemin Notre Dame). In winter there are frequent ice-fishing excursions in this area.

PETIT SAGUENAY
pop 850
It's worth stopping in this languid village to take the 4km gravel chemin du Quai to the pier for one of the many stunning views onto the fjord. A 10km hiking trail to L'Anse St Jean also starts from here. There are many lovely spots along the rivière Petit Saguenay, which descends from the rivière Saguenay. At the **Site Récréopatrimonial de la Rivière Petit Saguenay** (☎ 272-1169, 877-272-1169, 100 rue Eugène Morin), you can try your hand at salmon fishing (from $57 per person), go canoeing on the relatively calm waters (from $30 per person), or stay overnight in no-frills, rustic, two-to-eight-person cabins ($46 to $127) or in your tent ($17).

L'ANSE ST JEAN
pop 1250
Considered one of the loveliest villages in Québec, this is also the departure point for some scenic cruises along the fjord as well as the home of one of the province's most unforgettable hostels.

Boating
The Croisière Personnalisée Saguenay (☎ 272-2739, W www.fjord-best.com/deesse, 15 rue du Faubourg) offers four types of **motorboat cruises**, including some island exploration and stopovers at Tadoussac or Ste

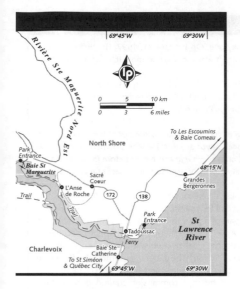

Anne du Rose, on their 24-foot vessel. Aventure Voile et Fjord (☎/fax 272-1200, 415 rue Ste Madeleine) offers personalized **sailing** excursions. Prices at both start at $30.

If you want to get your own oars wet, head to Fjord en Kayak (☎ 272-3024, **W** www .fjord-en-kayak.ca, 4 rue du Faubourg), which offers great excursions from three hours to five days. The staff are fabulous and are also used to dealing with kids. Prices start at $39 for the three-hour tour.

Horseback Riding

Horse lovers will be impressed with the facilities at the Centre Équestre des Plateaux (☎ 272-3231, 31 chemin des Plateaux). Perched on a hilltop is this incredibly peaceful farm and stables – the silence up there is so total it's creepy – which offers equestrian initiation courses and horseback rides through the surrounding nature. There are $10 pony rides for the younger critters, and $45 will get you a half-day excursion through the nearby fields and forest.

Places to Stay & Eat

Auberge Chez Monika (☎ 272-3115, 12 chemin des Plateaux) Dorm beds $10. Teeter-

ing atop a steep hill (even by car it's a challenge and if walking, prepare for a long, tough hike), this is a medicinal plant farm doubling as a hostel. Run like a commune by a multilingual herbalist and her students, there are also comfortable dorm rooms and a shared kitchen. Located in a sublimely peaceful area, this is the place to go for a respite – and to cure your ailing whatcha-macallits. The dreamy though languid surroundings will be heaven to some, a bit too unhurried to others, but memorable to all. The hostel is 4.7km from Rte 170; follow the signs for the Centre Équestre (which is almost next door).

Le Maringoinfre (☎ 272-2385, 212 rue St Jean Baptiste) Mains $11-21; open 5pm-11pm daily May-Oct. There's very fine dining here, where seafood and traditional First Nations dishes reign supreme. Their full-course meals are good deals and run from $17-31.

RIVIÈRE ÉTERNITÉ
pop 550

The town itself is somewhat moribund but there's a lot going on nearby. All the action is closer to the river at the Baie Éternité, the bay several kilometers from the town center (see the Parc du Saguenay map). Toward the river are main entrances to both the Saguenay-St Lawrence Marine Park and Parc du Saguenay (see later), through which are endless opportunities to engage in outdoor activities. Don't miss the **Halte des Artistes**, a free, roadside exhibition of sculptures on the west side of town. It's a drive-through exhibit of giant wood sculptures, some religious-themed, others of animals, and all crafted by locals. The life-size nativity scenes *(crèches)* are certainly a highlight.

In town there are more crèches inside the **Église de Rivière Éternité** (☎ 272-2807, 418 rue Principale; adult/child $5/2; open 9am-7pm daily July & Aug, 12:30pm-7:30pm daily end Nov–mid-Jan), which has some 250 different versions on view.

Another religious site in the area is the 8.5m **Virgin Mary statue**, perched atop Cap Trinité, the peak on the westernmost edge of the Baie Éternité. It looms ominously on

Mutiny in the Monarchy

It started off as a great idea, if a completely kooky one. On January 21, 1997, the first monarchy in North America was established in L'Anse St Jean. It was a municipal monarchy with fewer than 1300 subjects, but a monarchy nonetheless.

A hopeful wind was whipping up the snow in L'Anse St Jean that chilly day, when 68% of the town's village voted in a referendum in favor of being ruled by someone first dubbed the Illustrious Unknown, later self-titled as King Denys I (Denys Premier).

No, this is no joke. Keep reading.

King Denys I was actually Denys Tremblay, an environmental art professor at the Université de Québec in Chicoutimi before he replaced the local mayor as king. He was crowned in an official ceremony on St Jean Baptiste Day in 1997 amid cries of *Vive le roi*! Never before in North American history had someone so humble as a university professor risen to the highest title given by any society!

Politically, the idea was to try a hand at becoming sovereign while still united with both Québec and Canada, an odd attempt at fusing separatism and federalism. L'Anse St Jean was even to have its own flag and royal hymn. Practically, it was part of a plan to boost tourism in the area with a much-touted Millennium Plan. To distinguish L'Anse St Jean, the royal masterminds decided to carve an immense portrait of St Jean Baptiste out of the trees overlooking the village.

The price of putting L'Anse on the map? $1.1 million. The federal government offered up $275,000 (and people have the nerve to say the government squanders the taxpayers' money!) as long as the kingdom paid its share too. The $100,000 the royal commission granted for the project was deemed too much by a citizenry beleaguered by high unemployment.

The tide was starting to turn for Denys I. Many of his initial supporters started to turn against him and refused to support his expensive ideas. The whole affair was taking on Shakespearean dimensions of tragedy and betrayal, but thankfully the situation ended without blood being spilled into the lovely rivière Saguenay. Three years after his ascendancy, the king abdicated in January 2000, ending the continent's first monarchy.

Well, superstitious naysayers would say that he had it coming. After all, he chose to get elected King on the same day (January 21) that King Louis XVI was beheaded in 1793, abolishing monarchy for the first time in France. That's what you get for tempting fate.

one of the highest cliffs on the fjord, protecting the sailors and their boats that pass under it. It was erected in 1881 by Charles Robitaille, who had the previous winter narrowly escaped death after his horse broke through the ice over the waters below the cliff. He vowed to honor the Virgin Mary for having saved his life and commissioned the work from Louis Jobin, a well-known sculptor. It took over a week to cart and assemble the towering figure.

For **cruises** around Cap Trinité (which locals boast is the most beautiful spot on the entire fjord) Croisières du Cap Trinité (☎ 272-2591, 461 rue Principale; adult/child

$20/10) offers twice daily, 90-minute tours on their 96-passenger boat.

STE ROSE DU NORD
pop 430
There's a timelessness about this village that makes it instantly appealing. The rustling of leaves and the sounds of crickets take on added significance in a place like this. Located on the Saguenay River's less-frequented north side, 45km from Chicoutimi, there's a sense of remoteness here that complements the harmony one feels about how the village seamlessly blends in with the surrounding nature.

Aside from wandering around and letting the gentle pace of the village envelop you, there's not much to do here. The **Musée de la Nature** (☎ 675-2348, *199 rue de la Montagne; adult/student $4.50/2; open 8:30am-9pm daily*) is a sinister stuffed-animal exhibit with an even creepier, religious-themed B&B on the top floor (not recommended!). Most local fish and animal species are represented.

Québec Hors Circuit (☎ 545-3737, W www.Quebec-hors-circuits.com) is a Chicoutimi-based operation that organizes **adventure tours** in various regions of the province including several exploratory trips along the Saguenay. They offer a two- and five-day kayak trip from town as well as overnight camping and several nature hikes.

Explo Fjord (☎ 545-3737) has **boat excursions** on eight-person Zodiacs leaving from the pier three times daily. Call to reserve; they have no central office and also depart from other points along the fjord.

Places to Stay & Eat

Camping Descente des Femmes (☎ 675-2581, *154 rue de la Montagne)* Tent sites $12-17. Pitch your tent on a hill here and wake up to a view over the village and onto the fjord. This is one of the loveliest spots in the province for a campground, if you enjoy tranquility. The showers and toilets are in a converted grange, and the owner's a hoot.

La Nichouette (☎ 675-1171, *125 rue des Artisans)* Singles/doubles $60/80. This stately, two-story home has an air of old-fashioned elegance to it. Rooms are ample, and the rest area and dining room are sprawling, with a pretty river view.

Pourvoirie du Cap au Leste (☎ 675-2000, W www.capquebec.com, *chemin du Cap à l'Est)* Singles/doubles from $96/144. Situated at the end of a side road off Rte 172 between Ste Anne du Rose and St Fulgence, this outfitter is a perfect choice as an overnight stop in their sumptuous chalets or as base for outdoor activities. Perched atop a cliff, the spot offers dramatic views over a large stretch of the fjord. Excellent hiking trails snake through the surrounding forest, which has been left to grow wild. They can organize

canoe, kayak, skidoo, snowshoe and other sporting activities. Yet it's the genuine care that the friendly, young staff have in making the environment as pleasant and harmonious as possible that really sets this place above the rest. Be sure to check out the circular garden, where they grow vegetables for their kitchen's superb regional cooking (included in the price of a night's stay).

Café de la Poste (☎ 675-1053, *169 chemin du Quai)* Mains $5-12. This is a charming café with fresh, light meals, purr-inducing home-made pies, and strong espresso. It's nestled in a bend in the road just up from the pier.

ST FULGENCE
pop 2000

Most people stop here for the numerous nature-related attractions.

The **Parc du Cap Jaseux** (☎ 674-9114, *chemin de la Pointe aux Pins; adult/child $4/3; open 8am-9pm daily June-Sept)* is a small (10 sq km) but attractive park with very scenic walking and hiking trails buffered by maple and birch trees. There are explanation panels and botanical exhibits in their main pavilion explaining the area's microclimate. An on-site *campground* ($10 to $18) and several *dormitories* ($20) provide good alternatives for accommodations in unbeatably peaceful surroundings.

Located inside the park is Parcours Aventures (☎ 698-6673, 877-698-6653, W www.parcoursaventures.com), which offer **kayak excursions** from two hours ($25) to seven days ($710).

Another worthwhile stop is the **Centre d'Interprétation des Battures et de Réhabilitation des Oiseaux** (☎ 674-2425, W www.ville.st-fulgence.qc.ca, *100 rue du Cap des Roches; adult/child $5/2.50; open 9am-6pm daily May-Sept)*, a research center dedicated to the region's aviary life forms. Over 250 bird species call the area home. Short trails lead into the woods and nearby wetlands. Taking the free guided tour will increase your appreciation of what you see.

PARC DES MONTS VALINS

Great for year-round of activities is this park (☎ 674-1200, *360 rang St Louis; admission*

$3.50), 17km north of St Fulgence. The region's highest peaks are here, some reaching above 900m. The park's landscape is varied: numerous cliffs; a series of bulbous, oddly shaped mountains; rivers; waterfalls; and long, flat stretches between towering evergreens. Hiking, canoeing and cross-country skiing are perfect here.

LA BAIE
pop 20,900

This small but dynamic city is centered around an aluminum industrial plant. Its industrial look comes as an unpleasant shock if arriving from the pristine fjord, and gives the name Baie des Ha! Ha!, around which the city extends, an ironic, mocking quality. There isn't much of great interest for the visitor here, but a stop is recommended.

After all, you can't miss the **Pyramide des Ha! Ha!** (☎ *697-5050, rue Mgr Dufour; adult/ student $3/2; open 10am-7pm daily June–early Sept, 10am-7pm Sat & Sun early Sept– mid-Oct)*, a gigantic pyramid covered in aluminum-plated triangular plates (donated by Alcan, the area's aluminum giant). This was erected as a monument to people's endurance after the 1996 flood (see 'Black July') by local artist Jean Jules Soucy. There's nothing to see inside but a view of the surrounding area from the top, but it's worth getting a guided tour to hear about the artist's convoluted concepts regarding the symbolism of the structure. Occasional concerts are held inside it.

Located just 200m away is the **Musée du Fjord** (☎ *697-5077, 3346 boul de la Grande Baie Sud; adult/student $6/4; open 8:30am– 6pm Mon-Fri & 10am-5pm Sat & Sun late June–early Sept, 8:30-5pm Mon-Fri & 1pm– 5pm Sat & Sun early Sept–late June)*. There is no permanent exhibit here, as the museum's collection was washed away in the flood. However, their temporary exhibits are innovative, often focusing on an aspect of the local nature. If you plan to visit both the museum and the pyramid, you can buy a combined ticket (adult/student $6/4).

Several kilometers west of La Baie along Rte 170 is the **Bagotville Air Defense Museum** (☎ *677-4000, Rte 170; adult/student*

$4/3; open 9am-5pm daily mid-June–early Sept), on the premises of a sprawling military base. Built during WWII to protect the Alcan aluminum factory and hydroelectric plants in the area, the base became a central part of the NORAD system of US-Canada air defense in 1958. It is still an active training base from where troops are deployed on overseas missions. The mostly French-language museum has displays of technology and missions, and an amusing photo of

---

Black July

Locals refer to that fateful month in 1996 as 'Black July.' That was when part of downtown La Baie was washed away and thousands of homes in that town, in villages along the Saguenay and in Chicoutimi were destroyed in a devastating flood. After 155mm of rain fell in 24 hours, the Saguenay river swelled such that the Baie des Ha! Ha! overflowed into La Baie's downtown sector and got the last laugh. The Saguenay's waters swelled and joined with other inland rivers and lakes. Waters tore apart a bridge and carried away a farm, a gas station, a bank and hundreds of houses. In all, 3000 homes were destroyed in the area, and two children died.

The damages caused by the flood were estimated at $700 million. It also added to the pollution of the bay and the Saguenay river, as 9 million cubic meters of material and debris were dragged into them. The area in La Baie surrounding the present-day Pyramide des Ha! Ha! became completely inundated – it's easy to see where the flooding stopped by noticing where the new-looking houses suddenly end and older-looking ones continue. Today it's hard to imagine the devastation, so thorough has the re-building effort been.

While thousands of people lost their homes along with a lifetime of memories, locals say that a lasting effect of the flood has been a greater sense of cohesiveness between people. A sense of community and togetherness was fostered that will stay strong for a long time.

Queen Elizabeth II in the back hall. Massive CF-18s can be seen taking off on occasion. Guided tours (in English or French) are given at 9:45am and 2pm.

CHICOUTIMI
pop 63,300

This city is quite pleasant thanks to its pedestrianized port area (a magnet for cyclists and skateboarders) and young population (thanks to a university and Cégep). Originally the site of a 1676 fur-trading post, it became in the early 20th century, along with Trois Rivières, the world's pulp and paper capital; the world's largest pulp mill was here. Spread out along steep roads on both sides of the rivière Saguenay, the city's main center is on the south side, along rue Racine Est and the waterfront.

Administratively the city has been fused with Jonquière and is known alternately as Ville de Saguenay, though locals hate the new name.

The tourist office (☎ 698-3167, 800-463-6565) is at 295 rue Racine Est. To surf the Web, head to the very cool Cybernaute (☎ 543-9555) at 391 rue Racine Est ($3.50/hour).

Things to See & Do
La Pulperie (☎ 698-3100, 300 rue Dubuc; adult/student $8.50/6; open 9am-6pm daily late June–early Sept) was once the world's biggest pulp mill. Although it no longer operates, a guided tour and exhibition explains the mill's history and its role in the development of the city. It is located in the area of town dubbed the Bassin, and your tour will include most of the city's main sites, all on the same territory. All tours begin at the Chambre de Commerce (☎ 698-3100), 194 rue Price Ouest.

The tour will also include the **House of Arthur Villeneuve**. In the late 1950s when Monsieur Villeneuve retired as a local barber, he began painting. His depictions of the town and landscape along the river attracted a lot of attention and are now sold and collected around the world. The house, his former home, is a museum known not so much for the paintings it contains but for the painting it is. The entire house has been

painted inside and out like a series of canvases in Villeneuve's bright, naive folk style.

The **Petite Maison Blanche** (Little White House), which held steady against the floods of 1996 and was made famous around the world by news photographs, can also be seen on the same premises.

Across the street is the mid-19th-century **Église Sacré Coeur** (☎ 543-4302, rue Bossé; admission $3.50; open 10am-5pm daily), which contains a small exhibit on local history.

Those with a sweet tooth must stop at **Les Chocolats Lulu** (☎ 549-1203, 1806 boul Saguenay Ouest), on Rte 372 to Jonquière. This chocolate factory sells its wares at much reduced prices, including still-scrumptious 'defects' for a fraction of the usual cost. Try their sugarless chocolate bars – they are surprisingly delectable.

Organized Tours
Visites Forestières (☎ 690-2100, 540-9770) offers original excursions into the forests of the nearby Réserve Faunique des Laurentides to explore the **forestry industry** in Québec. You'll see the loggers in action and will be explained in detail the techniques of cutting and policies of reforestation as well as about the specificity of the local ecosystem. Half-day tours last five hours and cost $30; full-day, nine-hour tours are $60 including lunch and transportation.

Another unique excursion can be had by air. In one of the most reasonably priced **airplane tours** around, Exact Air (☎ 673-3522, chemin Volair) offer 45-minute flights above the fjord for $50 per person; another route flies over the rolling Monts Valin and the area's urban regions taking 30 minutes and costing $30.

From the redeveloped old harbor and market area, **tour boats** depart for trips down the Saguenay River. Croisière Marjolaine (☎ 543-7630) has a 400-seater that clunks down the Saguenay to Ste Rose du Nord. Prices vary from $15 to $35.

Places to Stay
Cégep (☎ 549-9520 ext 258, 534 rue Jacques Cartier Est) Singles/doubles $21/29 with bedding, $17/25 without bedding. Open

year-round, this is an adequate college dormitory 1.5km from the bus station. It's in the sinister gray building to the far left of the college's general entrance.

Auberge Centre Ville *(☎ 543-0253, fax 693-1701, 104 rue Jacques Cartier Est)* Singles/doubles $40/65. This is a good, central, no-frills place.

Hôtel Chicoutimi *(☎ 549-7111, 800-463-7930, 460 rue Racine Est)* Singles/doubles from $65/73. This is a reasonably priced, central and comfortable three-star hotel.

Places to Eat

Rue Racine Est has numerous cafés, bistros and bars. Chain restaurants are mainly on boulevards Talbot and Saguenay.

Bistro La Cuisine *(☎ 698-2822, 387A rue Racine Est)* Appetizers $4-12, mains $8-14. Mussels, pasta and burgers are doled out in a slick, relaxed atmosphere. Their specials are a good value.

La Piazzetta *(☎ 549-4860, 412 boul Saguenay Est)* Mains $7-16. Pizzas are the main attraction here, and they come in a large variety.

La Bougresse *(☎ 543-3178, 260 avenue Riverin)* Appetizers $3-10, mains $14-26. Fine French cuisine is fastidiously prepared and served in elegant surroundings.

Bar Shooters *(☎ 693-1003, 455 rue de l'Hotel Dieu)* At night this pub has a wide selection of beers, a pool table and big screen TV.

Getting There & Away

Intercar buses (☎ 543-1403), at 55 rue Racine Est, connect to Québec City (2½ hours, 5-6 daily), Montréal (6½ hours, 5-6 daily), Jonquière (25 mins, 9 daily), Tadoussac (1¾ hours, 1 daily), Alma (1 hour, 2 daily) and Dolbeau-Mistassini (3½ hours, 2-3 daily). CITS (☎ 545-2487) also runs local buses linking Chicoutimi, Jonquière and La Baie, and has service to Tadoussac. L'Autobus L'Anse Saint Jean (☎ 543-1403) runs a van down the Saguenay to L'Anse St Jean. Autocars Jasmin (☎ 547-2167) runs a van from Chicoutimi to the main towns around Lac St Jean.

Air Canada (☎ 692-0770, 800-630-3299) operates flights from Montréal to Chicou-timi (7-day advance purchase/no advance $419/629, 5 daily). The airport is located at Bagotville.

JONQUIÈRE
pop 57,000

West from Chicoutimi along Rtes 170 or 372, Jonquière is a friendly but nondescript place of limited interest. It is home to the enormous Alcan aluminum smelter and two paper mills. Just south of the city (follow rue Ste Dominique) is Lac Kénogami, surrounded by some 50km of scenic walking trails and several campgrounds.

The closest thing to a downtown core is rue St Dominique between boulevard du Royaume and boulevard Harvey. There are a number of tacky nightclubs, dive bars and some eateries there. From the end of June to early August, the street comes alive most days with street festivals and free, outdoor concerts in the evenings.

The tourist office (☎ 548-4004) is at 2665 boulevard du Royaume.

Set up in a displaced 1912 Presbyterian chapel is the **Centre d'Histoire Sir William Price** *(☎ 695-7278, 1994 rue Price; adult/student $5/4; open 10am-8pm daily mid-June–Aug, 10am-5pm Mon-Fri Sept-mid-June)*. Nicely displayed exhibits go through the history of the city, which Price influenced greatly through the construction of his Price Brothers Company pulp mill (now called Abitibi Consolidated). There are vintage film clips, antiques and old souvenirs, and bilingual explanation panels. The chapel was moved here in 1987 from its original site two blocks away to save it from destruction when local Presbyterians decided to construct a new one.

Worth a gander is the **Pont d'Aluminum** (Aluminum Bridge), bridging both banks of the rivière Saguenay at the end of route du Pont, near the Shipshaw hydroelectric dam. Built in 1950, its weight is one-third that of a comparably sized steel bridge and is apparently the only one of its kind in the world.

Places to Stay

Camping Centre Touristique *(☎ 344-1142, 9000 route Kénogami)* Tent sites $17-25.

Run by Sépaq, this a great campground south of Jonquière, on a small peninsula jutting out into Lac Kénogami. A number of activities are possible here, and canoes, kayaks and bikes are rented out.

Camping Jonquière (☎ 542-0176, 3553-122 chemin du Quai) Tent sites $23-26. There are more facilities here, though it's more crowded. A sandy beach makes it popular.

Cégep (☎ 542-2643, 2505 rue St Hubert) Singles/doubles $20/30 with bedding, $16/22 without bedding. In a very modern and clean college, this is a good bet. During summer, you're likely to run into swarms of English-speaking students from other provinces taking French immersion courses.

Gîte de la Rivière aux Sables (☎ 547-5101, 4076 rue des Saules) Singles/doubles $45/60. This pleasant B&B is located near the quiet banks of the rivière aux Sables, on the opposite side of downtown.

Places to Eat

Rue Ste Dominique is lined with a choice of eateries.

Le Trait d'Union (☎ 547-5525, 2509, rue Ste Dominique) Mains $4-9. A diner by any other name, but the grit is pretty good (smoked-meat sandwiches are their specialty) and very cheap.

La Vilaine (☎ 542-8106, 2166 rue des Étudiants) Mains $6-11. A restaurant-bar popular with a student crowd, it has decent food and, in the bar area, an atmosphere conducive for striking up a conversation.

Lac St Jean

The Lac St Jean region, shown on the Saguenay & Lac St Jean map, refers to the ring of towns surrounding the lake of the same name, whose coastline forms a wobbly, 210km-long circle. Fairly flat, the region is defined almost entirely by the 1053-sq-km lake. It may be less scenic or interesting than neighboring areas, but there are numerous worthwhile attractions.

Lac St Jean is known as the heart of Québécois nationalism and as the province's blueberry and meat pie (tourtière) capital, though all of these elements are found elsewhere in equally large quantities.

Blueberries are such a local trademark, that's what the locals are called – bleuets! In France, blueberries are called myrtilles, and bleuets is not Québécois slang. So where did the word come from? In 1613 Frenchman Samuel de Champlain took a trip up the Ottawa River on which he evidently made lots of munching stops; he started calling the berries bleuets, and it just stuck. A large forest fire in 1870 around Roberval led to an abundance of the berries a few years later, and they started being exported from the region. Locals like to say that the blueberries here are so big and juicy, only three are needed to make a pie.

Activities

Most visitors to the region simply like to drive around the lake. Just as a corner makes people want to peek around it or a long road instills the desire to see what lays at its end, so too has this lake borne the desire to circle it.

Driving is most people's choice, but **cycling** is another favorite. There are 256km of cyclable trails around the lake, together called the Véloroute des Bluets (Blueberry Bike Trail), and nearly every town along the way has some facilities to make the trip easier – rental and repair shops, B&Bs that cater to cyclists, and rest areas. There's even a minivan service (Gilles Girard; ☎ 342-6651) that will transport your baggage around the lake for $20 a trip. For maps and a list of rest areas, B&Bs and campgrounds along the way, contact the Véloroute (☎ 668-0849, 668-4541, Ⓦ www.veloroute-bleuets.qc.ca), at 1671 avenue du Pont Nord, in Alma. If you'd like to join in an annual bike marathon around the lake, the Tour du Lac St Jean (☎ 668-5211, 877-668-5211) is held for three days in early June.

To really experience the lake, instead of driving or biking around it why not try **swimming** across it? Each July, hundreds of hardy souls cross all or part of it (see Roberval for details).

ALMA
pop 31,000

This small, industrial town has a nice museum that serves as a good introduction to the region. The **Musée d'Histoire du Lac St Jean** (☎ 668-2606, 54 rue St Joseph; adult/student $3/2; open 9am-5pm Mon-Fri & 1pm-5pm Sat & Sun late June–Aug) chronicles the colonization of the area, blueberry picking, and the lake's importance in area's social and economic life. There's also a cute, small display of old-fashioned bicycles.

Bicycles can be rented for $20 a day through Vélo Jeunesse (☎ 662-9785, 1691 avenue du Pont Alma). This company donates a percentage of their sales to Tandem (☎ 480-1663), a local social services agency aiding troubled adolescents and their families.

At the end of August, downtown Alma erupts in world rhythms during the **Festival Multicultural Tam Tam Macadam** (☎ 668-5211). Musical artists from Africa and South America as well as local First Nation bands give live performances.

There's a **beach** at the Centre Plein Air les Amicaux (☎ 347-1212; adult/student $3.50/2), 16km north of Alma in Alma (quartier Delisle).

To get across the lake, a daily ferry travels to Roberval (☎ 668-3016; adult/child $19/12, bicycle $3 extra) from the marina, 1385 chemin de la Marina. The ferry operates Tuesday to Sunday; from Tuesday to Saturday, the ferries leave at various times; Sunday it leaves Alma at 8:30am and leaves Roberval at 3pm.

Places to Stay
Halte Touristique Delisle (☎ 347-1370, 3855 avenue Grande Décharge) Tent sites $17. A small campground north of Alma in quiet surroundings, this is your best bet for camping in the area. Call ahead to reserve.

Entre Deux Rivières (☎ 662-5531, 2865 rang Melançon) Singles/doubles $35/50. This decent B&B is 1km from the bicycle trail.

Motel Dequen (☎ 668-0088, 800 avenue du Pont Nord) Singles/doubles $55/75. On a main road with several motels to choose from, this one is adequate for a good night's rest.

PARC DE LA POINTE TAILLON
This Sépaq-run provincial park (☎ 347-5371, 825 rang 3 Ouest; admission $3.50) is the only one of its kind in the region. The highlights here are the long beaches, the best on the lake. There are also 45km of bike trails through wooded areas where you might come across a moose. For the beaches, enter just past the town of St Henri de Taillon. The campground (tent sites $18) is nearer another entrance, at Ste Monique.

PÉRIBONKA
pop 550

Aside from having the best – though only – hostel in the region, this village is also the birthplace of Louis Hémon, author of *Maria Chapdelaine,* one of the best-known Québec novels and a Canadian classic in its own right. Born in France, Hémon lived in this village for several years, and his descriptions of the locals he observed made their way into the book.

The **Musée Louis Hémon** (☎ 374-2177, 700 route Maria Chapdelaine; adult/student $5.50/3.50; open 9am-5pm daily June–Sept) is composed of several buildings, including an exhibition hall and his old residence. Not only does the museum chronicle the author's life and times in Péribonka, but there are also several hundred works of art donated by locals. The grounds are pleasant to wander around as well.

One of the best beaches is at the **Centre Touristique Vauvert** (☎ 374-2746, 472 route Vauvert), in the Dolbeau-Mistassini district but also easily accessed from Péribonka. The 7km beach has free access and is not crowded. A lifeguard is on duty during the day. Near the on-site restaurant are also places to pitch a tent for free, and no one minds people camping out on the beach as long as they're discreet and tidy. To get to the beach from Péribonka, turn left at chemin Vauvert (the first road outside the village, some 5km away) and continue for 10km. From Dolbeau-Mistassini, take route de Ste Marguerite Marie, then follow route de Vauvert all the way to the end.

Places to Stay & Eat

Auberge Île du Repos (☎ 347-5649, 🖃 *ilerepos@ globetrotter.net, 105 route Île du Repos)* Tent sites $15, dorm beds $17/19 member/ nonmember, singles/doubles from $45. Taking up an entire little island between Ste Monique and Péribonka, this HI resort features hostel dorms, kitchen facilities, private chalet rooms, camping, a rather pricey restaurant, bar with 'name' live music (also pricey) and a beach with swimming in murky water. There's no public transportation but it's popular with Québécois looking for some rest and recreation. The atmosphere depends a lot on who the other guests are.

La Volière (☎ 374-2360, 200 4-ème avenue) Mains $9-14. This odd little restaurant/B&B is famed for its tasty and heavy meat tourtières, made with three different meats. Definitely try their bean and barley soup. Decent doubles upstairs go for $45.

DOLBEAU-MISTASSINI
pop 15,400

Originally two communities now amalgamated, this area is heavily industrialized. The omnipresent smokestacks make a sometimes dramatic backdrop, sometimes a frightening one, particularly at sunset when they're set aglow.

The tourist office (☎ 276-7646) is in a lonely kiosk at 257 boulevard des Pères. Behind it is a shop called **Les Gâteries du Lac** (☎ 276-3000, 255A boul des Pères) selling chocolate products of the nearby Trappist monastery (see 'Chocolate-Dipping Monks').

To visit the **Notre Dame de Mistassini Monastery** (☎ 276-0491, 100 route des Trappistes; admission free), head 7km north of Dolbeau-Mistassini on the road toward St Eugène d'Argentenay/St Stanislas. There's a small gift shop but not much to see on the grounds themselves; the monastery does not encourage tourists unless they are male pilgrims who intend on staying for several days of meditation. This was the fourth Trappist monastery in Canada, built in 1892-93, and is affiliated with the Notre Dame du Lac head monastery in Oka.

GIRARDVILLE
pop 1350

People come to this small village, 39km northwest of Dolbeau-Mistassini, for only one thing: adventure. Aventuraid (☎ 258-3529), at 2395 rang de la Pointe, can ensure you a good, wet time **canoeing** or **kayaking** on the rivers nearby. There are some rough rapids to set the adrenaline in action – most visitors take a dunk at some point. The owner, Gilles Granal, inspires immediate confidence with his rugged appearance and expert control of the sometimes tough terrain; you'd think he was born in the nearby forests and raised by wolves, not in Marseille, as he was. In winter they also provide snowshoeing, skiing and snowmobile excursions. Count on paying about $35 for a half-day trip, though excursions can be as long as two weeks. They can also set you up with accommodations.

There's also a very nice walking trail (5km) here, which has great views onto the

Chocolate-Dipping Monks

Trappist monks are about the last people you'd expect to be making chocolates. Something refined and serious like cheese or even wine, OK, but something as fraught with frivolity, as tinged with decadence as chocolates?

It turns out that the monks at the Notre Dame de Mistassini Monastery have been engaged in the business since WWII, when they took over a bankrupt local business in an effort to generate funds for their survival. It caught on, their products have become known across Québec, and now about a dozen monks work full-time making them.

Still, visiting the almost clinically austere monastery gives little indication that somewhere within are hundreds of chocolate roosters and bunnies and lollipops in the making. Their most famous product is the chocolate-covered blueberry bar, a local delicacy also made by other chocolate makers throughout the region and in Charlevoix. These start appearing only around late July.

rivière Mistassini. Start from the **Domaine de la Pinède** (☎ 258-3345, *2235 rang St Joseph Nord; admission $3*).

Camping Lac des Coudes (☎ 258-3261, *2092 rang St Joseph Nord*) is a good campground near the hiking trails and activities. Tent sites cost $8 to $17.

ST FÉLICIEN
pop 11,000

This pleasant little town boasts a quirky park opposite the church on Rte 169, filled with statues of everything from Jesus to a black-spotted dog. With a fountain and a view onto the lake, it's a pleasant, if eccentric, place for a stroll.

The **Zoo Sauvage** (☎ 679-3647, 800-667-5687, *2230 boul du Jardin; adult/child 12-17/child 2-11 $18/12/6; open 9am-6pm daily mid-May–mid-Oct*) is a treat for the kids. You ride around in a caged car-train to see bears, cougars and other wild animals in their 'natural' habitat, get your feet wet visiting a beaver's den and get an up-close look at a polar bear through glass. Arrive well before closing time and count on at least 2½ hours.

The tourist office (☎ 679-9888) is at 1209 boulevard Sacré Coeur. Rte 167, the road that leads to the Réserve Faunique Ashuapmushuan and Chibougamou, starts here.

RÉSERVE FAUNIQUE ASHUAPMUSHUAN

This wildlife reserve (☎ 256-3806, 800-665-6527, *km 33 Rte 167; admission $3.50; open 7am-9pm daily May–Sept*) is mainly frequented by fishers but offers a great alternative as a place to stay the night or to enjoy the outdoors. One of the province's least-visited reserves, its 4487 sq km features wild scenery and the beautiful rivière Ashuapmushuan, a main artery of the historic fur trade. There are 1200 lakes here and a nice waterfall, Chute des Chaudières. You can rent canoes as well as kayaks ($28 per day), go on guided excursions, or just enjoy the peace and quite in one of their *campgrounds* ($19 to $24) or lakeside rustic *cabins*, a great deal at $25 per person.

ST PRIME
pop 2700

One of the nicest towns in the region, St Prime offers one of the best access points to the lake and is close to the interesting Innu reserve Mashteuiatsh (see below).

At **Vélo Touristes** (☎ 256-8242, *14-ème avenue*), right at the marina, you can rent boats of various sizes, paddleboats and bicycles. There's also a beach nearby and a place to pitch a tent ($10). The lake views here are among the most scenic in the region.

At the **Musée du Cheddar** (☎ 251-4922, *148 15-ème avenue; adult/student $6/5; open 9:15am-5:30pm daily June-Sept*) there's some sampling involved in a guided tour of what has been a cheese-producing factory since 1895. It's worth stopping in, even if it's just to buy some of their delicious products. They also double as a tourist information office and are used to answering queries from wayward travelers.

Places to Stay & Eat

Chez Claudie (☎ 251-1108, e enseignesabrina@ qc.aira.com, *549 rue Principale*) Singles/doubles $45/55. On the main road, next to a diner and bar, this B&B's decent rooms are fine for a brief stay.

Mi-Rage (☎ 251-1327, *13 14-ème avenue*) Appetizers $2-7, mains $3-12. In town are basically burger and *poutine* joints, but this place has the best variety, with spaghetti, rib steaks, seafood and vegetarian dishes. It's right at the marina and the surrounding area is pleasant to walk around.

MASHTEUIATSH (POINTE BLEUE)
pop 1950

The residents of this reserve call themselves the Pekuakamiulnuatsh ('the Indians of Lac St Jean') but it's simpler to remember that they're part of the Innu (Montagnais) nation. Many residents have retained some of their nomadic traditions by going on month-long winter hunting trips in the forests.

This is one of the best-organized First Nation reserves in terms of tourism potential. The **Musée Amérindien de Mashteuiatsh** (☎ 275-7494, w *www.autochtones*

CHARLEVOIX

Art gallery, Québec City

Flying the fleur-de-lis, Québec's flag

View from the river, Tadoussac

Thar' she blows, Tadoussac

Marcel Gagnon's concrete statues, Ste Flavie

All aboard for whale watching, Tadoussac

.com/musee_amerindien, 1787 rue Amishk; adult/student $6/4.50; open 10am-6pm daily mid-May–mid-Oct, 9am-noon & 1pm-4pm Mon-Fri mid-Oct–mid-May) is a well-designed exhibit with multimedia displays on the history and way of life of the Pekuakamiulnuatsh.

At **Tipi** *(☎ 275-5593, 2204 rue Ouiatchouan; adult/student $5/3; open 9:30am-6pm Mon-Sat & noon-6pm Sun May–mid-Oct)* you get a guided tour of a reconstructed native village. There's also a good arts and crafts souvenir shop on site, and they sometimes offer camping in birch-bark teepees. The staff here can answer general questions and help you find a local B&B.

The **Centre d'Interpretation de la Traite des Fourrures** *(☎ 275-7770, 1645 rue Ouitchouan; adult/child $4/3; open 10am-6pm daily late May–Sept)* gives a good idea of what an old-time fur trading station looked like. Five generations of traders and crafters have used this home to fashion fur clothes and crafts. They will also prepare a traditional First Nations meal if reserved in advance.

***Plage Camping Robertson** (☎ 275-1375, 2202 rue Ouiatchouan)* Tent sites $14-21. This sizeable, very pleasant campground right on the lakeshore has a beach (with lifeguard) and an outdoor game area for kids. There's also on-site kayak rental.

To get to the reserve from St Prime, follow the lakeshore road, rue Ouitchouan, for 6km – it's a faster and more interesting drive than along Rte 169.

ROBERVAL
pop 11,500
This nondescript town, 8km from Mashteuiatsh, is good for stocking up on supplies or as a base from which to take a pleasure cruise on the lake.

Since 1954 the city has hosted the **Traversée Internationale du Lac St Jean** (☎ 275-2851, web www.traversee.qc.ca), a 32km race in which hardy participants from around the world test their stamina and swim across the lake to Péribonka. (There are also 1km, 2km, 5km and 10km races for the mere mortals.) Considered one of the most physically challenging sporting com-petitions in the world, it's a very popular event and draws thousands of spectators.

Les Voiles du Lac St Jean (☎ 275-5208, croisierevoile@hotmail.com), at 854 rue Arthur, offers a number of **sailing** excursions, usually two to three hours in length, for $24 to $35. The Club Nautique Roberval (☎ 275-2574, W www.gitt.qc.ca), at the marina, also offer a number of cruises.

A daily ferry plies the lake to Alma; see that section for details.

VILLAGE HISTORIQUE VAL JALBERT
This is not a real village per se, but a ghost town come to life. Along with Village d'Antan in Drummondville, this is Québec's only other reconstructed village *(☎ 275-3132, 888-675-3132, Rte 169; adult/child 7-14/ child under 7 $12/5/free; open 9am-5pm daily mid-May–mid-June, Sept & Oct; 9am-7pm daily mid-June–Aug)*. Run by Sépaq, it re-creates life at the beginning of the 20th century in a town revolving around the pulp and paper industry. A pulp factory was opened here in 1901 and a little village grew around it, until it – and the village itself – was closed in 1927. It lay decomposing until the 1970s when conservation efforts began.

Today it's possible to visit the village and become a citizen of the past. There are many activities to choose from, and a lot of nature to see at the same time. As you visit the remains of the old mill, the old religious school and log dwelling houses, guides in period costume explain the history and really get into the act, singing old folk tunes, waving rulers like the strict old schoolteachers used to do and carting logs for a fire.

There are also a few waterfalls to see along the **walking** trails, the most impressive being the 72m Chute Ouiatchouan – a real stunner. There is even one incredible and well-marked 30km **hiking** trail from Val Jalbert to Lac Bouchette, farther south. There are overnight cabins ($23 per person) and rustic campgrounds ($19) along the way.

Activities like theatrical shows, symposiums and concerts are put on periodically throughout the summer.

The village has an on-site restaurant and many choices of accommodations. The *campground* ($20 to $26) has all facilities and room for 170 tents or campers. Mini *chalets* ($54) can hold up to four people and are equipped with a fridge and small stove – bring your sleeping bag. The *hotel* (singles/doubles $67/79) has private baths. There are also fully equipped log *cabins* ($102/night, $550/ week) for four people, which have two bedrooms, kitchen, bathroom and TV.

There is bike rental (☎ 275-7967) just before the main entrance ($6/hour, $25/ eight hours).

LAC BOUCHETTE
pop 1350

Twenty-six kilometers south of the town of Chambord along Rte 155 is this lovely town, which spreads out over both banks of the quaint Lac Ouiatchouan. On the west bank, across the bridge, lies the town's driving force, the **Ermitage St Antoine** (☎ 348-6344, W *www.st-antoine.org, 250 route de l'Ermitage; admission free; open 7am-11pm daily mid-Mar–Dec).* St Francis of Assisi is the patron saint of this Capucin monastery (which began as a chapel in 1907), a major Québec pilgrimage site and religious tourist attraction. Capucin monks are followers of a rather obscure branch of the Franciscans, founded by St Francis.

Sure, it has its 'religious Las Vegas' side (happy monk on huge roadside poster welcoming you, motorized cart hauling tourists around to snap photos, gaudy souvenir shop with a big Visa sign in the window). But the monastery is really a fascinating place, much more pleasant and, er, affirming than the basilica at Ste Anne de Beaupré. Much of this has to do with the scenic, peaceful surroundings and the series of walking trails around the area. Along these paths you'll come across statues, nativity scenes, outdoor confessionals, and even a miniature replica of the grotto in Lourdes! On one hill, the life of Jesus is depicted in a series of statues, some of which are missing limbs or heads.

Inside the small museum you can learn about all the apparitions of the Virgin Mary throughout the world and see an interesting collection of Virgin Mary statues and reproductions from different countries. You can also symbolically walk in St Francis of Assisi's steps in a cleverly designed exhibit which uses alpinism as a parallel to the steps needed to be made on the road to enlightenment, mainly reflection and self-questioning.

Accommodations are available on-site, though they tend to be filled up with elderly pilgrims in search of this elusive wisdom. Singles/doubles in simple *cabins* range from $32/38 to $46/56.

DESBIENS
pop 1175

A settlement has existed here since at least the 17th century, when the Innu (Montagnais) lived here. The first European to set foot in these parts was a Jesuit named Jean de Quen, who hoped to convert the natives to the 'right' religion (he also renamed Lac Piekouagami after his patron saint, into Lac St Jean). A full mission was set up in 1665, and in 1676 it became a fur trading post called Métabetchouane. After becoming part of the Hudson's Bay Company in 1830 the mission flourished until its closure in 1879, following a change in European fashion taste, when beaver skin garments had become *passé.*

The **Centre d'Histoire et d'Archéologie de la Métabetchouane** (☎ 346-5341, 243 rue Hébert; adult/child $4/2; open 10am-6pm daily late June–early Sept) is arguably the most interesting museum in Lac St Jean. It depicts the history of regional population and settlement, and displays many artifacts (up to 5500 years old) discovered in archeological digs in the area. There is a re-creation of a fur trading post general store. There are also temporary exhibits of local artists. The staff here can also set you up in local B&Bs.

Also highly worth a stop is **Trou de Fée** (☎ 346-1242, 7-ème avenue; adult/child $8/5; open 9am-5:30pm daily mid-June–early Sept) – if you want to descend into a 68m-deep hole, that is. Before being lowered into this underground cave to explore its unique geological structures, you follow a guided tour on a very scenic 2km trail along the rivière Métabetchouane, with its several cascades. Bring warm clothing. This tour is not recommended for claustrophobics or children under 4.

Places to Stay & Eat
Camping Plage Desbiens *(☎ 346-5436, Rte 169)* Tent sites $15-22. This large campground off the main road has a sandy beach and all the facilities.

Chez Mes 2 Fils *(☎ 346-1087, fax 849-7857, 1229 rue Hébert)* Singles/doubles $55/60. These friendly folks are used to accommodating cyclists and their gear in their comfy, smoke-free home – and to serving up healthy breakfasts.

Restaurant Desbiens *(☎ 346-1106, 1290 rue Hébert)* Mains $8-14. This is a fairly run-of-the-mill restaurant with the usual assortment of fish, meat and pasta dishes, but there's something to please everyone.

North Shore & Île d'Anticosti

☎ 418

The North Shore *(Côte Nord)* is composed of two large regions, Manicouagan (stretching from Tadoussac to just east of Godbout) and Duplessis (east to the Labrador border). Statistics here are a bit overwhelming. The two regions together encompass an awesome 328,693 sq km (the size of New Zealand, Belgium and Switzerland together) and 1250km of coastline. In this vast expanse live only some 106,800 hardy souls (1.4% of Québec's population), almost all along the coast, making the area's population density a meager 0.3 persons per sq km.

The farther east you go, the greater the distance between villages, the fewer people, the deeper the isolation and the wilder the nature. Inland is a no-man's land of hydroelectric power stations, outfitter resorts, dense forest and a labyrinth of rivers. This part of the Canadian Shield was heavily glaciated, resulting in a jumble of lakes and rivers; all of the latter flow south toward the St Lawrence River or east toward the sea. Relatively flat, the land rarely rises higher than the plateaus 500m to 900m above sea level (the Groulx Mountains, north of Baie Comeau, being the exception).

Whale watching is the buzzword in the area around Tadoussac, where the rivière Saguenay flows into the St Lawrence. While a spectacular activity in and of itself, it has, sadly, eclipsed the endless other possibilities for adventure tourism here.

Rte 138 is the spinal cord of the area, yet 138 itself reaches only as far as Natashquan, birthplace of famous nationalist singer-songwriter Gilles Vigneault. The 300km more to Blanc Sablon can be navigated only by boat or plane. Outside of Tadoussac, the region is relatively free of tourists, although there is much to see. Aside from a dull stretch between Forestville and Baie Comeau, the region is also brutally attractive. Visitors will have no trouble finding needed services, but the farther east you go, the less the official tourism infrastructure matters and the more down-to-earth person-to-person contacts get things done.

A definite highlight of the region is the Mingan Archipelago, a series of islands stretching from Longue Pointe de Mingan to east of Havre St Pierre. Their fanciful

Highlights

- Whale watching!
- Walk along the sand dunes in Tadoussac
- Cruise around the Mingan Archipelago at sunset
- Count white-tailed deer on Île d'Anticosti
- Say you've been to the end of the road at Natashquan
- Boat-hop along Québec's easternmost extreme

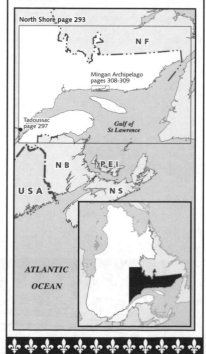

North Shore page 293

Mingan Archipelago pages 308-309

Tadoussac page 297

Gulf of St Lawrence

N F

N B

P.E.I

USA

N S

ATLANTIC OCEAN

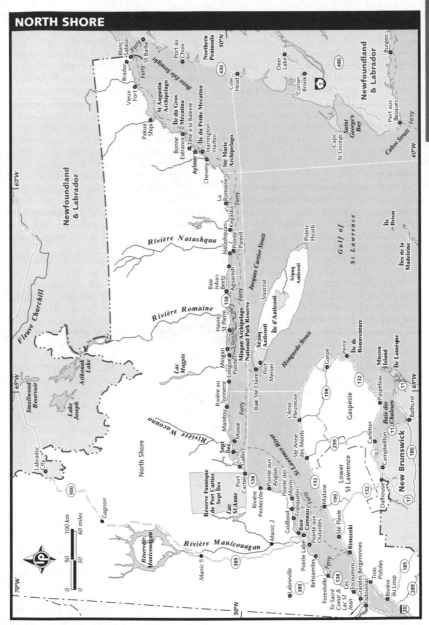

NORTH SHORE

geological shapes and the fact that they are a magnet for over 200 species of bird, including the striking-looking puffin, makes the archipelago one of Québec's major draws.

The region from Tadoussac to Natashquan is somewhat confusingly referred to as Haute Côte Nord (Upper North Shore) and east of Natashquan as Basse Côte Nord (Lower North Shore), in reference to their general elevation.

English is little spoken here, though tourist information offices should be able to answer your questions.

History

The region was inhabited by Native Canadians long before Basque, French and British fishermen frequented the region during fishing and whaling expeditions. Some of the oldest archeological findings in the US and Canada have been discovered in this area, some of which are between 7000 and 8250 years old. These have proved that ancestors of modern-day Inuits called the area home long before Jacques Cartier arrived (he dubbed the area of modern-day Havre St Pierre *Pointe aux Esquimaux*). Cartier even found an old French fisherman named Thiennot who had settled alone near what is today Natashquan.

Though the area did not become generally inhabited until the mid-19th century, a number of fur trading posts were set up in the area in the 17th century, in collaboration with the Algonquins living in the Manicouagan region. Tadoussac became the site of the first European fur trading post north of Mexico. The fur trade was the only interest on the part of France in this part of the Domaine du Roy, which in the 17th century also covered the Saguenay and Lac St Jean regions.

Hunting and fishing were the big businesses here until forestry redefined the region's existence in the 19th century. It was partly British forestry magnate William

Jacques Cartier

Price's pressuring of the government to break the British-owned Hudson Bay Company's stronghold on the region's resources that pushed Québec rulers to start colonizing the region in the 1840s. The Innus were pushed farther northeast. In 1859 the government placed a time limit on the Hudson Bay Company's exclusive rights to the hunting and fishing territories of the regions and later nationalized them – then promptly sold or rented them out again to rich American and Canadian businessmen who exploited the lands for profit.

As this territory opened up, a wave of Îles de la Madeleine inhabitants escaping poor conditions arrived to found several villages in Duplessis. In the 1870s immigrants from Newfoundland also moved to the Lower North Shore, making it an Anglophone-dominated area.

Forestry was the mainstay of the area in the 20th century. In order to feed the printing presses in Chicago and Boston, sawmills opened up, and the slashing of the inland forest was underway. Baie Comeau was founded partly to deliver on the high American demand for paper products.

Since the late 1950s the main industry here has become hydroelectricity. It took 30 years to complete, but the Manic-Outardes eight-megastation hydroelectric complex produces more than 6500 megawatts of electricity for the province, putting Québec among the world's leaders in hydroelectricity technology. Iron ore and mineral mines are mainly in the far north, near Fermont and Schefferville.

Today the region's survival hinges on the pulp and paper, aluminum, and mineral and metal mining industries, with tourism (especially in the area near the rivière Saguenay) playing an ever greater role in the economy. The Innus (Montagnais), who live in nine communities in the region, also play an active role in the cultural, political and economic life of the region.

Special Events
March & April
La Cabane à Sucre – Sugar shack fever hits the region and drenches everything in maple syrup. Call ☎ 877-236-4551 to find out where activities are being held.

June
Iceberg Festival – Held in Blanc Sablon every year to mark the dramatic passage of icebergs through the Strait of Belle Isle, the festival has concerts, fairs and general merrymaking.

Festival de la Chanson – In early June, this four-day song festival held in Tadoussac regroups singers and songwriters from across Québec.

July
Powwow – During the third weekend of July, the Innus hold their annual festival (☎ 233-2509) in Essipit. Music, traditional dance, and a moccasin race are part of the fun symbolically celebrating the return from the summer hunt.

Summer Festival – Mid-summernight as celebrated in Aguanish. For information call ☎ 533-2288.

August
Festival des Acadiens – Mid-month, this fest (☎ 538-2112) in Havre St Pierre celebrates Acadian culture.

Fête Nationale des Montagnais – Betsiamites comes alive on August 15th for this Innu festival (☎ 567-2265) of song, dance and sporting events.

TADOUSSAC
pop 910
This tiny village explodes with life in the summer, when thousands of people visit to catch sight of the main tourist draw here – whales. However, unlike other single-purpose tourist towns (Percé, for example), Tadoussac has much more to offer. Walks along sand dunes, boat trips up the rivière Saguenay, sea kayaking expeditions, several-day hikes and other adventure sports engage visitors. The attractive town (marred by tacky signs with whale fins advertising cruises) is also very good socially, with a wild youth hostel and several bars that ensure a great time relaxing or letting it all hang out after a day's activities.

Tadoussac, which in the Innu language means 'nipples' (no doubt referring to rocky shapes atop the surrounding hills), became the first fur trading post in European North America in 1600, eight years before the founding of Québec City. Here was the first permanent house built by Europeans north of Mexico. Yet even before that, Basque whalers had come here for frenzied hunting. The plankton rich waters, around the area where the dark hues of the Saguenay spill into the green-grays of the St Lawrence, have long been the perfect environment for feasting whales (see the whale watching special section in the Activities chapter).

When the Hudson Bay Company closed its doors in the mid-1850s, Tadoussac was briefly abandoned, only to be revived as a resort with the building of the garish Hôtel Tadoussac in 1864. The town was also reinvented as an important cog in the pulp and paper wheel, spun enthusiastically by British industrialist William Price.

At the beginning of June, the four day **Festival de la Chanson de Tadoussac** (☎ 235-1421, W www.fjord-best.com/festival-tadoussac) brings top-name acts from the province for kick-ass concerts ($10 to $20).

The tourist information office (☎ 235-4744, e ville@tadoussac.com, 197 rue des Pionniers) is open 8am to 9pm daily June through August, and 8:30am to 5pm weekdays September to May. All the sites and boat trips operate seasonally, and November to May, Tadoussac shuts down. If the place is too crowded for your liking in summer, consider using Baie Ste Catherine (see the Charlevoix, Saguenay & Lac St Jean chapter) as your base – it lies just across the Saguenay.

If approaching from the east, enter the village via rue des Forgerons if the line for the ferry is too long and blocks the other, more central turnoff.

Things to See & Do
The **Centre d'Interprétation des Mammifères Marins** (CIMM; ☎ 235-4701, W www.gremm .com, 108 rue de la Cale Sèche; adult/child $5.50/3; open 9am-8pm daily mid-June–late Sept, noon-5pm daily mid-May–mid-June & late Sept–late Oct) gives visitors excellent background information on local sea creatures. There are video clips and exhibits, and you

can listen to whale songs. It is located near the marina, and excellent, easy walking trails start from there around Pointe de l'Islet.

Chauvin Trading Post (*Maison Chauvin;* ☎ *235-4657, 157 rue de bord de l'Eau; adult/ student $3/2; open 9am-9pm daily mid-June–mid-Sept, 9am-5pm daily late May–mid-June & mid-Sept–early Oct*) is a replica of the country's first fur trading post and offers some history on the first transactions between Native Canadians and Europeans. A costumed guide will talk about the town's history, admitting bitterly how an English William Price was the founder of modern-day Tadoussac. Exhibits are in French, but ask for an English guidebook.

Built in 1747 by the Jesuits, **La Vieille Chapelle** (☎ *235-4324, rue du bord de l'Eau; adult/children $2/0.50; open 9am-9pm daily mid-June–mid-Oct*) is one of the oldest wooden churches in the country. It is also known as the Indian Chapel. The cemetery next door is worth a look too.

The **Pisciculture** (*Fishbreeding Station;* ☎ *235-4569, 115 rue du Bateau Passeur; adult/ child $5/4; open 10am-6pm mid-May–Aug*) is operated by the provincial government to provide fish for the restocking of Québec's salmon streams and rivers. You can see its operations and get a firsthand look at the fish. Some of the Parc du Saguenay's walking trails begin from behind the hatchery.

The specialized **Musée Maritime de Tadoussac** (☎ *235-4657, 145 rue du Bateau Passeur; adult/child $2/1; open 9am-5pm daily mid-June–early Sept*) outlines the maritime history of the area and of shipping on the St Lawrence with models, photographs and other artifacts.

Hiking

There are some fine green areas around town for hiking. From Pointe de l'Islet, a peninsular park at the southern edge of town, it's possible to spy whales from the shore. A walking trail beginning and ending from the rue du bord de l'Eau leads around the peninsula.

One of the entrances to the **Parc du Saguenay** is located in Tadoussac (see the Charlevoix, Saguenay & Lac St Jean chapter

for more information). Its **Maison des Dunes Interpretation Centre** (☎ *235-4238; adult/child $3.50/1.50; open 9am-5pm daily June–mid-Oct*) lies 5km out of town at the end of rue des Pionniers. There are trails down to the beach and to a small waterfall. An exhibit explains that what everyone calls 'dunes' in the area are actually marine terraces, which are formed by waves, not by wind as dunes are. Catch a screening of the very worthwhile 24-minute film by Richard Bach, *Mighty River*, a stunningly animated and lyrical work about the St Lawrence ecosystem.

There are many places in this area to climb atop the 'dunes' and suddenly find yourself on lunar-like terrain. You can also walk back to the village along a coastal trail, but only at low tide. A stroll on the shore here is virtually like being at the ocean, with salt air, seaweed and marine creatures to observe. Climbing the lovely sand hills along the beach is an aerobic challenge. The center has detailed maps of the entire park with hiking trails, camp sites etc.

For great views over the confluence of the rivers, take the trails around the hill beginning across the street from the Pisciculture (see Things to See & Do). There's free parking. Ask at the information office about longer trails, running north, that begin across the street from the Pisciculture. The Parc du Saguenay also includes the land around Lac de l'Anse à l'Eau, the lake just north of town. One of the walking trails beginning at the Pisciculture leads along the edge of this lake, which also provides good **swimming**.

The 42km hiking trail to Baie Ste Marguerite, which requires overnighting in the refuge huts, also begins at this lake. Contact the Parc du Saguenay before heading out.

Whale Watching

Even if you tried to, you couldn't possibly miss the multitude of different cruises and whale-watching expeditions on offer around town. Everywhere you turn – in a motel, gift shop or even café – there are tickets for sale. Check out the possibilities carefully – you want to get the kind that's right for you. The smaller the boat, the better. But for those who get too chilly or feel safer with crowds,

TADOUSSAC

PLACES TO STAY & EAT
2 Camping Tadoussac
4 Café du Fjord
5 La Maison Majorique
   Youth Hostel
7 La Maison Clauphi
10 Café Bohème
11 La Galouïne
15 Hôtel Tadoussac

OTHER
1 Bus Stop
3 Musée Maritime de
   Tadoussac (Maritime
   Museum)
6 Croissières AML
8 Tourist Information Office
9 City Hall

12 La Vielle Chapel (Indian
   Chapel)
13 Pisciculture (Fishbreeding
   Station)
14 Public Toilet
16 Chauvin Trading Post
17 Le Gibard
19 Centre d'Interprétation
   des Mammifères Marins
   (CIMM)

To Route 172,
Grandes Bergeronnes,
Les Escoumins & Baie Comeau

Rue des Frênes
Rue des Ormes
Rue des Bouleaux
Rue des Bois Francs
Rue du Bateau Passeur

1 Bus Stop
2 Camping

de la Montagne

Lookout

0   100   200 m
0   100   200 yards

Rue des Forgerons

Champlain
Champlain
Pont Gravé
Père Labrosse
de la Falaise

Lac de
l'Anse à l'Eau

Ruisseau Lac de l'Aqueduc

Rue des Jésuites
Morin
6
8
Rue des Pionniers
5
7
10
11
Hôtel de Ville
Chauvin
Jacques
Cartier
des Montagnais

12
9
Rue des Pionniers

To Maison Alexis,
Domaine des Dunes
& Maison des Dunes
Interpretation Centre

To Sacré Coeur
& Baie Ste
Marguerite
(43km)

138

Rue du Bateau Passeur

3
4

Rue du Bord de l'Eau

Trail

13
14   Trail

Rue Coupe de l'Islet

Lookout

Saguenay

15
16
17

Rue du Bord de l'Eau

Baie Tadoussac

Rue de la
Câle Sèche

18

19

Marina

Ferry to Baie Ste Catherine

Rivière Saguenay

Lookout

Pointe de l'Islet

St Lawrence River

big boats are the way to go. Only some of the choices are listed here. For each, count on at least $35 for a three-hour trip. See the special whale watching section in the Activities chapter for tips on how to make the most of your experience.

Croisières AML (☎ 235-4642, 177 rue des Pionniers) is the largest company in town and operates the largest boats, though they have Zodiacs as well. Count on at least $45 to $60 for adults, $20 to $35 for children. Tayaout (☎ 235-1056, W www.tayaout.com, 148 rue du bord de l'Eau), at the marina, is a better bet for the adventurous, offering whale-watching expeditions in sea kayaks.

Captain Claude Morneau runs Impacct (☎ 877-904-1964, e capitaineclahud@hotmail .com), a small charter company. He takes people in groups no larger than 12 on his 80-person fishing vessel and promises relaxed, personalized tours. Locally considered a black sheep for his strong critique of the big whale-watching companies, this knowledgeable, charismatic fisherman refuses to chase whales. Because of the decrease in the number of whales around Tadoussac, he mostly offers trips up the Saguenay to see the fjords. He charges $10 an hour per person, usually for three- to four-hour trips, but he's very flexible and open to spontaneity. He can also put you in contact with other fishermen along the North Shore and in Gaspé who can take you out on a personalized excursion.

Biking & Surfbiking

Nature Aventure (☎ 235-4303, 177 & 188 rue des Pionniers), the folks who run La Maison Clauphi (see Places to Stay), rent bikes and surfbikes (a super-cool paddleboat-like contraption that lets you bike on water), and organize a number of biking activities on land and in water.

Places to Stay

Camping Tadoussac (☎ 235-4501, 428 rue du Bateau Passeur) Tent sites $21. During summer its 200 sandy sites are full nightly; arrive early in the morning to get one. It's located on Rte 138, 2km from the ferry.

La Maison Majorique Youth Hostel (☎ 235-4372, 800-461-8585, 158 rue du Bateau Passeur) Dorm beds $15/18 members/ nonmembers, doubles $39, tent sites $6; open year-round. This big, red-roofed house is more than a hostel – it's an emporium of youthful energy. Anything goes here, and it usually does. Good, informal banquet-style dinners cost $6. Breakfast is cooked or you can use the kitchen yourself. The attached bar barely contains the eruptions of spontaneous dancing when a local band brings out the harmonica or spoons. It offers a minibus service ($7 for two) northwest to hiking trails up the Saguenay; you return on your own along the fjords. In wintertime, the owner arranges dogsledding trips.

Maison Alexis (☎ 235-4372, 389 rue des Pionniers) Dorm beds $15/18. Run by the hostel owners and only a three-minute drive from town, this place still feels eons away from the busy center, nestled in woods and haunted as it is. Yes, haunted. In 1930, Lumina, the woman who lived here, watched as her husband was killed by a falling tree. She never went outside again. She apparently still appears, long after her death. Aside from that, it's a quiet, creaky, great old place with rooms for four.

La Galouïne (☎ 235-4380, 251 rue des Pionniers) Singles/doubles $35/45. An excellent, centrally located B&B with very friendly owners, there's also a boutique on the 1st floor selling amazing sand-made objects from the Îles de la Madeleine.

La Maison Clauphi (☎ 235-4303, W www .fjord-best.com/clauphi, 188 rue des Pionniers) B&B singles/doubles $69/76, motel doubles $89. This is a one-stop shopping sort of place where everything is possible. Whether you want to stay at the central and efficient if nondescript motel, in a nearby B&B or in a more luxurious suite, these folks can also set you up with cruise tickets and more adventurous package trips including surfbiking and mountain-biking.

Hôtel Tadoussac (☎ 235-4421, 165 rue du bord de l'Eau) Doubles from $80, suites $150-255. Looking, feeling and (is it just imagination?) smelling like a sanitorium, this huge, seemingly out-of-place luxury resort was built in 1864 and renovated several times since. A walk through the lobby and around the grounds is an experience, though the clinical – almost surgical – ambience probably won't feel too inviting.

Domaine des Dunes (☎ *235-4843, 585 chemin Moulin Baude)* Chalets $100-120. The perfect place for families or several persons together, it offers lovely chalets surrounded by birch groves, with all the comforts.

Places to Eat

Café du Fjord (☎ *235-4626, 152 rue du Bateau Passeur)* Lunch buffet $13, dinner buffet $16; open 11am-3pm & 6pm-11pm daily. A convivial atmosphere and succulent food help make this *cabane-à-sucre*–style space a winner. There is only a buffet (all you can eat or by weight), but it's more than you could hope for. After the restaurant closes, the bar keeps rocking until the wee hours.

Café Bohème (☎ *235-1180, 239 rue des Pionniers)* Mains $4-9; open 7am-11pm daily. The best hangout in town aside from the hostel, this great bohemian café serves healthy sandwiches and quiches, delicious breakfasts and equitable coffee. Some evenings there are poetry readings or talks by naturalists.

Café-Bar Le Gibard (*135 rue Bord de l'Eau)* Open 10am-3am daily. Despite being smack near a number of tourist attractions, this little bar has retained a local feel. Light snacks are available, but it's really a place to sit around and pull back a few.

Getting There & Away

Tadoussac is just off Rte 138. The ferry from Baie Ste Catherine in Charlevoix is free, takes 10 minutes, and runs 24/7.

Intercar (☎ 235-4653) bus line connects Tadoussac with Montréal (7½ hours, 2 daily) and Québec City ($33, 4 hours, 2 daily) along the North Shore; it runs as far as Baie Comeau. The bus stop is at 433 Rte 138, opposite the campground. There's also service to Chicoutimi ($16, 1½ hours) Sunday to Friday.

SACRÉ COEUR
pop 2100
Even if you're heading east, this town might be worth a detour, especially if you've come with the kids. (For information on towns farther up the Saguenay, see the Charlevoix, Saguenay & Lac St Jean chapter.) Only 10km from Tadoussac along Rte 172, this area affords splendid views onto the fjord from the pier at **L'Anse de Roche**. The drive down to the pier is itself worth the trip. The **Domaine de Nos Ancêtres** (☎ *236-4886, 1895 Rte 172; adult/ child $20/10; open 10am-6pm daily mid-May–mid-Oct)* is a safari-like zoo where you observe black bears in their natural habitat. It gets good reports from our readers.

At the renowned **Ferme 5 Étoiles** (*Five-Star Farm;* ☎ *236-4551,* W *www.ferme5etoiles .com, 465 Rte 172),* there's a petting zoo where kids can play with and feed farm animals. It also organizes a variety of kayaking and fishing expeditions for the family. In winter you can build and sleep in igloos. Accommodations range from $45 to $120 per night.

About 10km beyond Sacré Coeur is another entrance to the **Parc du Saguenay** *(adult/child $3.50/1.50)* at Baie Ste Marguerite. From here you can take a scenic but long (43km) walk back to Tadoussac, with exceptional views onto the fjords, or do a 3km walk, mostly through woods, to a lookout with a grand vista where you might spot belugas. A campground is set to open here in 2002 and should be among the nicest in the region.

GRAND BERGERONNES
pop 750
With excellent whale-watching opportunities and two superb attractions, Grand Bergeronnes provides a quieter alternative for those who wish to avoid the bustle of Tadoussac, 22km southwest.

Archéo Topo (☎ *232-6695,* W *www.archeo topo.qc.ca, 498 rue de la Mer; adult/child $5.50/2.50; open 10am-5pm daily late May–mid-Oct)* is a research and exhibition center dedicated to archeological findings along the North Shore. There are multimedia displays and a film about the traditional seal hunt. Outside, trails lead down to the coast. Most evenings there are French-language 'theatrical interpretation' evenings.

A few kilometers farther east is the **Cap de Bon Désir Interpretation Centre** (☎ *232-6751,*

162 rue de l'Église; adult/child $5/2; open 8am-8pm daily June-Aug, 9am-6pm daily Sept), run by Parks Canada. A worthwhile stop, there are excellent marine life exhibits and scheduled activities. The real attraction is the large rocks by the shore from which you can almost always spot passing whales.

Camping Bon Désir (☎ 232-6297, 198 Rte 138) Tent sites $17-20. There are 122 sites here, some with a view onto the river, some isolated, some snug up against other sites. Ask to wander through and pick which you like. It's a nice place with biking and walking trails cutting through it; watch for whales.

L'Auberge la Bergeronne (☎ 232-6642, 65 rue Principale) Singles/doubles $40/50. The restaurant has a good reputation and serves up full-course meals nightly ($14 to $20). Rooms are simple and comfortable. Staff arrange whale-watching and sea-kayaking trips.

There's a *café* inside Archéo Topo that serves simple meals on the terrace.

LES ESCOUMINS
pop 2150

A pleasant town that's long been important for its maritime traffic control station, Les Escoumins is visited mainly by those who keep their heads up for bird-watching or down toward the seabed while diving. There are good eating and sleeping options here, too. Stop by the tourist information office (☎ 233-2663, 154 Rte 138).

On rue St Marcellin, just west of the bridge and next to the Pêcherie Manicouagan (see Places to Stay & Eat), the **Promenade du Moulin** leads to the rugged shoreline where you can watch for hundreds of birds. The small **Parc des Chutes**, on the north side of town at the end of rue de la Rivière, makes a pretty picnic spot by a modest waterfall.

Expert and wannabe divers should head to the Centre des Loisirs Marins (☎ 233-2860, 41 rue des Pilotes; adult/child $5/2.50; open 8am-7pm daily late June–Aug, 8am-4:30pm daily early–late June & Sept–mid-Oct). An exhibit opens the window to the underwater mysteries of the St Lawrence River, and activities are organized from here. If you want to uncover mysteries for yourself, Atlan (☎ 233-

3465), in the basement, has diving gear for rent and takes people on expeditions for about $30. Reservations are needed.

Essipit is the Innu (Montagnais) section of town, where some 200 Innus live in one of the best-organized Native Canadian reserves in the province. The main center (☎ 233-2202, 888-868-6666, 1087 rue de la Réserve) has an excellent crafts boutique selling locals' work (not counting the Norwegian fox fur wraps!) and makes reservations for stays in its campground and chalets (see Camping Le Tipi in Places to Stay & Eat). It also offers very good whale-watching cruises at slightly lower prices than those in Tadoussac. Your chances of seeing blue whales here are good. On the third weekend in July, the Innus host their annual powwow – anyone can join in on the festivities.

La Companie de Navigation des Basques (☎ 233-2266) runs a ferry between Les Escoumins and Trois Pistoles (for details, see the Trois Pistoles section of the Lower St Lawrence chapter).

Places to Stay & Eat
Camping Le Tipi (☎ 233-2266, 29 rue de la Réserve) Tent sites $14-19, chalets $95. For those who don't mind being cramped, this is a nice enough urban camping spot. The chalets have sea views, are fully furnished and fit up to six persons.

Auberge de la Plongée (☎ 233-3289, 118 rue St Marcellin) Dorm beds/singles $17/30. This lively, no-frills place is where divers congregate and swap tales of the day's plunges. A lot of English is heard here. Perched on an elevated portion of the city, it's a pleasant place with staff who can help organize diving, biking, kayaking and horseback-riding excursions.

Les Chalets au bord de la Mer (☎ 233-2213, 25 rue des Pilotes) 4-person chalet $100. These are spacious chalets with a superb view onto a rocky little bay, close to the marina.

Pêcherie Manicouagan (☎ 233-3122, 152 rue St Marcellin) This shop sells fresh and frozen local seafood, and there's always some hot soup, chowder or seafood subs ready to take away and enjoy on the nearby walking trail.

Bistrot Belge *(☎ 233-3724, 287 Rte 138)*
Mains $7-16; open 7am-10pm daily. A culinary oasis, this Belgian café serves big subs to go ($8), pasta dishes, Lebanese *shish taouk,* and great fries with mayo. Its breads and pastries, needless to say, are flaky bits of heaven. It even sells Belgian beer ($6) to wash the lot down.

STE ANNE DE PORTNEUF
pop 1000
This rather nondescript coastal village has pretty sandbanks that attract dozens of bird species including herons. Yet the best reason to stop here is to partake in what is perhaps the best **whale-watching** expedition in the entire region. There are several aspects unique to Crosières du Grand Héron (☎ 587-6006, 888-463-6006, Ⓦ www.iquebec .com/grandheron, rue du Quai), not the least of which is its unique nighttime bioluminescence tour (bring a bottle of champagne on board and watch the plankton light up!). At this distance from the rivière Saguenay, your one Zodiac (for up to 12 persons) is often the only boat in a vast expanse of water.

Though there may be fewer whales here than around Tadoussac, there are still many, and the advantages of being in the middle of the river, in a small boat that the whales recognize, outweigh the chances of seeing a couple extra. Captain Yvon Bélanger is personable, flexible about scheduling and knowledgeable about whales; he collaborates with the Swiss Whale Society (Ⓦ www.isuisse.com/ cetaces), which has set up a research camp nearby and runs two-week scientific expeditions. For about $1200 (course, accommodations and equipment included) you can join a 14-day bio-acoustic research project. See the Society's website for more details.

Capt Bélanger's tours cost $38 for adults and $25 for kids six to 13; kids under 6 go for free.

There's an area nearby where you can ***camp*** for free, and there is also an on-site ***café.*** A nice B&B in town is ***La Nichée*** *(☎ 238-2825, 46 Rte 138),* which has tidy doubles for $25 per person. The owners are gregarious, lots of fun and can give you suggestions on things to see in the area.

FORESTVILLE
pop 3900
As its name implies, this town was born and bred on the forestry industry; its decline is evidenced by the long, serpentine wooden 'slide' that winds its way along the road connecting Rte 138 with the ferry harbor. Until 1990, thousands of logs would spill down toward an awaiting boat. It now stands unused and dry; unfortunately there are no plans to turn it into a giant waterslide.

Although the section of town along the 138 is mighty ugly, there are some nice bourgeois houses in the wooded areas down toward the harbor. A ferry (☎ 587-2725) connects Forestville with Rimouski (see the Rimouski section of the Lower St Lawrence chapter for details).

BETSIAMITES
pop 2500
An Indian reserve since 1861, Betsiamites has the largest Innu (Montagnais) population in the province. However, there's not much to see – streets are lined with houses on which 'closed' signs cover broken windows, and the dusty, sidewalkless avenues leading to the shore call to mind Central American villages. It does, though, greatly resemble some other remote reserves in the province, and so holds interest to those unable to visit the others.

You'd be better to skip the **Centre de Villégiature de Papanachois** *(☎ 567-8863, 18 rue Messek; adult/student $5/3; open 10am-8pm daily year-round),* 8km east of Betsiamites. This re-creation of a traditional Innu village was designed to acquaint visitors with Innu culture. Many travelers, however, complain about cancelled activities and mysterious surcharges. Do check to see if things have improved, but otherwise, you'd be better off at Essipit (see Les Escoumins) and Uashat (see Sept Îles), where better-organized attractions inform about Innu culture.

PARC RÉGIONAL DE POINTE AUX OUTARDES
This tiny (one sq km) park *(☎ 567-4226, 4 rue Labrie Ouest; adult/student $4/3; open 8am-5pm daily June-Sept)* is reputed to be among

eastern Canada's best spots for bird-watching (there's some 175 species including plovers, Canada geese and Arctic skuas). The landscape is a mix of marsh, sandy beach (with swimming), small dunes and pine forest, and there are explanation panels. It's on a pretty peninsula, accessible via a 12km road off Rte 138 east of Chute aux Outardes.

BAIE COMEAU
pop 25,500
This unattractive city owes its existence to Robert R McCormick, owner of *The Chicago Tribune*, who, in 1936, decided to build a colossal pulp and paper factory to ensure a neverending supply of newsprint. This enterprise necessitated harnessing the hydroelectric power of the Manicouagan and Outardes Rivers, which in turn begot other hydro-dependent industries like aluminum processing. The immense Reynolds company still produces its famous foil here, among other products. A deep-sea port facilitated exporting processed goods.

The tourist information office (☎ 296-8178, 3503 boul Laflèche) is near the western limits of the city.

Baie Comeau is useful as a road gateway to Labrador. There are many services here, as well as canoeing, kayaking, swimming and biking possibilities, but to want to stay here you'd have to be interested in at times surreal and larger-than-life industrial landscapes. The **Parc de la Falaise**, in the city's west sector (where only factory workers used to live) and accessible from boulevard Joliette, has a good view of the confluence of the Manicouagan and St Lawrence Rivers.

If you're in town between September and March, it's worth checking out a hockey game. The Drakkar is a good Major League team that plays and practices at the Centre Henri Léonard (☎ 296-8484), in the eastern sector.

Also worthwhile is to gander at the southern end of boulevard Lasalle, in the east sector. This main street has a faded frontier-land feel: New cafés, closed shops and strip clubs stand aesthetically side by side. Only the strange odors from those surreal-looking factories nearby make you feel like leaving right quick.

There is a year-round ferry (☎ 294-8593) to Matane. See the Matane section of the Gaspé Peninsula & Îles de la Madeleine chapter for details.

Places to Stay
Camping Manic-2 (☎ 296-2810, 2 Rte 389) Tent sites $15-19. Near the Manic-2 hydro station (a 25-minute drive from the city center), this large campground is an exotic place to pitch for the night.

Le Grand Hôtel (☎ 296-2212, 48 Place Lasalle) Doubles $30-80. That's 'grand' as in 'big.' This is a no-frills place to crash and a pretty good deal for the cash. Some rooms have shared bathrooms.

Hôtel Le Manoir (☎ 296-3391, 8 avenue Cabot) Singles/doubles from $63/73, suites $160. A four-star hotel in a grand (with a capital G!) style, all comforts are assured, and there's a fine dining restaurant. It offers inexpensive winter package deals.

BAIE COMEAU TO LABRADOR
Rte 389 begins its 561km path to Fermont, on the Labrador border, through a wild area of dense forest (or at least it was, before clearcutting operations) and reservoirs, and past some of Québec's highest mountains.

Manic-2 (☎ 294-3923, 800-363-7443), only 22km from Baie Comeau, is worth the trip if you've never seen a hydroelectric dam, though **Manic-5**, 214km north of Baie Comeau, is the real stunner. It's the largest in the Manic-Outardes hydro complex, and

---

Beware of Meteorites!

North of Manic-5, the Île René Lavasseur and surrounding Réservoir Manicouagan are on the site of the world's second-largest crater formed by meteorite impact. Measuring 65km in diameter, it was formed 210 million years ago in a crash that supposedly wiped out up to 75% of the planet's life forms. The island is rich in minerals, especially nickel. In the middle, Mt Babel (952m) contains numerous semi-precious metals in its rock.

is the world's largest multiple arch and buttress dam. The dam itself is 1km long and 214m high (the visible portion is 165m). Montréal's Olympic Stadium would fit snugly at its base with much room to spare. The reservoir created for it alone measures 2000 sq km, twice the size of Lac St Jean.

Both are open and free of charge to visitors. From the end of June to early September, there are four daily 90-minute tours at each station. Reservations are not necessary, but call in advance to check on times. You can fly instead of making the three-hour drive; Air Satellite (☎ 589-8923) offers daily tourist flights from Baie Comeau to Manic-5 for $129 roundtrip, including a visit to the dam. It's a good way to see the entire hydro complex and surrounding forests. It's possible to spend the night at Manic-5.

From Manic-5, the road turns to gravel. After 124km there's a turnoff for hiking trails into the Groulx Mountains, which boast 30 plateaus topping 1000m. Contact the tourist office, listed above in the Baie Comeau section, if you wish to do overnight trekking in the area or to spend the night inside the dam complex at Manic-5.

Fermont
pop 3700
The town of Fermont is 350km northeast of Manic-5 on a mostly gravel road, passing by the now-closed town of Gagnon, razed after the local mine closed in 1985. Fermont owes its existence to the discovery and later exploitation of iron-rich land (reserves are estimated at four billion tons). The Québec Cartier Mining Company still generates the economy here. The town is famous for its 'wall,' a 1.5km connected series of buildings (with apartments, shops, banks, offices, a hotel and a school) that acts as a windbreaker for the rest of the town. People apparently disappear inside it for days on end during brutal winters.

For such a remote place, Fermont has a young, lively spirit. There are vast expanses for snowmobiling, cross-country skiing and trekking on the surrounding, low-lying hills. The tourist office (☎ 287-5822, 100 Le Carrefour) has more information.

Hôtel Fermont (☎ 287-5451, 299 Le Carrefour) Doubles from $81. This is the only game in town and it's pricey for what you get. Ask about specials, though, which include meals.

From the town of Fermont, Labrador City is just 35km away.

Schefferville
pop 255
There are no more roads going north in Québec, so to get to Schefferville you need to make about a 400km detour through Labrador, or take a train from Sept Îles (568km) (see 'Tracks in the Wilderness'). A train also runs from Wabush, near Labrador City, up to Schefferville.

A near ghost town, Schefferville was a booming iron ore mining town from the 1950s, before competition from Brazilian industries made world prices drop such that mining here was no longer lucrative. The town has been bled dry ever since, and plans are underway to destroy the old mining constructions. A number of other buildings have already been raised. It is still a base for hunters and fishers, however.

Two nearby Native Canadian reserves live in a tragic isolation. **Matimekosh** (pop 630) is an Innu village 1km from town; Nessipi Kantuet (☎ 585-3756) offers adventure trips in the region. **Kawawachikamach** (pop 500), farther north, is Canada's only Naskapi Indian reserve. The group used to live near Kuujjuaq on Inuit land before moving (more or less voluntarily, in hopes of getting jobs in the mines) to the Schefferville region in 1956. This town has existed only since 1982.

BAIE COMEAU TO SEPT ÎLES
East of Baie Comeau the landscape starts getting rugged, and the road dips up and down steep hills and passes over canyons and jagged, rocky cliffs. This is not the lyrical majesty of the Gaspésie; nature here is evidenced in its robust, brutish variety.

At picturesque Franquelin (pop 400), 31km east of Baie Comeau, you can visit **Village Forestier d'Antan** (☎ 296-3203, 27 rue des Érables; adult/student $5/4; open 9am-5pm daily late May–mid-Sept), an excellent reconstructed lumberjack village. Eight original

Tracks in the Wilderness

The most remote set of train tracks in the province follows the Sept Îles–Schefferville route. Once a week, the train rattles the 568km between the two, through a section of Labrador on its way to the tiny town. A separate service runs once or twice a week to Labrador City. The route through the merciless terrain was begun in 1950 and took 7000 people four years to finish – a dirty job. These workers had to be flown in, making the largest civilian airlift ever.

The train's passenger list is composed of adventure seekers off to an outfitter's for canoeing in the wild; hunters and fishers; employees of mining companies returning from shopping expeditions in Sept Îles or Innu; and Native Canadian Naskapis heading home.

The scenery is phenomenal. Cutting through forests of pine, birch and fir, the tracks pass over gorges, dip inside valleys, curve around waterfalls and rapids, dive through a section of mountain and jut along stretches of lakes, rivers, hills and forest as far as the eye can see. The train crosses a 900m-long bridge, 50m over rivière Moisie and past the 60m-high Tonkas Falls.

Every so often, the nearly spiritual vastness of it all is interrupted by what sounds like an earthquake. The train veers onto a secondary track and lets the planet's longest, heaviest cargo conveys pass. All day long, throughout the year, these 2km-long monsters, 67 wagons pulled by three diesel locomotives with 3500 horsepower, are filled with tons of iron and metal-rich soil destined for Sept Îles.

The train is also forced to a stop for herds of migrating caribou, or for black bears wandering along the tracks. This is the Great North, after all!

For more information, contact the QNS&L Railway (☎ 968-7808, 100 rue Retty, Sept Îles). Adult roundtrip tickets cost $138. Ask at the tourist information office for a list of outfitters operating in the area.

buildings have been restored and give a good idea of what life was like in many such towns. If you pass by at lunchtime from Thursday to Sunday, try the hearty, traditional lunches ($10). There's also **swimming** nearby.

Godbout
pop 390

Godbout (pop 390) occupies a lovely, sleepy, windswept spot on the St Lawrence. Originally a 17th-century trading post, it flourished for its salmon-filled Godbout and Trinité Rivers. It's still one of the best spots in the province for salmon fishing. At the intersection of Rte 138 and the turnoff for Godbout's harbor is the entrance to a ZEC fishing and hunting zone. You can buy an entrance ticket ($5) to watch spawning salmon from a suspended bridge.

The old general store serves as the tourist information office (☎ 568-7647, 100 rue Pascal Comeau), which has a small exhibit on local history and some great antiques. The **Musée Amérindien et Inuit** (☎ 568-7306, 134 rue Pascal Comeau; adult/child $3/2; open 10am-7pm daily June-Sept) has a nice collection of Inuit and Native Canadian sculptures. If you feel like a swim, dive into the rivière Godbout at the western end of the village.

The **Dépanneur Proprio** (☎ 568-7535, 156 rue Pascal Comeau), a convenience store, sells fishing permits for nonresidents and rents out plain, neat rooms on the second floor (singles/doubles $28/34).

La Maison du Vieux Quai (☎ 568-7453, 142 rue Pascal Comeau) Singles/doubles from $45/50. This fabulous house is on the site of the original salmon trading post (set up in 1670) and later the residence of the director of a local paper mill. Warm, spacious, elegant and with a down-home feel, this B&B is run by a friendly, smart young couple who is knowledgeable about the region.

A ferry (☎ 568-7575) links Godbout with Matane (for details, see Matane in the Gaspé Peninsula and Îles de la Madeleine chapter).

Pointe des Monts

This marks the point where the St Lawrence graduates from river to gulf. There is a 28m lighthouse (c 1830, the second oldest in

Québec) which has, despite its function, lorded over dozens of shipwrecks over the past century. It sits on a picturesque spit of land and has been converted into a **museum** (☎ 939-2400, W www.pointe-des-monts.com, 1830 chemin du Vieux Phare; admission $2.50; open 9am-7pm daily mid-June–mid-Sept) explaining the lives of the keepers and their families who lived inside it. It also tells the stories of the shipwrecked crews they used to play host to. There's an on-site **restaurant** serving first-rate local specialties, as well as a B&B offering good dinner/room/sea-excursion (or diving) packages for about $130 for two. This could make an exotic, relaxing and fun stop.

Pointe aux Anglais

A few kilometers east of this tiny village is a long public beach where people can pitch their tents for free in the wooded dunes that back it and spend a day sighting whales offshore. The beach is sandy, sprawling and clean – one of the finest on the North Shore – and while there are no services whatsoever here (not even a toilet), you can shower for $4 at the nearby restaurant *Le Routier de Pentecôte* (☎ 799-2600, 2767 Rte 138) from 6am to 9:30pm daily. You can also rent cheap rooms. There are two official *campgrounds* around the village of Rivière Pentecôte as well.

Port Cartier

pop 7000

This medium-sized industrial town was founded in 1958 as an exportation site of minerals extracted from near the border of Labrador, deep inland. There's not much of great interest here, but a little detour is worthwhile to walk a picturesque trail right downtown. The mouth of the rivière aux Rochers, streaming through the city, created several green islands that are now converted parklands. Boulevard des Îles leads to a parking lot just after the first bridge, from where a short, pretty jaunt will lead you to an observation point near some grand waterfalls. You'll pass a tiny wooden chapel, in which a faded poster of Pope John Paul II watches over the penitent.

The entrance of **Réserve Faunique Port Cartier-Sept Îles** (☎ 766-2524; admission $3.50;

open 8am-7pm daily late May–Oct) is 27km north of Port Cartier on chemin du Parc at Lac Walker. There are campgrounds, walking trails, canoe rentals (a 52km circuit is possible), fishing and hunting in this territory covering 6423 sq km. For more information, visit its office (24 boul des Îles, office No 109) in town.

SEPT ÎLES

pop 25,600

Sept Îles is the last town of any size along the North Shore and it boasts several worthwhile stops. A port city, international freighters make use of the docking facilities. Despite the rather isolated location, this is Canada's second busiest port measured by tonnage. The east-west streets from the Baie de Sept Îles to Rte 138 are arranged alphabetically (starting with rue Arnaud running along the waterfront).

There's a tourist information office (☎ 968-0022, 1401 boul Laure Ouest) with a smaller one at the Parc du Vieux Quai (port). For winter enthusiasts, contact Rapido (☎ 968-4011), a **cross-country skiing** club that's been promoting the sport in the area since 1974. It organizes many great treks.

There are two Innu reserves in the area, Uashat in the western sector of the city and Maliotenam 14km east. Though these look rather depressed and colorless, the Innu here are well organized and run several enterprises, including the large Les Galleries Montagnaises shopping center behind the Shaputuan Museum. A good place to buy Native Canadian–made souvenirs is the Innu-run Innu *Apakuai* (☎ 968-2066, 33 rue du Vieux Poste).

Things to See & Do

Musée Shaputuan This is a very good museum (☎ 962-4000, W www.museesha putuan.org, 290 boul des Montagnais; adult/ student $3/2; open 9am-5pm daily late June–early Sept, 9am-5pm Mon-Fri & 1pm-5pm Sat early Sept–late June) about Innu (Montagnais) history, culture, traditions – and superstitions (never enter a shaking tent; you'll be told lies inside). Temporary exhibits of local artists' work are also held in the circular exhibition hall, itself divided into four sections symbolizing the seasons.

Musée Régional de la Côte Nord At this modern museum (☎ 968-2070, 500 boul Laure; adult/student $3.25/2.25; open 9am-5pm daily late June–Aug, 10am-5pm Tues-Sun Sept–late June) you'll find a ho-hum, French-only (though English audio guides are available) history of the mining and hunting that characterized the city's history. However, its temporary exhibits are usually first-rate and have bilingual explanation panels. The gift shop is also excellent.

Le Vieux Poste An old fur trading post (☎ 968-2070, boul des Montagnais; adult/students $4/3; open 9am-5pm daily late June–late Aug), built in 1661, has been reconstructed into a walk-through series of buildings, each with its own exhibit to show the lifestyles of the hunters who used to call the forest home.

Île Grande Basque The largest island in a small archipelago off Sept Îles is a pretty spot to spend a day, walking on the 12km of trails or picnicking on the coast. The highest point is 150m, and there are several nice lookouts and even a *campground*. La Petite Sirène (☎ 968-2173) runs crossings from Sept Îles' port to/from the island 10 times a day (adult/child 6-13 $15/9; 10 minutes) and also organizes guided trips there. Tickets are available at the Parc du Vieux Quai (port), where other companies offer similar trips. Guided **kayak tours** of the islands are organized by Vêtements des Îles (☎ 962-7223, 637 avenue Brochu). Île du Corosol is a bird refuge.

Places to Stay & Eat

There are several motels along Rte 138 (boul Laure).

Le Tangon (☎ 962-8180, 555 avenue Cartier) Dorm beds $16/19 member/non-member, singles/doubles with shared bathroom $26/42, tent sites $10. This HI youth hostel has rooms with six to eight beds in the basement, while private rooms, often filled with fishermen, are on the second floor. The hostel area is fairly cramped and there's little room to socialize, but it's very clean.

Gîte des Îles (☎ 962-6116, 50 rue Thibault) Singles/doubles $40/50. This is a welcoming B&B in a quiet sector north of Rte 138.

Chez Jonathan (☎ 961-2207, 290 boul des Montagnais) Appetizers $3-12, mains $7-24, weekend brunch $13. Situated inside the Shaputuan Museum, this is a first-rate restaurant with delicious seafood and meat dishes, along with less expensive hamburgers and pizzas. Best is the last item on the menu, a traditional Innu recipe of grilled cod with onions and fried pork lard – sounds revolting but it's unforgettably delicious.

Pub St Marc (☎ 962-7770, 588 avenue Brochu) Appetizers $3-6, mains $8-17; open 11am-midnight daily. A very relaxed, pleasant atmosphere makes this pub-restaurant one of the best in the city to have a few drinks or a good meal – its pastas are great, and there are 20 kinds of salad.

Les Terrasses du Capitaine (☎ 962-6322, 295 rue Arnaud) Mains $7-16. For seafood, this is your best bet, right at the port so you can breathe in the sea air while eating out on the terrace. In the same building, there's also a fresh fish shop where you can get some of the local shrimp, tiny and sweet, or try another local fish, *bourgots* (whelks), though they're mighty rubbery.

Getting There & Away

Intercar (☎ 962-2126) runs a daily bus to/from Baie Comeau ($27, 3½ hours) and a daily bus to/from Havre St Pierre ($25, 2½ hours). The bus station is at 126 rue Mgr Blanche.

The *Relais Nordik* in Rimouski (☎ 418-723-8787, 800-463-0680, ✉ info@relais.nordik .desgagnes.com) sails along the Lower North Shore to Blanc Sablon once a week. From Sept Îles it leaves the Quai Mgr Blanche and travels to Île d'Anticosti. See the Lower North Shore section, later, for details.

Aviation Québec Labrador (☎ 962-7901, fax 962-9202) flies to Schefferville, Wabush (in Labrador) and many villages of the Lower North Shore to Blanc Sablon on their twin otters. The cheapest flight from Sept Îles to Natashquan costs about $350 roundtrip. Call the Sept Îles airport (☎ 962-8212), 15km east of Sept Îles, or the tourist office (see earlier) for more information. A taxi (☎ 962-9444) to the airport costs about $13.

SEPT ÎLES TO HAVRE ST PIERRE

As rugged as you might have found the landscape so far, nothing compares to the 355km east to the end of Rte 138 at Natashquan. Immediately east of Sept Îles, the scenery changes dramatically. Villages cease to appear with regularity, the trees become progressively smaller, some hilltops are rounded with lichen-covered rocks and lead to stretches of muskeg, and river after river reach their destination, some by creeping humbly, others by tumbling forcefully into the St Lawrence, sometimes off a rocky cliff, sometimes in torrential rapids.

The first potential turnoff after Sept Îles is **Moisie**, just 15km east. The road leads down to an abandoned military radar base set up in the 1950s to beef up North American security. Left rotting since 1988, some still live in what is now a very creepy-feeling ghost town. The Innu reserve of Maliotenam is also here. Farther on you pass over the famous **rivière Moisie**, one of Québec's richest salmon rivers.

About 80km east of Sept Îles, the road crosses over the spectacularly cascading **rivière Tortue**, worth a stop. Shortly after this, the **rivière Manitou** becomes a series of rapids that roadside trails lead to. There are information boards and picnic tables set up here.

At Rivière au Tonnerre (pop 350), some 35km beyond, is the unusual **Église St Hippolyte** (☎ 465-2842; admission free; open 9am-5pm daily year-round), a prim-looking, early-20th-century wooden church that exemplifies the tenacity of faith. It was built entirely by local volunteers who also carved out sacred images onto the 8m-high archway with their pocketknives.

At **Longue Pointe de Mingan** (pop 540) is the western entrance to the **Mingan Archipelago National Park Reserve** (see the following section for details). Several tour operators along the coast offer excursions to the western islands, interesting to bird watchers while less interesting geologically than those farther east. This was the site of a WWII US military base.

The **Minganie Research and Interpretation Center** (☎ 949-2126, 625 rue du Centre; adult/child $5/2; open 9am-6pm daily mid-June–early Sept) has bilingual exhibits on local sealife and provides a good introduction to the archipelago. This Parks Canada center works in collaboration with the **Mingan Island Cetacean Study Centre** (☎ 949-2845, 378 bord de la Mer), which conducts scientific studies on blue whales. It offers excellent whale-watching tours ($75, 6 hours) on which you can assist on research expeditions.

There are numerous motels and campgrounds here, but the village itself is not as interesting as those farther east.

Mingan (pop 430), 10km east, is definitely worth a stop. Populated by a dynamic Innu community (who call it Ekuanitshit), the village is a lovely spot where wind and waves have carved out strange monoliths and figures by the coast ('Mingan' might come from the Celtic 'Maen Cam,' meaning 'curved stone'). Not to be missed is the **Église Montagnaise** (☎ 949-2272, 15 rue de l'Église; admission free; open 8am-7pm daily year-round), a little church containing Native Canadian motifs, a striking mix of Catholicism and aboriginal culture. A teepee form enshrines the crucifix, and the stations of the cross are painted on animal skin parchment.

The **Centre Culturel Montagnais** (☎ 949-2234, 888-949-2406, 34 rue Mistamehkanau; admission free; open 9am-6pm daily mid-June–Aug) has a small photo exhibit about life in the region, and can inform you about Innu-organized fishing, hunting or boating excursions.

HAVRE ST PIERRE & MINGAN ARCHIPELAGO
pop 3700

This sizeable fishing town has a lot of charm, though its developed tourist industry feels anachronistic in the context of the region. It's also an industrial zone, where iron oxide and titanium-rich rock are extracted (in mines near Lac Allard) and then shipped to processing plants in Tracy-Sorel. If you're up early enough, you can catch the miners heading for their break-of-dawn train taking them 43km north to the mines.

Havre St Pierre was founded in 1857 by six Acadian families who had left the Îles de la Madeleine and set up here in traditionally

Inuit territory. Minke and fin whales are seen here too – most afternoons for many years, a friendly minke named Georgette has come to say hello near the ferry landing.

The tourist information office (☎ 538-2512) is at 957 rue de la Berge, where a small exhibit has been mounted in what used to be general store.

The region's main attraction is the **Mingan Archipelago National Park Reserve**, a Parks Canada–run protected zone, made up of an 85km-long string of 40 main islands near the coast. They stretch from Longue Pointe de Mingan to 40km east of Havre St Pierre. You can spot some 200 species of birds. The island's distinguishing character-istics are the oddly shaped stratified lime-stone formations, caused by erosion, along the shores. They are dubbed 'flowerpots' for the lichen and small vegetation that grow on top of them.

Perched atop the flowerpots might be the *macareux moine* (puffin), a striking mix between a parrot and penguin (see 'Curse of the Puffin' in the Facts about Québec chapter). You're most likely to spot them on Îles de la Maison, du Sanctuaire and aux Perroquets.

The landscape is spectacular here, partic-ularly at sunset, and the geology fascinat-ing. You'll see arctic vegetation (more than 150 kinds of moss, 190 kinds of lichen, 500 kinds of delicate plants and flowers) and may come upon a fossil of plants that thrived in the area's once tropical climate (which, as you'll notice, must have been oh-so-long ago).

The Visitor Reception and Interpretation Center (☎ 538-5264, 975 rue de l'Escale) is near the entrance to the town of Havre St Pierre. It has exhibits and information about scheduled activities and excursions. A second information office (☎ 538-3285, 1010 rue de la Promenade) is at the marina. To contact the park reserve's headquarters, call ☎ 800-463-6769.

Activities

Many visitors bring their own boats, but a variety of commercial boat trips run from the mainland, too. Some of the islands have hiking paths, picnic areas and/or wilderness camping sites. Ask about drinking water. There are several kiosks lined up at the marina offering excursions. Comparison shop to find the one that suits you. In

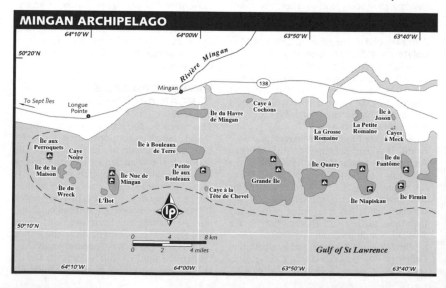

MINGAN ARCHIPELAGO

general, the smaller the boat, the better the experience. Count on $30 to $50 per person.

Expedition Agaguk (☎ 538-1588, W www .expedition-agaguk.com, 1062 rue Boréale) is run by a young, dynamic team who rent kayaks, canoes and bikes, and run excellent guided **kayak tours** of the archipelago. This is the best way to experience the islands. To go out alone, you'll need to take a short training session if you've never handled a sea kayak before – they tip over easily in rough waters.

Places to Stay & Eat

Camping ($6-$9) is allowed on some islands, but you must register first at the Visitor Reception and Interpretation Center.

Camping Municipal (☎ 538-2415, 1730 rue Boréale) Tent sites $17. This is a wooded campground on the eastern edge of town.

Auberge de la Minganie (☎ 538-1538, 3908 Rte 138) Dorm beds $15, tent sites $8. Inconveniently, this isolated hostel is 17km west of Havre St Pierre and there's no transport to town (the Orléans bus will stop if you ask, and you then walk the remaining 700m). However, it sits on a beautiful, quiet bay, surrounded by trails through woods. You can rent a canoe here and immerse yourself in

the surrounding serenity. Beds are in separate cabins, and there are laundry and kitchen facilities.

Auberge Boréale (☎ 538-3912, 1288 rue Boréale) Singles/doubles $46/56. This large B&B at the eastern end of town rents out bikes and boasts a pretty sea view (ask if your room has one).

Motel de l'Archipel (☎ 538-3900, 800-463-3906, 805 rue de l'Escale) Singles/doubles from $65/75. A comfortable hotel/motel right in town with a large selection of rooms, this is a good bet.

Restaurant La Promenade (☎ 538-1718, 1197 promenade des Anciens) Mains $5-16; open 5:30am-midnight daily. This glorified diner serves the usual fare but is good for a fill-up. If you're an early riser, you can sit with the miners who come in for a coffee before they head to work.

Chez Julie (☎ 538-3070, 1023 rue Dulcinée) Mains $7-18. Considered one of the best places to dine, its specialty is (guess what?) seafood.

Getting There & Away

Both Air Satellite (☎ 800-463-8512) and Anticosti Air (☎ 538-1600) have scheduled flights to Port Menier on Île d'Anticosti.

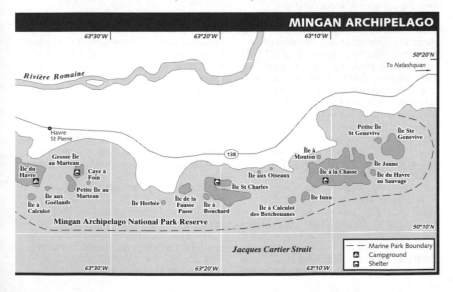

The *Relais Nordik* boat arrives here once a week from Rimouski and Sept Îles (see the Lower North Shore section, later, for more details).

ÎLE D'ANTICOSTI

Just in the past few years, this island's 7943 sq km of nature have begun to unfold their beauty before an ever-growing number of visitors. Until recently, the only people able to appreciate the land and its riches have been lazy deer hunters with good connections. Lazy because, with more than 120,000 deer on the island, it doesn't take much looking to find one, and good connections because for much of the island's modern history, it has been private land, open only to friends, business partners and those with enough money to pay for the privilege of coming here to hunt.

A French chocolate maker, Henri Menier, bought the island in 1895 to turn it into his own private hunting ground. He built a Victorian chateau for himself, stuffed it with expensive antiques (much of which were later destroyed in a fire), and lived like a king in his own fiefdom. He imported fox, beavers, moose and the Virginia white-tailed deer for hunting purposes – to this day hunters come from far and wide to shoot the deer.

In 1926, Anticosti (from the Innu language, meaning 'bear hunting territory') was resold to Wayagamack, a consortium of pulp and paper companies, and only in 1974 did the provincial government gain control over it. Repatriation didn't help much, as the government rented out the land to companies that continued to use it as their private stomping grounds. But in the past few years, since small portions of the island have been turned into a wildlife reserve and since tour groups started making organized visits, it's turned into a viable ecotourist option.

The heavily wooded, cliff-edged island has waterfalls, canyons, caves and good salmon rivers. The abundant deer here have wiped out many species of plants and now are content to also munch on conifer trees and even sea algae. Biologists suspect that because of their isolation and specific dietary habits, a new subspecies of deer may be now developing. The **hiking** and **biking** trails are limitless; the island is a paradise for outdoors adventurists.

Port Menier (pop 280), inhabited mainly by workers from the wildlife reserve and other island services, is the closest thing to a village on the island. It's from here that the island's lone road ventures to the interior. A tourist information office (☎ 535-0250) is on chemin des Forestiers.

In Port Menier, the **Écomusée d'Anticosti** *(☎ 535-0250, rue Dr Schmidt)* is a free exhibit of the flora and fauna found on the island and has photographs of Menier's chateau before the fire. The *Maison des Artisans (rue du Cap Blanc)* sells deerskin products. Nearby are some houses dating from Menier's time on the island.

Also in town on the east side of the island, the **Musée Henri Menier** *(☎ 786-5788, rivière auc Saumons)* displays wooden sculptures of the island's fauna and many of the ancient fossils found here. The **Chutes Vauréal** are the most impressive waterfalls (76m) on the island, appearing as if from a dream in a canyon 146km east of Port Menier. There's a deep cave that can be explored at rivière à la Patate, in the middle of the island.

Places to Stay & Eat

Safari Anticosti (☎ 538-1414, **W** www.safarianticosti.com) is probably the best bet. It runs very well-organized tours of two or more days that take in all the sites. The tours concentrate on the wilder eastern sector of the island, where most of the best sites are. Its helicopters depart daily from Havre St Pierre. Count on paying about $229 for two days.

Domaine du lac Geneviève (☎ 535-0294, 800-463-1777) offers a range of options, including camping if you want to save costs. This outfitter operates in the sector north of Port Menier. It can arrange transportation to the island (from Mont Joli, Québec City or Sept Îles) and offers excursions. Its chalets are rented out from $625 per week.

There are also a few restaurants and B&Bs in the Port Menier area, including Auberge Port Menier (☎ 535-0122, rue Menier), which offers singles/doubles for $65/80 and has two-night packages including transport from Havre St Pierre for $300 per person.

Though it's possible to get to the island yourself, camp, rent a bike or 4X4 and wander around, it requires much planning. One campground, *Camping Baie Ste Claire* (☎ 533-0155), is not far from Port Menier, but you don't want to get stuck in this sector of the island, and you'll need a vehicle because the distances to the eastern sector of the island are great. Nearly every visitor chooses to go with one of the many small-group package tours. Get more information at the tourist office on Havre St Pierre (see that section, earlier). Plan to stay a bare minimum of two nights. Note that Sépaq, who administers the island's wildlife reserve, also offers summer and winter packages, but they are among the most expensive of all.

Getting There & Away

See the Havre St Pierre section, earlier, for details on air travel.

The only regular boat service is the once-weekly boat from Havre St Pierre on the *Relais Nordik,* but it is not the most convenient. It arrives in Port Menier at midnight every Monday morning, and leaves again every Wednesday at 3:45pm.

BAIE JOHAN BEETZ
pop 100

This magnificently scenic village, 65km east of Havre St Pierre, is named after a Belgian aristocrat who saved the local population from an epidemic of the Spanish flu through his precautions and sound advice. Multitalented, Beetz was an artist and naturalist who fell in love with the region and, in 1898, built a villa there. He spent long winter nights painting, and summers collecting specimens. The tourist office (☎ 539-0125, 20 rue Johan Beetz) is underneath a convenience store. The folks there can inform you about nature excursions with the local anglers.

Maison Johan Beetz (☎ *539-0137, 17 rue Johan Beetz; adult/child $3/2; open 9am-6pm daily June-Sept)* is the yellow mansion standing proudly on a rocky tongue of land in the middle of the rivière Piashti, coursing

through town. This is where Beetz lived with the girl he fell in love with (when she was 14 years old; it was OK in those days). Some of those long winter nights produced more than paintings – they had 11 children together. Check out the delicate door panels he painted. Rooms are rented out for about $70 a night, making it one of the more extravagant B&Bs on the North Shore.

Auberge de la Baie (☎ *539-0184, 18 Rte 138)* is a B&B with singles/doubles for $45/50, and a double with private bathroom for $60.

NATASHQUAN
pop 600

There's a romance about wanting to see what's at the end of any road. This haunting little village, 780km from Tadoussac, does not disappoint quixotic expectations. However, people make pilgrimages to Natashquan for more than the exoticism of seeing the word *'fin'* (end) on Rte 138's signpost (and anyway, the 138 picks up again in the far east of the province, between Vieux Fort and Blanc Sablon, but pretend you didn't know). It's also the birthplace of Gilles Vigneault, a singer-songwriter of great stature in Québec, and many have traveled here to see the landscape that so inspired his songs (see 'Québec's Most Loved *Pays*an').

Natashquan is still getting used to its recent connection to the rest of the province. Rte 138 first connected it to Sept Îles in 1996, and only since 1999 has it been paved. Most villagers are not as excited about this development as you'd think. Young teens say life is harder now because the police patrol the area more often and it's not so easy to go joyriding, get drunk or have a fair scrap after a few drinks (before, police would fly in for one day a week, and the airport attendant would alert the rest of the community beforehand).

Others say that the huge influx of anticipated tourist dollars never arrived. Instead, many seasonal or temporary workers for provincial or federal offices and enterprises (Hydro Québec or Bell Canada, for example) who used to stay and spend money for weeks and months at a time now simply drive away. Industries that were supposed to open never materialized.

NORTH SHORE

Québec's Most Loved *Paysan*

A living legend throughout Québec, Gilles Vigneault is close to God-status in his hometown Natashquan, where he was born in 1928. After studying in Rimouski and the University of Laval, he turned his attention to his first love: poetry. Renowned composer Claude Leveillée set to music many of Vigneault's texts, passionate and lyrical love letters to his homeland, and soon Vigneault's concerts became phenomenons. His signature song, *Mon Pays* (My Country), written for a 1965 film, is today quoted across the province, particularly when it starts to get chilly: *Mon pays/Ce n'est pas un pays/C'est l'hiver* (My country/Is not a country/It's winter).

Vigneault's fervor for his country showed up in other songs like *Les gens de mon pays* and *Gens du pays*, which became the anthem of the sovereignty movement. In the 1970s he began writing heavily nationalist songs and in 1980 gave numerous concerts in overt support of the referendum on Québec independence. This link to separatism has alienated a younger generation from his music, but he still commands revered respect from most people.

In Natashquan, his presence is infused in the very air that rattles Vigneault name plates in front of some houses; the extended family is large and many of his relatives live here. One distant cousin, Jean-Paul Vigneault, has made a name for himself by widely proclaiming his association with the master. He plays guitar, accordion and violin, and does a pretty good vocal imitation of the real thing. A natural born *raconteur*, Jean-Paul will chew the ear off of anyone within listening distance, but he always has fascinating tales to tell; he's the kind of character one always remembers having met, a true *bon vivant!* He loves to pose for photos with tourists; if you're up for it, ask at the tourist office (or ask anyone on the street) where to find him.

There is a small tourist information office (☎ 726-3756, 33 allée des Galets), but the tourism infrastructure is not so well developed here. Your best bet is just to ask around if you'd like to go on a fishing, canoeing or kayaking trip. Just like in the 'old days,' things get done here via word of mouth and out of locals' genuine desire to be helpful.

Things to See & Do

You'll learn about how Acadian exiles from the Îles de la Madeleine founded the village in 1855 at the **Centre d'Interprétation bord du Cap** (☎ 726-3233, 32 chemin d'en Haut; adult/child under 12 $3.50/free; open 9am-5pm daily late June–Aug). Among the many antiques and odd objects on view at this local history museum, the creepiest is a wax nun who seems to follow your every move. There's also a Gilles Vigneault room-cum-shrine.

Les Galets is the name given to a small collection of small white houses with bright red roofs huddled together on a small peninsula. Where fishermen used to sort and dry their catch, it's now an abandoned, lovely area. Aside from enjoying the endless, sandy beaches, **hiking** inland is highly worthwhile. There are 15km of trails through unspoiled woods, where you can feel completely isolated and peaceful. There are numerous waterfalls, lookouts and obscenely beautiful spots to sit and picnic. Pick up a map at the tourist office. One entrance to the trails is right in the village. Another, more isolated path begins just west of the village. Look for the sign 'Sentier Pédestre Le Pas du Portageur,' and drive to the end of the dirt road.

Pointe Parent (pop 800), 15km east of Natashquan, is where Nutukuan, a dusty Innu reserve is located, and where Rte 138 ends. The town has easily distinguishable Native Canadian and non-Native sections. The indigenous tourism industry here is faltering, since a few innovative but badly organized organizations have folded. Check at the Innu Band Council (☎ 726-3529) to see if there are any new adventure tours operating.

Places to Stay & Eat

There are numerous B&Bs in town, all in the $35 to $70 range.

Gîte et Châlets Paulette Landry *(☎ 726-3206, 78 rue du Pré)* Singles/doubles $40/50, chalets $50. The two small furnished chalets with picture-picture sea views are great if you can get them, and a superb deal. The in-house B&B rooms are standard. The owners are great souls who can set up fishing trips.

L'Auberge le Port d'Attache *(☎ 726-3569, 70 rue du Pré)* Singles/doubles $50/65. If you can get rooms No 1 or No 2 in this seaside B&B, you're in luck (great views!). This comfortable place also offers dinners for about $15.

Restaurant John Débordeur *(☎ 726-3333, 9 rue du Pré)* Mains $8-16. This is your best bet in town, with everything from *poutine* and spaghetti to fine seafood meals. The owner was immortalized in one of Gilles Vigneault's songs.

LOWER NORTH SHORE

The string of tiny villages in the far eastern corner of the province remains an enigma for most Québécois, mere names on the weather report. As the only viable access is a weekly boat and because there are no roads connecting them to the rest of the province, the area remains a challenging destination for all but the most determined. Snowmobilists, however, can travel on a trail that links Natashquan with Blanc Sablon.

The *Relais Nordik* is the region's main lifeline, setting sail every week of the year (except from mid-January through early April) from Rimouski, bringing supplies, the odd curiosity-seeker and, for the few hours they remain docked in each port of call, a few hours of fresh conversation to the locals (see Rimouski in the Lower St Lawrence chapter for contact details and prices). During the two to three hours in port, passengers can disembark and sniff around (going toward Blanc Sablon, however, the boat pulls into Harrington Harbour after midnight; the return journey is done in daytime). Most of the villages spread around the port, but even the inland ones can be visited by hopping a lift with friendly locals.

After an all-too-brief stop at Port Menier on Île d'Anticosti, the *Relais Nordik* sails to Havre St Pierre and Natashquan before heading to the villages farther east.

Kegaska (pop 155) is an Anglophone village known for its crushed seashell-covered roads. There is one outfitter in the area, Pourvoirie Leslie Forman (☎ 726-3738), which sets up lobster-, crab- and scallop-fishing excursions. **La Romaine** (pop 250) and its Innu sister village of **Unamen Shipu** (pop 830) are located 5km inland. East of here the land becomes very rocky.

Harrington Harbour (pop 285) is next, and it's living eye candy. Considered one of Québec's ten prettiest villages, this Anglophone community has made much of its rocky terrain and small, wind-sheltered bay. All the houses are perched atop rocks and brightly painted in whites, reds, greens and blues. Except for the wooden sidewalks that link the houses, this village would look at home on the north coast of Norway. A popular place is ***Amy's B&B & Craft Shop*** *(☎ 795-3376)*.

Tête à la Baleine (pop 330) is a major seal-hunting area, where sealskin and fur products are crafted by locals. Toutes Îles (☎ 242-2015, 800-242-2015) offers overnight tours of Île Providence, 45 minutes away by boat, where there's a lonely chapel (1895).

Amid archeological digs in **Brador** (pop 150), 10km west of Blanc Sablon, what might have been the first road in New France has been uncovered. On the site of a French trading outpost abandoned in 1759, the 2.5km stretch of gravel road is intact and still used today.

Blanc Sablon (pop 1100) is the end of the line, 2km west of the Labrador border. A ferry (☎ 461-2056) links it in less than an hour to St Barbe in Newfoundland, and a paved road links it to several coastal villages in Labrador, meaning that the inhabitants are less isolated than are their neighbors farther west. A dynamic, mainly Anglophone fishing community lives here, in an area where numerous archeological digs since the early 1980s have shown a European presence since the 16th century and an aboriginal one stretching back more than 7000 years.

Scheffer Museum *(no ☎ ; admission free; open 8am-9pm daily)* is a small local history museum set up in the town's church. There are numerous B&Bs and restaurants.

Lower St Lawrence

LOWER ST LAWRENCE

☎ 418

This region, called Bas St Laurent in French, extends from La Pocatière to just west of Ste Flavie, at the start of the Gaspésie (Gaspé Peninsula). Tourists often zip along the coast through the region, making brief stops in Rivière du Loup or Rimouski, the last large population centers before the Gaspésie. Yet aside from the spectacular views of the North Shore's mist-covered, layered mountains seen from the region's coastline, there are surprises awaiting inland, particularly around Lac Témiscouata toward the New Brunswick border.

Traditionally the Lower St Lawrence has been an economically troubled region (the unemployment rate of 14.2% in early 2001 is double the national average). Still, information technology is a growing industry here, tourism has been slowly but steadily increasing and the government has promised to contribute over $70 million to reenergize the battered forestry industry.

High season here and in the Gaspésie begins after June 24th, St Jean Baptiste Day. Many tourist attractions open only after this date, but in an effort to extend the tourist season this is less true than it used to be. While July and August are the liveliest months, avoiding the crowds and visiting earlier or later should also be considered.

For information on the area just west of this region, see the Around Québec City section of the Québec City chapter.

KAMOURASKA
pop 700

The name alone of this small village (founded in 1674) conjures tales of mystery and imagination, thanks to an eponymous novel by Anne Hébert. Based on the true story of a woman and her doctor lover who conspired to kill her husband, the seigneur Achille Taché (a distant relative of Hébert's), *Kamouraska* was turned into a lyrical film in 1973 by Claude Jutra. Featur-ing epic windswept winter scenes and the haunting Geneviève Bujold, the film sealed tale and place forever as one in the collective consciousness of many Québécois.

Highlights

- Count razorbills and thousands of other birds off Rivière du Loup
- Tipple the alcoholic maple *aceritif* in Auclair
- Visit Québec's Timbuktu: St Louis de Ha! Ha!
- Try some saltwater lamb on Île Verte
- Have a go at a game of pelote in Trois Pistoles
- Find out about the worst maritime disaster after the Titanic at Pointe au Père

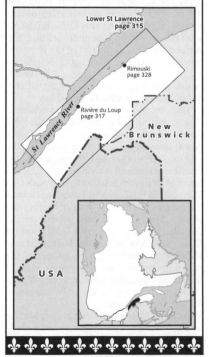

Two other personalities representing opposing political sympathies hail from this village: the author of the French lyrics to the national hymn ' O Canada,' Basile Routhier; and René Chalout, who designed the provincial flag.

There is indeed something special about Kamouraska and its enveloping serenity, which makes for a languid, peaceful overnight visit. It also makes an excellent lunch or picnic stop – buy some fresh fish from Gertrude (see below) and some baked goods from the boulangerie, and grab a picnic table along rue de la Promenade to bask in the seaside view.

A visit to the **Site d'Interprétation de l'Anguille** (☎ *492-3935, 205 avenue Morel; adult/child $4/3; open 9am-6pm daily mid-May–mid-Oct*) is recommended. True, you may not have come all this way to learn about eel fishing, but this place is an experience thanks to the vivacious owner, Gertrude Madore, who proudly states that she was the first woman in coastal Québec to receive a professional fishing license. She'll show you the nets she uses to capture the slimy creatures, 98% of which are exported to countries where people deem eel a delicacy. All the stuffed birds and sea life you see had the misfortune to be caught in Gertrude's nets – they now comprise one of the best exhibits of local fauna in the entire region. Another reason to visit is to sample her smoked eel and herring. She also sells her seafood products.

Places to Stay & Eat

Auberge des Aboiteaux (☎ *493-2495, 280 Rte 132*) Doubles $59/64 with shared/private bath, including breakfast and dinner. This must be one of the best deals in the province. Located in a little slice of paradise some 5km east of Kamouraska, the Auberge, in a stately house hidden behind apple trees, offers a delicious dinner in the price of your stay. The view of the river is your just desserts.

Motel Au Relais de Kamouraska (☎ *492-6246, 253 rue Morel*) Doubles $60. This great, mid-sized hotel overlooking the river is well worth a stop, even if only for a meal. They cater to families and offer childcare services. The on-site restaurant also has an

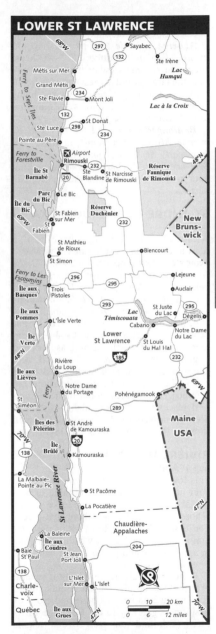

LOWER ST LAWRENCE

excellent reputation in the area – as expected, seafood is the specialty.

Auberge Foin de Mer *(☎ 492-7081, 85 avenue Leblanc)* Doubles $65-95. Most rooms have some view of the sea, though only the largest (and priciest) offers a head-on view of its magnificence. A large living room, small terrace and wood-paneled kitchen complete the picture.

Boulangerie Niemand *(☎ 492-1236, 82 avenue Morel; open 9am-6pm daily end June–early Sept, 9am-6pm Thur-Sun early Sept–late June)*, This bakery serves up melt-in-your-mouth fresh bread and yummy German pastries.

ST ANDRÉ DE KAMOURASKA
pop 600
Aside from the charming village itself, a reason to stop here is the **Salt Water Marsh Ecological Rest Stop** *(☎ 493-2604, 273 Rte 132; adult/child $2/1, guided tours $5 per person; open 10am-6pm Mon-Fri & 9:30am-8pm Sat & Sun late June–late Sept)*. Run by SEBKA, a local conservation group, this ecological park has 6km of well-marked trails describing the riches of the local environment – sea and marsh – as well as flora and fauna. Kayaks can be rented here and rock-climbers can scale nearby cliffs (ask for a pass). The views of the opposite shore are stunning. Best of all, this is one of the region's best places to spend the night – there's a great *campground* ($14 per night) with showers. Rivière du Loup is only 18km away.

RIVIÈRE DU LOUP
pop 17,800
This town has a way of weaving itself into your heart. While it boasts nothing of particular grandeur, visitors often leave saying, 'There's *something* I like about that place.' For its size it's a lively town with a pleasant atmosphere. The Cégep, which specializes in applied arts and photography, lends the town a culture edge.

Built on a rocky ridge (giving it several extremely steep hills) at the mouth of the Rivière du Loup, it has benefited from its position as gateway to the Maritime Provinces (Edmundston, New Brunswick, is 122km away). A ferry also connects it to Charlevoix, at St Siméon.

Founded in 1673, the city's development took off only after Scottish immigrant Alexander Fraser became seigneur and opened a sawmill here in 1802. A railroad (completed in 1860) connecting it to Montréal increased its importance, but it never grew bigger than its britches. Today Rivière du Loup is the perfect launching pad for exploring the beautiful islands just offshore or as a base for a bike or car trip down the Témiscouata region toward New Brunswick.

Orientation & Information
Rue Lafontaine is the main road, curving its way through the town's middle, and housing the main restaurants, bars, shops and, conveniently, banks and ATMs. It's as close to a downtown as you'll get. Both Hwy 20 and Rte 132 course through the town, the 132 becoming rue Fraser, another main artery acting as a motel strip.

The tourist information office (☎ 862-1981, 888-825-1981), at 189 boulevard Hôtel de Ville, is open year-round, from 8:30am to 9pm daily mid-June through August, and 8:30am to noon and 1:30pm to 5pm Monday through Friday from September through mid-June. There you can also see a small exhibit on the Saguenay-St Lawrence Marine Park. They also arrange one- to four-person, hour-long taxi tours of the city. The regional tourism association (☎ 867-3015, 800-563-5268) can also give information about the Lower St Lawrence, but by phone only.

The post office (☎ 862-6348) is at 140 rue Lafontaine and is open 8:30am to 5:30pm Monday through Friday. For Internet access go to the Centre Communautaire (☎ 867-5885), a community center in the Old Arsenal, at 26 rue Joly. They charge only $1 per hour and are open 9am to noon and 1pm to 4:30pm Monday through Saturday, and also from 6:30pm to 9:30pm Tuesday and Thursday.

To hire a cab, try Taxi Capitol at (☎ 862-6333).

Things to See & Do
Musée du Bas St Laurent This lively museum *(☎ 862-7547, 300 rue St Pierre; adult/*

student $5/3; open 10am-6pm daily early June–early Oct, 1pm-5pm Tues & Thur-Sun & 6pm-9pm Mon & Wed early Oct–early June) offers a good mix of regional history and contemporary art works in permanent and temporary exhibits.

Les Carillons Eccentricity is alive and well at the self-proclaimed largest museum in the world dedicated to bells *(☎ 862-3346, 393 rue Témiscouata; adult/child $5/2; open 9am-8pm daily late June–early Sept, 9am-5pm daily early–late June & early Sept–early Oct).* That's right, bells. Spread

out over sprawling gardens are some 200 bells saved from metal smelters. Bronze, pewter or cast iron, they come in all shapes and sizes (the largest weighing 1000kg) and date from 1718 to 1950. There's even a replica of the US Liberty Bell (1753) and another from a Pennsylvania plantation once used to call slaves (1760). You can ring most of them.

Parc des Chutes A few minutes walk from downtown is this small park *(admission free; open year-round)*, where some picnic tables and a 2.3km trail have been laid out to let

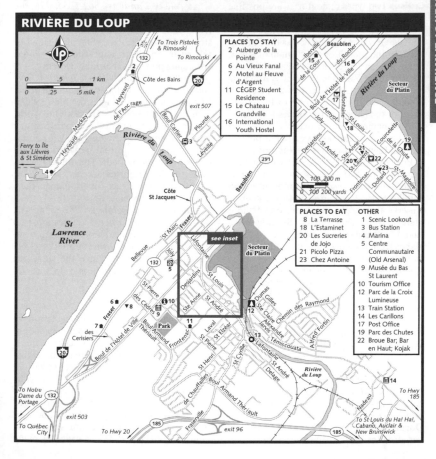

LOWER ST LAWRENCE

RIVIÈRE DU LOUP

PLACES TO STAY
2 Auberge de la Pointe
6 Au Vieux Fanal
7 Motel au Fleuve d'Argent
11 CÉGEP Student Residence
15 Le Chateau Grandville
16 International Youth Hostel

PLACES TO EAT
8 La Terrasse
18 L'Estaminet
20 Les Sucreries de Jojo
21 Picolo Pizza
23 Chez Antoine

OTHER
1 Scenic Lookout
3 Bus Station
4 Marina
5 Centre Communautaire (Old Arsenal)
9 Musée du Bas St Laurent
10 Tourism Office
12 Parc de la Croix Lumineuse
13 Train Station
14 Les Carillons
17 Post Office
19 Parc des Chutes
22 Broue Bar; Bar en Haut; Kojak

you admire the 30m waterfalls, which power a small hydroelectric power station.

Parc de la Croix Lumineuse A short drive up to the hilly areas of town leads you to this tiny park *(admission free; open year-round)*, where an illuminated cross guards a nice lookout. To get there from downtown, take rue Joly south until the underpass leading to rue Témiscouata. Make a left on chemin des Raymond, turn left at rue Alexandre, right at rue Bernier and then left at rue Ste Claire.

Cruises Two types of boat trips are possible from the marina at Rivière du Loup. AML (☎ 867-3361, 200 rue Hayward) offers 3½-hour whale-watching trips across the St Lawrence to the mouth of the Saguenay River. These are on large boats, often with large numbers of people (see the Whale Watching special section in the Activities chapter), but if you are not planning to go to the North Shore or to Gaspé – better places to observe marine mammals – you may want to do it from here. Prices are usually $40 per person; child and senior discounts are offered.

Better still are trips offered by La Société Duvetnor (☎ 867-1660, W www.duvetnor .com, 200 rue Hayward), a nonprofit group founded in 1979 by marine biologists keen to preserve the fragile ecosystem on offshore islands (see 'The Lower St Lawrence Islands'). They raised money to buy the islands from the government and have kept them free from major development. They offer a range of bird-watching and nature excursions lasting from a few hours to several days. Sighting belugas is common. Prices are about $20 for a 1½-hour trip to and around the Îles du Pot à l'Eau-de-Vie, $30/15 adult/child for a day trip to Île aux Lièvres, and $120 to $180 for overnight stays in cottages or an old lighthouse, including meals.

Places to Stay
International Youth Hostel (☎ 862-7566, fax 862-1843, e aubergeriviere-du-loup@ moncourtier.com, 46 rue Hôtel de Ville) Dorm beds $16.50/19 member/nonmember, doubles $21/22. Boasting a central lo-

cation in an old yellow house, this has a placid atmosphere as far as hostels go. Cheap breakfasts are served, and activities around the city are sometimes organized.

Cégep Student Residence (☎ 862-6903 ext 282, 325 rue St Pierre) Singles/doubles $20/40. Clean and quiet, here's where you can see how students live! Sparsely equipped kitchens are at your disposal.

Motel au Fleuve d'Argent (☎ 862-5315, 202 rue Fraser) Doubles in motel or chalet $65-70. Sparse but clean rooms and detached chalets overlooking the river. Chalets have a kitchenette and BBQ.

Au Vieux Fanal (☎ 862-5255, 170 rue Fraser) Double rooms $70/80 without/with river view. One of the best motels on the strip is this simple place with great views of the river (in the pricier rooms), heated swimming pool and charming owners.

Le Chateau Grandville (☎ 868-0750, 877-900-0750, W www.chateaugrandville.qc.ca, 94 rue Lafontaine) Singles/doubles $80/95, with breakfast $85/105. There's Old World elegance galore in this mid-19th-century grand home. Their highest-priced rooms, still a good deal, are real treats with wood floors and canopy beds. The three restaurants on the premises are also excellent, with an outdoor terrace (overlooking a busy street) and a cozy bar.

Auberge de la Pointe (☎ 862-3514, 800-463-1222, 10 boul Cartier) Doubles $85-140. This four-star complex, less than 2km from the marina, is well known for good service. Room prices depend on size, the view, and their numerous special offers.

Places to Eat & Drink
Les Sucreries de Jojo (☎ 862-2671, 340 rue Lafontaine) Mains $5-11, open 8am-6pm Mon-Wed, 8am-10pm Thurs & Fri, 9am-5pm Sat & Sun. This country-kitchen café is renowned for its sweets (pastries and Belgian chocolate) but their breakfasts are killer (oh, the things they think of to stuff on your plate!) and light meals taste fresh and healthy.

L'Estaminet (☎ 867-4517, 299 rue La-fontaine) Mains $6-10, open 10am to midnight or 1am daily. In a pub-like atmosphere (the more than 100 types of beer, including many local brews, reinforce this), good salads, paninis and pasta are served. Mussels with fries, their specialty, start at $7. People come just to hang out at the bar too.

La Terrasse (☎ 862-6927, 171 rue Fraser) Mains $7-14. The specialty of this restaurant inside the Hôtel Levesque, is what most everyone comes here for – the salmon, smoked by the owners, as succulent as its reputation. The other restaurant in the hotel, La Distinction, has similar dishes for higher prices.

Picolo Pizza (☎ 868-1671, 371 rue Lafontaine) Appetizers $3-10, mains $9-18. Despite the word 'pizza' in its name, make no mistake – this is fine cuisine. Their pastas and pizzas are creative (chicken-ginger pizza, two-salmon pasta), their specialties (seafood, pork) are well seasoned, and they do funky beer cocktails, mixed with cranberry juice or iced tea!

Chez Antoine (☎ 862-6936, 433 rue Lafontaine) Mains from $15-27. Considered the top dining spot in the city, with prices that prove it.

Broue Bar, Bar en Haut & Kojak (☎ 862-1101, 403 rue Lafontaine) Three bars in one building – take your pick! Broue Bar, in the basement, is mildly more grunge and alternative, and Kojak has a popular daytime terrace. The Bar en Haut, upstairs, is a standard disco that plays mostly pop.

Getting There & Away
Bus The bus station (☎ 862-4884), at 83 rue Cartier, has coin lockers. Orléans Express runs buses to/from Montréal ($68, 5½ hours, 3 daily), Québec City ($34, 2½–4 hours, 7 daily), Rimouski ($19, 1¼ hours, 6 daily), Edmundston ($18, 2 hours, 3 daily) and Halifax ($94, 11½ hours, 2 daily).

Train The train station (☎ 867-1525) is on the corner of Lafontaine and Fraserville, but don't bother going unless it's to catch your train – it's closed except for when trains arrive in the middle of the night. VIA Rail (☎ 800-361-5390) links Rivière du Loup to Montréal ($68, 3 weekly) to points along the southern coast of the Gaspésie (to Gaspé $65, 11½ hours) and to Halifax ($96, 14¼ hours).

Car Highway 20 (exit 503), Rte 132 and Rte 185 (to/from New Brunswick) lead directly into town.

Boat A 65-minute ferry service (☎ 862-5094, W www.travrdlstsim.com) runs between Rivière du Loup and St Siméon from mid-April until January 3. Throughout the summer, there are four or five departures a day. Tickets cost adult/child $11.30/7.50. An additional $29/4 for car/bike is charged. From mid-July through mid-August there's a 30% discount on first and last departures each day. All boats leave from the marina, 199 rue Hayward. Those wishing to take a three-hour roundtrip cruise can hope to spot belugas; the price is only marginally higher than for one-way.

LAC TÉMISCOUATA (LE TÉMIS)
Le Témis is the name affectionately given to a region concentrated around its main geographical feature, the 40km-long Lac Témiscouata. This area is relatively unexplored and holds a few surprises, particularly on the lake's east side, where several villages slated to be closed by the government (see JAL, later) took their fate in their hands and transformed themselves into busy and creative communities. For more info, see W www.tourismetemiscouata.com.

Petit Témis Interprovincial Linear Park
This very scenic bike and walking trail, mainly flat, runs 135km along an old train track nearly parallel to Rte 185, from Rivière du Loup to Edmundston, New Brunswick. The nicest part is where it meets Lac Témiscouata and southward toward the provincial border. Unfortunately users are required to buy a $10 access sticker (there are cyclist patrollers who'll try to get you to buy one, though they have no power to fine you). You can purchase stickers at Rivière du Loup's tourist office (☎ 868-1869, 189 rue Hôtel de Ville), the Société Aménagement in Dégelis (☎ 853-3593, 584 6-ème Rue) or at other places along the trail, at which time you will be given a map of the trail (free maps are also found in local tourist guides).

The Lower St Lawrence Islands

From Kamouraska to Rimouski, a series of small islands hug the coast. Many of these are mere dots on the map and accessible only by private boat, while others are protected areas of wildlife conservation able to be visited on a limited basis. To access many of these islands, contact the Société Duvetnor (see the Rivière du Loup section). For the Île aux Basques, see the Trois Pistoles section, and for the islands off the Parc du Bic, see the Le Bic section.

Near Rivière du Loup are several islands under the protection of the Société Duvetnor. All are important nesting and breeding grounds for birds, and are an ornithologist's paradise; razorbills (called *petits penguins*, 'small penguins,' because of their appearance), double-crested cormorants, great blue herons, black guillemot, goldeneyes and brants among others flock here.

The 7.5km-long **Îles des Pèlerins** (Pilgrim Islands), so named as they together resemble the shape of someone lying down, hands folded in prayer, are off-limits; they're home to the estuary's most important colony of kittiwakes. Common eiders, sometimes referred to as sea ducks, also nest there. Males have a striking black-and-white plumage, while the female's is striped with brown for better camouflage. Females pluck their own feathers into a down, used as a lining for their nests. This can be collected without harm to their young; the Société Duvetnor gathers a small quantity each year and exports it to Germany where it's stuffed into pillows.

The **Île aux Lièvres**, smack in the middle of the St Lawrence, is open to the public. There are some 40km of mostly scenic walking trails on this 13km-long, heavily forested island (some are off-limits until nesting is completed in mid-July). There are also three campsites ($22), making the island an excellent place to do take hikes, bird-watch (screech owls, goshawks and eagles sometimes make appearances), spot belugas and seals from the rocky shore, and then crash out for the night.

Smaller and lying near the Îles aux Lièvres are the **Îles du Pot à l'Eau-de-Vie**, where razorbills and cormorants are visible by the hundreds. It is also possible to stay here overnight in the refurbished lighthouse.

Farther east is **Île Verte**, off the coast of the village L'Isle Verte. The only island in the area to be inhabited (40 sturdy souls) and sporting the river's oldest working lighthouse (1809), this 11km-long island is characterized by petite, brightly painted houses (reminiscent of the ones on Îles de la Madeleine). Ornithologists and bird-watchers follow the flocks here as well.

Five kilometers off the coast of Trois Pistoles is **Île aux Basques**, which boasts 400 species of plant and 277 species of bird on its tiny territory (about 2km in length). It's protected by the Société Provencher but guided visits are possible. Finally, near Le Bic are several islands protected under the aegis of the Parc du Bic. Here the common eider is king, and they can be seen in swarms that sometimes defy the imagination.

If you get tired and want to cheat a bit, a taxi service can drive you from one place to another with your bikes; there's no shame in calling Taxi-Vélo (in Cabano ☎ 854-2630, in Notre Dame du Lac ☎ 899-2878, in Dégelis ☎ 853-3707).

St Louis de Ha! Ha!

Thanks to its name, this town (pop 1500) can be considered the Timbuktu of Québec –

somewhere to visit just to say you've been there. The origin of the town's odd name is uncertain. It could come from the Hexcuewaska language, referring to something unexpected, or it could be 15th-century French for 'dead end'; others say it reflects the exclamation of wonder and admiration the area's first colonizers uttered upon seeing such beauty. Considering the town itself, the first two explanations seem more likely.

James Bay hydroelectric station

Sidewalk café, Baie St Paul

Parc du Saguenay, Saguenay

One of the North Shore's mighty rivers

Lighthouse, Gaspé Peninsula

The legendary Pierced Rock, Percé

Aerial view, Îles de la Madeleine

There's not much to be gleaned in this arid, nondescript place save for the **Aster La Station Scientifique** (☎ *854-2172, 59 chemin Bellevue; adult/student $6/4; open noon-midnight late June–early Sept).* This mini planetarium hosts late-evening astronomical observations and has exhibits on local geology.

Cabano to Dégelis

This very pretty stretch of road follows Lac Témiscouata, which is largely in a natural state – heavily wooded and wild with game and fowl. In Cabano (pop 3200) there are panoramas of the lake and distant Mount Lennox, as well as a public beach. Here you can also visit **Fort Ingall** (☎ *854-2375, 81 chemin Caldwell; adult/child $6.50/4; open 9:30am-6pm June-Sept),* a 1973 re-construction of an 1839 British fort set up to keep out Americans who had set their sights on the St Lawrence's south shores. There's an exhibit here on Grey Owl, an eccentric Brit who immigrated to Canada in 1906 to work as a trapper and who later dressed like a First Nations man and fought against the killing of beavers. He was the subject of a Canadian film as well as a 1999 film by Richard Attenborough, who portrayed him as one of America's first environmental activists.

Notre Dame du Lac (pop 2200) is the area's resort town, with a popular beach. There's **boat and paddleboat rentals** at the marina (☎ 899-2776, 40 rue Ménard). Part of the Trans Canada Confederation Trail, for hikers, starts here and winds 105km south then north toward Trois Pistoles. There is also a ferry service across the lake to St Juste du Lac (☎ 899-2826; person/car $1.50/5), which runs June to September. For local history, check out the small **Musée du Témiscouata** (☎ *899-0072, 3 rue Hôtel de Ville; adult/student $4/2; open 1pm-5pm & 7pm-9pm Tues-Sun late June–early Sept).*

Just 15km from the border of New Brunswick is Dégelis (pop 3400), which means 'does not freeze' in archaic French. The tiny rivière Madawaska (a Micmac word for 'does not freeze'!), which courses through it at one point – you guessed it! –

never freezes due to strong currents. From here, take Rte 295 north to the eastern side of the lake and eventually to Trois Pistoles.

Places to Stay & Eat There is no shortage of campgrounds, motels, B&Bs and restaurants in the villages.

Centre de Plein Air Le Montagnais (☎ *853-2003, 750 Rte 295, Dégelis)* Tent sites $13. This small, quiet terrain offers varied activities such as hiking, canoeing, archery and rock climbing.

Centre de Plein Air (☎ *899-2776, 40 rue Ménard, Notre Dame du Lac)* Tent sites $14/22 no/full services. Near the marina and beach and situated at a rest stop along the bike trail, this is a great place to spend the night if you appreciate views of the lake.

Ranch du Soleil Levant (☎ *854-2983,* e *gitesoleillevant@globetrotter.net, 69 Rte 232 Est, Cabano)* Doubles $50. This B&B manages a rustic farm ambience on the lakeside.

L'Abrise du Lac (☎ *899-2508, 854 rue Commerciale, Notre Dame du Lac)* Doubles $50. This two-story B&B with a spacious attic room is right off the bike trail and is walking distance from the beach.

Boucherie Bégin (☎ *853-2976, 314 avenue Principale, Dégelis)* Meat lovers will appreciate the huge cow that sits atop this butcher's shop, which also sells ready-made meals ($4-7) and decent smoked meat.

JAL

JAL is an acronym for three little villages, St Juste du Lac, Auclair and Lejeune, that in the early 1970s formed a cooperative, with the support of the local clergy, to stand up to provincial powers that had decided to close them permanently. The cost of providing essential services was prohibitive, the powers argued. After winning a stay of execution, residents began a number of mini industries, including potato-seed production, lumber milling, maple tapping, and even coffin building. More recently, a unique medicinal herb garden has opened in the area, where you can also find the world's first producer of a sinfully delicious alcoholic beverage derived from maple sap!

In deciding to prove to the government that their community could be productive and profitable, residents sharply reversed their fate. In the process they created a community spirit approaching that of a commune – which is rare in Eastern Canada. Today these specks on the map in the middle of fields, forest and lakes have become one of the most dynamic areas in the province. Still, one must do more than scratch the surface to find out, so preciously has its bucolic charm been retained.

St Juste du Lac This village (pop 650) is composed of a few roads, the neighboring parish of **Lots Renversées**, a beach along the banks of Lac Témiscouata, and several hiking and mountain-bike trails. Part of the Trans Canada Confederation Trail passes through this region, along the lake.

Auclair Auclair (pop 550) lies in a scenic, hilly region of tall maples, so quiet that you could hear a leaf drop. Who could guess that heaven lies just around the corner at the **Domaine Acer** (☎ 899-2825, ⓔ *robert .vallier@simpatico.ca, 65 Rte du Vieux Moulin; guided visit $2; open 9am-5pm daily mid-March–Dec 24th, to 6pm July & Aug, shop only mid-Oct–Dec 24th)*? At this maple-grove-cum-ecomuseum you can get one of the best explanations about maple syrup production in the province on a guided visit (including bilingual signs), taste maple products and Belgian chocolates, and acquaint yourself with one of the country's most unique products – *aceritif.*

Since 1997 the country's first alcoholic beverage made from distilled maple sap, aged in oak barrels, has been produced here. The result is fantastic, particularly their two aperitif-like products. In 2001 they were granted permission to utilize their coined term, aceritif, to describe them, blending 'aperitif' with 'acer,' the Latin for maple.

Lejeune In Lejeune (pop 400), 9km from Auclair, you'll find other artisans and their wares, including **Viv-Herbes** (☎ 855-2731, *35 2-ème rang; guided tour adult/child $4/free; open July–early Sept or by appointment;*

tours at 1pm & 3pm daily), a medicinal herb garden and shop in beautiful, isolated surroundings.

Also impressive here is **Les Artisans Forestiers** (☎ 868-7438, ⓦ *www.chez.com/ chassegalerie, 23 2-ème rang; admission free; open by appointment)*, a workshop producing high quality First Nations crafts (clothes, jewelry, moccasins, and decorative objects) doubling as an adventure tourism organization. This is one of the best places to go dogsledding into the forest on wintertime excursions (around $120 a day). The animals are obviously well cared for by the owners, who infuse much passion into what they do. Camping in teepees is also possible in summer.

Places to Stay Accommodations choices are slim here but are rewarding in their simplicity and because of the region's quiet, pretty surroundings.

Camping d'Eau Clair (☎ 899-6093, *22 Rte 295)* Tent sites $13, cabins from $204/week. Truly one of the nicest public camping spots in the province, this is situated right on the banks of tranquil and clean Lac Grand Squatec, 2km east of Auclair. It's fully serviced (showers, laundry, cafeteria, playground) and, with 71 campsites, not big enough to feel too crowded. The cabins, for two to four people, overlook the lake and are good deals.

Le Prebytère (☎ 899-6695, *40 rue du Clocher)* Singles/doubles $50/60. This place offers rustic charm in a spacious house.

L'ISLE VERTE & ÎLE VERTE

Helpful hint: The one with the 's' refers to the village, the other one to the island. L'Isle Verte (pop 1050) shows its roots as a fishing village in the numerous places to buy fresh or smoked fish. The principal attraction is the small (406 hectare) but impressive **Réserve Nationale de Faune de la Baie de l'Isle Verte** (☎ 898-2757, *371 Rte 132; admission free, guided tours adult/child $5/2; open 9am-5pm daily mid-June–mid-Sept, tours Thur-Sat)*. This federally protected zone, which welcomes some 130 species of bird a year, was formed initially to protect the natural habitat of the American black duck.

It encompasses wetlands and marsh, and there are 5km of hiking/biking trails.

Just a few kilometers off the coast is **Île Verte** (pop 40), a dreamy 11km-long slice of the past. The island has a few attractions, namely the oldest **lighthouse** in the St Lawrence (1809), with a perky, newly painted red top. Yet pleasures here come in wandering along the rocky shore, hiking its trails, breathing in air sweetened by wild roses. So far the island remains relatively uncrowded; a boat has linked it with the mainland only since 1990, and so far only a couple thousand tourists a year make the trip.

The old way of life is slowly dying here: The fishing industry has dried up, arable soil on the island's south side has been bought by those seeking pleasant summer retreats, and it's only a matter of time before the lighthouse itself is closed. Locals concede that the island will eventually become a summer retreat overrun with cottages.

Places to Stay & Eat

There are several B&Bs and motels in L'Isle Verte and on Île Verte, any of which can help set you up with bike rental.

Les Capucines (☎ 898-3276, 31 rue Louis Bertrand) Singles/doubles \$40/55. This B&B in the village of L'Isle Verte has four simple rooms. They can arrange to cook dinners, too.

Les Maisons du Phare (☎ 898-2730, 28B chemin du Phare, Île Verte) Singles/doubles from \$45/55. Eight rooms in the lighthouse offer a perfect retreat – and an easy way to find your way back at night! This comfortable place is in a most exotic locale.

La Maison d'Agathe (☎ 898-2923, fax 898-3745, 68C chemin de l'Île, Île Verte) Doubles \$55. A place to feast on saltwater lamb (see 'Saltwater Lamb, Please') and to enjoy a view of the south shore. Meals are served three times a day in the restaurant, and an on-site *dépanneur* stocks everything else you might need.

Getting There & Away

A ferry (☎ 898-2843; adult \$5, child 7-16 \$2, child under 7 free, car/bicycle \$25/1) runs between L'Isle Verte and Île Verte from May to mid-November, making the 15-minute trip

'Saltwater Lamb, Please'

Tiny Île Verte boasts a culinary specialty found nowhere else in North America: saltwater lamb. Dominique Caron, the island's last shepherd, started raising sheep commercially with friends in 1999, the first new agricultural project on the island in years. The sheep are the only ones on the continent to be reared and fed on salty meadows; they spend four hours a day grazing during low tide, a sight odd enough to distract even the most avid bird-watcher or whale-spotter.

These sheep have more muscle mass, thus less fat, than regular sheep, and their meat is more tender and flavorful. The local B&Bs and restaurants all serve this delicacy (as does the Château Frontenac, in Québec City, though at a much higher price). Sadly these are the only places to sample the meat. The flock has about 100 animals and there are no plans to expand into mass production, as several American entrepreneurs have suggested that Caron do. The marshlands on the island cannot be overextended – and it keeps Île Verte all the more unique.

two to five times daily. It's best to reserve in advance. A Taxi Boat (☎ 898-2199) can be used around the clock, but for considerably higher prices.

TROIS PISTOLES
pop 3800

Just east of Rivière du Loup, Hwy 20 ends and, except during its brief reappearance around Rimouski, you must continue on Rte 132.

Legend has it that this town was named for a goblet worth three *pistoles* (an old form of French currency) lost by a sailor nearby. Fact has it that the town was founded in 1713 and that its imposing **Notre Dame des Neiges** (☎ 851-4949, 30 Notre Dame Est) was completed in 1887 (though legend has it that it was built on the spot that an August snowball from God landed – hence its name, Our Lady of the Snows).

Parc de l'Aventure Basque en Amérique

Examining the history of Basque fishermen in North America before European explorers arrived, this museum (☎ 851-1556, W www.icrdl .net/paba, 66 avenue du Parc; adult/student $6/3.50; open 9am-8pm daily June–mid-Oct) opens the door onto a part of history with which few are familiar. The exhibits are in French (an English booklet is available), and English tours can be booked in advance. On the first weekend in July they host the International Basque Festival with music, games (see 'Pelote, Anyone?') and a mini parade.

Cruises

Guided excursions to the Île aux Basques (☎ 851-1202, 11 rue du Parc; $15; open daily June–early Sept) touch upon the social history of the island (First Nations tribes lived here since at least AD 700; later Basque fishermen would extract oil from whale blubber here) as well as its present status as a protected bird sanctuary.

Also from the marina Les Écumeurs (☎ 851-9955, 888-817-9999, 11 rue du Parc) offer whale-watching cruises on the North Shore, from $35 per adult for a 2½-hour cruise.

A passenger ferry operated by Compagnie de Navigation des Basques (☎ 851-4676, e cnbasque@globetrotter.net, 11 rue du Parc) runs to/from Les Escoumins, on the North Shore, two or three times daily from mid-May to mid-October (adult $11.50, child 5-16 $7.25, child under 5 free, with car/ bicycle $29/4). It's best to reserve ahead.

Pelote, Anyone?

The most noticeable modern legacy of Basque culture in this region of Québec is no doubt the fronton found in Trois Pistoles. It's without question the most fun.

A *fronton*? It's a rectangular, marked court with a large wall on one end used to play Pelote Basque, one of the world's oldest ball games (it's even referred to in the Mayan creation story Popol Vuh). With a ball velocity of up to 300km/hr, it's also the world's fastest ball and bat game.

The fronton in Trois Pistoles is unique in Canada – indeed it's a rare sight outside Basque areas in Spain, where nearly every village sports one. In Canada and the US there is an indoor court in Montréal, an outdoor one on the French islands of St Pierre et Miquelon, and an outdoor one in Florida (there, a game colloquially termed Jaï Alaï is popular, although that's the name of the court used, which differs from a fronton; the game they play on it is Cesta Punta).

Though there are variations in the kind of Pelote Basque played on different styles of courts using different equipment, one element remains sacred: the small, hard ball, also called pelote. It's made with a tightly wound rubber center bound with cotton and strips of leather. Weighing only some 100 grams and measuring a mere 65mm in diameter, this little tiger can be a killer in the hands of experts. When a chistera or rebot (types of curved baskets) is used to hurl the ball, it whizzes around faster than the eye can see.

Commonly a heavy bat (like a huge ping-pong bat) is used for a game called Paleta Gomme. This is the Pelote variation enjoyed in Trois Pistoles, what enthusiasts travel from far and wide to play. Located just outside the Parc de l'Aventure Basque en Amérique, the fronton is used for several major pelote competitions every summer played by several hundred descendants from Basque families living throughout Québec, New Brunswick and Maine.

Visitors to the Parc de l'Aventure get to step onto the fronton and try the pelote for themselves (or rent the court for $10/hour). It's best not to begin overconfidently – this ain't ping-pong. The heaviness of the bat and hardness of the ball demand considerable force and precision timing, and there's a heck of a lot of running around. No matter how well you may do, keep in mind that experts often play with bare hands.

Places to Stay & Eat

Camping & Motel des Flots Bleus sur Mer
(☎ 851-3583, Rte 132, Rivière Trois Pistoles)
Tent sites $15; motel singles/doubles from
$40/$60. There are a couple of large, hard-
to-miss campgrounds in Trois Pistoles, but
this one, 5km west of town, on the banks of
the rivière Trois Pistoles, is much smaller,
quieter and in a nicer area. There are toilets
and showers on site. The neighboring motel
is bare-bones but the cheapest around and
decent enough.

Côté Mer (☎ 851-1255, 3 chemin Grève
Fatima) Doubles $60. This pleasant B&B
has nice views of the St Lawrence.

L'Ensoleillé (☎ 851-2889, 138 Notre Dame
Ouest) Mains $4-10, open 8am-midnight
daily. Excellent healthy food and seafood
served up in a country-kitchen atmosphere.
Their lunch specials are a good value.

ST FABIEN
pop 1800
The area between St Simon and Le Bic is
characterized by farms and peat moss operations, which together with the region's hills
might make you think you were somewhere
in Scotland.

The town of St Fabien and its smaller, residential sister town of St Fabien sur Mer are
the main stops in the area. St Fabien sur Mer
consists of fabulous country homes spread
out along chemin de la Mer, which wraps
itself around a fantastic bay. The mountainous ranges of the neighboring Parc du Bic
resemble fjords from here as they descend
into the sea, and the rocky shore, black with
chipped shale (referred to locally as 'toff'),
has a dramatic, barren look.

On chemin de la Mer Est there's a boat
ramp (☎ 750-1998, 869-2300) where worthwhile excursions in Zodiacs take you around
the Parc du Bic (see below), bird-watching
and to a 1919 shipwreck. Their schedule is
erratic, though, so best call first. Expect to
pay $25 to $30 per person. They also offer
charters.

Equestrian fans will be satisfied with the
various expeditions offered at **Ranch CR**
(☎ 869-3484, W www.ranchcr.qc.ca, 131 1-ère
rang Ouest; visits adult/child $2.50/2; open

May-Oct). There are horseback outings
ranging from a few hours to a few days long.
They're well prepared for child visitors.

PARC DU BIC
One of the smaller provincial parks is
nonetheless one of its most striking. At
times, especially with thousands of eiders
flying overhead, the landscape seems
surreal. Covering 33 sq km of islands, bays,
jagged cliffs, conical mountaintops, and
rocky shores covered with plump gray and
harbor seals, this park (☎ 869-3333, 33 Rte
132; adult/child $3.50/1.50; open year-round)
offers a plethora of activities. There are organized minibus tours, sea kayaking expeditions, specialized walks, and bike rental
($18/day). There are also hiking, biking,
skiing and snowshoe trails. Sunsets are particularly enjoyable from the Raoul Roy
lookout (entrance from St Fabien sur Mer)
and atop Pic Champlain.

The staff will delight in telling you the
meaning behind the names of all the park's
features, especially Île des Amours (Lovers'
Island). Connected to the mainland during
low tide, it becomes an island after the tide
comes in, and rumor has it that many
Casanovas of old used to take their dates on
walks only to be stranded there until low
tide returned the next morning.

An excellent option for **kayaking** is with
Kayak Rivi-Air Aventure (☎ 736-5252,
W www.rivi-air.qc.ca, 3257 Rte 132, Le Bic).
Friendly, flexible and knowledgeable staff
offer half-, full-day or sunset outings from
$30 to $60.

The park also runs a *campground* (☎ 736-
4711, 736-5035; tent sites $21) adjoining its
eastern end. Of its five sectors, the Guillemot
à Miroir is the least crowded and the most
remote. Unfortunately the campground,
while attractive enough, sits in a valley that
amplifies the truck traffic noise all night long.

RIMOUSKI
pop 32,400
Of limited interest to most tourists, Rimouski ('land of moose' in the Micmac language) nevertheless has its share of worthy
detours. The city is currently in a transitional

LOWER ST LAWRENCE

What's Wrong with Brigitte?

In Québec Brigitte Bardot is widely disliked for more than her performances in *Babette Goes to War* or *And God Created Woman*. In fact, the ex-sex kitten of 1960s French cinema is roundly hated in the fishing communities of Québec and throughout the Maritime Provinces. Fisherfolk say that her massive publicity campaigns against seal hunting helped result in chronic depletions of the fish stocks that sustained their livelihood.

No one knows for certain how many seals live in the St Lawrence but estimates range from five to eight million; the figure in the early 1980s was around three million. What is known is that adult seals eat up to 10% of their weight per day (depending on the type of seal, adult weight ranges from 85kg to 400kg). Harp seals alone eat an estimated seven million tonnes of prey a year, including 1.4 million tonnes of cod in the Maritime Provinces and Québec. Stocks of herring and cod, to name two seal favorites, have declined such that they no longer constitute an industry. Aside from overfishing, locals blame Brigitte Bardot for their plight.

It all started back in 1970 when Mme Bardot was appearing along with other superstars draped in soft mink coats in a huge pro-fur campaign photographed by Richard Avedon. (These ads can still be seen hung mockingly in the offices of Montréal furriers.) Before long, writer, academic, animal-rights activist and personal fan Marguerite Yourcenar recruited her to the other side. Bardot switched camps with a vengeance, taking on animal rights as her post–film career *raison d'être*.

In 1977 and 1978 she was the focal point in the most successful animal-rights campaign in history, choreographed and masterminded by Greenpeace. Between her enormous fan base and the campaign's effective tactics, attention was assured. She was flown out onto the icy banks of Labrador and the Îles de la Madeleine and was filmed giving motherly, tearful hugs of support to the baby seals lying there.

These were wildly captivating, highly emotional images, and soon public opinion swung around to the anti-fur side. Fur-wearers were being splattered with ketchup on the streets of Montréal and other cities across North America and Europe. In 1983 the European Community banned all baby-seal products. The Canadian government prohibited baby-seal hunting and curtailed the quota on hunting harp seals. Yet even without the quotas the seal hunting industry went bust as global demand and therefore sales withered.

By Bardot's second campaign, in the mid-'90s, the tide had turned again. Not only had ketchup been relegated back onto hot dogs but the pro-fur and pro-fishing lobbies had become much

phase. After experiencing a boom at the beginning of the 20th century thanks to successful lumber-finishing plants, Rimouski ended the century as the capital of one of the most depressed regions in Québec, thanks to the slow-down in the forestry industry. The city's economy has begun to look better, benefiting from development of the information technology and tourism sectors.

The city gives off alternating vibes as a consequence of these contrasting trends; at once there's a feel of both faded glory and of better days ahead. There's also a youthful energy thanks to the many educational institutions (if you are heading east, these might be some of the last youths you'll see for a while!), and residents are certain that theirs are the most beautiful sunsets in the country.

Orientation & Information

Central Rimouski spreads northeast from the meeting of rivière Rimouski and the St Lawrence. West of the river, Rte 132 is known as boulevard St Germain; after the bridge it splits into rue St Germain, the city's main street, with a downtown core running along it between avenues Rouleau and Belzile. It is dominated by the bulky

What's Wrong with Brigitte?

better organized. The government was increasing quotas again. This time Bardot and her attempts to politicize this campaign (she attacked Asian governments for trading in seal penises and called Canada's Prime Minister Jean Chrétien a murderer) were mercilessly mocked by the media, and her efforts fell flat. By 1995 the Canadian government was giving subsidies to encourage sealers to kill more.

'She missed a good opportunity to mind her own business,' says one fisherman in Tadoussac, a region where the harp seal has been hunted for several thousand years. 'Seals were never being tortured and murdered in the ways shown on the media.' Indeed, years after the fact, Greenpeace was accused of purposely skinning a baby seal alive just to broadcast the horrific images of it crawling bloodily along on the ice.

'I've read that she can't even take proper care of all the cats she lives with, and still she comes here to tell us what to do with our seals!' exclaims a Kamouraska fisher, who has seen her life change along with depleting fish levels. 'In the 1980s, on a good day, I'd catch over 1000 herring a day in my nets. Now on a good day there'll be about 100. Just forget about cod!'

A televised video filmed underwater showing how seals eat cod – playing with it until it dies, then carefully extracting its heart and liver, leaving the rest to rot on the seabed – enraged fishing communities. They say the seal population must be controlled, and consensus is growing. In exhibitions and museums along the Lower St Lawrence, on the Gaspé coast, on the Îles de la Madeleine and along the north shore you can find information about the usefulness of such a control.

The issue remains controversial. Animal-rights groups point to Canada as engaging in the world's largest marine-mammal cull (killing with the purpose to deplete a population) by refusing to lower its quota of 275,000 harp seals a year. They also note that illegal methods of killing are used every year (including skinning seals alive) to show the country as not serious about its commitment to animal welfare. The government counters that by fining offenders and claiming that they need to protect depleted fish stocks, that the seal population is not in danger.

As for Bardot, she still keeps her watchful gaze upon Canada. In late 2001 she wrote a letter to the director of the Granby Zoo, imploring him to reverse his much-attacked decision to go ahead with an attraction allowing visitors to swim with dolphins. (For details see 'The Wrath of Flipper' in the Eastern Townships chapter.)

Cathédrale St Germain (1826) and is home to everything from Mr Muffler to spiffy boutiques. Avenue de la Cathédrale splits the streets into east (Est) and west (Ouest).

Parc Beauséjour, which hosts many summer concerts and is a good place for summer or winter outdoor activities, is on the eastern banks of the rivière Rimouski.

The tourist office (☎ 723-2322, 800-746-6875), open year-round, is at 50 rue St Germain Ouest. The post office is at 136 rue St Germain Ouest. For Internet access there's a monitor at Café des Halles ($2.50 for 30 minutes; see Places to Eat). There are

several ATMs and banks along boulevard St Germain.

Taxis Touristes (☎ 723-3344) has eight guided taxi tours of the city or surrounding areas to choose from, costing from $35 to $50 for up to four people.

Things to See & Do

Musée Régional de Rimouski Each year there are rotating, permanent exhibits at this local history museum (☎ 724-2272, 35 rue St Germain Ouest; adult/student $4/3; open 10am-9pm Wed-Sat & 10am-6pm Sun-Tues June-Sept, noon-5pm Wed-Sun Oct-May), so the results can be hit or miss. There is usually a display of local, contemporary art. It's housed in a pretty stone church (1826).

Institut Maritime In summer this naval college (☎ 724-2822, Ⓦ *www.imq.qc.ca, 53 rue St Germain Ouest; adult/student $2/1; open 9am-noon & 1pm-5pm Wed-Sun June-Aug)* opens its doors and gives tours of the facilities, where some 350 students study mechanics, diving, architecture and navigation. There are some simulators on hand. Tours are given on the hour and can be in English (best to reserve this in advance).

Places to Stay

Cégep Residences (☎ 723-4636, 800-463-0617, Ⓦ www.cegep-rimouski.qc.ca/residenc, 320 rue St Louis) Students singles/doubles $18/25, without bedding $12/18; non-students singles/doubles $21/28. This college rents rooms year-round on a daily, weekly or monthly basis. It's a standard residence with paper-thin walls; ask for as quiet a floor as possible.

La Maison Bérubé (☎/fax 723-1578, 1216 boul St Germain Ouest) Singles/doubles $40/50. A farmhouse on Rte 132, halfway between Le Bic and Rimouski, this charm-

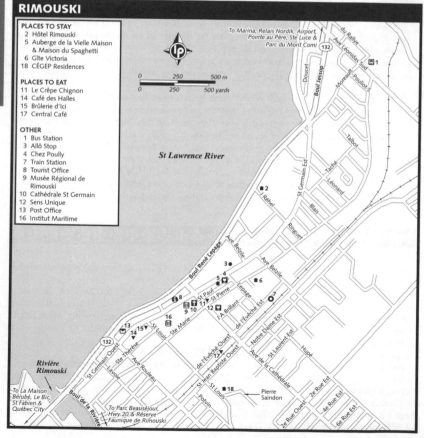

RIMOUSKI

PLACES TO STAY
2 Hôtel Rimouski
5 Auberge de la Vielle Maison & Maison du Spaghetti
6 Gîte Victoria
18 CÉGEP Residences

PLACES TO EAT
11 Le Crêpe Chignon
14 Café des Halles
15 Brûlerie d'Ici
17 Central Café

OTHER
1 Bus Station
3 Allô Stop
4 Chez Poully
7 Train Station
8 Tourist Office
9 Musée Régional de Rimouski
10 Cathédrale St Germain
12 Sens Unique
13 Post Office
16 Institut Maritime

St Lawrence River

To Marina, Relais Nordik, Airport, Pointe au Père, Ste Luce & Parc du Mont Comi

Rivière Rimouski

To La Maison Bérubé, Le Bic, St Fabien & Québec City

To Parc Beauséjour, Hwy 20 & Réserve Faunique de Rimouski

Pierre Saindon

ing place offers a bit of country living near the city. Your host will love to chat, can rent out bikes and cooks up a mean breakfast while listening to your life story.

Auberge de la Vieille Maison (☎ 723-6010, fax 723-9223, 35 rue St Germain Est) Singles $45-60, doubles $55-70, all with shared bath and breakfast. Somewhere between a B&B and hotel, this large, country home–style house on the main street has eight comfortable rooms, all with hardwood floors and lots of privacy. Breakfast is included.

Gîte Victoria (☎ 723-4483, 77 rue St Pierre) Doubles $55-75. Three quiet rooms in the city center, each decorated in a tasteful pseudo-Victorian style.

Hotel Rimouski (☎ 725-5000, 800-463-0755, Ⓦ www.hotelrimouski.com, 225 boul René Lepage Est) Singles/doubles $89/125. One of the city's biggest, of the Holiday Inn variety. Many special fares are offered, including access to local sights, sea kayaking excursions or even a massage.

Places to Eat
Le Crêpe Chignon (☎ 724-0400, 140 avenue de la Cathédrale) Mains $5-10. A bright light on the Rimouski dining scene, with delicious meal and dessert crêpes, quesadillas ($8), fair-trade coffee and lunch specials ($6-9), all in a relaxed, friendly atmosphere.

Central Café (☎ 722-4011, 31 rue de l'Évêché Ouest) Mains $7-13. Off the main street is the city's best hangout, a great bistro in an old two-story house with a terrace shaded by maples. The food is standard (pasta, smoked meats, burgers) but tasty.

Maison du Spaghetti (☎ 723-6010, 35 rue St Germain Est) Appetizers $3-8, mains $8-14. A Rimouski institution for 20 years, this places serves up the city's best pasta dishes in copious portions. Definitely get the garlic bread ($4), done on pizza crust.

Café des Halles (☎ 725-5411, 121 rue St Germain Ouest) Mains $6-14. Essentially a fancy diner, this is a good place for breakfast or a quick sandwich, meat or fish dish. It's part of a complex with a deli and other shops.

Brûlerie d'Ici (☎ 723-3424, 91 rue St Germain Ouest) Sandwiches $3-5. This is the city's top coffee shop – go for a pastry.

Entertainment
Chez Pouly (☎ 723-3038, 284 rue St Germain Est) A cavernous pickup disco where single guys in muscle shirts glare at gangs of heavily made-up girls, who smile and giggle in return. It's the most popular place in town.

Sens Unique (164 avenue de la Cathédrale) This is the closest you'll get to an alternative scene, with a mildly counterculture feel to its dark interiors. Occasional bands give rousing shows, but otherwise it's likely to be empty. Too bad – it's the only space with an edge compared to the reigning pop scene here.

Getting There & Away
Air Air Satellite (☎ 722-6161) flies from Rimouski to Baie Comeau twice a day Monday to Friday.

Bus The bus station (☎ 723-4923) is at 90 rue Léonidas Sud. Buses link Rimouski with Montréal ($80, 7-7½ hours, 3 daily), Rivière du Loup ($19, 80 minutes, 5 daily) and Québec City ($38, 4 hours, 5 daily). There are also four buses a day to Gaspé ($36), two each along the south (9 hours) and north (7 hours) coasts of the peninsula.

Train The VIA Rail train station (☎ 722-4737, 800-361-5390) is at 57 rue de l'Évêché Est. It's open only when trains pull in, usually past midnight. There are six trains a week to/from Montréal ($81, 8 hours).

Car Rimouski is on Rte 132's path. Hwy 20 makes a brief and final appearance here, curling around the back (south) area of the city. Allô Stop (☎ 723-5248, 106 rue St Germain Est) hooks up members needing lifts to Québec City or Montréal. They're open 10am to 5:30pm Saturday through Wednesday, and 10am to 9pm Thursday and Friday.

Boat All ferries leave from the marina, just north of the city.

A ferry service (☎ 725-2725, 800-973-2725) links Rimouski with Forestville, on the north shore. From late April to early October there are two to four boats daily (one-way adult/child $14/9, car/bicycle extra $34/4, 55 mins).

The *Relais Nordik* (☎ 723-8787, 800-463-0680, ⓔ info@relais.nordik.desgagnes.com, 17 avenue Lebrun) takes passengers on its weekly cargo ship to Sept Îles and villages along the North Shore. It departs Rimouski every Tuesday from early April to mid-January at 12:30pm and gets to Blanc Sablon Friday at 7pm. There are different classes of cabins and prices vary accordingly. From Rimouski to Blanc Sablon roundtrip in a four-berth cabin with three meals a day is $745. A Natashquan–Blanc Sablon roundtrip in the same class is $356.

AROUND RIMOUSKI
Pointe au Père
Just 5km east of Rimouski in this riverside village is the **Musée de la Mer** (☎ 724-6214, ⓔ *museep@globetrotter.qc.ca, 1034 rue du Phare; adult/student $6/4; open 10am-5pm daily June & late Aug–mid-Oct, 9am-7pm daily July–late Aug)*, which tells the story of the sinking of the *Empress of Ireland* in 1914. After the *Titanic*, this was the worst disaster in maritime history. In the 14 minutes it took the *Empress* to sink after being rammed inadvertently by a Norwegian boat, 1012 people lost their lives. You'll see found objects from diving expeditions, a tacky 3-D film about the accident, and great 1960s promo videos for trans-Atlantic ocean liners. You also get to climb an on-site lighthouse with the friendly staff, for an impressive view.

Ste Luce
This is where Rimouski's sun-worshippers come to soak up rays in summer, when this quiet village (pop 1400), 13km east of the city, turns into party central. The beach is enveloped in a small bay, with B&Bs and pizza joints lining the main road. The water may be a tad nippy, but the enthusiasm of the other bathers will convince the timid.

Parc du Mont Comi
Heading 12km southeast from Ste Luce on Rte 298 you'll come to St Donat and the Parc du Mont Comi (☎ *739-4858; admission free, day lift pass adult/student $24.50/22.50)*, which offers summer activities but is more popular in winter for its 22 downhill ski trails and 18km of cross-country ski trails. During the summer the park is open daily, but skiing takes place only 9am to 4pm Wednesday through Friday and 8am to 8pm Saturday and Sunday.

Portes de l'Enfer
For hiking, mountain biking and a view of a canyon and waterfalls from the province's highest suspended bridge (62m), head to this park (☎ *735-6063, chemin Duchénier)*, in St Narcisse de Rimouski, some 30km south of Rimouski along Rte 232.

Réserve Faunique de Rimouski
Hugging the border of New Brunswick, this 774-sq-km wildlife reserve (☎ *735-5672, 800-665-6527, 112 Rte de la Réserve Rimouski; admission $3.50; open June–early Sept)* comes replete with some nice Appalachian mountains. They're not as well set up for adventure tourism as other reserves in the province (hunters and fishers are their main clients), but it's possible to rent boats, and as part of the International Appalachian Trail passes through here, there's some good **hiking**. To get here from Rimouski, head south along Rte 232 and then farther south along Rte de la Réserve Rimouski.

Gaspé Peninsula & Îles de la Madeleine

Within Québec, you can hardly get much farther from Montréal than the Gaspé Peninsula and the Îles de la Madeleine, but for the extra time it takes to get there, the traveler will be rewarded with magnificent landscapes of dramatic mountains and valleys and deserted, windswept coastlines. While one of Canada's most easily recognized landmarks is here – the famous 'pierced' rock at Percé – memorable discoveries lie around every corner in these regions.

Many attractions and services are seasonal, starting up only in late June and closing in early September. This is less true than it used to be, however, as locals are making efforts to extend the tourist season; many say that it is the main chance for economic survival. While a summer visit will allow visitors to experience the area in its full splendor, winter tourism has gained ground in the last few years as cross-country ski expeditions in the Gaspésie and springtime seal-spotting excursions on the Îles de la Madeleine have become more popular.

Gaspé Peninsula

The rounded chunk of land that juts out north of New Brunswick into the Gulf of St Lawrence is known locally as 'La Gaspésie.' West of Matane the characteristic features of the region really become evident: The trees and woods become forests, the towns become smaller and farther apart, the North Shore slowly disappears from view, the wind picks up the salt air, and you sense remoteness more and more. The landscape, particularly on the north coast, also becomes breathtakingly spectacular, as rocky cliffs plunge into the sea, and layers of mountains and hills are visible for miles.

Some of the province's best hiking trails and possibilities for adventure tourism are here. Tourists will have no problem finding

Highlights

- Let your jaw drop at the scenery on the Gaspésie's north coast
- Climb the tall peaks in one of the province's jewels, Parc de la Gaspésie
- Throw yourself off Mont St Pierre – in a paraglider, that is
- See where the Appalachians plunge into the sea at Forillon National Park
- Walk around the rock that spawned a village, at Percé
- Discover why paradise is also called the Îles de la Madeleine

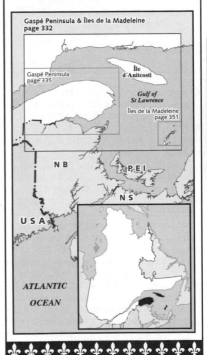

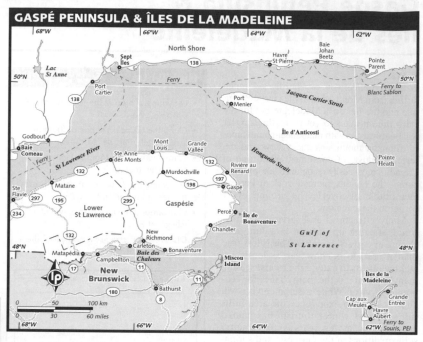

GASPÉ PENINSULA & ÎLES DE LA MADELEINE

services, though tourism is less developed than in the province's metropolitan centers. For the traveler who finds French a bit of a struggle, English communities at the eastern tip and around the south shore make a *petit* respite!

Socially the region feels static and at times listless – indeed, you'd be hard-pressed to spot anyone between the ages of 18 and 30, as so many youths have left the region to find fortune elsewhere. After the severe slowdown in the forestry, mining and fishing industries, the area is high in unemployment. Some locals note pessimistically that in 50 years the entire peninsula will become one huge provincial park. Some hope came in 2001 in the form of a $435 million government and forestry-industry investment toward reviving the Gaspésie, mainly for the opening of a new paper mill in Chandler.

The big question about getting around the peninsula has always been, to take the northern or southern route from Ste Flavie? Most people travel north toward Gaspé, then southward and around; in the past, when the roads were not in such good shape, people felt uncomfortable driving close to the shoreline. Now it's a matter of choice. Some people prefer to approach the Percé rock from the south, where it suddenly and dramatically appears around a corner; others like seeing it slowly unfold in grandeur approaching from the north. Here towns are listed going clockwise, partly because the south coast is relatively less scenic and impressive.

The best way of getting around is by car, but daily buses stop in nearly every town along the coasts. Despite the tough hills, it's also a popular destination for cyclists.

High-season prices are listed – before St Jean Baptiste Day and after Labour Day, expect accommodations prices to drop by about 30%.

STE FLAVIE
pop 950

In Ste Flavie on Rte 132 is a large, year-round information center for the Gaspésie. If you're here late in the season pick up one of the pamphlets that lists facilities that remain open until mid-October.

The **Centre d'Art Marcel Gagnon** (☎ 775-2829, W *www.centredart.net; 564 Rte de la Mer; admission free; open 8am-11pm daily May-Sept, 8am-9pm Oct-Apr*) is definitely worth a visit. It's an inn, restaurant, café and art school based on an exhibit of over 80 life-sized concrete statues by fecund sculptor, painter and writer Marcel Gagnon. The figures, all with different faces, march out to sea, appearing and disappearing with the tide. There is artwork on display and for sale.

The *Auberge* has comfortable singles/doubles from $50/100, including breakfast. They offer a good deal: A double room, full-course dinner, breakfast and entrance to the Jardins de Métis (see below) is $130 for two people.

GRAND MÉTIS & LES JARDINS DE MÉTIS
pop 270

One of the province's most revered attractions, the **Jardins de Métis** (☎ 775-2222, W *www.jardinsmetis.qc.ca; 200 Rte 132; adult/student/child 6-13/child under 5 $12/11/3/free; open 8:30am-6pm June–mid-Oct*) is highly recommended. Also known as the Reford Gardens (after Elsie Reford, who inherited the land from her uncle, Lord Mount Stephen, founder of the Canadian Pacific Railway), they take up 40 acres of immaculately tended grounds, boasting over 2000 varieties of plants. There are streams, paths, bridges, and a 37-room mansion doubling as a museum on the premises. Reford herself was the architect of the gardens, on which she worked for 33 summers. There are also floral exhibits every summer.

About 10km east of town are the villages of **Métis Beach** and **Métis sur Mer**, with nice sandy beaches. This area has traditionally been a country retreat for bourgeois, wealthy English families. It's worth a detour to drive into the towns to see the large houses with Anglo-Saxon names emblazoned on their front-lawn signs.

MATANE
pop 12,300

Matane, 42km east of Métis sur Mer, is a commercial fishing port known for its famous shrimp (the annual Festival de la Crevette, or Shrimp Festival, takes place around June 20th). Salmon go up the river here to spawn in June, and it's possible to go **salmon fishing** right from downtown. Take the Promenade des Capitaines road off Rte 132 and you'll see salmon fishermen in action. The area is also pleasant for strolling. There is a small interpretation center on rue St Jerome near the Hôtel de Ville.

Though pleasant, the town holds little of interest but is a good springboard to nearby wildlife reserves (see next entry) and to the ferry across to the North Shore. The tourist

---

Say a Prayer for Bathtub Mary

Despite the dropping attendance and declining influence of Québec's Roman Catholic Church, its iconography remains a pervasive part of the provincial landscape. Captivating, sometimes jarring images of the Virgin or a bloodied Jesus on the cross adorn both urban and rural settings. Inspirational statues embellish gardens, gaze out to sea and mark the entrances to quiet villages. These religious expressions make a striking addition to the province's considerable visual appeal.

One type to look for is the so-called Bathtub Mary, a folk-art tradition that graces the occasional roadside. An old-fashioned claw-foot bathtub is stood on end, usually one-quarter to one-half buried. With the arched top thus forming a sort of protective encasement, placed standing within the tub is a statue of Mary. Sometimes the edge of the tub is painted or otherwise adorned, and plants and flowers are grown around the bottom.

information office (☎ 562-1065) is at 968 avenue du Phare Ouest.

Absolu Aventure (☎ 562-8112, W www .absoluaventure.com) organizes one- to five-day guided hikes for beginners or advanced hikers along part of the **International Appalachian Trail** (see boxed text), which cuts through part of the Réserve Faunique de Matane.

There are several fish markets in town, where you can buy fish, fresh or smoked. Try *Poissonnerie Boréalis (☎ 562-7001, 985 avenue du Phare Ouest; open 9am-6pm daily year-round).*

Réserves Fauniques de Matane et Dunière

These two joined wildlife reserves *(☎ 224-3345, 562-3700, ℮ resmatan@globetrotter.qc .ca; admission $3.50; open 8am-8pm daily May-Oct)* can be reached via Rte 195, 40km south of Matane. It's a huge, wild and infrequently touristed area with camping, canoeing, hiking, fishing, boat rentals and abundant moose, fox and coyotes. There are some great, remote cabins available for rent here, like at Lac Joffre, 59km from the entrance on dirt roads. It's bloody far, but the view of Mont Logan is impressive.

Places to Stay & Eat

Camping de la Rivière Matane (☎ 562-3414, 150 Rte Louis Félix Dionne) Tent sites $13-19. Southwest of downtown Matane, this huge place (144 sites) has good, quiet camping in the woods. Follow the signs from the corner of rue Parc Industriel and the route for 3km.

Motel Le Beach (☎ 562-1350, 888-570-1350, 1441 rue Matane sur Mer) Singles/ doubles from $40/45. About 100m from Rte 132 and thus a bit quieter than the other hotels which line it, this motel has standard rooms but they boast a good view of the sea. It's very close to the ferry terminal.

Le Rafiot (☎ 562-8080, 1415 avenue de Phare Ouest, Rte 132) Mains $7-14. This yellow and white place is a casual sort of pub with a marine décor, plenty of seafood and good prices on shrimp dinners all summer long.

Getting There & Away

Buses (☎ 562-4085) arrive and depart the Irving gas station at 521 avenue du Phare Est (Rte 132), 1.5km east of the center. There are buses to Gaspé ($42, 5¼ hours, 2 daily) and Rimouski ($16, 1½ hours, 4 daily).

The ferry terminal (☎ 562-2500, 877-562-6560), about 2km west of the town center, provides the easternmost link to the North Shore. Passenger ferries carrying 126 cars run year-round to Baie Comeau (one or two times a day in summer) and Godbout (one to three times daily in summer); service is less frequent other times of the year. Both trips take about two hours and 20 minutes and cost $13/30/free for adult/car/bike.

CAP CHAT
pop 3000

A completely surreal sight awaits you here. The nearly 200km east of Rimouski reveal not much more than rocky coastline, scattered villages and forested hills. But suddenly, like an illusion, giant white windmills appear perched on hilltops, stoically twirling their propellers. This is the largest **windmill park** in Canada, with 133 of the dream-like critters producing 100 MW of electricity, used locally. It was the first experiment into harnessing wind power in the province, but the idea hasn't progressed much since they were installed. The world's largest vertical axe windmill (110m) is here too, alas broken, but freeze-frame it in a photo and your friends will never know!

It's possible to get close to the windmills, but if you'd like to take a tour of the biggest one and learn more about the project, contact **Éole Cap-Chat** *(☎ 786-5719; adult/ student $5/3; open 8:30am-5pm daily late June–Sept),* well sign-posted on Rte 132 just west of Cap Chat.

Camping au Bord de la Mer (☎ 786-2251) Tent sites $12-16. Right off Rte 132 east of the bridge at Cap Chat, this standard campground offers some nice views.

Gîte Vents et Marées (☎/fax 786-5065, 888-786-5065, 38 rue des Écoliers) Singles/ doubles from $40/55. This elegant B&B, off the main road, is perfectly comfortable and

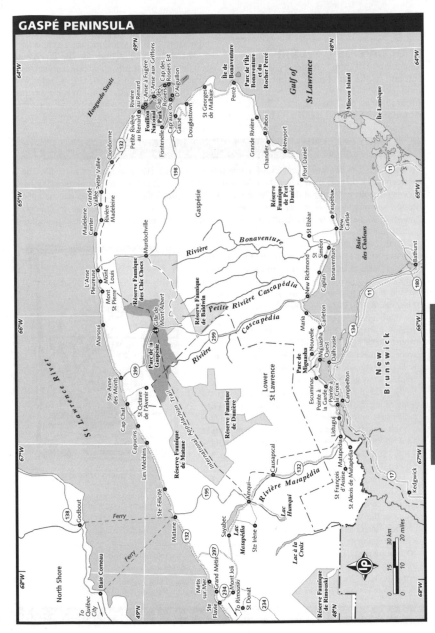

the owners can help arrange activities in the area year-round.

ST OCTAVE DE L'AVENIR

A speck on the map (but not even on most of them!) is the remnants of what was once a village (see 'The Rebirth of St Octave'). Situated near the base of the Chic Choc Mountains (Mount Logan's 1128 meters loom forbiddingly in the foreground), it has turned into a military base and a haven for adventurous skiers and mountain bikers.

The Relais Chic Chocs (☎ 786-2349, 800-530-2349, Ⓦ www.info-gaspesie.com/relaiscc, 1 rue Notre Dame Ouest, Cap Chat) is an outfitter for those interested in taking **cross-country skiing** or **mountain biking** trips into the stunning Mount Logan region of Parc de

---

The Rebirth of St Octave

It was 1929, the depression was in full swing, no end in sight; either struggle or succumb. The residents of a number of impoverished Gaspésie communities sought more promising solutions. Some residents of Cap Chat devised what may seem as an odd solution to combat poverty: Build a new community in the middle of the forest. At least the government would give small allotments of land and some cash for its construction. Later would come riches from the exploitation of the forest.

So that year, under the spiritual guidance of a priest, Monseigneur Caron, a score of volunteers cut a trail through thick forest, cleared land and built rudimentary houses, which their wives and children moved into to eke out their first long winter in the wilderness. They named it St Octave de l'Avenir *(avenir,* or future, for the bright prospects ahead). By 1934 there was a school, a chapel, a sawmill, a post office and several stores. Some agriculture had already begun, and cut wood was being sold. However, frequent fires, a punishing climate and a nagging sense of isolation still chipped away at residents' resilience.

By 1939 there were 900 people living with the hope of improving their lot in a place where 10 years earlier was nothing but trees and mosquitoes. More schools were built, plus a theatre, more sawmills and a bank. Electricity and television came. By the end of the 1940s, St Octave de l'Avenir looked the same as any other parish, and had over 1100 residents.

Ghost town! Where?

However, in the late 1950's the decline began: The earth had become infertile through mismanagement, good sections of the village had burned down (including the main sawmill), people were leaving to return to the 'mainland,' and in late 1971, the village itself was closed.

Forgotten in its ruins for several years, in the late 1970s the Canadian military decided to use it as a training camp for young cadets. To this day, every summer the place swarms with over 400 young teens with military aspirations. The old chapel is used as their mess hall. In winter, the former ghost town is a popular, if not exotic, draw for adventure tourists on ski or snowmobile expeditions.

So there was an *avenir* to St Octave after all, if not exactly the one it had foreseen.

la Gaspésie. There are chalets to refuge in on multi-day trips, and at Relais Chic Choc's base in St Octave de l'Avenir there's a comfortable auberge ($20 in dorm facilities, $40/50 for single/double rooms) and several chalets ($90 per room) to rent.

St Octave de l'Avenir is 19km south of Cap Chat. Take rue des Fonds just west of the bridge, veer left at Petit Fonds and follow Rte de St Octave de l'Avenir to the end.

STE ANNE DES MONTS
pop 7200

Ste Anne is not one of the prettiest towns, but it's a good place to stock up before heading into Parc de la Gaspésie. There are numerous restaurants, motels and shops. There's a summer tourist information bureau (☎ 763-5832, 90 boul Ste Anne Ouest) on Rte 132. The Orléans Express bus stop is next door.

L'échouerie (☎ 763-1555, 800-461-8585, e auberge.int.echouerie@globetrotter.nett, 295 1-ère avenue Est) Dorm beds $19. This converted school has a kitchen, a café, bike rental, transportation to Parc de la Gaspésie – the works. From the bus stop, cross the street, go east to Rte de Parc toward the church, then east along the river road. It's a 2km walk.

Riôtel Monaco (☎ 266-2165, 877-778-8977, 90 boul Ste Anne Ouest) Doubles from $79. The 46 rooms in this hotel offer standard comfort and not much more, but staying here has its advantages. Not only is the tourist office located inside it, but the Orléans bus stop is just outside, and a shuttle bus to the Parc de la Gaspésie leaves from here too (see the Parc de la Gaspésie section). As an extra perk, supper and breakfast are included in the room price.

PARC DE LA GASPÉSIE & RÉSERVE FAUNIQUE DES CHIC CHOCS

From Ste Anne des Monts, Rte 299 runs south to the excellent Parc de la Gaspésie (☎ 763-3181; admission $3.50; open year-round). Its 802 sq km of spectacular scenery is dotted by lakes and two of the province's most beautiful mountain ranges, the Chic Choc and McGerrigle, which together have

25 of the 40 highest summits in Québec. One of the province's best **camping** spots is here, as well as some of the best **hiking** (the International Appalachian Trail passes through). Another draw is the only herd of **caribou** south of the St Lawrence River, originally trapped on the south side during the formation of the waterway.

The **Réserve Faunique des Chic Chocs** (☎ 797-5214, 786-5715; admission $3.50, gem collecting expedition $20/10 adult/children under 14) surrounds and bleeds into the Parc de la Gaspésie, and both are administered by Sépaq (w www.sepaq.com). This reserve is used mainly for **hunting** and **fishing**, but geological expeditions are run. In general, the area is less impressive than at the Parc de la Gaspésie. The main entrance is some 12km south of the Gîte du Mont Albert (see Places to Stay, below) on Rte 299, then 1.5km east on the Rte du Lac Ste Anne toward Murdochville.

The Parc de la Gaspésie has an **Interpretation Centre** (☎ 763-7811; admission free; open 8am-8pm daily early June–late Sept), where attendants are extraordinarily helpful in planning a schedule to match your time and budget. They also rent out hiking equipment.

Mont Jacques Cartier

This is the highest peak (1270m) in this part of the country. It rises above the tree line and epitomizes the conditions of the Gaspé Peninsula: cold, windy and often wet at the peak.

Hiking it takes about 3½ hours roundtrip and is well worthwhile – the alpine scenery and views are fantastic, and it is fairly common to see some of the woodland caribou near the barren peaks munching on lichen. The trail is tightly regulated in order to protect the herd from being disturbed; access is permitted only between 10am and 4pm daily. These are the last of the caribou found this far south and conditions are very harsh. Do not approach or scare them. However, if you see some, you might try being quiet and raising your arms to form an antler shape. The curious and harmless caribou don't see too well and may actually walk toward you.

Mont Jacques Cartier hikers can drive to a designated parking area at the basic La Galène campground along one of two roads, each taking about 30 minutes from the Interpretation Centre. Alternatively, there's a bus from the Ste Anne des Monts tourist office (adult/child 6-12/child under 5 $6/3/free roundtrip; 8am daily) to the Interpretation Centre, where another bus ($13/6/free roundtrip) leaves at 9am daily (returning at 5pm). From La Galène, a shuttle bus ($5/3/free, 5 daily) runs hikers 4km to the beginning of the trail. The buses operate from the end of June through September.

Other Hikes

You can also climb **Mont Albert** (1181m), a steeper, more rigorous trail. Also excellent and not busy is the trail by Lac aux Americains up to **Mont Xalibu** (1135m), a fine half-day return walk with superb alpine scenery at the peak with mountain lakes and a waterfall in view on the way. An easier, two-hour roundtrip walk is on the newly opened trail up **Mont Ernest Laforce** (820m), which affords a splendid 360-degree panorama from its summit.

Places to Stay

There are *chalets* for rent from $80 a day throughout the park. Overnight *camping* is $23 in one of the four campgrounds. The busiest one is across the road from the Centre, but try for a spot at the 39-site campground at **Lac Cascapédia**. Its entrance is about halfway between Ste Anne des Monts and the Interpretation Centre, then 10km along the gravel Rte 11 (you can pay on-site, so no need to drive to the Centre first if arriving from Ste Anne des Monts). Though there are (spotless!) showers, there is no electricity; you are in pure nature here, near a lake of breathtaking beauty, with hills spilling gently into it. There is canoe and rowboat rental ($26 a day). Farther along Rte 11 is Lac Paul, where there's an observation stand to watch for caribou.

Gîte du Mont Albert (☎ 763-2288, 888-270-4483) Doubles $155, chalets from $100. This large, comfortable lodge next to the Interpretation Centre is for those who like their nature spiced with luxury. There's a pool (open to campers too) and a first-class restaurant. If you want to treat yourself, this is the place to do it.

Getting There & Away

The main road (Rte 299) enters the park at Ste Anne des Monts. Another, less busy, rougher access road from Mont St Pierre meets it inside the park. A loop through the park is possible using both access points as connectors to the coastal Rte 132. From mid-July to mid-August a bus runs from the Riôtel Monaco in Ste Anne des Monts to the Interpretation Centre once a day in time for the Mont Jacques Cartier shuttle.

MONT ST PIERRE
pop 300

East of Ste Anne des Monts the scenery starts to become ever-more spectacular: The North Shore disappears from view and the road winds around rocky cliffs and waterfalls, every curve unveiling an endless stretch of mountains cascading down toward the sea. Main roads according such views are rare in North America.

Mont St Pierre appears after a dramatic bend in the road and takes its namesake from the 418m mountain with a cliff off of which people regularly throw themselves. **Hang gliding** and **paragliding** enthusiasts come here in droves to enjoy one of the best spots on the continent for the sports. A microclimate and strong wind currents make it a challenging spot. At the end of July the international 10-day hang gliding festival, **Fête du Vol Libre** (☎ 797-2222, fax 797-5101), turns the skyline multicolored with hundreds of sails. A rough road goes to the summit of Mont St Pierre, where there are take-off stations and excellent views. A 4WD vehicle is required if you're not hoofing it up, which takes an hour.

If you feel like running off a cliff, your best bet is to do it with Pilot Yvon Volé (☎ 797-2896, @ delta@moncourrier.com, 34 rue Prudent Cloutier). It's a cool $100 per (10- to 15-minute) jump on a hang or paraglider. You're tandem with Yvon, but if you've never done it, it's worth it: The scenery over the valley and sea is breathtaking, and you'd be with an experienced glider whose bear-like appearance instills confidence in even the most timid.

Carrefour Aventure (☎ 797-5033, 106 rue Prudent Cloutier) offers tours of the area and rents hang gliders to first-timers! It also rents sea kayaks ($10/hour) and mountain bikes.

Just 6km east is the town of **Mont Louis**, where it's highly recommended to stop at the **Parc et Mer Mont Louis** (☎/fax 797-5270, e parcmer2000@hotmail.com, 18 10-ème rue Est; admission free; open 8am-10pm daily late June–Sept). A combo hip Internet café (the only place on the peninsula to sip espresso, read Wallpaper and surf the Web for $5 an hour), restaurant, nature trail, crafts boutique and concert hall (lively bands on weekends), it's also an ideal place to camp ($18 for one of 10 sites by the beach).

Parc de la Gaspésie can be reached by unsurfaced road (watch for logging trucks!) from behind Mont St Pierre but having a good map is helpful as the routes are not well marked.

Places to Stay

Camping du Pont (☎ 797-2951, 120 rue Prudent Cloutier) Tent sites $16. Of the two campgrounds in town, this place is smaller but slightly more pleasant, though near the main road.

Auberge les Vagues (☎ 797-2851, e lesvagues@globetrotter.net, 84 rue Prudent Cloutier) Dorm beds $15, singles/doubles $25/42, motel rooms $30/45. This hostel/motel has tiny rooms (the motel rooms are slightly more renovated than the others), but they have all you'll need. There's a restaurant/bar and communal kitchen.

MONT LOUIS TO FORILLON NATIONAL PARK

Heading east, the landscape keeps increasing in majesty. Unusual, even playful patterns etched by glaciers onto the planet's oldest rock accompany you as the road winds and then dips into and out of towering green valleys around Grande Vallée. Most of the villages on this stretch feel in perfect or near perfect harmony with nature; mankind

seems not to have attempted to conquer it, and in return it seems to have bent graciously to accommodate. There are many picnic stops – take advantage of them, as trying to take in the landscape from behind the wheel can be dangerous!

At L'Anse Pleureuse, turn off to **Murdochville** (pop 1600) for tours of its impressive yet somewhat unappealing copper mine (☎ 784-3335, 345 Rte 198; adult/child $8/5; open 10am-4pm daily mid-June–mid-Oct).

At **Madeleine Centre** (pop 450), the Site du Phare (☎ 393-3290, 4 Rte du Phare; museum and lighthouse admission $3/2 adult/child; open 9am-7pm daily mid-June–early Sept) operates as a makeshift tourist information center, Internet café ($6/ hour) and supply store. Climbing the lighthouse (1905) is worthwhile for the views, and the small museum has loads of antiques. They can also arrange a visit to an old hydro dam refitted to lift spawning salmon twice a day to let them keep swimming upstream.

The villages of **Grande Vallée** (pop 1450) and **Petite Vallée** (pop 225) are quite pretty, particularly the latter, which bursts to life at the end of June with the Festival en Chanson (☎ 393-2222, W www.festivalenchanson .com). Founded in 1982, this has become one of the most popular and important folk-song festivals in the province, launching the careers of popular singers Daniel Boucher and Richard Séguin. It usually lasts about 10 days and, despite its status, has retained an intimate feel – everyone from bold kids to the local butcher perform impromptu on stage.

La Maison Lebreux (☎ 393-2662, 2 Longue Pointe) is a great place to stay in Petite Vallée. Singles/doubles are from $40/60, and seaside chalets are $450 to $600 per week. At the bottom of a steep cliff on a lovely spit of land facing the sea, the grounds come alive during the Festival en Chanson. Inside is also a restaurant serving fresh fish and homemade bread; full-course meals are about $15.

East of **Cloridorme** is a good picnic site overlooking the Gulf of St Lawrence. **Rivière au Renard** is the largest fishing port in the Gaspé, and the processing plant can be toured via the Fishing Interpretation Centre (☎ 269-5292, 1 boul de Renard Est; adult/student $5/4.60; open 9:30am-5:30pm daily end June–Aug). A tourist office is also here.

For those not visiting Forillon National Park, Rte 197 runs southeast, cutting off at the end of the peninsula.

At **Cap des Rosiers**, the gateway to Forillon National Park, there's a graveyard on the cliff, which tells the town's interesting history: how the English came from Guernsey and Jersey; how the Irish settlers were Kavanaghs, O'Connors etc; and how both groups mingled with the French. Generations later, the same names live on.

FORILLON NATIONAL PARK

The park (☎ 368-5505, W www.parkscanada .gc.ca/forillon; adult/child 6-16/child under 6 $3.75/2/free; open 9am-9pm daily June–early Oct) lies at the extreme northeastern tip of the peninsula and is well worth a stop for its rugged seaside terrain and wildlife. Run by the ever-efficient Parks Canada, there are also a wealth of organized activities (at least one a day in English). In the woods there are moose, deer, fox and an increasing population of black bears (many tourists report sightings – take necessary precautions). The shoreline cliffs attract seabirds (including the Great Blue Heron), and offshore whales and seals are common.

There are two main entrances with visitors centers where you can pick up maps: one at L'Anse au Griffon (east of Rivière au Renard) on Rte 132, and another on the south side of the park at Fort Péninsule.

The park's northern coast consists of steep limestone cliffs – some as high as 200m – and long pebble beaches. **Cap Bon Ami** showcases the best of this topography. There is a telescope there for whale watching. The south coast has more beaches, some sandy, with small coves. **Penouille Beach** is said to have the warmest waters.

In the North Sector beyond Cap des Rosiers is a great picnic area with a small, rocky beach where limestone leans out toward the sea's expanse. Starfish are abundant here, sunning on rocks rounded out by

the waves. Please don't disturb the starfish; if you absolutely insist on taking one home as a souvenir, at least pick one that's already dead!

There are good hiking trails through the park, ranging from easy, 30-minute walks to a rigorous 18km one-way trail taking six hours. The hike along the southern shore to **Cap Gaspé** is easy and pleasant, with seashore views. The International Appalachian Trail ends here as the Appalachians plunge into the sea once and for all.

Two boat trips are offered. The MV *Felix Leclerc* (☎ 892-5629) departs from the quay at Cap des Rosiers ($18) and takes in rocky cliffs, seabirds, seal colonies and possibly whales. The *Zodiac Norval* (☎ 892-5500) departs the harbor at Grand Grave for longer cruises (adult/student/child $33/27/15) and focuses on whales. For both, inquire if the guide is bilingual (some are). Kayak trips also depart Grand Grave.

Places to Stay

Forillon Campgrounds (reservations ☎ 368-6050) Tent sites $16.50-20. There are 367 sites in four campgrounds within the park, and these often get filled to capacity. Petit Gaspé is the most popular organized campground as it is protected from sea breezes and has hot showers. The smallest (41 sites) is at Cap Bon Désir.

Auberge de Jeunesse de Cap aux Os (☎ 892-5153, 800-461-8585, 2095 boul Grande Grève) Members/nonmembers $15/17; open 24 hours May-Oct. This is one of the most established places in the province and has a fine view overlooking the bay. It's a friendly place that can accommodate 80 people. You gotta love Québec hostels – first they surprise people by often having co-ed dorms and then here they have condom machines in the washroom. Preventative or suggestive? (There are some rooms for families.) Breakfast and dinner are available, as are kitchen facilities. The bus from Gaspé stops at the hostel throughout summer months. A drawback for those without vehicles is that it's a long way to any of the hiking trails, although bicycles can be rented.

The International Appalachian Trail

The continent's longest, most ambitious hiking trail is the International Appalachian Trail (IAT), which stretches 4474km from Mount Springer in Georgia to Cap Gaspé, covering the mainland portion of the Appalachian Mountains, the world's oldest. With other trails joining it in the south, it's possible to walk on cleared trails from Key West, Florida to Cap Gaspé – 7616km! In the US, over 30 million people a year use their Appalachian Trail. In June 2001 the Canadian leg of the trail (making it 'international') officially opened, 672km of which courses through the Gaspé Peninsula.

Entering Québec from New Brunswick at Matapédia, the trail snakes along the Matapédia Valley and veers inland after Amqui, not to see another village for 240km. The trail's wildest spots go through the Réserve Faunique de Matane, where you're more likely to see large game than another human. It continues into the Parc de la Gaspésie and across summit after summit. This has widely been touted as the IAT's most spectacular and beautiful region.

Descending into a grand valley, the trail passes by Mont St Pierre enough to catch sight of a few hang gliders overhead. For the next 170km the trail sticks to the sea, sometimes descending onto the coast. The 32.7km stretch between Rivière au Renard and the south sector of Forillon National Park is considered the most dangerous of the Gaspé section, with steep rocky hills. The dessert at the end of the feast is the splendid panoramic view from atop Cap Gaspé.

Although portions of the IAT should be attempted only by experienced hikers, the trail is well-indicated, and there are 21 shelters along the way, as well as 18 campgrounds with some services. For those in need of more comfort, the Gîte du Mont Albert in Parc de la Gaspésie (see above) can provide a luxurious respite. For more info, see Ⓦ www.internationalat.org.

GASPÉ
pop 16,300

After a few hundred kilometers of tiny villages, Gaspé may seem like a mini-metropolis. Yet after hours of stunning scenery, it also feels dirty, dull, and run-down. Still, if you need some nightlife, there's a good choice here (much better than in Percé).

Where Gaspé now stands is where Jacques Cartier first landed in June 1534 and, after meeting with the region's Iroquois, boldly planted a wooden cross, claiming the land for the King of France. The area remained largely unpopulated for two centuries until French colonists arrived and began a fishing industry. Under General Woolfe, the British trashed the area twice, in 1628 and 1758. Descendants of the Loyalists who moved in afterward still live here.

The **Musée de la Gaspésie** (☎ 368-1534, 80 boul Gaspé; adult/student $4/3; open 9am-7pm daily end June–early Sept, 9am-5pm Tues-Fri & 1pm-5pm Sat & Sun rest of the year, closed mid-Dec–mid-Jan) depicts the difficulties of those settling the Gaspésie, some maritime exhibits, crafts and a section on traditional foods. It also familiarizes you with Cartier's voyages. Six bronze plates outside make up the **monument** commemorating his landing.

The **Cathédrale du Christ-Roi** (☎ 368-5541, 20 rue de la Cathèdrale) is the only wooden cathedral in North America. Remarkable stained glass inside commemorates Cartier.

At the **Site Historique Micmac de Gespeg** (☎ 368-6005, 783 boul Pointe Navarre; adult/student $4/3; open 9am-5pm daily mid-June–mid-Sept) you can learn about the disappeared Micmac Indian culture in a re-created village setting. There's also a good gift shop.

Places to Stay & Eat
Cégep de la Gaspésie (☎ 368-2749, 94 rue Jacques Cartier) Singles/doubles $22/37, rooms for six $74. This central, regional college is worth checking out for a cheap bed through the summer. There are laundry and kitchen facilities.

Motel Adams (☎ 368-2244, 800-463-4242, 20 rue Adams) Singles/doubles from $54/59. Standard hotel fare, but it's central and the rooms tend to be large. They can help arrange fishing expeditions. The Orléans Express bus stops just outside.

Café des Artistes (☎ 368-2255, 249 boul Gaspé) Mains $9-14. An upscale spot on the road in from Forillon, this place has excellent meals, fine cuisine (lobster in carrot and garlic sauce for $31), and a bathroom nice enough to move into.

Entertainment

The Cégep's student body gives the town several lively bars that attract a good deal of high-quality touring bands.

Brise Bise (☎ 368-1456, 2 côte Carter) On one side is a bistro serving good meals for under $13, on the other is a bar that's so popular it spills out into the back alley. Good bands from across Québec play here, and concerts often end up as a jam session in the wee hours.

La Voûte (☎ 368-1219, 114 rue de la Reine) This bar is filled with guys standing around awkwardly watching big-screen sports, but there are decent local cover bands after 10pm weekends.

Getting There & Away

A small airport south of town links Gaspé with Montréal and the Îles de la Madeleine daily with Air Nova (☎ 888-247-2262), an Air Canada regional airline. See Getting There & Away in the Îles de la Madeleine section, later, for more information.

The Orléans Express bus stop is at Motel Adams (see Places to Stay & Eat). Four buses a day travel to Rimouski: two along the north coast ($36, 7 hours), two along the south coast ($36, 9 hours) of the peninsula.

VIA Rail (☎ 368-4313) has service to Gaspé from Montréal ($118, 17½ hours, 3 weekly), going along the Matapédia Valley and along the south coast of the peninsula.

ST GEORGES DE MALBAIE

There's nothing here except a great view of both Forillon (43km north) and the Percé

rock (34km south), as well as an excellent campground.

Camping Tête d'Indien (Indian Head Camping; ☎ 645-3845, ⓔ campingtete@ netscape.net, 1669 Rte 132) Tent sites $22. An American ex-pat runs this fun campground with a friendly feel (free morning coffee may help with that). Even if you don't sleep here, walk through the grounds to the observation deck and see the rock that gave the place its name, as well a great view. There are kayaks for rent, a laundry room, a great walking trail and a volleyball court.

PERCÉ
pop 3850

This town's fortunes are owed entirely to a huge chunk of limestone with a hole in it. The **Rocher Percé** (Pierced Rock), at 88m high and 475m long, is one of Canada's best known landmarks and is truly stunning in person; photos could never do its majesty justice.

There are many activities possible and there's a killer new hostel – enough to warrant a several-day stay. Unfortunately the town's allure is greatly undermined by the sheer numbers of tourists who flock to it each summer. While commercialization has not taken on Niagara Falls proportions of bad taste, the crowded main street, lined with motels, tacky souvenir stores and 'art' galleries, feels tasteless compared to the natural beauty that surrounds it.

The rock itself is accessible from the mainland at low tide only (a timetable is posted at the tourist office and by the stairs leading down to the rock). Signs warning of falling rocks should be taken seriously – each year, some 300 tons of rock detach and tumble. In fact, there used to be two holes in it but one arch came crashing down in 1845. There are beautiful quartz veins coursing through parts of the rock, and the vertical layers you see are the result of crushing tectonic plates forced upward. Thousands of birds call the rock's top home. Take chemin du Mont Joli to the end and descend the staircase.

The tourist office (☎ 782-5448) is in the center of town at 142 Rte 132. It's open from 9am to 7pm daily from the end of May to the end of October. There's a laundromat at the wharf/shopping boutique complex, nearly across the street from the tourist office.

Things To See & Do

Highly recommended are the boat trips to green **Île Bonaventure**, an island bird sanctuary with over 200,000 birds including the continent's largest gannet colony (see 'Dive-Bombing Gannets') beyond Rocher Percé. Along Rte 132 you'll be accosted by many companies offering trips – select carefully, and ask if they tour the island or just

sail around it. If their boats are too big, they can't get close to the attractions.

Les Traversiers de l'Île (☎ 782-2750, ✉ homard99@globetrotter.net, 9 rue du Quai) offers good 90-minute cruises and stopover tours, with time to walk some of the island's beautiful 15km of walking trails. Best to leave early to make the most of it. Prices are $20 for adults, $15 for students and children 12 to 18.

Longer **whale-watching** boat tours are also available along the main strip. Prices for whale watching tours are $30 to $50. You

---

Dive-Bombing Gannets

Of all the hundreds of bird species living in Québec, none is closer to the hearts of Québécois than the northern gannet *(Fous de Bassans)*. This may be due to their sharing an important trait – both are known to fly south to Florida for the winter.

Île Bonaventure is home to about 60,000 northern gannets, North America's largest colony (the world's largest is in Scotland), but it's not their numbers alone that make them unforgettable to anyone who sees them. Adult gannets are of striking beauty, characterized by blazing white plumage highlighted by icy blue eyes surrounded by a black patch, jet-black wing tips and handsome gray-blue bills. During mating season their heads turn pale yellow, as if glowing from within.

The adults average 95cm long and their wing span is about 2m. Their flight is particularly graceful, as they're able to glide for long periods without a single flap. Socially they tend to mate for life (mates acknowledge each other by facing each other, slapping bills together and bowing) and live in large, crowded colonies. Both male and female take turns incubating their eggs, turning them over twice an hour to heat them uniformly.

Yet the most spectacular aspect of their behavior, which is possible to witness – if your timing is very, very lucky – only in the first few weeks of June and usually only in the waters between Gaspé and Percé, is how they dive-bomb over schools of capelin. Alone, or in groups up to several hundred, they fly above the water at a height of 18m to 30m and then plunge at great speeds, almost vertically, into the water when their binocular eyes spot their prey below. They strike at a velocity that sends spray 3m into the air, and can dive to a depth of about 5m. Their webbed feet help them shoot out of the water again. When large groups of them do this, it is coordinated and almost choreographed, as they form a huge circle above the water, descending in turn, one after the other, before retaking their position at the back of the queue again.

Efforts to conserve the gannet population have recently stepped up. Though it is illegal to hunt them (they were nearly wiped out of Eastern Canada because of relentless hunting in the 19th century), they are threatened by toxins they ingest via fish.

In the early 1970s traces of DDT were turning up in gannets – the pesticide dumped onto nearby forests had found its way into the sea, the fish and eventually the birds, and their numbers started to dwindle.

Aside from Île Bonaventure, gannet colonies are found on Île d'Anticosti and on the Îles de la Madeleine, and along the rocky coast of eastern Newfoundland. These are their only North American habitats – if you see them, enjoy!

may see minke, blue and humpback whales, but mainly dolphins, seals and fin whales frequent the area. If you won't get to see whales on the North Shore, try your luck here.

Better still are **diving** expeditions by the energetic, experienced folk at Club Nautique de Percé (☎ 782-5403, 199 Rte 132). They offer thematic dives to explore marine biology as well as underwater seal-observation tours and even whale-observation tours when possible. Count on paying about $75 for a full day with two dives, including equipment rental. They also rent kayaks ($55 for half-day), and there's an on-site pool for those who wish not to brave the seas.

The **Centre d'Interprétation** (☎ 782-2721, Rte d'Irlande; admission free; open 9am-5pm daily June–mid-Oct), 2km from the center (turn right onto Rte des Failles, then left onto Rte d'Irlande), is a good place to learn about the local flora and fauna in bilingual exhibits.

Behind town are some interesting walks, for which the tourist office's map is useful. Hike up to **Mont Ste Anne** for a great view and to see the cave along the 3km path, which begins behind the church. Another walking trail (3km) leads to the **Great Crevasse**, a deep crevice in the mountain near the **Camping Gargantua**.

Of all the art galleries in town, **Studio-Galerie** (☎ 645-2745, 1004 Rte 132; open 10am-8pm daily June-Sept) is one of the better ones. Artist Gilles Côtés art naïf canvases capture a warm, idealized spirit of the surroundings.

You might also see people searching for agate and jasper on the beaches around Percé. If you're interested, you'd do better at the beaches in Coin du Banc and l'Anse à Beaufils (9km north and south, respectively, of town).

Places to Stay

Accommodations here are fair bargains although prices can spike sharply upward during summer when traffic is very heavy. There are also numerous campgrounds close at hand. The tourist office can help you find a place: The choice is large.

Camping Gargantua (☎ 782-2852, 222 Rte des Failles) Tent sites $18, motel singles/

doubles $65/75. Perched at the highest point around Percé (if you're biking, it'll be quite a climb), there are great views here, walking trails nearby, and an excellent dining room in the motel section. Far from the touristy center, this is a great place.

Maison Avenue House (☎ 782-2954, 38 rue de l'Église) Singles/doubles from $25/$35. This B&B is in an excellent location, off the main street in the middle of town. The owner, Ethel, is adorable and discrete. The rooms have sinks and are comfy.

La Maison Rouge (☎ 782-2227, e rmasse@globetrotter.net, 125 Rte 132) Dorm beds $20, singles/doubles $40/60. The best place in town, it's composed of a converted red grange where three 10-bed rooms have been made, plus a central, stately home with fine and spacious rooms. Even inside the atmosphere is relaxed – no family lives in the house, so it's more private than a B&B but with a hostel feel. The owners rent kayaks and encourage guitar-playing and building bonfires.

Le Macareux (☎ 782-2414, 262 Rte 132) Doubles $25-80. There's nothing special about this motel, but its cheapest rooms (with shared bathroom) are all you need. Many types of rooms are offered. Register inside their tacky souvenir shop out front.

Gîte le Presbytère de Percé (☎ 782-5557, 47 rue de l'Église) Singles/doubles $50/60-80. On the same quiet street as the Maison Avenue House but closer to the church, this place has a peaceful, contemplative atmosphere.

Auberge au Coin de Banc et Chalets (☎ 645-2907, 315 Rte 132) Rooms $40-95. This place, several kilometers north of town, offers accommodations in small, comfy chalets and has a swimming pool and restaurant.

Hôtel La Normandie (☎ 782-2112, w www.normandieperce.com, 221 Rte 132) Singles/doubles $80/120-160. Resembling a grander motel but facing the famous rock, this place has neat rooms with huge beds and nice sea views.

Places to Eat

Resto-bar Le Matelot (☎ 782-2569, 7 rue de l'Église) Mains $7-15. You can get a very good evening meal at this candlelit place, which features seafood in the mid-price range (lobster's their specialty). Later at night it's also a place to just have a beer and catch the night's entertainment.

Les Fous de Bassans (☎ 782-2266, 162 Rte 132) Mains $9-16. This casual, recommended café is just off the main street. It's good anytime – for a coffee or a meal in a warm atmosphere. Seafood dishes are more expensive; the menu also has vegetarian items.

La Maison du Pêcheur (☎ 782-5331, 155 Place du Quai) Pizzas $10-21, mains $14-22. An obvious choice for a little splurge, this naval-themed dining room serves 16 types of fantastic pizza (even topped with octopus!) from its maple wood heated stove. Succulent dishes like grilled seal in fennel sauce, mussels, and poached salmon are also served. All this and a view of the rock – what more could you want?

There's also a **bakery** (9 rue Ste Anne).

Getting There & Away
Orléans Express (☎ 782-2140) buses link Percé to Rimouski ($46, 8½ hours, 2 daily). A bus also serves the south shore of the peninsula twice daily, reaching popular destinations like Carleton ($14, 3 hours). A ticket to Cap aux Os (Forillon National Park) requires a transfer in Gaspé. The Petro Canada service station and dépanneur (variety store) at the north end of the main street doubles as the bus station.

VIA Rail (☎ 782-2747, ☎ 800-361-5390) serves the south side of the peninsula three times a week from Montréal (via Charny at Québec City). The one-way fare from Charny to Percé is $92 (11 hours).

The station is 10km south of town at l'Anse à Beaufils; a taxi is about $11.

THE BAY SIDE
The south shore of the Gaspé Peninsula along the Baie des Chaleurs is quite different from the north coast. The land is flatter and less rocky, the weather warmer and villages are more run-down. There are a few Anglophone towns here where residents have charming accents, and pronounce Gaspé 'Gaspi' and Percé 'Percy.' Much of the French population is descended from the original Acadian and Basques settlers. The inland area is virtually uninhabited.

Port Daniel
pop 1690
Residents of this pretty, former Micmac settlement are of Scottish, Irish and Acadian descent.

Secondary roads from town lead to the **Réserve Faunique de Port Daniel** (☎ 396-2789, 396-2232) offering hunting, fishing and walking trails but no canoe rental.

Paspébiac
pop 3630
Descendants of Normans, Bretons and Basques live in this fishing town. The **Banc de Pêche de Paspebiac** (☎ 752-6229, 3-ème rue; adult/child $5/3; open 9am-6pm mid-June–end Sept), a waterfront historic site with restaurant and trade shops, is open daily throughout summer. It depicts the early life of the village as a fishing port; there are site tours by guides in period costumes. The church in town has a rare Casavant electropneumatic organ (see Ste Hyacinthe in the Montréal to Québec City chapter).

New Carlisle
pop 1460
One of the area's English towns, New Carlisle was founded by Loyalists and has some grand colonial homes. There are three protestant churches in town, recalling New England 19th-century architecture. In this atmosphere René Lévesque, the provincial premier who worked the hardest for separatism, was born. His natal home is at 16 rue Sorel. Oddly, long-standing plans to turn it into a museum have stalled indefinitely. A modest plaque is placed outside.

Hamilton House (☎ 752-6498, 115 rue Gérard Lévesque; adult/student $3.50/3; open 10am-4.30pm daily June-Sept) is a highlight of the area, a sheer delight. From 1852 this was home to the local member of Parliament and his family. Since 1983 it's blossomed into a museum in the hands of its dear owner, Katherine Smollett. The two-story mansion is lovingly stuffed to the brim with old photographs, scrapbooks, antiques and costumes of all kinds, placed thematically in the 14 rooms. Ask to play the old phonograph and check out the Dr Who–like Accelomatic machine to dry hair dye. Kids and adults will get a kick out of the Haunted Basement and the imagination it took to create it from scratch. Tea and scones are served most afternoons in the sitting room.

Bonaventure
pop 2940

A pleasant town founded by Acadians in 1791, Bonaventure has the region's most interesting attractions.

The **Musée Acadien** (☎ 534-4000, 95 ave Port Royal; adult/student $5/4; open 9am-6pm daily end June–early Oct, 9am-5pm Mon-Fri & 1pm-5pm Sun early Oct–end June), is worth a visit and has English booklets available to explain some of the tragic yet fascinating Acadian history. They host great Acadian music on Wednesday at 7:30pm. Next to the museum are several arts and craft stores worth visiting for local products, including items made of fish-skin leather – soft, supple and attractive and no, it doesn't smell. The cheap bookmarks make a good gift.

The new **Bioparc** (☎ 534-1997, 123 rue des Vieux Ponts; adults/students $10/8; open 9am-6pm June-Sept) houses a flora and fauna collection (with sea animals, mountain lions and lynx) taken from around the peninsula. Their full moon walking tours are good.

North of town is the **Grotte de St Elzéar** (☎ 534-4335, 198 Rte de l'Église; adults/children $37/27; open 8am-4pm June–mid-Oct), which gives four-hour tours of one of Québec's oldest caves. You descend into the cool depths (it's one way to escape summer heat, but bring warm clothes!) and view the stalactites and stalagmites. English tours must be booked in advance. To get there, take chemin de la Rivière and follow the signs.

Cime Aventure (☎ 534-2333, 800-790-2463, Ⓦ www.cimeaventure.com, 200 chemin Arsenault) is a well-run outfit offering a large variety of **canoe/kayak trips** – either a few hours along the scenic, tranquil rivière Bonaventure or several-day guided trips around the tip of the Gaspésie. Excursions cost $20-$1260, but day-trips cost under $70. On their site is a camping supply store (with vegetarian food), one of the province's nicest **campgrounds** ($20 per tent site; $40 in tee-pee) and even a sauna. They also rent bikes. Take chemin de la Rivière (which extends from avenue Grand Pré).

Places to Stay & Eat Bonaventure has some charming, if eccentric, places to stay, and a good selection of eateries.

Gîte du Foin Fou (☎ 534-4413, Ⓦ www .foinfou.qc.ca, 204 chemin de la Rivière) Singles/doubles $40/55. Ask the owner why he calls his B&B Crazy Hay: 'Because there's hay all around, and a nut in the middle – me!' You know you're in for something different when eggs descend from the ceiling as you enter. There are creative surprises to be found everywhere in this spacious house, which attracts a young, artistic, laid-back crowd. Anything goes here.

Auberge du Café Acadien (☎ 534-4276, 168 rue Beaubassin) Singles/doubles $50/60; mains $8-15. The specialty here is the owners' own smoked salmon (marinated in light maple sauce and smoked with maple wood) – it's delicious, and served in the restaurant as are other excellent, Cajun-styled meals. Upstairs are a few comfortable rooms with shared bathroom.

Bistro Bar le Fou du Village (☎ 534-4567, 119 ave Grand Pré) Mains $4-8. This pub serves good snacks, but the main focus is the live music on Thursday to Sunday nights (cover charge varies). It's a fun place with a lively atmosphere.

New Richmond
pop 4000

Nestled in the bay near the mouths of two rivers, New Richmond is another Loyalist center. The **British Heritage Centre** (☎ 392-4487, Ⓦ www.casa-gaspe.com, 351 boul Perron Ouest; adults/students $5/3.50; open 9am-6pm daily June-Aug) is a small re-created Loyalist village of the late 1700s. It consists of an interpretive center, houses, a general store, a lighthouse and other buildings. The center also covers the influence of later Irish and Scottish immigrants.

Carleton
pop 4300

Located at a pretty point on the water and backed by rounded hills with excellent views, Carleton also has a decent beach. This is where the people of the Gaspésie come for a day at the beach. There is a tourist office (☎ 364-3544, 629 boul Perron) in the central Hôtel de Ville.

From the docks there are **boat excursions** for fishing or sightseeing. At the central **bird sanctuary**, herons, terns, plovers and other shore birds can be observed along the sandbar. Walking paths and a road also lead behind the town to the top of **Mont St Joseph** (555m), which provides fine views over the bay and across to New Brunswick. The blue, metal-roofed oratory at the top can be visited, and after the climb the snack bar is a welcome sight. To avoid paying parking fees at the oratory, park at the first parking lot on your way up and take the 1.1km trail. Bilingual explanatory panels provide insight into the beginnings of Canada.

There is a network of 12 **hiking** trails between Carleton and Maria, 13km to the east, covering 30km of mostly intermediate-level forest paths. Get maps from the tourist office.

Places to Stay & Eat While they're not exactly unforgettable, there are decent B&Bs, motels and restaurants in town.

Camping de Carleton (☎ 364-3992, Pointe Tracadigash) Tents sites $14-18. Set on a jutting spit of land in front of town, there are miles of beach and swimming here too. Canoes can be rented nearby for birding and exploring the calm inner bay.

Gîte de la Mer et Montagne (☎ 364-6474, 711 boul Perron) Singles/doubles $35-50/50-65. This place is central and pleasant. Try for the top-floor room with a sea view from the balcony.

Le St Honoré (☎ 364-7618, 548 boul Perron) Mains $4-8, dinner specials $22. A succulent taste of France is available here (chocolate croissants, fresh salads), and their full-course suppers are a treat.

Mai (☎ 362-6652, 550 boul Perron) Mains $6-13. Good Vietnamese and Chinese cooking in a no-frills atmosphere. Their weekend buffets are a good value.

Getting There & Away The Orléans bus stops at 561 boulevard Perron. Tickets are available inside the restaurant Le Héron (☎ 364-7000). The train station is 1km from the center, back against the mountains on rue de la Gare. A bus to Rimouski from Carleton costs $35 (four hrs, twice daily), a bus direct to/from Montréal costs $112 (16½ hrs, twice a day) and a train between Carleton from Montréal costs $101 (12 hrs, three times a week).

Parc de Miguasha

The small peninsula south of Rte 132 near Nouvelle is renowned for its fossils, so much so that it is one of Canada's 13 Unesco World Heritage sites. Unesco describes the area as the most important fossil site in the world for illustrating the Devonian period (342 to 395 million years ago). In this small region are 'the greatest number and best preserved specimens found anywhere in the world of the lobe-finned fishes that gave rise to the first four-legged, air-breathing terrestrial vertebrates – the tetrapodes.'

The park (☎ 794-2475, 231 Rte Miguasha Ouest; adult/child $4/2; open 9am-6pm daily June–mid-Oct) and information center are set up around the Devonian period site. Guided walks take visitors through the museum and along a trail to the fossil-filled cliffs to look at fish and insects that existed here so long ago. Do *not* collect your own fossils!

For those headed to Dalhousie, New Brunswick, a ferry (☎ 506-684-5107; $12 car & driver, 2 min, hourly) is just down the road from the park.

Pointe à la Garde

There is no village here, just a castle. Yes, a castle – a modern one, built by someone fulfilling a life-long dream to live in one. Good news for others: It has been transformed into what may be Québec's most memorable hotel after Québec City's Ice Hotel (see that chapter). The *Chateau Bahia (☎ 788-2048,*

152 boul Perron) emerges through the trees as if from a dream, particularly if you are not expecting it. There is also an excellent, year-round HI hostel on the premises here.

All rooms have their own staircase and small balcony, allowing you your night in a castle tower. Doubles with toilet cost $59, with shared washroom $45, and shared rooms for three to five people are $20 per person, making it one of the best deals around. Hostel beds are $17 each. Built in 1983, it is still a work in progress, and the owner has made a 12km Poetry Trail through the forest, on which you can read poetry on your way to a summit with stunning views. As if that wasn't enough, there is a restaurant too, serving only stupendous banquet-style dinners ($12) at 8.30pm, often maple-cured ham or seafood, with home-baked cakes. The owner, Jean, loves to share with others his notion of the good life.

The Orléans bus will stop 100m from the door if you ask the driver.

Pointe à la Croix & Listuguj

The scenery become more lush and green at this point, while the bay slowly peters out in a swampy mix of mist-covered islands and weeds. Around Pointe à la Croix has always been and remains a largely Micmac community. There's a bridge over to Campbellton, New Brunswick. Some people live on New Brunswick time here (one hour ahead), and businesses tend to accommodate both time zones.

Listuguj is the Micmac part of town. The **Centre d'Art et Culture** *(☎ 788-1760, 2 Riverside Ouest; admission free; open 9am-8pm daily June-Oct)* displays local handicrafts (including fine basket work) and sculptures.

A few kilometers west of the bridge from Pointe à la Croix, the Parks Canada-run **Battle of the Ristigouche National Historic Site** *(☎ 788-5676, Rte 132; adult/child $3.75/2; open 9am-5pm daily June–early Oct)* details the 1760 naval battle of Restigouche, which finished off France's New World ambitions. An interpretive center explains the battle's significance to the British and has salvaged articles and even parts of a sunken French frigate. The last few years of the war for control of the country are neatly chronicled. Skip the animated film but speak to the well-informed guides.

MATAPÉDIA VALLEY

Between the village of Matapédia and the coast of the St Lawrence River is this peaceful, pretty valley, unlike any other portion of the Gaspésie. Alongside the rivière Matapédia and the railway line, Rte 132 passes through fertile farmland with a backdrop of green mountains for about 70km. The valley is covered with broad-leafed maple and elm trees, which add brilliant color in the autumn. The river is renowned for its salmon fishing for which expensive permits are required – in the past, Presidents Nixon and Carter managed to find the funds for

---

Scenic Drive – Southern Matapédia Valley

From Rte 132, it's recommended to make a loop inland. Cross the small bridge in Matapédia and head uphill, toward St Alexis de Matapédia. After 2km, on your left you'll see a pure-water source where locals fill up. After the pretty, winding road to St Alexis, turn left on what might be the deadest rue Principale in the province. Drive 4.5km to the lookout (a 300m walk from the parking lot), which affords incredible views of the valley and the winding rivière Matapédia from 230m up. Continue to St François d'Assise, passing by flat agricultural lands. There's an *Invasion of the Body Snatchers* feel to this little town in the middle of nowhere. Rejoin Rte 132 from here along rang du Moulin.

them. There are several smallish towns along the way and, around Lac Matapédia, a couple of picnic sites and a campground.

Matapédia
pop 700
This tiny village is the gateway into Québec from the International Appalachian Trail, and some beautiful expeditions can be had with the help of Nature-Aventure (☎ 865-2100, W www.members-tripod.com/nature, 9 rue du Vieux Pont). They offer a range of rugged and worthwhile canoe, kayak, mountain bike and hiking possibilities along and near the rivières Ristigouche and Matapédia.

Causapscal
pop 2700
This is a good place for a stop on the trip through the valley. It's a pretty town with a traditional look, a beautiful stone church and many older houses with typical Québécois silver roofs. Sometimes the odors of nearby sawmills make things unpleasant. There are over 25km of walking and observation trails in the surrounding hills. Salmon are king here, as you can tell by the outlandish salmon statue on the main road.

There are a couple of covered bridges south of town and, in the center, a pedestrian-only suspension bridge across the rivière Matapédia, from where you can see anglers casting their lines where the Matapédia and Causapscal meet. If you want to try your luck, a permit here only costs $35 per day; farther up the Causapscal, where salmon are plenty, you'll pay $200 a day, but still farther up the Matapédia it's only $5 per day (you get what you pay for!). Ask at the tourist office (☎ 756-6048, 53 rue St Jacques) for more information.

If fishing's not quite your gig, check out the interesting **Site Historique Matamajaw** (☎ 756-6099, 53c rue St Jacques; adult/student $4/3; open 9am-9pm daily June-mid–Oct). This museum was once a salmon-fishing lodge – the outbuildings and much of the riverfront property were all part of a private fishing estate built in 1870 by Lord Mount Stephen of Canadian Pacific Railway fame. It became a private club for the wealthy

before long. Take a look in the lodge, some of which remains much the way it was. Other rooms are devoted to the Atlantic salmon, the impetus for all this.

The Orléans Express bus, linking New Brunswick to the Lower St Lawrence, stops at 122 rue St Jacques.

Places to Stay & Eat The pickings here are slim, but the area so charming, it may well be worth an overnight stay.

Camping de Causapscal (☎ 756-5621, 601 Rte 132) Tent sites $16-20. This place is small (65 sites) and situated on attractive land; there are showers here too.

Auberge La Coulée Douce (☎ 756-5270, 888-756-5270, 21 rue Bourdreau) Singles/doubles $55-80/65-100. This place is on the hill opposite the historic site, and is a favorite among fishing enthusiasts. They also serve hearty meals in the evening (call ahead if you're not staying there).

Amqui
pop 6800
The largest town in the valley doesn't have much worth mentioning, aside from a range of services. Toward the end of summer you may see people standing by the side of the road waving jars. They're selling locally picked wild hazelnuts *(noisettes)*, which are not expensive.

Around **Lac Matapédia** there are some viewpoints over the lake and as well as picnic spots.

Îles de la Madeleine

pop 14,500
Its lack of higher temperatures and palm trees are the only things that separate this string of islands in the Gulf of St Lawrence from other of the world's island paradises. Arguably the province's most beautiful area, these islands bewitch the visitor with its sense of isolation and stretches of red cliffs, which burn into the memory of all who see them firsthand.

The Îles de la Madeleine (Magdalen Islands) are a dozen islands stretched out over some 100km, and are 215km southeast from Gaspé, 105km from Prince Edward Island. Six islands are linked over 65km by long sand spits. Where sandy beaches don't greet the Gulf, iron-rich red cliffs do, sculpted by nature's powerful forces of wind and sea into fantastic shapes that seem to take on new forms in changing light; one never tires of looking at them. Aside from a salt mine (the islands are formed on salt beds), there is no industry to pollute the wind, sand and sea. Sand covers 30% of the islands.

In complement to the landscape's unusual hues, many of the island's houses and fishing boats are painted in smart, audacious colors. A can of paint goes a long way here, where small, modern villages are alight in purples, yellows, greens and reds. The rhythm of life is laid-back and content. It's the kind of place where people don't lock their doors. Locals are not overly sociable or solicitous, but friendly and respectful of each other's privacy.

Most surprising of all is that in summertime, the place is seething with life. Where the Gaspésie is overwhelmingly beautiful but socially limp, the islands are teeming with the energy of young, free-minded travelers who come here for days or months at a time. In fact, the place has been a magnet for artists, hippies, drifters and free-thinkers since the 1960s, when beatniks are credited for having 'rediscovered' the islands. This influence is felt today, not only via the ones who decided to stay, but in a new generation of young, adventurous travelers who are into healthy foods, the outdoors and letting it all hang out in bars livelier than you'd find on rue St Denis in Montréal.

People come here not only for the landscapes, but also for the wind, which is nearly always very strong. Kitesurfing is popular, as are kite-buggying and windsurfing. Some former seal hunters now take tourists out on the ice in early spring to see and photograph baby seals. The Magdalens are considered the best place for this.

History

Vikings, Micmacs and Basque fishermen had all visited the islands, but the first major wave of people arrived after the great Acadian deportations of 1755. Several hundred Acadian families founded villages on the islands. After 1763, the islands became British territory, and Isaac Coffin became administrator, enforcing a near-feudal system of exploitation of the French inhabitants. Increasingly difficult living conditions pushed the Acadian 'Madelinots' into exile, and from there they founded several North Shore villages, notably Blanc Sablon (1854), Natashquan (1855) and Sept Îles (1872).

Supposedly the islands take their name from Madeleine Fontaine, the wife of the first French governor, in the late 17th century.

Population & People

About 95% of the population is Francophone, but each village has its own verbal particularities, which locals make much of (eg, people from the Havre aux Maison region don't pronounce their 'r's while those from the Havre Aubert region accent them). Anglophones with Scottish and Irish ancestry live on Île d'Entrée and Grosse Île, some descendants of shipwrecked sailors. Until very recently, these English communities mixed very little with the French, despite sharing only 222 sq km. This is changing slowly; there are reported sightings of English islanders socializing in Cap aux Meules, and even instances of intermarriage.

Information & Orientation

The tourist information office (☎ 986-2245) is at 128 chemin du Débarcadère, near the ferry terminal, and is open year-round.

The main road, Rte 199, runs through the six connected islands. L'Île d'Entrée is only accessible by boat. Except for Cap aux Meules, villages here are spread out and without traditional centers; names refer more to regions.

About 16km north of Grosse Île is **Île Brion**, an ecological reserve once but no longer inhabited by humans. It remains home to 140 species of birds and much interesting vegetation. L'Istorlet (see Places to

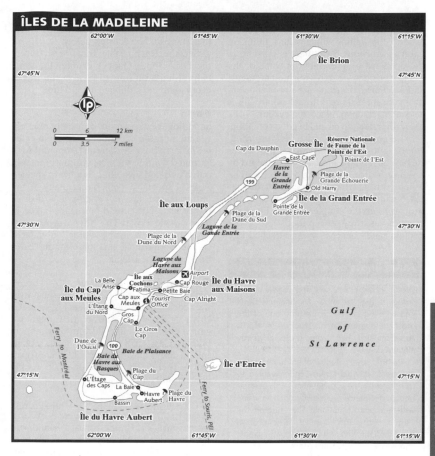

ÎLES DE LA MADELEINE

Stay & Eat in Île du Havre Aubert, below) organizes snorkeling trips there; check at the tourist office in Cap aux Meules for other ways to get and possibly overnight there.

The islands follow the Atlantic Time Zone, one hour ahead of mainland Québec.

Special Events

At Grande Entrée, the **Lobster Festival** (☎ 985-2277) is held in mid-July. In mid-August, watch for the **Sand Castle Contest** (☎ 986-6863) along a 2km stretch of beach on Havre Aubert. **Traditions Maritimes en Fête** focuses on the island's folklore and history in songs, races, shows and exhibits for three weeks beginning at the end of August.

The **Canadian Professional and Amateur Windsurf Competition** is usually held here in late August and early September. Also wind-related, the fun **Fête du Vent**, in mid-September, showcases islanders' inventions that run on wind power. There are other music, crafts and sporting festivals and events from mid-June through mid-September.

Activities

Most of the islands' activities and sights revolve around the sea. Beach-strolling and exploring lagoons, tidal pools and cliff formations can take up days, but so can poking around the fishing villages and going on nature excursions. **Swimming** is possible in the open sea or, preferably, in some of the shallow lagoons – water is warmest in August and September. Currents are strong and venturing far from shore is not advisable. This is also a spectacular place for **cycling** – the main roads are paved and in good condition.

Also popular on the island is **kitesurfing**, where you get pulled along the water surface on a board similar to a surfboard by holding onto a wind-driven kite. The island's strong winds also make **kitebuggying** possible – try to catch glimpses of the wide grins on the people strapped into little buggies, as they are pulled across the endless sandy beaches by an attached kite

---

Madelinots on a Flying Trapeze

While lobsters, mussels and road salt are some of the Îles de la Madeleine's best-known exports, few realize that one of the most innovative circus troupes in North America also hail from these elegantly aligned dots on the map.

In 1993 seven Madelinot graduates of the Montreal National Circus School wanted to form a circus new to Québec – an animal-free, performance-oriented circus more in line with European traditions. They birthed the Cirque Éloize (pronounced *EL-was,* local slang for lightning) and were met with almost immediate success. Since 1997, their second original piece, *Excentricus,* has played to packed houses in Europe, Australia, South America and across the US and Canada. They've staged over 800 shows in 200 cities worldwide.

It's their fusion of circus with theatre, dance, classical music and avant-garde performance that has won them acclaim and a chance to steal some of the limelight from Montréal's internationally renowned Cirque du Soleil. Their new piece, Cirque Orchestra, began touring in summer 2001.

---

flying above. To try on that kind of smile, contact Aerosport Carrefour d'Aventures in l'Étang du Nord, listed below.

See the Responsible Tourism section in the Facts about Québec chapter for some helpful hints on how to protect the fragile ecosystem and still have a good time.

Food

Sampling fresh seafood, especially mussels, is a memorable experience. The main catch is lobster, whose season runs from mid-May to mid-July. Snow crabs, scallops, mussels, perch and cod are other significant species. A local specialty available at many of the better restaurants is *pot-en-pot,* a dish of mixed fish and seafood in a sauce baked in its own pie crust. The adventurous may want to try dark, strong-tasting seal meat.

There are excellent restaurants and cafés throughout the islands.

Getting There & Away
Air The airport (☎ 969-2888) is on the northwest corner of Île du Havre aux Maisons. Air Nova (☎ 888-247-2262), an Air Canada regional airline, has flights from Montréal via Québec City ($578 roundtrip, 2 daily), Mont Joli (2 daily) and Gaspé ($170 roundtrip, 2 daily). There's also a once or twice weekly flight from Halifax.

Ferry The cheapest and most common way to get to the Îles de la Madeleine is by ferry from Souris, on Prince Edward Island, run by Traversier CTMA (☎ 986-3278, 888-986-3278, ☑ ctma@duclos.net). The boat, holding 300 passengers and 90 vehicles, makes the five-hour, 223km cruise from April through January. From July to early September there is daily, sometimes twice-daily, service; crossings are less frequent other times of the year. In mid-summer reservations are strongly recommended. Second best to booking ahead is arriving at least two hours ahead of time. Adults pay $37 for the trip and $10 for their kids ages five to 12. Cars and bikes are $70 and $9 extra, respectively.

CTMA also operates a weekly passenger service from Montréal via Québec City and

Monument to Jacques Cartier, Gaspé Peninsula

Church, Ste Anne des Monts, Gaspé Peninsula

Fishing boats off the coast, Gaspé Peninsula

Polar bear country – the harsh tundra of Whapmagoostui (Kuujjuarapik)

Hudson Bay, Nunavik

Deer in winter, Abitibi-Témiscamingue

Matane, with a whale-watching stop in Tadoussac. It takes about 48 hours for the journey, but is a great way of seeing the St Lawrence River and gives the opportunity of boating one way and returning by car. The year 2002 will inaugurate this route with their new, large boat. Prices were not available at press time; call CTMA for prices and schedules.

Getting Around

There is no public transport on the islands. MA Poirier (☎ 986-4467) runs a seven-hour guided bus tour of the islands leaving from the tourist office.

There's a Thrifty (☎ 969-9006, 800-367-2277) for car rentals near the airport, but it's essential to book as far ahead as possible.

Bike rental is available from some of the places mentioned later. In addition, Le Pédalier (☎ 986-2965, 365 chemin Principal, Cap aux Meules) will rent you a cycle for $18 per day.

ÎLE DU CAP AUX MEULES
Cap aux Meules
pop 1680

This is the busiest town of the islands, and with the ferry terminal is the archipelago's commercial center. It's quite modern, which can be a little disconcerting for those looking for something else. It is, however, atypical of the rest of the towns, villages and landscapes around the islands. Banking and shopping for supplies should be taken care of here, and there are a few killer entertainment spots.

It's recommended to find a place away from town in the beautiful countryside, but if you prefer the town, there are some good places.

Pas Perdus (*Lost Steps;* ☎ 986-5151, Ⓦ *www.pasperdus.com, 160 chemin Principal*) Doubles $70; meals in café $5-11; open 7am-10pm daily. Dropping in here is a big part of the Magdalen experience, whether you sleep in their upstairs rooms or not (and they can be noisy when things get wild downstairs). The relaxed, bohemian, wood-paneled café is the center of the islands' youth-culture scene. At some point everyone rolls through for a drink at the bar, to surf the Web ($6 per hour), read a book on a sofa, have breakfast (their $6 Eggs Benedict is renowned), grab a shark burger to go ($5, yes, real shark meat), or check out the art exhibits on the walls. On Monday nights the house kicks with their famous impromptu fusion jam sessions, when locals belt out jazz, rock or whatever else comes to mind.

Les Bons Garçons (☎ *986-5964, 460 chemin Petitpas*) Singles/doubles $55/65. This central, very neat and gay-friendly B&B is heavy on antiques. Their breakfast is buffet-style.

Café Théâtre Wendell (☎ *986-6002, 185 chemin Principal*) Mains $5-10. This is a perfect hangout, with light, healthy meals in a relaxed atmosphere where the accent is on theatre and film culture. The in-house Cinéma Parallel screens films most weekends at 9pm.

La Patio (☎ *986-8000, 455 chemin Principal*) Mains $6-13. This inexpensive place serves pizza, BBQ chicken and spaghetti.

La Table du Roy (☎ *986-3004, 1188 Rte 199*) Mains $11-25. Considered the finest dining on the islands, this intimate place uses fresh, mainly local ingredients in their succulent dishes.

Fatima, L'Étang du Nord & Around

These two 'towns' spread out over the rest of the island not taken up by central Cap aux Meules.

On the west side of the island are some excellent spots to see the red cliffs in their glory, particularly at **La Belle Anse**, where you can walk along them to gape at their erosion patterns. At **Cap du Phare**, the lighthouse is a popular gathering spot to watch sunsets. In the middle of the island is a high peak, **Butte du Vent**, which proffers a 360-degree panoramic view. The road leading there, chemin des Buttes, is also very scenic. At **Anse de l'Étang du Nord** there's a small harbor and a concentration of boutiques and cafés, a public square for festivities and an unusual sculpture of seven fishermen.

An excellent place run by young, enthusiastic sportsmen who ensure your outdoors

GASPÉ PENINSULA

thrills is Aerosport Carrefour d'Aventures (☎ 986-6677, ⓦ www.aerosport.ca, 1390 chemin Lavernière). Most popular are their **kayaking** expeditions, including cave visits, but when the wind is right, a more unforgettable experience would be trying out their power kites to sail along the beaches in a kite-pulled buggy, or go **kitesurfing**. A kite-pulled buggy, with lesson, is $40-50 for two hours for two people; kitesurfing is $200 per person for four hours; kite-pulled sea kayak is $80 for two hours for two people; wintertime kite-skiing is $60 per person for three hours. In winter, the fun keeps rolling with kite-skiing. They're used to initiating newcomers.

Places to Stay Many will find staying in this area convenient if they do not want to get too far from the ferry terminal, Cap aux Meules, and all the 'action' there.

Auberge Internationale des Îles (☎ 986-4523, 74 chemin du Camping) Dorm beds member/nonmember $23/25, doubles $46, tent sites $15-20. Now *this* is a hostel! With only 30 places, the feel is intimate and quiet, but there's a spacious gathering room for hanging out as well as a spotless kitchen and laundry room. The campground is the islands' prettiest. It's situated at Gros Cap, a small peninsula shaped like an inkblot, on the site of an old marine-biology laboratory. From the second floor there's a view onto a pierced rock in the shape of an elephant, and there are daily sea-kayaking expeditions; they also rent bicycles. It's due south of Cap aux Meules, accessible via chemin de Gros Cap from Rte 199.

Camping Le Barachois (☎ 986-4726, chemin du Rivage) Tent sites $15-20. The largest campground on the islands (180 sites) feels crowded and is popular with trailers.

Les Bons Garçons (☎ 986-5964, 56 chemin du Rivage) Singles/doubles $65/70, chalet $750 per week. This gay-friendly, tidy B&B is in Fatima, a stone's throw away from the sea. The chalet, big enough for four persons, has especially nice views.

Chalet-Maison à Edgar (☎ 986-5214, 49 chemin Thorne) Doubles daily/weekly $85-120/550-850. Located on a quiet stretch of road in Fatima, there are two separate housing units to choose from, both with all the conveniences.

Places to Eat There's a good mix of quaint cafés and diners here to satisfy all tastes.

Café La Côte (☎ 986-6412, 499 chemin Boisville Ouest) Mains $6-9. Right at the harbor in L'Étang du Nord, this is a great, colorful place for cappuccino, focaccia sandwiches and healthy, light meals. They also serve excellent breakfasts.

Salon de Thé Arthur (☎ 986-6526, 530 chemin Fougère, l'Étang du Nord) Attached to an art gallery, this airy tea salon has delicious pastries and cheeses to accompany their dozens of teas from around the world.

Decker Boy (☎ 986-4525, 618 chemin les Caps) Mains $7-15. This plain looking place in Fatima is cheap and good. There are hot dogs and *poutine,* but lots of inexpensive seafood dishes too.

La Factrie (☎ 986-2710, 521 chemin du Gros Cap) Mains $7-19. Its name is a play on the word 'factory,' as this is located in a lobster-processing plant (for proof, just peer through the huge window that overlooks the workings). Cafeteria-style, it serves up fresh seafood with no pretensions. It's a good place to try seafood appetizers like soup ($3) and *coquilles St Jacques* ($5).

ÎLE DU HAVRE AUBERT

South of Cap aux Meules, connected by long bars of sand at points barely wider than the road, this is the archipelago's largest island.

The most lively area of the town of **Havre Aubert** (pop 1050) is known as La Grave, an old section by the water at the southeastern tip of the island. The main street is lined with small craft and gift shops, some restaurants and many old houses. Here you feel the rustic charm of an old-time fishing community. From there it's highly worthwhile to drive to the west side of the island, either via chemin du Bassin, which follows the coast and ends up on a long beach of sandbars and dunes, or via chemin de la Montagne, which cuts through the middle of the island, where the forests and fields come as a contrast to the seascapes.

A must-see is the **Artisans du Sable** (☎ 937-2917, 907 Rte 199), a workshop and boutique specializing in creations made entirely of sand. Aside from their branch in Tadoussac, this is the only place in Québec to find items like vases, lamps, frames and clocks, all quite striking, made with compacted sand. It's interesting just to drop in and chat with the vivacious owners.

On any rainy day the interesting **aquarium** (☎ 937-2277, 146 chemin de la Grave; adult/child $4/2; open 10am-6pm daily June–mid-Oct) is packed with visitors disturbed from their seaside activities. Their 'petting pool' is popular. The **Musée de la Mer** (☎ 937-5711, 1023 Rte 199; adult/child $4/2; open 9am-6pm daily end June–Aug, 9am-5pm Mon-Fri & 1pm-5pm Sat & Sun Sept–end June) has displays on shipwrecks and various aspects of the islands' transportation and fishing history.

Places to Stay & Eat

L'Istorlet (☎ 937-5266, W www3.simpatico .ca/istorlet, 100 chemin de l'Istorlet) Singles/ doubles $20-30/25-35, tent sites $10-15. This complex rents bikes ($18 per day) and watersports equipment like snorkels, canoes, sailboards and kayaks ($10/hour or $30/ half-day). They give lessons and guided tours, including one where you dive with seals ($75 per person, 4-6 hours). You can stay inside the main complex in single or double rooms, pitch a tent or stay in their comfy wooden ones. Call to make sure it's not summer-camp week, or that place'll be overrun with little whipper-snappers.

La Maison de Camille (☎ 937-2516, e camille.vezina@sympatico.ca, 946 chemin de la Grave) Singles/doubles $45/55. Run by one of the original hippies who came to the islands in the 1960s, and still travels the world come wintertime, this B&B, in the heart of La Grave, is a real charmer. A garden out back lines the waterfront, the wood paneled interior exudes real warmth, and your laid-back (so laid-back that you might have to make your own breakfast), barefooted host is a true winner.

La Marée Haute (☎ 937-2492, e lamaree haute@sympatico.ca, 25 chemin des Fumoirs)

Doubles $60-75; mains $19-26. People come here equally for the incredible kitchen as for the sweet B&B upstairs. If main dishes like grilled mako shark and rabbit are out of your price range, try an entrée of seal paté ($5) or scallops and leek in sesame sauce ($7). The pies are also out of this world.

Café de la Grave (☎ 937-5765, 969 Rte 199) Mains $7-9. Your island experience wouldn't be complete without a visit to this grand ex-general store (there are still old posters and antiques) transformed into a blissful eatery serving nachos, sandwiches, soups, salads, daily specials and pot en pot. If you feel like tinkering on the corner piano, don't stop yourself – others don't!

ÎLE DU HAVRE AUX MAISONS

Probably the most scenic of the Magdalen Islands, Havre aux Maisons is an explorer's paradise. Heading north from Cap aux Meules, take the first left off Rte 199 to chemin de la Petite Baie and chemin des Cyr, which curves around **Butte Ronde**, a steep, high hill well worth the climb.

Even more impressive is the Havre aux Masions' east coast, following chemin de la Pointe Basse and chemin des Montants. Best approached from the north along chemin des Montants, the landscape is ridiculously scenic, with rolling hills, isolated houses, and a cute lighthouse guarding a dramatic view onto rocky cliffs and the rugged sea.

Auberge La Petite Baie (☎ 969-4073, 187 Rte 199) Doubles $60-75, suite $95; mains average $15, full-course meals average $20). This antique-filled rustic B&B sits atop a dining room open for dinner only.

Chalets les Sillons (☎ 969-2126, 436 chemin Dune du Sud) Chalets daily/weekly $55-100/375-650. A series of separate chalets of different styles and comfort levels are near a beach with huge sandstone arches.

ÎLE AUX LOUPS

pop 200

This tiny island community is in the middle of the long sand spits connecting the north and south islands. For a quick dip by the dunes, the water is warmer on the lagoon side. The **Maison du Héron** (☎ 969-4819, 21 chemin du Quai) is a boutique with a small archaeological exhibit on objects left by aboriginal inhabitants thousands of years ago.

GROSSE ÎLE

Scottish pioneers settled this, the principal English section of the islands. Despite generations of isolation, many of the local people barely speak a word of French, a touchy subject for the Francophone locals. Pointe de la Grosse Île, East Cape and Old Harry are the main communities. Old Harry (named in honor of Harry Clark, for a long time the area's only inhabitant) was where walruses used to be slaughtered for oil. Sea Cow Lane is the site of the former walrus landing.

The **Gateway to the East Interpretation Center** (☎ 985-2931, 56 Rte 199; admission free; open 10am-6pm daily May-Sept) has an excellent exhibit on the rare flora and geological peculiarities of the islands (and of Québécois – it explains why Québec is the world's largest consumer per capita of salt). It's located right near the salt mine, which excavates at a depth of over 200m below sea level.

In Pointe de la Grosse Île check out **Trinity Church**, known for its stained glass depicting Jesus the fisherman. Out through the windows the eye captures the graves, piles of lobster traps, some solitary houses and then the sea – the island's world in microcosm.

In Old Harry, at the **Council for Anglophone Magdalen Islanders** (☎ 985-2116, 787 Rte Principale; admission free; open 8am-4pm Mon-Fri, 1pm-4pm Sat & Sun year-round), you can visit an old schoolhouse that for 52 years housed grades one through six (take a look at what they used as a toilet!). There are other thematic exhibits about the English community.

Reflective of the local's insularity, you have to know people to find out who rents out rooms in private homes.

La Maison Burke (☎ 985-2501, 54 Gerry Lane) Chalet $80 for two. A comfy, quiet chalet is rented to up to six persons ($130). Weekly rates are available.

POINTE DE L'EST

Linking Grosse Île and Île de la Grande Entrée is this wild region, which boasts the archipelago's most impressive beach. From Pointe Old Harry, **Plage de la Grande Échouerie**, a curving sweep of pale sand, extends for about 10km. A short road with parking areas and trails stretching down to the beach begins near Old Harry's harbor. From Rte 199 (through Pointe de l'Est which, other than the beach, is entirely a national wildlife refuge area) a few turnoffs lead to hiking paths.

ÎLE DE LA GRANDE ENTRÉE

This island begins beyond Old Harry and leads to a beautiful, isolated, infrequently visited section of the archipelago. It has been inhabited only since 1870.

Just past Old Harry on Rte 199, stop in at **St Peter's by the Sea**, a beautiful, peaceful little church overlooking the sea and bounded by graves of the Clark and Clarke families. It's open to visitors and is well worth a visit. On a breezy day the inside offers a quiet stillness broken only by creaking rafters. The church is made entirely of wood, including a richly carved door honoring drowned fishermen.

The locus of activity on this island is the excellent **Club Vacances des Îles** (☎ 985-2833, ⓦ www.clubiles.qc.ca, 377 Rte 199). The center's main functions are ecotourism and research, and they offer a wide range of worthwhile daily activities, which can be participated in on their own, or in packages including accommodations. There are two- to 10km nature walking tours ($5 to $10) with knowledgeable guides; cave exploration excursions ($27) where you swim, in a wetsuit, through caves and grottos; ornithological expeditions in kayaks; and even mud baths are an option! All can be done in English, but best to ask ahead. There is a cafeteria open to all, but accommodations in the rooms for rent and the lovely campground are given only with tour packages.

Inside is also the **Seal Interpretation Centre** (admission free; open 10am-6:30 pm daily June-Sept), which has a range of exhibits about the beasties including references to the controversial annual seal hunt.

Places to Stay & Eat

Gîte L'Émergence (☎ 985-2801, 122 chemin des Pealey) Doubles $60. Right at the tip of the island in a remote sector near a beach and small harbor, this little B&B is comfortable and quiet.

Délices de la Mer (☎ 985-2831, 907 chemin Principal) Mains $6-15. One of the best restaurants on the islands is this unassuming but atmospheric diner at the end of Rte 199. Sit with the fishermen and try their delicious chowder or cod.

ÎLE D'ENTRÉE

This is the one inhabited island not interconnected by land with the others, and which receives fewer tourists too. The tourist office can tell you about other boat tour options.

The virtually treeless island has an English-speaking population of around 175 and is primarily a fishing community. It's about 4km long and less than 1km wide with walking trails leading over much of it.

The gentler western section supports some farms before ending in high red cliffs. The eastern section is mountainous with the highest point, Big Hill, at 174m above sea level. A trail from Post Office Road leads up to the views from the top. There are a couple of grocery stores and one basic snack bar.

Chez McLean (☎ 986-4541, no address) Doubles $50. This is the only official guesthouse on the island, with cooking facilities. You need to reserve in advance. For other home-stay options, ask at the tourist office.

A twice-daily ferry run by SP Bonaventure (☎ 986-8452, 986-5705; $16; 1 hour) links it to the port at Cap aux Meules from Mon-Sat. Board in front of the coastguard building. It's possible to leave Cap aux Meules at 8am, explore the island and return on the 4pm ferry.

Northern Québec

☎ 819

The area covered in this chapter is larger than many of the world's countries, and comprises Québec's 'final frontier.' Northern Québec is the name given to three distinct areas: Abitibi-Témiscamingue, containing the region's most populous settlements and itself an amalgamation of two distinct regions; James Bay, a vast land defined by one of the world's largest hydroelectric facilities and by its numerous Cree villages; and Nunavik, Québec's arctic region, home of the Inuit.

Abitibi-Témiscamingue

This sparsely populated area (in over 65,140 sq km there are only 155,000 people and over 100,000 lakes!) has a special place in the Québécois imagination. It was the last area to be settled and developed on a major scale and stands as a symbol of the settlers' dreams and hardships, all the while conjuring up the mythical ethos of man conquering nature.

The traditional land of the Algonquin, Abitibi-Témiscamingue is an amalgamation of two distinct areas, each named after different tribes – Abitibi to the north and the sparsely settled Témiscamingue to the south. The area was colonized following the usual pattern of resource exploitation. Before the 19th century, the only Europeans in the area were hunters and fur traders (the region's renown among hunters continued – even Laurel and Hardy came here regularly to go moose hunting).

Témiscamingue, the area bordering Lac Témiscamingue on the border of Ontario, was settled first by loggers and lumberjacks (and missionaries were never far behind them) after 1850. The thick forests were cut and sent as logs down rivers. Abitibi's turn for settlement came in the 1910s with the

Highlights

- Go canoeing or hiking among the splendid, rugged canyons of Parc d'Aiguebelle
- Become a gold miner for a day in Val d'Or or orther old-time gold-fever boom towns in Abitibi
- Venture to Québec's final frontier, the town of Radisson
- Experience the magical displays of the Northern Lights
- Discover traditional Inuit hospitality and the beauty of the tundra in Nunavik, Northern Québec

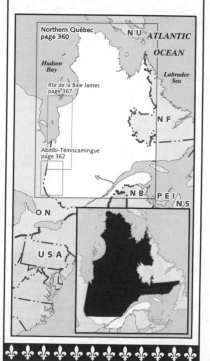

building of a railroad and the discovery of copper deposits just outside of present-day Val d'Or. However, many of the first colonists were up against a forbidding climate, relatively infertile soil and no infrastructure whatsoever.

Yet in the 1920s the desolate area was painted over in gold fever. The precious mineral was found first near present-day Cadillac and as thousands flooded the region in search of fortune, the first mine was opened in 1927. Other mines opened as more deposits were found (throughout the rest of the century, 96 gold and copper mines would open), sprouting boom towns in their wake. Many of these have closed; the larger ones of Val d'Or (meaning Valley of Gold) and Rouyn-Noranda survived.

In the 1930s an influx of immigrants from Eastern Europe, Russia, Poland and Ukraine arrived and helped build towns and do the dirty work in the mines. Mining was the mainstay of the area until a decline beginning in the 1980s, accompanied by layoffs and closings. Mining is still a major activity here, but could not prevent an exodus of many young people in search of more attractive opportunities in Québec's metropolitan regions.

Forestry has been the area's other economic backbone, as evidenced in the clearcut regions you may come across. The Association Forestière de l'Abitibi-Témiscamingue (☎ 762-2369) at 212 avenue du Lac in Rouyn-Noranda, can provide information on all the forestry-related sites that can be visited, free of charge, throughout the region.

Today this sector of Québec retains an exotic air, partially due to its remoteness. Most of Abitibi's terrain is flat, which makes the stunning valleys and cliffs of Parc d'Aiguebelle all the more striking in contrast. Témiscamingue is more diversified in its vegetation and landscape, with valleys and the majestic Lac Témiscamingue. Accessible only via northern Ontario and one long road south of Rouyn-Noranda, Témiscamingue does not see many tourists.

Special Events

February

La Sarre en Neige This is a month-long series (☎ 333-2294) of fun and games revolving around snow – there is everything from snow sculpture contests to rides in antique snowmobiles.

June

Festival Forestière de Senncterre Feel the importance of the forestry industry at this festival (☎ 737-2277) by fancying yourself a lumberjack and trying games like the axe throw and contests featuring chainsaws.

October

Festival du Cinéma International A non-competitive film festival (☎ 762-6212) held in Rouyn-Noranda at the end of October, this event's reputation has grown solid in the last few years.

Activities

The main activities in the region are **biking**, **snowmobiling** and **cross-country skiing**.

There are several major **cycling competitions and marathons** requiring lots of endurance. The Tour de l'Abitibi (☎ 825-5554) has been held in mid-July around Val d'Or since 1969 and features bicycle competitions for teens. The Raid des Conquérants (☎ 339-3300, ⓦ www.lesconquerantsdunord.com) happens at the beginning of August each year in La Sarre. It's a grueling two- or five-day mountain-bike ride. And the Vélo Tour 48-ème Nord (☎ 800-670-0499) is for participants ready to ride 400km in just four days. It happens in mid-July around Rouyn-Noranda.

Tourist offices have copies of the region's cycling trail guide, *À Vélo Sous le 48-ème Nord*.

An original and fun cross-country ski event is the Traversée du Lac Abitibi (☎ 339-3300), a five-day trek in March across the frozen lake near La Sarre.

Lovers of **downhill skiing** have just two small choices: **Mont Kanasuta** (☎ 279-2331, ⓦ www.kanasuta.com, chemin du Lac Kanasuta), in Arnfield, which has 10 slopes; and **Mont Vidéo** (☎ 734-3193, Rte Barraute-Québec-Lithium), which is in Barraute, with 14 slopes. Both places offer nighttime skiing.

NORTHERN QUÉBEC

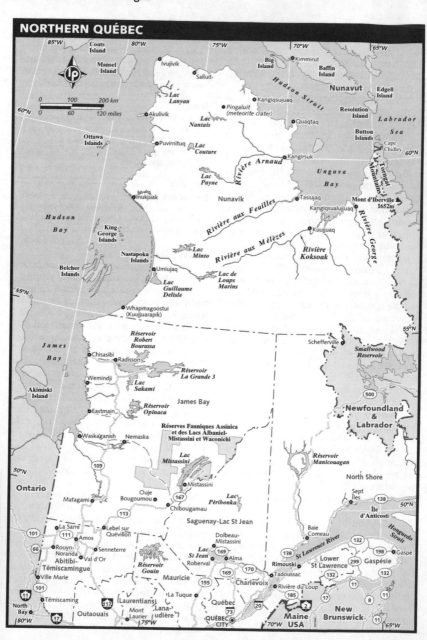

NORTHERN QUÉBEC

RÉSERVE FAUNIQUE LA VÉRENDRYE

Because of its immensity (13,615 sq km) and its remoteness, this provincial park (*☎ 736-7431, Rte 117; admission $3.50; open daily mid-May-mid-Sept*) offers some of the best wilderness opportunities in the province. Though the landscape may not be as grandiose and imposing as in other wildlife reserves, canoers and campers regale in the vast spaces, which put the *wild* back in wildlife. Much of this reserve was traditional hunting territory for the Algonquins of the Outaouais region, who in the 1920s had a 16,000-sq-km reserve here, called Réserve du Grand Lac Victoria. This reserve was slowly whittled down to zero thanks to the forestry industry's clearcutting operations, flooding (to create reservoirs), the construction of Rte 117 and the forming of this wildlife reserve.

Flora and fauna are abundant here – there are moose, black bears, foxes and wolves (and 35 other mammals), 150 species of bird,

Keep your eyes peeled for moose

and thousands of gray trout in the 4000 lakes. **Canoeing** is possible at $28 a day. The waterfalls at **Lac Roland** are also worth a visit.

There are four access points, all on Rte 117. Coming from the Laurentians, the Le Domaine information post (*☎ 435-2541*) is 58km past the village of Grand Remous.

During the 180km crossing of the reserve to Val d'Or there are no villages so make sure your tank is full.

There are several *camping* possibilities ($16) and *chalets* for rent inside the reserve. One of the several outfitters offering package deals in the area is Pavillon Cabonga (*☎ 449-2482, 800-880-2481, W www.pavcabonga.qc.ca*), which offers specials from $54 per person per day and covers a wide range of outdoor activities.

VAL D'OR
pop 24,700

Born in 1933 around the Sigma gold mine (which opened in 1927), Val d'Or today looks like a mining boom town of yesterday. There are wide avenues and a main street (3-ème Avenue), which still has a rough edge to it – one can easily imagine it being frenzied in the gold rush days. The Sigma mine is still open, though it's no longer the city's economic motor. The tourist office (*☎ 824-9646, 877-582-5367*) is at 20 3-ème Avenue (Rte 117), at the eastern end of town.

Things to See & Do

La Cité de l'Or (*☎ 825-7616, W www.citedelor.qc.ca, 90 avenue Perreault; adult/student $20/16; underground tours 8:30am-5:30pm daily late June-early Sept*) offers guided excursions 91m underground to show what gold mining's all about. On the same site is the **Village Minier de Bourlamaque** *(adult/student $10/8),* a restored mining village with 80 log houses. Call in advance to reserve a tour and bring warm clothes if you're going underground.

The **Native Friendship Centre** (*☎ 825-6857, 1272 7-ème Rue; admission free; open 9am-5pm Sat-Wed, 9am-9pm Thur & Fri*) is the Algonquin and Cree cultural center, with small exhibits and a gift shop. Sometimes you can taste traditional bread, called *bannik*, and Labrador tea. Cree and Algonquin peoples make up a sizeable percentage of the population here. The boutique *Wachiya* (*☎ 825-0434, 145 rue Perreault*) also sells many Cree arts and crafts.

For those interested in exploring First Nation traditions more deeply, Oscar

NORTHERN QUÉBEC

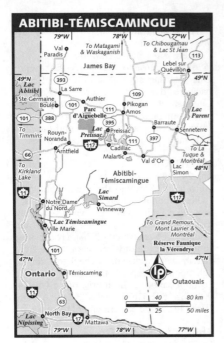

ABITIBI-TÉMISCAMINGUE

Aux 3 Tilleuls (☎ 825-4765, 106 rue Champlain) Doubles $50-60. This modern, comfortable B&B has an outdoor pool. Two rooms have a private bathroom.

Pizzadelic (☎ 824-7920, 810 3-ème Avenue) Mains $6-14. Incredible pizza – try the ginger shrimp! – in snazzy surroundings.

Getting There & Away

Air Val d'Or is well served by air. Air Creebec (☎ 800-567-6567, W www.aircreebec .ca) flies Sunday through Friday from Montréal ($282-670 roundtrip, 1½ hours, 1 daily) and from there serves reserves farther north. The cost of a roundtrip flight depends on when you fly. They only reserve six sale-price seats per flight, so book early. Air Canada flies from Montréal to Val d'Or (weekend/ weekday $300/200 roundtrip, 1¼-2¼ hours, 3-6 daily), direct or via Rouyn-Noranda.

Bus The bus station (☎ 874-2200) is at 851 5-ème Avenue. There are buses to/from Montréal ($72, 7 hours, 3 daily), Amos ($14, 1 hour, 2 daily), Rouyn-Noranda ($20, 1½ hours , 1 daily), Matagami ($38, 3½ hours, 1 daily) and Chibougamau via Senneterre ($107, 6 hours, 1 daily).

Train Senneterre, 50km northeast of Val d'Or, has the only train station in the region. Trains go there from Montréal ($125 11½ hours, 3 weekly), but you'd need to overnight there before catching a bus to Val d'Or the next afternoon.

PARC D'AIGUEBELLE

As the Abitibi landscape can be a tad on the dull side, the stunning scenery in this provincial park *(☎ 637-7322, 877-637-7344, 1737 rang Hudson; admission $3.50; open year-round)* comes as a doubly pleasant surprise. Suddenly there are canyons and gorges, massive rocky cliffs with fascinating geological formations and excellent, rugged **hiking** trails flanked by 200-year-old trees. One trail leads to the summit of the 566m Mont Dominant (the region's highest peak); another goes to a 64m bridge suspended 22m over the long, thin Lac La Haie, which runs through a magnificent canyon and is perfect

Kistabish (☎ 824-4871, e helenegodbout@ cablevision.qc.ca) gives occasional weekend workshops in the forests of the area (and throughout the province) incorporating ancient native ceremonies. You even get to build a traditional native sweat lodge.

Val d'Or is proud of their junior hockey team, Les Foreurs, who play at the **Palais des Sports** *(☎ 825-3078, 810 6-ème Avenue; adult/student $10/5)*. They won the Coupe du Président for the best junior team in Québec in 1998 and 2001. The schedule for their games and practices are just inside the main doors.

Places to Stay & Eat

Centre Plein Air Arc-en-Ciel (☎ 824-1414, 600 chemin des Scouts) Tent sites $14, dorm bed in chalet $17. South of town (follow chemin de la Baie Carrière), this complex features a pond where you fish for your trout meal (which they cook for you) and all the fresh air you can breathe.

for easy, pleasant **canoeing**. If you visit in August or September, you can gorge on fat blueberries, which grow wild here.

An interesting tidbit about this small park (only 268 sq km): The so-called water line that separates water flow runs through the park. Lakes and rivers north of here flow northward toward James Bay, and lakes south of here flow southward toward the St Lawrence.

The park has three entrances: via Mont Brun (well signposted on Rte 117 between Val d'Or and Rouyn-Noranda and the closest to the suspended bridge); via Destor (off Rte 101 between Rouyn-Noranda and La Sarre); and via Taschereau (south from Rte 111 between La Sarre and Amos). There are lovely campgrounds ($19) near all three, as well as canoe and kayak rentals ($25-30 a day).

ROUYN-NORANDA
pop 31,000

Rte 117 runs right through the area's most interesting town, which is made up of two distinct sectors. Successful mines were developed in Noranda, which was run, settled and organized by American and British industrialists. Rouyn, set up by the French as a frontier town, was chock-full of brothels, bars, hotels and shops. To this day you can see the difference between Rouyn's (located in the city's south-east sector) more helter-skelter setup in the city's south-east sector and Noranda's elite, orderly feel in the city's north-west sectors.

Founded in 1926 by prospector Edmund Horne, it still claims to be Canada's copper capital. Though the mines operate only according to the fluctuations of the world market, there is a successful smelter for copper processing. Tons of rock are sent here from abroad for refining and processing. There's still gold left in the area, but concentrations have decreased – it used to take three tons of rock to produce one ounce of gold, now five tons are required.

Your first stop should be at the **Maison Dumulon** (☎ 797-7125, 191 avenue du Lac; tour $3; open 9am-8pm daily late June–early Sept, 9am-5pm Mon-Fri early Sept–late June). The town's first general store and post office

opened here in 1924, and it later turned into a residence. A fun, guided tour by friendly (and costumed!) staff explains the town's interesting history. The house has charmingly recreated the look and feel of the old general store. The tourist office (☎ 797-3195) is also housed here. The folks that were there can give you free day-parking permits for the city.

Noranda Inc/Horne Foundry (☎ 762-7764, W www.noranda.com, 101 avenue Portelance; admission free; open 8:15am-4pm daily June-Aug) is the mine and foundry that has made Rouyn-Noranda famous since 1927. It offers free guided tours of the processing plant and mine.

A vestige of the town's multicultural heritage (see 'Promised Land') is seen in the **Église Orthodoxe Russe** (Russian Orthodox Church; ☎ 797-7125, 201 rue Taschereau; adult/child $3/1; open 1pm-6pm daily late June–early Sept). Built in 1955 by and for the 20 Russian families who immigrated here, this tiny church with onion domes closed in 1982 with the death of the last priest. Most of the descendants of these Russian families have long since moved out of the region. A brief tour familiarizes you with Orthodox traditions.

Promised Land

The success of the gold and copper mines in Rouyn-Noranda was largely due to an immigrant work force, whose treatment at the hands of big industry is a sad addition to the pages of Canadian history.

There were two main waves of immigration to the area. Fleeing WWI, Finns, Ukrainians, Italians, Slovaks and Czechs all easily found jobs in the mines here. They were nicknamed 'fro's' by the locals (from the word 'foreigner'). Yet working conditions were so poor that by 1934 the workers organized one of the biggest strikes ever in Canada. Workers were occasionally forgotten overnight inside the mine, had to breathe in toxic air, and dealt with improper cleaning facilities and long hours.

NORTHERN QUÉBEC

Places to Stay

There are a number of nondescript, cheap motels along avenue Larivière.

Cégep de l'Abitibi-Témiscamingue (☎ 762-0931 ext 5250, 555 boul de Collège) $20 per person. Located east of tiny Lac Edouard in the Rouyn sector of town, this college rents out its student rooms from mid-May to mid-August.

Le Passant (☎ 762-9827, 489 rue Perreault) Singles/doubles from $40/50. Close to downtown, this is a perfectly comfortable B&B made more charming by its affable owner.

Comfort Inn (☎ 797-1313, 800-465-6116, 1295 avenue Larivière) Doubles $85. This inn sometimes has worthwhile weekend specials.

Places to Eat

Pub O'Toole (☎ 762-2255, 258 boul Rideau) Mains $6-13. This spacious Irish pub's laid-back atmosphere is good for a relaxed beer and lunch and dinner specials. Their specialty is, of all things, Vietnamese cooking.

Pizzadelic (☎ 797-4461, 122 rue Principale) Mains $7-14. Reliable pizza and pasta dishes are served in this hip pizzeria.

Getting There & Away

The bus station (☎ 762-2200) is at 52 rue Horne. There are buses to/from Val d'Or ($20, 1½ hours, 2 daily Mon-Fri, 1 daily Sat & Sun). Monday to Friday there are buses to/from La Sarre ($14, 1 hour, 1 daily).

There's also a bus to/from North Bay, Ontario ($45, 3½ hours, 1 daily).

LA SARRE

pop 8350

This friendly, pleasant town, considered one of the forestry capitals of Canada, doesn't have too much to offer the visitor other than various visits to forestry companies and processing plants. The tourist office (☎ 333-3318), at 600 rue Principale, also has a good exhibit detailing the life of a lumberjack in 1930s Québec. Check out an exhibit of local artists' paintings and sculptures at the **Centre d'Art Rotary** *(☎ 333-2294, 195 rue Principale; admission free; open 9am-5pm & 7pm-9pm Mon-Fri, 1pm-5pm Sat & Sun).*

AUTHIER

pop 300

This tiny dot on the map, 29km east of La Sarre along Rte 111, has a very sweet, restored schoolhouse, the **L'École du Rang II** *(☎ 782-3289, 269 Rte 111; adult/child $3/2; open 9:30am-5:30pm daily late June–early Sept).* It brings home the reality of rural education in pre-Quiet Revolution Québec. Because of the distance between villages and the difficulties in transportation, small, one-room schoolhouses like these, in which one teacher would look after kids from six to 15 years old, were the norm – not exactly the breeding ground for *Dead Poets Society*

Scenic Drive – Rouyn-Noranda to La Sarre

Between Rouyn-Noranda and La Sarre is probably the region's prettiest corner, a series of small villages and settlements surrounding Lac Abitibi, most of which lies in Ontario. Heading north on Rte 101, veer west 34km north of Rouyn-Noranda toward **Duparquet** (pop 700), a 'boom town' founded around a gold mine in 1933. Farther on is the lovely village of **Rapide Danseur** (pop 250), just north of Rte 388. Here you'll see the most attractive example of the stone churches around Abitibi – these were community-built churches, with residents finding and carrying the stones from the surrounding regions. This one cost just $3000 to build in 1951. You can take a look around inside (admission free). From here, a scenic 6km gravel road leads to **Gallichan** (pop 500), sitting on a thin arm of the lake. Farms and rustic settlements surround the lake. Rte 393 will lead you to La Sarre.

NORTHERN QUÉBEC

enlightenment. This one was open from 1937 to 1958.

AMOS
pop 13,850

The first town to be founded in Abitibi (1910), Amos – named after the wife of Québec's premier at the time, Lormier Gouin – became a center of the forestry and agriculture industries. It's a pleasant, languid town that is lucky to have some of the cleanest water of any urban area in the world! A natural source of spring water emerging from a nearby glacier-formed esker constitutes the town's water source – it's so pure that it's bottled commercially under the name of Périgny in the same form as it pours from the city's faucets and taps.

If you doubt this claim, see for yourself at the **Puits Municipal** *(Municipal Wells; ☎ 727-1242; adult/child $4/1; open year-round),* which can be visited by making reservations at the tourist office (☎ 727-1242, 800-670-0499), at 892 Rte 111. It's open 8am-8pm daily mid-June to early September; from early September to mid-June it's open 8:30am to 4:30pm Monday to Friday and 10am to 4pm Saturday and Sunday. They are a particularly helpful office and can give lots of advice on things to do in the area.

The **Refuge Pageau** *(☎ 732-8999, 3991 chemin Croteau; adult/student/child 3-12 $10/8/6; open 1pm-5pm Tues-Fri, 1pm-8pm Sat & Sun late June–Aug, 1pm-5pm Sat & Sun Sept)* is a highly worthwhile stop, especially – though not only – for the kids. Before he opened his animal shelter in the 1970s Michel Pageau was a hunter and trapper. He had a change of heart, deciding to put his energies into nursing and helping wounded animals. His shelter takes in mammals and birds that have been hit by cars, wounded by hunters or fallen sick. The tour guides' knowledge of English is nonexistent, but there's a nice variety of animals and the reasons they're here add a touching component.

Places to Stay & Eat
Camping municipal du Lac Beauchamp (☎ 732-6963, 1402 chemin du Lac Beauchamp)

Tent sites $13-19. Under 10km west of town, this is a mid-sized campground by a small lake. In winter there's cross-country skiing here.

Hôtel-Motel Atmosphère (☎ 732-7777, 800-567-7777, W *www.atmosphere.com)* Singles/doubles from $63/80. There's nothing special about this hotel-motel complex with different room styles, but a big bonus is that they rent out bikes for free to their clients.

Hôtel des Eskers (☎ 732-5386, fax 732-0455, 201 avenue Authier) Doubles from $60/90. You know you shouldn't expect much from a place that lists hair dryers as one of its main features. Still, the rooms are decent enough and clean, and the bar-restaurant cozy in its own way. A buffet is served lunchtime, and there's a large dinner menu. Come evening, locals wander in and out of the bar.

O'berge de l'Harricana (☎ 727-2856, 7465 Rte 111 Est) Singles/doubles $35/45. This is a comfortable B&B that looks more like a mini motel.

PIKOGAN
pop 500

In this Algonquin village, 3km north of Amos on Rte 109, Bercé par l'Harricana (☎ 732-3350, fax 732-3358, 10 rue Tom Rankin) can organize several-day guided **canoe trips** down the rivière Harricana, sleeping in tents or teepees and feasting on traditional meals. These services are not done regularly, and you need to phone to inquire and reserve.

PREISSAC
pop 700

Rte 395 west and south from Amos joins Rte 117 halfway between Val d'Or and Rouyn-Noranda and passes through lovely countryside. The village of Preissac sits in an idyllic spot near Lac Preissac. There's nothing to do here but admire the nature or stop for a picnic at the roadside Parc des Rapides, a splash of green by some pretty rapids. You can run in for a quick dip here, but be mindful of the strong currents.

The *Domaine Preissac (☎ 759-3501,* W *www.domainepreissac.com, 1 chemin du*

Domaine), one of several outfitters in the area, has fully furnished, simple chalets in nice surroundings for rent (day/week per person $40/540) and offers many packages combining canoeing or fishing excursions.

James Bay

With a size of 350,000 sq km (nearly 1½times the size of the UK), James Bay (Baie James) is the largest administrative municipality in the world. Only 30,000 people live here, almost half of them Cree Native Canadians living in eight reserves separated by hundreds of kilometers in both the western section bordering James Bay and in the eastern sectors north and west of Chibougamau.

This truly represents Québec's final frontier. The near-mythic Rte de la Baie James ends at Radisson, a small village 1400km north of Montréal, 800km north of Amos. A 100km extension branches westward to Chisasibi, a Cree reserve near James Bay. This area is defined by the immense James Bay Hydroelectric project, a series of hydroelectric stations that produce half of Québec's energy resources.

The area was named after Thomas James, who in 1631 published a map of Hudson Bay, itself named after Sir Henry Hudson, one of the first European explorers of the region. In the 17th century the beaver fur trade was set up in this region, and within fifty years over 200,000 fur pelts were shipped annually to Europe to keep up with exacting fashion demands.

The region captivates on several levels. First and foremost is its sheer vastness. The seeming endlessness of boreal spruce forests giving way to the taiga (where trees become visibly shorter the farther north you go) and the fact that it appears completely unpopulated can be challenging realities to wrap your mind around. More sensitive visitors en route to Radisson have reportedly turned around, unable to cope with the unnerving sense of limitless space around them; a lifetime of city living will do that.

Moreover, its remote Cree communities provide glimpses of a way of life most find difficult to comprehend (see 'First Nations in Québec' in the Facts about Québec chapter). Finally, the romance of making it to the end of the road – if just to see what lies there – cannot be discounted. The adventurousness involved in going so far is a main reason why many Québécois head to Radisson each summer. Everyone knows the epic proportions of the James Bay Hydroelectric complex, one of the government's proudest, most ambitious achievements; the mere notion of visiting it combines adventure, romance and patriotism.

There are a surprising number of Americans who also make the trip, interested in being able to drive so far north on a paved road, curious about the wide, open spaces.

The landscape is neither impressively rugged like the North Shore, nor majestic and mountainous like the Laurentians. This is the beginning of true North. Aside from powerful rivers, a sky that goes on forever and lots of trees, there's not that much to *see*. Yet it's through the sense of isolation and remoteness that one discovers the beauty here.

It goes without saying that while temperatures have been known to pass 30°C here in July or August, it is essential to bring warm clothes to protect from chilly summer evenings. The usual July daytime temperature is around 17°C. in winter – which can come as early as October – the temperatures are often below -15°C and can reach -40°C at night.

Orientation

The usual access point to the region is via Abitibi-Témiscamingue. Rte 109 runs 183km north to Matagami, the last town before Rte 109 becomes the Rte de la Baie James and continues 620km to Radisson. To reach the eastern sector, where Chibougamau is the largest town, the easiest access is via the Lac St Jean region; Chibougamau is 232km northwest of St Félicien. From there, a grueling 424km gravel road (Rte du Nord) joins the Rte de la Baie James at Km 274. It's also possible to drive from Senneterre to Chibougamau (351km) on the paved Rte 113, passing through several Cree villages.

MATAGAMI
pop 2300
For a dreary town in the middle of nowhere, several factors contribute to the busy feel of this place. Since 1963, when the town was founded, it has been the site of a copper and zinc mine. It's also Québec's most northerly forestry center. Both of these industries are still going strong here, and shift workers are always coming and going. Finally, most everyone on their way to Radisson stops here for the night. Because both workers and travelers all want a good night's rest, nightlife here is, to say the least, limited. Unless you consider 5am 'night,' as that's when diners and restaurants open for breakfast.

Places to Stay & Eat
Motel Le Caribou (☎ 739-4550, fax 739-4552, 108 boul Matagami) Singles/doubles $40/65. This one's a bit more run down than the Hôtel-Motel Matagami, but it's fine for a night. Each room has its own bathroom, and there's a dingy bar in front with long-faced, jowly clientele.

Hôtel-Motel Matagami (☎ 739-2501, fax 739-2139, 99 boul Matagami) Singles/doubles $72/82. Considered the top place in town, it's decent enough and always seems to be crowded – mainly for the restaurant, open from 5am to 10pm daily.

Getting There & Away
There's one bus a day Sunday to Friday to/from Val d'Or ($24 3½ hours), and it stops at the Hôtel Matagami.

RTE DE LA BAIE JAMES
This road, an extension of Rte 109 heading *way* north, was built in the 1970s to facilitate the construction of the James Bay Hydroelectric project. As such, the road is paved, wide and kept in good shape. Monster trucks carrying cut logs also thunder down the southern reaches of the road, where the trees are still big enough to be commercially viable. Many side roads up until Km 257 will lead to clear-cut areas (around Km 60,

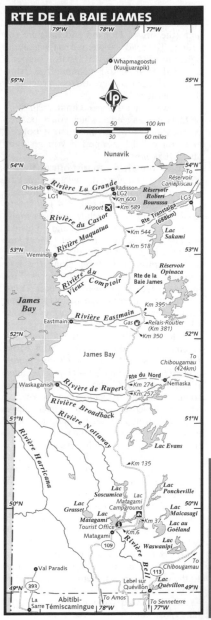

RTE DE LA BAIE JAMES

for example). The forestry industry owns 72,000 sq km of territory in the James Bay area (the size of Holland and Belgium together). The road was opened to the general public in 1984. As part of Hydro Québec's deal with First Nations communities living in the region, roads were also constructed to their remote villages.

Be aware that the speed limit is 90km/hr on this road, a speed at which you appear to be crawling. However, the road is policed and you will be stopped if you go over about 105km/hr.

At **Km 6** there's a tourist office (☎ 739-2030), open 24 hours a day year-round. You must at least slow down here and announce yourself through a speaker – for safety reasons, everyone traveling north is registered. It's worthwhile to stop and go inside, as they have several booklets and pamphlets of interest that detail the geological and geographical features along the way and give information about the forest fires that destroyed huge swaths of land. There are bilingual information panels all along the road and emergency telephones at Kms 135, 201, 247, 301, 361, 444 and 504.

At **Km 10** there's a rough trail following an electric line leading up the 480m Mont Laurier. At **Km 37** is the route's only *campground* (reservations ☎ 739-4473; $20 per site). It's by the shores of Lac Matagami, which has some of the purest water in the province. There's a beach, if you care for a frigid dip, as well as showers and toilets. There are other areas to pitch a tent along the road, but this is the only campground with services.

The robust rivière de Rupert displays its rugged glory at **Km 257**, where picnic tables have been set up. The many rapids and waterfalls here, separated poetically by small islands, show the impressive force of nature. Sadly these will be reduced to a trickle in the coming years as a recently signed, 1300 MW Hydroelectric project will harness the energy of the mighty rivière Rupert.

At **Km 274** the Rte du Nord stretches east to the Cree reserve of **Nemaska** (also called Némiscau by the Cree) and Chibougamau.

Another road (opened only in 2001) leads westward to the Cree community of

Waskaganish (pop 1550). The first trading post of the north was established there as Fort Rupert in 1668. It was handed over to the Cree in 1942. There is an active native artistic community here, and overnight, cultural stays are organized by the Band Council (☎ 895-8650).

Eastmain (pop 490) is another coastal Cree village, 103km down a gravel road from **Km 350**. There was a fur trading post here from 1690 until 1932; it's been populated again since 1949. Wilderness excursions and overnight stays are possible here. Contact the local Band Council (☎ 977-0211, 888-818-8580, W www.eastmain-nation.ca).

Everyone needs to stop at **Km 381**, the so-called *Relais Routier*, the only **gas station** and service stop on the road. It's open 24 hours a day. There's a *cafeteria (☎ 638-7948)* serving food better than you'd expect (or else it just tastes good after driving all day!), at prices that introduce you to the high cost of living in the north – a club sandwich costs $12. There's a *motel* of sorts (singles/doubles $56/81). For reservations call the cafeteria.

At **Km 395** is the puny rivière Eastmain. Note, however, that this used to be just as majestic as rivière Rupert but its diversion for the James Bay Hydroelectric project has caused it to trickle to just 10% of its original flow. If you get out and walk under the huge bridge, signs of its original depth are evident.

A gravel road shooting west from **Km 518** leads to the Cree community of **Wemindji** (pop 1000). This was the site of another trading post; the village was moved to its present location in 1959. Some ecotourist possibilities exist here – you can contact the Band Council (☎ 978-0264, W www. wemidji-nation.qc.ca).

At **Km 544** another unimaginably long road extends east: The *Rte Transtaïga* is 688km of grueling gravel that leads to the most distant Hydro power stations. There are two **gas stations** along this road.

At **Km 600** a paved road heading west leads to the power station **LG1** (62km away) and to the Cree village of **Chisasibi** (see below). Continue on Rte de la Baie James another 20km and the shock of a lifetime arrives – the tiny village of Radisson.

RADISSON

pop 350

Named after explorer Pierre-Esprit Radisson, the village was set up in 1973 to house the workers on the James Bay Hydroelectric project (also called *La Grande*). Radisson looks and feels larger than its population would suggest, as it was built to accommodate fluctuating numbers of workers (who work there for eight days, then fly home for six) and because about 20 families have decided to settle permanently here and create a real village.

Despite its remote location there's a warmth to the town and a feeling of expansion. It also feels fresh and new – it may be one of the only villages in the province with no cemetery! The 80 school-age children attend one school that encompasses kindergarten through grade 11.

The scenery around Radisson is spectacular, with the majestic rivière La Grande visible thanks to the built-up area around the larger-than-life **Robert Bourassa hydroelectric power station** (named after the Québec premier who oversaw its construction; also called LG2) just outside town. On some elevated areas surrounding the Belvedère de la Tour observation tower, the vegetation becomes tundra with tiny flowers and lichen covering a mostly rocky terrain, and blueberries growing wild. As of mid-August, on clear, cold evenings you can observe the Aurora Borealis from anywhere in town, but a good vantage point is from this lookout.

There's a very good native arts and crafts shop in town, *Inquis (☎ 638-6969, 96 rue Albanel).*

Information

The tourist office (☎ 638-8687), at the village's entrance at 198 rue Jolliet, is run by an energetic resident who'll infuse you with her love of the area. Here you can get maps and information on local outfitters who can organize fishing and hunting excursions. The office is open 8am to 8pm daily June through September. At other times contact the Town Hall (☎ 638-7777), at 101 Place Gérard Poirier.

Power Stations

Everyone who makes it up here takes a free, guided tour of the **LG2 power station**. The main offices of Hydro Québec (☎ 638-8486, 800-291-8486, W www.hydro.qc.ca) are in the Pierre Radisson Complex. After an introduction to hydroelectricity (97% of Québec's energy needs are met by it, and Québec exports up to 19% of its energy output to northeastern US and boasts some of the cheapest electricity costs in North America), you'll be taken inside and outside the massive LG2. This, together with **LG2A**, the world's largest underground power station (the generating station itself, as tall as a 15-story building, is 140m deep in the bedrock), produces one quarter of the province's energy and ranks as the third-largest hydroelectric plant in the world.

There are eight power stations stretched out over the 800km length of rivière La Grande, thus the same water is used eight times. It took 20 years, 185,000 laborers and 70 million work hours to complete construction at the cost of some $23.5 billion. The total energy output is 15,244 MW. Over 9600 sq km of traditional Cree and Inuit hunting territory was flooded to make reservoirs. The 1975 signing of the James Bay and Northern Québec Agreement between the government of Québec, Hydro Québec, and the Cree and Inuit offered compensation for this land (see 'First Nations in Québec' in the Facts about Québec chapter).

Backed by the enormous Réservoir Robert Bourassa, which is three times the size of Lac St Jean, is the most impressive aspect of the entire complex: the Robert Bourassa spillway. Stretching out almost 1km in length, this 'giant staircase' is a series of 10 steps blasted out from rock, each 10m high with a landing the size of two football fields. Its enormous proportions are hard to grasp – its height is equivalent to a 53-story building – even if standing right in front of it.

A free, four-hour tour is given once a day, but reservations are strongly recommended, especially if you want an English-speaking guide.

NORTHERN QUÉBEC

Parc Robert A Boyd

On the site of the original workers' camp is this park (☎ 638-6969; admission $2; open daily May-Nov), accessible via boat or a newly opened hiking trail. It's essentially a reconstructed village near where rivière Mosquito tumbles into rivière La Grande. Taking a guided tour helps understand how people lived and worked here. Pourvoirie LG2 (☎ 638-6673, Ⓦ www.sshr.qc.ca), at 65 avenue Des Groseillers, offers daily, two-hour excursions (adult/student & child $5/3 plus $1 each for the boat ride). They also offer boat cruises ($26.50 per person) on the La Grande, which make stops here.

Places to Stay & Eat

Camping Radisson (☎ 638-8687, 198 rue Jolliet) Tent sites $15-17. Located on a hill behind the tourist office, it also has modern toilet and shower facilities.

Motel Baie James (☎ 638-7080, 877-638-5400, 99 rue Belleau) Singles/doubles $65/70. This is a standard motel in a quiet corner of town. They can also arrange canoe rental.

Carrefour La Grande (☎ 638-6005, 53 avenue des Groseillers) Singles/doubles $75/82. This motel's nondescript rooms are overshadowed by its lively and rowdy bar, mostly frequented by Cree residents of Chisasibi.

Auberge Radisson (☎ 638-7201, 66 avenue des Groseilliers) Doubles $92. The top place in town has comfortable, large, simple rooms in a well-managed hotel. Clients can use the pool in the adjacent sports complex. Their restaurant has good dinner specials for $25 and the relaxed bar inside is popular with the locals. From September to June their prices drop 20%. Package deals are offered year-round.

Les Entreprises du Lagopède (☎ 638-5978, 21 rue Iberville) This organization sells Caribou meat and frozen filets of Arctic char, and makes 'lunchboxes' ($8) with a sandwich, fruit and drink – good to take along on a picnic.

Getting There & Away

By car (or hitching) is the main way to get here and to Chisasibi. No buses go farther north than Matagami. There is an airport at Km 589 of the Route de la Baie James called La Grande. Air Creebec (☎ 800-567-6567) flies here once a day from Montréal Monday to Friday (no flights on the weekend) (5½ hrs). They also fly to a small airport in Chisasibi once a day from Montréal Sunday to Friday (4½ hrs). Expect prices to both airports to be about $1000 return.

CHISASIBI
pop 2900

Located near where rivière La Grande meets la Baie James, 100km west of Radisson, Chisasibi is a Cree village well worth visiting, and tour operators offer interesting excursions in the area. The surrounding nature – windswept taiga doused by the Arctic breezes from James Bay – is haunting.

The town as it looks now has existed only since 1981. Before this the residents lived on the island of Fort George, 10km from town, where the Hudson's Bay Company had set up a fur trading post in 1837. Catholic, and especially Anglican, missionaries had a strong hand in the development of the community, which became divided into two halves along religious lines. With the impending hydroelectric projects threatening to flood the island, the community voted to move out of the village.

Thus a modern town replaced the traditional one. A vestige of their traditional way of life is evidenced by the many teepees seen in backyards – mainly these are used for smoking fresh fish.

Sadly, Chisasibi has a well-deserved reputation as a rough town with many social problems (alcoholism, domestic violence and suicide), caused mainly by the sudden adoption of modern lifestyles, an abrupt connection with the outside world with no accompanying social-support infrastructure and alcohol availability. There's a checkpoint outside the village to ensure that no alcohol is brought in, however some residents drive to Radisson to carouse, then make a treacherous return trip (not all successful – note the stone and flower memorials on the side of the road). Things are much calmer here than they were in the late 1980s, and it's a safe place for tourists to visit.

Things to See & Do

Margaret and William Cromarty (☎ 855-2800, 855-2626, Ⓦ www.fortgeorgeisland tours.com) offer excellent guided excursions to the island of **Fort George**, where most of the original structures, including churches, schools and cemeteries, remain. Their tours can be as short as two hours ($25 per person) or include an overnight stay on the island ($120 per person, including three traditional meals of Labrador tea, bannik bread, caribou and other Cree treats). In August, hundreds return here for several weeks of a nostalgic powwow.

The Mandow Agency (☎ 855-3373, fax 855-3374, Ⓦ www.mandow.ca) also arranges excursions to Fort George, as well as **fishing and canoe trips**, with snacks included. Expect to pay about $60 per person per outing, though the different guides they work with charge different prices. They also offer winter activities and act as middlemen to nearby outfitters.

LG1, another hydroelectric station, is 19km east of Chisasibi, toward Radisson. While it's less monumental than Robert Bourassa (LG2), enough concrete went into its construction to pave a road from Montréal to Miami. There are five lookouts near the complex providing stunning views of rivière La Grande. Contact Hydro Québec in Radisson (see above) to take a tour of LG1.

Places to Stay

The one place to stay in town, *Chisasibi Motel (☎ 855-3089, Center Road)* is inside the Chisasibi Center, a shopping mall in the middle of town, which is filled with children no matter what time of day. It's near the enormous teepee, *the* town landmark, which doubles as a cultural center. Their advertised prices are $90/140 for standard but comfortable singles/doubles, but if you ask for the tourist rate or book via the Mandow Agency (see above), they cost $65/85.

CHIBOUGAMAU
pop 8650
Built around a series of copper and gold mines, Chibougamau is a dreary place indeed, but, as northern Québec's largest settlement, it offers a number of services. At 800km east of Radisson and 232km north of the Lac St Jean region, it is lodged in a remote area shared by several Cree villages, notably **Oujé Bougoumou** (pop 400) and **Mistassini** (pop 2500), 90km north near the banks of the largest freshwater lake in the province, Lac Mistassini.

There are two tourist offices in town. One office (☎ 418-748-7276), at 512 Rte 167 Sud, is open June to September only. Open year-round is the Economic and Tourist Commission (☎ 418-748-6060), at 600 3-ème Rue. In Mistassini, the Band Council (☎ 418-923-3461, Ⓦ www.nation.mistissini.qc.ca), at 187 rue Principale, can help organize adventure tourism excursions in the area and visits to the mines.

The Summer Cultural Festival (☎ 748-7195), held in early August, regroups native and Québécois singers and musicians for a four-day series of concerts.

Things to See & Do

A few public **parks** in town highlight the area's geological formations, such as stratified blocks of lava polished by glaciers (in Parc Allard) and fossils of ancient algae (in Parc du Souvenir). There are several great **hiking** trails starting from the public beach (accessed via 3-ème Rue), the most interesting being the one leading to Mont Chalco, which passes by unusual rock formations and leads to a great view of several lakes and distant mountains. The tourist office has maps of other trails in the area.

Several outfitters and organizations offer wilderness excursions in the area. Ayak Ayak Aventures (☎ 748-7747, chemin du Lac Dorés) has many **canoe/kayak trips** available for beginner or advanced paddlers.

The **Réserves Fauniques Assinica & des Lacs Albanel-Mistassini et Waconichi** (☎ 748-7748, Rte du Nord; admission $3.50), two adjacent wildlife reserves north of

Chibougamau, are truly wild places. There are **chalets** to rent (2 persons $43) and sites for rustic **camping** (sites $19-26), as well as canoe rental. You can register at the Centre du Plein Air du Mont Chalco (☎ 748-7162; open 7am-10pm daily June-Sept), 4km north of Chibougamau on Rte 167.

Getting There & Away

The bus station (☎ 748-2842) is at 501 4-ème Rue. There's service to/from St Félicien ($34, 3 hours, 1 daily) and Val d'Or ($107, 6 hours, 1 daily)

Nunavik

The territory of Nunavik stretches from the 55th to the 62nd parallel, bordered by Hudson Bay to the west, the Hudson Strait to the north and Ungava Bay and the Labrador border to the east. At 507,000 sq km, it's a tad smaller than France, yet fewer than 10,000 people live there in 14 villages separated from each other by several hundred kilometers of mainly tundra, with no roads to join them. Almost 90% of the population are Inuit; the remainder are Cree and Naskapis, and white Québécois.

Though much of Nunavik is classified as tundra, there is a great diversity to its ge-

ography. Even tundra has many rich shades of beauty – the region is far from just desolate plains of snow and ice. In the southwest there are sandy beaches and large dunes that stretch as far as the eye can see. In the northeast are the formidable Torngat mountains, extending in a series of bare, rocky peaks and untamed valleys 300km along the border of Labrador. The province's highest peak, Mont d'Iberville (1652m), is also here.

Of the 144 known meteorite-formed craters on earth, five of them are in Nunavik. The largest, indeed one of the largest on the planet, is called Pingualuit, 88km south of Kangiqsujuaq. It's 1.4 million years old, has a diameter of 3.4km, in parts is 433m deep (the height of a 145-story building), and the lake that has formed inside it is 267m deep. Its water is considered among the purest in the world and in terms of transparency is second only to Japan's Lake Masyuko.

Floating above this terrain are the magical Northern Lights (Aurora Borealis), which can be seen an average of 243 nights in the year.

Socially, the villages hold great interest. The Inuit are generally friendly and approachable – and it's their adaptability that has helped them make such a radical transition in their lifestyles in so short a time. It is much easier to make fast friends with Inuit than other First Nations, who approach strangers with more caution.

The communities are also organized quite differently from urban North American ones and visiting them is somewhat of a culture shock for the unprepared. The villages range in population from an unimaginable 159 (Aupaluk) to 2050 (Kuujjuaq). That half of the population are under 18 is very evident in the sheer number of little ones running around, most under a minimum of parental supervision. Though dire poverty is not an issue, serious social problems of domestic violence, alcoholism (even though most villages are 'dry') and drug abuse are plainly a part of the modern-day social fabric. There are 4.4 persons per household in Nunavik, compared to 2.6 in the rest of the province.

Speaking Correctly

The Inuit used to be called Eskimos, a First Nations word meaning 'eater of raw meat.' The term is considered pejorative and no one uses it anymore. Inuit is the plural of the work *inuk*, which means 'person' in their language, Inuktitut.

From 1927 to 1978 the Nunavik was called Nouveau Québec (New Québec). Both *nunavik* and *nunavut* mean 'our land' in different dialects of Inuktitut. Yet don't confuse Nunavik – in northern Québec – with Nunavut, the enormous territory in northern Canada that became an autonomous region, self-governed by the Inuit, in 1999.

Because Nunavik can be accessed only by plane, few casual tourists make it out there. The ones who do are often unexpectedly moved and vow to return. It's that famous Northern bite: Once bitten, it's for good. The majority of whites there are either contract workers for federal or provincial bodies (including medical and social counseling clinics) or they're rich American or European adventure-seeking tourists and hunters. Yet, once arrived, independent travel is possible in the region for those willing to make their own local contacts.

One should still be prepared for stellar prices for goods and services, however. On average, food prices are 69% higher here than in Québec City. A liter of milk costs $5.65 here; a 24-can case of Coke is $33 (versus $7 elsewhere). Don't expect your precious ISIC card to be of help here!

After Inuktitut, the second language in Nunavik is English. More youngsters are learning French than their parents did, and very few elders can speak anything other than Inuktitut.

History

It is believed that the Inuit's ancestors arrived in North America after the last Ice Age some 12,000 years ago. Three waves of these peoples settled in present-day Nunavik – the paleo-eskimos (3000-500 BC), the Dorset (AD 0-1000) and the Thule (from AD 1000), who are the direct ancestors of modern Inuits.

Extensive contact with white Europeans started only in the 18th century with the establishment of fur trading posts along the Hudson Bay coast – the first was opened in 1731 at Fort Good Hope, later called Fort Chimo, near present-day Kuujjuaq. Many more posts were opened in the 19th century, and the resulting trade together with the religious conversions by missionaries significantly altered the natives' lifestyles.

Still, their way of life was more or less preserved until the federal government started implicating itself in their daily lives in the early 1950s. Social and administrative

---

The Inukshuk

The figure of the *inukshuk* (*inukshuiit* in the plural) is omnipresent in Inuit tradition. It is an arrangement of stones resembling a human figure – the word itself means 'looks like a person.' These can be seen standing several meters tall and proud along the shoreline and elsewhere in many Inuit communities, and have become a symbol of Inuit culture. Many Québécois have adopted them as a trendy fashion, placing mini versions outside their country homes, and little souvenir inukshuiit are sold in tourist shops everywhere.

Though gift-shop vendors in Old Montréal like to link these striking figures to something deeply spiritual, they were originally an important part of the caribou hunt, before rifles made hunting easier. Large inukshuiit were erected on a vast plain creating a funnel to guide the near-sighted caribou (who mistook them for humans) to an impasse, or toward a body of water where they could more easily be hunted. They would also be used as landmarks or as places where meat would be stored and easily found again during a long hunting expedition.

---

services were dispensed, and enforced schooling began. The goal was to move the Inuit into permanent villages – at that time, they were living in 700 small and scattered settlements.

The provincial government entered the game briefly in the 1960s, doing surveys for their massive hydroelectric projects. Before then they had shown no interest in this section of Québec. In the 1970s, however, the signing of the James Bay and Northern Québec Agreement gave the Inuit $90 million in exchange for some of their traditional hunting grounds for the government's hydro project.

Using this capital, the Inuit have created the infrastructure necessary to govern their own economy, mainly via the

NORTHERN QUÉBEC

Makivik Cooperative. They've also created an airline (Air Inuit), commercialized caribou meat and set up a national distribution system for their artists. The regional government is called Kativik and is hoping to work toward a system of self-government by 2005, like the one now a reality for their northern brothers and sisters in Nunavut.

Information

The Nunavik Tourism Association (☎ 964-2876, 888-594-3424, Ⓦ www.nunavik-tourism .com) is headquartered in Kuujjuaq, the region's administrative capital. They can give you the phone numbers for the mayor's office of each village, which could provide more specific information.

Another good source of information is the Fédération des Coopératives (☎ 514-457-9371, 800-363-7611), who have been organizing Arctic adventures in the region since 1967.

Throat Singing

The most distinctive and (to Brittany Spears–infested ears) unusual musical tradition among the Inuit is throat singing. Done exclusively by women, usually in pairs, this is less singing than imitation of sounds occurring in nature (birds and animals). The sounds come from as deep in the throat as possible and the results are arresting – occasionally amusing, sometimes disturbing, but always transfixing.

The tradition of throat singing (called *katajaq*) originates from a game that used to be played between women when their husbands had gone off hunting. Two gal pals would face each other, utter these sounds and try to out-do the other without laughing. The first to laugh would lose. It has evolved into a rarefied art, however, one gaining notoriety and respect abroad.

In 2001 Björk asked Nunavut throat singer Tanya Tagaq to join her on her worldwide tour after hearing her work for an Icelandic documentary.

Kuujjuaq
pop 2050

Lying on the shores of the rivière Koksoak, the 'capital' of Nunavik, is considered by many Inuit residents of other communities to be too big and busy for their liking. There is a lot of air traffic moving in and out of here, and because it is a transportation hub as well as the headquarters for major Nunavik administrative bodies, there are some hotels and restaurants.

It was 5km from Kuujjuaq where the first European fur trading post was set up and where the US army held an air base from 1942 to 1945.

Pat's Parts (☎ 964-2383) rents out ATVs ($10/hour) and snowmobiles ($150/day). Johnny Jr May (☎ 964-0015) organizes dogsled expeditions from a half-day to several days long.

Whapmagoostui (Kuujjuarapik)
pop 1200

In several ways this is one of Nunavik's most interesting villages, located 175km north of Chisasibi. It is the only one shared between two communities, the Inuit and the Cree, who each have their own names for it. The Cree name, Whapmagoostui, is pronounced wop-maks-du. The Inuit name is Kuujjuarapik. Traditionally the Cree and the Inuit have not gotten along, however the one village and a number of social services are shared between them and in recent years more mixing has occurred.

As Nunavik's southernmost community, it lies on the vegetal border between taiga and tundra, featuring patches of forest, sand dunes and lichen-covered rocky hills. It lies on the spot where James Bay gives way to Hudson Bay, a vast body of water the size of the Gulf of Mexico. The village represents the northern limit for small mammals like squirrels and the southern limit for animals like polar bears and walruses.

For rentals of ATVs or taxi service, contact William Koapit (☎ 929-3607). He rents out ATVs ($10/hour, $50/day), which are great for tearing it up on the nearby sand dunes and across the long stretches of

beach. The town's best-known soapstone sculptors are Lucy Meeko and her husband Noah. Some local works are for sale at the Coop store.

Activities

There is an endless array of activities possible here: joining some Inuit on long-journey hunting expeditions, boating to nearby islands, snowmobile excursions, wildberry picking, exploring the delicate resilience of tundra vegetation on hiking treks

ANDRE-A. G.
272-2361
11

CHRISTINE COSTE

Ice fish in (crooked) comfort

and meeting with Inuit artists and soapstone sculptors. Hunting and fishing, however, remain the main sports of interest to tourists, and it's what the outfitters cater to. The region has the world's largest caribou population, estimated at one million head.

There are a number of tour operators working in the region, but here more than elsewhere it pays to do your homework to find the one best suited to your desires. Many are geared toward Europeans or Americans who agree to pay from $2000-5000 per week, per person, without airfare,

for wilderness forays. The trick is to get into direct contact with locals who are able to provide excursions or lend equipment (snowmobiles, snowshoes, skis, ATVs, canoes and kayaks) for much more reasonable prices. Getting in touch with the mayor's office and asking via those channels well beforehand can be a good idea.

In Whapmagoostui call the Cree Band Council (☎ 929-3384, 929-3364) to hire a reasonably priced guide for boat excursions, hiking or fishing trips, and ATV expeditions.

Special Events

Puvirnituq is host to the **Snow Festival** in early April, where there are sporting events on the sea-ice and where artists from across Nunavik come to create splendid ice sculptures.

In Kuujjuaq every mid-August is the **Aqpik Jam**, where singers and musicians from Nunavik, Nunavut and Greenland gather to wow the crowds.

Places to Stay & Eat

There are hotels in many of the villages, though the prices are rarely below $125 per person per night, with no special rates. The Coop often run lodging slightly cheaper than commercial hotels. Again, however, you can save lots of money by doing your homework. In most villages some residents will be willing to accommodate a visitor in their homes for $30 to $50 a night. Call the mayor's office of the village in question first. In Whapmagoostui (Kuujjuarapik) call the Cree Band Council (☎ 929-3384, 929-3364), which can arrange for homestays for $30 per night.

Qilaluqak Hotel (☎ 929-3374, fax 929-3062) Singles/doubles $120/195. Near the airport at Whapmagoostui (Kuujjuarapik), the accommodations are quiet and simple. Their bar, in a separate building, is the most popular in town – and not only because it's the only one! They also serve food, but it's $10 for a hamburger.

Kuujjuaq Inn *(☎ 964-2903, fax 964-2031)*
Singles/doubles $200/250. The top place in
town, but it's nothing special. The rooms are
decent-sized, however, and the service is
friendly.

There are cafés and fast-food restaurants
in all the villages, as well as convenience
stores. You may be invited to partake in a
traditional Inuit meal, including caribou
and seal meat. Beluga whales are also
hunted here, and their skin is cut into foul-
tasting strips, which are then chewed like
bubble gum.

Getting There & Away

Unless you're willing or able to make a long
snowmobile trek north of Radisson, the
only way to get to Nunavik is by plane. First
Air (☎ 800-267-1247, W www.firstair.com)
provides service between Montréal and
Kuujjuaq. Full fare is $2210 roundtrip, with
seven-day advance $1440, and on their oc-
casional seat sales, half of that.

Air Inuit (☎ 800-361-2965, W www.air
inuit.com) flies from Montréal to Puvirnituq

($1544 roundtrip with seven-day advance or
$2560 full fare) and from there to other vil-
lages, though they're pricey – a roundtrip
flight to Whapmagoostui (Kuujjuarapik)
from Puvirnituq costs $1000! Their Mon-
tréal to Kuujjuak fares are similar to First
Air's. If you're planning on visiting several
villages, contact their head office (☎ 800-
361-5933) to inquire about possible package
deals.

Air Creebec (☎ 800-567-6567) flies into
Whapmagoostui (Kuujjuarapik). Aeroplan
frequent flyer points can be used on First
Air and Air Creebec flights.

An Air Creebec roundtrip flight from
Montréal to Whapmagoostui would cost
$888 with seven-day advance, $1720 full
fare. A return flight from Val d'Or to Whapmagoostui is $832.

There are a number of smaller companies offering charter flights between villages
as well – contact the tourist office in Kuujjuaq for more details. The prices for these
flights can sometimes be as expensive as
traveling from North America to Europe.

Language

English and French are the two official languages of Canada. You'll notice both on highway signs, maps, tourist brochures and all types of packaging. In the west French isn't as prevalent, but in Québec, English can be scarce. Roadside signs and visitor information will often be in French only, though in certain regions (such as the Eastern Townships) they're in both languages. Outside Montréal and Québec City, the use of some French, or your own version of sign language, will be necessary at least some of the time.

Many immigrants use their mother tongue, as do some indigenous groups. In some First Nation communities, though, only older members retain their native language. Few non-aboriginals speak any Native Canadian or Inuit language, but some crossover words such as igloo, parka, muskeg and kayak are commonly used.

The Inuit language Inuktitut is interesting for its specialization and use of many words for what appears to be the same thing. For example, the word for 'seal' depends on whether it's old or young, or in or out of the water. And there are up to 20 or so words for 'snow,' depending on its consistency and texture.

New Brunswick is, perhaps surprisingly, the only officially bilingual province in Canada. French is widely spoken there, particularly in the north and east. It is somewhat different from the French of Québec *(Québécois)*. Nova Scotia and Manitoba have significant Francophone populations as well, and there are smaller pockets in most provinces.

CANADIAN ENGLISH

Canada inherited English primarily from the British settlers of the early and mid-19th century. This form of British English remains the basis of Canadian English. There are some pronunciation differences; for example, Britons say 'clark' for clerk, Canadians say 'clurk.' Grammatical differences are few. The Canadian vocabulary has been augmented considerably both by the need for new words in a new land and by the influence of the First Nations languages as well as the pioneering French.

Canada has never developed a series of easily detectable dialects such as those of England, Germany or even the USA. There are, however, regional variations in idiom and pronunciation. In Newfoundland, for example, some people speak with an accent reminiscent of the west country of England (Devon and Cornwall) or Ireland, and some use words such as 'screech' (rum) and 'shooneen' (coward).

The spoken English of the Atlantic Provinces, too, has inflections not heard in the west, and in the Ottawa Valley you'll hear a slightly different sound again, due mainly to the large number of Irish who settled there in the mid-19th century. In British Columbia some expressions reflect that province's history; for example, 'leaverite' (a worthless mineral) is a prospecting word derived from the phrase 'Leave 'er right there.'

Although Canadians and Americans may sound the same to many non-North Americans, there are real differences. Canadian pronunciation of 'ou' is the most notable of these; words like 'out' and 'bout' sound more like 'oat' and 'boat' when spoken by Western Canadians. Canadian English has been strongly influenced by the USA, particularly in recent years via the mass media and the use of US textbooks and dictionaries in schools. Most spellings follow British English, such as 'centre,' 'harbour' and 'cheque,' but there are some exceptions, such as 'tire' ('tyre') and 'aluminum' ('aluminium'). US spelling is becoming more common – to the consternation of some people. Perhaps the best-known difference between US and Canadian English is in the pronunciation of the last letter of the alphabet. In the USA, it's pronounced 'zee' while in Canada it's pronounced 'zed' (like both the British and the French).

Canadian English has also developed a few distinctive idioms and expressions. The most recognizable is the interrogative 'eh?' tag-word that to American ears seems to appear at the end of every spoken sentence, as in: 'This is great beer, eh?' It is Canadians' most-mocked trait. Canadian English has also added to the richness of the global English language, with words like kerosene (paraffin), puck (from ice hockey), bushed (exhausted) and moose and muskeg from anglicized Native Canadian words.

English in Québec

While stringent language laws in Québec have reflected a fear of English subsuming the French language, it can be argued that French has altered the English spoken in the province almost as much. In fact, as of 1997, the *Oxford Dictionary of Canadian English* has classified Québec English as a separate dialect.

Three regional English accents have been identified in the province – a standard Canadian intonation, a working-class accent in which consonants are crisply enunciated, and an Americanized twang heard in the Eastern Townships regions closest to the border. However, what really distinguishes the English heard in Québec from that spoken in other provinces are the French or Francicized words in daily use, which may baffle English-speakers from other provinces. Many of these have come into current use in the last 25 years after the enforcement of Québec's language laws.

For example, a Torontonian might have trouble deciphering this sentence from a Montréal counterpart: 'They're announcing rain for tomorrow, so the animator driving in for the fête might have some trouble on the autoroute.' English Québecers often use 'announce' instead of 'predict' or 'call for' in weather forecasts, from the French verb *annoncer*; in French an *animateur* is someone who organizes an event; *fête* is often used as both a verb or noun for 'party;' and *autoroute* is an accepted synonym for 'highway.'

Sometimes French words are used in place of English ones; other times English words are used with a French meaning when the two sound alike. In addition to this, a number of people liberally pepper their English speech with *bien placées* (well placed) French words or phrases.

Another example of uniquely Québécois English is the use of the word 'coordinates' to mean 'essential personal data' – in French, *coordonées* is what you'd ask someone for if you wanted to get in touch with them later. A *dépanneur,* used equally by Anglophones and Francophones, is a convenience store. Also, an 'allophone' is an immigrant living in Québec whose first language is neither English nor French.

CANADIAN FRENCH (QUÉBÉCOIS)

For the most part, French speakers from Québec and France would be perfectly able to understand one another – they would merely find each other's accents quaint or mildly amusing. Locals say they speak Québécois, a French dialect with a rich vocabulary of words and phrases unknown to people from France. Several dictionaries of Québécois slang attest to this fact. Many who hold nationalist political views consider it a separate language.

Though you're unlikely to hear a very heavy Québécois accent in downtown Montréal, you'll notice regional inflections as you cross the province. The word for yes, *oui* (pronounced wee), will be pronounced 'why,' often with a nasal *bien* (behn, meaning 'well') thrown in front of it for good measure. Instead of the words for you and me – *moi* and *toi,* respectively – being pronounced 'mwah' and 'twah,' they will be pronounced 'mwuay' and 'twuay.'

Sometimes final consonants, which often remain silent in spoken French, will be emphasized. For example, *au bout* (to the end) is usually pronounced 'oh bou,' but in Québécois it will sound like 'o buit.' The word for bed, *lit* (pronounced li) will come out as the English 'lit.' Québécois is also characterized by contractions (*il est aller* becomes 'y'est aller'; *peut être* becomes 'p'tête') and tag words like *bien* (well) and *là* (there, then) are frequently used.

Another characterization of Québécois is its incorporation of many English words into its lexicon. Car parts, for example, are usually described by their English terms, which might save you on the side of a highway one day. Indeed the word *char* (shahr) for car may be heard. Hitchhiking is known not as *autostop* but as *le pousse* (the thumb). Some English words are used verbatim, with only a le or la article thrown in front of it *(la machine shop)*, while others get a twist in pronunciation *(un lecteur* is slang for a lighter).

Other English incursions into Québécois include *feeler* (fee-lay), meaning to feel and *checker* (check-ay), meaning to check out, watch or verify. *Last call, deadline* and *fake* all are used with their English meanings.

Other differences between French from France and the Québec version worth remembering (because you don't want to go hungry!) are the terms for breakfast, lunch and dinner. Rather than *petit déjeuner, déjeuner* and *dîner,* you're likely to see and hear *déjeuner, dîner* and *souper.*

As you'll have noticed, language is often a politically contentious issue in Québec; the Québécois dialect is no exception. Many people have an ambiguous relationship to it, feeling at once that it represents Québécois as a people and reflects solidarity, yet that it's not as cultured or refined as the French from France. There are as many people who consider a heavy Québécois accent an element of cultural pride as there are those who feel that it is not 'proper' French. Some feel a Parisian accent denotes snobbism, others see it as reflecting culture and education.

The Québécois dialect is sometimes known as *joual,* a pejorative term invented by intellectual Québécois journalists in the 1960s to describe the way people from the rural regions spoke, enunciating as if they were chewing at the same time. To them the accent was a result of colonization, a symbol of the repressed, uncultured working class. The word comes from the French for horse, *cheval – joual* is what you'd get if you 'chewed' the original. A 1960 article in *Le Devoir* attacked the way French Canadians spoke as resembling the sounds a talking horse would make. However, others felt that *joual* was to be an assertion of national pride of the Québécois people, particularly as the accent actually resembles the affected inflections of Parisian nobility of the 17th and 18th centuries.

For more information about French language laws in Québec, see the Language section in the Facts about Québec chapter.

USEFUL WORDS & PHRASES

The following is a short guide to some French words and phrases that may be useful for the traveler. The combinations 'ohn/ehn/ahn' in the phonetic transcriptions are nasal sounds – the 'n' is not pronounced; 'zh' is pronounced as the 's' in 'measure.' Stress in French is much weaker than in English. All it really does is lengthen the final syllable of the word, so it is important to make an effort to pronounce each syllable with approximately equal stress.

For a far more comprehensive guide to the language, get a copy of Lonely Planet's pocket-size *French phrasebook.*

Civilities & Basics

Yes.	*Oui.*	wee
No.	*Non.*	nohn
Please.	*S'il vous plaît.*	seel voo pleh
Thank you.	*Merci.*	mehr-see
You're welcome.	*Je vous en prie./de rien*	zhe voo-zohn pree/duhree-en
Hello. (day)	*Bonjour.*	bohn-zhoor
Hello. (evening)	*Bonsoir.*	bohn-swar
Hello. (informal)	*Salut.*	sa-lew
Goodbye.	*Au revoir.*	oh rev-wahr
How are you?	*Comment ça va?* (or *Ça va?)*	com-mohn sa vah?
I'm fine.	*Ça va bien.*	sa vah bee-ahn
Welcome.	*Bienvenu(e).*	bee-ahn ven-oo
Excuse me.	*Pardon.*	par-dohn
Pardon/What?	*Quoi?* (slang) *Comment?*	kwah? com-mohn?
How much?	*Combien?*	kom-bee-ahn?

Language Difficulties

I don't understand.	*Je ne comprends pas.*	zhe neh com-prohn pah
I understand.	*Je comprends.*	zhe com-prohn
Do you speak English?	*Parlez-vous anglais?*	par-lay vooz ang-lay?
I don't speak French.	*Je ne parle pas français.*	zhe neh parl pah frohn-say

Getting Around

bicycle	*vélo*	veh-loh
bus	*autobus*	oh-toh-booss
train	*train*	trahn
plane	*avion*	a-vee-ohn
train station	*gare*	gar
platform	*quai*	kay
bus station	*station d'autobus*	sta-seeyon d'ohtoh-booss
one-way ticket	*billet simple*	bee-yay sam-pluh
return ticket	*billet aller et retour*	bee-yay a-lay eh reh-tour
boat cruise	*croisière de bateau*	kwa-zyeh de ba-toh
gas (petrol)	*essence/gaz*	eh-sohns/gaz
self-serve	*service libre*	sair-vees lee-br
highway	*autoroute*	oh-to-root
Where is...?	*Où est...?*	oo eh...
What time does the... leave/arrive?	*A quelle heure part/arrive le...?*	a kel ur pahr/ah-reev le...?

Directions

I want to go to...	*Je veux aller à...*	zhe vuh a-lay a
left	*à gauche*	a goshe
right	*à droite*	a dwaht
straight ahead	*tout droit*	too dwah
near	*proche*	prosh
far	*loin*	lwahn
here	*ici*	ee-see
there	*là*	lah

Around Town

bank	*banque*	bohnk
beach	*plage*	plazh
B&B (Bed & Breakfast)	*gîte de passant*	zhit de pass-ahn
the bill	*l'addition/le reçu*	la-dis-yohn/le reh soo
bridge	*pont*	pohn
city hall	*hôtel de ville*	o-tel de vil
convenience store	*dépanneur*	day-pahn-nur
department store	*magasin*	mag-a-zahn
grocery store	*épicerie*	ay-pee-sree
museum	*musée*	mew-zay
opening hours	*horaires*	oh-rair
post office	*bureau de poste*	bew-roh duh post
the police	*la police*	la po-lees
show/concert	*spectacle*	spek-tahk'l
toilet	*toilette*	twah-let
tourist office	*bureau du tourisme*	bew-ro doo too-rees-muh

Food & Dining

bakery	*boulangerie*	boo-lohn-zhe-ree
beer	*bière*	bee-yair
a bottle of	*une bouteille de*	oon boo-tay duh
bread	*pain*	pahn
homemade bread	*pain de ménage*	pahn de may-nazh
a cup of	*une tasse de*	oon tass duh
cheese	*fromage*	fro-mahzh
pancakes	*crêpes*	kraip
a glass of	*un verre de*	uhn vair duh
breakfast	*le (petit) déjeuner*	luh (puh-tee) day-zhuh-nay
lunch	*le dîner*	luh dee-nay
dinner	*le souper*	luh soo-pay
dish of the day	*le plat du jour*	luh plah dew zhoor
fixed-price (prix fixe) menu	*le table d'hôte*	luh tab doht
fresh fish store	*poissonnerie*	pwa-sohn-e-ree
fruit	*fruit*	fwee
honey	*miel*	mee-el
main course	*le plat principal*	luh plah pran-see-pal
maple syrup	*sirop d'érable*	si-ro day-rab
meat pie	*tourtière*	tor-tee-air
milk	*lait*	lay
pork pâté	*crêtons*	kre-tohn
red wine	*vin rouge*	vahn roozh
restaurant	*restaurant*	rest-uh-rohn
snack bar	*casse croûte*	kass kroot
soft drink	*liqueur*	lee-ker
steak	*steack/bavette biftek*	stayk/bah-vet beef-tehk
vegetables	*légumes*	lay-gyoom
Waiter!	*Monsieur!/Mademoiselle!*	muh-syuh/mad-mwa-zel
water	*eau*	oh
white wine	*vin blanc*	vahn blohn
wine	*vin*	vahn
wine list	*la carte des vins*	la cart day vahn

I would like (to order)…
  je voudrais (commander)   zhe voo-dray (ko-mahn-day)

I'm a vegetarian.
  Je suis végétarien/végétarienne (male/female)   zhe swee veh-zheh-teh-ryahn/ryen

Other Useful Words

big	*grand*	grond
small	*petit*	peh-tee
much/many	*beaucoup*	boh-coo
too much/too many	*trop*	troh
cheap	*bon marché/pas chère/*	bohn mar-shay/pa sher/
	c'est cheap	seh cheap
expensive	*cher*	share
before	*avant*	ah-vohn
after	*après*	ah-preh
tomorrow	*demain*	de-mahn
yesterday	*hier*	ee-yehr

Numbers

1	*un*	uhn
2	*deux*	duh
3	*trois*	twah
4	*quatre*	cat'r
5	*cinq*	sank
6	*six*	sease
7	*sept*	set
8	*huit*	weet
9	*neuf*	nerf
10	*dix*	dees
15	*quinze*	cans
20	*vingt*	vahn
21	*vingt et un*	vahn-teh uhn
25	*vingt-cinq*	vahn sank
30	*trente*	trohnt
40	*quarante*	car-ohnt
50	*cinquante*	sank-ohnt
60	*soixante*	swa-sohnt
70	*soixante-dix*	swa-sohnt dees
80	*quatre-vingt*	cat-tr' vahn
90	*quatre-vingt-dix*	cat-tr' vahn dees
100	*cent*	sohn
500	*cinq cents*	sank sohn
1000	*mille*	meel

Glossary

Acadians – The first settlers from France who lived in Nova Scotia.

Amérindien – A French term for Native Canadians

aurora borealis – Also called the northern lights, these are charged particles from the sun that are trapped in the earth's magnetic field. They appear as otherworldly, colored, waving beams. Generally, they can be seen in high northern latitudes in late fall and throughout the winter, however, they have appeared in areas as far south as the Laurentians on cool evenings throughout the year. They are best viewed as far away as possible from city lights.

beaver fever (giardiasis) – This disease affects the digestive tract and can be avoided by boiling drinking water. The bacteria that causes it is found in many freshwater streams and lakes.

boîtes à chanson – Cheap, casual and relaxed folk clubs, popular in Québec. They are usually small, cozy, and feature folk-style entertainment.

boondoggle – A futile or unnecessary project or work.

boreal – Refers to the Canadian north and its character, as in the boreal forest, the boreal wind etc.

brewpub – A pub that brews and sells its own beer.

BYOW – An acronym for Bring Your Own Wine, also used in French; it designates restaurants that do not have a license to serve alcohol but permit customers to bring it on the premises.

cabin fever – A traditional term still used to indicate a stir-crazy, frustrated state of mind due to being cooped up indoors over the long northern winter.

calèche – Horse-drawn carriage that can be rented around parts of Montréal and Québec City.

calleurs – A Québécois slang term for 'callers,' the people who lead square dancing evenings by calling out instructions such as 'Swing your partner to the right!'

Canadian Shield – Also known as the Precambrian or Laurentian Shield, this plateau of rock was formed 2.5 billion years ago and covers much of Canada's north.

Cégep – Québec's equivalent of 'college,' a Cégep is a two year-long school, which students attend before university and after completing 11 years of primary and secondary education. It is not compulsory.

chansonnier – A folk singer. The term is usually applied to singers and guitarists who play folk music in small clubs called 'boîtes' (*buat*, literally, boxes).

clear-cut – An area where loggers have cut every tree, large and small, leaving nothing standing; *coupe à blanc* in French.

CLSC – Centre Local de Santé Communautaire, or local community health center. You'll see green-and-white CLSC signs in almost every Québec town or urban district.

correspondence – A transfer slip, like those used between the Métro and bus networks in Montréal.

côte – This French word for 'side' is also an old Québécois term meaning 'hill' (eg, the Montréal street côte du Beaver Hall).

coulées – Gulches, usually dry.

dépanneur – Called 'dep' for short, this is a Québécois term for a convenience store, often open 24 hours.

dome car – A two-level, glass-top, observation train car.

l'Estrie – Québécois term for the Cantons de l'Est (Eastern Townships), a former Loyalist region southeast of Montréal toward the US border.

filles du Roi – socially disadvantaged single girls (mostly illegitimate offspring of bourgeois women, orphans and prostitutes); literally, King's daughters.

First Nations – A term used to denote Canada's indigenous peoples. It is often interchangeable with Native Canadians.

flowerpots – Unusual rock formations created by erosion from waves. Examples can be seen at Tobermory, in Ontario, and at The Rocks, in New Brunswick.

Front de Libération du Québec (FLQ) – A radical, violent political group active in the 1970s that advocated Québec's separation from Canada. In 1970 a renegade cell of the FLQ kidnapped and murdered Québec health minister Pierre Laporte.

fruit leather (cuir de fruits) – A blend of fruit purees dried into thin sheets and pressed together, common among backpackers and hikers.

gasoline – Petrol, commonly known as gas (*gaz* in Québécois). Almost all gasoline in Canada is unleaded and comes in regular and more costly higher-octane versions.

gîte du passant – A Québécois term often used for bed and breakfasts (B&Bs).

Grande Noirceur – The term 'Great Darkness' is sometimes used to describe the period of the Duplessis government in Québec (1936–39 and 1944–59).

Group of Seven – A group of celebrated Canadian painters from the 1920s.

Haligonians – Residents of Halifax, Nova Scotia.

Hudson Bay Company (Compagnie de la Baie d'Hudson) – An English enterprise created in 1670 to exploit the commercial potential of the Hudson Bay and its waterways The department store the Bay (La Baie) is the last vestige of Canada's oldest enterprise.

igloo – Traditional Inuit houses made from blocks of ice.

Innu – Another name for the Montagnais people.

inukshuk – Inuit preferred to trap caribou in water, where they could be hunted from a kayak. For this reason they built large, stone human like figures called inukshuks next to lakes to frighten the animals into the water.

interior camping – This refers to usually lone, individual sites accessible only by foot or canoe. You must pre-register for those in provincial or national parks (for your own safety).

Je me souviens – This Québécois motto with a nationalist ring appears on license plates across the province; 'I remember' in English.

joual – *See* Québécois.

loon – A fish-eating diving bird of the genus *Gavia*.

loonie – Canada's one-dollar coin, so named for the loon stamped on one side.

Lotto 649 – The country's most popular, highest-paying lottery.

Loyalists – Residents of the USA who maintained their allegiance to Britain during the American Revolution and fled to Canada.

Mennonites – Members of a religious utopian group originating in Europe, mostly found in the Kitchen-Waterloo region of southern Ontario.

Métis – Canadians of French and First Nations stock.

Mounties – Royal Canadian Mounted Police (RCMP).

mukluks – Moccasins or boots made from sealskin and often trimmed with fur; usually made by Inuit people.

muskeg – Undrained, boggy land, most often found in northern Canada.

NAFTA – North American Free Trade Agreement; an accord that eliminated a range of trade barriers among Canada, the USA and Mexico. The French acronym is ALENA.

Newfie – A slightly pejorative term applying to residents of Newfoundland, or 'The Rock' as it is sometimes known.

no-see-um – Any of various tiny biting insects that are difficult to see and that can annoy travelers when out in the woods or along some beaches. No-see-um netting, a very fine mesh screen on a tent, is designed to keep the insects out.

Nunavut – Official territory of the Inuits in northern Québec since 1999, a vast area encompassing 350,000 sq km.

permafrost – Permanently frozen subsoil that covers the far north of Canada.

petroglyphs – Ancient rock paintings or carvings.

piastre – Québécois term for a Canadian dollar.

portage – The process of transporting boats and supplies overland between navigable waterways. Also the overland route used for such a purpose.

pot-en-pot – An Îles de la Madeleine specialty dish of mixed fish and seafood in a sauce baked in its own pie crust then topped with processed cheese curds and thin, brown gravy.

pourvoirie – A forest area with lakes and rivers granted by the Québec government to a private group or association for commerce and tourism. Often, the owners of pour-voiries act as semi-adventure tour companies, offering fishing, hunting and other wilderness activities. In recent years some owners have switched to animal protection and observation.

public/separate schools – Canada's two basic school systems. Both are free and essentially the same, but the latter is designed for Catholics and offers more religious education.

qiviut – Musk ox wool that was traditionally woven into garments by Inuit in the far north.

Québec nationalism – Against federal jurisdiction and governance in provincial, 'national' affairs. The term nationalism in this province refers to the idea of Quebec as a separate or sovereign nation, and not to Canada as a whole.

Québécois – The local tongue of Québec, where the vast majority of the population is French; also known in street vernacular as *joual*. The term also refers to the residents of Québec, although it is applied only to the French, not English 'Québecers.' It is also used as an adjective to describe anything originating from the province.

Refus Global – The radical manifest of a group of Québec artists and intellectuals during the Duplessis era.

ringuette – A sport played on ice, similar to hockey but with a ring instead of a puck and a straight stick with no flat or angled end.

rock hounds – Rock collectors.

rubby – A derelict alcoholic who is often homeless. The term comes from rubbing alcohol, which is often mixed with cheap wine for drinking.

RV – Recreational vehicle (a motor home).

SAQ – Société des Alcools du Québec, a state-run agency whose branches are authorized to sell beer and wine.

screech – A particularly strong rum once available only in Newfoundland, but now widely available (in diluted form) across Canada.

seigneury – Land in Québec originally held by grant from the King of France. Thus a seigneur is a holder of a seigneury.

649 – *See* Lotto 649.

Ski-Doo – Snowmobile. This machine, invented and developed in Valcourt, Québec, was originally dubbed a Ski Dog; the word 'skidoo' came about as that's how it sounded when 'Ski Dog' was said quickly.

sourdough – Refers to a person who has completed one year's residency in northern Canada.

sous – Québécois currency term used for cents.

spelunking – The exploration and study of caves.

steamies – Hot dogs in Québec; they get their name from the method by which they are cooked.

sugar-making moon – A former Native Canadian term for the spring date when the maple tree's sap begins to run.

sugar shack – A place where collected maple sap is distilled in large kettles and boiled as part of the production of maple syrup; *cabane à sucre* in French.

taiga – The coniferous forests extending across much of subarctic North America and Eurasia.

toonie – Sometimes spelled 'twonie,' this is a Canadian two-dollar coin introduced after the 'loonie,' or one-dollar coin.

tourtière – A meat pie with a flaky crust, prepared with several kinds of meat and potatoes, as well as spices such as nutmeg. Though it is available throughout Québec, the Lac St Jean region lays claim to being its homeland and the tastiest varieties are said to be made in this region.

trailer – In Canada, as well as in the USA, this is a caravan or a mobile home (house trailer). Also a vehicle used for transporting goods.

trap line – A marked area along which a trapper will set traps to catch fur-bearing animals.

tundra – The vast, treeless Arctic plains, north of the treeline and with a perennially frozen subsoil.

voyageur – A boatman employed by one of the early fur-trading companies. He could also fill the function of a woodsman, guide, trapper or explorer.

Lonely Planet Guides by Region

Lonely Planet is known worldwide for publishing practical, reliable and no-nonsense travel information in our guides and on our Web site. The Lonely Planet list covers just about every accessible part of the world. Currently there are 16 series: Travel guides, Shoestring guides, Condensed guides, Phrasebooks, Read This First, Healthy Travel, Walking guides, Cycling guides, Watching Wildlife guides, Pisces Diving & Snorkeling guides, City Maps, Road Atlases, Out to Eat, World Food, Journeys travel literature and Pictorials.

AFRICA Africa on a shoestring • Botswana • Cairo • Cairo City Map • Cape Town • Cape Town City Map • East Africa • Egypt • Egyptian Arabic phrasebook • Ethiopia, Eritrea & Djibouti • Ethiopian Amharic phrasebook • The Gambia & Senegal • Healthy Travel Africa • Kenya • Malawi • Morocco • Moroccan Arabic phrasebook • Mozambique • Namibia • Read This First: Africa • South Africa, Lesotho & Swaziland • Southern Africa • Southern Africa Road Atlas • Swahili phrasebook • Tanzania, Zanzibar & Pemba • Trekking in East Africa • Tunisia • Watching Wildlife East Africa • Watching Wildlife Southern Africa • West Africa • World Food Morocco • Zambia • Zimbabwe, Botswana & Namibia
Travel Literature: Mali Blues: Traveling to an African Beat • The Rainbird: A Central African Journey • Songs to an African Sunset: A Zimbabwean Story

AUSTRALIA & THE PACIFIC Aboriginal Australia & the Torres Strait Islands • Auckland • Australia • Australian phrasebook • Australia Road Atlas • Cycling Australia • Cycling New Zealand • Fiji • Fijian phrasebook • Healthy Travel Australia, NZ and the Pacific • Islands of Australia's Great Barrier Reef • Melbourne • Melbourne City Map • Micronesia • New Caledonia • New South Wales • New Zealand • Northern Territory • Outback Australia • Out to Eat – Melbourne • Out to Eat – Sydney • Papua New Guinea • Pidgin phrasebook • Queensland • Rarotonga & the Cook Islands • Samoa • Solomon Islands • South Australia • South Pacific • South Pacific phrasebook • Sydney • Sydney City Map • Sydney Condensed • Tahiti & French Polynesia • Tasmania • Tonga • Tramping in New Zealand • Vanuatu • Victoria • Walking in Australia • Watching Wildlife Australia • Western Australia
Travel Literature: Islands in the Clouds: Travel in the Highlands of New Guinea • Kiwi Tracks: A New Zealand Journey • Sean & David's Long Drive

CENTRAL AMERICA & THE CARIBBEAN Bahamas, Turks & Caicos • Baja California • Belize, Guatemala & Yucatán • Bermuda • Central America on a shoestring • Costa Rica • Costa Rica Spanish phrasebook • Cuba • Cycling Cuba • Dominican Republic & Haiti • Eastern Caribbean • Guatemala • Havana • Healthy Travel Central & South America • Jamaica • Mexico • Mexico City • Panama • Puerto Rico • Read This First: Central & South America • Virgin Islands • World Food Caribbean • World Food Mexico • Yucatán
Travel Literature: Green Dreams: Travels in Central America

EUROPE Amsterdam • Amsterdam City Map • Amsterdam Condensed • Andalucía • Athens • Austria • Baltic States phrasebook • Barcelona • Barcelona City Map • Belgium & Luxembourg • Berlin • Berlin City Map • Britain • British phrasebook • Brussels, Bruges & Antwerp • Brussels City Map • Budapest • Budapest City Map • Canary Islands • Catalunya & the Costa Brava • Central Europe • Central Europe phrasebook • Copenhagen • Corfu & the Ionians • Corsica • Crete • Crete Condensed • Croatia • Cycling Britain • Cycling France • Cyprus • Czech & Slovak Republics • Czech phrasebook • Denmark • Dublin • Dublin City Map • Dublin Condensed • Eastern Europe • Eastern Europe phrasebook • Edinburgh • Edinburgh City Map • England • Estonia, Latvia & Lithuania • Europe on a shoestring • Europe phrasebook • Finland • Florence • Florence City Map • France • Frankfurt City Map • Frankfurt Condensed • French phrasebook • Georgia, Armenia & Azerbaijan • Germany • German phrasebook • Greece • Greek Islands • Greek phrasebook • Hungary • Iceland, Greenland & the Faroe Islands • Ireland • Italian phrasebook • Italy • Kraków • Lisbon • The Loire • London • London City Map • London Condensed • Madrid • Madrid City Map • Malta • Mediterranean Europe • Milan, Turin & Genoa • Moscow • Munich • Netherlands • Normandy • Norway • Out to Eat – London • Out to Eat – Paris • Paris • Paris City Map • Paris Condensed • Poland • Polish phrasebook • Portugal • Portuguese phrasebook • Prague • Prague City Map • Provence & the Côte d'Azur • Read This First: Europe • Rhodes & the Dodecanese • Romania & Moldova • Rome • Rome City Map • Rome Condensed • Russia, Ukraine & Belarus • Russian phrasebook • Scandinavian & Baltic Europe • Scandinavian phrasebook • Scotland • Sicily • Slovenia • South-West France • Spain • Spanish phrasebook • Stockholm • St Petersburg • St Petersburg City Map • Sweden • Switzerland • Tuscany • Ukrainian phrasebook • Venice • Vienna • Wales • Walking in Britain • Walking in France • Walking in Ireland • Walking in Italy • Walking in Scotland • Walking in Spain • Walking in Switzerland • Western Europe • World Food France • World Food Greece • World Food Ireland • World Food Italy • World Food Spain **Travel Literature:** After Yugoslavia • Love and War in the Apennines • The Olive Grove: Travels in Greece • On the Shores of the Mediterranean • Round Ireland in Low Gear • A Small Place in Italy

Lonely Planet Mail Order

Lonely Planet products are distributed worldwide. They are also available by mail order from Lonely Planet, so if you have difficulty finding a title, please write to us. North and South American residents should write to 150 Linden St, Oakland, CA 94607, USA; European and African residents should write to 10a Spring Place, London NW5 3BH, UK; and residents of other countries to Locked Bag 1, Footscray, Victoria 3011, Australia.

INDIAN SUBCONTINENT & THE INDIAN OCEAN Bangladesh • Bengali phrasebook • Bhutan • Delhi • Goa • Healthy Travel Asia & India • Hindi & Urdu phrasebook • India • India & Bangladesh City Map • Indian Himalaya • Karakoram Highway • Kathmandu City Map • Kerala • Madagascar • Maldives • Mauritius, Réunion & Seychelles • Mumbai (Bombay) • Nepal • Nepali phrasebook • North India • Pakistan • Rajasthan • Read This First: Asia & India • South India • Sri Lanka • Sri Lanka phrasebook • Tibet • Tibetan phrasebook • Trekking in the Indian Himalaya • Trekking in the Karakoram & Hindukush • Trekking in the Nepal Himalaya • World Food India **Travel Literature:** The Age of Kali: Indian Travels and Encounters • Hello Goodnight: A Life of Goa • In Rajasthan • Maverick in Madagascar • A Season in Heaven: True Tales from the Road to Kathmandu • Shopping for Buddhas • A Short Walk in the Hindu Kush • Slowly Down the Ganges

MIDDLE EAST & CENTRAL ASIA Bahrain, Kuwait & Qatar • Central Asia • Central Asia phrasebook • Dubai • Farsi (Persian) phrasebook • Hebrew phrasebook • Iran • Israel & the Palestinian Territories • Istanbul • Istanbul City Map • Istanbul to Cairo • Istanbul to Kathmandu • Jerusalem • Jerusalem City Map • Jordan • Lebanon • Middle East • Oman & the United Arab Emirates • Syria • Turkey • Turkish phrasebook • World Food Turkey • Yemen **Travel Literature:** Black on Black: Iran Revisited • Breaking Ranks: Turbulent Travels in the Promised Land • The Gates of Damascus • Kingdom of the Film Stars: Journey into Jordan

NORTH AMERICA Alaska • Boston • Boston City Map • Boston Condensed • British Columbia • California & Nevada • California Condensed • Canada • Chicago • Chicago City Map • Chicago Condensed • Florida • Georgia & the Carolinas • Great Lakes • Hawaii • Hiking in Alaska • Hiking in the USA • Honolulu & Oahu City Map • Las Vegas • Los Angeles • Los Angeles City Map • Louisiana & the Deep South • Miami • Miami City Map • Montréal • New England • New Orleans • New Orleans City Map • New York City • New York City City Map • New York City Condensed • New York, New Jersey & Pennsylvania • Oahu • Out to Eat – San Francisco • Pacific Northwest • Rocky Mountains • San Diego & Tijuana • San Francisco • San Francisco City Map • Seattle • Seattle City Map • Southwest • Texas • Toronto • USA • USA phrasebook • Vancouver • Vancouver City Map • Virginia & the Capital Region • Washington, DC • Washington, DC City Map • World Food New Orleans **Travel Literature:** Caught Inside: A Surfer's Year on the California Coast • Drive Thru America

NORTH-EAST ASIA Beijing • Beijing City Map • Cantonese phrasebook • China • Hiking in Japan • Hong Kong & Macau • Hong Kong City Map • Hong Kong Condensed • Japan • Japanese phrasebook • Korea • Korean phrasebook • Kyoto • Mandarin phrasebook • Mongolia • Mongolian phrasebook • Seoul • Shanghai • South-West China • Taiwan • Tokyo • World Food Hong Kong • World Food Japan **Travel Literature:** In Xanadu: A Quest • Lost Japan

SOUTH AMERICA Argentina, Uruguay & Paraguay • Bolivia • Brazil • Brazilian phrasebook • Buenos Aires • Buenos Aires City Map • Chile & Easter Island • Colombia • Ecuador & the Galápagos Islands • Healthy Travel Central & South America • Latin American Spanish phrasebook • Peru • Quechua phrasebook • Read This First: Central & South America • Rio de Janeiro • Rio de Janeiro City Map • Santiago de Chile • South America on a shoestring • Trekking in the Patagonian Andes • Venezuela **Travel Literature:** Full Circle: A South American Journey

SOUTH-EAST ASIA Bali & Lombok • Bangkok • Bangkok City Map • Burmese phrasebook • Cambodia • Cycling Vietnam, Laos & Cambodia • East Timor phrasebook • Hanoi • Healthy Travel Asia & India • Hill Tribes phrasebook • Ho Chi Minh City (Saigon) • Indonesia • Indonesian phrasebook • Indonesia's Eastern Islands • Java • Lao phrasebook • Laos • Malay phrasebook • Malaysia, Singapore & Brunei • Myanmar (Burma) • Philippines • Pilipino (Tagalog) phrasebook • Read This First: Asia & India • Singapore • Singapore City Map • South-East Asia on a shoestring • South-East Asia phrasebook • Thailand • Thailand's Islands & Beaches • Thailand, Vietnam, Laos & Cambodia Road Atlas • Thai phrasebook • Vietnam • Vietnamese phrasebook • World Food Indonesia • World Food Thailand • World Food Vietnam

ALSO AVAILABLE: Antarctica • The Arctic • The Blue Man: Tales of Travel, Love and Coffee • Brief Encounters: Stories of Love, Sex & Travel • Buddhist Stupas in Asia: The Shape of Perfection • Chasing Rickshaws • The Last Grain Race • Lonely Planet…On the Edge: Adventurous Escapades from Around the World • Lonely Planet Unpacked • Lonely Planet Unpacked Again • Not the Only Planet: Science Fiction Travel Stories • Ports of Call: A Journey by Sea • Sacred India • Travel Photography: A Guide to Taking Better Pictures • Travel with Children • Tuvalu: Portrait of an Island Nation

LONELY PLANET

You already know that Lonely Planet produces more than this one guidebook, but you might not be aware of the other products we have on this region. Here is a selection of titles which you may want to check out as well:

Montréal
ISBN 1 86450 254 1
US$15.99 • UK£ 9.99

Canada
ISBN 1 74059 029 5
US$ 24.99 • UK£ 14.99

French phrasebook
ISBN 0 86442 450 7
US$ 5.95 • UK£ 3.99

Toronto
ISBN 1 86450 217 7
US$ 15.99 • UK£ 9.99

Canada's Maritime Provinces
ISBN 1 74059 023 6
US$ 16.99 • UK£ 10.99

New England
ISBN 1 74059 025 2
US$ 19.99 • UK£ 12.99

Available wherever books are sold.

Index

Text

Bold indicates maps.

Bold indicates maps.

Bold indicates maps.

Bold indicates maps.

Boxed Text

MAP LEGEND

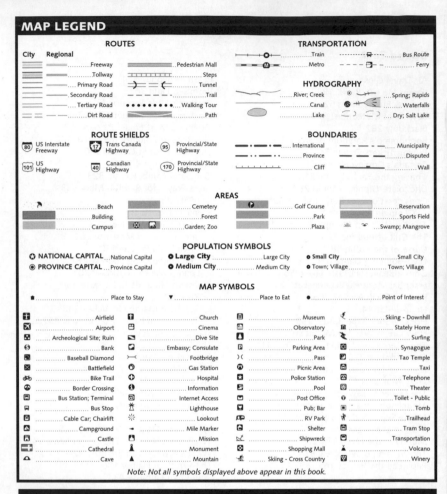

ROUTES

City   Regional

- ....Freeway
- ....Tollway
- ....Primary Road
- ....Secondary Road
- ....Tertiary Road
- ....Dirt Road

- ....Pedestrian Mall
- ....Steps
- ....Tunnel
- ....Trail
- ....Walking Tour
- ....Path

TRANSPORTATION

- ....Train
- ....Metro

- ....Bus Route
- ....Ferry

HYDROGRAPHY

- ....River; Creek
- ....Canal
- ....Lake

- ...Spring; Rapids
- ....Waterfalls
- ...Dry; Salt Lake

ROUTE SHIELDS

- **80** US Interstate Freeway
- **17** Trans Canada Highway
- **95** Provincial/State Highway
- **101** US Highway
- **40** Canadian Highway
- **170** Provincial/State Highway

BOUNDARIES

- ....International
- ....Province
- ....Cliff

- ....Municipality
- ....Disputed
- ....Wall

AREAS

- ....Beach
- ....Building
- ....Campus

- ....Cemetery
- ....Forest
- ....Garden; Zoo

- **⊙** ....Golf Course
- ....Park
- ....Plaza

- ....Reservation
- ....Sports Field
- ...Swamp; Mangrove

POPULATION SYMBOLS

- **◎ NATIONAL CAPITAL** ...National Capital
- **◉ PROVINCE CAPITAL** ... Province Capital
- **● Large City** ....Large City
- **● Medium City**...............Medium City
- **● Small City** ....Small City
- **● Town; Village** ....Town; Village

MAP SYMBOLS

- ▪ .... Place to Stay
- ▼ .... Place to Eat
- ● ....Point of Interest

.... Airfield	.... Church	.... Museum	.... Skiing - Downhill
.... Airport	.... Cinema	....................Observatory	.... Stately Home
...... Archeological Site; Ruin	.... Dive Site	..........................Park	.... Surfing
.... Bank	.... Embassy; Consulate	..................Pass	.... Synagogue
.... Baseball Diamond	.... Footbridge	.... Picnic Area	.... Tao Temple
..................Battlefield	.... Gas Station	..............Police Station	........................Taxi
.... Bike Trail	.... Hospital	.......................Pool	.... Telephone
.... Border Crossing	.... Information	.... Post Office	.... Theater
.... Bus Station; Terminal	.... Internet Access	.... Pub; Bar	.... Toilet - Public
.... Bus Stop	.... Lighthouse	.... RV Park	.....................Tomb
.... Cable Car; Chairlift	.... Lookout	.... Shelter	....................Trailhead
.... Campground	.... Mile Marker	.... Shipwreck	.... Tram Stop
.... Castle	.... Mission	.... Shopping Mall	...........Transportation
.... Cathedral	.... Monument	.... Skiing - Cross Country	.....................Volcano
......................Cave	.... Mountain		.....................Winery

Note: Not all symbols displayed above appear in this book.

LONELY PLANET OFFICES

Australia
Locked Bag 1, Footscray, Victoria 3011
☎ 03 8379 8000 fax 03 8379 8111
email talk2us@lonelyplanet.com.au

USA
150 Linden Street, Oakland, California 94607
☎ 510 893 8555, TOLL FREE 800 275 8555
fax 510 893 8572
email info@lonelyplanet.com

UK
10a Spring Place, London NW5 3BH
☎ 020 7428 4800 fax 020 7428 4828
email go@lonelyplanet.co.uk

France
1 rue du Dahomey, 75011 Paris
☎ 01 55 25 33 00 fax 01 55 25 33 01
email bip@lonelyplanet.fr
www.lonelyplanet.fr

World Wide Web: www.lonelyplanet.com *or* AOL keyword: lp
Lonely Planet Images: lpi@lonelyplanet.com.au